The Mrożek Reader

SŁAWOMIR MROŻEK

The Mrożek Reader

Edited by Daniel Gerould

Grove Press
New York

Published simultaneously in Canada
Printed in the United States of America

FIRST EDITION

Library of Congress Cataloging-in-Publication Data
Mrozek, Slawomir.
 [Selections. English. 2004]
 The Mrozek reader / Slawomir Mrozek ; edited by Daniel Gerould.
 p. cm.
 Contents: Ten stories from The elelphant—The police—Out at sea—Charlie—Striptease—Tango—Vatzlav—Emigrants—The hunchback—Four one-act animal plays—On foot—A summer's day.
 ISBN 0-8021-4066-1
 1. Mroçek Sławomir—Translations into English. I. Gerould, Daniel Charles, 1928– II. Title.
PG7172.R65A2 2004
891.8'527—dc22   2003067760

Grove Press

841 Broadway

New York, NY 10003

04 05 06 07 08   10 9 8 7 6 5 4 3 2 1

CONTENTS

Chronology of the Life and Work of Sławomir Mrożek

1930 June 29 born in Borzęcin, a small village forty miles from Kraków.

1933 Mrożek's father, a postal employee, moves the family to Kraków.

1939 At the outbreak of World War II, the family returns to Borzęcin. Experiences the war and occupation as an "ontological abyss" destroying all previous certainties and questions the values, modes, and codes he was born into. Experiences the operational excellence of communism in the power game.

1944 Finishes the local elementary school (first two first grades completed in Kraków).

1945 Back in Kraków with his family after the war, Mrożek attends the Nowodworski Lycée. Active in the Boy Scouts (banned in 1948). Drafted into a paramilitary youth work camp, "Service to Poland."

1949 Graduates from the Lycée; studies architecture at the Polytechnic Institute, but quits after three months. Death of his mother.

1950 Wins a prize for his cartoons in a competition organized by the satirical weekly, *Pins*. Enrolls at the Kraków Academy of Fine Arts, but soon abandons his studies to take a job at the newspaper, *The Polish Daily*. From 1950 until 1953 falls under the spell of Stalinism, in whose dogmatic ideology he becomes a fervent believer.

1951 Works as a journalist and cartoonist, publishing satirical sketches in various publications. Becomes a member of the Polish Writers' Union. To avoid compulsory military service, enrolls at the Jagiellonian University in Oriental studies, which he abandons in 1952 after receiving a deferment.

1952 Publishes his first two volumes of satirical stories: *Tales from Bumblebee Hill* and *Practical Half-Armor Plates*. Receives the Silver Cross of Merit for journalistic excellence in advancing the official ideology.

1953 Receives the Julian Brun Award for journalism, named after a communist theoretician.

1955 Sent as a reporter to the World Rally of Democratic Youth in Warsaw. Begins writing theater reviews and working collaboratively with several satirical theaters and cabarets in Kraków and Warsaw as well as with the Gdańsk student theater Bim-Bom (headed by Zbigniew Cybulski). His satirical novel *Little Summer* is serialized in *The Polish Daily*. Quits his job at the newspaper to become a freelance writer.

1956 The bloodless October Revolution brings liberalization and semi-autonomy in the arts, now freed of socialist realism. Mrożek's first short play, "The Professor" (playing time nine minutes), is staged as part of Bim-Bom's second program, *Joy in Earnest*. First trip abroad to the Soviet Union (Odessa, Crimea, Moscow, Kiev). Writes newspaper columns and theater reviews. *Little Summer* is published in book form.

1957 *The Elephant*, a collection of forty-two stories, an instant success and wins a prize. Receives a scholarship for a two-month visit to France. Stops writing theater reviews.

1958 Appears as principal actor in Janusz Majewski's short surrealist film, *Rondo*. *The Police*, a drama in three acts, published in *Dialog* (Poland's leading theater journal in which almost all his plays appear) and presented at the Warsaw Dramatic Theatre and elsewhere. Troubles with censorship leads to a temporary ban.

1959 Marries Maria Obremba, a painter, and moves to Warsaw. Publishes a collection of stories, *Wedding in Atomice*, and wins second prize in a television drama contest for *The Martyrdom of Peter Ohey*. Comes to the United States to attend the Harvard University Summer School International Seminar directed by Henry Kissinger.

1960 Travels to Italy and Yugoslavia. Begins a series of feuilletons and cartoons, "Seen through Sławomir Mrożek's Glasses," for the Kraków journal *Cross-Section*.

1961 Travels to London. *The Turkey* staged in Kraków; *Charlie, Out at Sea*, and *Striptease* in Gdańsk. A humorous children's story with illustrations, *Flight to the South*, published.

1962 Receives a literary award in Geneva. Travels in Europe.

1963 June 3 leaves on a tourist visa with his wife for Italy, where he stays until 1968. Lives in Chiavari, a small town on the Italian Riviera. Continues to publish his plays in Poland. Writes *Tango*.

1964 *Tango* is published in *Dialog*. Receives Alfred Jurzykowski Foundation Award in New York and French "L'Humeur Noir" prize.

1965 *Tango* is first staged in Belgrade, then in Bydgoszcz, Warsaw, and throughout Poland and the world, becoming Mrożek's greatest success.

1966 *Tango*, in Tom Stoppard's adaptation of Nicholas Bethell's translation, is directed by Trevor Nunn at the Royal Shakespeare Company, London.

1968 Moves to Paris. His letter protesting the Soviet-led Warsaw-pact invasion of Czechoslovakia published in *Le Monde* and the Paris émigré journal *Kultura*. When the Polish authorities order his immediate return home and Mrożek requests political asylum in France, all publication and performance of his works come under a ban in Poland that lasts five years. In the summer writes *Vatzlav*, the first of his plays not to be published and performed in Poland. The final opening of a Mrożek play takes place in June 1968, and productions already in the repertory soon disappear. His latest book, a volume of cartoons entitled *Seen through Sławomir Mrożek's Glasses*, appears in bookstores in July.

1969 Despite the ban, on International Theatre Day a long excerpt from *Tango* is shown on Polish National Television, indicating that Polish censorship is applied selectively. Mrożek's wife dies of cancer.

1970 *Vatzlav* receives its world premiere in Zurich and is published in German. The English-language premiere takes place in August at the Stratford Festival in Ontario.

1971 Resigns from the Polish Writers' Union.

1972 Receives the Austrian State Award for European Literature.

1973 In the spring Mrożek's new plays gradually start to appear again in *Dialog* and in theaters throughout Poland. Receives a grant from Pennsylvania State University and travels in the United States and South America from December to March 1974.

1974 In West Berlin on a grant from the Deutsche Akademische Austausch-
−75 Dienst, writes a scenario, *Island of Roses*, filmed by Franz Peter Wirth in 1976.

1975 *The Hunchback* staged in Łódź and in Kraków. *Emigrants* widely performed to great acclaim in Poland and abroad. Polish authorities let it be known that Mrożek would be welcomed back if he chose to return.

1977 Publishes *The Tailor, Philosopher Fox, Fox Hunt,* and *Serenade*. Writes and directs the film *Amor* for West German Television Süddeutsche Rundfunk.

1978   Obtains French citizenship. Requests readmission to the Polish Writers'
       Union and visits Poland for the first time since 1963.

1979   Polish premiere of *Vatzlav* in Lódź. Writes and directs the film *The
       Return* for Süddeutsche Rundfunk. For the opening of *Emigrants* goes
       to Mexico City, where he meets assistant director Susana Osorio
       Rosas, his future wife.

1980   Publishes *On Foot*.

1981   Visits Poland. Polish premieres of *The Ambassador* and *On Foot*.
       After the military takeover and imposition of martial law on 12/13
       December 1981, writes an open letter to *Le Monde* and to the *Inter-
       national Herald Tribune* protesting Jaruzelski's dictatorship and ridiculing
       the spurious rationalizations used to justify it. Refuses to allow pub-
       lication of his work in the Polish press or the showing his plays on
       Polish television. Polish theaters continue to perform his plays, al-
       though *Ambassador*, *Vatzlav*, and *Alpha* are prohibited by the censor.

1983   Publishes *A Summer's Day*. In Moscow, Teatr Chelovek presents an
       underground production of *Emigrants* that becomes their signature
       work.

1984   First Polish publication of *Vatzlav*, in a volume with *The Ambassa-
       dor*, by Paris *Kultura*. Directs *The Ambassador* in Munich. Polish text
       of *Alpha* published in France, and premiere of *Alpha* in Polish in
       London.

1987   Marries Susana Osorio Rosas. For the first time since the imposition
       of martial law in 1981, returns to Poland to be with his dying father.
       Premieres of *Contract* and *Portrait*, and *The Ambassador* returns to the
       Polish stage.

1988   Takes part in a symposium held by the Nobel Foundation and the
       Royal Dramatic Theatre, Stockholm. *Portrait* given at the Moscow
       Art Theatre.

1989   Spring, moves from Paris to Mexico. Buys a ranch, La Epifania, in
       the mountains between Mexico City and Puebla near the village of
       Tlahuapan.

1990   Summer, takes part in two-week Mrożek Festival in Kraków to cele-
       brate his sixtieth birthday, where he is given honorary citizenship.
       Builds a tower on his ranch. In December falls gravely ill with aneu-
       rysm of the aorta and undergoes heart surgery.

1991   Suffering from partial amnesia, disorientation, and depression, spends
       a year in convalescence. Receives a grant to appear at the Playwrights'
       Center in Minneapolis.

1992 January–April, writes *Widows,* which he directs in March at the Dionisia Festival in Siena (in Polish with Polish actors) and at the European Month of Culture in Kraków. Stages *Widows* for friends at the Teatro de Epifania in Tlahuapan. Autumn, visits Poland.

1993 Publishes *Love in the Crimea,* a pastiche of Chekhovian themes.

1994 Premiere of *Love in the Crimea* in Kraków and in Paris. *Collected Works* begins to appear in Polish. Susana goes public with her homemade jams, "Mermeladas y Conservas LA EPIFANIA fabricacion artesanal." *Widows* premiers in Moscow as *Banana,* a knock-about farce.

1995 *Love in the Crimea* at the Moscow Art Theatre. Unemployment, banditry, and corruption in Mexico lead the Mrożeks to feel besieged and betrayed by servants and staff. They hire bodyguards and sleep armed.

1996 Forced to leave the ranch by fears of attack, returns to Kraków. Begins to publish in serial form *The Journal of My Return,* a new column of essays. Writes *The Reverends* in English.

1998 Writes *A Beautiful View.* Jerzy Jarocki's production, *A History of People's Poland According to Mrożek,* based on a montage of the author's plays, reaffirms Mrożek's preeminence as a chronicler of life in communist Poland.

2000 Publishes *The Reverends* and *A Beautiful View.* Receives *doctor honoris causa* from Jagiellonian University (Kraków).

2001 Premiere of *The Reverends* at the Teatro Duse in Genoa.

2002 *The Reverends* staged in Kraków.

2003 French ambassador to Poland presents Mrożek with the Medal of the Legion of Honor.

INTRODUCTION

Mrożek for the Twenty-First Century

I

For the past half century Sławomir Mrożek has been the preeminent playwright-satirist of Eastern Europe. During the years of communist censorship, he developed a parable form of drama that had great resonance—political and moral—for audiences in Poland and throughout the entire Eastern bloc. In East Germany and the Soviet Union, where for the most part his works were officially banned until the late 1980s, daring groups staged unauthorized performances. Listening between the lines of his plays, spectators in the iron-curtain countries found pointed allusions to the tyranny of the state under which they suffered. The laughter of derision unleashed in the theater was liberating, demystifying arbitrary power and dispelling fear by revealing its sources.

Whereas in the East, politics seemed to define Mrożek's work as dissident and antiregime, in the West the Polish playwright was hailed as an exponent of the theater of the absurd and lumped with Beckett, Ionesco, and Pinter.

From the perspective of the twentieth-first century, both these labels may be discarded as obsolete. The cold war is over, and the theater of the absurd has receded into the past as a trend of the '50s and '60s, but Mrożek's plays seem as fresh as ever, open to new interpretations and innovative stagings. The reason is simple. Mrożek is a writer of imaginative dramas and tales that can be read in different ways at different times in the course of one's own life and in the history of the world.

After the collapse of communism and the dismantling of the old Soviet bloc, Mrożek's studies of tyranny and exile have lost none of their satirical bite, and have in fact acquired new meanings. In their obsessive concern with conspiracy, terrorism, and paranoia, and their exposure of the hidden links between culture and power, his plays seem strikingly contemporary.

As long as humanity is caught in mechanisms of dominance and submission and forced to play masked games imposed by the wielders of authority, his works will find responsive audiences. Like all effective parables, his plays are cast in universal forms that leave the determination of particular meanings to the spectator.

Short-story writer, cartoonist, essayist, filmmaker, and playwright, Mrożek is hard to categorize as either an artist or a person. Having lived half his life abroad as an outsider, displaced person, and exile—in Italy, France, Germany, America, and Mexico—he has now returned to Poland.

Mrożek is too much his own man to be enrolled in any school, of either the East or the West. His spirit is one of contradiction; his entire work challenges slogans and ridicules stereotypical thinking, opposing the complexity of human experience to simplistic reasoning and absolutist solutions.

Seen through Sławomir Mrożek's Glasses is the title of one of his early collections of cartoons that reveals his highly personal vision of the world. To the Polish public, Mrożek's persona as a hawk-eyed satirist is familiar: rimless glasses with metal frames, beaklike nose, long, svelte silhouette, quizzical stance, and furled umbrella. It is a studied, controlled appearance—the silhouette of a man standing apart and alone, coolly viewing the follies and vices of mankind with scorn, sarcasm, and even a touch of compassion.

Mrożek has always been obsessed by history: his own history and that of his country and his age. In his short autobiography (written and published in English in 1989) he tells us he has long sought for a way out of history. It is both his nemesis and his muse. "I have not only been enslaved by the monster but also fascinated by it," Mrożek confesses.

The entire body of his creative output reveals the composite self-portrait of an era scarred by catastrophic social upheavals. Individual works, written at various points in his career, present different segments of the picture, detailing the wounds inflicted on the victims of history: oppression, flight, uprootedness, and exile. Mrożek is above all a chronicler of the fears and anxieties that first arose in the early 1900s as old empires began to crumble, then grew to nightmare proportions with the violence of twentieth-century wars, revolutions, and dictatorships, and that still haunt us today, perhaps more insidiously than ever.

The itinerary of Mrożek's creative journey is the subject of this introduction. According to the author himself, the course of his life has been shaped, from the outside, by the impact of history and, from within, by two competing pulls: his desire for adventure and his need for order. My approach to Mrożek's stories, plays, and drawings is to trace their origins and explore their meanings at the point of collision between history and his own inner imperatives. Although I devote considerably more attention to the works included in the reader, I also examine briefly other examples of his writings necessary for an understanding of the development of his art.

II LIFE 1930–57

Born in a small town in southern Poland and educated in nearby Kraków, Mrożek has his cultural roots in the old Austro-Hungarian Empire, to whose traditions and values he has always felt an heir. He grew up in newly independent Poland at a time when it was veering toward right-wing authoritarian rule and menaced with extinction by its two totalitarian neighbors, Nazi Germany and Bolshevik Russia. Nine when the Second World War started, he was a member of a lost generation of those too young to fight but whose lives were ravaged by the war, German occupation, and harsh imposition of communism crushing any hopes for a better future.

But as Stalinism started to falter in the early 1950s, a crack in the ice, known as the Polish pre-Thaw, offered a tiny opening through which the bold could make their way toward the light. Here Mrożek's story is representative of a small group of highly talented and intensely ambitious young artists in their twenties (such as Andrzej Wajda, Zbigniew Cybulski, Roman Polanski, and Jerzy Grotowski) who, driven by a long-suppressed desire to get ahead and break out of the gloomy stagnation, burst on the cultural scene almost simultaneously. Hunger for stylish clothes, an affluent lifestyle, and perhaps someday even an automobile fired creative dreams, and devotion (real or feigned) to Marxist-Leninist ideology provided opportunities and rewards.

Mrożek has explained his own deluded infatuation with Stalinism from 1950 to 1953 as an aberration of youth. Although he never actually became a party member, getting aboard the communist bandwagon satisfied a need to rebel against his conservative rural Polish background and, at the same time, enabled him to obtain choice journalistic positions and embark on a meteoric career at a very young age.

Gifted with a perfect ear for mimicking styles, Mrożek was able to turn out feature articles and columns that were paradigms of socialist realist prose (then the reigning dogma)—so good they almost seem to be parodies. His reverence for Stalin was exemplary; he praised the workers' brigades that outdid their quotas and denounced capitalist America for its imperialist war with North Korea. At twenty-three he joined the Writers'

Union and received state awards and distinctions usually reserved for hacks who had long served the propaganda machine dutifully.

Gradually, however, Mrożek started to distance himself from the official line and develop his own individual voice in satirical sketches about sleepy old Hapsburgian Kraków with its venerable skeletons in the closet. Now Mrożek wore tapered black pants and wrote about the need for style in life and in the arts. By the mid-fifties, he abandoned journalistic reporting and devoted himself entirely to writing entertaining stories and novels and, for a short period, theater criticism.

Mrożek's stint as a theater critic—from 1955 to 1957—coincided with the remarkable rebirth of the Polish avant-garde. He saw Tadeusz Kantor's opening production at Cricot 2, *The Cuttlefish* by Stanisław Ignacy Witkiewicz—which constituted the playwright's posthumous rediscovery—as well as other works designed by Kantor, such as *St. Joan, Measure for Measure,* and Jean Anouilh's *Antigone.*

In his reviews, Mrożek articulated an aesthetic for the theater that would help to shape his own practice. He objected to realism and to historical accuracy in the handling of time and place, preferring instead plays that dealt metaphorically with contemporary issues of interest to a broad public. Suspicious of an abstruse and dogmatic avant-garde, he valued clarity, intelligibility, and humor, although he admits that history, with its wartime traumas, has robbed the members of his generation of natural gaiety and made their laughter bitter, ironic, and despairing. And, championing the prerogatives of the creator, he questions the right of the director and designer to refashion the playwright's work and of the critic to pass judgment on it.

Saying good-bye forever to dogmatic ideology, Mrożek now discovered a new sense of freedom in writing that sprang from his own imagination, not the dictates of a political doctrine. The stories, drawings, and soon plays that he began to produce revealed a skewed, cockeyed perception of life and quirky nonchalance that appealed vastly to a public sick and tired of socialist realism's preposterously idealized pictures of a glorified future that was just around the corner.

III   *THE ELEPHANT* 1957

Mrożek first made his name as an original artist with *The Elephant* (1957), a collection of forty-two very short satirical stories about People's Poland, in which a straight-faced narrator recounts the odd and unnerving things that happen in the provincial backwaters when Marxist dogma encounters local superstition. The real and the fabulous, civilized and barbarous, human and animal—each is inextricably implicated in its opposite.

In his tales, Mrożek serves as cultural archeologist, cutting through rock surfaces to reveal diverse strata of civilization jutting into one another in odd-shaped formations. Time warps bring together different historical eras and their incompatible mentalities. Small-town officialdom and rule-ridden bureaucracy swallow wholesale the wonders of modern technology and spout ideological slogans promising miracles.

In such a communal world, where everyone watches everyone else, the highest civic virtue is to conform. Not calling attention to oneself becomes the order of the day. The writer whose stories don't fit prescribed categories, the actor who grows too big for his roles in a theater of midgets—anyone who stands out is suspect and subject to surveillance. The lion in the Coliseum plays it safe by refusing to eat the Christians for fear they may eventually come to power.

Although Mrożek depicts the darkest Stalinist days in Poland, the atmosphere in these fables is more *Alice in Wonderland* than *1984*. Instead of unmasking naked power, Mrożek parodies nonsensical modes of thought, ridiculous cultural clichés, and distorted ways of perceiving the world that dialectical materialism has fostered. The landscape of these tales is a familiar one, alive with celebrations, festivities, and institutional gatherings in town parks and squares dotted with statues and brass bands. Willingness to believe in the fantastic is deeply entrenched in superstitious minds.

On a heavy diet of ideology, the civic life of the community has grown totally neurotic. To save money for fulfilling industrial quotas, a rubber elephant at the zoo is inflated with gas—accidentally, the simulated mammal takes off until, punctured by a cactus, it fizzles in the botanical garden, shattering the school children's belief. In these stories Mrożek's satire is whimsical and surreal; he is concerned with the collective follies of a tradition-bound people, primitive yet cunning, trapped in dead social formulas at a point of transition to new pseudo-scientific values. In the final and longest story, "The Chronicle of a Besieged City," hatred of an imagined enemy leads to the spread of terror. The short-sighted old man intent on hunting down the foe and invariably shooting the wrong people will soon reappear in Mrożek's plays, and the narrator who discovers that he himself is in fact the proscribed enemy is the victim hero of many of the playwright's future works.

IV   LIFE: PLAYWRITING—BIM-BOM

When Mrożek turned to theater, he used many of the same themes and characters as in his sketches and stories, which had often been monologues perfectly suited to the stage. It is fair to say that he was naturally drawn to the dramatic form. But to discover the roots of his playwriting, we need to go back for a moment to his early work as cartoonist, which had sharpened his satirical vision and given him a formidable dramatic technique. With a few bold strokes of the pen, he had learned to make the sort of rapid synthesis of abstract and concrete that captures the essence of a situation or a concept. He called this kind of drawing an ideogram, and it became the basis of his theatrical style.

Because of his success as a humorist, Mrożek was invited in the mid-1950s to work with the Gdańsk student theater Bim-Bom, one of the new amateur troupes gaining prominence in the growing quasi freedom of pre-Thaw Poland. Directed by two professional actors (who would soon become film stars) Zbigniew Cybulski and Bogumił Kobiela, Bim-Bom drew its inspiration from the popular arts of circus, carnival, music hall, and film. By staging poetic images and loving parodies of popular culture, all timed to the split second, Bim-Bom brought a bit of gaiety and bright color to the gray, regimented lives of their fellow students.

In 1956, Mrożek served a six-month theatrical apprenticeship in Gdańsk, when he participated in Bim-Bom's second program, *Joy in Earnest*. Celebrating the Chaplinesque little man, all the numbers illustrated one central theme: the contrast between two paired but opposite human types found everywhere—roosters and organ-grinders—whose images were projected on the curtain even before the show began. Roosters appear as self-important, soulless, overbearing officials, always crowing or showing their tails, whereas organ-grinders are uncertain dreamers and poets of everyday life, playing what is in their hearts.

Mrożek's nine-minute skit for Bim-Bom, "The Professor," is a tightly organized, precisely structured orchestration of sights and sounds. To put off the daily mathematics lesson, students in the gymnasium class get the old professor to recall his one visit to Vienna years ago and tempt him to impersonate the orchestra conductor at the Burgtheater. The sudden entry of the school director, a bureaucratic rooster, cuts short a magnificent performance by the professor, who embodies the lost values of the past.

Bim-Bom taught Mrożek his craft. There he learned the importance of rhythm and tempo, acquired a sense of economy and exact timing, and adopted a cabaret aesthetic of direct communication with the audience. Bim-Bom also gave him the catalytic device of a pair of ideologically opposed characters and confirmed in him his preference for parody as the truest of voices.

But Mrożek was temperamentally unsuited to belonging to any group. He soon tired of the communal life of a theater collective like Bim-Bom and sought his own road to fame by writing plays in a new mode that was analytical rather than lyrical and sentimental (like *Joy in Earnest*).

V POLICE, OUT AT SEA, CHARLIE, STRIPTEASE

Mrożek's sardonic humor filled a real need in a beaten-down society and was enthusiastically adopted by the Polish public. His stories and plays gave audiences a way of laughing both at the regime and at themselves as victims of the system. It was the self-ironic shared laughter of the abused acknowledging their own comical helplessness and loss of dignity in the face of the daily absurdity of their lives.

Utilizing the same fantastic postulates as in his stories, Mrożek conceived of a new mode of drama not as an imitation of reality, but rather as the construction of model situations revealing cultural, social, and historical processes. The dramatic technique is that of testing of a hypothesis.

In his early cabaret-style plays—*The Police, Out at Sea, Charlie,* and *Striptease*—he starts with a suddenly imposed dilemma of a drastic nature and then develops this absurd premise to its logical consequence. These plays examine the operation of power in closed monolithic totalitarian regimes. The language—the jargon and pseudo-logic—is imposed on the characters by the system to conceal the brute force and violence underneath that sustain it.

In *The Police,* when the last political prisoner finally abandons his opposition to the regime, the police are forced to recruit from their own ranks a sergeant volunteer to play the role of a freedom-loving revolutionary and then to imprison him in order to ensure their own continued existence. Interrogated as to his terrorist plans, the sergeant now starts to think as though he were an anarchist and, given a bomb to test his intentions, he throws it at the general. Now the police have plenty of work to do again. Mrożek's first drama, set in a mythical Austro-Hungarian realm, shows that the self-perpetuation of the police state is due to every one's complicity. On the higher levels of power, the chief of police and the former prisoner, who has become the general's aide-de-camp, manipulate reality through spurious reasoning and mythologies of the common good, while at the bottom of the hierarchy the sergeant willingly sacrifices himself to keep the system going.

In *The Police* and three one-acts, which are swift and telegraphic in the unfolding of their action, the absence of psychological motivation renders the characters passive victims, puppets that respond to the demands of the model situation. Identity is imposed from outside and confirmed by acquiescence to circumstances. These efficient, economical works, which combine clarity of form with the resonance of parable plus great technical mastery of theatrical effect, proved striking in performance and immediately established Mrożek as an original new voice in Polish drama. Audiences understood the game that was being played and immediately took on the part that was assigned them of deciphering the code.

But here an important question of interpretation arises. Do Mrożek's parables contain allusions to actual events and people contemporaneous to their composition, or are they autonomous structures, reflecting abstract and general processes, without exact parallels or analogues outside themselves?

In the "Author's note on the production of *The Police*," Mrożek categorically rules out extrinsic readings of his text, calling for a strict theatrical presentation: "The play does not contain anything except what it actually contains." The rest of the "Author's Note" consists of a series of negations, disallowing the play to be committed to any genre or style, and concluding with the following theoretical principle: "While I know what this little play is not, I do not know what it is, and it is not my duty to explain what it is. This must be discovered by the theater." This mistrust of conceptual imposition from above will be the playwright's enduring credo.

Mrożek's characteristic method of definition is by opposition, exclusion, and rejection. Bred on the lies of communist propaganda, he has a purely negative conception of truth and knows only what is not true. For example, the playwright's brief letter of protest published shortly after the imposition of martial law in Poland is entitled "What It Was Not" (*International Herald Tribune*, 18 December 1981). In this ironic sketch, Mrożek points out that the Polish army is not a third force between the party and Solidarity, and that only if General Wojciech Jaruzelski (the strongman who seized power) arrested himself would this proposition become credible. Such a paradoxical notion is the fundamental line of reasoning of the general in *The Police*, who realizes that for exposing himself to attack he should be under arrest. Mrożek's application of one of his own model situations to a subsequent political event indicates that, no matter how purely conceptual these theatrical mechanisms may have been at their origin, history constantly supplies new referents and analogues.

In *The Police* Mrożek doesn't attack the system directly, but shows the flaws in the reasoning that supports it by appealing to experience and common sense. When ideological or verbal constructs are confronted with reality, the characters themselves can see the falsity of the intellectual claims. Mrożek unmasks the hidden contradictions, magic thinking, and false causality behind the official language and the ideology that props it up.

In the ingeniously schematic one-act plays *Out at Sea* (1960), *Charlie*, and *Striptease* (both 1961), the victims of ideological entrapment—defined by the arbitrary situations in which they find themselves—feel compelled to invent reasons for their own victimization. The structure of these tragifarces is neatly symmetrical, and the dialogue rich in circular reasoning, rhetorical self-deception, and logical quibbles. Starting from absurd premises, these short plays develop a single action to its logical conclusions. The dramatic rhythm accelerates as the human puppets succumb to the social pressures masquerading as historical necessity.

In *Striptease*, Mrożek turns an erotic nightclub act into a political and philosophical metaphor for exploring human self-delusion and cowardice in the face of arbitrary power. An opposed pair—aggressive doer and passive thinker—respond to pressure from above by struggling for dominance between themselves, the aim being to gain power and bring about the "other's" submission. Oppression works its way down the hierarchy of superior/inferior. Both are victims of a superior force, which assumes the shape of a hand and imposes an official language, which shapes their identity and determines the nature of their struggle against it. The partially open door suggests that the victims are more caught up in the discussion of freedom than in the possibility of escape from the room. Mrożek traces the comic growth of terror as abject victims, confronted with what they imagine to be historical necessity, hasten to conform to the demands of absolute power.

In *Charlie*, the tracking down of an invisible enemy—known only as Charlie—gives rise to fear and paranoia. The witch hunt takes the form of a visit to an oculist's office, which becomes a hunting field. Sight and sighting are the central issues. The hunter-patients need good glasses; with the "right" lenses, everyone looks like Charlie. At first a horrified witness to the terror unleashed in his office, the oculist gradually becomes first a reluctant participant and then an active and willing collaborator.

As often happens, Mrożek returns to the same theme later in *Vatzlav*, where General Barbaro orders the castration of all camels, without ever defining who is a camel. Everyone becomes suspect as a potential enemy of the state and subject to liquidation; any political, racial, or social group or class can be identified as "camels" and hunted down. In *Charlie,* Mrożek analyzes how hatred, transformed into fanaticism, gives rise to repression and terrorism.

In *Out at Sea,* three civilized men shipwrecked on a raft in the middle of the ocean decide to electioneer as to who will be the first meal. The message to those on different steps of the social ladder is "eat or be eaten"— saving one's own skin means devouring someone else's. Both eaters and eaten are impelled to find ideological justifications in history for their participation in society's cannibal dinners. Even when a can of beans is discovered, Fat and Medium conceal it, because Thin is so convinced of the necessity of his own martyrdom that it would be a shame to stop him.

Out at Sea bears comparison with "Cannibalism in the Cars," a story from 1875 by Mark Twain, a pessimistic satirist and professional humorist with whom Mrożek has more in common than might be imagined. In Twain's story, a group of men going by train from St. Louis to Chicago are caught in a terrible blizzard and, a week later, with starvation staring them in the face, they make nominations and conduct political campaigns as to who will be eaten at each meal. Whereas Twain simply delights in the glee with which political man eats his fellow man, the Polish playwright lets the eaten celebrate being consumed.

Mrożek reveals himself as a master of dramatic construction in short plays with two or three characters. His craftsmanship, sense of timing, and ability to distill complex ideas into terse dialogue make his plays occasions for virtuoso performance.

VI *TANGO*

Premiered a year after Mrożek's departure from Poland, *Tango, or The Need for Order and Harmony* (1964) enjoyed international success and became the most widely performed Polish play of the decade.

The culmination of Mrożek's first period of playwriting, *Tango* takes the family as a microsociety, or scale model, for studying the history of modern Europe. The disintegration of the three different generations of the farcical Stomil clan, each representing a further step in the historical debacle, charts the decline and fall of European civilization from turn-of-the-century liberalism through interwar avant-garde experimentation to the present-day triumph of totalitarianism.

By the use of parody and allusion (citations come from Shakespeare and the Polish romantic and modernist traditions), Mrożek creates a multi-layered work—a museum of modern European art, manners, and morals—which serves as a prism for viewing the relations of culture to power and for assessing the intelligentsia's responsibility for glorifying force as the ultimate value.

Arthur, the young son, can find no meaning in the world his elders have created for him; his avant-garde parents—products of the rebellious 1920s, who dabble in experimental theater—have left him nothing to rebel against. Seeing the chaos all about him, Arthur concludes that there has been enough freedom; now convention must be reestablished and cultural memories reawakened. To clean up the mess at home and to impose order, the young hero realizes that he must have a wedding, following the mythic precedents set in plays by Stanisław Wyspiański (*The Wedding*) and Witold Gombrowicz (*The Marriage*). Only such a formal ceremony can revive old traditions and restore former disciplines. For Mrożek, fashion is a central metaphor for civilization, and the attempted manipulation of its disguises is a grab for creative power.

As a result of Arthur's domestic coup d'état—a minor counterrevolution against the license and anarchy of his parents' avant-garde generation—everyone is forced to dress neatly in old-fashioned gowns and suits, but the disillusioned young hero soon sees that he is creating form without content and that it is impossible to reinstate the absolutes of tragedy once the values of the past have eroded.

Abandoning his futile efforts to bring about a spiritual rebirth in his family, Arthur arrives drunk at his ridiculous formal wedding (complete with Mendelssohn's music and posed group photographs). The entire performance, which Arthur has staged, has failed in its desired effect and is as absurd as his father's avant-garde posturing. Ala, Arthur's new bride, with whom he has been sleeping for some time, has been deceiving him with Eddie, the sleazy semiliterate goon who has been lurking in the background and fraternizing with the hero's mother.

In search of any imperative as long as it is absolute, Arthur—inspired by alcohol and disgust—discovers the idea of death-dealing power as the only value that can exist in a world of chaos and nullity, but he is too weak and too much an intellectual to put his own brilliant principle into practice. Instead, it is the gross boor Eddie who preempts the idea and suddenly kills its inventor with two sharp blows on the back of the neck with the butt of Arthur's own revolver. Thereupon the thug assumes command in the crumbling, decadent family. Within Arthur's abortive coup, a second, genuine shift in power takes place with surprising speed. The elite's admiration for the strongman who restores order leads to a brutal dictatorship that despises intellectuals.

Tango ends with a striking scenic effect that encapsulates the dramatic action in a final telling image, whose components are clothing and dance. Asserting that at last there will be order in the household, Eddie puts on Arthur's coat, which is too small for his broad shoulders, and Great-uncle Eugene, muttering that he submits to brute force although he despises it in his heart, unlaces his new master's shoes. Then Eddie plays a recording of a tango (Mrożek specifies that it is to be "La Cumparsita")—the dance that for Arthur's parents symbolized liberation and rebellious abandon—on an old wind-up gramophone with a large horn and forces the great-uncle, pitiful relic of once elegant old Europe, to dance with him. Here Mrożek makes another allusion to Wyspiański's *Wedding,* which ends with a famous somnambulistic dance of hopelessness and stagnation suggesting the vicious circle of death-in-life.

In the original staging of Mrożek's play in Warsaw, the compelling music of the tango did not stop even after the curtain fell, but continued out in the street as the audience left the theater. Eddie, the new man, keeps on tangoing cheek to cheek with old Europe, the doddering humane tradition that always capitulates to brute force and dances to its tune.

The crude boor—juxtaposed to the insecure intellectual—is one of Mrożek's essential character types. A barbarian within, he remains on the periphery of the action until at the very last moment he seizes power—like Fortinbras after Hamlet's death. The members of Arthur's family, blind to the danger posed by Eddie, respond to his "otherness" by praising him as natural man unconstrained by civilization—an identity that will come back to plague them.

For Polish and Eastern European spectators, there was little doubt as to what Eddie stood for in general: He was the sinister tide of violence that brought to power and maintained totalitarian regimes. Who he actually was became a subject of speculation. Western European countries with powerful communist parties and discontented masses also understood the menace. But British and American theater artists and spectators had difficulty grasping the class dynamics of a role that had little counterpart in their own experience. Since the fall of communism, new stagings of *Tango* have had to rethink the problem of Eddie's otherness. More recent historical events have constantly enlarged its possible meanings and permitted new interpretations. A 1990

Leningrad production, for example, made Eddie a mafioso and changed "La Cumparsita" to a theme from the film *Once Upon a Time in America.*

Tango found favor with actors, directors, and audiences through its absurd humor, grotesque characterization, and precise movement and gesture, making Mrożek the most widely performed contemporary Polish playwright, a position he retained for the next twenty-five years despite his émigré status, antiregime stance, and occasional brushes with censorship.

After *Tango,* Mrożek, now living abroad, left behind the closed circle of repressive regimes to examine the refugee's flight into the unknown, the paradoxes of freedom, and the ironies of exile. He enlarged the scope and variety of his work and tempered its paradigmatic quality with detailed interplay among human characters and their everyday experiences.

VII EXPATRIATION 1963–75

By the time he turned thirty-three, Mrożek was a celebrity in Poland; he had fame, money, and a growing international reputation; he was widely published and performed in both the East and West. The high status traditionally accorded to writers in Poland was exploited by the communist regime, which gave its famous artists all sorts of privileges and material benefits, even allowing them a certain amount of leeway to dissent. In return, all the artists were asked to do was consent to be a display in the regime's propaganda showcase. Realizing that assured success for life within a stifling closed system was a dangerous temptation, Mrożek refused to play the game. His two-month visit to America in 1959 had already opened his mind to the limitless possibilities awaiting him in the unpredictable world of freedom, where history was less of a burden.

The playwright left Poland for the West early in his career while on a trip to Italy in May 1963. This was a deliberate and carefully thought-out decision, brought about in large part by his desire to prove to himself that he could be an independent artist on the free market and discover his own cultural identity, rather than have it given him by the state. But, paradoxically, although he found it necessary to live and write in a free environment, he continued to compose his plays for audiences in Poland, where—except for the period from 1968 to 1973—they have been constantly and successfully performed. Thus Mrożek was able to become the most popular and well paid of all twentieth-century Polish playwrights, even while living abroad. His experience has been quite unlike that of the Czech or Russian émigré playwrights during the same time, who were denied any hearing on the stages of their homelands.

Reluctant to become part of the émigré community, Mrożek considered himself a Polish writer living abroad rather than an expatriate. He claimed he chose a rootless state of existence because it corresponded to his psychic nature as an outsider, not because he subscribed to the Polish national mythology of exiled writers.

Yet in Italy he was still obliged to maintain his Polish citizenship and forced constantly to apply for passport extensions and visas, making him feel, he admitted, "what all foreigners of uncertain legal status feel [a considerable part of the world population by now]." He knew firsthand the humiliations of exile and its paranoiac fears of homelessness and loss of cultural identity.

Driven by a perpetual need for adventure, Mrożek moved to Paris in February 1968 just in time to witness the student revolution of May, whose socialist ideals left him unmoved and whose anarchistic attacks on Western bourgeois society aroused his fears of disorder, even though he professed no attachment to the world of consumerism.

But for all his apolitical detachment, Mrożek flew into a rage when the Polish army took part in the Warsaw Pact invasion of Czechoslovakia in the summer of 1968. The sight of one slave kicking another to please their common master, Russia, caused him to write a sarcastic letter of protest that he published in *Le Monde* and in *The International Herald Tribune*. The Polish government reacted predictably with denunciations of the author as a turncoat and capitalist lackey. No longer able to straddle the fence, he was finally compelled to become a refugee and apply for political asylum in France, which he was readily granted under the circumstances. It all worked out quite well for the writer, except for the fact that his works were banned at home.

After the death of his wife and his open break with communist Poland, Mrożek found himself completely free and alone. He attempted to realize his vision of himself as an adventurous loner by traveling widely, directing, and making films, as well as by writing, until his new identity as an existential outlaw grew repetitious and boring.

Then, because both the communist authorities and the theater world needed him back as their star playwright, Mrożek was resurrected as a Polish writer, his plays were again performed everywhere in the country, and he returned home privately for visits in the late 1970s. From this point on Mrożek became fully accepted by the Polish government. Although he wrote satirical pieces against the regime after the workers' movement was crushed, he never joined the Solidarity bandwagon, doubting that writers should meddle in public affairs to the detriment of their art.

VIII *VATZLAV*

Vatzlav (1970) begins Mrożek's cycle of émigré plays about a former slave in quest of a new life and cultural identity. Written shortly after Mrożek sought political asylum in France, *Vatzlav* is a transitional work about a hero in transit by an author himself in transit. The play was first published and performed in German and English, and because of censorship (caused less by the play's content than by the author's status as refugee), it could not appear in Poland until almost ten years later in somewhat altered form.

A pastiche of eighteenth-century French philosophical tales like Voltaire's *Candide* and the Marquis de Sade's *Justine,* the play takes the panoramic shape of a series of picaresque adventures. The seventy-seven scenes are cinematographic in the fast deployment of brief tableaux, indicating that Mrożek once thought *Vatzlav* could be adapted as a film. The use of episodic open form represents a departure from the playwright's previous practice of creating closed circular structures, built on model situations that mirror a repressive political regime.

Vatzlav opens under a lowering sky, with thunder and lightning, as the shipwrecked hero is tossed by the sea onto an alien shore. Permitting his double—former self, brother, past history, fellow countryman—to drown, so that he can start a new life without any witness to what he once was, the ex-slave, now a free man in a free world, sets out on a series of adventures in which he attempts to improve his lot and achieve wealth, fame, and honor.

Journeying from country to country, the gullible newcomer grows progressively disabused by his experiences of feudalism, capitalism, and a kind of communism. All his preconceived notions are shown to be false. The freedom of exile proves to be an empty promise, while the pressures of history continue unabated.

Vatzlav, it seems, has been cast adrift in a land of anti-utopia where reason is prostituted to justify the vices of society; where equality is proclaimed, but injustice rules; and where the ultimate argument is always the clenched fist of coercion and violence. But for all these iniquities, Vatzlav is only passing through a chaotic world from which it is still possible to flee for another unknown destination.

The conclusion of Vatzlav is symmetrical; the hero's journey starts over again. After failing to realize his materialistic self-seeking goals, he finds himself back at his starting point: on the coast, retreating into the sea and hoping to reach a distant shore. The sea is a source of both death and birth. By his decision to take along Justine's child (whom she would drown), the ex-slave saves his second double and is reborn, giving life to another whose future may be brighter than his.

Vatzlav has seen the same abuses of power and authority in the free world as in the slave regime; the two systems have much in common and mirror each other in their hypocritical pretenses to equality for all. But the taste of freedom, however empty it proved in practice, has made it possible for the ex-slave to think and to choose an identity for himself, rather than have it imposed by the regime.

The hero of Mrożek's play has a Polish name, *Wacław,* but it is spelled (in the Polish text as well as in translation) *Vatzlav,* in a Westernized phonetic transcription. Starting a new life abroad, Vatzlav sheds an earlier self (much as he let his double drown) and assumes a fresh identity—with a changed orthography facilitating assimilation—that will replace that of ship-wrecked slave.

Mrożek has described Vatzlav in these terms:

"His name suggests that he is Slavic. Yet Vatzlav is the representative of the lower half of humanity in general, of humanity making its way up toward material prosperity, full of longings and complexes. Humanity is in an undefined, transitional phase. Subject to corruption, leading a marginal existence, a potential opportunist of great vitality. His outspokenness is childlike rather than cynical. His craftiness is more a consequence of an instinct for self-preservation than of ill will. At the end of the play he permits himself disinterested reflection, which indicates the ability to grow. A complex character."

Vatzlav is natural man in two senses: He is driven by self-interest and the desire to survive, and he is an innocent open to experience and capable—perhaps—of learning. According to Mrożek's description of his hero in the cast, Vatzlav is "a healthy extrovert, rather stocky"—a mark of his plebeian origins.

This modern everyman, cut off from his roots, wandering homeless, and ready to make every compromise in order to survive, has lost the sense of belonging conferred by serfdom and has left behind the security of prison. He now must face the cruelly competitive and lonely world of freedom.

A perpetual stranger, Vatzlav stands totally apart from the society in which he finds himself. The shipwrecked ex-slave is frequently alone, communing only with himself—and the audience—in lengthy monologues. As an exile, he suffers from the alienation caused by his isolation from contact with his own kind.

The secondary characters in Vatzlav—a colorful mixture of stereotypes with generic names, animal names, real names, and names taken from literature—are what the author calls "theatrical ideograms," by means of which the playwright advances the debate about freedom and equality, nature and civilization, power and morality.

For example, the bloodsucking capitalist Bats are iconographic figures derived from the stereotypical poetics of the propaganda posters from the early period of the Russian revolution. Starting from a privileged position, the Bats' son Bobby rebels against his own class and parents and becomes a bear. The emigrant Vatzlav, on the other hand, fascinated with material things, defends dogs because they protect private property; otherwise wild forest animals would take over. A have-not hoping to become a have, the ex-slave Vatzlav sides with the hunters, not the hunted, with civilization and its laws rather than with the forces of anarchy represented by the Bear and the forest. The episodes involving Bobby and the Bear reflect Mrożek's reactions to the French student revolution of May 1968 and in Western Europe gave rise to attacks on *Vatzlav* as a reactionary work, causing the playwright to feel as rejected by leftist theatrical circles as he already had been by the Polish censor.

In *Vatzlav,* Mrożek exposes the dangers of abstract thought, of which the Genius is the standard-bearer in his demented plans to reform society through reason alone. He represents the optimistic eighteenth-century philosopher who believes in nature as the basis for a civilized and ethical social order, but his daughter Justine, sprung from his head, is his ultimate misconception, personally embodying the refutation of his ideals in the harsh world of experience. Justine—"the just one"—calls to mind the heroine of the Marquis de Sade's novel *Justine, or The Misfortunes of Virtue,* in which goodness is invariably punished and vice rewarded. Mrożek's Justine, like Sade's, is brutally violated, offering a paradigm of the fate of justice in the real world, where the state of nature means perpetual warfare of the strong against the weak.

Vatzlav's display of Justine's naked body in an ideological striptease for paying customers degrades the virtue of justice in the manner of a Sadean voyeuristic spectacle. As Justine, the biological counterpart of abstraction, strips, Vatzlav quotes verbatim from a key text of the French Revolution, "The Declaration of the Rights of Man and the Citizen," passed by the French National Assembly on 27 August 1789. (Perhaps at this point Mrożek was reading French history as he prepared to become a French citizen and enjoy the rights of man.)

If *Vatzlav* can rightly be called Mrożek's homage to the *conte philosophique*, its first Polish production in 1979 was surely a salute to eighteenth-century theater. When Kazimierz Dejmek was finally able to stage the play, he chose the rococo style of performance, with spectacular visual effects, painted scenery that moved before the eyes of the spectators, and elegant period costumes.

After the accords signed by the Polish government with Solidarity in August 1980, leading to a new spirit of freedom and the relaxing of censorship, *Vatzlav* was at last shown as part of the Warsaw Theatre Encounters in January 1981, where it was enthusiastically received. With its biblical reference to Moses leading the children of Israel through the Red Sea to the promised land, Vatzlav's direct address to the audience in his final speech had special meaning for a people who in 1981 expected miracles and hoped that they could pass to the other shore.

IX *EMIGRANTS*

Following *Vatzlav, Emigrants* (1974) depicts a further stage in the journey of the displaced: the limbo of exile. In explaining the play's theme, Mrożek states that the loss of identity of those who settle abroad but remain strangers in another country is a dilemma that he knows firsthand and that has also become a problem for a large number of people, not only Eastern Europeans.

I share the opinion of many that *Emigrants* is Mrożek's most deeply comic and profoundly moving work for the stage. The universality of its theme of expatriation and loss of national roots is now more strikingly evident than it was when written. Because it is an extremely simple play with only two characters and a single set, it is easy and inexpensive to stage. For all these reasons, *Emigrants* has become the author's best known and most accessible work.

Emigrants has also seemed to many to be a new departure for Mrożek— toward a more naturalistic form of drama dealing with real characters in a real situation located in actual time and space. Declaring it the best play ever written on the subject, Martin Esslin—on the basis of his own memories as a Hungarian expatriate—claimed that Mrożek describes the experience of emigrants in an almost clinically accurate way.

The "real" situation is as follows: A haughty intellectual, AA, and a primitive boor, XX—opposite halves of a composite national type—are emigrants who share a grimy basement in a large city, totally isolated from the surrounding foreign world in their self-made prison. To save money to impress the neighbors when he returns home, XX slaves as a day laborer running a pneumatic drill that destroys his health. AA, a political refugee, imagines that he will write a book about human liberty and slavery, although once he has left behind his oppressive homeland, he no longer has any impetus to do so.

When it is said that, with *Emigrants,* Mrożek begins to create "real people," we should remember that realism is only another set of dramatic conventions, one among many modes available to the playwright. In *Emigrants,* Mrożek adopts a number of the conventions of realism, but the names of the characters, AA and XX, and the schematic and parabolic antitheticalness of their temperaments come from a different dramatic tradition. "Motivation" is added to *Emigrants* as another theatrical component, but it does not serve as an overarching principle as would be the case in realistic psychological drama. The characters are still ideograms serving the play's argument.

AA and XX are two halves of a whole, parts of the same language, although at opposite ends of its alphabet. In the old country, they would never have met. Divided by temperament and life experience, they are united by their need for a home and a country, a place to which they can belong. Instead they have become refuse, discarded scraps, which have lost both names and identities. To pass the time, they must play games, make up stories, tell self-aggrandizing lies—or hang themselves. *Waiting for Godot,* part of the cultural memory upon which Mrożek draws, is a central text parodied in *Emigrants.*

The realism of the setting is highly selective, not designed to create a naturalistic environment, but to provide a visual counterpoint to the emigrants' tragic isolation. Mrożek maintains extreme precision and economy of scenic details. Sounds and sights—the gurgling pipes, the sink, the water, the electricity—help to establish the basement as a nether region, subterranean prison, lower intestine, or tomb. Sounds alone convey the outside world from which they are cut off: the steps on the stairs, the noise from the neighbors above, the hum and clang of the city outside, and at midnight the tolling of the church bells.

The duo of worker and intellectual are sustained in their lonely and alienated lives abroad by a symbiotic relationship of mutual antagonism. To satisfy longings for an absent homeland, the rootless pair has created a surrogate family. It is New Year's Eve, a very special occasion that awakens all their cultural memories. As midnight approaches and the sounds of celebrating drift down from above, the two expatriates decide to give a party to usher in the new year, all the while discussing an ever present obsession: their absent native country. As in Wyspiański's *Wedding,* where an upperclass poet marries a peasant girl as a symbolic act of integration, so in *Emigrants* a festive celebration is invoked to unite the divided social classes.

Like Arthur in *Tango,* the intellectual A is a theorist attempting to impose his ideas on the chaos that confronts him. Through an examination of the concept "being free," he conducts an experiment on himself and on his loutish companion. AA's Great Idea is that the primitive boor is a "perfect slave" wedded to meaningless pursuit of material things, while he, an intellectual who has renounced everything for freedom, is perfectly free. But the unpredictable happens, when AA's theory is confronted by the reality of XX's nature; the perfect slave—his human dignity affronted—tears up his hard-earned money. All illusions are stripped away from both the worker and the intellectual. The absolute pursuit of freedom is as insanely destructive as the absolute pursuit of material things—both are forms of slavery.

The bankruptcy of their illusions leaves the two emigrants alone in the void of their freedom. All that is left them is a human bond between two people who have nothing in common and cannot stand one another. Is this a point of departure, or of no exit? The mutual interdependence of AA and XX can be seen as the emergence of a new set of values in Poland—foreshadowing the alliance of the worker and intellectual in Solidarity and reflecting a compromise between classes that can lead to a new middle-class mentality and serve as the basis of postcommunist democracy. The play provides no answer; it ends not with words but with pure sounds: a comic snore and a tragic sob.

X   THE HUNCHBACK

Premiered at the same time as *Emigrants, The Hunchback* (1975) deals with the breakdown of identity in times of crisis and moral chaos, when fears of conspiracy and terrorism grip the psyche. Here Mrożek approaches the theme of social disintegration in a distanced manner.

Cast in the mold of a fin-de-siècle comedy of manners, *The Hunchback* takes place in an isolated resort on the periphery of the decaying Austro-Hungarian Empire. In Mrożek's social history of the modern era, *The Hunchback* presents an early stage of decline, when revolution is only a storm gathering on the horizon at the turn of the century. But it is ominously the beginning of the end of the old order.

Beneath the picturesque operetta setting with its stylized "ancient regime" banter there lurk apocalyptic fears of disaster. The stereotypical characters, who come in pairs, are engaged in trivial sexual intrigues but seem to be playing more sinister hidden roles, creating a clash between form and content productive of the grotesque.

The mood in *The Hunchback* is one of loneliness, alienation, and growing terror. The Stranger, a double agent with a perverse hankering for the revolutionary Student, observes: "In the times which are coming upon us, the question of identity, ladies and gentlemen, becomes increasingly difficult to resolve satisfactorily. . . . We are being confronted by another world: a world of antithetical identity." The barbarians are not at the gates, but are within the structure of society itself. Not far below the veneer of civilization, violence is waiting to break out, and spreading paranoia gives rise to theories of conspiracy and fear of terrorism.

Seemingly about the past and out of step with its own time, *The Hunchback* is a "retro" comedy that calls attention to its own literary and theatrical ancestry. Theatrical styles quoted by Mrożek come from Ibsen and the symbolists, comedy of manners circa 1900, Gorky, and Chekhov (one of his favorite authors and sources for pastiche). For Mrożek, parody is form of historical consciousness and a means of carrying on a dialogue with the past.

Theatrical artifice is the dominant characteristic of Mrożek's fin de siècle: For the dramatis personae of *The Hunchback,* life is a performance, and each attempts to be the author or director of the scenario that they are enacting.

The concept of the barbarian is the key to the enigma of *The Hunchback*. The social group defines itself in relation to the threat posed by the other, barbarian or outsider. In his essay, "Needed: A Shark," Mrożek writes: "We are tormented by ourselves. We need not so much a Moses as an Enemy. The appearance of a common Enemy for all mankind, from outside humanity, perhaps could put an end to our destruction of ourselves by ourselves."

The Hunchback is the central figure around whom all events unfold; his presence leads to the dissolution of all the other characters' stable identities.

The guests at the inn react in self-revealing ways to the innkeeper's "abnormality" or "otherness" that threatens them and unleashes their aggression. Their dread of this "monster" gives rise to pretense, lying, and fraud. Here Mrożek echoes Witold Gombrowicz's *Ivona, Princess of Burgundia,* in which the heroine's ugliness and deformity arouse the cruel hostility of the entire court and define the courtiers' own moral misshapenness.

Mrożek has explained the mysteriousness of his looming protagonist this way: "The Hunchback can be understood as synonymous with 'existence.' . . . He can represent different kinds of minorities: racial, social, biological. He represents all those who are 'different than us' and thus 'must be worse.'" Those who fear and despise him have their own "psychic hump" or interior "crookedness" in the form of psychological impairments and neuroses; beneath its fine clothing, the entire Belle Époque is revealed to be hunchbacked. Like Eddie in *Tango,* the ubiquitous Hunchback is an ambiguous, menacing figure, silently performing his duties as host of the inn and suddenly appearing out of nowhere with his "huge, curved gardening knife." His true identity is never resolved. Although the guests read their own anxieties into him, the Hunchback is simply what he is, never taking the audience into his confidence or disclosing his inner self. He is constant and unchanging in a world of flux, speaking only of what is real and actual.

Like everyone in the play, the Hunchback has his double: the mountain bearing his name, where satanic rites were once practiced and an old mill is blown up: a symbol of revolution, the Stranger announces, the work of the new barbarians. Is the Hunchback-innkeeper one of them, or is he to be their victim?

The course of events has no clear direction. The action leads nowhere, and there is no resolution, simply a dissolution of ties and ultimately dispersal. As in Chekhov's *Cherry Orchard,* the denouement of *The Hunchback* takes the form of departures. One by one the characters leave in panic until the stage is empty—except for the Hunchback. A process of progressive reduction has left only a series of negations: no newspapers, no telephones, no coffee, no horses, no peasants, and finally no guests.

The visitors have had to fend for themselves and leave "on foot." Emptiness and nothingness prevail. The norms of civilization have broken down; the expectations of the audience have been frustrated. Yet, until the very last the Hunchback has gone about his duties and attended to his daily routine as an innkeeper. Then he closes his establishment and disappears into the house. A sense of impending disaster engulfs the stage.

Unlike *Tango,* which is a self-contained private world functioning allegorically, *The Hunchback* is a drama that refers directly to an outside world, from which the guests arrive and into which they depart. Mrożek explained that the play "shows that beyond the stage of our personal life, History is unfolding and one day enters our life." Reports are heard from outside—sometimes literal reports, as with the sound of distant explosions (which may be thunder, fireworks, or the beginning of Armageddon). Thus the stage picture in *The Hunchback* is part of the larger world rather than a replica of it. The Stranger, an emissary from that outside world, discloses, "We are being poisoned by conspiracies, secret societies, plots. . . . There are terrorists." But who are the terrorists? The real terror lies in our inability to answer that question.

We cannot help thinking that the actions of the misshapen innkeeper and the approaching social upheaval are in some mysterious way connected. But these suspicions about the Hunchback may only be our own warped response to the one truly normal character (despite his physical impairment). As spectators we are made to experience the guests' inability to know themselves or others, which proves to be a far worse deformity than any hump. This is a disturbing play about the roots of paranoia and violence in the human psyche.

XI   ANIMAL FABLES

Man and beast analogues, so essential to satirists and moralists from Aesop to Thurber, are plentiful in Mrożek's stories, plays, and cartoons. Animal protagonists are well suited to reveal the bloody fangs beneath the masks of culture and to comment on the hunt as a fundamental activity of all supposedly civilized societies.

The bear sequence in *Vatzlav,* in which the hero is forced to become game in the woods, uses the conventions of the animal fable to demonstrate the mechanism governing the sacrifice of the individual for the good of the community. In the 1970s and '80s, Mrożek also wrote a number of very short prose tales with three characters, "the Fox, the Rooster, and I," who engage in whimsical speculations and quibbles about their daily activities.

In a tetralogy of dramatic parables—*Serenade, Philosopher Fox, Fox Hunt,* and *Aspiring Fox* (1976–78)—the characters, both animal and human, while actively pursuing their predatory existence in a cannibalistic social order, use ingenious arguments to justify their conduct or to improve their standing in the evolutionary hierarchy. These cautionary tales, warning of the dangers of overstepping the laws of nature, are among the playwright's wittiest and most engaging works, displaying his technical virtuosity and mastery of the short form. In the tradition of La Fontaine and German fabliaux about Renard, Mrożek's animal fables are variations on serious themes revolving around twin poles of nature and nurture, barbarism and civilization. And even these lighthearted comedies are permeated with fear, and three out of four have violent bloodstained endings,

As literary tradition dictates, the Fox is a crafty gentleman, used to getting his own way and having the run of the woods—thanks to his fast-talking charm. But change is in the air; the old order is threatened by the coming of the barbarians. Through cracks in the veneer of civilization, the brute force that maintains it can now be distinctly seen. Ironically, it is the Fox who laments being tied to the cruel laws of nature and who experiences existential anxiety causing him to seek a new self-definition.

Aspiring Fox and *Philosopher Fox* are monologues addressed to a silent listener. In the first, after encountering a monkey who seems almost human and several species above him, the Fox longs to rise on the evolutionary ladder, but the light of dawn reveals that the monkey is only a mannequin tied to a hurdy-gurdy and that the body of the organ-grinder (Bim-Bom's poet-dreamer) is hanging from a lamppost.

In the second, the Fox, troubled by the worldwide loss of faith, seeks a return to tradition and asks forgiveness for bringing suffering into the world by following his base instincts and eating his fellow animals. After turning to the Bishop for remission of sins, the Fox is shocked to discover that His Holiness is a woman nursing her baby. Although the carnivore is unable to put off his nature, the Bishop can change roles and even gender, because the masks of culture are ever shifting. The Fox now must live in a world without moral absolutes or any firm conviction about his own position in it; culture has given animals an inferiority complex. The last wild and free creature, the Fox sees that the march of civilization is encroaching on his territory.

In *Serenade,* Mrożek juxtaposes the Fox's instincts as a killer to his artistic talents as a stylish deceiver. The bohemian artist plays a sonata on his cello in front of the henhouse as a way to lure the ladies into his clutches. Art has no scruples whatsoever in accommodating the lower drives of nature. But the Rooster, a perfect bourgeois husband, is outraged by the musician's immorality and sends his wives back to the henhouse. He himself falls for the Fox's ruses when he comes out of the henhouse to listen to a whispered secret. After the lights come up, the Fox finishes his sonata to the applause of the three hens dressed in black as widows. When the Fox bows to his audience, we see that his face and hands are smeared with blood.

The last fable in the series and the most complex of the four, *Fox Hunt* is a richly allusive parable about shifting tides of power and the fate of those caught in the crosscurrents. The setting, like that of all the other animal fables, is a refuse heap of civilization, littered with scraps of papers and old tin cans. Humankind has despoiled and depleted the world of nature. In a new egalitarian regime, all the people—and not simply the king and nobles— have the right to hunt; in fact, everyone is required to go hunting, even Uncle, a sick old man in a wheelchair, who does not know how to shoot and would prefer to stay home. The result of such "democratic" hunting on a mass scale is that there are no more wild animals left in the forest, except for one last fox desperately trying to save his hide. This Fox—a clever farm- yard bandit—has, therefore, brought with him into the woods a rooster— a petty henhouse tyrant—to serve as a decoy, hoping to convince the hunters that domestic animals would make good prey. The hunters are ready for the chase and urge the dogs on, the latter being bureaucrats with briefcases who keep careful count of the exact number of times they bark. Suddenly, in a surprising coup d'état as the denouement, the terrifying howling of a pack of wolves can be heard offstage—evidently, not all wild animals are extinct. As the wolves draw closer and closer, the hunters rush for home in panic, and Uncle, abandoned by all, wildly fires his shotgun twice, acci- dentally killing both the Fox and the Rooster who had concealed them- selves in a tree. The Fox's place in the world is no longer assured once wolves replace dogs. Fear and paranoia grow rampant when the customary social hierarchy of top and bottom is suddenly upset by the arrival of a far more brutal force.

XII *ON FOOT*

On Foot (1979) is both a concrete historical drama taking place in early 1945 and a metaphorical fable about the human condition. It is one of the great modern works about war. Even though the action covers only a single night and the following morning, the play presents a vast apocalyptic panorama of catastrophic displacement, social upheaval, and collapse of values during the last days of World War II.

Polish audiences immediately recognize that the scene is Poland at the blank moment in history just before the communists replaced the Nazis as the masters imposing a new order, but no external historical events are ever mentioned either in the dialogue or in the stage directions. The playwright sticks to the particulars of personal experience in order to reach the universal. *On Foot* is above all a play about homelessness and helplessness, and a probing exploration of identity in times of crisis, combining the tale of a young boy's initiation into adult life with the story of a war-weary people's fears of coming political disaster and an allegory of mankind's waiting for a train that never comes.

Mrożek creates a sense of the public cataclysm and its epic dimensions not through reference to actual happenings, but only by showing the impact of these events on a small group of characters, precisely described as to class and age and given historically authentic costumes. The audience is offered less a slice of observed wartime experience than a private recapitulation, a synthetic replica or miniature that draws upon the techniques of parable and parody, not those of realistic historical drama.

The pathos and pomposity of national drama, so characteristic of the Polish theater, are rigorously excluded. The word "Poland" never once occurs within the drama except in a "French" joke in which local moonshine is called "eau de Pologne."

All the violence of history is internalized in the brutality of the members of the group toward one another. We witness the war solely in the reactions of the dramatis personae—and in the inventive use of sound, including music and popular songs, almost as though Mrożek were writing a radio play. Although the war is offstage out of view, it is never out of hearing.

There are nine characters (plus one mute figure) in the dramatis personae of *On Foot*—only two more than in *Tango* or *The Hunchback*—schematically arranged by class and profession as well as by the "road" they are taking on their journey into the future. They constitute a cross section of society. All await the coming of peace and the "new life" that they imagine it will bring—as they don new clothes and hope for an escape from history.

Mrożek uses parody as an activator of cultural memory in order to carry on a conversation with the national heritage. Here lies the special Polishness of *On Foot*. Prominent as an underlying geological formation shaping the landscape of the play is Wyspiański's *Wedding*, which Mrożek had already utilized extensively in *Tango*. From *The Wedding*, Mrożek appropriates powerful techniques of mood and structure: the long night of expectation, the half-dreaming states, and the phantasmagoric atmosphere as characters appear and disappear in shifting pairs. The futile waiting for the phantom train that passes in the night unseen (but distinctly heard, an echo of the Holocaust) also has its genealogical source in *The Wedding,* as does the ghostly fiddler playing for the drunken dance and his dead-soldier double.

An embodiment of death or fate, Mrożek's fiddler calls to mind the living-dead soldier-musician in another memory play composed at exactly the same time. I am thinking of Uncle Staś, the returned Siberian exile in Tadeusz Kantor's *Wielopole, Wielopole.* Of different generations and formations, but both from the Kraków region and both implicated in their Austro-Hungarian antecedents, Mrożek and Kantor are true kinsmen.

A further link to tradition, leading to another stratum in *On Foot,* comes in the form of a citation from Polish literature and theater of the interwar years. Here Mrożek alludes to the Polish avant-garde not by parodying a work, style, or set of conventions, but by directly introducing a figure who is both a double for Witkacy (pen name for the playwright Witkiewicz, 1885–1939) and like a character out of one of Witkacy's plays. Mrożek's Superius is sufficiently similar to the actual Witkacy to make the reference clear, but he is an autonomous character in a Mrożek play, not a historical personage—hence the fictitious name and deliberate departures from biographical truthfulness.

The rites of passages in *On Foot*—the death and birth of regimes and of individual lives to which the characters bear witness—are marked by a ceremony in the manner of Wyspiański's *Wedding,* but Superius and the Boy, however, remain mere spectators to the ensuing drunken orgy (derived partially from Gombrowicz's *Marriage*), in which all the other characters participate.

From his parodic and synthetic interweaving of Wyspiański, Witkacy, and Gombrowicz, Mrożek creates a crucible in which to probe the questions of identity—personal, cultural, and national—that haunt the entire dramatis personae. Old ties of community have been broken—between man and wife, father and child, citizen and society. Delivered from the burden of imposed social identity for the brief moment when neither old nor new order exists, the characters in *On Foot* engage in self-fabrication and undergo sudden metamorphosis, shedding old skins and adopting new ones. As Superius observes, "Only war can give ordinary people freedom. They cease to be what they are or even what they're not."

As the group disperses, impelled by the centrifugal force of history, the clever and opportunistic seek advantageous new roles to play. Only the peasant Father and his Son wish to return "home," maintaining their traditional identity as a pair despite generational antagonisms. The Father gives the boy his boots to wear and the old-fashioned advice "to be honest," as they set off down the road on their lonely journey through a blighted landscape.

Frightened by what he has seen, yet full of hope for the future, the Son in *On Foot* is the focal figure in a drama of expanding consciousness and undergoes a metaphoric initiation into manhood: recognition of the complexity of the human condition. The Boy's spiritual mentor is Superius, his antithetical double. As the weary elite intellectual exits the scene of past defeat, the youthful Son of coarse stock enters the stage of approaching victory. But what victory? The Son reluctantly puts on his Father's shoes.

Mrożek wrote *On Foot* in 1979 when the rise of Solidarity already signaled the beginning of the end for the communist regime. The ultimate temporal perspective of *On Foot* is the author's vantage point in the present, from which he remembers the past and looks back to the beginnings of the world that shaped him and his entire generation as adolescents. From the ruins of the past—the "inertia, entropy and anarchy" that constitute a repeated national ordeal—came the new communist order giving Poland and its inhabitants false identities for the next forty years, until that regime, too, disintegrated.

Mrożek's return to his roots makes the author's presence felt in *On Foot*. When Jerzy Jarocki staged the play at the Kraków Theatre School in January 1981, the actor playing the Son resembled the young Mrożek; the wire-rimmed glasses that he wore and the deep penetrating eyes were almost those of the playwright. Both the Son and his creator were fourteen years old in 1945. And the meeting of the Son with Superius, who initiates him into the nature of reality, affirms the continuity of Mrożek with Witkacy.

XIII   POLITICAL PLAYS

During the politically explosive years 1980–81 as the battle between Solidarity and the communist regime intensified, Mrożek was at the height of his popularity in the Polish theater. In a single season, eighteen of his plays had forty-five premieres, accounting for 982 performances seen by almost a quarter of a million spectators.

The political drama being enacted in Poland led Mrożek to abandon his usual distance from the topical and to attempt to write in a more involved way about the current situation, which he viewed from his apartment in Paris. Mrożek's next two plays were among his most political, but not his most satisfying aesthetically. I shall describe them briefly.

Set in the embassy of a Western democracy located in the capital of a communist totalitarian state (unmistakably the USSR), *The Ambassador* (1981) pits the representatives of the two governments and their opposed philosophies against each other in an ideological duel centering on a political refugee who has sought asylum in the building. The Ambassador of the liberal regime that respects the rights of individuals discovers that his government no longer exists; the ruthless communist Deputy, who advocates the power of terror and hatred to build a better future for mankind, is willing to maintain the fiction that the democratic government is still a reality in order to have a hated enemy, provided that the Ambassador turn over the political refugee. The Ambassador refuses, deciding to keep his word and maintain his honor in what is perhaps a losing battle.

Alpha (written in 1983, published and performed in the West in 1984 but banned in Poland) deals with a national hero patterned after Lech Wałęsa although in the details of his life he is kept deliberately unhistorical. He is identified simply as the leader of a popular national uprising that has been crushed by a military coup. Imprisoned in comparative luxury, Alpha is visited by his captor Beta, the colonel who claims to have saved the country from supposed anarchy—and by his friends and colleagues as well as by representatives of the Church and foreign press. While presenting Alpha in a favorable light as an enemy of abstraction (the root of all evil), Mrożek uses the situation to demystify the notion of the hero and the national myths associated with his deification, in order to show the divisions within a society that cannot hold together in an organic unity.

Realizing that he will be attacked for mixing the historically true and the imaginatively fictional and for desecrating what should be held sacred, the playwright has written a preface "To the Readers," in which he explains that the acceleration of history has turned a human being into a legend, a national myth and a symbol during his own lifetime. Mrożek's aim is to present "the dilemma of a human being who has become a symbol without ceasing to be a human being."

These two plays show the difficulties Mrożek experienced when he attempted to write about actual historical figures and situations and to create characters that are in some ways admirable examples of political courage.

XIV *A SUMMER'S DAY*

After experimenting with topical political plays, Mrożek turned to a subject that engaged him on a different and perhaps deeper level. Eros and Thanatos are the ultimate themes of *A Summer's Day* (1984), which portrays a beautifully choreographed confrontation at the seashore between two antithetical yet complementary types, the man with all the luck and the man without any luck, both planning to commit suicide and both competing to win the favor of an attractive woman whose path crosses theirs. One is reduced to despair because he never wins; the other is bored to death because he never loses. Drawn as cartoon characters or comics in a cabaret skit, Sux and Unsux, like all Mrożek's diametrically opposed pairs, contest one another's positions and provoke trials of strength. Their contrasting temperaments and worldviews wind the spring that drives the clockwork plot.

A virtuoso exercise in its intricate symmetry of construction, *A Summer's Day* was designed as a vehicle for bravura performance. Written for two actors at the Royal Dramatic Theatre in Stockholm in appreciation for the outstanding production of *The Ambassador* in 1982, the play is, ostensibly, a light comedy, an elegantly crafted trifle about nothing, a vacation adventure of two men and a girl at a seaside spa, with parasols and old-fashioned bathing suits. But beneath its bright sunlit surface, *A Summer's Day* is a bitter, brooding play harboring mysterious and unspoken thoughts. Danger and anxiety are the constant subtext.

At the end of the day, transformed by his love for the Lady, the naive and romantic Unsux strides off into the ocean for a swim, exclaiming, "I want to live." Regrettably incapable of learning to swim, he slowly disappears in the water, ironically fulfilling his initial goal of killing himself. The refined, good-mannered, Sux—an expert swimmer—looks on indifferently without stirring (much as Vatzlav had watched his double drown). His poetics of success has left him coldhearted. He readily accepts the unfairness of fate, which permits him to manipulate reality to be rid of his rival. With the rhythmic ebb and flow of the waves as background music, the triumphant and bored Sux confesses to the Lady that it is comforting to think there is always time to commit suicide.

Even though at first sight the comedy appears to lacking any cultural context, *A Summer's Day* is a further stage in the drama of expatriation. Here Mrożek revisits the storm-swept shore of Vatzlav's emigration, now transformed into a seaside resort of pastel colors, where an émigré from the East meets his counterpart from the West. When Mrożek wrote the play in 1984, the gauche underprivileged Unsux could be seen as a newly arrived refugee confronting a well-established cousin who has already made good in the free world. Ten years later after the fall of the Berlin Wall, Unsux might appear as an awkward East German in an ill-fitting suit admiring his elegantly dressed, self-assured West German relative.

Embodiments of East and West, Unsux and Sux are halves of a single self, which through living simultaneously in two realities has produced a split personality drawn toward suicide. They are doubles at odds with one another, one of which must be killed to preserve the cultural identity of the other.

History has now been replaced by a woman, a femme fatale standing in for fate. And death has become the ultimate destination. In an intricate pas de deux, in which first one, then the other follows his partner's steps, Unsux and Sux do a dance of suicide and seduction. They reach a point where there is no exit except through the water. The ocean into which Vatzlav finally plunged was the route to another shore. In *A Summer's Day,* it is the way to the other world.

XV   THE OLD WORLD AND THE NEW

In the pages that remain, I wish to indicate briefly the writer's continuing evolution. In his final plays from the 1980s, Mrożek returns to two of his major themes: the East-West dialectic, from which there seems to be no synthesis except death, and Stalinism, for which he can now write an epitaph.

Contract (1986), set in the lobby of an elegant old-world hotel, sets forth the bizarre pact made between the aging writer Magnus, bored with life and running out of funds, and the feral young Eastern European night clerk Moris, who agrees to murder the older man at an unexpected moment and spare him the bother of committing suicide. The clash between these two different realities and mentalities is pervaded by a deep anxiety about the stability of Europe. The cultured West is senile and moribund, waiting for a nudge from the barbarian East to topple over and die.

In *Portrait* (1987), Mrożek settles accounts with Stalin's poisoned heritage and assesses the human costs of its liquidation. A fitting obituary for the death of communism, *Portrait* demythologizes the rationalizations used to justify submission to historical necessity. Two former colleagues—the one a former believer in Stalinist ideology, the other an opponent denounced by his friend and imprisoned—meet in the 1960s and try to overcome their guilt and pain. The title refers to a picture of the Soviet dictator, but more figuratively the playwright paints the picture of an entire generation that was crippled by fanaticism in the cause of utopian abstractions.

The fall of the Polish communist regime in 1989 appeared to confirm that the playwright had said his last word on these now definitively settled issues. All the walls were down, a democratic era had opened in no longer divided Europe, and Mrożek was about to embark on a new life and career.

In June 1990 the writer came to Kraków to attend the two-week Mrożek Festival held to commemorate his sixtieth birthday. The welcome home was a high-spirited celebration of freedom. Censorship was abolished that very month, officially ending forty-five years of state control of the arts. Now all of Mrożek's work could for the first time be publicly shown and honestly interpreted without recourse to the Aesopean subterfuges and forced hypocrisies of the previous decades. There were twenty different productions of his plays by a dozen theater companies from Poland, the Soviet Union, Hungary, France, Italy, Germany, Switzerland, and the United States.

But the Mrożek Festival was only a hail and farewell for the playwright. He had already started a new life with his Mexican wife Susana on the North American continent, where he finally hoped to reconcile the conflict between order and adventure, go beyond European values, and achieve freedom from history which had weighed so heavily on his existence.

In 1989, Mrożek bought La Epifania, a small ranch in the Mexican mountains whose garden and fruit trees made it seem a paradise. He built a tower with a view to serve as his study, while his wife went into business making jam. In setting out for that distant shore, the writer thought that he had embarked on his last adventure and found his final identity as a rancher. But forces of chaos and disorder were gathering quietly in the background.

The first menace was a life-threatening illness. In late 1990, Mrożek was diagnosed with an aneurysm of the aorta. Emergency eleven-hour surgery miraculously saved him, and after a difficult convalescence of almost a year, he made a full recovery—only to confront new dangers.

First, brush fires threatened La Epifania, then an earthquake caused the tower to tilt, and finally by 1995 banditry and public lawlessness had become so widespread in Mexico that the Mrożeks felt under siege and hired bodyguards, carried weapons, and slept armed. Fear and paranoia grew until they eventually fled La Epifania and returned to Kraków, where the playwright resumed newspaper work, writing feuilletons and drawing cartoons (as he had half a century earlier), while Susana opened a Mexican restaurant.

Mrożek's dramatic output has slackened over the past decade; his four plays of the 1990s are expressions of quite varied creative impulses. They indicate a desire to address contemporary issues in the postcommunist world.

Set in a coffeehouse and presided over by a waiter who serves as master of ceremonies, director, and playwright, *Widows* (1992) is an existential dance of death in slapstick style for two men and two women. Death appears as a silent, black-clad female figure whose mysterious presence brings all the males to their destruction. A farcical parable pushed to burlesque and self-parody, *Widows* reflects Mrożek's recent brush with death, his obsession with mortality, and his exposure to the Mexican Day of Death with its folkloristic humor about the dead.

Subtitled a "Tragic Comedy," *Love in the Crimea* (1993) is one of Mrożek's longest and most ambitious works and the culmination of a lifelong fascination with Poland's powerful neighbor. Panoramic in scope, the play, which runs four hours in performance, is a pastiche of borrowed themes and motifs covering eighty years of modern Russian history, starting with a Chekhovian first act in 1910, going through a Bolshevik second act in 1928, and ending with a postcommunist third act in 1991. The setting always remains a seaside resort in the Crimea—a place that Mrożek regards as crucial in Russian history, culture, and self-imaging. Through the passage of time and the succession of different regimes, the playwright poses the problem of identity in dissolving structures. As the social fabric unravels, love is the only source of constancy. Although some of the characters age, the hero and heroine remain unchanged according to the imperatives of the heart.

Mrożek's point of departure in *Love in the Crimea* is Chekhovian drama, whose scenic codes and linguistic signs he parodies with great skill. The entire drama is a complex web of allusions to Russian literature, history, and culture. The best of Mrożek's late plays, *Love in the Crimea* is primarily of interest as a contribution to the growing literature of Chekhov sequels and elaborations.

When first published, *Love in the Crimea* was accompanied by an author's afterword that contains ten injunctions forbidding directors to make even the slightest departure from the printed text. It is worth citing these stipulations in full as a satirical manifesto by means of which the playwright attacks some of the reigning stage conventions of avant-garde theatrical performance.

Jokingly referred to as Mrożek's "Decalogue," the ten commandments attached to *Love in the Crimea* specify that: (1) nothing will be cut from or added to the text; (2) there will be no change in the sequential ordering of events; (3) the stage design will be executed as given; (4) there will be no additional music beyond that indicated; (5) the songs sung by the performers will be those referred to by the author; (6) the age and gender of the actors will correspond (age approximately, gender absolutely) to the age and gender of the characters whom they are portraying; (7) the passage of time between acts 1 and 2 and between acts 2 and 3 will be marked only as the author has made explicit—some characters age, others do not, and all are played by the same performers throughout; (8) the action will take place only on the stage and the actors will not enter or exit through the auditorium; (9) the acts will begin and end with the rise and fall of the curtain, and scene changes will take place behind the lowered curtain; (10) the theater must print the above items in the program under a title such as "The Author Has Gone Mad" or "The Last of the Mohicans."

As yet unstaged, *A Beautiful View* (1995) consists of two one-act plays with two characters: first, a man and a woman staying in a deserted hotel somewhere in southern Europe; then a woman and a guard in a small, provincial museum. The atmosphere is menacing, full of intrigue and danger. Secret agents and terrorists may be involved, but only gradually is it revealed that the "beautiful view" is of the Balkans during the recent wars—or is it a disguise for Mexico?

Set in nineteenth-century New England, *The Reverends* (1996), which Mrożek wrote in English and translated into Polish, presents ethical dilemmas that result when two competing reverends arrive at the church of a small village, both claiming to be the pastor—one is a woman, the other Jewish. The play is unfinished and without any resolution. Here Mrożek has gone back to the situation of his early play *The Prophets* (1967), where rivalry between two prophets leads to disaster for the claimants to the title.

XVI CONCLUSION

On my first trip to Poland in 1965, I saw *Tango* in the celebrated Warsaw production directed by Erwin Axer. Never, before or since, have I been in a theater auditorium as charged with excitement or seen an audience react to a play with such intellectual and emotional intensity. I realized that something unusual was taking place between playwright, play, performers, and spectators—a shared experience of a different kind than that provided by great theatrical performances in Western theaters, where we are deeply moved, made to laugh uproariously, and filled with awe and admiration. Here, there was rather a sense of complicity, an engagement of the psyche, an intricate mental interplay. Since that September evening in Warsaw almost forty years ago, I have followed Mrożek's work closely, captivated by the special attractions that his plays provide for both spectators and readers.

Given the opportunity to present a selection of his work to the English-speaking public in *The Mrożek Reader,* I have chosen fourteen plays (out of a total of thirty-four), plus ten stories. The plays are those, which—in addition to being my personal favorites—seem to me to be most accessible to non-Polish readers and most viable in the theater. They also represent a wide spectrum of the author's mastery of styles and illustrate the development of his talent over many decades.

Although almost all of Mrożek's plays have been translated into English, until now only his early work has been published in English versions, with the result that the entire second half of his career remains virtually unknown to the Anglo-American public. *The Mrożek Reader* addresses this lack; the last seven plays in the volume appear for the first time in versions by Mrożek's British translator, Jacek Laskowski, who has completed translations of all the playwright's later works for the stage. We should not be deceived by the seeming simplicity of Mrożek's dialogue; it is richly allusive, parodic, and full of humor and verbal fireworks—and therefore a challenge to the translator who must retain the concision and brisk tempo while attempting to capture the resonances.

Looking at his long career, I am struck by the fertility and variety of Mrożek's imagination, by his artistic and intellectual independence, and by the hidden personal dimension of his work. As an exile, having lost a national mission, he renewed himself, refusing to stand still and repeat old formulas. Displaced, he became a playwright of displacement. He moves from a drama of models dealing with political reality to an existential drama of personal experience. His later plays address the precariousness of one's place in the world, given the collapse of old traditions, the paper-thin veneer of civilization covering over barbarism, and the terrorism darkening every corner. He excels at portraying the games that frightened lonely people play with one another and the lies they tell, showing how feelings of inferiority on the part of outsiders lead to the violence of resentment. History has been his teacher and taskmaster; these are the lessons that he conveys.

Mrożek's work forms a coherent whole that is unified by a strong authorial presence and vision, but the shapes that it assumes are bewilderingly different. The playwright displays great mastery of dramatic form without committing himself to any single style. He plays with conventions, modes, and traditions; through pastiche and parody he avails himself of an entire cultural heritage but refuses to be enrolled under any fashionable banner, whether it be black humor, the grotesque, or the absurd. Like most satirists, an upholder of tradition, he has been hostile to the post-1968 avant-garde, its antitextual bias and its leftist ideology.

He goes against the current of late-twentieth-century stage practice in asserting the primacy of the word in the theater and denying the director the right to go counter to the author's wishes expressed in his eloquent and precise stage directions. Despite that several of Poland's finest contemporary directors—Erwin Axer, Kazimierz Dejmek, and Jerzy Jarocki—have given his theater much of their best work.

A rationalist and a moralist, Mrożek defends the individual against the state and takes aim at social norms and cultural stereotypes, which he exploits and ridicules. Rejecting the notion of total theater and theater of cruelty as subjugation by paroxysm, he has created a drama that is addressed to the mind and the imagination. Mrożek's theater—didactic but never dogmatic—has a cognitive function, enabling both readers and spectators to draw conclusions, form judgments, even make decisions.

—Daniel Geroud

The Mrożek Reader

TEN STORIES FROM
THE ELEPHANT

❦

Translated by Konrad Syrop

1

❦

From the Darkness

In this remote village of ours, we are in the grip of terrible ignorance and superstition. Here I am, wanting to go outside to relieve myself, but at this moment hordes of bats are flying about, like leaves blown by an October wind, their wings knocking against the windowpanes, and I am afraid that one of them will get into my hair and I will never be able to get it out. So I am sitting here, comrades, instead of going out, repressing my need, and writing this report for you.

Well, as far as the purchase of grain is concerned, this has been falling ever since the devil appeared at the mill and took off his cap in an elegant greeting. His cap was in three colors: red, white, and blue, and on it was embroidered *Tour de la Paix*. The peasants have been avoiding the mill, and the manager and his wife were driven by worry to drink until one day he splashed her with vodka and set her on fire. Then he left for the People's University, where he is going to read Marxism so that, as he says, he has something to put against those irrational elements.

And the manager's wife died in the flames and we have one more ghost.

I have to tell you that at night something howls here; howls so terribly that your heart almost stops beating. Some say that it is the spirit of poor Karas, who never had a bean, cursing the rich kulaks; others say that it is wealthy Krywon, complaining after death about the compulsory deliveries. A proper class war.

My cabin stands on the edge of the forest, alone. The night is black, the forest is black, and my thoughts are like ravens. One day my neighbor, Jusienga, was sitting on a tree stump by the forest, reading *Horizons of Technology*, when something got at him from the back so that for three days he never stopped staring vacantly.

We need your advice, comrades, because we are alone here, miles from anywhere, surrounded only by distance and graves.

A forester has told me that, at full moon in the clearings, heads without bodies roll about, chase each other, knock at each other's cold foreheads as if they wanted something, but come dawn they all disappear and there are only trees left to murmur, not too loudly because they are afraid. Oh my God, nothing will make me go outside, not even the greatest need.

And it is the same with everything. You talk about Europe, comrades, but here. . . . No sooner do we pour our milk into jugs than hunchback dwarfs appear from somewhere and spit into it.

One night, old Mrs. Glus woke up swimming in sweat. She looked at her eiderdown and what did she see? The small credit, that had been given to us before the elections (so that we could build a bridge here) and died suddenly without Extreme Unction, that credit was sitting on her eiderdown, all green and choking with laughter. The old woman started to scream but nobody came to see what was the matter. Can one be sure who is screaming and from what ideological position?

And at the spot where we were to have the bridge an artist got drowned. He was only two years old, but already a genius. Had he grown up he would have understood and described everything. But now all he can do is to fly about and fluoresce.

Of course, all those happenings have changed our psychology. People believe in sorcery and superstition. Only yesterday they found a skeleton behind Mocza's barn. The priest says that it is a political skeleton. They believe in ghosts and things, and even in witches. True, we have one woman who takes milk away from the cows and gives them fever, but we want to get her to join the Party and in this way deprive the enemies of progress of at least one argument.

How those bats flap their wings. Christ! how they fly and squeak "pee pee" and again "pee pee." There is nothing like those big houses where everything must be inside and there is no need to go into the bushes.

But there are even worse things than that. As I am writing this the door has opened and a pig's snout has appeared. It is looking at me very queerly, it is staring at me . . .

Have I not told you that things are different here?

3

☙❧

The Elephant

The director of the Zoological Gardens has shown himself to be an upstart. He regarded his animals simply as stepping-stones on the road of his own career. He was indifferent to the educational importance of his establishment. In his zoo, the giraffe had a short neck, the badger had no burrow, and the whistlers, having lost all interest, whistled rarely and with some reluctance. These shortcomings should not have been allowed, especially as the zoo was often visited by parties of schoolchildren.

The zoo was in a provincial town, and it was short some of the most important animals, among them the elephant. Three thousand rabbits were a poor substitute for the noble giant. However, as our country developed, the gaps were being filled in a well-planned manner. On the occasion of the anniversary of the liberation, on 22nd July, the zoo was notified that it had at long last been allocated an elephant. All the staff, who were devoted to their work, rejoiced at this news. All the greater was their surprise when they learned that the director had sent a letter to Warsaw, renouncing the allocation and putting forward a plan for obtaining an elephant by more economic means.

"I, and all the staff," he had written, "are fully aware how heavy a burden falls upon the shoulders of Polish miners and foundry men because of the elephant. Desirous of reducing our costs, I suggest that the elephant mentioned in your communication should be replaced by one of our own procurement. We can make an elephant out of rubber, of the correct size, fill it with air, and place it behind railings. It will be carefully painted the correct color and even on close inspection will be indistinguishable from the real animal. It is well known that the elephant is a sluggish animal and it does not run and jump about. In the notice on the railings we can state that this particular elephant is exceptionally sluggish. The money saved in this way can be turned to the purchase of a jet plane or the conservation of some church monument.

"Kindly note that both the idea and its execution are my modest contribution to the common task and struggle.

"I am, etc."

This communication must have reached a soulless official, who regarded his duties in a purely bureaucratic manner and did not examine the heart of the matter but, following only the directive about reduction of expenditure, accepted the director's plan. On hearing the ministry's approval, the director issued instructions for the making of the rubber elephant.

The carcass was to have been filled with air by two keepers blowing into it from opposite ends. To keep the operation secret, the work was to be completed during the night because the people of the town, having heard that an elephant was joining the zoo, were anxious to see it. The director insisted on haste also because he expected a bonus, should his idea turn out to be a success.

The two keepers locked themselves in a shed normally housing a workshop, and began to blow. After two hours of hard blowing they discovered that the rubber skin had risen only a few inches above the floor and its bulge in no way resembled an elephant. The night progressed. Outside, human voices were stilled and only the cry of the jackass interrupted the silence. Exhausted, the keepers stopped blowing and made sure that the air already inside the elephant should not escape. They were not young and were unaccustomed to this kind of work.

"If we go on at this rate," said one of them, "we shan't finish before the morning. And what am I to tell my missus? She'll never believe me if I say that I spent the night blowing up an elephant."

"Quite right," agreed the second keeper. "Blowing up an elephant is not an everyday job. And it's all because our director is a leftist."

They resumed their blowing, but after another half hour they felt too tired to continue. The bulge on the floor was larger but still nothing like the shape of an elephant.

"It's getting harder all the time," said the first keeper.

"It's an uphill job, all right," agreed the second. "Let's have a little rest."

While they were resting, one of them noticed a gas pipe ending in a valve. Could they not fill the elephant with gas? He suggested it to his mate.

They decided to try. They connected the elephant to the gas pipe, turned the valve, and to their joy, in a few minutes there was a full-sized beast standing in the shed. It looked real: the enormous body, legs like columns, huge ears, and the inevitable trunk. Driven by ambition, the director had made sure of having in his zoo a very large elephant indeed.

"First class," declared the keeper who had the idea of using gas. "Now we can go home."

In the morning, the elephant was moved to a special run in a central position, next to the monkey cage. Placed in front of a large real rock, it looked fierce and magnificent. A big notice proclaimed: "Particularly sluggish. Hardly moves."

Among the first visitors that morning was a party of children from the local school. The teacher in charge of them was planning to give them an object lesson about the elephant. He halted the group in front of the animal and began:

"The elephant is a herbivorous mammal. By means of its trunk it pulls out young trees and eats their leaves."

The children were looking at the elephant with enraptured admiration. They were waiting for it to pull out a young tree, but the beast stood still behind its railings.

". . . The elephant is a direct descendant of the now extinct mammoth. It's not surprising, therefore, that it's the largest living land animal."

The more conscientious pupils were making notes.

". . . Only the whale is heavier than the elephant, but then the whale lives in the sea. We can safely say that on land the elephant reigns supreme."

A slight breeze moved the branches of the trees in the zoo.

". . . The weight of a fully grown elephant is between nine and thirteen thousand pounds."

At that moment, the elephant shuddered and rose in the air. For a few seconds, it swayed just above the ground but a gust of wind blew it upward until its mighty silhouette was against the sky. For a short while, people on the ground could still see the four circles of its feet, its bulging belly, and the trunk, but soon, propelled by the wind, the elephant sailed above the fence and disappeared above the treetops. Astonished monkeys in the cage continued staring into the sky.

They found the elephant in the neighboring botanical gardens. It had landed on a cactus and punctured its rubber hide.

The schoolchildren who had witnessed the scene in the zoo soon started neglecting their studies and turned into hooligans. It is reported that they drink liquor and break windows. And they no longer believe in elephants.

6

✻

The Trial

At long last, the aim has been achieved and a tremendous amount of work and effort has borne fruit. All the authors have been put into uniform and awarded suitable ranks and distinctions. In this way, chaos, lack of criteria, unhealthy artistic tendencies, and the obscurity and ambiguity of art have been removed once and for all.

The design of the uniforms had been worked out centrally; the division into districts and formations, as well as the system of ranks to be awarded to individual members, were the result of long preparatory work in the Supreme Council of the Writers' Association. From then on every member had to wear a uniform consisting of wide mauve trousers with piping of a different color, green jacket, belt, and peaked hat. Thus the basic uniform was simple, but it allowed for a great variety of rank. Members of the Supreme Council wore two-peaked hats with gold braid, but members of regional councils were entitled only to silver braid. Chairmen wore swords, vice-chairmen stilettos.

All the writers were assigned to appropriate formations according to their genre. Two regiments of poets were set up, three divisions of practitioners in prose and one firing squad composed of various elements. The greatest changes took place among the literary critics; some of them were banished to the salt mines and the remainder incorporated in the gendarmerie.

Everybody was given a rank within a scale ranging from private to marshal. The deciding factors were the number of words published by each author during his lifetime, the angle of his ideological spine in relation to the floor, his age, and his position in local or national government. Flashes of different colors distinguished the various ranks.

The advantages of this new order were self-evident. First of all it was clear to everybody what he should think of any author; a writer-general could not possibly write a bad novel and, obviously, the best novels had to come from the pen of a writer-marshal. A writer-colonel might make mistakes but, even so, he must be much more talented than a writer-major.

The work of editorial offices was greatly simplified; it was easy to calculate quickly and accurately how much more suitable for publication was the work of a writer-brigadier than that of a writer-lieutenant. In the same way the question of fees was settled automatically.

It became impossible for a critic-writer-captain to commit to paper any adverse views on the work of anyone holding the rank of writer-major or above and only a critic-writer-general could find fault with something coming from the pen of a writer-colonel.

The advantages of the new order were not confined to the literary profession. Before the reform processions and public ceremonies were marred by the dreary appearance of the writers who compared unfavorably with the sportsmen. Now the writers' detachment presented a gay and colorful spectacle. The glitter of gold and silver braid, the multicolored flashes and piping, the peaked hats, all this appealed to the crowd and led to a great increase in the popularity of the writers among the people.

It must be admitted that certain difficulties were encountered in connection with the classification of one eccentric writer. Though he wrote prose, his works were too short to be described as novels and too long for short stories. Moreover, rumor had it that his prose had a poetic quality and a satirical bent, and that he wrote articles which were indistinguishable from stories and also bore the characteristics of critical essays. It was thought improper to assign this writer either to a prose or to a poetry detachment and it was clearly impracticable to create a special formation for one man only. There were suggestions that he would be expelled, but in the end a compromise was reached; he was given orange-colored trousers, the rank of a private, and was left to his own devices. The whole country could thus see that he was really a blot on the profession. Had he been expelled this would not have been without precedent. At an earlier stage several writers who, because of their build, did not look good in uniform had been removed from the association.

Within a short time the country discovered that leaving the eccentric in the ranks of writers had been a serious mistake. It was he who was the cause of a scandalous affair which undermined the beautifully simple principles of authority.

One day, a well-known and respected writer-general was taking a walk along a boulevard in the capital city. Approaching him from the opposite direction was the eccentric writer-private in orange trousers. The writer-general threw him a contemptuous glance and waited for the private's salute. Suddenly he noticed on the private's hat the insignia of the highest rank, a small red beetle, which only writer-marshals were entitled to wear. Respect for authority was so deeply embedded in the writer-general that, without pausing to consider the unusual nature of his discovery, he immediately adopted a most respectful attitude and saluted first. The astonished writer-private returned the salute, and as his hand went up to his hat, the large ladybird that had been sitting there opened its wings and flew away. Gripped by anger because of this humiliation, the writer-general immediately summoned a patrolling critic who took away the private's fountain pen and escorted him to the guardroom in the House of Literature.

The trial took place in the marble hall of the Palace of the Arts. Judges and other dignitaries sat behind a large mahogany table, their glistening epaulettes and golden insignia reflected in the dark, mirrorlike surface.

The eccentric writer-private was accused of illegally wearing insignia to which he was not entitled by his rank. However, luck was on his side. On the eve of the trial, during a meeting of the Council for Culture, strong criticism had been voiced of the soulless attitude to the artist and of the way art was being administered. Echoes of this debate could be heard the following day when the critic-writer-marshal himself rose to speak during the trial.

"We must on no account," he proclaimed, "adopt a bureaucratic attitude to this case. Our task is to get to the very bottom of this affair. Without doubt the case we are trying here today concerns the violation of those rules which, in spite of some mistakes, have led to an unprecedented flowering of our literature. The question we must ask, however, is this: 'Is the accused a conscious and active criminal?' We must probe deeply in search of the answer, we must expose not only the effects of this act but also its causes. Let's consider first of all who brought the accused to his present sorry condition. Who has depraved him, who has exploited his initial lack of social consciousness? What sort of creative atmosphere could have led to this crisis? To whom must we mete out punishment so as to prevent similar trials in the future?

"No, comrades. It's not the accused who is mainly responsible. He was only a tool in the hands of the ladybird. There can be no doubt whatsoever that the ladybird, motivated by hatred of our new hierarchy, incensed by the achievements of our system of absolutely precise criteria and by the perfect organization of our association . . . the ladybird with treacherous deliberation alighted on the hat of the accused and imitated a marshal's insignia. It's the ladybird who has tried to undermine our hierarchy. Let's punish the hand and not the blind tool."

The speech was greeted as a profound exploration of the very roots of evil. The writer-private was rehabilitated and a proper indictment was prepared against the ladybird.

A platoon of critics found the ladybird in a garden, sitting on a lilac leaf and plotting. When the ladybird realized that it had been unmasked, it offered no resistance.

The new trial took place in the same marble hall. All those present were straining their eyes to see the little red spot on the shiny table. Under a glass saucer, which prevented its escape, the ladybird sat still and unrepentant in its crime, preserving a disdainful silence to the very end.

The execution took place at dawn the following morning. Four thick and well-bound volumes of the latest novel by the writer-marshal of literature were the chosen instrument. They were dropped one by one from the height of four feet. It is reported that the condemned did not suffer long.

When the writer-private in orange trousers heard about the verdict, he cried and asked that the ladybird be set free in a garden. This brought him under suspicion once more of having been at least an accomplice in this crime; his attachment to the ladybird was thought to be highly suggestive.

8

❦

Tiny

There was once a theatrical company of dwarfs which appeared under the name of "Teeny Theater." It was a reliable, permanent troupe which performed at least four times a week and bravely tackled all problems. Small wonder that, in due course, the Ministry of Culture raised it to the rank of a model Lilliputian theater and gave it the official name of "The Central Teeny Theater." This guaranteed excellent conditions to the company, and to join it became the ambition of every dwarf actor, be he amateur or professional. However, the troupe already had all the actors it needed, including some outstandingly gifted performers. Among its leading lights was a midget who was always entrusted with leading roles because he was the smallest of them all. He earned good money and the critics always stressed his excellent technique. On one occasion he even reached such a degree of excellence in the part of Hamlet that even though he was on the stage the spectators did not see him, so small, so exquisitely and perfectly small was he. Intellectually he was one of us; in appearance he belonged to Lilliput. The success of the theater was largely due to him.

One day, when he was putting on makeup in his dressing room before the first night of a historical play in which he naturally was to act the leading part of the king, he noticed that he could not see in the mirror the reflection of the golden crown he was wearing on his head. Later, as he was going out into the corridor, he did not realize that the door was too low and the crown was knocked off his head and rolled away with a loud metallic clatter. He picked it up and went on the stage. After the first act, as he returned to his dressing room, he instinctively lowered his head in the door. The building of the "Central Teeny" had been designed especially on the scale of the actors, the state subsidy paying for the marble and the artificial clay imported from as far as Novosibirsk for the construction of the theater.

Performances of the historic play continued one after another and the diminutive actor got used to lowering his head on entering and leaving the dressing room. On one occasion, however, he noticed the old theater barber watching him intently. The barber was also a dwarf, but taller than the others and thus considered unsuitable for acting; this condemned him to work behind the scenes and filled his heart with hatred and envy. The barber's gaze was thoughtful and sinister. An unhappy feeling gripped the tiny actor and it would not leave him for a long time. In vain did he try to dismiss this feeling; it was there when he went to sleep and when he woke up. He tried to ignore it and to suppress the suspicion which started to develop in his mind. Time brought no relief. On the contrary. The day came when he had to bend in the door of his dressing room even though he wore no headgear. In the corridor he passed the barber.

That day he decided to face the truth. Even the superficial measurements he made behind the drawn curtains of his elegant apartment left no room for doubt. He could cherish no more illusions. He was growing.

That night he sat almost paralyzed in his easy chair, a glass of grog by his side, staring at the photograph of his father, also a dwarf. The next day he removed the heels from his shoes in the hope that his predicament was only temporary, that perhaps he would eventually shrink to his original size. For a time the removal of the heels did the trick. But one day, because of the presence of the barber, he left his dressing room fully erect and nearly knocked himself out in the doorway. He could not help noticing the scorn on the face of the barber.

Why was he growing? Why should his hormones wake up from their sleep after all those years? In desperation his mind fastened on an idea. He remembered the frequent propaganda slogan: "Here people grow . . ." Ordinary people? Yes, but dwarfs? Just in case, he stopped listening to the radio, gave up reading newspapers, and deliberately neglected his ideological education. He tried to persuade himself that he was an antisocial being, he even tried to overcome his natural disgust and became an apologist of imperialism, but all this was artificial and of no avail. His irrepressible class instinct, inherited from his pauper dwarf father, proved stronger. He threw himself into the other extreme, went on sprees in kindergartens and drank by the thimbleful in an attempt to drown his sorrow. Meanwhile time mercilessly but almost imperceptibly kept on adding to his size.

Did his colleagues know? On several occasions he caught the barber whispering with the actors in the wings. As soon as he approached, the whispering gave way to an exchange of banal remarks. He watched his comrades' faces but could read nothing in them. In the street less and less frequently was he stopped by women asking: "Have you lost your mommy, boy?" On one occasion he heard for the first time in his life someone say to him: "Excuse me, sir." After that incident he hastily went home and threw himself on his divan. For a long time he lay motionless, staring at the ceiling, but finally he had to change his position because of the cramp in his legs which were hanging over the edge of the already too short divan.

In the end he could have no doubt about his colleagues at the theater. They knew or they guessed the truth. He also noticed that the critics were no longer enthusiastic about his performances and even favorable mentions became rare. Or was it perhaps his excited imagination playing tricks on him, discovering everywhere derision or compassion? Fortunately there was no change in the attitude of the management. His success in the historical play was, after all, considerable, even if not as sweeping as in the part of Hamlet. Without hesitation he was given the leading part in the forthcoming production.

He suffered much during the rehearsals but somehow reached the first night without any special difficulty. Before the curtain rose he was sitting in his dressing room, already made up, facing the mirror but avoiding his own reflection. He was ready. On the summons of the callboy he rose heavily; his head hit the ceiling light and broke it. He turned toward the open door and in the brightly lit corridor he saw practically the whole company standing in a semicircle with the barber in the center. Next to the barber was his chief rival, another leading actor, who hitherto had always been an inch or so taller than himself.

There was no way out; he had to give up acting. As he grew taller, he tried various occupations. For a while he was an extra in crowd scenes at the children's theater, later a messenger boy, a switchman for the municipal streetcar . . . From time to time, because he could not earn enough to support himself, he sold some of the possessions he had accumulated during his years of glory. And then he grew a little more and stayed like that, a man of medium height.

What did he feel? Did he suffer much? His name, covered by the dust of time, had long since disappeared from the billboards. He took a clerk's job in the State Insurance Department.

One Saturday, several years later, trying to occupy his free evening, he found himself in a theater watching a performance by a company of dwarf actors. Sucking mints, he laughed at the jokes on the stage, fairly amused, fairly interested. When it ended, comfortable in the knowledge that supper was awaiting him at home, he said to himself:

"Yes, those tiny ones are quite fun."

9

The Lion

The emperor gave the sign. The iron grille, enclosing the entrance to the tunnel, rose, and from the darkness came a crescendo of menacing roars. In the center of the arena a group of Christians drew closer together. The spectators were on their feet. Excited chatter, cries of fear, and the roar approaching like an avalanche. From the tunnel emerged the first lioness moving swiftly and silently. The spectacle had begun.

Armed with a long pole, the keeper of the lions, Gaius, was checking if all the beasts had gone into the arena to take part in the terrible entertainment. He was about to give a sigh of relief when he noticed that one lion had stopped just short of the entrance and was calmly chewing a carrot. Gaius swore. One of his duties was to ensure that no beast remained idle. He approached the lion as far as safety and health regulations permitted and prodded the animal's rump with his pole. To his surprise, the lion only turned his head and swung his tail. Gaius prodded again, harder this time.

"Oh, leave me alone," said the lion.

Gaius scratched his head. The lion had made it crystal clear that it did not wish to go into the arena. Gaius was a kind man but he was afraid that if the supervisor caught him neglecting his duties he would soon find himself among the victims in the arena.

On the other hand he did not feel like arguing with the lion. He tried persuasion.

"Perhaps you'll go out just for my sake?"

"I'm no fool," replied the lion and continued to eat his carrot.

Gaius lowered his voice.

"I'm not saying that you have to jump at one of those wretches and tear him to pieces. Just go and run around a little and roar. That'll give us an alibi."

The lion swung his tail.

"Man, I've told you that I'm no fool. They'll see me and remember me. Later nobody will believe that I didn't eat one of them."

The keeper sighed and asked with an accent of complaint: "And why don't you want to?"

The lion looked at him attentively.

"You've yourself used the word 'alibi.' Hasn't it occurred to you why all those patricians there don't run into the arena and themselves tear the Christians to pieces, but instead rely on us, the lions?"

"Oh, I don't know. They are mostly old men. Short of breath, you know. Asthma. . . ."

"Old men," purred the lion mockingly. "You know a lot about politics. They simply want to have an alibi."

"Why?"

"Because of the new truth that is gaining ground. One has always to watch what's new and growing. Has it never crossed your mind that the Christians could come to power?"

"They—to power?"

"Yes. One has got to be able to read between the lines. It looks to me as if Constantine the Great is likely to come to terms with them sooner or later. And then what? Investigations and rehabilitations. Then those up there in the amphitheater will be able to say: 'It wasn't us, it was the lions.'"

"Really, I never thought of it that way."

"There you are. But never mind them. I want to save my own skin. When it comes to it there will be witnesses to say that all I did was to eat a carrot. Mind you, it's filthy stuff, this carrot."

"But all your comrades," said Gaius not without malice, "they are all gobbling up the Christians with great gusto."

"Stupid beasts. Shortsighted opportunists. No tactical sense at all. From darkest Africa—"

"I say," interrupted Gaius.

"Yes?"

"Should those Christians, you know . . ."

"What about them?"

"Should they come to power . . ."

"Well?"

"Will you then testify that I didn't force you to do anything?"

"*Salus Respublicae summa lex tibi esto,*" said the lion sententiously and returned to his carrot.

16

꿰

The Monument

We have in our town a monument to the Unknown Fighter of 1905. He died at the hand of the tyrant during the revolution, and his fellow citizens made a little mound to commemorate him. Fifty years later a stone plinth was placed on the mound with a carved inscription, "Eternal Glory." Above the plinth rose a statue of a young man breaking his chains. The unveiling of the statue in 1955 was performed with great ceremony. Lots of speeches. Masses of wreaths and flowers.

Sometime later eight pupils from a local school decided to pay their homage to the unknown hero. Their eloquent history master had moved them so deeply with his description of the revolution that, after school, they pooled their money and bought a wreath. Forming a small cortege, they walked toward the monument.

When they turned the corner of the street, they met a short man in a navy blue overcoat. He looked at them and started following them at a distance.

They passed the old town square. People paid no attention to them. Processions are not unusual.

Few people live in that part of the town. There is St. John's Church, but the old houses surrounding it have been converted into offices and museums.

When they reached the monument, the man in the overcoat approached them quickly.

"Good evening," he called. "Paying your homage? Very nice. Very nice indeed. It is the anniversary? One is so snowed under by work that one cannot remember . . ."

"No, it isn't the anniversary. We just felt like it," answered one of the boys.

"What do you mean, 'just felt like it'?" The man's voice rose in surprise. "What do you mean by this?"

"We simply wish to honor the memory of a revolutionary who gave his life in the fight for the freedom of the people."

"Ah, so you are from the district committee of the party."

"No, we are from the school."

"You mean, there's no one with you from the committee?"

"No."

He thought for a while. "Perhaps the school ordered you?"

"No, we decided by ourselves."

He went away. The boys were placing the wreath on the plinth when one of them called out: "He's coming back."

Indeed, the man in the overcoat had appeared again. This time he stopped a few paces away and asked: "Is it by any chance the month devoted to the deepening of respect for unknown revolutionaries?"

"No," they shouted back in unison, "we've decided by ourselves."

He walked away. The boys deposited the wreath and were about to go when the stranger returned. He had a policeman with him.

"Your identity cards, please," demanded the policeman.

They produced their school cards. He examined them and saluted.

"They are in order. Everything seems to be in order."

"Not at all," protested the man in the overcoat and, turning to the boys, he asked: "Who told you to lay that wreath?"

"No one."

He beamed. "So you admit it?" he cried. "So you admit that this demonstration in honor of the Unknown Revolutionary has been organized neither by your school, nor by the Praesidium of the Association of Polish Youth, nor by any committee of the party?"

"Of course it hasn't."

". . . That this ceremony has not been initiated either by the League of Women or by the Society of Friends of 1905?"

"No."

". . . That it's neither the anniversary nor the special month, nor anything like that?"

"No."

". . . That you've had no directive at all? That you've done this all by yourselves?"

"Yes, we have."

He mopped his brow with his handkerchief.

"Officer," he said, "you know who I am. Remove this wreath. And you: Go home!"

The boys left in silence. The policeman went off carrying the wreath. The activist in the navy overcoat was left alone by the monument. He was eyeing the statue with suspicion.

It started to rain. Small drops fell on his navy coat and on the stone jacket of the revolutionary. The clouds brought twilight in their wake. Silver drops were flowing down the face of the statue, hesitating on the earlobes like earrings, glistening in the granite eye sockets.

And so they stood, facing each other.

17

❧❧

The Background to an Era

My new lodgings were in a street which for some fifty years had been one of the city's main arteries. The high ceiling of my ground-floor room seemed to be supported by a pair of exceedingly tall and narrow windows and a similarly elongated door with an ornate brass handle. Persistent twilight filled this room, defying the sunshine outside; only at noon would it recede momentarily into the corners and under the canopy of the ceiling, returning soon to occupy the whole room triumphantly. All I could see through my windows was a row of similar windows on the opposite side of the street, blind ones because of the gloom that filled the rooms behind them.

Just outside my windowsill the headgear of passersby was floating about; it seemed as if the city had been flooded and the waters were carrying an endless stream of men's and women's hats, mementos of their drowned owners. The constant rustle of footsteps that reached me through the closed windows kept on reminding me of a river.

One day, among the usual multitude of floating hats, I saw one quite unlike all the others: a black bowler. It passed my window and disappeared. The river flowed on. A minute or so later, when I answered the doorbell, I saw the bowler again; it was on the head of an elderly man who was wiping his feet carefully, though the weather had been dry for a week and there was no mat outside my door. Raising his hat, the stranger inquired if he might come in. Once inside he looked around, took out of his pocket a folded newspaper, and announced, "I've brought the solution."

"What solution?"

He passed me the newspaper. It was the color of old ivory dominoes. The type was of a style that had gone out of use a long time ago; the letters had long anemic legs and their feet and heads were marked by thin horizontal lines. My eye caught the beginning of a dispatch: "Sixth June 1906. The current week in Baden-Baden. . . ."

"The puzzle," he pointed, seeing my lack of comprehension.

On another page there was the puzzle and, next to it, the solution written out in a careful hand in a mauve indelible pencil, which had been licked in the process.

"I see."

"I've got the complete solution."

"Yes."

"I've brought it here as it says in the instructions. I could have posted it, but I thought I'd rather bring it myself. But is this the editorial office?" he asked, looking doubtfully at the furniture.

"No. It no longer is. It's now a private apartment."

"Pity. I've solved it all. And where is the editorial office now?"

I shrugged my shoulders.

"When I moved in it was already a private apartment."

"And before that?"

"I don't know."

"Great pity! I've solved it all by myself."

"Perhaps there was an editorial office here once," I said, "but it must have been a long, long time ago."

He nodded.

"Yes, fifty years ago."

The stupid man was beginning to irritate me.

"What do you want with your puzzle? Don't you know that a lot has happened since then?"

"I can't help it that I'm not an intellectual," he said in an offended voice, "but I've solved it all by myself."

We were both silent for a moment. It was only then that I noticed the name of his newspaper and became really indignant.

"Do you realize that your newspaper was a perfidious organ of a monarchy that followed a policy of dividing national minorities?"

"It happened on a Sunday," he said. "My uncle came to see us. He had this paper in his pocket. It was a hot day and we were sitting in the garden. Father and Uncle decided to play cards. I wanted to join them, but Father wouldn't let me. He said I was too young and I would have enough time for playing cards when I was grown up. Then they took off their jackets; they left their waistcoats on. My uncle's jacket was hanging on a branch of a cherry tree, and when they started playing I took the paper out of his pocket. That's how I started on the puzzle."

"And you've only just finished," I added with irony.

"Yes. It was a very difficult puzzle. Do you know the word 'adequate'? And there were even worse ones."

"But what about the First World War?" I said.

"I was in a reserved occupation."

"You're funny! All those changes, upheavals, the republic, the referendum . . ."

"Do you think it was easy? Back in 1910 we didn't really know what a zeppelin was. I couldn't figure it out. Only after I got 'zip' and 'pelt' and 'in,' and that took some working out—only then did I begin to see daylight."

"You are impossible. The 1929 Depression, and you still at your puzzle. . . ."

"Perhaps I'm not very clever. Maybe you think I had too much time. But I had to work, my dear sir, I had to earn my living. Only in the evenings could I get down to the puzzle."

"And what about the Spanish Civil War? What about Hitler? What were you doing then?"

"Haven't I told you? I've had to solve it all by myself. Lots of foreign words. It wasn't easy. Still, I've got a head on my shoulders."

"You are a wizard." I was mocking him. "Probably you spent the Second World War working on your puzzle. You are an Einstein, but you didn't invent the atom bomb. You didn't know how."

"The bomb is a different matter. That wasn't my responsibility. But do you think it's easy for an old man? One's forgotten all one's learned at school. And there are so many worries. But I never gave in."

I laughed loudly and derisively. He was offended. He rose and said: "You shouldn't laugh. I haven't invented the bomb, but there's nothing one can do about it. In 1914 I was in a reserved occupation, but even before the war broke out I'd been hit in the head by a ricochet bullet. It was in Montenegro that it happened. You're laughing, but one should respect human thought. Here's the puzzle. Human thought isn't dead."

21

A Drummer's Adventure

I loved my drum. I carried it suspended from a wide strap across my shoulders. It was a big drum. I used oak sticks to strike its matte, yellow membrane. With time the drumsticks had acquired a polish from my fingers, testifying to my zeal and diligence. I carried the drum along roads white with dust or black with mud; the world on either side was green, golden, brown, or white according to the season. Wherever I went the landscape reverberated with a rat-a-tat-tat, for my hands did not belong to me but to the drum and when the drum was silent I felt ill. Thus one night I was drumming gaily when the General came up to me. He was incompletely dressed in his uniform jacket, which was unbuttoned, and his long underpants. He greeted me, hemmed and hawed a little, praised the government and the state, and at last said casually: "And you just go on drumming, do you?"

"Yes, sir," I shouted, striking the drum with redoubled force. "To the glory of our country."

"Quite right," he agreed, but somehow his voice sounded a little sad. "And how long will you go on?"

"As long as my strength lasts, sir," I shouted back gaily.

"Good boy," he said, scratching his head. "And will your strength last much longer?"

"To the very end, sir," I said proudly.

"Well, well. . . ." The General sounded surprised. For a while he seemed to be deep in thought and then he went off on a tangent.

"It's late," he said.

"It's late for the enemy, never for us," I shouted back. "The future belongs to us!"

"Very good, very good . . ." said the General, but he sounded cross. "When I said it was late, I meant that the hour was late."

"The hour of battle has struck! Fire the guns, ring the bells!" I shouted with the enthusiasm becoming a true drummer.

"Oh, no, not the bells," he said quickly. "I mean, let the bells ring, but only from time to time."

"Quite right, comrade General," I agreed with passion. "We don't need bells if we have our drums. Let the roll of my drum silence the bells!" To underline my point, I struck a loud roll.

"Never the other way around? What?" asked the General. He sounded uncertain of himself and he was covering his mouth with his hand.

"Never, sir," I shouted back. "You can rely on your drummer, sir. He'll never allow his drum to go silent." I was carried away by a burning wave of zeal.

"Our army can be proud of you," the General said without enthusiasm. A cold fog had come down on our camp and he was shivering. All I could see in the gray mist was the top of the General's tent. "Yes, proud," he went on. "We shall never stop, even if we have to march day and night, even if . . . Yes, each step . . ."

"Each step will be an endless victory roll," I interjected, drumming for all I was worth.

"Well, well," murmured the General. "Yes, just that . . ." and he went toward his tent. I was left alone. Solitude stimulated my desire for self-sacrifice and my sense of responsibility as a drummer. You've gone, General, I thought, but your faithful drummer is alert. With your brow furrowed you're working on your strategic plans, placing little flags on the map to mark the road to our joint victory. Together, you and I shall conquer the future, and on your and my own behalf I shall announce the victory with a roll of drums.

I was overcome with tenderness toward the General, and with such a will to give myself to the cause that, if it were possible, I would have drummed even louder. In the depth of the night, fired by my youthful enthusiasm, animated by our great ideal, I devoted myself to my honorable task. From time to time, in between drumbeats, I could hear from the direction of the General's tent the creaking of mattress springs as if somebody, unable to sleep, were tossing in bed. At last, about midnight, a white figure loomed in the mist by the tent. It was the General in his nightshirt. His voice was hoarse.

"I say, so you're going to continue drumming, are you?" he asked. I was really moved that he should have come to me in the middle of the night. A true father to his soldiers!

"Yes, sir. Neither cold nor sleep will defeat me. I'm ready to go on as long as my strength lasts, obedient to the call of my duty and of the cause we're fighting for. My honor dictates it. So help me God!"

In saying these words I was not motivated by a desire to appear as a stickler for my duty or by a wish to suck up to the General. This was no empty boast on my part, calculated to bring promotion or any other reward. It never even crossed my mind that such an interpretation could have been put upon my attitude. I have always been a sincere, straightforward and, damn it, let me say it, a good drummer.

The General gnashed his teeth. I thought he was cold. Then he said: "Good, very good," and went away.

A few minutes later I was arrested. The patrol assigned to this task surrounded me silently. They took my drum away; they removed the drumsticks from my cold and tired fingers. Silence filled the valley. I could not talk to my comrades who surrounded me with their rifles pointing at me; that was not allowed by regulations. They led me out of the camp. On the way one of them whispered that I had been arrested on the General's orders. The charge was treason. Treason!

Dawn was breaking. A few pink clouds floated in the sky. They were greeted by healthy snoring which I heard as we passed the General's tent.

36

🕸

Spring in Poland

That year, April was exceptionally warm. Early in the month, just before noon one day, the crowds milling on the pavements of the main Warsaw thoroughfares witnessed a most unusual happening. Floating above the rooftops like a bird was a man. He was dressed in an ordinary gray raincoat and hat; under his arm, a briefcase. He was not using any mechanical aids, but slight movements of his hands and arms were enough to keep him flying.

The man circled above the building of the International Press Club, and then, as if having noticed something in the road, he dived. Astonished passersby stopped dead. He was now flying so low that they could see the glint of the ring on his finger and examine the condition of the soles of his shoes. With a loud and penetrating wail, the man soared again, circled majestically above the city center, and flew away in a southerly direction.

It is fully understandable that the event gave rise to a great deal of talk. The news was withheld from the press and radio because the political attitude of the bird-man was not known, but all the same the whole country was soon aware of the strange occurrence. There can be no doubt that this happening would have been long remembered were its memory not erased by further and even stranger developments which took place a few days later: Two other men, also with briefcases, were observed flying through the clouds above the center of Warsaw. They too disappeared in a southerly direction.

The advance of the spring brought in its wake even warmer weather. Above Warsaw, later also above the provincial cities, and even above the smaller district towns, the sight of men with briefcases flying in twos and threes, but more often singly, became a daily occurrence. They all floated gracefully and performed aerobatics, but in the end they always flew away toward the south.

The nation demanded to be told the truth. There seemed to be no point in trying to hush it all up, and a communiqué was issued, announcing that, as the result of rising temperatures during the mild spring weather and the opening of windows in government offices, many civil servants, yielding to their eagle nature, had been leaving their desks and flying out of the windows. The communiqué ended with an appeal to civil servants and all other government employees to remember the lofty aims of the five-year plan, to conquer the urge of their blood, and to remain at their posts. During the following days, mass meetings of civil servants were held at which they gave pledges to fight their nature and not to fly away. This led to tragic conflicts. In spite of their will to stay, the numbers flying above the capital and other cities did not diminish. They could be observed diving in and out of white cumulus clouds, turning somersaults in the blue skies, wallowing in sunsets and, drunk with the power of flying, racing ahead of spring storms. Sometimes they would come down almost to ground level only to soar again to a height which made them invisible. In the streets passersby found spectacles, spats, and scarves raining from the sky, lost in the mad flight. In the emptying offices, work was grinding to a halt.

From the Tatry Mountains in the south came alarming reports. The mountain guards had observed masses of civil servants settling on crests and peaks, flying about and causing damage to the wildlife of the national park. Complaints from the population started coming in thick and fast. In the Nowy Targ district, twenty-eight lambs disappeared without trace, and at Muszyna an eagle, which was later identified as the deputy director of a government department, made a particularly daring raid and flew away with a pig. They descended from the skies like lightning.

May was on the way, and in all the offices windows were wide open. The situation was made even more serious by the fact that most cases of reversal to eagles took place among the central authorities. In fact, the higher the authority the larger the percentage of officials turning into birds of prey. All this adversely affected the reputation of the state, especially that again and again people saw high officials, known to them only from photographs and public appearances, floating above their heads, waving their legs, and turning like balloons.

A decree was issued ordering windows in all public offices and institutions to be kept shut—in vain. The windows remained closed, but a true eagle can escape even through a small skylight.

Various other measures were tried. Lead weights attached to the shoes of civil servants proved of no avail—they escaped in their socks. Those suspected of wanting to fly away were tied to their desks with ropes but they always managed to undo the knots. And so, now and again, a civil servant would sigh, struggle for a few minutes with his sense of duty, allow his true nature to assert itself, climb the windowsill, give an embarrassed cough, and fly away, often finishing his sandwiches and tea while already airborne.

In these circumstances, the execution of any form of official business became very complicated indeed. The escaping civil servants usually took with them all the papers on which they had been working. I managed to get one matter settled only because a friendly forester had informed me that he had seen the official concerned fighting with a mountain goat near a well-known lake in the Tatry. Some people organized expeditions into the mountain regions where they expected to find the nests or hunting grounds of the officials dealing with their applications. In this way mountaineering flourished, but the administration of the country was disorganized.

The foresters and mountain guards were issued with new orders: They were to catch the fugitive officials. But who can catch a bird that flies like an arrow! Only one method produced surprisingly good results: nets around the offices of cashiers on payday. On that day, whole flocks of flying civil servants, driven by an instinct stronger than their will, circled above the pay offices, pressing against each other and issuing excited shrieks. But payday over, they disappeared again, and those who had been caught either wasted away or escaped once more.

In this manner the spring passed, followed by a hot summer, bursting with freedom, soaring with frequent flight. Then imperceptibly, like a sickness, autumn appeared and damped down the fire of the sun. Finding food in the mountains became difficult. The day came when a party of schoolchildren on an excursion to a mountain peak saw in a crevasse a senior civil servant who did not fly away on their approach, but stood there dejectedly looking at them. His beard was hidden under the collar of his tattered coat in which he had flown away in the spring. Only when the children were almost next to him did he clumsily run a few steps and with a hoarse cry fly heavily away into the mist.

The first snow came. Its damp flakes fell silently on peasant roofs up and down the country. Under those roofs a folk song could be heard, a song full of wonder. A song about various officials, those leaders of ours—true eagles.

42

⁘

The Chronicle of a Besieged City

The city is under siege. Peasants cannot bring their produce in, and prices of milk, butter, and eggs have rocketed. There is a cannon in front of the town hall. Municipal commissionaires are dusting the cannon carefully by means of hares' legs and feather dusters. Someone advises wiping it with a wet rag. But who will listen to advice amid the turmoil of the siege? Everyone who, hastening through the city center, notices this cannon, finds his heart gripped by anxiety. Some people shrug their shoulders: People don't clean their shoes, and here . . . But afraid of informers they pretend that their backs are itching and they scratch between their shoulder blades. They try to make their behavior appear to be of no importance.

As for myself, I don't regret anything. The limitations of my fate have tied me to my poky room, they have tied me to this city, and I know that I am not a count and shall never become a field marshal. The old chap who lives at the bottom of the stairs is absolutely delighted. All his life he has considered himself a first-class shot. Now he will be able to show them. Since the morning he has been polishing his metal-rimmed glasses. He suffers from conjunctivitis.

In the afternoon, a shell fell through the open door of a suburban house and killed two goldfish in an aquarium. A state funeral was ordered for them. Through the night, candles were burning around the black catafalque in the cathedral. On the catafalque rested a coffin and in it the two goldfish; one had to look close to see them at all, lying at the bottom of the black box, as if down a precipice. Later, the six horses harnessed to the hearse, feeling the lightness of their load, kept on running away. The man from the town hall, who was in charge of the funeral, tried to explain to them that for the good of the city they should move slowly and with dignity. The grooms surreptitiously gave them a beating, but this was also in vain.

The archbishop, standing in front of the open grave, delivered a fiery oration, but he tripped on his robe and fell in. They buried him by mistake because nobody had noticed his fall, even though all the faces seemed full of concentration. However, he was soon unearthed and the grave-diggers had to apologize to him. He was in a sufficiently bad mood. In spite of all this, the general hatred of the enemy increased appreciably after the funeral.

That evening the old man shot the attendant who goes around at dusk and lights the gas lamps. He blamed the poor light, because, he said, he had been aiming straight at the enemy. He swore that his conjunctivitis would soon pass.

During the night there was a loud noise in the cellar of our house. Bottles of fermenting wine were exploding. We placed a guard there.

When the noise brought us all running into the cellar, I noticed that my neighbor on the landing was wearing a nightdress in a pattern resembling small autumn leaves. I mentioned it to her. It immediately brought autumn into our minds and made us feel so sad that, though everybody else went back to sleep, the two of us sat on the back steps leading into the garden and talked about that unpleasant season. Then I remembered that I had an eiderdown in a pattern of gay spring flowers. I brought it down and wrapped it around my neighbor. At once we both felt more cheerful.

In the morning—sensation. One of the patriots found a torpedo in his breakfast coffee. He reported it at once. The coffee was poured away. We now have an instruction to drink coffee only through a straw. Especially now that all yogurt has been mined. It is said that these are, in fact, our own countermines.

The newspaper calls for increased efforts. It appeals for deeds that will bring glory and promotion. "A general in every house" is the slogan of the day. I increased my efforts and stretched my muscles; my suspenders gave way. My landlady keeps on grumbling: "What do I want a general for. He won't wipe his feet, he won't even take off his hat. . . ." In a shop window, three streets away from us, they are showing a model general. I heard that one can also get herrings there. But I can't go out because of my suspenders.

I tried to read, but opposite my window the old boy took up his position, the one who is so delighted that at last he has a chance of giving everything he's got. With his first shot, he shattered my lamp. I took refuge under the sofa, where, in relative safety, I can devote myself to my books. I am reading *Sindbad the Sailor*. It occurs to me, however, that this is not a text worthy of the times we are witnessing. I crawl to the shelves and pull out a slightly yellowed volume: *The Triumphant Progress of the Centrifugal*

Pump in Public Utilities. Bullets clang against the springs of the sofa. The springs respond with a long vibrating note.

About noon, the old man either exhausted his ammunition or went to see an eye specialist. My landlady came back with the news that the police had confiscated all the pictures of bearded men in photographers' windows. She could not explain why. She repaired my suspenders.

I could not get the puzzling news about the photographs out of my mind, and my recent reading about pumps had stimulated my inquiring spirit. I put on a false beard and went out. Two field policemen stopped me at the very first street corner. They took me to a photographer and took a picture of me, developed it, and instantly confiscated it.

That night it was difficult to sleep because an armored car was patrolling on our roof and checking the documents of the cats which always prowl there. I was told that only one cat had his papers on him but he too was arrested. After all, an ordinary cat carrying authentic personal documents is enough to arouse justified suspicion.

My neighbor went out today wearing a green polka-dot dress.

Since this morning, thirty men have been working on the shiny dome of the town hall and painting it black. That dome used to shimmer even on cloudy days, but a siege is a siege. As I was watching, one of the painters slipped and fell to the pavement. He broke his leg. As they were lifting him, he shouted: "For the Fatherland!" On hearing this, a citizen passing by grabbed a stick from another man and broke his own leg. "I also want to make my sacrifice!" he shouted. "I'll do my bit!" These cries excited him even more and for good measure he also broke his glasses.

In the circus, from today, they will be showing only patriotic numbers, and not all of them at that.

The family of our caretaker is showing signs symptomatic of the food difficulties in a besieged city. On coming home, I passed the open window of their basement and heard the caretaker say to his little son: "If you don't behave I'll eat your dinner." His voice was full of ill-disguised covetousness. I shrugged my shoulders. Why shouldn't a father admit frankly that he is hungry. Surely, the child would understand. I was indignant at this hypocrisy.

The landlady greeted me with another piece of news.

"Do you know," she said, "that there will be no Christmas this year? All the Christmas trees are to be sent to the barricades!"

"Oh, don't you worry about Christmas trees," I interrupted. "You'll hang your decorations on the asparagus fern."

"On the asparagus! Holy Mother," she wailed. "Nobody has ever done a thing like that!"

"My dear lady, better on the asparagus than on nothing at all."

She reflected over my words.

"Yes, you are right," she admitted, "but what if they take all the asparagus to the barricades, too?"

I had no answer to that one.

In the streets, messenger-dachshunds are running about. Clearly something has happened.

The first meeting of the general staff: It is reported that there was a difference of views on the possible use of the cannon outside the town hall. There is general agreement that the cannon should be fired at the enemy but some want to do it on a state holiday, others on a church holiday. There is also a group of the center which recommends as the best solution that a new state holiday should be proclaimed on a day which also happens to be a church holiday. The left has immediately split into two groups; one which wishes to consider the motion proposed by the center, the other regarding the proposal as wholly opportunist. Soon the extreme left splintered still further, with one group demanding the passing of a condemnatory resolution, while the other recommended that general reservations should be formulated in a noncommittal form, primarily for internal reasons. A similar division also developed within the wing that wanted the cannon fixed on a church holiday and different groups within it have adopted different attitudes to the proposal from the center.

In the afternoon, my suspenders broke once more. I was ashamed to ask my landlady to repair them again. After all, the woman has some right to a private life. So I stayed at home and made notes from "The Triumphant Progress."

In the evening, I felt tired. After my intensive intellectual labors, I needed some distraction. The darkness in the street (the man responsible for lighting the lamps was still in the hospital) emboldened me; nobody could see that my suspenders were torn. I slipped into a bar, where I met a nice man. He turned out to be the gunner responsible for our cannon. He confessed that he had no idea how to fire it; his real occupation was growing silkworms and he had been assigned to the cannon because of a clerical error. I had to hold up my trousers with my left hand while raising my glass with the right.

Time passed quickly. Soon we were friends and we were embracing each other. Alas, I couldn't embrace him with both arms and I was afraid that he would think of me as a cold, standoffish, and reserved person. On my way back, I had to crawl along the walls because the old shortsighted man had obtained some more ammunition and bullets were whistling along the street.

The landlady had bolted the door from the inside. Undecided what to do, I went into the garden and looked into the windows. Some people's lights were still on, among them my neighbor's. I saw her. She was so scantily dressed that she was shivering from the cold. I nearly cried out of compassion. How can one be so careless about one's health?

As I had gone to bed late, I slept till noon. When I got up I heard the important news. There had been a second meeting of the general staff, and the center group started splitting because of the different views adopted by its members on the positions taken by the groups of the left and the extreme left and the three groups of the right. The next item of news concerned the town hall. A ceremony had taken place there during which our old man, in recognition of his voluntary and vigilant fight against the enemy, was awarded a decoration and given a new rifle with a telescopic sight. I ran straight to the chemist and bought some bandages and iodine. I shall always have them with me. I heard also that the ceremony had not passed without a scandal. Because of his short sight, the old boy had pinned his decoration upside down. When his attention was drawn to it, he replied with bullets and, shouting that he would not allow a single enemy to escape, ran out into the streets. His decoration strengthened his readiness to sacrifice. What nobility! What zeal!

Life in the city tires me. I feel that it is time to make an excursion, to lie somewhere on the grass, with only clouds above my head. Will the weather hold? There are so many beautiful cathedrals and monuments in my city. The seasons change so miraculously, as if nature wished to give us a permanent spectacle with a subtly changing decor. I am sure that if one went to the outer fortifications and climbed a wall, one could look southward and see an unlimited world. Is there anything lovelier than to stand on the seashore at five o'clock on a summer morning, to stand by the sea on which we shall soon sail southward and southward? I am sure there is, and this very certainty makes us hop gaily and wander farther and farther. Of course, these were only my thoughts. I was gravely handicapped by the absence of serviceable suspenders. My ignorance of practical matters prevented me from finding a remedy, and a feeling of shame did not allow me to seek help. In any case, every minute brought new developments. An official communiqué announced that the cannon would be fired at the enemy the following day.

Preparations for the event were most elaborate. According to official orders, everybody had to find a helmet for himself. This helmet could be worn during the rest of the siege, but it was compulsory on the Day of the Firing. The orders caused a great deal of confusion. My landlady got busy with her scissors, needle, and thread and then entered my room wearing a helmet made of felt taken from her old school hat, which, having spent half a century in the loft, smelled strongly of mothballs.

"Is that all right?" she asked uncertainly, as if ashamed of something.

I was surprised. Contrary to her normal custom, she had done all the work in silence, without the loud grumbles and complaints she always voiced when complying with any official instructions. Thus I had had no warning.

"Fine," I said. "Most becoming. It makes you look young. But, you know, perhaps it isn't quite stiff enough. A helmet should be hard."

"Oh, what shall I do?" She was distressed. "I've darned it as well as I could."

"It isn't that," I tried to explain gently. "You know, it's just in case. Anyway, you must have a piece of sheet metal somewhere, a baking pan or even an old, unwanted kettle. . . ."

As far as I was concerned, the solution of the helmet problem was simple. As soon as my landlady left my room, I threw out the asparagus fern and put the pot on my head. This did not afford me much protection, even from splinters, but I was not worried. All I wanted was to avoid trouble with any police inspection. Just for one moment I was not entirely happy with the thought that we may really need the fern for Christmas.

In the evening, after a day filled with preparations, I decided to seek some relaxation by taking a walk in the cemetery. I found there what I wanted: peace and silence, so soothing after the streets filled with excited crowds, most of them already wearing helmets. Everybody was in a hurry to complete his shopping before the holiday, when everything would be closed. Walking slowly along a path I came to an unfinished obelisk marking the official grave of the two goldfish, which were killed on the first day of the siege. Out of habit I am referring to the "goldfish," though this description does not tally with what is written on the tombstone.

To my surprise I met my neighbor, who, like me, must have slipped out of the hubbub and confusion in search of some peace. A lock of her hair had escaped from under a small helmet made of corrugated tin. I felt bashful.

"How quiet it is," I said, standing in front of her.

"Yes, very quiet," she agreed.

"They will fire the cannon tomorrow."

"So I hear."

She took out her mirror and adjusted the helmet.

The firing of the cannon was not successful. My landlady reported this to me. There was no official communiqué. I thought that the gunner I had met must have told me the truth, but I also heard that the failure was not his fault. Possibly there were other reasons. In any case there was a great deal of talk about it. Later I was preoccupied with other matters because I wanted to make my excursion to the walls. As you know, at that time I did not go out much because of my suspenders. I lied to my landlady and told her that my feet hurt and I had too much work at home. To reinforce my point, I showed her the open volume on *The Triumphant Progress of the Centrifugal Pump in Public Utilities* and my notes on it. As for my excursion, I counted on the fact that in the outskirts there would be hardly anyone about, especially that I was planning to set out in the late afternoon. I spent the rest of the Day of the Firing at home, planning my excursion and dreaming about it. Having switched off the light, I stood for a long time by my window.

When I woke up the next day, I heard my landlady crying in the kitchen. As I lay in bed, I wondered what could have upset her. At last she brought my breakfast, the newspaper, and the sandwiches I had ordered for my excursion. She left them all on the table and fled in tears. My photograph was on the front page of the paper and with it an announcement that the person responsible for everything has been and is—me.

I was less surprised by it than I expected. After all, how can one be absolutely sure that one is not responsible for everything? I stayed indoors, glad for once that the broken suspenders compelled me to do so. I would not have liked to show my face to other people if it was all my fault and they were convinced of it.

It was a pity that the pleasure of my excursion should have been marred. When at last I left the house, one of my hands was holding up my trousers; with the other I shook the caretaker's hand. I gave all my books, including *Sindbad the Sailor* and *The Triumphant Progress of the Centrifugal Pump in Public Ulilities,* to my landlady. She asked me to write to her from time to time.

I was glad that dusk was already gathering. The man who used to light the lamps had not yet recovered. I went down into the yard hoping to catch a glimpse of my neighbor through the window. I did not see her, but I heard her talking to someone. I recognized the voice of my friend, the gunner.

I made off in a southerly direction. I did love my city. Its walls exuded the gentle, deep warmth that stones give up at the end of a sunny day. I have always admired true architecture, everything that is wise and simple, that follows naturally, everything that is great and beautiful because it owes its existence to a reflex of nature. That is why I enjoy living, when it is possible.

I had thought of going to the old citadel, which has long been deserted. I was walking toward its ancient but still tall walls on which high green grass was waiting to be cut. I had left behind me the noise of the streets and was making my way between the deserted bastions that age had given the shape of round humps. All their military meaning had deserted them, leaving idyllic mounds that still carried a slight aura of uneasiness.

I was glad that my excursion was going according to plan. I had hardly met a soul and I could, without embarrassment, hold up my trousers with one hand, while carrying the sandwiches in the other.

Feeling somewhat tired by my rapid march, I sat down for a while in the valley between two high parallel walls that were stretching into the distance. I had followed the bottom of this defile for quite a time and now, in the deepening dusk, I could only see a strip of the aquamarine sky. Staring at that sky, I noticed a sharply defined silhouette of a man cleaning a rifle. On his chest glittered the disc of a medal.

Of course it was the old man with conjunctivitis, so intent on chasing the enemy. His devoted voluntary service must have taken him to the outskirts, where he was now holding guard. Though full of admiration for his persistent devotion, I was nevertheless afraid that however good his intentions may be, a mistake on his part could not be ruled out.

Fortunately he did not notice me. Trying to make no noise, I resumed my walk along the defile. Soon I left him behind. I could have moved much faster were it not for my falling trousers, which I had to hold up all the time. If only I had some serviceable suspenders! Those silly inhibitions did not desert me even there. I was alone. There was no one to embarrass me.

Then, after all, he fired. Lying on the grass with my face touching the earth, I felt in my heart a pain, a blunt, dull, stupid pain.

THE POLICE

Translated by Nicholas Bethell

Characters

CHIEF OF POLICE

PRISONER, A former revolutionary, later the General's Aide-de-Camp

SERGEANT, An agent-provocateur

WIFE [of the Sergeant-Provocateur]

GENERAL

POLICEMAN

Acts I and III take place in the Chief of Police's office.

Act II takes place in the house of the Sergeant-Provocateur

AUTHOR'S NOTE
ON THE PRODUCTION OF
THE POLICE

This play does not contain anything except what it actually contains. This means that it is not an allusion to anything, it is not a metaphor, and it should not be read as such. The most important thing is to present the naked text, as exactly as possible, with a firmly underlined sense of logic in the opinions and scenes. The play, provided it is in fact staged, will demand intense concentration on the part of the audience because of its structural compactness. So unless the production is clear and pure, the play will be a tiring one.

The statement that this play is not a metaphor, but is simply what it is (within its own area and time of duration), entails the following consequences:

No scenographic tricks must be added to the play, either for the sake of humor or for the sake of decoration (decorativeness). Nothing need be "emphasized," and "atmosphere" should be treated with great care. No overcontrived action should be added to the play. In a word, nothing should be done to detract from the transparency of the production, which must be stern and static, clean, and "snake in the grass"-like. Bitter experience shows that any attempt at exaggerated "emphasizing," "interpreting," or overacting this author's texts will be an artistic failure.

Nor is the play (God forbid) a comedy, which means that the jokes in it must not be overaccentuated. Whatever jokes the play may contain, they are not the sort of jokes to be told in a voice that implies, "Pay attention! I am about to tell you a joke." If my advice is ignored, the result will be a failure. It will be inelegant, if not tasteless.

Neither is this a "modern" or an "experimental" play. It is certainly neither of these. I do not think I need expand on this.

I imagine that what I have just written will lay me open to the charge that I do not understand theatricality. This is not the point. Perhaps I do not understand theatricality. Perhaps I do not even feel it. But one thing I do know, and that is that certain elements of so-called "theatricality" and of theatrical thought have become entirely banal. They have made themselves shallow and a fetish, and have entered somehow into the arsenal of a thought that is thoughtless and automatic. Apart from anything else, the reading of plays as metaphors, which is capable of being creative and new, is also capable of being transformed into yet another pattern of thought. (All the more so since the little play in question can provoke one to "make life easier" by applying such labels as "metaphor," "comedy," "modern," and suchlike.)

While I know what this little play is not, I do not know what it is, and it is not my duty to explain what it is. This must be discovered by the theater. And if anyone imagines that these author's remarks and 'nots' limit the producer or leave him without a job to do, it means that the person has no true respect for the theater. The theater is not so cramped and poverty-stricken as he thinks.

THE AUTHOR

ACT I

In the CHIEF OF POLICE's office, which has a desk, two chairs, and all
other essential, props. The office door is in a prominent position and there are two
pictures on the wall. One is of the Infant King (a baby in an old-fashioned
carriage or a child dressed in the style of the nineteenth-century bourgeoisie) and
the other of the Regent (a frightening-looking old man with a mustache). All
those in any way connected with the police have big mustaches. The
PRISONER-REVOLUTIONARY has a pointed beard like those of
nineteenth-century progressives. All the policemen have jackboots, swords, and
high, stiff collars. The interrogator has a civilian jacket, short and close-fitting.
The uniforms, which are all navy blue, have very shiny metal buttons.

CHIEF OF POLICE (*Standing up and reading the end of some document*)
"... and so with feelings of shame and disgust I renounce my crimes,
and the only desire I have is to serve our government with all my
strength and with the deepest veneration and love for the rest of my
life." (*Sits down, folds up the document.*)

PRISONER   Don't put it away. I'll sign it.

CHIEF   You'll sign it! What?

PRISONER   I'll sign it and that's that.

CHIEF   But why?

PRISONER   What do you mean, why? For ten years you examine me,
interrogate me, keep me in prison. Every day for ten years you give
me that form to sign. When I refuse, you threaten me with dreadful
punishments and try to talk me around. Finally I agree to sign so that
I can get out of prison and serve the government, and you look
surprised and ask me why.

CHIEF   But it's so sudden, and without warning.

PRISONER   Colonel, I am undergoing a drastic change.

CHIEF   What change?

PRISONER   A drastic change of heart. I don't want to fight the
government anymore.

CHIEF   Why not?

PRISONER   I'm fed up with it. If anyone wants to fight the government, let them. I don't know who's going to do it. Spies for a foreign power, perhaps? Secret agents? But not me anymore. I've done my bit.

CHIEF (*Sadly*)   I'd never have expected this of you. Stop fighting the government? Become a conformist? You're a fine one to talk like that. The oldest prisoner in the country.

PRISONER   Exactly, Colonel. Is it true that I am the last man still in prison?

CHIEF (*Hesitatingly*)   Yes . . .

PRISONER   You see? Sometime ago it became obvious to everyone that we have the best political system in the world. My former colleagues confessed their guilt, received their pardon, and went home. Now there's nobody left to arrest. I am the last remaining revolutionary; but what sort of a revolutionary? In my heart of hearts I'm a stamp collector.

CHIEF   That's what you say now, but who threw the bomb at the general?

PRISONER   Ancient history, Colonel. And the bomb didn't even explode. It's not worth raking that up.

CHIEF   Honestly, I can't believe my ears. For ten years you've refused to make a statement. You've held out splendidly. Time and time again you've been ordered to sign, but you never broke down. Instead you would stand up in disgust and spit at the picture (*Gets up from his chair and stands to attention.*)   of our Infant King and his uncle the Regent. (*Sits down.*)   We've got used to living here together. Everything's nicely settled and now suddenly you want to destroy it all.

PRISONER   I tell you, there's just no point. If only I hadn't been so ideologically abandoned perhaps I could have gone on longer. But to think that the whole population of our beautiful, peaceful, and fertile country has for so long been singing the praises (*Gets up and stands to attention.*)   of our Infant King and his uncle the Regent, that all the prisons are empty and that I alone, just me . . . No, Colonel, I promise you. I've given up my former beliefs. If the whole people supports the government and is against me, then there must be something in it. In fact, we've got a very good government, and that's that.

CHIEF Hmmm . . . hmmm . . .

PRISONER I beg your pardon?

CHIEF (*Gets up and adopts an official tone of voice*) While accepting with sincere joy and satisfaction the prisoner's confession, bearing witness to a change of heart which has come about under the corrective influence of imprisonment, I nevertheless consider it my duty to ascertain to what extent his new, favorable, and entirely rational opinions are deep-rooted and lasting. (*Sits down. In a different tone.*) Why then, if I may ask, do you consider that our government is good?

PRISONER You've got eyes, Colonel. Never before in history has our country reached such a high stage of development. You know, sometimes I move my plank bed against the window of my cell and put my latrine bucket on top of it upside down; then I can stand on the bucket on tiptoe and gaze out at a most beautiful meadow. Every spring it bursts into flower with different colored blossoms. Then at haymaking time the farmworkers come to the meadow and cut the grass. During the last ten years I have watched their faces light up with a happiness and satisfaction which grows in strength every year.

CHIEF Do you realize that it is against the prison rules to look out of the window?

PRISONER But for ideological purposes, Colonel, in the cause of corrective education. And that is not all. On the other side of the meadow there's a small hill, and on the other side of the hill during the last seven years an industrial building has been constructed. I can see a chimney, and sometimes there's smoke coming out of it.

CHIEF To be strictly accurate I think I should tell you that that is a crematorium.

PRISONER Why should they always bury dead people in the ground, like they've been doing for centuries and centuries? Don't atheists have the same right as believers to dispose of their bodies in the way they wish, with the sort of funeral they like. What you say only confirms what I've always felt, that this country of ours is a land of the broadest tolerance, even in religious matters.

CHIEF   Yeees . . .

PRISONER   Take culture and art. The hours I've spent walking up
and down my cell—down the length of it, that is, because it's
rectangular—all the time getting more and more excited.

CHIEF   Well yes. You've got to admit it.

PRISONER   You see, I'm right.

CHIEF   I am a civil servant and I can't settle this matter myself. That is
to say, I can't accept your change of heart too readily. I must first of
all investigate that there are no doubts or hesitations left in your mind.
It may be you are looking at things through rose-tinted spectacles.
Take the economic situation, for example, are you not overlooking
certain specialized matters like, say, the railway?

PRISONER   Even the most fanatical enemy of our state system could not
deny that the railway, as a phenomenon, exists in this country.

*Pause. The Chief of Police and the Prisoner look at each other. The Chief of
Police gets up, walks out from behind his desk, and marches up and down the
room in silence. Then he stops. For a moment he gazes at the pictures of the
Infant King and his uncle the Regent. The Prisoner watches him the whole time.*

CHIEF   Yes, and what about them? (*Points to pictures.*)   I suppose you
never had the slightest intention of . . . (*Impatiently.*)   No, really! It's
impossible!

PRISONER   I don't understand, Colonel.

CHIEF   Honestly, talking to you anyone would think you threw a
tomato at the general, not a bomb, and that it never entered your
head that (*Stands to attention.*)   our Regent, the uncle of our Infant
King, is an idiot. (*Stands at ease.*)

PRISONER (*Leaping to his feet in indignation*)   Colonel!

CHIEF   No, all right, that's enough, obviously he isn't. (*Goes on walking
up and down.*)   That is to say, as far as his intellect is concerned. But
you must admit that even the most powerful brains have their little
weaknesses; lower down, that is, among their habits, tastes.

*He gets up, stares at the Prisoner, and winks at him. The Prisoner does not react.
The Chief of Police comes nearer, winks again very meaningfully and emphati-*

cally, moving his whole head and even his neck, as if he wanted to throw his eye at the Prisoner. The Prisoner turns around as if the wink were directed not at him, but at someone behind him. Pause.

PRISONER   Why are you winking at me, Colonel?

CHIEF (*Violently unbuttoning his tunic collar*)   You ought to be ashamed of yourself! You, an old revolutionary, asking such a question.

PRISONER   It's all this educational effect of prison life that you were talking about. I give you my word, I've simply forgotten what that wink might mean. Is it some sort of an allusion? Is it something unpleasant connected with the persons of our Infant King and of his uncle the Regent?

CHIEF   You don't think, then, that our Regent is—an old pervert?

PRISONER   Him? That pure old man?

CHIEF (*Again starts walking round the room*)   All right, very good . . . As representative of the High Command I congratulate you on your progress. (*Offers his hand, which the Prisoner takes.*)   But this does not mean that we can give ourselves up to a sudden burst of rejoicing. It is a matter of great concern both to you, since you have undergone what we hope is a genuine change of heart, and to me, who must not accept your story too trustingly. You say that you do not believe that our Regent is a—a you know what. But psychologists tell us that often a man gives the impression that he is not thinking something, while in fact he is thinking it all the time. What have you got to say to that?

PRISONER   You're right, Colonel. That's exactly the point. Sometimes it seems to us that we think we're not thinking, but we are thinking— while all the time we're not thinking at all. Thought is a powerful weapon, Colonel.

CHIEF (*Pompously, sternly, suspiciously, and testingly*)   But only in the service of mankind!

PRISONER   That is true.

CHIEF (*Unwillingly*)   Very well. Now please take a look at this picture of our Infant King. Small, isn't he?

PRISONER   Like all children.

CHIEF You mean he's a shortarse, eh?

PRISONER You know, Colonel, if it wasn't for your uniform and high
rank I might begin to think that you were right. But if the chief of
police himself says that our infant leader is a shortarse, then obviously
such an opinion could never, never be the right one. If a shopkeeper
had told me that, or a bricklayer out in the street, perhaps I'd have
had my doubts. But the chief of police! No, this only confirms me in
my great admiration and reverence for the person of our Infant King
and—as a natural consequence—of his uncle the Regent.

*The Chief of Police sits down again. Then the Prisoner gets up, walks toward
the desk, and takes up the initiative.*

PRISONER (*cont.*) Please believe me. I've finished with my former
mistaken antigovernment point of view. The reasons for my change of
heart fall into two categories: There are the external ones and the
internal ones, and it is this double conviction which is the guarantee
of the depth and permanence of my evolution—a thing which you,
Colonel, for my own good are naturally concerned about. The
external reasons are those we've already mentioned: the universal
progress that our country has made. You only have to pick up a
newspaper to be convinced of it. Look around you, Colonel. Don't
hide your head in the sand in the face of these achievements. Is there
anything wrong with the country? You've only got to look at your
salary, Colonel; that in itself is enough to show how groundless are
complaints of this sort. Anyway, I've become a keen government
supporter, and I don't mind admitting it.

*The Prisoner sits down and pulls his chair up nearer the desk. His tone is more
confidential.*

PRISONER (*cont.*) However, if you have any doubt that the
emotions of nature are strong enough to make sure that I won't go
back on my conversion, I'll show you that there are other emotions,
internal emotions, which I feel more personally. You see, when I
was a child I had no idea about law and order, about discipline and
having an aim in life. All the time it was freedom and freedom.
This—sort of—monotony in my spiritual diet could only satisfy part
of my personality. Feelings of revolt against the established order, a
desire to oppose all restrictions and authority—I had plenty of those.
But in the course of time I began to feel a certain dissatisfaction. I

came to the conclusion that I was in some way handicapped. I, a free rebel, a model revolutionary, began to feel a curious nostalgia. How is this? I asked myself. Why has Fate tormented me, deprived me of the joyful sensation of agreement, subservience, and loyalty; the delightful feeling of unity with authority; the blissful capacity to carry out political inevitabilities; as well as the added delight of, without needing to be summoned by these inevitabilities, yielding myself up to them voluntarily, and having at the same time a complete, self-elevating confidence in myself as a man of action? I was a man unfulfilled, Colonel, but at last I understood that it was not too late. And it was then that the time came when my first me, rebellious and always complaining, perished as a result of overindulgence, and a second me awoke, with a loud voice demanding the nourishment that was its due—a joyful and calm conformity, an eager hope in the future, and the peace which flows from full submission to authority. The joyful knowledge that the government of our Infant King and his uncle the Regent (*Both stand, then sit.*) is just as good, wise, and virtuous as we ourselves, arouses within us feelings of sheer delight unknown to those poor individuals, so imprisoned in their own negative outlook and so unfulfilled in their relationship with mankind. Only now, Colonel, have I achieved real fullness. So here I am—the last political prisoner in a country that is now flourishing and entirely loyal; the last dark cloud in the blue sky of the rule of our Infant King and his uncle the Regent; one single crow, with the blackness of his wings marring the pure rainbow of our statedom. It is only on my account they still keep the police force going. If it wasn't for me they could send all the judges and guards off home. The prison would stand empty and could be turned into a preparatory school. Because of me, Colonel, you've got to hang around in this stuffy office. Otherwise you could get out far into the fields and meadows with a gun or fishing rod and throw off your suffocating uniform. I tell you, Colonel, you've won at last. The police have brought their mission to a close. The last man to oppose the government lays down his arms and his only desire is to join the chorus of citizens singing hosanna to our Infant King and his uncle the Regent. For the first time in the world's history the ideal of law and order in a state has been achieved. When I leave here the last obstacle will be gone. Today should be a great occasion in your life, Colonel. It is the day of final victory. The task at which you have labored your whole life and for which you were ordained has been crowned by success. Today I sign the paper that you have been trying to persuade me to sign for ten years. I will then go out into the free world and support the government. What is more, I will send an open letter to our Infant King and his uncle the Regent—the most humble letter that has ever been written, filled with the deepest devotion and love.

CHIEF   You remember that stamp collection you were so proud of?

PRISONER (*Startled*)   Yes, what's that got to do with it?

CHIEF   Just reflect for a moment whether you really want to leave us. Perhaps you could think it over once more and strengthen your convictions. Look before you leap, as they say. Meanwhile we could give you a hand in your stamp collecting. We've got secret agents in many interesting foreign countries who send us reports. We could soak the stamps off and give them to you for your album. Outside it's not so easy to get good stamps.

Enter a POLICEMAN.

POLICEMAN   Sir, the sergeant's back.

CHIEF   Tell him to come in.

Enter the SERGEANT. *He is broad and red-faced, with a mustache twice as long as the others. He has one black eye and is limping. He comes to attention before the pictures of the Infant King and his uncle the Regent, and then flops into a chair. He is wearing a raincoat and a green hat with a narrow brim.*

CHIEF (*cont.*)   Well, Sergeant, how did it go? My God! You're a sight! What happened?

The Sergeant groans.

CHIEF (*cont.*)   Does it hurt?

The Sergeant nods his head, takes out a handkerchief, and applies it to his eye. The Chief of Police motions to the Policeman to leave the room.

CHIEF (*cont.*)   You can tell me now.

SERGEANT   Sir, as part of my duties as agent-provocateur I was trying to shout antigovernment slogans—and they beat me up.

CHIEF   Who beat you up? No, you don't really mean that they . . . you were beaten up by . . .

SERGEANT   Unfortunately, yes. I was beaten up by the loyal population.

CHIEF   (*Mutters gloomily to himself*)   I expected as much.

PRISONER   You see, Colonel. It bears out my theory.

CHIEF   (*Sharply*)   Please don't interfere. Give me the details, Sergeant.

SERGEANT   Sir, immediately upon receiving your instructions I proceeded to carry them out. First of all, I acquired a civilian suit, although if there's one thing I hate it's civilian clothes. To improve my disguise, I obtained a green hat with a narrow brim and a raincoat. I then went out into the street. For a short time, I conducted myself defiantly opposite the government office of weights and measures, but nobody paid any attention. So I went to the square and made faces in front of the statue of our Infant King and his uncle the Regent. (*Gets up, sits down.*)   Again nobody saw me because, as you know, Colonel, everybody's in a hurry there. Then I went off and stood in line at a stand where they were selling beer. I looked around and saw that in front of the stand and all around me there was a collection of simple, ordinary citizens, in the thirtieth or thirty-eighth wage bracket, I should say. This is fine, I thought to myself. The line moved forward and all the time I was wondering what to do about it. At last I had an idea, and when my turn came I said to the man in my normal voice, "Two half pints, please, in quick succession." You see, Colonel, as if it was the royal succession that had brewed the beer, or something, and they were giving short measure, etc., etc. Well, either he didn't understand—he looked pretty stupid—or else he didn't want to understand—anyway he just asked me: "Mild or bitter, sir?" So then I let him have it straight. I said to him: "Our whole farming system's down the drain, and anyone who doesn't steal will die of starvation." Then the people who were standing in line with me came in closer and one of them asked if I was making any allusion to life in the present day, because he was an employee of the state, and he would not tolerate the state being insulted. So then I gave them the lot: the agricultural situation, foreign trade, then a few words about the police, especially the secret police. Then a young man in a cloth cap came out of the group and walked toward me. "You leave our police alone," he says. "I suppose next

thing you'll start on the army; you'll want to cut down national
service or get rid of it altogether, and next autumn I'm due to go
before the recruiting board." And then some old bag who was
standing a bit farther off yelled out: "Oh, so he doesn't like the police,
eh? Why, only last week, they sent me a summons to arrange to have
my house searched, and this so-and-so's going to get in the way, I
suppose. After a search you always feel more comfortable and loyal,
and if you don't have your house searched you get an uneasy feeling."
I realized things were heating up. But you know me, Colonel, I've
been in the police since I was a child, and this job as agent-
provocateur, it's something sacred to me, although it's hard work and,
as I say, I'm sick of wearing these civilian clothes. Anyway, I didn't
pay any attention and went on with all the usual things—the income
tax, the health service, and then a lot of stuff about our Infant King
(*Stands up.*)   and his uncle the Regent (*Sits down.*)   "So!" they all
shouted. "You're one of those, are you? You're going to stand here
and slander our beloved rulers." And then they all got together and
beat me up.

PRISONER   Bravo, what a fine set of men.

SERGEANT   And you know, Colonel, when they were beating me
up there were two conflicting feelings in my mind: a feeling of sadness
and a feeling of joy. I was sad that I had not carried out your order, that
I could not provoke anybody to be disloyal, and that once more there's
nobody we can arrest. But I was glad that love and reverence for the
government and for the persons (*Stands up.*)   of our Infant King and
his uncle the Regent (*Sits down.*)   are so widespread and strongly felt
by the population, as you can tell by my black eye.

PRISONER   (*Half to himself, enthusiastically*)   What a wonderful country!
Wonderful people!

CHIEF   What you need is some steak on that eye.

PRISONER   Colonel! What the sergeant has said makes me even more
convinced. I desire this instant to renounce my former ideals. They
disgust me whenever I think of them. I will now sign the declaration
of loyalty. Can I have a copy of it please, and pen and ink?

CHIEF (*Sadly*)   Is your mind made up, then?

PRISONER   Nothing can alter my decision now. When I leave this building, with all its memories and recollections, I shall straight away apply to work for the state. Give me the paper, please.

CHIEF   You don't mind about the stamps?

PRISONER   Why should I think about postage stamps when I can join the service of our Infant King (*Stands up.*)   and his uncle the Regent? (*Sits down.*)   The passion of a collector is nothing compared to the spirit of service. Of what use are my stamp albums when I can give myself up to the delights of loyalty, which I have discovered for the first time in my life after such a long phase as an anarchist?

CHIEF   All right, then. I won't press you anymore. Here is a pen, ink, and paper. If that's what you want, you can have it. (*Angrily puts the paper in front of the Prisoner.*)

PRISONER   At last! (*Signs it.*)

The Chief of Police takes the paper from him, blows on it, and dries it. He rings the bell. Enter the Policeman.

CHIEF   Bring his things in here. (*Exit the Policeman. To the Prisoner.*)   You have disappointed me. I thought you'd hold out longer. It was so impressive the way you never broke down . . .

The Policeman brings in the Prisoner's things: a cape, a mask, and a bomb.

CHIEF   It is my duty to return you the things that were found on your person at the moment of your arrest.

PRISONER   Ghosts of the past!

Takes the conspirator's cloak from the Policeman, throws it over his arm, and puts the mask in his pocket. The Policeman then hands him the bomb.

PRISONER (*cont.*)   Oh no! I don't want that. I've finished with that forever. Colonel, I would be so pleased if you would accept this bomb as a present from me and as a souvenir of our happy times together. It can be a mark of the fatherly triumph that you have achieved over me. It is all that remains of the last revolutionary. You can have the mask too. (*Takes the mask from his pocket.*)

CHIEF   Just as you like.

Unconcernedly takes the bomb and mask from the Prisoner's hand and puts them in a drawer.

PRISONER   Allow me to congratulate you, Colonel. The last revolutionary is dead. A new citizen has been born. In your place I would order the rockets to be sent up and give my staff three days' holiday. And why only three days? From now on there will be nothing left for them to do. Good-bye all and thank you for everything.

CHIEF   Don't mention it.

The Prisoner kisses the hand of the Chief of Police, then that of the Sergeant and of the Policeman. He walks out of the door. The Policeman makes a regulation about-face and also walks out. The Chief of Police and the Sergeant are left in silence. Suddenly a piercing shout is heard through the window from the Prisoner who is now in the street.

PRISONER   (*Offstage*)   Long live our Infant King and his uncle the Regent!

CHIEF   (*Hides his face in his hands and breaks down completely*)   My God! My God!

SERGEANT   (*Dreamily*)   I wonder if I could provoke him to be disloyal . . . ?

ACT II

The action takes place in the home of the agent-provocateur. On the wall are the well-known pictures of the Infant King and his uncle the Regent. There is a wedding photograph of the agent-provocateur sergeant and his WIFE. *A door and a window are in clear view, and there are two chairs, a table, and a tailor's dummy dressed in a very elaborate uniform of a police sergeant with a large number of medals. Nearby is a small screen, under which a pair of jackboots can be seen. There is a fig plant, or possibly a palm, and a small table carrying a pair of dumbbells. The agent-provocateur's Wife is onstage, as is the Chief of Police, who is dressed as in act 1 but disguised with a coat and hood thrown over his uniform. He is wearing his sword.*

CHIEF OF POLICE (*His hood pulled over his eyes*) Good morning. Is your husband at home?

WIFE No, I'm afraid he's not back from work yet.

CHIEF Not back from work? Today's his day off, isn't it?

WIFE He doesn't like days off. What do you want to see him about?

The Chief of Police moves into the center of the room and throws off his hood.

WIFE (*cont.*) Colonel! I didn't recognize you.

CHIEF Shhh . . . Not so loud! Did your husband say when he'd be back?

WIFE No. He went into town to do some voluntary provoking. I don't know when he'll be here.

CHIEF Please don't let me interrupt you. You're sewing, I see.

WIFE (*Ashamedly putting down her work*) Er . . . yes. It's just some gold braid for my husband's underpants. He feels so terrible in civilian clothes these days and always likes to wear some tiny piece of military dress, even if it's underneath everything. (*Suddenly changing her tones, imploringly.*) Colonel!

CHIEF Yes. What is it?

WIFE I wish you'd take him off this job. Don't make him do any more provoking in civilian clothes.

CHIEF Why not?

WIFE You've no idea how thin and pale he's got since he's had to go about in civvies. He can't exist out of uniform. He's withering away.

CHIEF I'm afraid that's just too bad, madam. Provoking is always done in civilian dress.

WIFE Couldn't he just wear his helmet? He always used to feel much better then.

CHIEF No, madam. A helmet would attract attention.

WIFE (*In a confidential tone*) Oh yes, of course. It's such a long time since he's had anyone to arrest. He probably doesn't show it in front of you, Colonel, but at home he's become moody and quite intolerable. One new arrest would put him right again.

CHIEF (*Pompously*) You can't make arrests without an agent-provocateur.

WIFE (*Dully and sadly*) I'm afraid I've just given up hope.

CHIEF *You* don't know anyone that we could arrest?

WIFE No! All the people I know are as loyal as hell. And if there was anyone, my husband would be the first person I'd tell, just to give him some peace of mind. He's always asking me.

CHIEF Any neighbors, then? Any distant relatives?

WIFE No. They're all law-abiding citizens. There was an old man on our street who used to complain, but with him it was the gout, not the government. He's just died, probably of being too careful.

CHIEF Yes, nowadays it's all so peaceful, all so quiet. Tell me, how did you first meet your husband?

WIFE Oh, that was ages ago, Colonel. He reported me to the secret police and I reported him. That's how we got to know each other.

CHIEF Have you got any children?

WIFE Two. But they're locked up now. Shall I get them down?

CHIEF No, please. I don't want to inconvenience anyone. I just dropped in to have a word with your husband.

WIFE   He may be back by now. He always listens at the doors on the way upstairs. I'll go and have a look.

Exit. Light footsteps are heard on the stairs. The window opens and through it enters the Sergeant in civilian clothes. He is carrying a raincoat and a small green hat.

SERGEANT   Colonel! Fancy seeing you in my house. How wonderful!

CHIEF   Psst! I'm here unofficially. I'll tell you why later. Why didn't you come in through the door?

SERGEANT   I was walking on the tops of the houses. When it was time to come home, I thought I'd come back across the roofs. It's one way of getting here, and there could have been something going on. Anyway, down in the street it couldn't be quieter.

CHIEF   What did you find?

SERGEANT   Nothing at all, Colonel. Just a few birds. Is my wife here?

CHIEF   She went out onto the staircase. She thought you were there.

SERGEANT   She always listens at the doors when she goes down those stairs. You don't mind if I change now, do you, Colonel? I feel naked without my uniform on.

CHIEF   No, do change if you like. You're in your own home, and it's your day off, anyway.

SERGEANT   (*Going behind the screen*)   Yes, I know. But you see, I thought maybe today would be my lucky day, and I went out. I did a bit of provoking before lunch, but as usual it was no good. They just said hello and walked on.

CHIEF   Sergeant, if it hadn't been for you perhaps we'd never have lived to see this alarming drop in the crime figures. That is to say, I mean, thanks to you we now have this perfect state of law and order. I must recommend you for promotion.

SERGEANT   (*All this time changing into uniform behind the screen*)   It's nothing, Colonel. I just felt I had to go and try once more. I like doing it, really. (*Pause. The Sergeant finishes changing.*)

He comes out in full uniform with sword and medals. He stretches himself luxuriously.

SERGEANT (*cont.*)   Ah, what a relief. At last I feel I can relax. Coming home from work, changing into uniform, you've no idea how marvelous it is. Oh . . . er, excuse me, Colonel. (*Realizes he has been behaving a little too informally. Comes to attention.*)   This is what comes of working in civvies. Civilian clothes are very bad for morale. You see, sir, I've got to take a grip on myself.

CHIEF   Oh, don't worry about that. I've got an important matter to discuss with you. Find some excuse to send your wife off; she mustn't come in here. I'm sure she's quite reliable, but what I have to talk to you about is most secret.

The Sergeant exits. His footsteps die away on the stairs. The Chief of Police takes off his coat and sits down. More footsteps. Enter the Sergeant.

SERGEANT   I sent her off to get some waterproof glue.

CHIEF   Couldn't you think up a better pretext than that?

SERGEANT   It wasn't a pretext, Colonel. I really need it. My raincoat got torn when they beat me up last time.

CHIEF   Oh, all right. Has she gone far?

SERGEANT   She won't be back for three quarters of an hour.

CHIEF   I suppose you're surprised by my visit.

SERGEANT   Just as you say, sir.

CHIEF   You're surprised, then?

SERGEANT   Yes, sir. The chief of police here in my house! I'd sooner have expected a revolution.

CHIEF   No wishful thinking now, Sergeant. And a keen sergeant must always be prepared for a revolution. No, I didn't really mean that. Your service record is irreproachable.

SERGEANT   But of course, Colonel.

CHIEF   Still, in your exemplary conduct there is something more than ordinary conscientiousness and sense of duty. (*The Sergeant comes to attention.*)   No, don't bother about that. Sit down.

SERGEANT   With your permission, sir, I'd rather do my exercises for a bit—that is if you don't mind, Colonel.

CHIEF   Your exercises?

SERGEANT   Always at this time, as soon as I get home, I do a little weight lifting or spring exercises. I must be able to cope with any situation that crops up. They're good for my muscles. (*Bends his biceps.*)   You want to try them?

CHIEF   No thank you. I can see from here. If you want to do your exercises, do them.

The Sergeant tucks up his sleeve, takes the dumbbell from the table, and returns to his place in front of the Chief of Police. All the while listening to his boss, he performs a few rhythmical lifts of the dumbbell every now and again. Every now and then he checks his biceps to see if they have hardened. He then tries the other arm. All this time he is engaged in conversation with the Chief of Police.

CHIEF (*cont.*)   As I said, you are not only an excellent policeman. I have found that you are something more than that.

SERGEANT (*In a very disciplined manner*)   Sir!

CHIEF   I find that you have given me an idea.

SERGEANT (*As before*)   Sir! Yessir!

CHIEF   You put on civilian clothes, do you not, when your job requires it, even though you can't stand wearing them?

SERGEANT   Yessir! Anything for my job, sir.

CHIEF   Exactly, in other words you sacrifice your personal likes and dislikes on the altar of service to the state. But that's not important. In examining your case I have come to the conclusion that your keenness, readiness, and devotion to duty are quite out of proportion to the tasks you fulfill so admirably, even though these tasks are certainly not easy.

SERGEANT   Yessir!

CHIEF   You give me the impression of a Hercules who spends his time cutting wood and carrying water. Of course, this sort of work is difficult and useful, but it is not the work of a Hercules. In you there is a strength, Sergeant, a strength which is only partly finding its outlet in ordinary work. For you are something more than a civil servant. You are inspired by the idea of order and general discipline. You are the mystic of the police force, the saint of the police. Why have you got so thin lately, Sergeant?

SERGEANT   It's my insomnia, Colonel.

CHIEF   Oh, I see. Tell me, do you have dreams?

SERGEANT   Well, I do sometimes, but they're silly.

CHIEF   Tell me about them.

SERGEANT   Often, I don't know why it is, but I dream that there are two of me.

CHIEF   Bravo! Bravo!

SERGEANT   One in uniform and another in civilian clothes. We are walking across a big field; the birds are singing, it's warm—and then I, that is, both of us, or both of me, feel in my soul that I am being carried far, far away . . . and somewhere out there . . . and there's a smell of fresh grass, you know, like in the spring—and then I feel such a desire, such a longing to arrest someone, to arrest someone even if it's just a hare sitting under a ridge, or a little bird. Then I look, or rather, we look, all around the field; we strain our eyes and there's nobody there, nobody to arrest, and then I throw myself on the soft earth, beat my head, and the tears pour out. And it's then that the stupidest part of my dream comes.

CHIEF   (*In great suspense*)   Tell me! Tell me!

SERGEANT   Then I dream that I arrest myself. That is to say—the I that's in uniform arrests the me that's in civilian clothes. Then I wake up covered in sweat.

The recounting of the dream has been a severe effort for the Sergeant. While he is telling it, he stops doing his gymnastics.

CHIEF   This is very interesting, what you say, very interesting. Now, Sergeant, when was the last time that you made an arrest?

SERGEANT   (*Heavily, despondently*)   Oh, Colonel. I'm ashamed to tell you.

CHIEF   Well, listen carefully to what I say.

SERGEANT   Yessir.

CHIEF Do you realize that we shall never have the chance to arrest anyone again?

SERGEANT (*Letting the weight fall from his hand*) What did you say, sir?

CHIEF (*Gets up from his chair and begins to walk about the room*) I'll tell you something else. Not only will we never arrest anyone ever again, but your son, your grandson, and your great-grandson—they won't arrest anyone either. The whole police force is standing on the edge of a precipice, on the eve of a catastrophe. What is the function of a policeman? It is to arrest those who offend against the existing order. But suppose there aren't any people like that left. Suppose that as a result of the operations of our improved and reconstituted police force the last trace of rebelliousness in our people has disappeared and that they have become universally enthusiastic for the regime. Suppose that they have formed once and for all a permanent love for our (*Stands at attention.*) Infant King and his Uncle the Regent. What is there for the police to do then? I did my best to improve matters and that is why I advised you to carry on provoking people to criticize the government but, as you see, even this last resort has come to nothing. Not only were you unable to provoke anyone, but when you started on your antigovernment slogans, they beat you up.

SERGEANT That's nothing. It's healed up already.

CHIEF That is not the point. We are dealing here with more general matters. For a long time I have been expecting and dreading the moment which has now arrived. Our last political prisoner has just signed the act of allegiance, has been released from prison, and has begun to serve our Infant King and his uncle the Regent. I tried to keep him back; I promised him stamps for his collection, it was no good. Do you know what this means? It means that we have beautiful prisons constructed at great expense; we have a highly trained, devoted staff; we have courtrooms, offices, and card indexes—and we now have not one single prisoner, not one single suspect, not one single clue to follow up. The people have become wildly, cruelly, bestially loyal.

SERGEANT That's true, Colonel. That's a fact. I'd . . .

CHIEF Soon, the time will come when we'll have to take off our uniforms; and then you'll toss and turn in bed at nights, longing hopelessly for one little interrogation. Your gold braid sewn onto your underpants won't be much good to you then. Already you're suffering from insomnia, and for the moment you've still got your job. Think what it'll be like soon, eh?

SERGEANT   No, no!

CHIEF   But yes, yes! They'll take away your uniform; they'll give you some sort of sports jacket, walking shoes, and a pair of flannels. You'll be able to go out into the fields or onto the water with a fishing rod or a shotgun if you like, and enjoy your spare time exactly as you wish. You'll be able to arrest hares and sparrows, so long as it isn't the mating season.

SERGEANT   Is there nothing we can do, Colonel?

CHIEF   (*Putting his arm around his shoulder, warmly*)   I have come to you not only in my capacity as chief of police, not only as your superior officer. At this dreadful time we are both of us just simple constables. In the face of the ruin that is facing our life's work, we must give each other our hands and offer brotherly advice for its solution.

Gives the Sergeant his hand. He is very much moved and squeezes it, at the same time wiping away a tear with his left hand.

CHIEF   (*cont.*)   And now listen to me. The man who can even now save the situation—is you.

SERGEANT   Me?

CHIEF   Yes, you. Pay attention to what I'm saying. What do we need? What we need is one person we could lock up, whom we could arrest for something that could in some very slight degree be described as antigovernment activity. Having several times attempted to find this man, it has become apparent that we shall not find him in the ordinary course of events, or in what we might call a natural manner. We must, so to speak, compose this man ourselves. My choice has fallen on you.

SERGEANT   I don't understand, sir.

CHIEF   What don't you understand?

SERGEANT   What I have to do.

CHIEF   Exactly the same as you've been doing all along: Shout something against the government, but with this difference—this time we won't let you off; we'll lock you up.

SERGEANT Me?

CHIEF I assure you that the fulfillment of the task I have set you is far more admirable from the point of view of police morality than simply provoking any old citizen to criticize the government and arresting him. That would simply be carrying out your ordinary daily work. Here it is a question of fulfilling an act that is not without a certain poetry of its own, an act which belongs only to a policeman who is specially selected, inspired, pierced right to the marrow of his bones with the spirit of the police force. This is what I was thinking of when I said that I saw in you the fire of a policeman's vocation, something that is rare even among the best of us. I said that there was something in you that had not found its proper outlet, that had been eagerly awaiting the assignment that I can only now reveal to you. You are going to be our sergeant redeemer.

SERGEANT Colonel, I'll always—anything I can do, sir—sir, I've got a headache.

CHIEF Don't worry about that. Now change back into civilian clothes.

SERGEANT What, again? What for?

CHIEF You can't act as your own provocateur wearing uniform.

SERGEANT All right, shall I change now? This minute?

CHIEF Yes, of course, we've no time to waste. When you've changed we'll open the window so they can hear you better from the street. Then you can stand by the window and shout out something as loud as you can against our Infant King and his uncle the Regent. (*Both stand to attention.*) Then I'll draw my sword, arrest you, and that's that.

SERGEANT My God, but I'm supposed to be a policeman!

CHIEF You are more a policeman than anyone else in the world. To be a member of the police and to pretend to others that you're not a policeman—that makes you a double policeman; but to be a policeman and to pretend to *yourself* that you're not a policeman—that makes you a policeman deep down, luxuriously, in the depths of your heart. We might say that you're a super-policeman, unlike any other policeman, even a double-police policeman.

The Sergeant goes behind the screen. There, groaning and sobbing, he changes into civilian clothes. The screen is low so that his head is visible and, at the bottom, his calves too.

CHIEF (*cont.*)   Before today is out I shall send a report to the general. Tomorrow morning our Infant King and his uncle the Regent will be informed that we have discovered and arrested a revolutionary. We shall be saved.

SERGEANT (*Doing up his buttons*)   What do I have to shout?

CHIEF   Haven't you got anything prepared from your previous experience?

SERGEANT   Shall I say that our Regent, the uncle of our Infant (*Stands to attention.*)   King, is a swine?

CHIEF   That's not direct enough. It must be something strong and forceful, with no understatement, so that I can arrest you one hundred percent.

SERGEANT   Well then, what about—dirty swine?

CHIEF   That's much better. We'll open the window. (*They open the window.*)   Now—one . . . two . . .

SERGEANT   Just a minute!

Runs away from the window and takes out a brush from behind the screen. With one careful movement he removes a speck of dust from the uniform which is now hanging again on the tailor's dummy. Puts down the brush and returns to the window.

SERGEANT (*cont.*)   All right, now! (*Fills his lungs with air.*)

CHIEF   One . . . two . . . three . . .

SERGEANT (*Shouts*)   Our Regent, the uncle of our Infant King, is a dirty swine!

CHIEF (*Drawing his sword, loudly*)   I arrest you in the name of our Infant King and his uncle the Regent.

SERGEANT'S WIFE (*Enters the room suddenly*)   Good heavens! Still trying to provoke people. Can't you ever take a rest?

CHIEF   Silence, woman! At last he's made a success of it!

ACT III

The Chief of Police's office, as in act one. A Policeman is nailing up some garlands made of leaves or something. He is preparing the decorations for the visit of the GENERAL. *The Chief of Police and the Sergeant are sitting opposite each other; the Chief behind the desk and the Sergeant where the Prisoner sat in the first act.*

CHIEF So—you've been trying to saw through the bars of your cell window. And you kicked one of the wardens. This is the second time it's happened.

SERGEANT I don't know what's come over me, really, Colonel.

CHIEF Is there anything you need?

SERGEANT (*Sadly*) No, thank you.

CHIEF Still, you look as if there's plenty you need. You're so pale, silent.

SERGEANT Maybe that's because I'm locked up in prison, sir.

CHIEF Every day, I send reports about you to the general. Thanks to you, we've been granted funds for rebuilding the prison, recruiting new personnel, and strengthening the patrols. The general has become personally interested in your case. He says you're a very dangerous man and that it's extremely fortunate I got you in time. (*The Sergeant shrugs his shoulders.*) Don't look so glum. If I didn't know you better I might think you were displeased with all this. The general says that today he will attend your interrogation in person.

SERGEANT He—he—he . . .

CHIEF Are you ill? Aren't you sleeping properly?

SERGEANT Not very well.

CHIEF Are you having dreams?

SERGEANT Now and again.

CHIEF What dreams?

SERGEANT I dream I'm walking through a great big field . . .

CHIEF   The birds are singing, eh?

SERGEANT   How do you know?

CHIEF   Are you wearing uniform or civilian dress?

SERGEANT   Civilian dress! An overcoat and plus fours.

CHIEF   And what else?

SERGEANT   I walk on and I look upward. There's a tree. And you, sir, are sitting on one of the branches and eating cheese.

CHIEF   I am sitting and eating cheese?

SERGEANT   Yes. I am standing under the tree and you open your mouth to arrest me, sir, and the cheese falls out of your mouth onto the ground.

CHIEF   And you pick it up?

SERGEANT   No. I don't like Gorgonzola.

CHIEF (*Displeased*)   A very stupid dream.

SERGEANT   Yes, Colonel.

CHIEF   Would you like a drink?

Without waiting for an answer, wishing to improve an unpleasant situation, he reaches toward the desk, takes out a bottle of beer and glasses, pours.

SERGEANT   Thank you. (*Drinks. Suddenly he puts down the glass.*)   No, really, Colonel, I mustn't drink with you.

CHIEF   Why not?

SERGEANT   Because I'm just an ordinary . . . Colonel, can you tell me, what am I?

CHIEF   What a question! You're yourself.

SERGEANT   But what does that mean, Colonel: I'm myself? I just don't know what I am now, a policeman or a prisoner. And another thing, if I'm a policeman, am I myself, or if I'm a prisoner, am I myself; and since I must be myself, am I a policeman or a prisoner?

CHIEF   I explained all this to you at the time of your arrest. Why start all over again?

SERGEANT It was all quite clear then, sir, because that was just the beginning and I still knew what I was—an ordinary police sergeant in the secret service. But things really started to go wrong earlier, when I was working as an agent-provocateur. Please don't be angry, sir, but I see now that it was then that it all started, and if I'd known at that time I'd have asked you to put someone else on this provoking job. It wasn't just an idle whim that I was so upset at having to wear civvies. A policeman should never take off his uniform, under any circumstances.

CHIEF Still, it never entered your head to make a complaint. And when it was your day off you went out to work of your own free will.

SERGEANT But, sir. It wasn't anything like as bad as it is now. I didn't have the remotest idea, sir. Even when you came to my house yourself and talked about my golden future and said I reminded you of Hercules, even then it was pretty awful, but at least I knew that I was a first-class policeman and, as you said, Colonel, far better than all the others. It only really began to get bad when you arrested me and I started my time in prison. Prison has a terrible effect on a man, sir. From the moment I was arrested everything started getting more and more confused.

CHIEF What do you mean?

SERGEANT Well, sir, to start with I remembered everything just as you explained it to me. Then I began to have attacks and blackouts. I got frightened and started repeating to myself over and over again: "I am a sergeant in the secret service. I am a sergeant in the secret service," or rather in the top-secret service. But then . . .

CHIEF What happened "then"?

SERGEANT Then I stopped repeating it. I didn't see the sense. And it reached the point, Colonel, that . . . Oh, anyway, what I meant was that I am just an ordinary . . .

CHIEF An ordinary what, damn it?

SERGEANT Either an ordinary policeman or an ordinary prisoner, and whichever I am . . .

CHIEF Why do you have to bring out these stupid, childish arguments. This is what comes of giving responsible jobs to people with no higher education. In your place a man with any intelligence . . .

SERGEANT   What I was going to say was that whichever of the two I am I do not think I should drink with you, sir. If I am to be a policeman, then I cannot condone your drinking with a prisoner—that is to say with me, because I am in fact under arrest. And if I am a prisoner, a revolutionary feared by the general himself and by the government of the country, there again I should not drink with you.

CHIEF   Why not?

SERGEANT   Because if I am a prisoner I must conduct myself according to the moral code of an imprisoned revolutionary, and I cannot drink with the chief of police, a representative of authority.

CHIEF   Have you gone mad?

SERGEANT   No, Colonel, this is something stronger than me. Are you in a position to release me from prison? No, you are not. So I've got to stay here. And if I have to stay in prison, the effect of that environment upon me becomes stronger and stronger. I've tried to fight it, but I feel that every day I spend in prison does something horrible to me—something I don't quite understand.

CHIEF   Maybe you *are* ill. Have you ever had trouble with your lungs?

SERGEANT   No, it's not that, Colonel. I couldn't be more healthy. You saw me yourself doing my dumbbell exercises, and I only wish you could have seen me doing my push-ups. This is something quite different. Do you know that since the time that you arrested me, I have started to develop certain new ideas?

CHIEF   Be careful what you say.

SERGEANT   No, sir, I want you to know about it. For example, before this I used to travel quite often by train, and I've never thought about it particularly. But when a man's in prison he becomes, I think, much more critical, and you know what I've decided?

CHIEF   How should I know? Tell me at once.

SERGEANT   That our railway system is atrocious.

CHIEF   Do you realize what you're saying? I warn you, I shall have to report this.

SERGEANT   Do make a report, sir, please. This sort of thing gets a hold on a man and he just can't stay silent any longer. Take art and culture, for example. Will you tell me, Colonel, why did we have to torment and persecute those poor artists . . . ?

CHIEF   (*Writing quickly*)   A little slower, please. What were those last two words?

SERGEANT   I said "those poor artists."

CHIEF   . . . tists. Right. (*Taking his eyes from the paper and stopping writing.*)   No, I don't believe it. You, with your record of loyal service, do you really hold these opinions? We've worked together for so many years; everything's always gone smoothly, and all the time you were . . . Do you really think that things are so bad in this country? Think it over.

SERGEANT   What is there to think over? Listen: If I move my plank bed against the wall, put the bucket on it upside down, and stand on it, I can see out of the window of my cell. There's a field there and just now it's full of farmers because it's harvest time. When I examine them closely I can't help thinking—and I wish you could see it, sir— what sour expressions they've got on their faces, the general dissatisfaction that's painted on them.

CHIEF   This is an entirely subjective outlook on your part. Quite apart from the conclusion to which it leads, whether they're loyal or disloyal, subjectivism as a method is entirely opposed to our party program. I would have had to punish you even if you hadn't mentioned this so-called dissatisfaction. And besides, it's against the rules to look out of the window.

SERGEANT   But not for someone who's fighting against the government, Colonel. Someone like that would not deprive himself even of the most trivial act of rebellion. On the contrary, he would consider it part of his duty, to bring his mission to fulfillment, not to mention the satisfaction it would give him. And another thing, when I look out of the window, I can see a newly built crematorium on the other side of the field, and that also gives me food for thought. It is a nonproductive investment.

CHIEF   Would you deny atheists the right to dispose of their bodies as they like, with their own sort of funeral? If you are against religious tolerance how can you have the nerve to criticize the government's record in that respect?

SERGEANT　Those people are dead, and your argument is not valid. And even if I hadn't looked out of the window, there are writings scratched on the walls in my cell. A man sits there with nothing to do, so he reads. Some of them make you think. They aren't so stupid.

CHIEF　What, for instance?

SERGEANT　"Down with tyranny," Colonel.

CHIEF　So! That's the way it is! It's reached that stage. And I suppose our Regent (*Comes to attention.*)　the uncle of our Infant King (*The Sergeant, however, remains seated.*)　is an idiot.

SERGEANT　(*Sadly*)　I'm afraid so, Colonel.

CHIEF　And I suppose our Infant King is a shortarse.

SERGEANT　I'm afraid so, Colonel.

CHIEF　(*Choking with anger*)　Umph!

The Policeman is walking around the room all this time, but not in such a way as to interrupt the dialogue. He carries in a Christmas tree, hangs garlands on it, leaves the room, and returns. Everything is done most discreetly. At this moment he enters the room.

POLICEMAN　Sir! The general's arrived, sir.

The Chief of Police runs to put away the bottle and straightens his uniform. Shortly afterward the former prisoner and revolutionary enters the room in the uniform of an aide-de-camp. He has no beard but has a policeman's mustache. He stands at attention in front of the door, facing the audience, with his side toward the door where the General is going to enter. The Chief of Police and the Policeman are also at attention. The Sergeant stands up reluctantly. Enter the General in suitable regalia, with a mustache, of course. He walks up to the Sergeant and stands in front of him, inspecting him.

GENERAL　So! This is the man . . .

CHIEF　Yessir, that's him.

GENERAL　He looks to me like the ringleader. Have you managed to find the rest of his gang?

CHIEF Not yet, but we're interrogating him systematically.

GENERAL A dangerous bird. Did you find any explosive materials on him?

CHIEF Not so far. But we haven't given up hope.

GENERAL (*Gives a whistle*) Hmmm. He's more dangerous than I thought. He's dishonest. Good, straightforward revolutionaries always have a couple of pounds of dynamite on them. It looks to me as if we've caught their key man. What do you think, Lieutenant?

AIDE I agree, sir. If he's been searched and nothing's been found on him it means there's more to this than meets the eye.

GENERAL Oh, Colonel, allow me to present to you my aide-de-camp. I've just chosen him as my special adviser on revolutionary affairs and antigovernment activity. He's an expert on that subject.

CHIEF Sir! No, it's impossible, sir.

GENERAL What's the matter with you?

CHIEF Your Excellency, you must allow me to speak, sir. You have become the victim of a mistake, sir, or of a deliberate trick. This man . . .

GENERAL Speak up, man.

CHIEF He was the one who threw the bomb at you, sir.

GENERAL Who?

CHIEF Your present assistant and my former prisoner.

GENERAL Yes, Colonel, please continue.

CHIEF I swear to you, sir, I am not mistaken. I know him well. For ten years I used to interrogate him here in my office—on this chair, sir. It is impossible that Your Excellency should have such an assistant.

GENERAL What have you got to say, Lieutenant?

AIDE The colonel's right, of course. I am his former prisoner. The fact that he recognized me in this uniform and with a different hairstyle is a great tribute to his keenness and professional skill.

CHIEF Why, you impertinent . . .

AIDE   I am your former prisoner, Colonel, naturally. But you seem to have forgotten that I signed the act of allegiance and was released. His Excellency is perfectly well aware of all this.

GENERAL   Calm yourself, Colonel. I knew it all along, really. And you can see that if I introduce the lieutenant as an expert in matters concerning the fight against subversive activity, it is not without justification.

CHIEF   But the bomb . . . the bomb . . . I've still got it in my drawer.

GENERAL   My dear Colonel, everybody sometime has to throw some bomb at some general or other. The organism of the body demands it. The sooner you get it over the better. As for me, I have complete confidence in my new assistant precisely because he has all this behind him. There are so many people who have still not satisfied this natural urge. You mustn't be angry if I ask you, Colonel, but have you ever thrown a bomb at a general?

CHIEF   Your Excellency!

GENERAL   You see. Neither have I. And therefore, if you'll forgive my saying so, I have more confidence in my assistant than I have in you, or even in myself. I promise you, Colonel, that if you want to be thought of as the ideal chief of police, part of your job should consist of taking precautions in case I throw a bomb at myself. Have you thought about that?

CHIEF   No, sir.

GENERAL   You see. You should think about it. The person of a general is the property of the state and the government, not of the individual who holds the rank. So any attempt of this sort, even on my part, must be considered an attack against the uniform of an officer and, so, indirectly, against the state. And if ever you should have to arrest me on this account, I trust you will remember that it was I who reported myself to you and brought this vital information to the notice of chief of police, and in my trial this will be considered as an extenuating circumstance. That is the situation.

The Chief of Police comes to attention.

GENERAL (*cont.*)   To revert to our discussion about the lieutenant, I will tell you something else. He entered the service not long ago and came to us from a situation that was, I need hardly tell you, extremely different from our own. Already he has achieved the rank of an officer. This requires some effort, as you can imagine. We must congratulate him on his keenness and hard work. We, Colonel, are the old guard, and have acquired our qualities of loyalty little by little. In him a love for the government has exploded suddenly, fresh and pure, and has been concentrated by his long years of antigovernment activities. And as regards his qualifications for this present job, I can assure you that he is second to none in combating these same activities. Therefore in expressing your dislike of him you lay yourself open to the charge—groundless, I am sure—of being jealous of him because of his lightning success.

CHIEF I can promise you, sir . . .

GENERAL All right. Don't worry. I brought him here specially because I knew we had a tricky case on our hands with this enemy of (*Stands to attention.*) our Infant King and his uncle the Regent. It'll be quite a business, you can be sure. Shall we begin?

They take their places and sit down ready for the interrogation. There is an air of expectation, as before a stage performance.

GENERAL (*cont.*) Proceed, Lieutenant, if you please.

CHIEF Allow me to suggest . . .

GENERAL What, you again? You ought to be ashamed of yourself. This aversion of yours toward our young people is beginning to look suspicious.

AIDE I'm afraid you're going to be disappointed, Your Excellency, both you and the chief of police. The matter will be quite short and simple.

CHIEF Oh, you think so do you, young man?

GENERAL I agree with the Colonel; you are overestimating the simplicity of the case. We know that as a result of the accused's incredible treachery and low cunning we have no evidence of any substance against him. The extent of his subversive activity is borne out by his outburst concerning our Regent (*They stand, then sit.*) the uncle of our Infant King, the outburst which immediately unmasked the criminal and became the grounds for his summary arrest. And if the criminal shouted out things like that at the top of his voice, how much more terrible must be the things that he has been carrying on in silence. Still, we do not possess the materials that would enable us to discover what the criminal has done. I need only mention the fact that no explosives were found on him. On what ground, then, do you consider that the case is short and simple?

AIDE I do not intend at this time to point to any hostile acts that the prisoner has committed openly. But I can state quite categorically that such acts are to be found lurking in their full baseness in the personality of the accused, and that even if they have not yet been carried out, they exist with the same reality as if they had been carried out. For we know, do we not, that time is one, and that it is not to be divided into time past and time present? And from the point of view of the investigation it is the most clear and damning truth.

CHIEF If you will allow me, General, two words . . .

GENERAL But of course! Please!

CHIEF I do not deny that we have to deal with an exceptionally dangerous criminal, and that those who have been claiming that the police have nothing to do deserve simply to be pitied, if not actually arrested. It seems to me, though, that the method employed by my colleague the lieutenant is the sign of an engaging though, perhaps, overrash belief in his own abilities—typical of the inexperienced.

GENERAL Colonel, I thought I asked you . . .

AIDE As far as I know the criminal began his unusually intensive enemy activity after a long period of loyalty and even of cooperation with the government.

CHIEF That is so, my young friend.

AIDE We have then to deal with an exceptionally dangerous individual. It is a process analogical with the one that you, General, were so kind as to outline a moment ago when you were evaluating my career— that is to say a process of contrary direction. This man, at a comparatively late age—which leads to a sharpening of the symptoms—achieved his first sensual pleasures with the feeling that he was being persecuted. As you know, this feeling gives one an illusion of one's own importance and dignity, the same, in fact, in intensity as the feeling of God-fearing loyalty and agreement with the prevailing viewpoints, although entirely different from it in its detail, of course, and this is why it is so extraordinarily attractive to people who have not yet experienced it.

CHIEF   I do not agree. This man is an abominable sort of criminal, that is obvious, but I do not see in what way he is worse than other such people who . . . who throw bombs at generals.

GENERAL   That damn bomb again!

Consternation, muttering. Chief of Police puffs through his mustache.

AIDE   I can assure you, Colonel, that this man is capable of throwing a bomb at three generals without batting an eyelid.

CHIEF   (*Impulsively, to the Sergeant, in his old superior-officer tone of voice*) Attention!

The Sergeant instinctively draws himself up to attention.

CHIEF   (*cont.*)   Speak up now! Would you throw a bomb at the general?

GENERAL   Answer frankly and truthfully, Sergeant. Don't take any notice of us.

SERGEANT   Well—er—no, sir. Of course I might have a few strange ideas, I admit, about the railways and the agriculture and things like that; but to throw a bomb at the general . . .

CHIEF   (*Triumphantly*)   You see, gentlemen.

AIDE   (*To the Sergeant, pressingly*)   Imagine that you are taking a stroll on Sunday afternoon and it so happens that you have a bomb with you. You've taken it from your house, though you don't quite know why. All around you there are people, beautiful women—and suddenly you see a general . . .

SERGEANT   A real one?

CHIEF   (*Sharply*)   Behave yourself, Sergeant.

AIDE   Right! The general is walking straight toward you. He doesn't turn aside, just keeps on walking straight ahead. His medals are sparkling, his jackboots are shining. You feel that now you can pay him back for everything; that such a beautiful general won't come your way a second time.

SERGEANT The bastard!

CHIEF For the last time . . .

AIDE Well? Well?

Silence.

SERGEANT (*Struggling with himself. At last, with a heavy sigh of resignation*) No, I can't. (*Everyone relaxes.*)

CHIEF I hope you're satisfied, General.

GENERAL To be quite frank, I am beginning to wonder why you are obstructing the investigation.

CHIEF Me? Obstructing the investigation? Me?

GENERAL That's how it looks to me. How important is it to you that nothing be proved against this man?

CHIEF I protest . . .

GENERAL It seems clear to me that you are trying to hinder my assistant in his final unmasking of the criminal, in his laying bare of the full baseness of the man. I warn you that I may feel it my duty to discuss your position with the Regent, the uncle of our Infant King. (*They stand, then sit.*)

CHIEF And for my part I should like to inform His Excellency that I possess adequate means to demonstrate to His Excellency the unprofitability of this sort of interference.

GENERAL Are you threatening me?

CHIEF I would not presume to do so, sir. I merely state that I am washing my hands of the whole affair and that I will accept no responsibility for the further development of the matter in hand.

GENERAL Very well. We shall return to our interrogation.

AIDE May I ask that the prisoner be removed for a moment?

GENERAL Certainly. Colonel, will you . . . ?

CHIEF (*Rings a bell. Enter the Policeman.*) Take him out into the corridor. Bring him back when I ring. (*The Policeman takes the Sergeant out.*)

AIDE I still maintain that basically the accused is guilty of a bomb attack on the general. The problem is simply that he is a man of low intelligence and has too little imagination. But I have a plan.

GENERAL We are listening.

AIDE In the colonel's desk there is a bomb—the same one that at a certain time in the past I threw at the general. The bomb does not work, the best proof of which is the fact that the general is still here among us. I propose that we call the suspect in and give him this bomb. We will open the door, the general will go out into the corridor, and then I guarantee that when he has the bomb in his hands and sees the general standing opposite him, all his libertarian and anarchist instincts will be aroused. Unable to resist them any longer, he throws the bomb. In this way we will acquire a dazzlingly clear proof of his extreme evil intentions and crimes in conditions as closely as possible approaching the natural.

GENERAL But this is madness. What do you think about it, Colonel?

CHIEF I think, sir, that your assistant, your chosen expert on these questions and an officer of great promise in spite of his short record of service, is quite right. You should not lightly reject the idea of this experiment, General, and obstruct the investigations.

AIDE I repeat, the bomb is harmless. The detonator didn't make contact. At least, last time it didn't.

GENERAL So, Lieutenant, you think that . . .

AIDE I am carrying out my duty and suggesting what I consider to be the most effective means of unearthing antigovernment activities. I am an officer in the service of (*They all stand, they all sit.*) our Infant King and his uncle the Regent.

GENERAL I think you may be a little bit too smart, young man.

CHIEF As a friend of yours, General, I would not advise any slackness in your conduct of this investigation. I may tell you in confidence that in the reports which I send *directly* to (*They stand, then sit.*) the

Regent, the uncle of our Infant King, I shall be forced to describe in detail your relationship with and attitude toward the police service, and in particular your enthusiasm for unmasking the enemies of our (*They all stand, they all sit.*)   Infant King and his uncle the Regent.

GENERAL (*Dejectedly*)   Show me the bomb. I must think.

The Chief of Police goes to the desk and brings the bomb over to the General. He hands it to the Aide-de-Camp who returns it to the Chief of Police.

AIDE   Yes, it's the same bomb.

GENERAL   Definitely?

AIDE   Quite definitely.

CHIEF   Well then, General, do you agree?

GENERAL   Are you suggesting, Colonel, that I'm being uncooperative? Please explain the situation to the prisoner.

The Chief of Police rings the bell. The Policeman brings in the Sergeant.

CHIEF   You can go, Constable. (*Exit Policeman.*)   You are going to throw this bomb at the general.

SERGEANT   What, just like that?

CHIEF   The general will stand in the corridor and you will be in here.

GENERAL   Can't we put it off until tomorrow?

CHIEF   Just as you like, General. Shall we consult the opinion of the government on this matter?

GENERAL   Oh, no, no. I'm going.

Closes the door behind him. The Chief of Police positions the Sergeant, gives him a demonstration of how to throw and hands him the bomb. The idiocy of the situation grows clearer.

AIDE   Just a moment, General.

GENERAL (*Opens the door slightly*)   What?

AIDE   Leave the door open, please. Otherwise he can't throw the bomb at you.

GENERAL   Oh, of course. (*Leaves the door open.*)

AIDE   Give him my mask. It should be there in the drawer with the bomb. The illusion must be complete. (*Gives the mask to the Sergeant.*)

CHIEF (*Stepping back*)   Ready. Right, Lieutenant, over to you.

AIDE   OK. Now, you are strolling along . . . There are beautiful women . . . Over here where the colonel is standing, the sun is blazing in the sky, and there (*Points to the corridor.*)   there is the general. His medals are sparkling, his jackboots are shining, and now you think to yourself, at last you'll pay him back for everything. You can see the general . . .

The Sergeant throws the bomb. The lights are extinguished for a second. A flash and an explosion. For a second, it stays dark and then normal light. The Chief of Police and the Aide-de-Camp stand opposite one another in silence.

CHIEF   I suppose you liked the general. As your superior officer he always treated you with great courtesy.

AIDE   Quite the opposite from the way in which he treated you. He seemed to ignore the fact that you have been the chief of police for years and years.

CHIEF   What would you say if I were to place you under arrest. You must admit that that little matter of the bomb is, to say the least, doubtful.

AIDE   Yes, I have to admit that. Doubtful to the extent that your part in it is extremely obscure. In that case we would find ourselves in the curious situation of mutual arrest.

CHIEF   Young man, you will go far, but not so far as you think, and not toward my position, that of chief of police, but in precisely the opposite direction. I arrest you. (*Draws his sword and arrests the Aide-de-Camp.*)

AIDE   Fine. I'm afraid, though, that by acting in this way you have brought your career to a very sharp close. I must point out, sir, that your laughable attempts to charge me with the bomb attack can only turn themselves automatically to your disfavor.

CHIEF   And why should that be, my friend?

AIDE   Very simply, old boy, you are accusing me of opposing the government and of attempted murder. They will ask you where you were when that certain lieutenant signed the act of allegiance and was released from prison. What sort of a chief of police would you be if the meanest convicted prisoner was able to pull the wool over your eyes? What sort of a security officer were you if you failed to spot his little game and simply released him from custody. And if you argue that you were right to release me, because my repentance was genuine, you would be quite correct since I really was and am sincere in my loyalty and entirely devoted to the government. However, in this way you would bring to nothing your accusation against me of attempted murder, and would place yourself in the ludicrous situation of a squalid intriguer. But to return to the point. What would you say if I were to arrest you?

CHIEF Please do not think that the police are above arrest. On the contrary, arrest is above us. It is above everything. I am a policeman with a long record of service. So, if you think that you can establish a case . . .

AIDE Of course I can. This is how I see the situation: One of the most elementary duties of the head of the police is to protect generals against attacks by bombs. And what did you do? You personally pressed the bomb into the hands of the arrested revolutionary; you personally showed him how to throw it. It's frightful.

CHIEF Have you gone mad? The whole thing was your suggestion.

AIDE . . . Which you adopted with suspicious eagerness.

CHIEF But only under pressure from you. It was you who wanted to do it. It was you who were so keen on that experiment with the bomb.

AIDE But I am not the head of the police. I repeat: What is the most elementary duty of the chief of police? Any fool will tell you: to protect generals against bomb attacks.

CHIEF But the bomb ought never to have gone off. You told me yourself it was useless.

AIDE I've got nothing to do with it. You had no right to believe me.

CHIEF And you assured me a moment ago that you were speaking the truth and that you are loyal to the government.

AIDE   That is correct. I am loyal to the government. But you as the chief of police ought to know that the fact that something is correct does not necessarily have any special meaning. It can eventually have, or perhaps does have, an opposite meaning, depending on certain circumstances. You see, in spite of your record of long service, you can still only understand the most primitive arguments.

CHIEF   (*Resigned*)   All right. We will remain under mutual arrest until the situation is cleared up.

The Aide-de-Camp draws his sword and arrests the Chief of Police. Enter the General.

CHIEF   (*cont.*)   General! You're alive!

GENERAL   I'm not such a fool. I went and hid in the lavatory.

AIDE   I must point out that the chief of police's outburst a moment ago must be considered as extremely incriminating. The astonishment expressed in the sentence "General! You're alive!" shows that the chief of police was expecting, if not actually counting on, something else.

GENERAL   I'm afraid that I am forced to arrest both of you. There are two possibilities: Either it was an accident or else one of you three wound up the detonator. Unfortunately, even we are not yet able to arrest accidents, so we are left with the second possibility. The prisoner doesn't count because he is already under arrest, and so I am left with you two gentlemen.

CHIEF   Precisely. The lieutenant's past record will doubtless give the tribunal plenty to think about.

AIDE   The members of the court of inquiry will doubtless see the chief of police's motives as a classic example of their type. Leaving aside for the moment the real, more serious charges that he must face, I imagine that he intends to compromise the general's assistant. It is an understandable desire, but it arises from feelings that are purely personal and have nothing in common with the service of our government.

CHIEF   I regret to inform you, General, that in the name of this government of yours, I must place you under arrest.

GENERAL   Me? What for?

CHIEF   For irresponsibly exposing the uniform of a general to attacks by bombs. You are under suspicion of condoning subversive conduct. It was you who aroused my sense of duty in this matter, and that will be regarded as a mitigating circumstance at your trial.

AIDE   We still haven't sorted out the question of whether a policeman who has arrested an individual with whom he finds himself in a state of mutual arrest, like the chief of police is with me, is able to arrest a third individual, by whom he has at some time previously been arrested together with the first individual to whom he is united by the first double action of arrest.

CHIEF   Persons under arrest are not permitted to express an opinion.

AIDE   The same to you, Colonel.

GENERAL   It looks, gentlemen, as if the police now have plenty of work on their hands.

The Sergeant has up to now been standing modestly apart from the others. He now utters a high-pitched cry and raises one arm in the air. The rebel in him has come completely to the fore.

SERGEANT   Long live freedom!

OUT AT SEA

❦

Translated by Nicholas Bethell

CHARACTERS

FAT

MEDIUM

THIN

POSTMAN

BUTLER

The action takes place in a single act and with a single set, which represents a raft out at sea. Three shipwrecked men, in smart black suits and white shirts, with their ties correctly tied and white handkerchiefs sticking out of the top pockets of their jackets, are each sitting on a chair. There is also a large trunk on the raft.

FAT   I am hungry.

MEDIUM   I could do with some food.

THIN   Are the provisions entirely exhausted?

FAT   The provisions are entirely exhausted. There is not the tiniest morsel.

THIN   I thought there was one more can of sausages and baked beans?

FAT   There are no more cans.

MEDIUM   What I want is something to eat.

THIN   I want something too.

FAT   "Something"? Gentlemen, we must be realistic. What we want is more like . . .

MEDIUM   I don't care what it is.

THIN   You said the provisions were exhausted. So what have you got in mind?

FAT   We must eat not something, but someone . . .

MEDIUM   (*Looking behind, to right, and to left*)   I can't see . . .

THIN   I can't see anyone either, except . . . (*Suddenly stops talking. Pause.*)

FAT   We must eat one of us.

MEDIUM   Fine! Let's start.

THIN   (*Agreeing with undue haste*)   Yes, let's start!

FAT   Gentlemen, we must not be children. Allow me to point out that we cannot all join in a cry of "let's start." In such a situation one of us must say, "If you please, gentlemen, be so kind as to help yourselves."

MEDIUM   Who?

THIN   Who?

FAT   That is exactly the question I was going to ask. (*There follows an awkward silence.*)   I appeal to your sense of loyalty and to your good breeding.

MEDIUM (*Suddenly points to the sky, as if he had just spotted something amazingly interesting*)   Look! There's a seagull! A seagull!

THIN   I'm sorry to have to admit this so frankly, but I am an extremely selfish man. I have always been an egoist. Even when I was a schoolboy, I used to eat my lunch quite alone. I never shared it with anyone.

FAT   How very unpleasant. In that case we shall have to draw lots.

MEDIUM   Fine.

THIN   That is the best solution.

FAT   We shall draw lots in accordance with the following system. One of you two gentlemen will declare a number. Then the second gentleman will choose another number. Finally I too shall declare a third number. If the sum of all three numbers is odd, the lot will fall upon me. I shall be eaten. However, if it so happens that the sum is even, one of you two will be eaten.

Pause.

MEDIUM   No . . . I don't think I approve of gambling.

THIN   What happens if you make a mistake?

FAT   I am sorry if you don't trust me.

MEDIUM   We'd better find another way. We are civilized men. Drawing lots is a remnant of the Dark Ages.

THIN   It's superstitious nonsense.

FAT   Very well. We can organize a general election.

MEDIUM   Not a bad idea. (*To Fat.*)   I suggest you and I form an electoral alliance. That will simplify the campaign.

THIN   Parliamentary democracy is out of date . . .

FAT   But there's no other way. If you'd prefer a dictatorship, I'd be happy to assume the supreme power.

THIN   Oh no. Down with tyranny.

FAT   Free elections, then.

MEDIUM   And secret ballot.

THIN   And no electoral alliances. Every candidate must campaign separately.

FAT   (*Stands up, opens the trunk, and takes out a top hat*)   Here is a hat. Into it we shall put our voting slips with the name of the candidate.

THIN   I don't have a pen.

MEDIUM   I would be happy to lend you one.

FAT   (*Taking a fountain pen from his pocket*)   Here is a pen!

MEDIUM   (*Rubbing his hands*)   Hurrah for the elections!

THIN   One moment. If we are going to arrange these elections like civilized men, we cannot leave out the preelection campaign. Everywhere in the cultural world the campaign precedes the voting.

FAT   If you insist . . .

MEDIUM   All right, let's make it quick.

FAT   (*Gets up from his chair and walks to the center of the raft*)   The campaign is now open. Who will be the first to speak?

MEDIUM   (*To Thin*)   What about you?

THIN   I'd rather speak later. I was never a good orator.

FAT   But it was your suggestion.

MEDIUM   Exactly, all this electioneering and politicizing was your idea. So you must be the first to speak.

THIN   Of course, as you gentlemen wish . . . (*Stands on his chair, as if on the rostrum. The two other castaways arrange themselves in front of him. Fat takes from his pocket a cloth banner with two handles, one of which he hands to Medium. They hold the banner above their heads. It reads:* WE WANT FOOD.)   Ha-hmm . . . gentlemen!

MEDIUM (*Interrupting him*)   Don't you soft-soap us! We're simple people!

FAT   I quite agree. Down with idle phrases. We want the whole truth.

THIN   My friends, we are gathered here . . .

MEDIUM (*Interrupting him*)   Get to the point!

FAT   We haven't got all day!

THIN   We are gathered here to discuss the burning question of food supplies. My friends, it would be wrong for you to consider me as a candidate. I have a wife and children. Many a time, at sunset, I have sat in my garden, watching my children swinging away on their swing, my wife knitting, and the darkness gathering. Gentlemen! Friends! Can you visualize this serene, beautiful picture? Does it not touch you?

MEDIUM   That's no argument. When it's a matter of the public good, sentiment is out of the question. Your children can swing on their own.

FAT   Better, probably.

THIN   My friends! When I was a boy, I had such wonderful plans for the future. True, I did not work hard enough. I never achieved my dreams. But it is still not too late. All this can be changed, I assure you. I am not going to neglect my duty any longer. I've had my troubles, it's true—lack of self-confidence, laziness—but I shall improve, I swear it. I shall exercise my will, shape my character, acquire knowledge, and finally achieve everything that lies in store for me. I shall become someone.

MEDIUM   Louder!

THIN   I shall become someone!

FAT   Selfish!

MEDIUM   We want food!

FAT   All together now: one, two, three . . .

FAT AND MEDIUM (*Simultaneously*)   We want food! We want food!

THIN (*Breaking down, almost in tears*)   No. It's no good . . . it's no good . . . (*Comes down from the tribune.*)

MEDIUM (*Hands him his end of the banner and mounts the rostrum himself*)   Fellow diners!

FAT   Hear, hear!

Thin begins clapping his hands, but not very enthusiastically.

MEDIUM   I am not an orator and I do not intend to speak for long. Action is my motto. Ever since my childhood I have been passionately interested in the art of cookery. It's not so much the actual food—oh no! I'm a man of modest appetites and quite frankly I don't like eating. All I need is—that is to say I eat very little, almost nothing, in fact. What am I saying? I don't eat anything at all. Two years ago, maybe I ate a little piece here and there, every two or three days, but now? Not a thing! I've finished with food once and for all. However, the preparing of food has become the joy of my life. As a cook I know nothing more exciting than to watch other people eating what I have made with such careful effort and enjoying it. That is the only reward I desire. Let me add simply that I am a specialist in meat dishes. My sauces are without equal. That is all I have to say.

FAT   Bravo! (*Applauds. Thin is apathetic, and hardly reacts at all. Medium descends from the rostrum and Fat takes his place.*)

MEDIUM   Hurrah!

He stops. Fat stands with arms akimbo. For a moment he looks about him in all directions, as if surrounded by a vast crowd.

FAT (*Suddenly extends his hand in a fascist salute*)   Hungry men, I salute you!

MEDIUM (*Enthusiastically*)   Hurrah! Hear, hear!

FAT (*Silences him with an authoritative gesture of his hand*)   My speech will be brief—one soldier to another. First, I do not want to influence your opinions. You must decide for yourselves. I am your servant, and your will is sacred to me. I eat what I am given. Second, there's no point in denying it, I am indigestible. I have always been weak, bony, and leathery. I have two metal ribs, an amputated liver, and one leg shorter than the other. Why should I hide it? Third, I do not wish to be a demagogue. I prefer straight talking. If I am not chosen, I shall give the other man the rump and the sirloin all to himself. I shall be happy with what's left over, and the tongue. Let any man with aggressive intentions beware. I shall not surrender the tongue!

MEDIUM   Bravo, bravo! Long live our leader!

FAT   That's all. No more chattering or philosophy. Forward to battle!

MEDIUM   Bravo! Hear, hear! Encore! Three cheers! Hurrah!

Fat comes down from the rostrum. Thin and Medium roll up their banner.

FAT (*To Thin*)   Are you satisfied?

THIN   You were wonderful! Only . . . it's just that . . . that I can't eat sirloin. It's bad for me. If it doesn't make any difference to you . . .

MEDIUM (*Standing at attention in front of Fat*)   Sir! My congratulations. Your speech moved me deeply. In the matter of the tongue I am entirely on your side.

FAT   Well, that's the end of the campaign. Now we shall vote.

Fat puts down the top hat in the middle of the raft. The men go to three separate corners of the raft and start to write on their cards, their backs turned to each other. Fat and Medium snatch glances at Thin. Fat creeps up to Thin and peeps over his shoulder. Thin notices him in time and hides his card. Then he gives the pen back to Fat.

THIN   Thank you very much.

FAT   Don't mention it. Anything else I can do for you, I am at your disposal.

Fat walks off to another corner of the raft. Now Fat and Medium fill in their cards. All the time Thin is standing with his back to them, gazing at the sea. Then they all turn around at the same time, walk into the middle of the raft, and put their slips into the top hat.

FAT (*cont.*)   Now we shall count the votes.

MEDIUM   It's very exciting. Voting certainly sharpens the appetite.

THIN   You might be more tactful.

Fat puts his hand into the top hat. Then he raises his head and gazes silently at Thin. A long pause.

THIN (*cont.*)   What's the matter? What has happened?

MEDIUM   What's the result?

FAT   Gentlemen, we must annul the elections.

MEDIUM   Why? I'm hungry.

THIN   Are you trying to sabotage our free, democratic elections?

FAT   In the top hat there are four cards. Four!

As before, Fat looks suspiciously at Thin; so does Medium.

THIN (*Innocently*)   I said parliamentary democracy was out of date.

MEDIUM   What happens now?

FAT   This is a cabinet crisis. Maybe it would be simpler to nominate a candidate?

THIN   Who will do the nominating?

FAT   I should be happy to oblige.

THIN   Exactly. Just as I thought. No! Out of the question.

MEDIUM   A very bad business. Democracy doesn't work. Dictatorship is unacceptable. We've got to think of something.

FAT   At such moments the only one who can help us is a man of devotion and inspiration who will offer *himself*. When the normal forms of behavior fail, it is the volunteers who so often save the situation. (*Preparing once again for an oration.*)   My dear friend . . .

THIN   Oh no! I won't listen to you.

MEDIUM   Listen to him!

FAT   My dear friend! We know that characteristics such as devotion to duty, love of one's neighbor, and loyalty cannot be concealed. From the moment of our meeting, my friend and I saw that in you there was something that separated you from us. I refer, of course, to your innate nobility, your unswerving desire to assist the common good, your readiness to . . . Isn't that right, my friend?

MEDIUM (*Eagerly*)   In all my life I never met a better man.

FAT We are happy that at last society can provide you with the chance to fulfill your pure, though hidden, longing: your yearning to be remembered by us as a man who was modest, loyal, warmhearted, delightful, succulent . . .

THIN No! I don't want to.

MEDIUM What's that? You don't want to volunteer?

THIN No.

FAT Will you betray your fellow men? Surely you must . . .

THIN No.

MEDIUM That's disgraceful!

FAT You absolutely refuse?

THIN I refuse categorically. I have no call to greatness.

MEDIUM I don't think I want to speak to you ever again. I thought you were a man of honor, the patriot of our raft. And you have shown yourself to be a scoundrel. Good-bye.

Walks away and turns his back on Thin.

FAT We are very disappointed. Clearly honor means nothing to you. However, maybe you can suggest some other way out? Can you?

THIN (*With increasing faith*) Yes! Certainly! The only thing I require is justice. Justice in everything—no more and no less.

FAT You amaze me.

THIN Why?

FAT How can you be sure that justice will not decide against you—that is to say, in your favor, in you as a candidate?

THIN It's quite simple. I've had such a miserable, unfortunate life. Even as a child, nothing ever worked out for me. Circumstances fought against me, so . . .

FAT So you consider that universal justice will compensate for your hitherto lack of happiness?

THIN Yes.

FAT It's an extraordinary thing how the only people who complain about lack of justice are the irresponsible elements. They demand justice, simply because they wish to profit from the success of others.

THIN No, I won't withdraw. I agree to anything, on condition that the decision is a just one.

FAT You mean on condition that you're not eaten.

THIN Now you're making insinuations. Justice first, if you please.

FAT Let us sit down, gentlemen. I know this is difficult, but it has to be done.

MEDIUM I'm not talking to him.

They all take up places as at the beginning.

FAT (*To Medium*) My dear friend, is your mother alive?

MEDIUM (*Hesitatingly*) I . . . don't know, boss . . . What about yours?

FAT (*Raising his eyes to the sky*) Unfortunately, I became an orphan very soon after my birth. My poor parents!

MEDIUM (*Hastily*) That's just what I was going to say. Quite frankly, I have no parents at all.

FAT (*To Thin*) What about you?

THIN I have a mother. At this moment she mourns me in her loneliness. Poor Mother!

FAT It appears to me that from the point of view of justice the affair is simple. Surely it would be against your conscience to harm an orphan? Even savages consider orphanhood one of the most terrible of misfortunes. No, my dear sir, if one of us two orphans were to be eaten, it would be a slap in the face to elementary justice. Isn't being an orphan enough, without being eaten as well?

THIN (*In confusion*) But . . .

FAT No, my dear sir. It is as clear as the day. You possess a mother, things have been better for you on earth, don't you think it is now time to repay this moral debt to the orphans of this world—all those who have never known a mother's care, the warmth of a home, and

food in abundance? Especially since, as you admitted just now, your
mother is *already* mourning your death.

THIN (*Desperately searching for an answer to this argument*) I don't know,
maybe my mother has died. She was feeling very weak last time I saw
her. I haven't been home for ages.

FAT Now you're talking like a child. How on earth could we prove
such a thing?

MEDIUM Yes, what about proof, eh?

THIN All I say is she was not feeling well when I left home. There's so
much talk about illness in modern civilization . . .

FAT Artistic fantasies . . . pure imagination. Clearly your mother is
enjoying excellent health, and may God grant her a long life. While as
for our parents . . . (*To Medium.*) Do you remember those long
autumn evenings when we were barefooted children, wandering
about selling matches to the passersby?

MEDIUM Please, don't talk about it. There are some things it is better to
forget.

FAT And do you recall the distant relative, the mean despot who took
away our last piece of cheese because he wanted to bait a mousetrap?

MEDIUM (*Groaning*) Nightmares of the past.

*Fat stands silently with hands outstretched in front of Thin, as much as to say,
"You see, there's nothing we can do."*

THIN Excuse me, I thought I heard someone talking out at sea. (*Listens.*)

FAT You're changing the subject. Of course. Human suffering arouses
no feeling in your heart. You're all the same; selfish sons of
mothers . . .

A voice is heard, weak and in the distance.

MEDIUM (*Accusingly*) He spent his childhood playing with toys!

FAT That's right. Toys and teddy bears.

The same voice, nearer this time.

VOICE Help! Help!

THIN   I did not! Aha, I definitely heard it that time.

VOICE   Help!

FAT   Yes, there's someone swimming toward us. Orphans always have the worst of the luck.

MEDIUM   (*Standing up and looking out to sea*)   It could be someone with some food, boss. I can see better now; he's only swimming with one hand. The other one's holding something.

Fat and Thin also get up from their chairs and walk to the edge of the raft where Medium is.

THIN   Yes, yes, that's quite possible. A farmer on his way to market falls into the water with his pig. And then as he swims he uses one arm to hang on to the pig, his only possession . . .

FAT   There, I can see him!

MEDIUM   It's someone in uniform.

VOICE   (*Quite near*)   Help!

A POSTMAN climbs out of the sea, complete in his uniform, cap, and with his leather bag slung around his neck. Medium gives him his hand and pulls him onto the raft.

POSTMAN   Thank you very much.

FAT   Have you got anything to eat?

POSTMAN   Absolutely nothing. I wouldn't mind a bite myself. I haven't had a thing since breakfast. (*Notices Thin.*)   Good God, it's you! What an extraordinary coincidence!

FAT   (*Suspiciously*)   You know each other?

POSTMAN   Of course we do! I've delivered his mail for ten years. I had no idea I'd find you in the middle of the ocean. Things have turned out very well, as it happens. I've got a telegram for you.

THIN   Telegram for me?

POSTMAN   Yes. I was walking toward your seaside house to deliver it, when a wave washed me away. It's lucky I'm a good swimmer. (*Looks in his bag.*)   Here it is.

THIN (*Moving to one side to open and read his telegram*) Excuse me, please.

FAT (*Suspiciously, to the Postman*) Is that uniform genuine?

POSTMAN It's genuine, only it's wet. You see, when it goes in the water . . .

THIN Hurrah!

FAT What's happened?

THIN (*Pondering*) Gentlemen, I have suffered a terrible tragedy. My mother has died.

MEDIUM That's done it!

THIN And while we're on the subject, allow me to point out that now I am an orphan as well as you, and therefore we must reopen the discussions and once again consider the matter of one of us being eaten.

FAT I protest! It's a trick. You fixed it all up with the postman!

POSTMAN (*Pompously*) Are you insulting a civil servant in the execution of his duty?

FAT How much did you pay him? I suppose you were at school together.

THIN Your accusation is quite groundless. Please ask the postman whether I conspired with him.

FAT Fine. We'll ask him. If he says yes, if he pleads guilty, we'll eat you without leave of appeal. If he denies it, we'll eat the postman.

POSTMAN What's that about eating me? I've only just arrived!

FAT That's the reason. You must be fresh—you'll do perfectly.

MEDIUM Boss, do you think we ought to eat both of them? One of them fried and the other with salad or stewed fruit? Or we could marinate them, or put one on top of the other . . .

THIN (*Hopefully*) Maybe the postman isn't an orphan? Here we are, the three of us—homeless, abandoned . . . We ought to ask him, don't you think?

FAT (*Still thinking about the menu*) No, I'd rather make wine out of the other one. Only how can we make Burgundy out of a postman?

POSTMAN (*Joining in eagerly*)   Yes, quite. I'm a first-class postman but a very poor Burgundy.

THIN (*To the Postman*)   If you give false testimony that we were in collusion, I'll report you to the department of posts and telegraphs.

POSTMAN   Don't worry about that! I have served thirty years—without blemish.

FAT   We're wasting time. Were you in collusion with this man? Yes or no? If the answer's yes and the news of the death of his mother is false, we will give you the kidneys and perhaps part of the rump. However if the information is true, then we three orphans will eat you for the simple reason that you are a postman. The post office is an institution of public utility, and as such it must serve everybody.

THIN   Please, do not destroy your good reputation.

POSTMAN   There's no fear of that. For years I have been an honest postman; I can't be bribed with a few kidneys.

FAT   We could perhaps offer you the knee bone in addition, but I warn you, that's as far as we'll go.

POSTMAN   No, sir. (*Pointing at his uniform.*)   You see these two crossed trumpets? The honor of these trumpets I value more than anything else. I wish you good-bye. (*Jumps into the water.*)

THIN   No, no, don't go away. Tell them I'm innocent first. Wait! (*Waving the telegram.*)   Now, my friends, you can see, from the justice point of view our situation is identical. We are all orphans.

FAT (*Matter-of-factly, to Medium*)   Would you please lay the table. The things are in my trunk.

THIN   What? My fellow orphans, preparing to . . .

FAT   You are forgetting that there exist other sorts of justice. For instance, historical justice.

THIN   What do you mean?

MEDIUM (*Who has meanwhile been opening the trunk*)   Boss, do we need the colander?

FAT   The fact that we are all without parents does not place us all on the same level. The question must now be considered: Who were our parents?

THIN   Good heavens, they were . . . just parents.

FAT   Ha ha! And who was your father?

MEDIUM   What about the rolling pin?

THIN   My father? He was an office worker. What about yours?

POSTMAN   (*Emerging from the sea, leaning against the edge of the raft*)   Excuse me, I forgot the receipt. All that talk about eating people, I lost my head.

THIN   Where shall I sign?

POSTMAN   Here, please. (*Thin signs the receipt.*)   Good-bye. (*Swims away.*)

FAT   So your father was an office worker? Just as I expected. You know what my father was?

THIN   No.

FAT   He was a simple, illiterate woodcutter. My friend, of course, never had a father. His mother conceived him as a result of extreme worry, poverty, and distress. You see, while your father filled in office forms as a servant of the aristocracy, sitting comfortably in a warm, clean office, my father was felling fir trees for pulp, so that your father could have paper to write his notices to quit, which he would then send to the mother of my poor friend here, who never had a father. I hope you're ashamed of yourself.

Medium has been removing from the trunk certain kitchen implements, which he places on the raft. Now he takes out a meat grinder, which he puts to the test by turning the handle several times.

THIN   (*Understanding what Fat's insinuations are leading up to, tries to defend himself in the same idiom*)   But I had nothing to do with that!

FAT   That is why the justice which now decrees that you should be eaten is called historical justice.

VOICE FROM THE SEA   Your Grace! Your Grace!

FAT   For God's sake, now what's happening?

Alongside the raft appears the head of an old family BUTLER *with hoary sideburns.*

BUTLER   Your Grace, how wonderful that I've found you.

FAT   What are you saying?

BUTLER   (*Almost crying with emotion*)   Don't you recognize me, Your Grace? Don't you remember how I taught you to ride a pony, when Your Grace was only a little viscount.

FAT   Go away!

BUTLER   How wonderful that my old eyes should behold you once again, Your Grace. Everyone in the palace is so worried. When the news arrived that your ship was sunk, I could not restrain myself. I said to myself, Where he goes, I go. His fate is my fate. So I jumped into the sea and here I am, Your Grace. What luck, eh?

FAT   John, will you please leave the raft and drown.

BUTLER   Certainly, Your Grace. What luck, how wonderful! (*Vanishes.*)

THIN   No, no, my good man, don't leave us! Come here, please . . . He's drowned.

FAT   (*In a tone as if nothing had happened*)   As I was saying, you can see that historical justice . . .

THIN   (*Becoming excited*)   I see, do I? I see that you used to live in a palace, and you took pony lessons . . .

FAT   Pony? My father couldn't even afford a Shetland pony! You're thinking about your own sordid childhood.

THIN   This is the end! Are you trying to say it was me, me who rode a pony?

FAT   Certainly. You said so yourself a moment ago.

THIN   No, this passes all understanding! I declare categorically that I have had no connection whatever with any pony.

FAT   No more have I. My poor father didn't even know the word "pony." He was illiterate.

MEDIUM (*Has meanwhile been watching the scene, standing over the various kitchen implements, with a saucepan in his hand*)   Poor little pony. Nobody wants him. (*To Thin.*)   Don't you feel any pity for the animal? Whatever's happened, you owe him the happiest moments of your childhood.

THIN   But that butler . . .

FAT   What butler? (*To Medium.*)   You, did you see any butler?

MEDIUM   Of course not.

FAT   My dear chap, I'm afraid I have nothing more to say to you in this discussion. You are suffering from hallucinations.

MEDIUM   You're a madman!

FAT   And so, as a man who is not responsible for his actions, you would do best to put yourself under the guidance of people who know what they want. You must be eliminated from society, and the best way is for society to eat you. (*To Medium.*)   Would you mind laying the table?

MEDIUM   Shall I put out teaspoons?

FAT   Of course. It's a proper dinner.

Medium lays out the teaspoons.

MEDIUM   One or two knives?

FAT   Two.

Medium puts out the knives.

MEDIUM   Napkins?

FAT   Naturally. Everything must be just so. We are men of culture.

During this exchange, Thin retreats to the edge of the raft, drags one of the chairs after him, and hides behind it. Medium lays a clean white tablecloth across the middle of the raft and carefully lays two places. Fat stops watching Thin. Instead he observes Medium and from time to time makes signs to him about where various things should be put. Soon the table is properly laid. Thin watches them, horror-struck, from behind the chair.

THIN (*Timidly*)   Excuse me . . .

FAT (*Paying no attention to him*)   Move the cutlery a little to the right.

THIN   I think I ought to tell you . . . I'm poisoned . . .

FAT   The fruit bowl in the center . . .

THIN   I promise it's true. I didn't want to tell you before. I would be very bad for you.

FAT (*Picks up one of the forks and looks at it*)   Clean this.

THIN   I'm not trying to be difficult, I just don't want to hurt you. I like a good meal myself and I know what greed can do to a man. If I wasn't poisoned I wouldn't object, I promise. But as things are, it is clearly my duty . . .

FAT   Let us begin.

MEDIUM   As you say, boss.

Takes out of the trunk a big carving knife and a sharpening steel. Both these props must be genuine. He sharpens the knife, making an authentic, unpleasant, rhythmical sound.

THIN (*Retreating still farther right to the very edge of the raft*)   I don't say it's incurable. No, all you have to do is wait a bit, and it'll go away. A day or two's rest and I'll be depoisoned. I'll lie down here in the corner so as not to disturb you. As soon as I'm depoisoned I'll tell you. I won't make any excuses then.

Medium is still rhythmically sharpening the knife. Fat looks at the "table" once more, inclines his head, considers it, walks up to the trunk, and removes from it a vase and some flowers. He puts the flowers in the vase and the vase on the tablecloth. Then he takes a few steps to the side and observes the general effect. Only now is he satisfied.

THIN (*Becoming less and less sure of himself*)   Well, maybe two days is a bit too long. One day at the most. You know the proverb, "What you have to eat today, eat rather tomorrow"—ha, ha, ha!

Medium tries the sharpness of the knife with his finger.

THIN (*cont.*)   I think a few hours should be enough. One hour even.

FAT   It's time to start.

Medium takes a step forward in the direction of Thin.

THIN (*Hastily*)　All right, all right! I agree. Only let me give you a word of advice. For your own sake.

FAT　What about?

THIN　Gastronomic advice. Advice that is exactly to the point. Don't . . . don't, you think it would be better if I washed my feet?

Medium looks inquiringly at Fat.

FAT　Certainly, I never thought of that. (*To Medium.*)　What do you think?

MEDIUM (*Doubtful*)　I don't know . . . He might be a bit gritty . . . Maybe he ought to wash.

THIN (*Quickly rolling up his trouser leg*)　Yes, yes, you're quite right. Hygiene is the foundation of a healthy existence. (*Scratches his leg.*) Bacteria are invisible to the naked eye, and I can feel them itching.

FAT　Very well. Personal cleanliness never did anyone any harm. On the contrary, it ensures a long and healthy life. One second and I will find you a towel.

Thin sits down on the edge of the raft and dangles his legs in the sea. He washes and splashes.

THIN　So, you two are absolutely determined to . . . to . . .

FAT　I thought we had made that clear.

THIN　You mentioned something about self-sacrifice . . .

FAT　Yes. I said self-sacrifice was a noble idea.

THIN (*Listening intently*)　Yes? Tell me more.

FAT　I don't think there's anything I can add. Self-sacrifice, the readiness to dedicate oneself . . .

THIN　Yes, I know, that's all true.

FAT (*Standing over him with a towel*)　Do you understand now? You refused to believe me before.

THIN　I must have been very immature and inexperienced . . . But now I see there's something in what you say.

FAT (*Encouragingly*) You still have time to reform.

THIN I behaved disgracefully. I rejected all your arguments.

FAT But deep down you are not entirely cynical, judging by the noble feeling I can see beginning to emerge. Don't you think that's enough on the left one?

THIN No, I must do between the toes. So, to get back to the subject, I must tell you that within me a new, better man is beginning to awake. Er, by the way, are your minds made up irrevocably?

FAT (*Impatiently*) My dear sir!

THIN No, no, of course they are! So what was I talking about? Aha, a new, better man. Of course it is one thing to be eaten as an ordinary human sacrifice, and something quite different to be eaten as a new, better man, who out of his own dedication . . . In other words, to be eaten with one's own internal consent and noble inspiration. You promise me, do you, that everything is decided?

FAT My word of honor.

THIN Ha! Too bad. Well then . . . What was I saying? Aha, so it gives one a feeling of satisfaction, a sense of freedom and libertion . . .

FAT At last you're seeing our point of view. (*To Medium.*) My friend, would you pass me the soap?

THIN (*Feverishly*) Because you mustn't think I'm a mere slave.

FAT Rest assured, we do not think of you in this way. On the contrary, you will go down in our stomachs—I mean in our memories—as a hero, as a luminary of disinterested dedication. I think the left leg's all right now, don't you?

THIN (*Even more feverishly*) Of course it's all right. The right leg's all right too. Hand me the towel and I'll come out of the water.

FAT No, I think you ought to do the right leg a bit . . .

THIN Just as you like.

FAT I think it would be better.

THIN Yes, I was the first man to make this great decision. I was the first man to stand up and sacrifice myself for others . . .

MEDIUM (*Looking at Thin critically*)   I think you need some detergent.

FAT   No, there's nothing wrong with soap. We can wait a few seconds longer.

THIN   Wait? When my friends are hungry! Never! (*Tries to get up, but Fat holds him in the sitting position.*)

FAT   A few moments on the right leg and you're finished.

THIN   My feet seem so pointless now that I've seen the light. They might as well be dirty.

FAT (*Handing him the towel*)   There we are, and here's the towel.

Thin stands up and walks to the center of the raft.

THIN   Gentlemen, I thank you. At last I have become a real man. I have found I am a man of ideals.

FAT   Don't mention it.

THIN   I have found my self-respect. After all, what is the situation? We are three men, and out of them I am the only one who is saving the other two. I should like, if I may, to make a short speech on the subject of freedom.

FAT   Is it long?

THIN   No, just a few words.

FAT   All right, go ahead.

THIN (*Pulls one of the chairs over to the side of the raft and climbs onto it, in the same way as during the speeches at the beginning of the play*) Freedom—means nothing at all. It is only *true* freedom . . . that means anything. Why? Because it is true and therefore better. In which case, where are we to search for true freedom? Let us think logically. If true freedom is not the same thing as ordinary freedom, where are we to find this true freedom? The answer is simple: True freedom exists only in the place where there is no ordinary freedom.

MEDIUM   Where's the salt, boss?

FAT   Don't interrupt! Honestly, what a time to . . . (*Very quietly.*)   At the bottom of the trunk.

THIN   And therefore I have decided . . .

Medium goes over to the trunk and looks inside it. Then he hurries over to Fat.

THIN   And therefore I have decided . . .

He repeats these words and goes on repeating them like a stuck gramophone record, only not monotonously, but interpreting them in different ways, as if he were desperately searching for what it was he wanted to say.

MEDIUM (*With great emotion, in a semiwhisper, but extremely clearly*)   Boss, I've found that can of baked beans and sausages.

FAT   Shhhh! Hide it this instant!

THIN   . . . And therefore I have decided . . .

MEDIUM   To be quite frank I'd prefer baked beans. What do you think, boss?

FAT   I don't want baked beans. And anyway . . .

THIN   . . . And therefore I have decided . . .

MEDIUM   Anyway what?

FAT (*Pointing at Thin*)   Can't you see? He's happy as he is!

CHARLIE

❧

Translated by Nicholas Bethell

CHARACTERS

GRANDPA

GRANDSON

OCULIST

Onstage there are two chairs, a cupboard, and a telephone. On the wall there is a white sheet of paper with printed lines of letters and numbers of different sizes as used in eye tests. The OCULIST, a middle-aged man in glasses, is lying on a sofa reading a book. There is a knock at the door and the Oculist rises.

OCULIST   Come in!

Enter GRANDSON and GRANDPA. Grandson, a man of thirty, strong and angular, comes in first, followed by Grandpa, a slight, little old man with a white beard. He is carrying a double-barreled shotgun over his shoulder.

GRANDSON   Good morning, Doctor. May I present my grandfather?

OCULIST   Come in, please. Your grandfather? He looks remarkably young for his age.

GRANDSON   I've brought him to see you, specially.

OCULIST   Why, what's happened? A shooting accident? Somebody shot in the eye?

GRANDSON   Oh no! Grandpa hasn't started shooting yet.

OCULIST   Ah! You mean the accident will happen later. You've come as a precautionary measure.

GRANDSON   There won't be any accident. Grandpa is going to shoot, and that's the end of it.

OCULIST   Is that really necessary?

GRANDSON   Doctor, Grandpa has to shoot.

OCULIST   If he observes the safety rules of shooting, I see no reason to object. Old age has its rights.

GRANDSON   Exactly. But the problem is—glasses.

OCULIST   Trouble with his sight?

GRANDSON   Grandpa can't see very well. When he gets some glasses, he'll shoot.

OCULIST   I see, I see. You mean he's going to shoot at a target?

GRANDSON   Exactly. Look, Doctor, he's searching for one now.

Grandpa, who has up to now been standing quietly, begins to search the room, yard by yard, bent double, with his face almost on the floor, like a man suffering from terrible shortsightedness.

OCULIST   What's he looking for?

GRANDSON   (*Without answering the Oculist*)   Grandpa! Calm down! He's not here.

OCULIST   Precisely, there's nobody here except us.

GRANDSON   Grandpa's very vindictive. I know him.

OCULIST   A patriot?

GRANDSON   Among other things. But this time it's Charlie.

OCULIST   What Charlie?

GRANDSON   We'll soon see what Charlie.

OCULIST   Is he a friend of yours?

GRANDSON   That's what we've got to find out.

OCULIST   How?

GRANDSON   Grandpa has got to get some glasses. Then he'll recognize him.

OCULIST   And when he recognizes him?

GRANDSON   Then he'll shoot him. He needs glasses first to recognize him and then to shoot him. That's why we've come to you, Doctor.

Meanwhile Grandpa looks under the sofa and under the chairs, searches everywhere, but at no time takes his shotgun off his shoulder.

OCULIST   Has—er—Mr. Charlie done anything wrong?

GRANDSON   How are we supposed to know? Grandpa hasn't got any glasses and he can't recognize him.

OCULIST   So you don't know him at all?

GRANDSON   I've been trying to explain; we're looking for him.

OCULIST   Your grandpa doesn't know him either?

GRANDSON   Without glasses? You're joking!

OCULIST Why do you want to meet somebody you don't know?

GRANDSON Because we can't know him until we meet him. It's quite simple.

OCULIST But why a man called Charlie?

GRANDSON Do you want us to shoot the first person who comes along? Sadist! You've got to have some sort of justice.

OCULIST In that case, why shoot anybody?

GRANDSON Doctor, you said yourself, Grandpa's got to shoot. Old age has its rights.

OCULIST But he could shoot targets, into the air, birds, maybe . . .

GRANDSON What?

OCULIST Birds, targets . . .

GRANDSON Who?

OCULIST What do you mean, who?

GRANDSON I said, who's supposed to shoot at targets?

OCULIST Well, your grandpa.

GRANDSON (*Unbelievingly*) Grandpa?

OCULIST Yes, Grandpa.

GRANDSON You don't know him.

OCULIST In that case, you'd better take his gun away.

GRANDSON (*In even greater disbelief*) Whose?

OCULIST (*Less definitely*) Grandpa's.

GRANDSON (*In amazement*) Grandpa's?

OCULIST Well yes, I thought . . .

GRANDSON Did you hear, Grandpa?

GRANDPA (*For a moment interrupting his search, puts his hand to his ear*) Eh?

GRANDSON He says, take away your gun.

GRANDPA (*Taking his gun off his shoulder*)   Where is he?

GRANDSON   There he is, by the chair. Shall I get him for you?

OCULIST (*Hastily crossing over to the side of the stage*)   Well, anyway it's your private affair; I'm not interfering.

GRANDSON   Now you're talking sense. The gun's been loaded for twenty years; it just can't go on.

OCULIST   Why can't it?

GRANDSON   Ask Grandpa. Grandpa, this fellow . . .

OCULIST (*Interrupting*)   No, no . . . If it can't, it can't. Of course it can't.

GRANDSON   I'll ask him why not. Grandpa, this man . . .

OCULIST (*Interrupting again*)   No, I believe you. After all, if you've got a gun . . .

GRANDSON   Exactly. You've got to shoot. Before Grandpa's day, his father, my great-grandpa, used to shoot, and before him his father's father. All of them shot, all the time.

OCULIST   Hm . . . yes . . . In that case perhaps we can start examining your grandfather.

GRANDSON   Now you're talking. Grandpa, come on, Grandpa, a little closer.

OCULIST   Would you be so good as to take a seat.

Grandpa sits down in the chair offered to him, throwing his shotgun across his shoulder.

GRANDSON   Now, Grandpa, listen to the doctor. *Pif-paf* later.

OCULIST   Perhaps we could put the gun down there for the moment.

Uncertainly, he touches the gun. Grandpa objects violently.

OCULIST (*cont.*)   No? All right, all right, just as you like.

GRANDSON   Grandpa never parts with his gun. He cleans it every day. We and our family—we know what our duty is.

OCULIST (*Going up to the sheet of paper with the eye tests, points to the smallest row of signs*)   Can you read this?

GRANDPA (*Dreamily*) Ah! I remember my old father—he let him have it, half a pound of shot right in the middle of the belly. From sixty yards, I tell you.

OCULIST Please try and concentrate. Now then, does reading these letters cause you any difficulty?

GRANDPA (*After long hesitation*) Ah! Maybe it wasn't quite sixty. Fifty.

GRANDSON Later, Grandpa, later. Now you must listen to what the doctor's saying.

OCULIST Let's try again. Can you read this?

GRANDPA Errr, no.

OCULIST And this?

GRANDPA No, not a thing. Where's Charlie?

GRANDSON Be patient, Grandpa. You must listen to the doctor, otherwise there won't be any *bum-bum* at Charlie.

GRANDPA I'll show him.

OCULIST Can you read this?

GRANDPA Er, no.

OCULIST (*Consolingly*) The situation is still not hopeless. We'll carry on testing. Can you read this?

GRANDPA You know, I'd rather put a bullet in it.

OCULIST Or this?

GRANDPA Oh! Doctor, you really . . . No, I can't.

OCULIST Hm. The weakness of vision is really considerable. Now let's try again. Can you read this?

GRANDPA I haven't got my glasses.

OCULIST (*To Grandson*) That we shall try to remedy. May I know in what circumstances your grandpa lost his keenness of vision?

GRANDSON Through being on guard. Grandpa was always watching to see if the enemy was walking about. And, you see, our windows are dirty.

OCULIST   Yes, that strains the eyes.

GRANDSON   More than once we've told him. If only, Grandpa, you'll put off watching until Easter, the windows will be cleaned. But he was in too much of a hurry. He was on watch even in his sleep. That's the sort of man he is.

OCULIST   Let's get back to the patient. (*Pointing to the largest row of letters.*)   What about this?

GRANDPA   What?

OCULIST   Can you read it?

GRANDPA   Read it?

OCULIST   Yes.

GRANDPA   No.

OCULIST   One moment.

From behind the sofa he pulls out a roll of white paper, unrolls it, and fastens it to the wall. On it a single, huge letter A is printed in black ink, almost as large as a man.

OCULIST (*cont.*)   Now can you?

GRANDPA   I'm hungry.

OCULIST   Stick to the point. Can you read it now?

GRANDPA   Oh, what the hell!

OCULIST (*Takes from the cupboard a box full of pairs of glasses, puts a pair on Grandpa. The following questions are spoken at high speed.*)   And now?

GRANDPA   No.

OCULIST (*Changes them for another pair*)   Now?

GRANDPA   No.

OCULIST (*As above*)   Now?

GRANDPA   No.

OCULIST (*As above*)   Now?

GRANDPA (*Chuckling*)   No.

OCULIST (*As above*) Now?

GRANDPA (*Chuckling even more*) No.

OCULIST (*Losing his patience, takes Grandpa by the back of the neck and leads him right up to the sheet with the large letter* A) Now?

GRANDPA (*Doubling up with laughter*) Oh dear!

OCULIST What the devil are you laughing at?

GRANDPA It tickles.

OCULIST (*Takes off the last pair of glasses and crosses his arms. To Grandson*) Unfortunately, there is nothing I can do.

GRANDSON Why?

OCULIST This is an extraordinary case.

GRANDSON You're taking the wrong approach. Grandpa can't read.

OCULIST You mean he's illiterate?

GRANDSON That's right. Any objections? You're literate, and so what? Are we afraid of you? No, it's you that's afraid of us.

OCULIST But . . . it never entered my head.

GRANDSON What?

OCULIST I simply wanted to find out whether . . . whether reading lies among the sphere of activities practiced by your progenitor and . . .

GRANDSON Doctor, you're forgetting yourself! Maybe your grandpa was a progenitor, but not mine! There has never been any venereal disease in our family! We're shooting men—exclusively!

OCULIST You're missing the point! I quite simply wanted to find out whether your grandpa reads, reads, is in the habit of reading.

GRANDSON (*With pride*) My dear sir, neither my grandpa nor I have ever read anything. Is that clear? (*Pointing to the huge letter* A.) And you wanted to force a poor old man, and exhaust him mentally, and give him a pain in the head, eh?

OCULIST (*Explaining*) No, I was simply thinking of all our plans for universal education.

Meanwhile Grandpa resumes his search.

GRANDSON I've got an idea.

OCULIST Oh, I'm sure you have.

GRANDSON Let me see that.

OCULIST Let you see what?

GRANDSON Don't play the fool. (*Taking a step toward the Oculist.*) Give them to me.

OCULIST (*Stepping back*) I don't understand.

GRANDSON Let me see your glasses.

OCULIST (*Trying to turn it all into a joke*) Ha ha ha! You're a funny one! I remember we used to make jokes like that at school. I remember once we put a thumbtack under the math teacher's . . .

GRANDSON Stop fooling about! Take your glasses off. Come on!

OCULIST (*Stiffening*) I won't put up with this sort of behavior. My glasses are my private property.

GRANDSON We'll give you private property. Grandpa!

OCULIST (*Terrified*) No, don't!

GRANDSON Well?

OCULIST There's no need to upset an old man. In his excitement he might forget himself, get carried away. I understand that.

GRANDSON I hope I make myself clear.

OCULIST Maybe after all I can lend you them just for a moment. But just for a moment. Without my glasses I am almost blind. I can hardly see anything.

GRANDSON All right, all right, that's unimportant.

Oculist takes off his glasses and hands them to Grandson. He turns them around for a moment in his hand and looks at them.

GRANDSON (*cont.*) Beautiful.

OCULIST Zeiss lenses.

GRANDSON   Shall we try them?

OCULIST (*After taking off his glasses he becomes defenseless. His movements are uncertain. Every now and then he takes a step or two in some direction, but uncertainly, as if after every step he was sure he had taken the wrong direction.*)   My glasses!

GRANDSON   Grandpa! Here! Come here!

GRANDPA (*Has already resumed his search and taken his gun off his shoulder, and is holding it at the ready and peering into the corners. He gets up and, with the haste typical of an old man, trots over to his Grandson.*)   Where? Where is he? Is he there?

GRANDSON   Calm down, Grandpa. Let's put these glasses on.

GRANDPA   Oh, I'm getting so excited!

GRANDSON   Stand up straight, Grandpa. That's it, you put them on your ears, like the doctor. (*Stepping back a pace.*)   Now, what do you say?

GRANDPA (*Loses his trembling fever and becomes motionless and more important-looking. He looks about himself with deliberation and surprise.*)   Good! Good!

GRANDSON (*Excited*)   What? Good, did you say?

GRANDPA (*Has found just what the Oculist has lost: confidence in his movements and keenness of vision. With growing satisfaction in his voice*)   Good!

OCULIST   Can you really see better?

GRANDPA (*Looking at him carefully*)   Who's that?

GRANDSON   That's the doctor.

GRANDPA (*Without taking his eyes off the Oculist*)   Doctor?

OCULIST   Doctor . . . of medicine.

GRANDSON   A doctor, and he didn't know how to give an old man a pair of glasses.

OCULIST (*Justifying himself*)   This is an extraordinary case, I could never have imagined . . .

GRANDPA (*Still not taking his eyes off the Oculist, approaches him more closely*) Do you know, it looks to me as if . . .

GRANDSON I suppose it's just bad breeding . . .

OCULIST (*Nervously smoothing back his hair, adjusting his dress*) I am delighted, sir, that you have recovered your keenness of vision. Delighted.

GRANDSON What is it, Grandpa? (*Pause.*)

GRANDPA (*Takes a step backward. All the time gazing intently at the Oculist, he signs to Grandson to come nearer.*) You know what I think?

GRANDSON (*Running up*) What can you see?

OCULIST (*Gets up violently from his place. Walks about the room, gesticulating nervously*) For the true man of science, there is no greater joy than to witness the triumph of one's own methods. To organize the blind forces of nature, to set some harmony to the free play of the elements, such achievements produce their own true reward. May I ask you to return my glasses? I am shortsighted, and my head is beginning to ache . . . Furthermore, wearing somebody else's glasses may turn out harmful for you in the long run. (*Stops walking and tries to listen in on Grandpa and Grandson's conversation.*)

GRANDPA Something tells me . . . (*Whispers.*)

GRANDSON (*Astounded*) Good lord! Really?

Grandpa points his finger at the Oculist listening in. The latter realizes he has been caught in the act and starts walking, pretending that he is occupied in expounding his opinions.

OCULIST Only in the society of today have men of science received the recognition due to them. I ask you not to forget that our power has grown immeasurably since the time of Paracelsus. We are now hacking out new paths for the human race. Please return my glasses immediately.

Grandpa leans over and whispers something in Grandson's ear.

GRANDSON Impossible! (*Grandpa whispers something else.*) Are you absolutely sure?

GRANDPA Ho, ho!

OCULIST Who can foretell what future discoveries may transform our life, in what direction particular branches of science may extend? Thought, that property which places even an uneducated man on so infinitely higher a level than that of the beasts, lies at the root of these achievements. And at the head of this great progress of humanity, this procession marching in state through the history of nature, this crusade of reason to the land of chaos and accident, go the priests of science, go we, true leaders of an army in the service of mankind. Excuse me, I must go outside for a moment.

During this speech the Oculist has been maneuvering himself as near as possible to the door. Meanwhile Grandson has cut him off from the way out.

GRANDSON Why have you gone so pale?

For a moment they stand opposite each other in silence.

OCULIST I've gone pale? Extraordinary.

GRANDSON White as a sheet. Or maybe we'd better say—ha! ha!— white as a corpse!

OCULIST Metaphorical.

GRANDSON Could be. We're uneducated. We shoot.

OCULIST Where's the door? I can't see properly . . . There's such a mist in front of my eyes. I want to go outside. You admitted I was pale.

GRANDSON That doesn't matter to us. I'd like to ask you a few questions.

OCULIST I am not ready for them. Anyway, what about?

GRANDSON Who about, you mean!

OCULIST I know nobody, I've done nothing. I don't know any addresses. I won't tell you anything.

GRANDSON And if I ask you nicely?

OCULIST What do you want to know?

GRANDSON Why did you want Grandpa to shoot at targets and birds?

OCULIST   In the name of humanity and of the preservation of moral laws of coexistence among men.

GRANDSON   And why did you want to take Grandpa's gun away?

OCULIST   I thought . . . I thought it might become dangerous and therefore . . .

GRANDSON   Dangerous? Who for?

OCULIST   Whatever you say, he's an old man. Very honest, I'm sure, but tired by life. Weakened sense of responsibility. Still, I could be wrong.

GRANDSON   I said, dangerous for who?

OCULIST   Well, in general, for everybody.

GRANDSON   For everybody? You look at me. Am I afraid of this danger? No, and shall I tell you why?

OCULIST   How should I know? . . . Maybe, lack of imagination . . .

GRANDSON   I'm not afraid because I am not . . . Do you know who I'm not? Well? Oh . . . Oh . . . Come on!

OCULIST (*Stammering*)   Ch . . . Ch

GRANDSON   Well, Cha, Cha, Char . . .

OCULIST   Char . . .

GRANDSON   Charlie . . . lie . . .

OCULIST   Charlie.

GRANDSON   You see. (*Pause.*)

OCULIST (*As if to himself*)   You must be joking.

GRANDSON   No man on earth who's honest and straightforward has any objection to Grandpa shooting. Those who have clear consciences can sleep in peace. But Charlie, oh he's trembling with fear, and rightly because he knows that we shall recognize him anywhere, and especially now that Grandpa's got these glasses.

OCULIST (*Hysterically*)   Why won't you let me go outside? It's not democratic.

GRANDSON   So much the better. At this moment millions of simple, quiet people in the world are coming in and going out whenever they want. If it was an ordinary door, on hinges, with bolts, or a swing door, or even a bead curtain, the creak and rustle of these doors would resound uninterruptedly, freely, and joyfully. Only you, you do not belong to these happy kingdoms. Is that our fault?

OCULIST   What have you got against me?

GRANDSON   You are Charlie.

OCULIST   No!

GRANDSON   Who protested when I said his gun had been loaded for twenty years and that something had to be done about it? Who wanted to force Grandpa to read?

OCULIST   Nonsense!

GRANDSON   Who didn't want to give glasses to a poor old man? You are Charlie!

OCULIST   No! I swear I'm not. (*Feverishly searching in his pockets.*)   I've got my identity card, I'll show you my identity card.

GRANDSON   Your identity card doesn't mean a thing. Grandpa recognized you, Charlie!

OCULIST   Grandpa may be mistaken!

GRANDSON   Grandpa! Let's start!

Grandpa takes off the safety catch.

OCULIST   Gentlemen, wait, there must be a mistake, a tragic misunderstanding. I do not claim that Charlie is innocent. On the contrary, he is probably an exceptionally disgusting type, but why me? Grandpa, take a look around. There's always time for me. I take surgery every other day between two and six. You've got me, gentlemen, as it were, in the bank. Meanwhile you'd do well to have a look around; really, you would. And all this time the real Charlie is sitting cozily somewhere, drinking his milk, and laughing in your face, gentlemen, the rotten swine! Hasn't this occurred to you?

GRANDSON   It has indeed. Perhaps you aren't the only Charlie in the world. There may be two, or three. Grandpa, when we've done this one, we'll carry straight on looking for the others.

OCULIST   Two? Three? Ten, a hundred, maybe they're all Charlies, all of them, but not me. And you're wasting all this time on that one person who is not Charlie, and meanwhile all the others are running around, free!

GRANDSON   That's an idea, Grandpa. Who said there was only one of them? Have you got the ammunition?

GRANDPA   Ho ho! There's enough, enough for them all.

GRANDSON   (*Rubbing his hands*)   Fine, fine. (*Runs up to Grandpa and kisses him in joy.*)   What a grand idea, Grandpa. We'll have a real shooting match.

OCULIST   Yes, shoot, shoot, but not at me!

GRANDSON   I think we'll do him with buckshot first, and then with a bullet.

GRANDPA   Good idea.

OCULIST   No, no. (*Throws himself on to the floor, runs on all fours to the sofa and crawls under it. His voice now comes out from under the sofa. Grandson and Grandpa bend down to try to spot him there.*)   There's no need to bother about me. I am not against shooting at all. Shooting is very good for the lungs; it's a fine sport. Not at targets or birds or anything—a true man doesn't shoot at nonsense like that. I understand, I'm on your side. I am simply surprised that the older gentleman has only got one shotgun and that it only has two barrels. If he had eight guns, and each one had three barrels, that would still not be excessive. It's not a question of too many, he's got to have them. Wait, listen to me!

GRANDPA   (*Going down on to all fours with his gun pointing under the sofa*)   It's dark, damn it.

GRANDSON   Shall I move the sofa?

OCULIST   I don't want anything. I don't even want the glasses. Grandpa can keep them for himself. But I want justice, I demand it! Not me but Charlie!

GRANDPA   Light a match for me, and I'll get him.

Grandson lights a match and brings it close to the sofa. The Oculist's head appears; he blows, puts out the match, and vanishes again under the sofa.

OCULIST   Gentlemen, allow me to raise the cry, "Hurrah for shooting!" But I cannot agree that the beautiful and noble idea of shooting should be defiled by a fatal shooting accident. Gentlemen, I'm not the one who should be shot at.

GRANDPA   It's no good, I'll shoot blind.

GRANDSON   (*Leaning to one side*)   Aim more in the middle, Grandpa.

GRANDPA   I had him there. (*Prepares and takes aim—a pause. The Oculist's hand appears from under the sofa, waving a white handkerchief.*)

GRANDSON   That's good. It means he'll come out now.

GRANDPA   Ah, today's youth!

OCULIST   (*Crawls out from under the sofa and stands up in front of Grandpa and Grandson*)   All right, I'll tell you everything.

GRANDSON   Well?

OCULIST   He's coming here.

GRANDSON   Who?

OCULIST   Charlie. The real Charlie.

GRANDPA   When? When?

OCULIST   Any moment. He should be here now.

GRANDPA   Shall I shoot?

GRANDSON   In a minute, Grandpa. (*To the Oculist.*)   How can you prove to us that the man that's coming is a greater Charlie than you?

OCULIST   Because of various things he said about you.

GRANDSON   What things?

OCULIST   Various things.

GRANDSON   What does that mean?

OCULIST   Shall I repeat them?

GRANDSON   Yes.

OCULIST   He said that you are murderers.

GRANDSON   Oh, he said that, and what else?

OCULIST   That your grandpa is a bloodsucking old idiot . . .

GRANDSON   What?

OCULIST   I'm just repeating what I heard. As for you, he said you're an unbelievable fool and a pervert and a typical product of your nauseating family. Shall I go on?

GRANDSON   Everything.

OCULIST   He said that the very fact of your existence is sufficient proof of the senselessness and rottenness of the world, to such an extent that to be murdered, even by you, would be a merciful relief, and a splendid way of ceasing to share with you what is common to humanity.

GRANDSON   Did you hear that, Grandpa?

GRANDPA   Charlie! As if I heard his very words! That's Charlie.

GRANDSON   And what else?

OCULIST   And he also said, I don't know whether it's true, that you . . . I can't say it . . .

GRANDSON   I tell you, don't conceal anything.

OCULIST   No, I really can't.

GRANDSON   Tell me at once!

OCULIST   He said that you belch. (*Pause.*)

GRANDSON   The swine! Why didn't you tell me this before?

OCULIST   Because I've only just realized. I must admit that before you came here the idea of Charlie was quite new to me. But this discussion has opened my eyes. I am not Charlie; you don't believe me—too bad. But I cannot bear the idea that I will die and that the real Charlie will be walking about and laughing in your face. For what guarantee have I that, having once made a mistake about me and

taken me for Charlie, you won't in turn make a mistake about Charlie
and take him for me, for an innocent person? It's not so much a
question of my life as of justice. You said yourself that there must be
some justice, that one can't just shoot at anybody in the street. So,
when I was lying under the sofa I thought to myself, My God, how
tragic that these two gentlemen, instead of just resting, are spending
their time chasing this Charlie, little knowing that their efforts will be
quite wasted. So, I decided to rebel; I rejected the rest of my former
pseudomorality and resolved to tell all.

GRANDSON   Listen. The fact that you're Charlie is another matter.
Grandpa recognized you, and he doesn't make mistakes. But it's true
that there may be more than one Charlie. We shall wait here. If he
doesn't come, we'll do you in and go. If he does come, we'll do him
in and then think about it. It's quite possible that you know the whole
organization. Why is he coming here, anyway?

OCULIST   He's my patient. Like you.

GRANDSON   Let's ambush him, Grandpa.

*Grandson puts the chair opposite the door. Grandpa kneels behind the chair with
the gun pointing at the door. Grandson stands well back in the stage behind the
cupboard. The Oculist, completely exhausted, sits on the sofa and wipes his
forehead with a handkerchief. He covers his face with his hands. Grandpa and
Grandson, having taken up their positions, begin to wait. The stage grows
slightly darker.*

GRANDSON   I can't see him.

OCULIST   He's not a young man. He walks slowly.

Pause. Silence.

GRANDSON   He ought to be here now.

OCULIST   He'll come. He's sure to come. He's always punctual, and so
well mannered.

Pause. Silence.

GRANDSON   There's something I don't like about this.

OCULIST   Why? The weather's nice . . . a beautiful sunset.

GRANDPA   I'm bored.

OCULIST   Shall I read something? (*Without waiting for an answer, he opens a book and reads, holding it very close to his eyes.*)   ". . . the traveler who attains the valley from the direction of the southeast will be greeted by a most impressive landscape. The vine-covered slopes promise that not only the marvelous vistas, purity of the air, and colorfulness of the different flowers comprise the feast with which the surrounding district regales the newcomer. In truth, both spiritual and other advantages await in abundance all those who do not recoil before what is good and beautiful. The local inhabitants, though generally of moderate height, are attractively built . . ."

GRANDSON   Enough!

OCULIST   Just as you say. (*Close the book.*)

GRANDSON   How much longer do we wait?

OCULIST   The whole fun of the hunt is waiting. (*Changing the subject.*)   Shall I make you some coffee?

GRANDSON   No need. We don't drink coffee.

Pause. Silence. The Oculist remains motionless. Suddenly he gets up again and begins to creep about the room. It continues to get just perceptibly darker.

GRANDSON   What is it?

OCULIST   A fly. (*He performs the usual waves of the hand, closing his fist, preceded by a quiet creeping noise. The fly keeps getting away.*)

GRANDSON   (*With interest*)   Got it?

OCULIST   Missed it. Ah, there it is!

Pause. Grandpa stops looking at the door; in spite of himself he is drawn into the fly hunt.

GRANDSON   Now! Left hand!

A longer pause in which the Oculist carries on his pantomime. He is enthralled, rapt, his mind completely concentrated on the chase. He alternately creeps along and then hurls himself forward. Being deprived of his glasses he guides himself more by ear. At a certain moment the fly settles on the gun of Grandpa, who has been kneeling down all this time and following the hunt simply by the motion of his head. Grandson, leaning out from behind the cupboard, watches the scene intently. Oculist approaches the gun and hovers menacingly over it. This is the moment of sharpest tension. Then suddenly he performs a lightning sweep of the hand along the barrel and stays motionless with closed fist. He looks first at Grandpa and then at Grandson, then very slowly opens his hand.

OCULIST   Missed!

Footsteps are heard on the other side of the door coming nearer and nearer. It is getting darker and darker.

GRANDSON   (*Exclaims triumphantly*)   He's coming!

GRANDPA   (*Lets out something that resembles a joyful yodeling noise*)   Halla— lii . . . !

Oculist throws himself desperately onto the sofa and covers his head with a cushion.

GRANDSON   (*Blissfully*)   Now's your chance!

GRANDPA   Like my father!

GRANDSON   And your grandfather!

GRANDPA   Forward! Charge! (*A knock at the door. Grandpa, questioningly to Grandson.*)   Now?

GRANDSON   Just a minute. (*Draws from his bosom a bugle and plays a few notes of a rousing song. Renewed knocking.*)   Now!

The door opens slowly. Grandpa fires both barrels. Silence.

GRANDSON   (*Runs out from the corner behind the cupboard and gazes at the door which is still open*)   Got him!

GRANDPA   (*Slowly puts down his gun and stretches his limbs*)   Well, that's a relief.

GRANDSON   (*Yawning*)   A tense moment.

GRANDPA   (*Pointing at the Oculist who is still lying motionless covered with a cushion*)   And what about him?

OCULIST   My glasses!

GRANDPA   That's a great load off my mind.

GRANDSON   You see, Grandpa, the world is not so wicked.

OCULIST (*Slowly sitting up on the sofa*)   Is it all over?

GRANDSON (*Clapping him on the shoulder*)   It looks like you were telling the truth. He's lying there, on the floor.

OCULIST (*Lethargically*)   Yes, yes . . . And how is Grandpa feeling now?

GRANDSON   Grandpa? Grandpa has never felt better in his life. You've cured him, Doctor. Charlie was what he needed.

OCULIST (*All the time as in a dream*)   I am very happy, very happy.

GRANDSON   And we must be off now. Grandpa has got to load both barrels.

OCULIST   Again?

GRANDSON   Then we'll be back. (*Pause.*)

OCULIST   Then . . . then you're going to go to all this trouble again.

GRANDSON   I'm afraid so. It could be that some Charlie is going to come here again, and even if he doesn't . . .

OCULIST   But I thought . . .

GRANDSON   You thought we weren't coming back, did you? Well, you needn't worry. There's enough ammunition. He's got his glasses. All he needs is his good health.

OCULIST   So when can I expect you?

GRANDSON (*Threatening him jokingly with his finger*)   Eh, eh! Don't you be so curious. We could be here tomorrow, in two days, or maybe in ten minutes. Any time's a good time to shoot Charlie, as our saying goes.

OCULIST (*Resignedly sitting on the sofa with his head in his hands*)   So I'll have to . . .

GRANDSON   Come on, Grandpa. Present arms and forward march. How much do we owe you?

OCULIST   Oh, nothing. We'll put it down to national insurance.

GRANDSON (*Giving him his card*)   This is our telephone number. If ever anything . . .

GRANDPA   Straight between the eyes, my friend. And remember an old man's advice: Tea should be hot, an *i* should have a dot, and Charlie should be . . .

GRANDSON (*Impatiently*)   Come on, Grandpa, let's go. (*They leave the room. Grandson lets Grandpa pass through and moves back from the door toward the Oculist.*)   And if you know anybody else . . .

OCULIST   Yes? (*Pause. They look at each other.*)

GRANDSON   Because we'll be back. (*Leaves the room. He stops in the doorway and, looking down at what is lying on the floor outside, says to himself:*)   So he said I belch . . . (*Really goes out this time.*)

The Oculist sits still for some time, as before. It has got much darker but now stops darkening. Then he gets up slowly, goes out, and drags into the room an inert figure. It is a dummy, of course. The corpse is not played by a live actor. He places the dummy on the sofa, lays its hands on its chest, then examines its eyes, turns back the eyelids, and looks at the eyes according to the rules of eye tests.

OCULIST   Incurable separation of the cornea. Of course, the shock of the blast may have hastened the onset of the disease, but who can guarantee that tomorrow he wouldn't have fallen down the stairs, and then his cornea would have become separated completely? In any case there was nothing I could do for him. (*Pause.*)   He didn't have to come either. His appointment wasn't for today. I was taking a chance. (*Pause.*)   I'm shortsighted too and I'm still alive. (*The telephone rings. The Oculist lifts the receiver.*)   Hello! . . . Yes, can I help you? . . . Yes, speaking . . . Between two and six . . . Whenever it's convenient . . . Four o'clock? All right, tomorrow at four. Don't you worry, we'll soon fix you up. Can I have your name? (*Pulls a notebook and pencil out of his pocket. Begins to write.*)   I must write it down in the appointment book . . . Hello! Yes. Now then . . . name—Charlie. Till tomorrow then. Good-bye. (*Replaces the receiver. Walks away from the telephone, looks at his watch, glances at the door, listens through the keyhole, then suddenly opens the door to check that nobody's listening. Reflects for a moment. Suddenly he runs to the telephone and hurriedly dials a number.*)   Hello, hello! Who's speaking? Grandpa? Grandpa, this is the doctor. Yes, the doctor. What do you mean, what doctor? (*Ingratiatingly.*)   Don't you recognize my voice? Don't you recognize your own doctor? . . . Well then, Grandpa, tomorrow at four. Yes, tomorrow at four. He'll be here. Who? What do you mean who? Charlie, of course. Well, bye! Till tomorrow! Good-bye! (*Pause. The Oculist replaces the receiver, walks up to the sofa, lifts the dummy off it, and pushes it underneath. He himself lies down on the sofa, opens his book, and begins to read it just like at the beginning of the play.*)

STRIPTEASE

᭺᭺

Translated by Lola Gruenthal

CHARACTERS

MR. I

MR. II

The stage is bare except for two chairs. Two doors, one stage left and one stage right, should be in clear view of the audience. When the curtain rises there is no one onstage. One can hear strange rattling and rumbling noises that may sound vaguely familiar but cannot be identified. The door on stage left opens and MR. I *comes rushing in. He is middle-aged, neatly but conventionally dressed, and carries a briefcase. Obviously he is not interested in his present environment but is rather preoccupied with something that has just happened outside. He should convey the impression that he has not entered the stage of his own will. He finally looks around and adjusts his suit. The door remains slightly ajar. A few moments later* MR. II *rushes in through the door on stage right. He looks like an exact replica of Mr. I and also carries a briefcase. The second door is not completely closed either.*

MR. I   Extraordinary!

MR. II   Incredible!

MR. I   I was walking along as usual . . .

MR. II   Not a care in the world . . .

MR. I   When suddenly . . .

MR. II   Like a bolt from the sky . . .

MR. I   (*As though just becoming aware of the presence of Mr. II*)   How did you get here?

MR. II   Why don't you ask what brought me here, or who brought me here?

MR. I   (*Again following his own thoughts*)   Outrageous!

MR. II   (*As though slightly mimicking Mr. I*)   Preposterous!

MR. I   I was simply walking, or perhaps, rather, hurrying along . . .

MR. II   Yes, that's right! You were certainly heading for a particular destination.

MR. I   How do you know?

MR. II   It's obvious. I was walking along too, or rather, hurrying along, heading for my destination.

MR. I   You took the words right out of my mouth. As I said, I was heading for this destination when suddenly . . .

MR. II   And remember, this was a destination that you yourself had chosen.

MR. I   Exactly! And with conscious intent, mind you, with full conscious intent . . .

MR. II   Obeying the dictates of your conscience, motivated by faith and reason.

MR. I   You're reading my very thoughts. As I was saying, I followed the path most appropriate for my chosen destination when suddenly . . .

MR. II   (*Confidentially*)   They beat you?

MR. I   Oh, no! (*Also confidentially.*)   And you?

MR. II   God forbid! I mean, I don't know a thing. That's all I can say.

MR. I   What was it then?

MR. II   That's hard to say for sure. It was like a gigantic elephant blocking the street. Or were there riots? First I had the impression of a flood, then of a picnic. But being in such a fog . . .

MR. I   That's true! It's so foggy today you can hardly see a thing. Still, I was trying to reach my particular destination . . .

MR. II   Which you yourself had freely chosen . . .

MR. I   That's God's honest truth! Nothing was left to chance. I had prepared everything down to the last detail. My wife and I often spend long hours planning ahead, planning our entire lives.

MR. II   I also had it all mapped out in advance. Even as a child . . .

MR. I   (*Confidentially*)   Did you hear a voice?

MR. II   I certainly did. There was a voice.

MR. I   Something like a saw . . . a persistent sound . . . no, actually an intermittent one.

MR. II   A gigantic buzz saw.

MR. I   But where the hell could a saw come from?

MR. II   Perhaps it wasn't a saw. Something threw me to the ground.

MR. I   But what?

MR. II   The worst part is this uncertainty. Was it really to the ground?

MR. I   Where else if not to the ground?

MR. II   But was I really thrown? What a jungle of riddles! I can't even tell if this was a "being-thrown" in the exact, classical sense, deserving of the name. Though I had the sensation of being thrown down, lying on the ground, I was perhaps—

MR. I (*Tensely*)   More overthrown than thrown down?

MR. II   Precisely! And to tell the truth, I really have no complaints. Did you see any people?

MR. I   Are there any at all?

MR. II   I suppose there are, but with all this fog . . . it doesn't seem likely.

MR. I   The worst of all is this lack of assurance.

MR. II   What color was it?

MR. I   What?

MR. II   It's so hard to figure out anything. It was something bright . . . a sort of rose color shot through with lead.

MR. I   Nonsense!

MR. II (*Moving over to Mr. I, after a pause*)   And still they hit you in the jaw.

MR. I   Me?

MR. II   Me too.

Pause.

MR. I   Well, anyway, now I can't get there on time anymore.

MR. II   How about just walking out? Right now! As though nothing had happened?

MR. I   No, no!

MR. II   Are you afraid?

MR. I Me? Why should I be? I'm just a little nervous. I just can't see . . .

MR. II That's because of the fog.

MR. I Did they say we must not leave the room?

MR. II Who?

MR. I Whom were you thinking of?

MR. II Never mind!

MR. I I've decided to stay put. The situation will clear up by itself.

MR. II But why? It may be quite possible for us to leave this room, unimpeded, and to continue on our way. After all, we can't really tell what's going on. Perhaps we ourselves went astray.

MR. I Are you blaming yourself? Us? We both knew where we were going, each of us heading for his specific destination.

MR. II Then it was not our own fault?

MR. I No, unless . . .

MR. II Unless?

MR. I How do I know? Let's drop the subject! I, for one, feel most strongly that we should not leave this room.

MR. II If you're so sure about it . . .

MR. I Definitely! We have to use sound reasoning in dealing with this matter.

Both sit down.

MR. II Perhaps you're right. (*Listens*)   There's nobody there.

MR. I Actually, there's no cause for concern, is there?

MR. II No obvious cause, I would say.

MR. I Are you implying that there is a cause . . . an obscure one?

MR. II You have a mind of your own.

MR. I Let's establish the facts.

MR. II All right, go ahead.

MR. I Very well, then: Each of us left his house according to plan and walked, or rather hurried, as you observed correctly, in the direction of his goal. The morning was brisk, the weather fair, the existence of wife and children an established fact. Each of us knew whatever there was to be known. Of course, we had no exact idea about the kind of molecules, not to speak of atoms, that our bedside tables are composed of, but, after all, there are specialists who deal with such matters. Basically, everything was perfectly clear. Well-shaved, carrying our practical and indispensable briefcases, we set out purposefully toward our goal. The respective addresses had been thoroughly committed to memory. But to be quite safe we had also noted them down in our notebooks. Am I correct?

MR. II On every point.

MR. I Now listen carefully! At a certain moment, as we were pursuing our course, a course that we had mapped out in detail and that was, so to speak, the end result of all our rational calculations, something happened that . . . and this is a point I must stress . . . came entirely from the outside, something separate in itself and independent of us.

MR. II With regard to this point, I must register some doubt. Since we are unable to define the exact nature of the occurrence, and since we cannot even agree as to its manifestations . . . due to the fog or to whatever other causes . . . we are in no position to state with any degree of certainty that this something came exclusively from the outside or that it was entirely separate in itself and independent of us.

MR. I You are discomposing me.

MR. II I beg your pardon?

MR. I You're interrupting my thoughts.

MR. II I'm sorry.

MR. I Unfortunately, we are not able to determine the exact nature of the phenomenon, and . . .

MR. II That's just what I said.

MR. I If you wish to go on, don't mind me!

MR. II The words just slipped out. It won't happen again.

MR. I (*Continuing*)   We cannot even determine with any appropriate degree of accuracy what particular elements constituted this something. (*Pause.*)   I beg your pardon?

MR. II   I didn't say a thing.

MR. I   I, for instance, perceived something that seemed to have the shape of an animal, but still I cannot be absolutely sure that it was not at the same time a mineral. Actually, it seems to me that it involved energy rather than matter. I think all this may be best defined as a phenomenon hovering on the borderline of dimensions and definitions, a connecting link between color, form, smell, weight, length, and breadth, shade, light, dark, and so on and so forth.

MR. II   Do you still feel any pain? Mine is almost all gone.

MR. I   Please don't reduce everything to its lowest level!

MR. II   I was just asking.

MR. I (*Continuing his train of thought*)   This much is certain: We were helpless in the face of the phenomenon, and, partly of our own will, as we were looking for shelter, partly due to external pressure, we happened to find ourselves in these strange quarters, which at that critical moment were close at hand. Fortunately, we found the doors open. Needless to say, our original intentions have thus been completely upset and, as it were, arrested.

MR. II   I fully agree. What are your conclusions?

MR. I   This is just what I was coming to. Our main task now is to preserve our calm and our personal dignity. Thus, it would seem to me, we still remain in control of the situation. Basically, our freedom is in no way limited.

MR. II   You call this freedom, our sitting here?

MR. I   But we can walk out at any moment . . . the doors are open.

MR. II   Then let's go! We've wasted too much time anyway.

Again the same strange noise is heard as in the beginning.

MR. I   What . . . ? What's that?

MR. II   I told you we should go.

MR. I   Right now?

MR. II   Are you afraid?

MR. I   Not at all.

MR. II   First you insist on preserving your personal dignity by asserting your freedom, and then you don't even want to leave while there is still time.

MR. I   If I left right now I would limit the idea of freedom.

MR. II   What do you mean?

MR. I   It's quite obvious. What is freedom? It is the capacity of making a choice. As long as I am sitting here, knowing that I can walk out of this door, I am free. But as soon as I get up and walk out, I have already made my choice, I have limited the possible courses of action, I have lost my freedom. I become the slave of my own locomotion.

MR. II   But your sitting here and not walking out is just another way of making a choice. You simply choose sitting rather than leaving.

MR. I   Wrong! While I'm sitting, I can still leave. If, however, I do leave, I preclude the alternative of sitting.

MR. II   And this makes you feel comfortable?

MR. I   Perfectly comfortable. Unlimited inner freedom, that is my answer to these strange happenings. (*Mr. II gets up.*)   What are you doing?

MR. II   I'm leaving. I don't like this.

MR. I   Are you joking?

MR. II   I'm not trying to. I believe in external freedom.

MR. I   And what about me?

MR. II   Good-bye.

MR. I   Please wait! Are you crazy? You don't even know what's out there!

Both doors close slowly.

MR. II   Hey! What's going on now?

MR. I   Don't close them! Don't close them!

MR. II   All because of your babbling! We should have made up our minds right away.

MR. I   You don't have to blame me. If you had sat still, the doors wouldn't have closed. It was your fault.

MR. II   Now there's no way of finding out.

MR. I   It's all because of you. Thanks to your behavior we've lost our chance to get out.

Mr. II goes to one of the doors and tries unsuccessfully to open it.

MR. II   Hey! Open up right now!

MR. I   Shh! Be quiet!

MR. II   Why should I be quiet?

MR. I   I don't know.

MR. II   (*Goes to the other door, knocks, and listens*)   Locked!

MR. I   Do me a favor and sit down!

MR. II   Well, where is it now, your precious freedom?

MR. I   I have nothing to blame myself for. My freedom remains unaffected.

MR. II   But there's no way to get out now, is there?

MR. I   The potential of my freedom has remained unchanged. I have not made a choice; I have in no way confined myself. The doors were closed for external reasons. I am the same person I was before. As you may have noticed, I did not even get up from my chair.

MR. II   These doors are upsetting me.

MR. I   My dear sir, while we are unable to influence external events, we must make every effort to preserve our dignity and our inner balance. And with regard to those, we command an unlimited field, even though the infinite variety of choices has been reduced to two alternatives. These, of course, exist only as long as we do not choose either of them.

MR. II   What else could happen?

MR. I   Do you think it may get worse?

MR. II   I'll try to knock on the wall . . . perhaps somebody is there.

MR. I   It is regrettable that you have no regard for the inviolable nature of your personal freedom. I, too, could knock on the wall, but I won't. If I did, I would preclude other possibilities, such as reading the papers I have in my briefcase or concentrating on last year's horse races.

Mr. II knocks on the wall several times and listens; he repeats this for a while. Then he takes off one shoe and bangs it against the wall. One of the doors opens slowly, and in comes a Hand of supernatural size. It resembles the old-fashioned printer's symbol: Hand with pointing index finger and attached cuff. The palm should be brightly colored to make it stand out clearly against the scenery. With bent index finger the Hand makes a monotonously repeated gesture in the direction of Mr. II, beckoning to him.

MR. I   (*The first to notice the Hand*)   Pssst! (*Mr. II has not yet seen the Hand; he keeps banging with his shoe and listening.*)   Pssst! Stop it, please! Don't you see what's going on?

Mr. II turns around. Mr. I points to the Hand.

MR. II   Something new again!

The Hand continues beckoning to him. Mr. II walks over to it. The Hand points to the shoe he is holding, then it reaches out in an ambiguous gesture that may be either begging or demanding. Hesitantly, Mr. II puts his shoe into the Hand. The Hand disappears and returns immediately without the shoe. Mr. II takes off his other shoe and gives it to the Hand. The Hand leaves the room, returns, and repeatedly touches Mr. II's stomach with its index finger. Guessing what this means, Mr. II takes off his belt and hands it over. The Hand withdraws, returns without the belt, and begins to beckon to Mr. I

MR. I   Me? (*He slowly walks over to the Hand; stopping at every other step. While he is talking, the Hand continually beckons to him.*)   But I didn't knock . . . There must be a misunderstanding . . . I didn't make a choice . . . no choice whatsoever . . . I did not knock, though I must admit that when my colleague knocked I was hoping that someone might hear it and come in, that the situation might be cleared up and that we would be allowed to leave. This much I admit, but I didn't do any knocking. (*The Hand points to his shoes.*)   I protest. I repeat once more: The knocking was not done by me. I don't understand why I should hand over my shoes. (*Bends down to untie the laces.*)   I value my inner freedom. A little patience, please! Can't the Hand see that there's a knot here? . . . Personally, I don't hold anything against the Hand, because my own conscience is clear. I am determined to save my inner freedom, even at the cost of my external freedom . . . quite the opposite to my colleague here. But I'm not holding anything against him either, because, after all, what he does is his own business. I request only that we be treated as individuals, each according to his own views . . . Just a moment, I'm getting it. There's no fire, is there? (*Giving the Hand his shoes.*)   Glad to oblige! (*The Hand points to his stomach.*)   I'm not wearing a belt . . . I prefer suspenders. All right, I'll give up the suspenders, too, if necessary. (*Takes off his jacket and unbuttons his suspenders.*)   Peculiar methods they have here! All right, here they are . . . Somebody's fingernails could use a good cleaning, if I may venture an opinion. (*The Hand disappears, the door closes slowly.*)   At least I'm wearing a fresh pair of socks. I'm glad about that.

MR. II   Bootlicker!

MR. I   Leave me alone! I'm not bothering you.

MR. II   What can I use now to knock with?

MR. I   That's your problem. I'm going to sit down. (*Returns to his chair.*)

MR. II   You're in good shape now with your inner freedom. You're losing your pants.

MR. I   What about yours? They won't stay up either without a belt.

MR. II   Well, what do you make of all this?

MR. I   I can only repeat what I said before: First the dear Hand interfered with my free movement in space and then with my ability to wear trousers. This is true, and this I'm willing to admit. But what does it matter? All these are externals. Inwardly I have remained free. I have not become engaged in any action; I have not made any gesture. I haven't even moved a finger. Just sitting here I am still free to do whatever lies in the realm of possibility. Not you, though. You did something . . . you made a choice . . . you knocked against the wall and made a fool of yourself. Slave!

MR. II   I could slap your face, but there are more important things to be done.

MR. I   Right. But why do they deal with us like this?

MR. II   It's always the first thing they do . . . take away your shoelaces, belt, and suspenders.

MR. I   What for?

MR. II   So you can't hang yourself.

MR. I   You must be joking! If I'm not even getting up from my chair, how can I hang myself? Of course, I could if I wanted to, but I won't. You know my views.

MR. II   I'm sick and tired of your views.

MR. I   That's your problem. But listen to this: If the dear Hand doesn't want us to hang ourselves, this means that it wants to keep us alive. That's a good sign!

MR. II   This is just what bothers me. It means that the Hand thinks of us in terms of categories . . . Life and the other . . . what's it called?

MR. I   Death?

MR. II   You said it.

Pause.

MR. I   I am calm.

MR. II   Tell me, what could you do now, if you felt like doing something? Of course, taking into account the fact that you had to relinquish your shoes and suspenders.

MR. I   Oh, quite a few things. I could, for instance, put on my jacket inside out, roll up the legs of my trousers, and pretend to be a fisherman.

MR. II   And what else?

MR. I   I could sing.

MR. II   That's enough. (*Turns up the legs of his trousers, puts on his jacket inside out, and takes off his socks.*)

MR. I   Are you crazy? What are you trying to do?

MR. II   I'm pretending to be a fisherman, and I'm going to sing, too. In contrast to you, I want to explore all the possibilities of action. Maybe the Hand is partial to fishermen and lets them return to freedom. Who knows? One should not neglect any possibility. I've asked you because you have more imagination than I. For instance, I could never have thought up all those things about inner freedom.

MR. I   It's all right with me. But please remember that I'm not moving from this chair.

MR. II   You don't have to. (*He climbs on the chair and sings Schubert's "The Trout." One of the doors slowly opens.*)

MR. I   (*Who has been anxiously watching the door*)   Now you've done it!

The Hand appears.

MR. II   How do you know? Perhaps I'll be allowed to go and you'll keep sitting. (*The Hand beckons to him.*)   I'm coming, I'm coming. What's it all about? (*The Hand indicates that it wants his jacket.*)   But I was just—Is there a law against fishing? (*The Hand repeats its gesture.*) I was just pretending. I'm not really a fisherman. (*Gives the Hand his jacket. The Hand disappears, comes back, and now obviously requests his trousers.*)   No, I won't give up the trousers! (*The Hand forms a fist and slowly rises.*)   All right. (*He takes off his trousers.*)

MR. I   (*Getting up*)   Me too?

After waiting for an answer, which he does not receive, Mr. I voluntarily removes his jacket. Meanwhile Mr. II has given the Hand his trousers, and he now stands there in striped knee-length underpants. The Hand carries the trousers backstage, returns immediately, and beckons to Mr. I.

MR. I   (*cont.*)   All right, here it is. I'm not resisting, and I beg the Hand to take this into consideration. (*He gives his jacket to the Hand, which takes it out and returns immediately.*)   I'm always willing to oblige . . . may I keep my trousers in return? (*The Hand makes a negative gesture.*)   All right, I won't protest.

He takes off his trousers and stands up in his underpants, identical to those of Mr. II. The Hand disappears, the door closes.

MR. I (*cont.*)　You can go to hell with your idea about fishermen.

MR. II　It seems to me that it was your idea.

MR. I　But you carried it out. It's cold in here.

MR. II　It's quite possible that we might have been ordered to hand over our clothes anyway, idea or no idea.

MR. I　No! I'm convinced it was you who got us both into this predicament with your idiotic masquerade. It was you who attracted the Hand's attention to our clothing. If at least you had not rolled up your trousers, they would not have caught its eye.

MR. II　But fishermen always roll up their trousers.

MR. I　What good does that do you now?

MR. II　You can't keep ignoring the fact that we differ in our views. You do nothing so that you can feel free to do anything—of course, within the range of what is permitted—while I try to do everything I am permitted to do. But apparently wearing trousers is not permitted.

MR. I　You yourself have brought this down on your head.

MR. II　An anatomical inaccuracy! Besides, let me repeat this once more: We don't know whether the removal of our clothes was provoked by my action or whether it was part of a predetermined plan.

MR. I　At least now you should realize that my basic attitude is superior to yours. Don't you see: I didn't knock, I didn't sing, I didn't roll up my trousers, and still, here I am, looking just like you. Even our stripes are the same.

MR. II　Where is your superiority then?

MR. I　No waste of energy; same results. Plus, of course, my sense of inner freedom, which . . .

MR. II　One more word about inner freedom and that will be the end of you.

MR. I (*Backing up*)   You're unfair! After all, everyone has a right to choose the philosophy that suits him best.

MR. II   Never mind! I can't stand this anymore!

MR. I   I'm warning you: I won't defend myself. Defending oneself involves making a choice, and for me this is out, in the name of . . .

MR. II   What? Go on! In the name of what?

MR. I (*Hesitantly*)   In the name of inner free—(*Mr. II throws himself at him. Mr. I runs all over the stage.*)   Keep your hands off!

The door opens and the Hand reappears, beckoning to both. Mr. I and Mr. II come to a sudden halt.

MR. II   Me?

MR. I   Or me?

MR. II   Maybe it's you . . .

MR. I   You started this fight. Now you'll get your just deserts.

MR. II   Why me? Do you still believe that your idiotic theory is better?

MR. I   And you believe that your vulgar pragmatism, this lack of any theory, will stand up to such a test?

The Hand beckons to both.

MR. II   We'd better go over! It wants something again.

MR. I   All right, let's go! We'll soon find out who is right.

They go over to the Hand, which links them together with a pair of handcuffs. The Hand disappears and the door closes. Mr. II drags Mr. I along with him by the chain of the handcuffs and collapses on his chair. Silence.

MR. I   What does this mean? (*Anxiously.*)   Aren't you feeling well? Do you believe that this time it's serious? Say something, please!

MR. II   I'm afraid . . .

MR. I   Of what?

MR. II   So far the Hand has limited only our freedom of movement in space. But what assurance is there that soon we won't be limited in something even more essential?

MR. I   In what?

MR. II   In time. In our own duration.

Pause.

MR. I   I don't know either. (*Pedantically.*)   You, of course, being an activist, will exhaust your energies more rapidly. I, on the other hand, conserve mine . . .

MR. II (*Imploringly*)   Not again!

MR. I   I'm sorry. I didn't mean to hurt your feelings. Do you have a plan?

MR. II   There is only one thing we can do now.

MR. I   What?

MR. II   Apologize to the Hand.

MR. I   Apologize? But what for? We haven't done anything to the Hand. On the contrary, it should . . .

MR. II   This is completely irrelevant. We have to apologize all the same . . . in general, for no reason. To save ourselves . . . for whatever good it may do.

MR. I   No, I can't do that. I don't suppose I have to explain my reasons.

MR. II   You're right, I know them by heart. To apologize to the Hand would mean to make a choice, which again would limit your freedom, and so on and so forth.

MR. I   Yes, that's how it is.

MR. II   Do as you please! In any case, I am going to apologize. One has to abase oneself. Perhaps that is what it expects us to do.

MR. I   I would like to join you, but my principles . . .

MR. II   I have nothing more to say.

MR. I   I think I can see a way out. You're going to force me to apologize with you. In that case there is no question of choice on my part. I'm simply going to be forced.

MR. II   All right, consider yourself forced.

The door opens.

MR. I   I think it's coming. (*The Hand appears.*)   If only we had some flowers! (*Whispering.*)   You start!

Both run over to the Hand. Mr. II clears his throat in preparation for his apology.

MR. II   Dear Hand! I mean, Dear and Most Honorable Hand! Although well aware of the fact that the Hand is not here to listen to us, we still beg permission to speak to the Hand from the heart . . . I mean, we would like to hand the Hand a confession, although somewhat belated, nevertheless with full conscious awareness, we sincerely beg to apologize for . . . for . . . (*Whispering to Mr. I*)   For what?

MR. I   For walking, for going ahead, for everything in general . . .

MR. II   For walking, for going ahead, for . . . I'm expressing myself poorly, but I simply wish to apologize in general . . . for having been . . . for being . . . begging forgiveness from the depth of my heart for whatever the Honorable Hand knows that we don't know . . . for how are we to know what there is to be known? Therefore, whatever the case may be, I humbly apologize, I beg the Hand's forgiveness, I kiss the Hand. (*He ceremoniously kisses the Hand.*)

MR. I   I wish to join my colleague, though only in a certain sense, having been forced . . . The Hand knows my principles . . . Therefore, though being forced, I nevertheless sincerely apologize to the Hand on principle.

He ceremoniously kisses the Hand. Meanwhile the other door opens and through it appears a Second Hand, completely covered by a red glove. It beckons to both. Mr. II notices it first. Both turn their backs to the First Hand.

MR. II   There! Look!

MR. I   Another one!

MR. II   There are always two.

MR. I   It's calling us.

MR. II   Should we go? (*The First Hand covers his head with a conical cardboard hood.*)   I can't see anything!

MR. I It's calling us. (*The First Hand covers his head with an identical hood.*) It's dark.

MR. II When you're called, you have to go.

Handcuffed to each other and blinded by the hoods, they move toward stage center. Constantly stumbling and swerving, they gradually come closer to the Second Hand.

MR. I The briefcases! We forgot our briefcases!

MR. II Right! My briefcase! Where's my briefcase?

They grope blindly for their briefcases, left standing next to the chairs, then pick them up and follow the Second Hand through the door.

Blackout.

TANGO

Translated by Ralph Manheim and
Teresa Dzieduszycka

CHARACTERS

EUGENIA

EDDIE

EUGENE

ARTHUR

ELEANOR

STOMIL

ALA

ACT I

*A large, high room. The wall on the right ("right" and "left" are always taken
from the point of view of the audience) is not visible. This gives the impression that
the room extends beyond the edge of the stage. The wall on the left does not reach to
the front of the stage but forms a right angle a few steps behind it and continues
leftward along the proscenium. Between this corner of the wall and the left edge of
the stage, there is a door leading into a second room. This produces a kind of corridor
leading offstage to the left and into the main room on the right. At the left and right
of the rear wall, two more doors. The doors all look the same: double doors, high,
painted a dark color, and ornamented in a style befitting old, solidly middle-class
houses. Between the two doors in the rear wall, an alcove covered by a curtain. In
the room: a table with eight chairs, armchairs, a couch, small tables, a large mirror
on the left-hand wall. The furniture is arranged haphazardly as though the family
had just moved in or were about to move out. Great confusion. In addition, the
whole stage is full of draperies, hanging, lying, or rolled, adding to the impression of
confusion and blurring the outlines of the room. The room seems to be covered with
spots. At one point on the floor draperies are thrown into a heap, forming a kind of
bed. An old-fashioned black baby carriage on high, thin wheels. A dusty wedding
dress. A derby hat. The velvet tablecloth is shoved half-aside. Three persons are seated
at the uncovered part of the table. The first, who will be called* GRANDMA *for
the present, is an elderly but well-preserved and lively lady, who suffers only
occasionally from senile absentmindedness. Her dress, in a garish-colored flower
pattern, has a train attached; she wears a jockey cap and sneakers. She seems to be
nearsighted. A gray-haired, extremely polite* OLD GENTLEMAN. *He is
wearing glasses with thin gold rims, but his dress is disordered, and he seems dusty
and intimidated. Swallowtail coat, dirty stiff collar, a wide tie with a pearl stickpin,
but khaki-colored shorts, Scotch plaid knee socks, torn patent leather shoes, bare
knees. The third* PLAYER, *who gives the impression of being crude and shady,
wears baggy, light gray rumpled pants and an ugly checked shirt, open at the chest.
His shirtsleeves are rolled up. He habitually scratches his fat behind. Long greasy
hair, which he frequently combs with a comb that he takes from his back pocket.
Small, square mustache. Unshaven. A watch with a shiny gold wristband. All three
are deep in their card game. On the velvet tablecloth: dishes, cups, carafes, artificial
flowers, scraps of food. But also a few incongruous objects: a large, empty, bottomless
birdcage; a lady's shoe; a pair of riding breeches. Even more than the rest of the
furnishings, this table gives an impression of haphazardness, eccentricity, and
disorder. Each plate comes from a different set, each object is of a different period and*

style. From the right enters a YOUNG MAN *of twenty-five at the most: imposing and pleasant appearance. Neat, freshly pressed, ready-made suit that fits him perfectly, white shirt, tie. Under his arm he is carrying books and papers. He stands still and observes the scene. The three card players do not notice him. The table is quite far to the left. The person temporarily known as Grandma is sitting with her back to the young man, her profile to the audience. The elderly gentleman is facing her. At the head of the table the third player, with his back to the audience. The young man who has just come in is to one side of him.*

PERSON TEMPORARILY KNOWN AS GRANDMA (*Throwing a card on the table with exaggerated gusto*)   Three of spades. Razor blades.

PLAYER WITH MUSTACHE (*Throwing down a card*)   Down on the table goes old Aunt Mabel. (*He drinks beer from a bottle standing beside his chair.*)

OLD GENTLEMAN (*Timidly clearing his throat; speaks with a visible effort*)   Indeed, yes. I mean. . . . Well, plunk! (*He throws down a card.*)

PERSON TEMPORARILY KNOWN AS GRANDMA (*Waits for a moment, then with disapproval*)   Plunk! Oh come on, Eugene! Plunk what?

OLD GENTLEMAN OR EUGENE (*Stuttering helplessly*)   Plunk . . . plunk. . . .

PLAYER WITH MUSTACHE   The old gentleman's not in form today.

He takes a swig from the bottle.

PERSON TEMPORARILY KNOWN AS GRANDMA   Eugene! If you're going to play with us, you've got to do it right. Plunk's all right, but then what?

EUGENE   Well, just plain plunk!

PERSON TEMPORARILY KNOWN AS GRANDMA   Good Lord, you're blushing again!

EUGENE   Well then, plunk—trunk. Will that do?

PERSON TEMPORARILY KNOWN AS GRANDMA   Certainly not. Why don't you help him out, Eddie?

PLAYER WITH MUSTACHE OR EDDIE   With plunk? That's a tough word to work with. How about: Scram, Sam. We're on the lam.

EUGENE   Splendid! Splendid. But if you'll excuse my asking, what does it mean? Who's on the lam?

EDDIE It's what they say, that's all.

PERSON TEMPORARILY KNOWN AS GRANDMA Eugene. Eddie knows best.

EUGENE (*Throwing the same card on the table again*) Scram, Sam. We're on the lam.

PERSON TEMPORARILY KNOWN AS GRANDMA See, with a little effort you can do it too.

EDDIE The old gentleman is a bit bashful.

PERSON TEMPORARILY KNOWN AS GRANDMA Thank you, Eddie dear. I don't know what we would do without you.

EDDIE Don't mention it. (*He sees the Young Man and quickly hides the bottle under the table.*) I'd better be leaving.

PERSON TEMPORARILY KNOWN AS GRANDMA What? Why? What's got into you? Right in the middle of our game?

YOUNG MAN Good morning!

PERSON TEMPORARILY KNOWN AS GRANDMA (*Turns around, annoyed*) Oh, it's you.

YOUNG MAN Yes, me. What's going on here anyway?

PERSON TEMPORARILY KNOWN AS GRANDMA What do you mean? We're just having our little game.

YOUNG MAN I can see that. But with whom?

PERSON TEMPORARILY KNOWN AS GRANDMA With whom? Don't you recognize your Uncle Eugene anymore?

YOUNG MAN I wasn't asking about Uncle Eugene. I'll settle with him later. Who is this individual? (*He indicates Eddie.*)

EDDIE (*Stands up*) I'll just be running along now: Madam, the pleasure was mine.

PERSON TEMPORARILY KNOWN AS GRANDMA Edward! Stay!

YOUNG MAN Out! Out!

EDDIE (*Reproachfully to Grandma*) Dear lady, didn't I tell you we shouldn't have played today?

EUGENE (*Pointing to Grandma*)   It's her fault. Entirely her fault. I didn't even want to play.

YOUNG MAN (*Stepping up to the table*)   I said Out!

EDDIE   Easy, aces. I'm going!

On his way out he comes close to the Young Man. He takes one of the books from under his arm and opens it.

YOUNG MAN (*Rushing toward the table*)   How often have I told you never to let this happen again?

He runs around the table in pursuit of Grandma, who tries to evade him.

PERSON TEMPORARILY KNOWN AS GRANDMA   No! No!

YOUNG MAN   Oh yes, oh yes! And right now too!

EDDIE (*Leafing through the book*)   Fabulous!

PERSON TEMPORARILY KNOWN AS GRANDMA   What do you want of me anyway?

YOUNG MAN (*Running after her*)   You know very well what I want.

EUGENE   Arthur, have you no pity for your own grandmother?

YOUNG MAN OR ARTHUR   Oh, so you're talking back again are you, Uncle?

EUGENE   Not at all. I simply wanted to say that even if Eugenia may have forgotten herself a bit . . .

ARTHUR   Then I'll just have to remind her. And you too, Uncle. Pity! How can you talk about pity? Do any of you have any pity for me? Does she ever try to understand me? Oh, but this time, Uncle, you're going to get what's coming to you. Why aren't you working? Why aren't you writing your memoirs?

EUGENE   I did write a bit this morning, but then they came barging into my room, and . . .

PERSON HITHERTO KNOWN AS GRANDMA, OR EUGENIA   Eugene! Traitor!

EUGENE (*Hysterically*)   Why can't you all just leave me in peace?

ARTHUR   Oh, we will. But you've got to be punished too. (*He puts the bottomless birdcage over Eugene's head.*)   Now sit there until I let you out.

EUGENIA   Serves him right.

ARTHUR   Don't think you're going to get off free. (*He pulls back the curtain over the alcove, revealing a catafalque covered with a discolored black cloth and surmounted by several candelabra.*)   Hup! Up you go!

EDDIE (*Looking through the book with increasing interest*)   Terrific! (*He sits down off to one side.*)

EUGENIA   Again? I don't want to!

ARTHUR   Not another word!

Eugenia humbly approaches the catafalque; Eugene attentively offers her his arm.

ARTHUR (*cont.*)   Up you go.

EUGENIA (*Icily*)   Thank you, Judas!

EUGENE   Your cards were no good anyway.

EUGENIA   Fool!

ARTHUR   This ought to cure you of your disgusting frivolity. (*Tapping his pockets.*)   Matches! Who's got a match?

EUGENIA (*Lying down on the catafalque*)   At least spare me the candles, Arthur.

ARTHUR   Quiet, or I'll think up something really grim.

EDDIE (*Without taking his eyes off the book, produces a box of matches*)   Here!

Arthur takes the matches, lights the candles. Eugene takes the artificial flowers from the table, places them beside Eugenia, takes a few steps back to examine the effect, adjusts the flowers again.

EDDIE (*cont.*)   Great pictures! (*He giggles.*)

EUGENIA (*Raising her head*)   What's he looking at?

ARTHUR   Lie down!

EUGENE (*Steps up to Eddie and looks over his shoulder*)   Handbook of Anatomy.

EUGENIA   Just what he needs!

EDDIE   Is Mr. Arthur studying medicine?

EUGENE   He's studying for three different degrees. One in philosophy.

EDDIE   Is there something like this for philosophy?

EUGENE   Don't be ridiculous! They don't illustrate philosophy.

EDDIE   Too bad. It might be good.

EUGENIA   (*Sitting up*)   Let me see!

ARTHUR   Lie down!

EUGENIA   To think that you're the youngest one of us all! Why don't you enter a monastery?

ARTHUR   Why do you simply refuse to understand me, Grandmother?

EUGENE   Yes, I've been wondering about that myself. Why do you refuse to understand him, Eugenia?

ARTHUR   I just can't live in a world like this!

ELEANOR *enters from the door on the extreme left. She has definitely crossed the threshold of middle age. She is wearing slacks with suspenders in the style of the 1930s.*

ELEANOR   What kind of world? What *are* you people doing?

ARTHUR   Good morning, Mother.

ELEANOR   Mama! On the catafalque again?

EUGENIA   A good thing you've come, Eleanor. Now you can see for yourself how he treats me.

ARTHUR   How *I* treat *you*? She had to be disciplined.

EUGENIA   He's trying to educate me.

ARTHUR   She really goes too far.

ELEANOR   What did she do?

ARTHUR   She knows.

ELEANOR   But why the catafalque?

ARTHUR   To remind her of eternity. Let her lie there and look within.

ELEANOR (*Seeing Eddie*)   Ah, Eddie.

EDDIE   Hi!

ARTHUR   You mean you know each other?

EUGENE (*To himself*)   Here we go.

ELEANOR   Everybody knows Eddie. Why not?

ARTHUR   I'm going mad. I come home and what do I find? Laxity, chaos, shady characters, ambiguous relationships. And on top of all that, it turns out that even you . . . No! No! Why does all this have to happen? Where is it all going to end?

ELEANOR   Perhaps you'd like something to eat?

ARTHUR   Eat? No. All I want is to get the situation under control.

ELEANOR   Oh Lord. I sleep with Eddie from time to time. Don't I, Eddie?

EDDIE (*Absently*)   What? Oh yes. Of course. (*He unfolds some color plates inserted in the book.*)   Look at that! And all in color!

ARTHUR   What's that? What did you say, Mother?

ELEANOR   I'll get you something to eat. I won't be long.

She goes out through the right rear door. Arthur sits down distraught.

EUGENE (*To himself*)   She did put that a bit bluntly. I must say. (*To Arthur.*) May I take this off now? (*Silence.*)   Arthur? (*Silence.*)   Arthur! (*Silence.*) Arthur, I say, may I take this thing off now?

ARTHUR   Take it off. (*To himself.*)   Nothing matters now.

EUGENE (*Taking the birdcage off his head*)   Thank you! (*He sits down next to Arthur.*)   What's wrong, Arthur?

EUGENIA   Christ, this thing is hard!

EUGENE   I can understand that this business about your mother must be rather upsetting. I can well understand that. I'm an old-timer. (*Pause.*)   Eddie's not a bad sort. He has a good heart even if he doesn't look very bright. (*More softly.*)   Between you and me, he's not quite all there . . . (*Louder.*)   But what can you expect, my dear boy? Life must be taken as it is . . . (*More softly*)   . . . or must it?

(*Louder.*)   Now, now, Arthur. Chin up! Eddie has his good points, and after all, my goodness . . . we've got to face up to it: Your mother isn't quite what she used to be. (*More softly.*)   You should have seen her when she was young, before you were born, of course. Even before Stomil came along . . . (*Ponders, moves his chair closer to Arthur; very softly.*)   What are you planning to do about Eddie anyway? Frankly, he's a thoroughly bad sort. His fingernails are always so dirty. A sleazy type, wouldn't you say? And I'm convinced that he cheats at cards. He smacks his lips when he eats and he goes around here as if he owned the place. I wouldn't even shake hands with him if I weren't afraid of offending Eugenia. You know what he did yesterday? I go to Eugenia and I say: "Look here, it's fine with me if Eddie doesn't brush his teeth, but if he has to borrow my toothbrush, I wish he'd brush his teeth with it instead of his shoes." And what does he say? "There's nothing wrong with my teeth. They're white. They're sharp. But sometimes my shoes get dirty." That's what he says and then throws me out. I wouldn't want to influence you one way or another, but if I were you, I'd get rid of him. How about throwing him down the stairs? Hm?

ARTHUR   Oh, that wouldn't really solve anything.

EUGENE   Or maybe a left hook right in the face?

ARTHUR   That, too, would leave the basic situation unchanged.

EUGENE   Just a small one right in the face? It couldn't do any harm. If it's all right with you, I'll tell him to get ready for one.

Eugenia has meanwhile sat up and is listening. As soon as Eugene notices this, he moves away from Arthur. Louder.

EUGENE (*cont.*)   Eddie is simple, yes, simple and very decent. I have never in all my years met a simpler man.

EUGENIA   What's wrong with him?

EUGENE   I don't know. He just doesn't react anymore.

EUGENIA   What are you whispering in his ear?

EUGENE   Me? Nothing. I've just been telling him about the life of the bees.

ELEANOR (*Brings in a tray with a cup and cookies*)   Breakfast is ready, Arthur!

ARTHUR (*Waking out of his thoughts; automatically*) Thank you, Mother.

He sits down at the table. Eleanor sets the tray down in front of him, roughly shoving other objects aside. Arthur stirs his coffee. The tray is tilted up. He pulls a woman's shoe out from under it and heaves it angrily into the corner.

EDDIE Could you let me have this until Tuesday?

ARTHUR I'm afraid not. I've got an exam on Monday.

EDDIE Too bad. Some terrific pictures in here.

ELEANOR Mother, get down off that thing, will you? You look like a character out of Edgar Allen Poe.

EUGENIA A who, out of what?

ELEANOR Oh, just like somebody on a catafalque. It's all so terribly old-fashioned.

EUGENIA (*Motioning toward Arthur*) But what will he say?

ELEANOR He's eating now. He won't say anything.

EUGENIA Arthur, may I get down?

ARTHUR It's all the same to me. (*He drinks.*) This coffee's bitter.

ELEANOR We're all out of sugar. Eugene ate it.

EUGENE I beg your pardon. All I ate was the jam. It was Eddie who ate up the sugar.

Eugenia comes down from the catafalque.

ELEANOR And blow those candles out, will you? We've got to economize. (*Looking at the cards.*) Who's winning?

EUGENIA Eddie.

EUGENE There is something positively unnatural about Edward's good luck.

ELEANOR Eddie, have you been cheating?

EDDIE Me? Never.

ELEANOR You haven't? But you promised you'd lose today, remember? I need the money for groceries.

EDDIE (*Throwing up his arms*)   I must be a born winner. Tough luck!

Enter STOMIL, Arthur's father. In pajamas, sleepy. Yawning and scratching himself. He is a large, corpulent man with gray hair like a lion's mane.

STOMIL   I smelled coffee. (*Catching sight of Eddie.*)   Hello, Eddie.

Arthur thrusts the tray aside and observes the scene with tense interest.

ELEANOR   I thought this was your day to sleep until noon. The bed will be occupied after lunch.

STOMIL   I can't sleep. A whole new idea suddenly came to me. Who's drinking coffee anyway? Oh, it's you, Arthur . . . (*He steps up to the table.*)

ARTHUR (*Disgustedly*)   Good God, Father, can't you at least button up your pajamas?

STOMIL   What for?

ARTHUR   What for? What do you mean, what for?

STOMIL   I mean: What for? Such a simple question and you can't find an answer.

ARTHUR   Because . . . because one just doesn't appear like that.

STOMIL (*Drinking Arthur's coffee*)   You see? Your answer is meaningless. It's pure convention. It won't stand up under the scrutiny of the intellect.

ARTHUR   Isn't that enough?

STOMIL   Not at all. Not for me. I'm the kind of man who goes deeper. If we're going to discuss this, we've got to take the imponderables into account.

ARTHUR   Oh Lord, Father, can't you button your fly first and then talk it over?

STOMIL   That would be a complete reversal of the logical thought process. The effect would precede the cause. Man should never act without thinking, never act like an automaton.

ARTHUR   I take it then that you will not button your pajamas.

STOMIL   No, son. Anyway, I can't. No buttons.

He takes a swallow of coffee. He sets the cup down on the table. Unnoticed, Eddie has crept up behind Arthur.

ARTHUR I might have expected as much.

STOMIL Not at all. In this case at least, matter springs from the mind.

Eddie reaches over Arthur's shoulder for the cup and drinks.

ARTHUR That's precisely what I wanted to talk to you about, Father.

STOMIL Later, boy. Later. (*Takes a swallow out of the cup which is now in front of Eddie. Looks toward the catafalque.*) Isn't anybody ever going to remove that thing?

ELEANOR Why?

STOMIL Well, I have nothing against it on purely formal grounds. Actually it enriches reality, stimulates the imagination. But I could use the space for my experiments.

ELEANOR But you've got the whole house.

EUGENIA I'd be glad, too, if you got rid of it. Then Arthur couldn't torture me.

ARTHUR (*Pounding the table with his fist*) You see? What's going on in this house? Chaos, anarchy, entropy! How long has it been since Grandfather died? Ten years! And all that time nobody's ever thought of ridding the house of that catafalque. Incredible! We should be grateful, though, that you at least took Grandfather out of the house.

EUGENE We couldn't keep Grandfather any longer.

ARTHUR I'm not interested in the details. It's the principle of the thing.

STOMIL (*Drinking coffee, bored*) Really?

ARTHUR (*Jumps up and runs across the stage*) But it's not only Grandfather. I was born twenty-five years ago and my baby carriage is still standing here. (*He kicks the baby carriage.*) Why isn't it up in the attic? And what's this thing? Mother's wedding dress. (*He pulls the dusty veil from under a pile of rubbish.*) Why isn't it put away in a closet? And Uncle Eugene's riding breeches. What are they lying around here for when the last horse he ever rode died forty years ago?

No order, no sense of reality, no decency, no initiative. You can't move in this place, you can't breathe, you can't live!

Taking advantage of the confusion, Eddie empties the cup at one gulp.

ELEANOR (*Aside to Eddie*)   How beautifully you drink, Eddie!

STOMIL   My boy, tradition doesn't interest me in the slightest. Your indignation is absurd. You know very well we attach no importance to these monuments of the past, these relics of family tradition. That's why everything's lying around like this. We live in freedom. (*He looks into the cup.*)   Where's my coffee?

ARTHUR   No, no, Father, you just don't understand me. That's not what bothers me. No, that's not it.

STOMIL   Then kindly explain yourself more clearly, will you, boy? (*To Eleanor*)   Isn't there any more coffee?

ELEANOR   No, there won't be any until the day after tomorrow.

STOMIL   Why the day after tomorrow?

ELEANOR   How should I know?

STOMIL   All right. Never mind.

ARTHUR   Listen to me! It's not this particular tradition that bothers me. It's a fact that in this family there's no frame of reference at all. All that's left is bits and pieces, fragments, rubbish. You've destroyed everything but you go on destroying; you've gone on so long you've finally forgotten why you began in the first place.

ELEANOR   He's right. Stomil, do you still remember how we shattered tradition? How, in protest against tradition, I gave myself to you with Mummy and Daddy looking on? In the first row of the orchestra at the opening night of *Tannhäuser*. What a gorgeous scandal that was! Where are the days when people were still shocked by such things? And then you proposed to me.

STOMIL   As I recall it was at the National Museum's first avant-garde exhibition. The critics gave us rave reviews.

ELEANOR   No. It was at the opera. At the exhibition it wasn't you, or maybe it wasn't me. You're getting everything mixed up.

STOMIL Possibly. (*With enthusiasm.*)   The days of revolt, the time of the great leap forward. Liberation from the fetters of the old art and the old way of life. Man coming into his own, man overthrowing the old gods and putting himself on the pedestal. The seed burst open, the chains snapped. Revolution and release. That was our slogan then. Away with outmoded forms, down with convention! Long live the dynamic! Life as creation, an incessant striving toward new frontiers! Movement and struggle! All form transcended!

ELEANOR Stomil! You've been drinking at the fountain of youth! I hardly recognize you.

STOMIL Yes, we were young once.

ELEANOR What do you mean? We haven't grown any older. We've never betrayed our ideals. Why, even now our motto is still "Forward! Ever forward!"

STOMIL (*Without enthusiasm*)   Yes. Yes. That's right.

ELEANOR Do we have any prejudices? Do conventions mean anything to us? Aren't we still fighting against the old? Aren't we free?

STOMIL The old what?

ELEANOR Well, the old times. Don't you remember? Don't tell me you've forgotten what we were just talking about? All those fetters, those rusty chains of religion, morality, society, art. Especially art, Stomil. Art!

STOMIL Yes, of course. But when was all that actually?

ELEANOR Just a minute. Let me figure it out. We were married in 1900 . . . no, just let me think . . . Arthur was born in 1930, or . . . oh, be quiet, will you? Or was it 1940?

STOMIL Oh, *then.* I see. (*He stops in front of the mirror, passes his hand over his face.*)

ELEANOR Don't interrupt me. You're getting me all mixed up . . . (*Figures in an undertone, thoroughly absorbed.*)   1914 . . . 1918 . . . 1921 . . .

STOMIL (*At the mirror*)   We're young. Eternally young . . .

ARTHUR Father's right.

STOMIL   What do you mean?

ARTHUR   It's all dead and gone now. All in the past.

Eleanor runs across the stage, whispering dates, becoming more and more entangled in her calculations.

STOMIL   What's gone?

ARTHUR   All those fetters and chains! They're all gone now, unfortunately.

STOMIL   Unfortunately? You don't know what you're saying. If you'd lived in those days, you'd know how much we've done for you. You have no idea what the world was like then. Can you imagine how much courage it took to dance the tango? Do you realize that in those days there were hardly any fallen women? That the only recognized style of painting was naturalism? That the theater was utterly bourgeois? Stifling. Insufferable. You couldn't even put your elbows down on the dinner table! I can still remember a youth demonstration on that very issue. Why, it wasn't until after 1900 that the boldest, the most advanced spirits, stopped giving up their seats to elderly people. No, we didn't spare ourselves in our struggle for these rights and if you today can push your grandmother around, it's to us your thanks are due. You simply can't imagine how much you owe us. To think how we struggled to give you this freedom which you now despise!

ARTHUR   And what did you do with it? What did you produce? This bawdy house, where nothing works because everyone can do what he pleases, where there are no laws and no violations?

STOMIL   I know only one law: Don't hesitate, do what you feel like. Every man is entitled to his own kind of happiness.

ELEANOR   Stomil, I've got it! I've figured it out! It was 1928.

STOMIL   What was?

ELEANOR   (*In consternation*)   I've forgotten.

ARTHUR   You've poisoned the generations before you and after you with your freedom. Look at Grandmother! She's completely addled. Haven't you noticed?

EUGENIA I just knew he'd drag me into it.

STOMIL There's nothing wrong with Mama. What do you mean?

ARTHUR Naturally you're not shocked by her senile demoralization. Once she was a dignified, self-respecting grandmother. And now? Now she plays poker with Eddie!

EDDIE I beg your pardon. We also play bridge, you know.

ARTHUR I wasn't talking to you.

STOMIL Each has the right to do what he wants and with whomever he chooses. Old people, too.

ARTHUR That's not a right. It's a moral obligation to be immoral.

STOMIL You astonish me. Your opinions are so terribly outdated. When we were your age, we considered every kind of conformity disgraceful. Rebellion! Rebellion alone had any value for us.

ARTHUR What value?

STOMIL A dynamic and therefore positive value, though sometimes in a negative way. I trust you don't think we were merely blind anarchists? Certainly not. We were a column marching off to the future, a movement, a historical process. History is indebted to us. What is rebellion? The rock on which progress builds its temple and the greater the scope of the rebellion the grander the temple will be. Believe me: The scope of our rebellion was prodigious.

ARTHUR But if that's the case . . . why these misunderstandings? If you, too, are trying to do something constructive, why can't we build together?

STOMIL Impossible. What I said just now was purely objective. I described our historical role, but said nothing of our intentions. Well then, what were our intentions? Why, to do what we wanted, go our own ways, each for himself. We have always pursued our own inclinations. But by opposing everything, we paved the way for the future.

ARTHUR What future?

STOMIL That's not my affair. My job was to shatter existing forms.

ARTHUR   In other words, we're still enemies?

STOMIL   Why take it so tragically? All you need to do is stop worrying about principles.

ELEANOR   Yes. What I still can't understand is why you, the youngest of us all, should be the one to harp on principles. It used to be the other way around.

ARTHUR   Because I'm starting out in the world. But what a world! If I want a world, I've got to make one.

STOMIL   But you're young, Arthur. Don't you want to be modern? At your age?

ARTHUR   That's just the point. These modern times of yours. Even Grandmother has grown old in this world that has lost its standards. That's how modern your era is. What's more, you've grown old in it.

EUGENE   If you'll allow me to put in a word, I should like to call your attention to certain achievements; for instance, the right to wear short pants . . . ah, the fresh feel of the breeze . . .

ARTHUR   Oh, keep quiet, Uncle. Don't you realize that, precisely because everything is possible, nothing is possible anymore? If you were at least bucking convention with your short pants. But all convention was broken ages ago. By the time you came along it was all taken care of. The whole thing is absurd.

STOMIL   Well, what *do* you want then? Tradition?

ARTHUR   An orderly world!

STOMIL   That's all?

ARTHUR   . . . and the right to rebel.

STOMIL   That's it. That's what I've been telling you all along: *Rebel!*

ARTHUR   Don't you see that you've deprived me of every last chance to revolt? You've been nonconformists so long that there aren't any conventions left to rebel against. You've left nothing for me . . . nothing! Your only norm is the absence of all norms. The only thing left for me to rebel against is you . . . you and your immorality.

STOMIL   Go right ahead. Did I ever tell you not to?

EUGENE That's the stuff, Arthur. You'll show them.

ELEANOR Maybe it would calm you down. You've been so jittery lately. . . .

Eugenia makes signs to Eddie; they come to an understanding behind Arthur's back and pick up the cards.

ARTHUR (*Falls into an armchair with resignation*) Impossible!

ELEANOR Why?

EUGENE We're all in favor of it.

ARTHUR Rebel against you? What are you, anyway? A formless mass, an amorphous blob, an atomized world, a mob without shape or structure. Your world can't even be blown up; it's disintegrated all by itself.

STOMIL You mean we're no good for anything?

ARTHUR Exactly.

ELEANOR But couldn't you just try?

ARTHUR There's nothing to try. It's hopeless. You're all so disgustingly tolerant.

STOMIL Yes, that could be irritating, I suppose. Still, I don't like to see you feeling so left out.

ELEANOR (*Stands behind him and strokes his hair*) Poor little Arthur. You mustn't think your mother's heart is made of stone.

EUGENE We all love you, Arthur. We want to help you.

EUGENIA (*To Eddie*) I pass.

ARTHUR It's hopeless. This nonconformism you're pushing me into is only a new kind of conformism. But I can't be a conformist forever. I'm twenty-five. My friends are all laughing at me.

STOMIL But what about art, Arthur? What about art?

ELEANOR Exactly. You've taken the words out of my mouth.

ARTHUR What art?

STOMIL Well, art in general. I've devoted my whole life to art. Art is eternal rebellion. Why don't you give it a try?

EDDIE   Bring your bedding. Skip the wedding.

EUGENIA   Crash, smash, I'm out of cash.

ARTHUR   Father, you bore me. I want to be a doctor.

ELEANOR   A disgrace to the whole family! I've always dreamed of his becoming an artist. When I was carrying him in my womb, I ran through the woods stark naked, singing Bach. All for nothing!

ARTHUR   Maybe you sang out of tune.

STOMIL   All the same, don't give up hope. You still don't understand the value of art. I've just had an idea for a new experiment. You'll see.

ELEANOR   (*Clapping her hands*)   Eugenia, Eddie. Stomil has come up with something new.

EUGENIA   Again?

STOMIL   Yes. It came to me this morning. It's absolutely original.

ELEANOR   You'll put it on right away, won't you, Stomil?

STOMIL   I'm ready.

EUGENE   Heaven help us!

ELEANOR   Eugene, move the table. Make room.

Eugene shoves the table aside with a good deal of crashing and thumping. Eugenia and Eddie pick up the cards and step to one side. Under the mound of draperies suggesting a bed, something starts to move. Finally Cousin ALA's head comes to light.

ALA   (*A girl of eighteen with a good figure and long hair. She blinks in the light and yawns.*)   Where am I? First all that shouting and now they're moving furniture . . . What time is it anyway?

ARTHUR   Ala!

ELEANOR   I forgot to tell you, Ala has been here since six o'clock this morning.

STOMIL   This is marvelous, Ala. You're just in time for the show. (*To Eugene*)   That's fine. Now the catafalque.

ARTHUR   But why didn't you tell me? If I'd known, I'd have kept them quiet . . .

He notices that Eddie is approaching Ala with interest.

ARTHUR (*cont.*)   Back Eddie. Face to the wall.

Eddie steps back obediently and stands with his face to the wall.

ARTHUR (*cont.*)   Did you sleep well?

ALA   So-so.

ARTHUR   How long can you stay?

ALA   I don't know. I told Mother I might never go back.

ARTHUR   And what did she say?

ALA   Nothing. She wasn't there.

ARTHUR   Then how could you tell her?

ALA   Maybe I didn't. I don't remember.

ARTHUR   You've forgotten?

ALA   It was so long ago.

ARTHUR   How about some breakfast? Oh! We're out of coffee. May I sit beside you?

ALA   Why not?

Arthur gets a chair and sits down beside the pile of draperies.

ARTHUR   You're very lovely.

Ala laughs loudly.

ARTHUR (*cont.*)   What are you laughing about?

ALA (*Suddenly stops laughing. Gloomily*)   Me? Laughing? I'm not laughing.

ARTHUR   But you *were*.

ALA   Are you trying to pick a fight?

ARTHUR   I've been thinking about you a lot, Ala.

ALA (*Loud and coarse*)   Go on.

ARTHUR   I thought about meeting you!

ALA   Go on.

ARTHUR   And sitting down beside you . . .

ALA   Go on.

ARTHUR   . . . and talking with you . . .

ALA (*Gradually growing excited as though watching a boxing match*)   Go on.

ARTHUR   . . . about one thing and another . . .

ALA   Go on.

ARTHUR (*Louder*)   About different kinds of things.

ALA   Go on! Go on!

Arthur picks up the book that Eddie has left on the chair and throws it at Ala. She dodges and hides under the covers.

ARTHUR   Come out!

ALA (*Sticking her head out*)   What's wrong with you?

Arthur says nothing.

ALA (*cont.*)   Why did you do that?

Arthur says nothing.

ALA (*cont.*)   What do you want anyway?

ARTHUR   That's what they all keep asking me.

ALA   Never mind. I don't need to know.

STOMIL   Kindly take your seats. Kindly take your seats.

The stage is set for Stomil's experiment. To one side, the table. Nearer the proscenium, four chairs are lined up with their backs to the audience. Eugenia, Eleanor, and Eugene sit down from left to right. Eddie picks up his bottle of beer, still half-full, and tries to tiptoe away. Eugene sees him and points him out to Eleanor.

ELEANOR   Eddie, where are you going?

EDDIE　Be back in a minute.

ELEANOR　You stay right here!

Eddie turns around with resignation, sits down on the chair to the right of Eugene, intentionally stepping on his foot. Stomil goes into the room opening into the corridor on the left-hand side of the stage.

ELEANOR (*cont.*)　Arthur, Ala, what are you doing? We're waiting for you.

ALA　What's going on?

ARTHUR　Experimental drama. You know my father.

He gives her his hand. Ala jumps up. She has on a long nightgown that reaches the floor. It should not be transparent—this is called expressly to the attention of directors who like to make things easy for themselves. The cut and ruching make it look almost like a dress. They stand beside the chair on the extreme right. Eddie stretches out his arm and takes Ala by the waist. Arthur changes places with her.

STOMIL　(*Who has meanwhile come back with a big box and gone behind the catafalque so that only his head can be seen*)　Ladies and gentlemen, your attention please. Here are the principal characters of our drama. (*In the tone of a circus director introducing the next number.*)　Adam and Eve in paradise! (*Over the catafalque, which serves as the stage, two puppets manipulated by Stomil are seen: Adam and Eve, with the apple in her hand.*)

EUGENE　We've had that.

STOMIL　(*In consternation*)　When?

EUGENE　At the beginning of the world.

STOMIL　That was the old version. This is a new one.

EDDIE　Where's the snake?

ELEANOR　(*Whispering*)　Shhh!

STOMIL　The snake is in our imagination. We all know the story. Attention please! Here we go! (*In a deep voice.*)
　　So this is Paradise.
　　I'm Adam and before me lies
　　A world of possibilities.

But now it starts. From Adam's bone
Eve steps upon the earth.
To what will *she* give birth?
O Destiny, 'tis known
To you alone.

In a soprano:

Adam was first, but he
Did not exist until
I also came to be.
He walks so proudly still.
Doesn't the poor man see
For all his intellection
That there is no perfection
Except in what is not?
Where does the darkness go
When the sun comes out?
O Destiny!

A loud report and all the lights go out.

ELEANOR'S VOICE Stomil, Stomil, what's happened? You're not dead, are you?

EUGENE'S VOICE Fire! Fire!

Arthur lights a match and then the candles over the catafalque. Stomil appears; he is holding an enormous revolver.

STOMIL Well, what do you say? Not bad, eh?

ELEANOR Stomil, you frightened us so!

STOMIL Every experiment must shock. That's my first principle.

EUGENE If that's what you were after, it was a success all right. My heart's still pounding.

ELEANOR How did you do it, Stomil?

STOMIL I unscrewed the fuse and fired the revolver.

ELEANOR Marvelous!

EUGENE What's so marvelous about it?

STOMIL   Don't you understand?

EUGENE   No, I don't.

ELEANOR   Don't mind him, Stomil. Eugene has always been slow.

STOMIL   How about you, Eugenia?

EUGENIA   Huh?

STOMIL (*Louder*)   Did you understand the experiment, Mama?

ELEANOR   The experiment has made her deaf.

EUGENE   That doesn't surprise me.

STOMIL   Let me explain. The shock method creates an immediate unity of action and perception. See?

EUGENE   Yes, but . . .

STOMIL   Yes, but what?

EUGENE   But what's that got to do with Adam and Eve?

ELEANOR   Eugene, do try to concentrate.

STOMIL   What we are dealing with here is an intrinsically theatrical phenomenon, the dynamics of sense perception. That means something to you, doesn't it?

EUGENE   Frankly, I don't think it does.

STOMIL (*Throws the revolver on the catafalque*)   I give up.

ELEANOR   Don't be discouraged, Stomil. Who's going to experiment if you lose heart?

All stand up and put the chairs back in their places.

EUGENE   A flop, friends.

EDDIE   Give me the movies.

ELEANOR   Well, now what should we do?

ARTHUR   Clear out! All of you. Out!

STOMIL   What's got into you?

ARTHUR   All of you! I can't bear the sight of you.

STOMIL   Is that a way to treat your own father?

ARTHUR   I used to have a father. Not anymore. I'll have to make myself a father.

STOMIL   You? *You* make *me*?

ARTHUR   You and the whole lot of you. I'm going to make you all over. And now get out. This minute!

STOMIL   That boy's going just a bit too far.

ELEANOR   Never mind, Stomil. Thank God, we're enlightened.

STOMIL   You think I should really go?

ELEANOR   Why not? After all, you're not really interested in anything but your experiments.

STOMIL   Ah yes, art! Modern art! Give me God and I'll make an experiment out of him.

ELEANOR   There. You see!

They all go out through the left rear door.

EDDIE   (*To Eugenia*)   Come on, Grandma.

EUGENIA   Don't forget the cards.

Eddie picks up the cards and goes out with Eugenia.

EDDIE   (*Turning around again, to Arthur*)   If you need anything . . .

ARTHUR   (*Stamping his foot*)   Get out!

EDDIE   (*Conciliatory*)   Okay, okay!

He goes out left with Eugenia.

EUGENE   (*After making sure that the others are gone*)   You're absolutely right, Arthur. Between you and me, they're a bad lot.

ARTHUR   You too. Out!

EUGENE   Certainly. Certainly, my boy. I'm going. I only wanted to tell you that you can count on me.

ARTHUR   What do you mean?

EUGENE   Never mind. Just do what you think right. But remember. I can be useful to you. I'm not as far gone as the rest of them. (*More softly.*)   I'm an old-timer.

ARTHUR   Glad to hear it. But now leave us alone, will you?

EUGENE   (*Goes out left, turns around again, and says with emphasis*)   An old-timer. (*Exits.*)

ALA   Now what?

ARTHUR   Now I'll explain everything.

ACT II

The same scene as in act one. The only light comes from a simple standing lamp. Arthur is sitting in an armchair. Someone enters from the right.

ARTHUR Who's there?

FIGURE Me.

ARTHUR Who's me?

FIGURE Your Uncle Eugene.

ARTHUR Password?

EUGENE New life. Countersign?

ARTHUR Rebirth. (*Pause.*) All right. Come in.

Eugene steps into the light. He sits down facing Arthur.

EUGENE Oof. I'm exhausted.

ARTHUR Is everything ready?

EUGENE I've brought everything I could down from the attic. You should see the moths! You think it will work?

ARTHUR It's got to work.

EUGENE I'm worried, worried. They're so demoralized . . . Think of it. A whole lifetime in this bawdy house . . . I beg your pardon, I meant this atmosphere of moral disintegration. You see, it's contagious. Forgive me.

ARTHUR Forget it. What's my father doing?

EUGENE He's in his room, working on a new production. Don't you feel sorry for him sometimes? After all, he actually believes in that art of his.

ARTHUR Then why do you discourage him?

EUGENE For spite. To get his goat. But the fact is, those experiments of his don't mean a thing to me. What do you make of them?

ARTHUR I've got other problems. And Mother?

Eugene stands up, goes to the left rear door and looks through the keyhole.

EUGENE Can't see a thing. Either she's turned the light out or hung something over the keyhole. (*He goes back to his former place.*)

ARTHUR And Grandmother Eugenia?

EUGENE Probably sitting at her mirror, putting on makeup.

ARTHUR Good. You may go now. I have an important appointment in a few minutes.

EUGENE (*Stands up*) Any further orders?

ARTHUR Be vigilant. Eyes open, mouth shut, and ready for action.

EUGENE Yes, sir. (*On his way out.*) God protect you, Arthur, my boy . . . Maybe we'll manage to bring the good old days back again yet.

Goes out to the right. Ala enters by way of the corridor right. She is still wearing her nightgown.

ALA (*Yawning*) What did you want me for?

ARTHUR Shh . . . quiet.

ALA Why?

ARTHUR This is private—between you and me.

ALA You think they care what we do? We could climb up the walls and sleep on the ceiling for all they care. (*She sits down, wincing as though in pain.*)

ARTHUR What's wrong?

ALA Stomil pinched me twice today.

ARTHUR The rotter!

ALA Arthur, he's your father!

ARTHUR (*Kissing her hand gallantly*) Thank you for reminding me.

ALA It sounds so old-fashioned. Nobody calls his father a rotter nowadays.

ARTHUR What *do* you call him then?

ALA Nothing. You just ignore him.

ARTHUR (*Disappointed*)   Then I was mistaken.

ALA   Well, it's your headache that he's your father. Personally, I think
he's great.

ARTHUR (*Contemptuously*)   An artist!

ALA   What's wrong with that?

ARTHUR   Artists are a plague. They were the first to contaminate our
society.

ALA (*Bored*)   Oh, who cares? (*Yawns.*)   What did you want me for? It's
cold in here. I'm practically naked. Hadn't you noticed?

ARTHUR   Well, what do you say? Have you thought it over?

ALA   You mean will I marry you? But I've already told you. I don't see
the point.

ARTHUR   You mean the answer is no?

ALA   Why do you get so worked up about it? I mean—I don't care—if
it means so much to you, we can get married tomorrow. We're
already cousins.

ARTHUR   But I *want* you to care! I want you to realize that marriage is
something very important.

ALA   Important? Why? I don't get it. If I'm going to have a baby it'll be
with you, not with the minister. So what's the problem?

ARTHUR   Well, if it's not important in itself, then we've got to make it
important.

ALA   What for?

ARTHUR   Nothing is important in itself. Things in themselves are
meaningless. Unless we give them character, we drown in a sea of
indifference. We have to create meanings, because they don't exist in
nature.

ALA   But what for? What for?

ARTHUR   Well, if you must have a reason, let's say "for our own
pleasure and profit."

ALA   Pleasure?

ARTHUR   Yes. We derive pleasure from profit and we only profit from doing things we attach importance to—difficult things, the unusual things that seem rare and precious. And that's why we have to create a system of values.

ALA   Philosophy bores me. I think I prefer Stomil. (*She sticks her leg out from under the nightgown.*)

ARTHUR   You only think that. Kindly remove that leg.

ALA   You don't like it?

ARTHUR   That has nothing whatsoever to do with the subject.

ALA (*Obstinately*)   You really don't like it?

ARTHUR (*With difficulty takes his eyes off her leg*)   Oh, all right, show your leg if you want to. Anyway, it only proves my point.

ALA   My leg? (*She examines her leg closely.*)

ARTHUR   Yes. Do you know why you're showing your leg? Because I don't leap all over you like my artist father and everybody else does. That worries you. You were pretty bewildered this morning when we were all alone. You thought you knew what I wanted from you.

ALA   That's not true.

ARTHUR   Not true? Ha. You think I didn't see how upset you were when I proposed marriage instead of just picking you up and throwing you down on the bed?

ALA   I had a headache.

ARTHUR   Headache? Go on. You just couldn't figure out *what* was going on. You thought I wasn't attracted, that you must be losing your charms. If I suddenly started acting like my father, it would be a relief, wouldn't it? Yes. Except you'd run away, just to get even with me.

ALA (*Stands up with dignity*)   I'm running all right.

ARTHUR (*Takes her by the hand and pulls her down into the chair.*)   Sit down. I haven't finished yet. All you care about is your sex appeal. You're so primitive! You can't think about anything else. You don't know anything else!

ALA   Are you suggesting that I'm backward? (*She tries again to stand up.*)

ARTHUR (*Holding her down*)   You stay right here. You've confirmed my theory. My behavior was atypical; that baffled you. The unusual is a value in itself. See? I have given meaning to an encounter that would otherwise have meant nothing. I!

ALA   Well, if you're so terribly clever, what do you need me for? If you're so awfully superior, why don't you just live all by yourself?

ARTHUR   You don't have to be so touchy.

ALA   We'll see how far you get alone. Or with Uncle Eugene. (*She resolutely draws her nightgown over her knees, buttons it up to the neck, and wraps herself in a steamer rug. She puts on the bowler and draws it down deep over her forehead.*)

ARTHUR (*Shyly*)   Don't be angry.

ALA   What do you care?

Pause.

ARTHUR   Aren't you too warm . . . in that blanket?

ALA   No.

ARTHUR   Uncle Eugene's hat doesn't look very good on you.

ALA   I don't care.

ARTHUR   Suit yourself. Where were we anyway? Oh yes, a system of values . . . (*He moves his chair closer to Ala.*)   Now, generally speaking, a system of values is indispensable to the proper functioning both of the individual and of society. (*He seizes Ala's hand.*)   Without the right kind of values we can never hope to create a harmonious world or establish the necessary balance between those elements commonly termed good and evil—though of course I use these words in their larger rather than strictly ethical sense. Now in this connection our task is twofold: We must, one, restore the practical relevance of these concepts and, two, formulate rules of conduct which . . .

He flings himself at Ala and tries to kiss her. She struggles free; they wrestle. Eddie enters with his towel around his neck and a hairnet on his head.

EDDIE (*With the pretentious enunciation typical of the semiliterate*)   Oh, do excuse me.

ARTHUR (*Lets Ala go as if nothing had happened. Ala straightens her hat and rubs her shoulder demonstratively.*)   What are *you* doing here?

EDDIE   I was just going to the kitchen for a drink of water. I beg your pardon, I didn't know you were conversing.

ARTHUR   Water? Water? What for?

EDDIE (*With dignity*)   Because I'm thirsty, sir.

ARTHUR   At this hour? In the middle of the night?

EDDIE (*Offended*)   If that's the way you feel about it, I can go without.

ARTHUR (*Furious*)   Drink and get out!

EDDIE   As you wish. (*He goes majestically to the door left rear.*)

ARTHUR   Just a minute.

EDDIE   Yes, sir?

ARTHUR   The kitchen is on the right.

EDDIE   There? Impossible.

ARTHUR   I believe I know where the kitchen is in my own house.

EDDIE   You just can't be sure of anything these days. (*He changes his direction and goes out through the door right rear.*)

ARTHUR   That idiot! I'll have to take care of him once and for all.

ALA (*Icily*)   Have you finished taking care of me?

ARTHUR   It's all his fault.

ALA   I suppose it was his fault you nearly twisted my arm off.

ARTHUR   Does it hurt very much?

ALA   What do you care?

She affects a cry of pain. Arthur, troubled, tries to examine her shoulder.

ARTHUR   Where does it hurt? (*He touches her shoulder, but not with his original purpose.*)

ALA (*Uncovering her shoulder*)   Here . . .

ARTHUR   I'm terribly sorry.

ALA (*Uncovering her back*) . . . and here . . .

ARTHUR (*Dismayed*) Really, I didn't mean to . . .

ALA (*Thrusts her leg forward*) . . . and here . . .

ARTHUR How can I ever make it up to you? . . .

ALA (*Lays her forefinger on her rib*) . . . and here too!

ARTHUR Forgive me. I didn't mean to . . .

ALA Now you've shown what you really are—a brute. First a lot of talk and then the usual. (*She sinks tragically into an armchair.*) We poor women! Is it our fault we have bodies? If we could only check them somewhere like a hat or a coat. Then maybe we'd be safe from our sweet-talking cousins. Frankly, I'm surprised. You with your noble ideals.

ARTHUR (*Confused*) But really, I . . .

ALA No excuses! You don't think I like a good conversation too? But that calls for a nice restful atmosphere. How can I converse when some philosopher is clutching at my legs? But never mind. What were we talking about? It was just beginning to be interesting when you . . .

Behind the door through which Eddie has passed a sound of gushing water is heard. Then gargling.

ARTHUR This is too much. Do you seriously think I wanted to rape you?

ALA (*Alarmed*) Didn't you?

ARTHUR Certainly not. I was only teaching you a lesson.

ALA Thanks. I know that subject.

ARTHUR You can only think about one thing. Then why did you resist? Come on. Why?

ALA You're vulgar.

ARTHUR Science knows no shame. Why?

ALA Well, why did you attack me?

ARTHUR Attack you? I was sacrificing myself.

ALA   What?

ARTHUR   Yes, sacrificing myself in my effort to make certain things clear to you. It was a pure exercise in sexual pragmatics.

ALA   Pig! Scientific pig! Pragmatics? What is it anyway? Some new kind of perversion?

ARTHUR   There's nothing new about it. I'm sure we'll always be friends. Yes, women will follow me.

ALA   Women? Which women?

ARTHUR   All women. Women throughout the world will be my allies. And once the women are convinced, the men will soon come around.

ALA   What women? Anybody I know? Anyway, do what you like with them. I couldn't care less.

ARTHUR   Look here. The central fact of history is the total enslavement of women, children, and artists by men.

ALA   I thought you didn't approve of artists.

ARTHUR   That's beside the point. The reason men don't like artists is that artists aren't men. That's what has always brought artists and women together—unfortunately. The ideas men have dreamed up— like honor, logic, progress—have always been foreign to women and artists. It's only very recently that the male has even begun to suspect the existence of such things as ambiguity, relativity, forgetfulness—in short, the glamour and poetry of this world, the exact opposite of what he had originally invented in that thick soldier's skull of his and tried to impose on women, children, and artists.

ALA   But what about you? Aren't you a male?

ARTHUR   I transcend myself; I take an objective view. That's essential if I'm to carry out my plan.

ALA   Can I trust you?

ARTHUR   It was only to make up for their lack of imagination that men invented the concept of honor. And, at the same time, of effeminacy. Why? To guarantee male solidarity. Anyone who dared question the code of manly virtues was immediately accused of being effeminate. The result was that, in self-defense, women, children, and artists

closed ranks to form a single community. They had no choice. . . .
Just a second.

The gargling is still heard from the kitchen. Arthur goes to the kitchen door.

ALA   Maybe he's washing.

ARTHUR   Him? Not likely! (*He goes back to his place.*)   Let's get back to
the subject.

ALA   I just don't believe you. I see what you're getting at. You can't
fool me.

ARTHUR   I have no desire to fool you. I'm simply trying to make you
aware of your own interests as a woman.

ALA   What does that mean? You want me to strip?

ARTHUR   Oh, don't be tedious. Once you've finally come to see that
our interests coincide, you'll be willing to work with me. What do
men want? They want to abolish all conventions relating to sex. And
why? To make life easier for *them,* to do away with all barriers
between desire and satisfaction.

ALA   You've got something there. They jump you like a bull. Like you
did just now.

ARTHUR   I can't deny that as an individual I'm subject to natural drives.
But I have a higher goal. Taking advantage of the general breakdown
in values, men have done everything they could to do away with the
last remaining rules governing sexual behavior. I can't believe that
women really like it, and that's the basis of my plan.

ALA   I like it fine.

ARTHUR   That's a lie. You *can't.*

ALA   Yes, I like it. It means I'm free, I can do as I please. For instance,
if I take my clothes off right now, what can you do about it? (*She
throws off the steamer rug and removes her hat.*)

ARTHUR   Stop it. This is a serious discussion.

ALA (*Undoing the ribbons of her nightgown*)   Why should I? Who's going to
stop me? You? My mother? God? (*She bares her shoulders.*)

ARTHUR   Cover yourself this minute! Pull up that nightgown. (*He tries desperately to look away.*)

ALA   I will not. It's my nightgown.

Eddie's head is seen in the doorway.

ALA (*cont.*)   Oh, hi, Eddie. Come on in.

ARTHUR (*Pushing Eddie away*)   Get out or I'll kill you. Taking your clothes off in front of this . . . Have you no shame?

ALA   He may not be very cultured, but he has marvelous eyes.

ARTHUR   Eyes like a pig.

ALA   *I* like them.

ARTHUR   I'll kill him.

ALA (*Sweetly*)   You wouldn't be jealous by any chance?

ARTHUR   I am not jealous.

ALA   First he's brutal. Then he's jealous. You ought to be ashamed of yourself.

ARTHUR (*Furious, face-to-face with Ala*)   Go on then. Undress! I'm not stopping you.

ALA   I don't feel like it anymore.

ARTHUR   Suit yourself.

ALA (*Retreating*)   I've changed my mind.

ARTHUR (*Following her*)   Oh, you don't feel like it anymore? Tell me, why don't you want to anymore! Tell me why you wanted to before.

ALA   My God, what a lunatic!

ARTHUR (*Seizes her by the arm*)   Why?

ALA   I don't know.

ARTHUR   Tell me!

ALA   What should I say? I don't know, I just don't know. Let me go.

ARTHUR (*Letting her go*)   You know perfectly well. It's because you only pretend to like all this absence of rules, this debauchery, this promiscuity.

ALA   Oh, I only pretend, do I?

ARTHUR   Of course. You really hate it, because it's not to your advantage. This lack of forms and norms cuts down your freedom of choice. There's nothing left for you to do but take off your clothes and put them back on again.

ALA   That's not true.

ARTHUR   Then why this sudden modesty?

Pause.

ALA   Now you're being logical. You just said that logic was nonsense.

ARTHUR   I said that?

ALA   Yes, only a minute ago. I heard you.

ARTHUR (*Disgruntled*)   You must have heard wrong.

ALA   I heard you quite clearly.

ARTHUR   Well, let's not bicker. But I still don't believe you. I'm convinced that the convention of unconventionality goes against your grain. You didn't make it up.

ALA   Who did then?

ARTHUR   Men! You only pretend to like it. And now you're stuck with it, and nobody likes to admit he's just following the herd.

ALA   But if I don't like it why should I go along with it?

ARTHUR   For fear of losing your attractiveness. To keep up with the fashion. Admit it!

ALA   No.

ARTHUR   No? All right. At least you admit there's something to admit. Come on. Why all these lies? Can't you see that important issues are at stake? I simply refuse to believe that you want to go to bed with every man in the world. Wanting to attract them is something else again. You want to be able to choose for yourself. But how can a woman choose when there are no conventions? Tell me that.

ALA I'm free. I know exactly what I want.

ARTHUR But you're weak by nature. What chance do you have when you're all alone with a strange man who's stronger than you and there's no convention to protect you? Let's assume, for instance, that you don't care for me. If Eddie hadn't butted in, you'd have been sunk, because I'm the stronger.

ALA I could always take up judo.

ARTHUR You take everything so literally. Can't you women ever understand a general idea?

ALA Lots of girls study judo. I'd have you begging for mercy.

ARTHUR Excellent. You're getting there. You're coming around. Don't you see? Why does it have to be judo when conventions are quite effective? I'd be kneeling at your feet with a bouquet in my hand begging you to take pity on me, to grant me a ray of hope. Behind a solid wall of conventions, without any wrestling, without even getting your hair mussed, you'd have me at your mercy. Wouldn't that be better than judo?

ALA You really mean it? Down on your knees?

ARTHUR Certainly.

ALA Okay. Go ahead.

ARTHUR Go ahead and what?

ALA Down on your knees!

ARTHUR Impossible.

ALA (*Disappointed*) Why?

ARTHUR Because there are no conventions left. Now do you see what a fix you're in?

ALA Isn't there anything we can do about it?

ARTHUR Yes.

ALA What?

ARTHUR   Establish new conventions or bring back the old ones. And
that's exactly what I'm going to do—with your help. Everything's
prepared. All I need is your help.

ALA   Great! And you'll really get down on your knees?

ARTHUR   I will.

ALA   All right. Now what can I do to help?

ARTHUR   Marry me. That's the first step. No more promiscuity, no
more dolce vita. A real marriage. Not just dropping into city hall
between breakfast and lunch. A genuine old-fashioned wedding with
an organ playing and bridesmaids marching down the aisle. I'm
especially counting on the procession. It will take them by surprise.
That's the whole idea. And, from then on, they won't have time to
think, to organize resistance and spread defeatism. It's the first shot
that counts. Catching them off guard like that, we can force them to
accept conventions they'll never break out of again. It's going to be
the kind of wedding they'll have to take part in, and on my terms. I'll
turn them into a bridal procession, and at long last my father will be
forced to button his fly. What do you say?

ALA   And I'll get to wear a white wedding gown?

ARTHUR   White as snow. Everything strictly according to the rules.
And at the same time you'll be helping all the women in the world.
The rebirth of convention will set them free. What used to be the first
rule of every encounter between a man and a woman? Conversation.
A man couldn't get what he wanted just by making inarticulate
sounds. He couldn't just grunt; he had to talk. And while he was
talking, you—the woman—sat there demurely, sizing your opponent
up. You let him talk and he showed his hand. Listening serenely, you
drew up your own order of battle. Observing his tactics, you planned
your own accordingly. Free to maneuver, you were always in
command of the situation. You had time to think before coming to a
decision and you could drag things out as long as you wanted. Even if
he gnashed his teeth and secretly wished you in the bottom of hell,
you knew he would never dare hit you. Up to the very last minute
you could move freely, securely, triumphantly. Once you were
engaged, you were safe, and even then, traditional avenues of escape
were open to you. Such were the blessings of conversation! But

nowadays? Nowadays a man doesn't even have to introduce himself—and you will admit it's handy to know who a man is and what he does for a living.

Eddie tiptoes from the kitchen door to the door right. As he disappears in the doorway, Arthur sees him and goes after him.

ALA Was somebody listening?

ARTHUR (*Coming back*) No.

ALA I had the feeling there was.

ARTHUR Let's settle this matter once and for all. Do you consent?

ALA I don't know yet.

ARTHUR You don't know? You mean I haven't convinced you?

ALA Yes.

ARTHUR Yes? Then you consent?

ALA No . . .

ARTHUR Yes or no?

ALA I've got to think about it.

ARTHUR But what is there to think about? It's as plain as day. I've got to rebuild a world, and for that I must have a wedding. It's perfectly simple. What don't you understand?

ALA The whole thing, I guess.

ARTHUR What do you mean?

ALA Wait . . . Give me time.

ARTHUR No, I can't wait. There just isn't time. I'll stay here while you go think it over. When you've made up your mind, come back and give me your answer. It's sure to be yes. I've explained everything.

ALA And you really have nothing else to say? There's really nothing else you want to tell me?

ARTHUR Run along now. I'll see you later.

ALA You're throwing me out?

ARTHUR   No, I have a little private business to attend to.

ALA   Can't I stay?

ARTHUR   No. This is a family matter.

ALA   All right. Then I'll have my little secrets too. Just wait. You'll see.

ARTHUR (*Impatiently*)   Yes, yes, but run along now. Remember, I'll be waiting for you here.

Ala goes out right. Arthur listens at the door left rear and then goes to the door in the corridor. He knocks softly.

STOMIL'S VOICE   Who's there?

ARTHUR (*Rather softly*)   Me. Arthur.

STOMIL   What do you want?

ARTHUR   Father, I've got to talk to you.

STOMIL   At this time of night? I'm busy. Come back tomorrow.

ARTHUR   It's urgent.

Pause.

STOMIL   But I've already told you, I'm busy. You can speak to me tomorrow.

Arthur tries the door and sees that it is locked. He shoves with his shoulder. Stomil opens. He is in pajamas as usual.

STOMIL (*cont.*)   Are you mad? What's going on?

ARTHUR (*In an ominous whisper*)   Not so loud, Father.

STOMIL (*Whispering, too, in spite of himself*)   Why aren't you in bed?

ARTHUR   I can't sleep. It's time to take action.

STOMIL   In that case, good night.

He starts for his room. Arthur holds him back.

ARTHUR   I only wanted to ask you, Father, doesn't it bother you?

STOMIL   What?

ARTHUR   This thing with Eddie.

STOMIL   Eddie? Oh yes, I remember the man.

ARTHUR   What do you think of him?

STOMIL   He's amusing.

ARTHUR   Amusing? He's repulsive.

STOMIL   Oh I wouldn't say that. Eddie's an unusual type. A very modern, very authentic type.

ARTHUR   Is that all you have to say about him?

STOMIL   You see, our trouble is that we're still too conscious, too cerebral. Enslaved by centuries of culture. Of course we've been doing our best to throw culture off, but we're still a long way from nature. But Eddie's lucky. He was born with what the rest of us can acquire only by art and effort. He interests me as an artist. I admire him the way a painter admires a landscape.

ARTHUR   Some landscape!

STOMIL   But don't you know there's been a complete revolution in aesthetics and morality? You keep making me remind you of things that ought to be self-evident. If Eddie shocks us now and then, it's because we're decadent. Sometimes I can't help feeling guilty toward Eddie. But I fight it down. We've got to get rid of these atavistic attitudes.

ARTHUR   And that's all you have to say?

STOMIL   I've been perfectly frank with you.

ARTHUR   Then I'll have to start all over again. Why do you tolerate him in your house?

STOMIL   Why not? He enriches our environment, he gives it a new tone, he adds a dash of authenticity. He even stimulates my imagination. We artists need an exotic touch now and then.

ARTHUR   Then you really don't know?

STOMIL   No, I don't know a thing.

ARTHUR   You're lying. You know perfectly well.

STOMIL   I repeat—I don't know. I don't want to know.

ARTHUR   He sleeps with Mother.

Stomil starts pacing.

ARTHUR (*cont.*)   What do you say to that?

STOMIL   My dear boy. Let's assume what you say is true. Sexual freedom is the cornerstone of human freedom. What do *you* say to that?

ARTHUR   But it's the truth! They *do* sleep together!

STOMIL   I said we'd assume it's true. What follows? Nothing.

ARTHUR   Then you insist on treating it as an abstract hypothesis?

STOMIL   Why not? I'm a modern man. On the intellectual plane we can envisage any hypothesis, even the most ticklish. Without such hypotheses human thought would mark time. So do speak freely. I trust we can discuss this business without prudery. Now, what's your opinion?

ARTHUR   My opinion? I haven't got any opinion and I refuse to treat this matter as a theoretical exercise. This isn't a philosophical problem. It's the naked truth. Can't you see that? It's life. They've put horns on you. Long ones! And arguing isn't going to make them go away.

STOMIL   Horns! Horns! Horns are a primitive image, not an instrument of analysis. (*Nervously.*)   Let's not descend to that low level.

ARTHUR   Father, you're a cuckold.

STOMIL   Hold your tongue. I forbid you to talk to me like that.

ARTHUR   You can't stop me. You're a cuckold.

STOMIL   I don't believe it.

ARTHUR   Ha! Now I've got you where I want you. Want me to prove it? Open that door. (*He points to the door left rear.*)

STOMIL   No!

ARTHUR   Are you afraid? Of course it's easier to perform theatrical experiments. When it comes to experiments you're a giant. In real life you're a midget.

STOMIL   Me?

ARTHUR   A hero in pajamas! A pint-sized Agamemnon!

STOMIL   I'll show you. You say they're in there?

ARTHUR   Look for yourself.

STOMIL   I'll show them. I'll show you. I'll show the whole lot of you! (*He runs to the door, stops.*)   Or you know what I'll do? I'll take care of this whole thing tomorrow. (*He turns around.*)

ARTHUR (*Barring the way*)   No you won't. You're going in there right now.

STOMIL   Tomorrow! Or by mail. A letter. What do you say?

ARTHUR   Phony!

STOMIL   What did you say?

Arthur makes horns on his forehead and laughs sardonically.

STOMIL (*cont.*)   All right then. Here I go!

ARTHUR (*Stops him*)   Just a second.

STOMIL (*With a martial air*)   Let me at them.

ARTHUR   You'd better take this.

He takes the revolver which Stomil had left on the catafalque in act one and gives it to his father.

STOMIL   What's that?

ARTHUR   You can't go in there bare-handed.

Pause.

STOMIL (*Calmly*)   Now I see through you.

ARTHUR (*Pushing him toward the door*)   Get in there! There's not a minute to lose.

STOMIL (*Tearing himself loose*)   Now I understand. You want a tragedy!

ARTHUR (*Retreating*)   A tragedy? What do you mean?

STOMIL   So that's what you're after, you dim little runt of a brainstorm, you . . .

ARTHUR   What are you trying . . .

STOMIL   (*Throwing the revolver on the table*)   You want me to kill him?
And then her? And then myself? Right?

ARTHUR   Of course not. I was only joking. I just thought that in case
Eddie . . . he might do anything.

STOMIL   You'd love that, wouldn't you! The injured husband wiping
out his shame in blood. Where do you *get* such ideas? From romantic
novels?

ARTHUR   Father, you know I never . . .

STOMIL   I always knew the younger generation cared more about ideas
than life, but I never expected my own son to sacrifice his father to an
idea. Sit down!

Arthur sits down obediently.

STOMIL (*cont.*)   That's it. Now we'll have a little talk. You want to bring
back the old values. What for? Well, never mind that. That's your
business. I've let you talk, I've heard you out, but now you're going
just a bit too far. How fiendishly clever! So you need a tragedy! Tragedy
has always been the most perfect expression of a society with established
values. So you needed a tragedy and thought you'd drag me into it.
Instead of the art form—which demands time and effort—you wanted
the thing itself. Or, never mind if somebody's killed, never mind if your
own father goes off to prison. No, all you care about is your idea. Do
you want to know what I think of you? A formalist. A vulgar formalist.
That's what you are. Your father and mother mean nothing to you. We
can all die as long as form wins out. And the worst of it is that you
don't even care about yourself. You're a fanatic!

ARTHUR   Maybe my motives aren't as formal as you think.

STOMIL   You dislike Eddie?

ARTHUR   I hate him.

STOMIL   Why? Eddie is necessity. He's the pure truth we've been
searching for so long because we always thought it was somewhere
else. Eddie is a fact. You can't hate facts. You've got to accept them.

ARTHUR   What do you want me to do, hug him?

STOMIL Good Lord! You talk like a petulant child. I can only see one explanation. Maybe you've got an Oedipus.

ARTHUR A what?

STOMIL An Oedipus complex. Have you consulted an analyst?

ARTHUR No. Mother's wonderful, but that's not it.

STOMIL Too bad. Then at least we'd know where we were at. Anything is better than sheer lunacy. I guess you're just a formalist.

ARTHUR I am not.

STOMIL Oh yes you are. And an insufferable and dangerous one at that.

ARTHUR It may look that way to you, but the truth is that I . . . I just can't go on like this. I can't live with you people.

STOMIL I see. That's more like it. In other words, you're an egoist.

ARTHUR Call it whatever you like. That's the way I am, that's all.

STOMIL But suppose you succeeded in making me kill him, in packing me off to prison for life, what good would that do you?

ARTHUR Something would be accomplished. Something tragic. You're right. Please forgive me. Tragedy is a form so vast and powerful that reality can never escape its grip.

STOMIL You poor devil. You really believe that? Don't you realize that tragedy isn't possible anymore? Reality erodes all forms and that goes for tragedy too. Suppose I actually killed him. What would be the good of it?

ARTHUR It would be something irrevocable, masterful, classical.

STOMIL Not for a minute. It would be a farce. In our time only farce is possible. A corpse won't change anything. Why can't you face facts? Actually, a farce can be very nice too.

ARTHUR Not for me.

STOMIL Lord, you can be stubborn!

ARTHUR I can't help it. I've got to find a way out.

STOMIL Regardless of reality?

ARTHUR   Yes. At any cost.

STOMIL   That's not so easy. I'd like to help you, but I don't see how.

ARTHUR   Couldn't we give it a try?

STOMIL   Give what a try?

ARTHUR (*Pointing to the door left rear*)   With them.

STOMIL   You still have illusions?

ARTHUR   Even if you're right about farce . . . (*Gradually he resumes his aggressiveness.*)   It's only because you people are such cowards. You complain, but you're stuck in a farce because no one has the courage to rebel. Why can't you free yourself by one act of sheer violence? You're so logical, so analytical, you see everything in the abstract. Instead of changing anything, you make diagrams. You've come a long way, but what have you actually done? Sat in a chair and discussed. But this situation calls for action. If tragedy has become extinct it's only because you don't believe in it. You and your damned compromises.

STOMIL   But why should we believe in tragedy? Come here, Son. I want to tell you something. All right. Eleanor is unfaithful to me with Eddie. What's so bad about that?

ARTHUR   But, Father, don't you know?

STOMIL   So help me, when you come right down to it, I don't. Maybe you can explain.

ARTHUR   I've never been in such a situation . . .

STOMIL   Try.

ARTHUR   It's obvious . . . Let me think . . .

STOMIL   Think away. Actually, I'd be delighted if you could convince me.

ARTHUR   Really?

STOMIL   To tell you the truth, I don't much care for this kind of thing either. In fact, I detest it. Only the more I think about it, the less I know why.

ARTHUR   So if I could convince you . . .

STOMIL   . . . I'd be very grateful.

ARTHUR   And you'd . . .

STOMIL   Go in and make a scene they'd remember as long as they lived. But I need a rational justification.

ARTHUR   Then you'd go in? Without being pushed?

STOMIL   I'd be delighted to. I've had it in for that bastard a long time. Believe it or not, nothing would please me more than to settle his hash. Except that my reason doesn't tell me why.

ARTHUR   Father, let me hug you.

They hug each other.

ARTHUR (*cont.*)   To hell with reason!

STOMIL   But what can we do? It won't let go of us. You were talking about compromise. It's reason that makes us compromise.

ARTHUR   Well, then, Father, shall we give it a try? What have we got to lose? If the worst comes to the worst, you'll shoot him.

STOMIL   Think so? If I could only be sure.

ARTHUR   Certainty comes later. The main thing now is to make up your mind.

STOMIL   Hm. Maybe you're right.

ARTHUR   I know I'm right. You'll see. We'll have our tragedy!

STOMIL   You've given me back my strength. The enthusiasm of youth untrammeled by the skepticism of the times. Ah, youth, youth!

ARTHUR   Shall we go in?

STOMIL   Yes. With you beside me, I feel better.

They stand up.

ARTHUR   Just one more thing. Give up those experiments of yours, will you? They only speed up the process of disintegration.

STOMIL   Well, but what can we do? Tragedy impossible, farce a bore—
what's left but experiments?

ARTHUR   They only make things worse. Give them up, Father.

STOMIL   I don't know . . .

ARTHUR   Promise.

STOMIL   Later. Now we go in.

Arthur puts the revolver back into Stomil's hand.

ARTHUR   I'll wait here. If you need any help, just shout.

STOMIL   That won't be necessary. If anybody yells, it'll be him, not me.

ARTHUR   Father, I've always had confidence in you.

STOMIL   With good reason, my boy. I was the best shot in my
regiment. Farewell! (*He goes to the door right rear.*)

ARTHUR   No, that's the kitchen.

STOMIL   (*Irresolute*)   I could use a drink.

ARTHUR   Later. When it's all over. No time now.

STOMIL   Right! I'll kill him on the spot. (*He goes to the left-hand
door, puts his hand on the knob.*)   That scoundrel! Now he's going to
pay!

*He enters the room cautiously, closes the door behind him. Arthur waits tensely.
Total silence. Arthur paces nervously back and forth. Grows more and more
impatient. Looks at his watch. Finally he makes a decision and flings both wings of
the door open, so that the whole room can be seen. Under a bright, low-hanging
lamp Eleanor, Eddie, Eugenia, and Stomil are sitting at a round table, playing
cards.*

ARTHUR   What's Eddie doing here? Why isn't Eddie . . . ?

STOMIL   Shhh! Take it easy, boy!

ELEANOR   Oh, it's you, Arthur? Are you still up?

EUGENIA   I told you he'd find us. He sticks his nose into everything.

ARTHUR   Father! . . . You . . . with them!

STOMIL That's how it worked out . . . It's not *my* fault.

ELEANOR Stomil turned up just in time. We needed a fourth.

ARTHUR Father, how could you!

STOMIL I told you it would end in a farce.

EDDIE Your play, Mr. Stomil. What you got?

STOMIL Here you are. (*To Arthur.*) A harmless pastime. You see the situation. What could I do?

ARTHUR But, Father, you promised!

STOMIL I promised nothing. We'll just have to wait.

ELEANOR Instead of talking so much, would you please put your mind on the game, Stomil?

ARTHUR For shame!

EUGENIA (*Throws down her cards*) I simply can't play under these conditions. Can't anybody throw this little twerp out of here?

EDDIE Easy, Grandma. Take it easy.

ELEANOR Arthur, you ought to be ashamed, upsetting your grandmother like this.

EUGENIA I told you we should lock the door. He's always looking for some way to pester me. You'll see. He'll put me back up on the catafalque!

ELEANOR Oh, no he won't! We've got to finish this rubber first.

ARTHUR (*Pounding the table with his fist*) Stop it!

ELEANOR But we've just started.

EDDIE You'd better listen to your mother. She's right. Look at the score cards, they're practically blank.

ARTHUR (*Tearing the cards out of their hands*) Now you listen to me! I've got something to tell you. Now! This minute!

STOMIL But Arthur, that was strictly between the two of us. Don't shout it from the rooftops.

ARTHUR   I pleaded with you. You wouldn't listen. Now I'm going to use force. Stop the game!

ELEANOR   What's going on?

EDDIE   What's got into you anyway? If I were your father, know what I'd do? I'd give you a good hiding.

ARTHUR   You shut up. (*Calmly but firmly.*)   Father, the revolver.

EDDIE   A guy can still make a joke, can't he?

ELEANOR   A revolver? For God's sake, Stomil, don't give it to him. Talk to him. Do *something*. After all, you're his father.

STOMIL (*Trying to take a severe tone*)   Now see here, Arthur, you're not a child. I'm sorry to have to speak to you like this, but . . .

Arthur takes the revolver from Stomil's pajama pocket. All jump up.

EUGENIA   He's gone mad. Stomil, why on earth did you make this child? Criminal negligence—that's what I call it.

EDDIE   Look here, Mr. Arthur . . .

ARTHUR   Silence! Into the living room, everybody.

One after another they go to the center of the stage. Arthur remains standing at the door. As Stomil passes him.

ARTHUR (*cont.*)   I'll talk to you later.

STOMIL   What's wrong? I did my best.

ARTHUR   Your best!

Eugenia sits down on the sofa, Eleanor in an armchair. Eddie stands in the corner, takes a comb from his back pocket, and runs it nervously through his hair.

STOMIL (*Facing Eleanor, raises his arms*)   I did everything I could to quiet him down. You saw me . . .

ELEANOR   Idiot. And you call yourself a father. Oh, if I were only a man!

STOMIL   That's easier said than done.

Eugene runs in.

EUGENE (*To Arthur*) Has it started yet?

ARTHUR Not yet. I'm still waiting for an answer.

EUGENE I thought it had started. I heard a noise and I came running.

ARTHUR That's all right. I'm glad you've come. Stay here and keep an eye on them. I'll be back in a second.

He gives him the revolver.

EUGENE Yes, sir.

ELEANOR Am I dreaming?

ARTHUR (*To Eugene*) Don't let anybody make a move.

EUGENE Yes, sir.

ELEANOR Have you both gone mad?

ARTHUR If anybody does move, shoot to kill. Understand?

EUGENE Yes, sir.

ELEANOR It's a plot! Mama, your brother's a gangster!

EUGENIA Eugene, do put that thing away. People don't play cowboys at your age. (*She starts to stand up.*)

EUGENE Stay where you are!

ELEANOR (*Astonished*) Eugene, it's me—your sister Eugenia.

EUGENE When I'm on duty, I have no sister.

EUGENIA What duty? Don't be a fool.

EUGENE I have enlisted in the service of an ideal!

ARTHUR Splendid. I see I can rely on you. I'm going to leave you for a moment.

STOMIL But, Arthur, can't you tell me, at least, what's going on? I thought we'd just become friends.

ARTHUR I'll tell you everything in due time.

He goes out. Eugene sits down with his back to the wall, holding his revolver in readiness. He aims it vaguely but menacingly at each in turn.

ELEANOR (*After a pause*)   So that's it . . . Eugene, you've betrayed us.

EUGENE   Silence! (*Then justifying himself.*)   That's not true. I haven't betrayed anybody.

ARTHUR'S VOICE (*Off*)   Ala! Ala!

ELEANOR   You've betrayed your generation.

EUGENE   No, you're the traitors. You've all betrayed our good old days. I'm the only one who hasn't.

ARTHUR'S VOICE (*Off*)   Ala! Ala!

ELEANOR   All you are is the tool of a mad pack of young zealots. With a missionary complex. You think you're so clever. They'll use you and then kick you out like a dog.

EUGENE   We'll see who uses whom. I've been waiting a long time for someone like Arthur to come along.

ELEANOR   Now at least you've shown who you really are. All these years you've been wearing a mask, you hypocrite.

EUGENE   Yes, I have. And all these years I've suffered. I hated you for your degradation but I kept quiet because I had to, because you were the stronger. Now at last I can tell you what I think of you! What a pleasure!

ELEANOR   What are you going to do to us?

EUGENE   We're going to give you back your dignity. We're going to turn you degenerates back into human beings with decent principles—that's what we're going to do.

ELEANOR   By force?

EUGENE   If we can't do it any other way, yes.

STOMIL   This is a counterreformation.

EUGENE   But for you it's salvation.

STOMIL   Salvation? From what?

EUGENE   From your damnable, diabolical freedom.

ARTHUR (*Enters*)   Uncle!

EUGENE   Sir?

ARTHUR   She's gone.

EUGENE   Look for her. She must be somewhere.

ARTHUR   Yes. She's got to be. I'm still waiting for her answer.

EUGENE   What? You mean she hasn't consented yet?

ARTHUR   She's got to. Everything else is ready now. She can't leave me in the lurch at a moment like this.

EUGENE   I don't mean to criticize you, Arthur, but haven't you rushed things a bit? I mean, shouldn't you have made sure of *her* before starting in on (*He points to the others with his pistol barrel.*)   these people?

ARTHUR   The time was ripe. I couldn't put it off.

EUGENE   Well, that's how it is with a coup d'état. Always some unforeseeable factor. Still, we can't back out now.

ARTHUR   Who could have dreamed of such a thing? I was so sure I had convinced her. (*He calls.*)   Ala, Ala! (*Irritably.*)   All because of some dumb cousin. Incredible! (*He calls.*)   Ala, Ala.

EUGENE   Women have been the ruin of kingdoms and empires.

ALA (*Enters*)   Gosh, are you all still up?

ARTHUR (*Reproachfully*)   At last! I've been looking all over for you.

ALA   What's going on? Uncle with a gun? Is it real? Is Uncle real?

ARTHUR   That's none of your business. Where have you been?

ALA   Out for a walk. Anything wrong with that?

EUGENE   Yes! At this solemn hour, there is.

ARTHUR   Steady, Uncle. You're on duty, remember. (*To Ala.*)   Well?

ALA   Well, what? It's a lovely night.

ARTHUR   I wasn't asking about the weather. Do you consent?

ALA   I think I need a little more time, Arthur.

ARTHUR   I need an answer immediately. You've had plenty of time.

Pause.

ALA   Yes.

EUGENE   Hurrah!

ARTHUR   Thank God! Now we can start!

He gives Ala his arm and leads her to the sofa where Eugenia is sitting.

ARTHUR (*cont.*)   Grandmother, your blessing.

EUGENIA (*Starts up from the sofa in a fright*)   Oh, leave me alone. I haven't done anything to you.

ARTHUR   But Grandmother, everything's changed now. I'm going to marry Ala. Give us your blessing.

EUGENE (*To the others*)   On your feet, everybody! Can't you see this is a solemn occasion?

ELEANOR   My goodness, is Arthur going to get married?

STOMIL   Is that any reason to make such a fuss?

EUGENIA   Get that boy out of here! He's going to torture me again.

ARTHUR (*Menacingly*)   Grandmother, your blessing.

STOMIL   A tasteless joke. It's gone on long enough now.

EUGENE (*Triumphantly*)   The jokes are over now. You've been having your jokes for fifty years. Stomil, button your pajamas immediately! Your son has just plighted his troth. The day of the wide-open fly is past. Bless them, Eugenia.

EUGENIA   What should I do, Eleanor?

ELEANOR   Give them your blessing if it means so much to them.

EUGENIA   Can't they do without it? It makes me feel so old.

EUGENE   A good old-fashioned engagement. Give them your blessing, or I'll shoot. I'm going to count to three. One . . .

STOMIL   This is incredible. If a man can't be comfortable in his own house . . . (*He tries to button his pajamas.*)

EUGENE   Two . . .

EUGENIA (*Lays her hand on the heads of Ala and Arthur*)   My blessing upon you, dear children . . . and now go to hell!

EUGENE (*Moved*)   Just like old times.

ARTHUR (*Stands up and kisses Eugenia's hand*)   We thank you, Grandmother.

EUGENE   Stomil has buttoned his fly! A whole new era has begun!

STOMIL   Eleanor! You're crying?

ELEANOR (*Sobbing with emotion*)   Forgive me . . . But Arthur's getting engaged . . . and after all he is our son . . . I know I'm being terribly old-fashioned, but it's so moving. Forgive me.

STOMIL   Oh, do what you want, all of you! (*He runs out of the room in a rage.*)

EDDIE   If you'll permit me, on this joyous occasion I would like to wish the young couple all the best for the days to come and especially . . .

Holds out his hand to Arthur.

ARTHUR (*Not taking his hand*)   You! To the kitchen!

He points dramatically to the kitchen door. Eddie saunters out.

ARTHUR (*cont.*)   And stay there until you're called.

EUGENE   To the kitchen.

ELEANOR (*In tears*)   When's the wedding?

ARTHUR   Tomorrow.

EUGENE   Hurray! We've won!

ACT III

Daylight. The same room, but with no trace now of the former disorder: a conventional middle-class living room of about fifty years ago. None of the previous confusion and blurred contours. The draperies, which had been lying about giving the impression of an unmade bed, are now hung in orderly fashion. The catafalque is still in its old place—the curtain in front of the alcove is drawn back—but it is covered with napkins and knicknacks, so that it looks like a buffet.

Onstage are Eleanor, Eugenia, Stomil, and Eugene. Eugenia is sitting on the sofa in the middle of the room. She is wearing a bonnet and a dark gray or brown dress buttoned up to the neck and adorned with lace cuffs and ruching. She has a lorgnette, which she frequently raises to her eyes. To her right sits Eleanor with her hair done up in a chignon; she is wearing earrings and a striped violet- or burgundy-colored dress gathered at the waist. Both sit bolt upright, immobile, their hands on their knees. Beside them stands Stomil, his hair combed, pomaded, and parted in the middle. His stiff collar forces him to stretch his head as though looking into the distance. He is wearing a brown suit that is obviously too tight for him, and white spats. He is resting one hand on a little round table on which stands a vase with flowers; the other is braced on his hip. One foot is balanced nonchalantly on the tip of his shoe. In front of the group near the proscenium, a large camera on a tripod, covered with black velvet. Behind the camera stands Eugene. He is still wearing his black swallowtail coat but his khaki shorts have been replaced by long black trousers with pinstripes. A red carnation in his buttonhole. In front of him on the floor, his top hat, white gloves, and a cane with a silver knob. He fusses with the camera while the others hold their pose. Eugenia says "ah . . . ah" several times and sneezes loudly.

EUGENE Don't move!

EUGENIA I can't help it. It's the mothballs.

EUGENE Hold it!

Stomil removes his hand from his hip and scratches his chest.

EUGENE (*cont.*) Stomil, your hand.

STOMIL But I'm itching all over.

ELEANOR Why should you be itching?

STOMIL Moths.

ELEANOR   Moths! (*She jumps up and runs across the stage, chasing moths, occasionally clapping her hands.*)

EUGENE   At this rate we'll never get a picture. Sit down, Eleanor.

ELEANOR   (*Reproachfully*)   The moths come from Mama.

EUGENIA   They do not. They come out of this old rag.

EUGENE   Let's not quarrel. They come from the attic.

EDDIE   (*Enters dressed as a valet, in a crimson vest with black stripes*)   You called, Madame?

ELEANOR   (*Stops clapping her hands*)   What? What is it now? Oh yes. My salts, Edward!

EDDIE   Salts, Madame?

ELEANOR   Those smelling salts . . . you know . . .

EDDIE   Certainly, Madame. (*He goes out.*)

STOMIL   (*Looking after him*)   I must admit it's a relief to see that fellow put in his place.

EUGENE   You haven't seen anything yet. Everything's going splendidly. You won't regret a thing.

STOMIL   (*Tries to loosen his collar*)   If only this collar weren't so damn tight!

EUGENE   That's the price you've got to pay for having Eddie wait on you. Everything has its price.

STOMIL   And my experiments? Will I have to give them up?

EUGENE   I couldn't say. Arthur hasn't announced his decision on that point yet.

STOMIL   Maybe he'll let me go on with them. He hasn't said anything?

EUGENE   There hasn't been time. He went out early this morning.

STOMIL   Perhaps you could put in a good word for me, Uncle?

EUGENE   (*Patronizingly*)   I'll speak to him when the opportunity arises.

STOMIL   At least once a week. After all these years I can't just suddenly stop. You ought to realize that.

EUGENE   That will depend entirely on your conduct, Stomil.

STOMIL   But I'm on your side. What more do you want? I'm even putting up with this collar. (*He tries again to loosen it.*)

EUGENE   Well, I can't promise.

Eddie enters with a tray on which a bottle of vodka is very much in evidence.

EUGENE (*cont.*)   What is that?

EDDIE   The salts for Madame, sir.

EUGENE (*Menacingly*)   Eleanor, what is the meaning of this?

ELEANOR   I can't imagine. (*To Eddie.*)   I asked for my smelling salts.

EDDIE   Madame no longer drinks?

ELEANOR   Take it away immediately!

EUGENIA   Why? As long as he's brought it . . . I don't feel too well.

EDDIE   As you wish, Madame.

He goes out. On the way he takes a good swig from the bottle. Only Eugenia, looking after him longingly, notices.

EUGENE   Don't let it happen again!

EUGENIA   God, am I bored!

EUGENE   Back to your places!

Eleanor, Stomil, and Eugenia sit up and freeze as at the beginning of the act. Eugene ducks under the velvet cloth; the ticking of the timer is heard. Eugene reaches quickly for his stick, top hat, and gloves, and takes a stance beside Eugenia. The ticking stops. Relieved, they all relax.

STOMIL   Can't I unbutton these buttons for just a second?

EUGENE   Certainly not! The wedding is at twelve!

STOMIL   I seem to have put on weight. The last time I wore these things was forty years ago.

EUGENE   You have only your experiments to blame for that. Experimental art pays so well these days.

STOMIL   That's not my fault, is it?

ELEANOR   When will that picture be ready? I think I blinked. I know I'm going to look simply awful.

EUGENE   Don't worry. The camera hasn't worked for years.

ELEANOR   What? Then why take the picture?

EUGENE   It's the principle of the thing. It's a tradition.

STOMIL   You begrudge me my innocent experiments but is an old-fashioned, broken-down camera any better? You know what I think of your counterrevolution? It's a fiasco.

EUGENE   Watch your tongue.

STOMIL   I bow to superior force, but I can still say what I think.

ELEANOR   (*To Eugenia*)   What do you say, Mother?

EUGENIA   I say we're in one hell of a mess and this is only the beginning.

EUGENE   It can't be helped. Our first job is to create the form. The content comes later.

STOMIL   You're making a colossal mistake, Eugene. Formalism will never free you from chaos. You'd be better off if you could just accept the spirit of the times.

EUGENE   That's enough out of you. Defeatism will not be tolerated!

STOMIL   All right, all right. I can still have an opinion, can't?!

EUGENE   Of course. As long as it agrees with ours.

ELEANOR   Listen!

Bells are heard in the distance.

STOMIL   Bells!

EUGENE   Wedding bells.

Ala enters. She is wearing a wedding dress with a long veil. Stomil kisses her hand.

STOMIL   Ah, here comes our dear little bride!

ELEANOR   Oh, Ala, it's so becoming!

EUGENIA   My dear child!

ALA   Isn't Arthur back yet?

EUGENE   We're expecting him any minute. He had a few final formalities to attend to.

ALA   These damned formalities.

EUGENE   But the spirit of life can't run around naked. It must always be dressed with taste and care. You mean Arthur hasn't discussed that point with you yet?

ALA   For hours on end.

EUGENE   And rightly so. Someday you'll understand and be grateful to him.

ALA   Oh, stop making such an ass of yourself, Uncle.

ELEANOR   You mustn't talk like that, Ala dear. Today is your wedding day and no time for family quarrels. There'll be plenty of time for that later.

EUGENE   Don't worry. No offense. I quite understand.

ALA   So old and so stupid. I can understand it in Arthur. But you, Uncle . . .

ELEANOR   Ala!

STOMIL   He had it coming.

ELEANOR   Forgive her, Eugene. She's so excited she doesn't know what she's saying. After all, this is a big day in her life. I remember the day I was married to Stomil . . .

EUGENE   I can tell when I'm not wanted. But don't delude yourselves. You can laugh at me as much as you like but childish insults won't change a thing. Stomil, come with me. I have a proposition to make to you.

STOMIL   All right. Just don't try to brainwash me!

They go out.

ELEANOR   Mama, you might go for a stroll too.

EUGENIA   Anything you say. It's all the same to me. Either way I'll be bored to death. (*She goes out.*)

ELEANOR   There. Now we can talk. Tell me, what's happened?

ALA   Nothing.

ELEANOR   Something's bothering you. I can see that.

ALA   Nothing's bothering me. This veil doesn't fall quite right. Help me with it, will you, Mother?

ELEANOR   Of course. But you don't have to take that tone with me. With the others it's different. They're such fools.

ALA   (*Sits down at the mirror; the bells are still ringing*)   Why do you all despise each other?

ELEANOR   I don't know. Maybe because we have no reason to respect each other.

ALA   Yourselves or each other?

ELEANOR   It comes to the same thing. Shall I fix your hair?

ALA   It's got to be done all over again.

She takes off her veil. Eleanor combs her hair.

ALA (*cont.*)   Are you happy, Mother?

ELEANOR   I beg your pardon?

ALA   I asked if you were happy. What's so funny about that?

ELEANOR   It's a very indiscreet question.

ALA   Why? Is it a disgrace to be happy?

ELEANOR   No, I wouldn't say that.

ALA   Then you're not very happy, are you? Because you're ashamed. People are always ashamed about not being happy. It's like having pimples or not doing your homework. It makes them feel guilty, almost criminal.

ELEANOR   "It is the right and duty of all to be happy, now that the new era has set us free." Stomil taught me that.

ALA   Oh. So that's why everybody's so ashamed nowadays. But how do *you* feel about it?

ELEANOR   I've always done as much as I could.

ALA   To make Stomil happy?

ELEANOR   No. Myself. That's the way he wanted it.

ALA   Then in a way it was for him?

ELEANOR   Of course it was for him. Oh, if only you'd known him when he was young . . .

ALA   It's not right yet on this side. Does he know?

ELEANOR   What?

ALA   Don't be like that. I'm not a baby. Your affair with Eddie.

ELEANOR   Of course he knows.

ALA   And what does he say?

ELEANOR   Nothing, unfortunately. He pretends not to notice.

ALA   That's bad.

Eddie comes in with a white tablecloth.

EDDIE   May I set the table now?

ELEANOR   Sure, Eddie. (*She corrects herself.*)   Yes, Edward, you may set the table.

EDDIE   Yes, Madame. (*He lays the cloth on the table and takes the camera out with him.*)

ALA   What do you see in him?

ELEANOR   Oh, he's just so simple . . . like life itself. He can be rough, of course, but that's the secret of his charm. A man without complexes—it's so refreshing. He just wants what he wants. Wonderful. And the way he sits—nothing unusual about it, but it's real, honest-to-goodness sitting. And when he eats, when he drinks! His stomach becomes a symphony of nature. I just love to watch him digest. It's so simple, so direct. It's like the elements. Have you ever noticed how divinely he hitches his trousers up? Stomil admires authenticity, too.

ALA I know. It doesn't fascinate me very much, I'm afraid.

ELEANOR You're too young. You haven't had time to learn the value of genuine simplicity. You will. It takes experience.

ALA I'll certainly try. Tell me, Mother, do you think it's a good idea for me to marry Arthur?

ELEANOR Oh, Arthur is something else again. He has principles.

ALA But Stomil has principles too. You said so yourself. All that stuff about the right and duty to be happy.

ELEANOR Oh, those were only opinions. Stomil has always detested principles. Arthur, on the other hand, has cast-iron principles.

ALA And that's all he has.

ELEANOR Ala, how can you say a thing like that? Arthur's the first man in fifty years to have principles. Doesn't that appeal to you? It's so original! And it's so becoming to him!

ALA You really think principles are enough for me?

ELEANOR Well, I admit, they're rather old-fashioned. But so unusual these days . . .

ALA I'll take Arthur with principles if I have to, Mother. But principles without Arthur—no.

ELEANOR But didn't he propose to you? Isn't he going to marry you?

ALA Not Arthur.

ELEANOR Then who? What are you talking about?

ALA His principles!

ELEANOR Then why did you accept?

ALA Because I still have hope.

ELEANOR That, my dear, is fatal.

Eddie enters with a stack of plates.

EDDIE   May I continue?

ALA   Clatter away, Eddie boy. (*Corrects herself.*)   I mean, yes, Edward, clatter away. I mean, do continue, Edward.

ELEANOR   Tell me, Eddie, does it depress you? All these changes thought up by a bunch of fools?

EDDIE   Why should it depress me?

ELEANOR   Didn't I tell you? He's as free and natural as a butterfly. Oh, Eddie, you set the table so gracefully.

EDDIE   I'm not knocking myself out, that's for sure.

ALA   Eddie, come here.

EDDIE   At your service. What can I do for you, miss?

Suddenly the bells fall silent.

ALA   Tell me, Eddie, have you got principles?

EDDIE   Principles? Sure.

ALA   What kind?

EDDIE   The best.

ALA   Tell me one. Please.

EDDIE   What's in it for me?

ALA   Well, can you or can't you?

EDDIE   If I have to, I guess. Just a sec. (*He puts the plates down on the floor and takes a little memo book from his pocket.*)   I've got one written down here somewhere. (*He leafs through the book.*)   Here it is! (*He reads.*)   "I love you, and you're sound asleep."

ALA   That's all?

EDDIE   "You made your bed, now lie in it."

ALA   Oh, come on, Eddie. Read.

EDDIE   I did read. That's a principle.

ALA   Then read another!

Eddie giggles.

ALA (*cont.*)   What's so funny?

EDDIE   Well, there's one here . . .

ALA   Read it! . . .

EDDIE   I can't, not in mixed company. It's too good.

ALA   And those are your principles?

EDDIE   Actually, no. I borrowed them from a friend who works for the movies.

ALA   You haven't got any of your own?

EDDIE   (*Proudly*)   No.

ALA   Why not?

EDDIE   What do I need them for? I know my way around.

ELEANOR   Oh yes, Eddie. You certainly do.

Stomil rushs in, pursued by Eugene carrying a laced corset. Eddie goes on setting the table.

STOMIL   No, no! That's asking too much!

EUGENE   Take my word for it. You'll be glad once it's on.

ELEANOR   Now what's wrong?

STOMIL   (*Running from Eugene*)   He wants to strap me into that thing.

ELEANOR   What is it?

EUGENE   Great-grandfather's corset. Indispensable. Pulls in the waist, guarantees a perfect figure for every occasion.

STOMIL   No, no, no. I'm wearing spats, I've got this collar on. What are you trying to do—kill me?

EUGENE   Now, Stomil, let's not do things by halves.

STOMIL   I've gone far enough. Let me live!

EUGENE   You're falling back into your old habits, Stomil. Come on. Stop making such a fuss. You admitted yourself you'd been putting on weight.

STOMIL   But I want to be fat! I want to live in harmony with nature!

EUGENE   You just don't want to be bothered. Come on. Don't fight it. It won't do any good.

STOMIL   Eleanor, save me!

ELEANOR   You don't think it might improve your looks?

STOMIL   My looks? What for? I'm a free, fat artist.

He runs into his room. Eugene following. The door closes behind them.

ELEANOR   These perpetual scenes. And you say you still have hope?

ALA   Yes.

ELEANOR   And if you're only deluding yourself?

ALA   What difference does it make?

ELEANOR   (*Tries to take her in her arms*)   My poor Ala! . . .

ALA   (*Freeing herself*)   You don't need to pity me. I can take care of myself.

ELEANOR   But what if things don't work out?

ALA   That's my secret.

ELEANOR   You won't tell even me?

ALA   It will be a surprise.

STOMIL'S VOICE   Help!

ELEANOR   That's Stomil.

ALA   Uncle Eugene is really overdoing it. Do you think he has any influence on Arthur?

STOMIL'S VOICE   Let me go!

ELEANOR   I doubt it. It's probably the other way around.

ALA   Too bad. I thought it was all Uncle's fault.

STOMIL'S VOICE   Get out of here!

ELEANOR   I'd better go see what they're up to. I have a feeling something awful is going to happen.

ALA   So do I.

STOMIL'S VOICE   Murderer! Let me go!

ELEANOR   Good God, how will it all end?

STOMIL'S VOICE   No, no! I'll burst! I'll explode! Help!

ELEANOR   Eugene's going too far. But you, Ala, do be careful.

ALA   Careful?

ELEANOR   Don't go too far—like Uncle Eugene. (*She goes into Stomil's room.*)

ALA   Eddie, my veil!

Eddie hands her the veil and stands behind her. From Stomil's room, screaming and the sound of a struggle are heard. Arthur enters. Ala and Eddie don't notice him. Arthur's coat is open. He looks gray. His listless, unnatural movements show that he is having great difficulty keeping himself going. He carefully removes his coat and throws it down somewhere. Sits down in an armchair and sprawls out his legs.

STOMIL'S VOICE   Damn you!

ARTHUR   (*In a low, dull voice*)   What's going on?

Ala turns around. Eddie dutifully picks up Arthur's coat and goes out.

ALA   (*As though merely making an observation*)   You're late.

Arthur stands up and opens Stomil's door.

ARTHUR   Let him go.

Stomil, Eugene, and then Eleanor come out of the room.

EUGENE   Why? It would have given him that final polish.

ARTHUR   I said let him go.

STOMIL   Thank you, Arthur. I'm glad to see you're not completely devoid of human feeling.

EUGENE   I protest!

Arthur grabs him by the tie and pushes him back.

ELEANOR   Arthur, what's happened? He's as pale as a ghost!

ARTHUR   Your whited skeleton!

EUGENE   Arthur, it's me, it's your Uncle Eugene! Don't you know me? You and I together . . . the new life . . . saving the world. Don't you remember? You're choking me. You and I . . . together . . . Don't . . .

ARTHUR   (*Pushing him back step by step*)   You stuffed zero, you synthetic blob . . . you worm-eaten false bottom!

ELEANOR   Do something! He's choking him!

ARTHUR   You fake . . .

Mendelssohn's "Wedding March" resounds, loud and triumphant. Arthur lets Eugene go, picks up a carafe from the table, and hurls it offstage where it lands with a loud crash. The march breaks off in the middle of a measure. Arthur sinks into an armchair.

EDDIE   (*Enters*)   Do you wish me to change the record?

ELEANOR   Who told you to put that on?

EDDIE   Mr. Eugene. His orders were to put it on as soon as Mr. Arthur entered the room.

EUGENE   (*Gasping for air*)   My orders. Yes, that's right.

ELEANOR   We won't need any music right now.

EDDIE   As you wish, Madame. (*He goes out.*)

ARTHUR   It's a fraud . . . The whole thing . . . a fraud! (*He collapses.*)

STOMIL   (*Leans over him*)   He's dead drunk.

EUGENE   That's a slander, an infamous slander. This young man knows his duty. He's the soul of moderation.

ELEANOR   I can't believe it either. Arthur never drinks.

STOMIL   Take it from me. I'm an expert.

ELEANOR   But why today of all days?

STOMIL   His last hours as a free man.

Ala pours water into a glass and feeds it to Arthur.

EUGENE   There must be some misunderstanding. It would be unwise to draw premature conclusions. The truth will soon be known.

STOMIL   Yes. If we wait just a minute, he'll explain. He was just getting started.

ELEANOR   Shh . . . he's coming to.

ARTHUR (*Raises his head and points to Stomil*)   What on earth is that?

ELEANOR   He doesn't know his own father. Ohhh! (*She bursts into tears.*)

ARTHUR   Quiet, you females! It's not my parents I'm asking about. What's the meaning of this masquerade?

STOMIL (*Looking at his legs*)   These . . . these are spats.

ARTHUR   Oh . . . yes, of course. They're spats. (*He sinks into thought.*)

EUGENE   Arthur's a little tired. Conditions will return to normal in a moment. Take your places. Attention! There will be no change in the program. (*To Arthur in a very friendly tone:*)   Ha ha, well, Arthur, my boy, you were just joking, weren't you? Putting us to the test, you little devil! Don't worry. We won't abandon our positions. Here we are, all buttoned up from top to toe, once and for all. Stomil was even going to put on a corset. Cheer up, my boy. A little rest, and then . . . on with the wedding!'

STOMIL   Same old song and dance! Can't you see, you ghost of the past, that he's stewed to the gills? His father's son all right.

EUGENE   That's a lie! Quiet! Come on, Arthur. It's time for action now. Everything's ready. Just one last step.

ARTHUR (*Goes down on his knees to Stomil*)   Father, forgive me.

STOMIL   What's this? Some new trick?

ARTHUR (*Dragging himself after Stomil on his knees*)   I was insane! There's no going back, no present, no future. There's nothing.

STOMIL (*Evading him*)   What is he now? A nihilist?

ALA (*Tearing off her veil*)   What about me? Am I nothing?

ARTHUR (*Changing direction and dragging himself after her*)   You, too . . . forgive, me!

ALA   You're a coward, that's all you are. A child and a coward and impotent!

ARTHUR   No, please don't say that. I'm not afraid, but I can't believe anymore. I'll do anything. I'll lay down my life . . . but there's no turning back to the old forms. They can't create a reality for us. I was wrong.

ALA   What are you talking about?

ARTHUR   About creating a world.

ALA   And me? Isn't anybody going to say anything about me?

EUGENE   This is treason!

ARTHUR   (*Changing direction again and heading for Eugene*)   You must forgive me too. I raised your hopes and I've let you down. But believe me, it's impossible . . .

EUGENE   I refuse to listen to this kind of talk. Pull yourself together. Stand up and get married. Raise a family, brush your teeth, eat with a knife and fork, make the world sit up straight. You'll see, we'll do it yet. You're not going to throw away our last chance, are you, Arthur?

ARTHUR   There never was a chance. We were wrong. It's hopeless.

EUGENE   Stomil's right. You're drunk. You don't know what you're saying.

ARTHUR   Yes, drunk. When I was sober I let myself be deceived, so I got drunk to dispel my illusions. You'd better have a drink too, Uncle.

EUGENE   Me? Certainly not. . . . Well, perhaps just a little one. (*He pours himself a shot of vodka and downs it in one gulp.*)

ARTHUR   I had cold sober reasons for getting drunk. I drank myself sane again.

STOMIL   Nonsense. You got drunk out of despair.

ARTHUR   Yes, despair too. Despair that form can never save the world.

EUGENE   Then what can?

ARTHUR   (*Stands up, solemnly*)   An idea!

EUGENE   What idea?

ARTHUR   If I only knew. Conventions always spring from an idea. Father was right. I'm a contemptible formalist.

STOMIL   Don't take it so hard, Son. You know I've always been indulgent. Frankly, though, I've suffered plenty from your ideas. Thank God, that's all over now. (*Starts taking off his morning coat.*)   Where are my pajamas?

ARTHUR   (*Rushes over to him and prevents him from taking off his coat.*) Stop! A reversion to pajamas is equally impossible.

STOMIL   Why? Are you still trying to save us? I thought you'd got over that.

ARTHUR   (*Aggressively, going from one extreme to the other as drunks do; triumphantly*)   Did you think I was going to cave in completely just like that?

STOMIL   Just a minute ago you were acting like a human being. Don't tell me you want to be an apostle again.

ARTHUR   (*Releasing Stomil, with emphasis*)   My sin was reason . . . and abstraction, the lewd daughter of reason. Now I have drowned my reason in alcohol. I didn't get drunk the usual way. Though my aim was mystical, I drank most rationally. The firewater cleansed me. You've got to forgive me because I stand before you purified. I clothed you in vestments and tore them off again because they proved to be shrouds. But I will not abandon you, naked, to the gales of history; I'd rather have you curse me. Eddie!

Eddie enters.

ARTHUR   (*cont.*)   Shut the door.

ELEANOR   Yes, Eddie, shut the door, there's a draft.

ARTHUR   Don't let anybody leave.

EDDIE   Okay, boss.

STOMIL   This is a violation of civil rights!

ARTHUR   You want freedom? There is no freedom from life, and life is synthesis. You'd analyze yourselves to death. Luckily, however, you have me.

EUGENE   Arthur, you know I don't agree with Stomil. But aren't you going a little too far? I feel it's my duty to warn you. In spite of everything, I stand by the freedom of the individual.

ARTHUR   Good. Now what we need is to find an idea.

STOMIL (*Simultaneously with Eugene and Eleanor*)   Is this any way to treat your father?

EUGENE   I wash my hands of the whole business.

ELEANOR   Arthur, lie down for a while. I'll make you a nice cold compress.

ARTHUR   Until we come up with an idea, nobody leaves this room. Eddie. Guard the door!

EDDIE   Yes, sir.

Pause.

ELEANOR   Find him an idea, somebody, so he'll leave us alone. If I don't go to the kitchen, the cake will be burned to a crisp.

EUGENE   Better humor him.

ARTHUR   What do you suggest, Uncle?

EUGENE   Search me . . . God, maybe?

ARTHUR   That's been done. Lost his appeal.

EUGENE   True. Even in my time there wasn't much you could do with God. I grew up in an age of enlightenment and exact science. I only mentioned him for the sake of form.

ARTHUR   Forget about form. What we're after now is a living idea.

EUGENE   How about sports? I used to ride horseback.

ARTHUR   Everybody goes in for sports nowadays. A lot of good it does them.

EUGENE   Sorry. Maybe Stomil has an idea.

STOMIL   Experiment. There's an idea.

ARTHUR   Please, this is serious.

STOMIL   Well, I'm serious too. Blazing trails, opening new frontiers! Man is always looking for new worlds to conquer and conquest comes from experiment. From trial and error. But always with an aim in view: the new life, radically new!

ARTHUR   A new life! I don't even know what to do with the old one.

STOMIL   Well, everything is still in the experimental stage, that's why.

EUGENE   Eleanor, have you got an idea?

ARTHUR   There's no sense asking a woman.

ELEANOR   I had an idea, but I've forgotten. I'm supposed to look after everything. Why don't you ask Eddie? He's got a good head on his shoulders, and when he does say something, you can depend on it.

STOMIL   That's right. Eddie is the collective mind.

ARTHUR   Well, what do you say then, Eddie?

EDDIE   Well, if anybody were to ask me, I'd say progress, sir.

ARTHUR   Meaning what?

EDDIE   Well, just that, sir: progress.

ARTHUR   But what kind of progress?

EDDIE   The progressive kind, the kind that goes right ahead.

ARTHUR   You mean forward?

EDDIE   Right. With the front moving forward.

ARTHUR   And the back?

EDDIE   The back moving forward too. Right out there in front.

ARTHUR   Then the front is in back?

EDDIE   Depends on how you look at it. If you look from back to front, the front is in front, though somehow or other it's also in back.

ARTHUR   That doesn't sound very clear to me.

EDDIE   No. But it's progressive.

Eugenia enters, leaning on a cane.

EUGENIA (*Timidly*)   There's something I must tell you . . .

ELEANOR   Not now, Mother. Can't you see the men are discussing politics?

EUGENIA   Just two words . . .

ARTHUR   No, I don't like it. I need an idea that naturally, inevitably, leads to form. Your kind of progress leads nowhere.

EUGENIA   Please listen to me, my darlings. I won't take much of your time.

STOMIL   What is it now?

ELEANOR   I don't know. Something's wrong with Mama.

STOMIL   Later. We're busy now. (*To Arthur.*)   I still say we should get back to experiments. Then the idea will come by itself.

Eugenia takes the knicknacks and napkins off the catafalque.

ELEANOR   What are you doing, Mama?

EUGENIA (*Matter-of-factly*)   I'm dying.

ELEANOR   Mother! That's not very funny, you know.

Silently Eugenia tidies up the catafalque. She wipes away the dust with her sleeve.

ELEANOR (*cont.*)   Mother says she's dying.

EUGENE   What? Dying? Can't she see we're busy?

ELEANOR   Did you hear that, Mama?

EUGENIA   Help me.

Involuntarily Eleanor gives her her arm. Eugenia climbs up on the catafalque.

ELEANOR   But don't be silly, Mama. There's going to be a wedding today. You wouldn't want to spoil everything by dying, would you?

STOMIL   Dying? What's all this about death? I never thought about that . . .

ARTHUR (*To himself*)   Death? Excellent idea! . . .

EUGENE   This is ridiculous, Eugenia. Pull yourself together. This is no way to behave.

ALA   It wouldn't be normal, Grandmother.

EUGENIA   I don't understand you people. You're all so intelligent, but if somebody wants to do something as simple as dying, you don't know what to make of it. Really, you are very strange people. (*She lies down on her back and folds her hands over her breast.*)

ELEANOR   Look at her. Do something . . . Maybe she's really . . .

EUGENE   Eugenia, this is carrying eccentricity too far. This sort of thing isn't done in our family.

STOMIL   It's sheer hypocrisy.

EUGENIA   You'll find the key to my room on the table. I won't need it anymore. I'll be able to come and go as I please. The cards are in the drawer. All marked . . .

ARTHUR   Death . . . the supreme form!

STOMIL   Not exactly viable, though, is it?

ARTHUR   Why not? When it's somebody else's death.

He seems to have had a revelation, beats his forehead.

ARTHUR (*cont.*)   Grandma, you're brilliant!

ELEANOR   You ought to be ashamed of yourself! You all ought to be ashamed of yourselves.

EUGENE   Eugenia, lie properly at least. You're all hunched up. Elbows at your sides. Or get up this minute. Dying is no way to behave in society. Death is irrational.

STOMIL   Death is final and therefore no good as an experiment. An experiment has to be repeatable. Of course, if you're only rehearsing, that's something else again. But even so, there's not much point in it.

ALA   Stop! Can't you see what's happening?

EUGENIA   Come closer, my children.

All except Eddie go over to the catafalque.

EUGENIA (*cont.*)   Eddie, you too!

Eddie joins the others.

EUGENIA (*cont.*)   Who are you?

EUGENE   We're . . . it's just us.

Eugenia starts giggling, first softly, then loudly.

EUGENE (*cont.*)   Now she's insulting us. Did I say something funny?

STOMIL   I'm not feeling so well myself. Must be a headache. (*He steps aside, feels his pulse, takes a mirror out of his pocket, and looks at his tongue.*)

ARTHUR   Thank you, Grandmother, I'll make use of your idea.

STOMIL (*Putting the mirror away*)   Nothing serious, I guess. Must be these tight clothes.

Eugenia dies.

ELEANOR   Try again, Mama.

ARTHUR   She's dead. Strange. She was always so frivolous.

ALA   I can't stand it!

EUGENE   I don't understand.

STOMIL   I don't want to have anything to do with this.

ELEANOR   I never dreamed . . . Stomil, why didn't you warn me?

STOMIL   Of course, it's all my fault. Frankly I don't see that this changes anything at all. My collar's as tight as ever.

ARTHUR (*Drawing the curtain in front of the catafalque*)   Eddie, come here.

Eddie comes over and stands at attention. Arthur feels his muscle.

ARTHUR (*cont.*)   You pack a good punch, don't you?

EDDIE   Not bad sir.

ARTHUR   And if necessary, you could . . . ? (*He runs his finger across his throat.*)

EDDIE (*Phlegmatically, after a pause*)   You ask me a question, Mr. Arthur? I'm not sure I heard you right.

Pause. Arthur laughs, unsure of himself, as though waiting to see. Eddie laughs with a similar "ha ha." Arthur laughs once again more loudly and with more assurance. Whereupon Eddie utters a resounding laugh. Arthur slaps him on the shoulder.

ARTHUR   Eddie, I like you. I've always liked you.

EDDIE   And I've always thought we'd understand each other someday.

ARTHUR   Then you do understand?

EDDIE   Eddie understands all right.

STOMIL   This business has rather upset me. I'm going to lie down for a while.

ARTHUR   Stay right where you are, Father.

STOMIL   Oh, stop ordering me around, you little punk. I'm tired. (*He starts for his room.*)

ARTHUR   Eddie!

Eddie bars Stomil's way.

STOMIL   Who do you think you are? (*Furiously pointing at Eddie; to Eleanor.*)   And you've been having an affair with this flunky?

ELEANOR   For God's sake, not now. Not with Mama lying, there.

Eddie pushes Stomil into an armchair.

ARTHUR   Just a bit more patience, please. It's all quite clear to me now. I shall show you the way to a better future.

EUGENE (*Sitting down with resignation*)   I just don't seem to care anymore . . . I must be getting old. We're just not as young as we used to be, are we, Stomil?

STOMIL   Speak for yourself. You're almost as old as Eugenia was, you old hypocrite. I feel fine. By and large. (*Pleading.*)   Eleanor, where are you?

ELEANOR   Here, Stomil, right beside you.

STOMIL   Come here.

ELEANOR (*Resting her hand on his forehead*)   How do you feel?

STOMIL   I don't know what's wrong, but not well at all.

ARTHUR   Uncertainty and indecision are behind us now. Now the road lies before us, straight and clear. From now on there will be only one law and one herd.

STOMIL   What's he jabbering about now? . . . Oh, my head!

EUGENE   Something about a new legal code for livestock.

ARTHUR   Don't you see the logical conclusion? Ah, creatures of flesh, caught up in your glandular secretions and terrified at the thought of your death, *are you incapable of all understanding?* But I understand! Unthinking cattle, behold your redeemer! I have risen above this world, and I will draw you all up after me, because I alone have a brain freed from the snares of the bowels.

EUGENE   Instead of insulting us, my dear great-nephew, kindly express yourself more clearly.

ARTHUR   Won't you ever understand, you whose lives rot away like mushrooms? You're like blind puppies that would walk in circles forever if they had no master to lead them. Without form or ideas, you would crumble to chaos and be consumed by the void if I weren't on hand to save you. Do you know what I'm going to do with you? I'm going to create a system in which rebellion will be combined with order, nonbeing with being. I will transcend all contradictions.

EUGENE   It would perhaps be better if you'd just leave the room. You've disappointed me. It's all over between us. (*To himself.*)   I'll probably return to writing my memoirs.

ARTHUR   Let me just ask you this: If nothing exists and if even rebellion is impossible, then what *can* be raised up out of this nothingness and made to exist?

EUGENE (*Takes out a watch with a little chain.*)   It's late. We could all do with a bite to eat.

ARTHUR   Isn't anybody going to answer me?

STOMIL   Eleanor, what are we having for lunch today? I'd like something light. My stomach's a bit queasy. It's high time we took better care of it.

ELEANOR   You're right, Stomil. From now on we'll look after you. A little nap after lunch, a little stroll after napping. The morning will be for experiments.

STOMIL   And everything cooked in butter, or maybe cut out fats entirely.

ELEANOR   Yes. We'll sleep better that way too.

ARTHUR   What? Silence? All right, I'll tell you. (*He puts his chair on the set table, climbs reeling onto the table, and sits down in the chair.*)

ELEANOR   Careful of the dishes, Arthur.

ARTHUR   The only possible answer is power.

EUGENE   Power? What power? We're your family, remember?

STOMIL   He's raving. Don't pay any attention to him.

ARTHUR   Power alone can exist in a vacuum. Now I am up here above you, and you are beneath me.

EUGENE   Brilliant, isn't he?

ELEANOR   Arthur, come down. You're getting the tablecloth all dirty.

ARTHUR   You grovel beneath me in dust and ashes.

EUGENE   How long are we going to put up with this?

STOMIL   Let him talk. We'll take care of him after lunch. It's beyond me where he gets these tendencies. Must be his upbringing.

ARTHUR   Everything depends on being strong and decisive. I am strong. Look at me then. I am the answer to your dreams. Uncle Eugene, there will be order. Father, you have always rebelled, but your rebellion consumed itself in chaos. Now look at me. Power, too, is rebellion. A revolution in form and order, the revolt of the top against the bottom, the high against the low. The mountain needs the plain and the plain needs the mountain; otherwise each would cease to be what it is. Power resolves the paradox of opposites. Neither synthesis nor analysis, I am the act, the will and the way. I am power. I am above, within, and beside all things. Give thanks to me for fulfilling the dreams of your youth. This is my gift to you. Yet I have a gift for myself as well: the form I have always longed for. For I can now create and destroy not just one but a thousand possible forms. I can incarnate and disincarnate myself. I have here within me—everything. (*He beats his breast.*)

EUGENE   Poor boy. Sad to see a thing like this happen.

STOMIL   Oh, don't take it so seriously. Adolescent foolishness. Words, words, words. What power has he got over us?

EUGENE   Right! What does all his talk amount to anyway? We're united by blood, not by abstractions. He can't do a thing to us.

ARTHUR   It's very simple. I can kill you.

STOMIL   (*Rises from his chair and falls back again*)   I absolutely forbid you . . . There are limits.

ARTHUR   Limits can be transcended. *You* taught me that. Power over life and death. What greater power can there be? A simple but profoundly important discovery!

EUGENE   Nonsense! I'll live as long as I please. That is, I mean, as long as it pleases. . . . I don't know whom, do you, Stomil?

STOMIL   Well . . . Nature?

EUGENE   Exactly. Nature or fate.

ARTHUR   No. *Me!*

EUGENE   (*Jumping up*)   Don't make me laugh!

ARTHUR   But suppose I become your fate, Uncle?

EUGENE   Eleanor, Stomil, what does this mean? I won't stand for it. He's your son, after all.

ELEANOR   Look what you've done, Arthur. You've frightened your uncle. He's white as a sheet. Don't get up, Stomil. I'll get you a pillow.

ARTHUR   Did you really think I'd start something I couldn't finish? Each one of you has a death shut inside you like a nightingale locked in a cage. All I have to do is let it out. Well, do you still think I'm a utopian, a babbler, a dreamer?

EUGENE   Ha ha! There's no getting around it, Arthur—you've got a head on your shoulders. You've thought this whole thing out very nicely. Nothing like a good university education, I always say.

Hopeless to argue with you; you'll always win. But while we talk, time is flying and though there's nothing I enjoy more than a philosophico-scientific discussion, especially with the younger generation, we've talked long enough. Our horizons have been expanded, but now it's time for something concrete. Enough theory. Let's have something to eat. What do you say, Eleanor?

ELEANOR   I wanted to suggest that some time ago, but I couldn't get a word in edgewise. Enough now, Arthur, come down. Or at least take your shoes off.

ARTHUR   You're right, Uncle, it's time for something concrete. Eddie, my dark angel, are you ready?

EDDIE   Ready, chief.

ARTHUR   Then grab him.

EUGENE (*Trying to escape*)   What are you going to do?

ARTHUR   First we're going to rub out Uncle Eugene.

ELEANOR   Rub out? Where on earth did you pick that up?

STOMIL   And now of all times, with my blood pressure skyrocketing!

EUGENE (*Still trying to reach the door*)   Why me?

Eddie bars the way.

ARTHUR   So I'm all just theory, am I? Eddie, show him he's mistaken. You trash! What do you take me for?

Eddie tries to catch Eugene.

EUGENE   This isn't a system. It's mob rule.

ARTHUR   Do your duty, Eddie.

EUGENE (*Running from Eddie, who follows him with sure, catlike movements*)   What does this ape want of me? Keep your hands off me!

ARTHUR   He's not an ape. He's the right arm of my spirit, my word made flesh.

STOMIL (*Tearing his collar open*)   Eleanor, I feel awful. Eleanor!

ELEANOR   Look, your father's fainted.

EUGENE (*Still running away*)   Madman! Murderer!

ARTHUR (*Stands up and stretches out his arm*)   No! A man who has seen
the one possibility and doesn't shrink from it. I am as pure as nature. I
am free. Free!

ALA   Arthur! . . .

ARTHUR   Wait. First we've got to save the world.

ALA   I've been unfaithful to you. With Eddie.

*Eddie and Eugene suddenly stop still and look at Arthur and Ala. Eleanor is
busy slapping Stomil's checks, trying to rouse him from his faint.*

ARTHUR (*Slowly lowering his arms, after a moment of silence*)   What?

ALA   I didn't think you'd mind. After all, you only wanted to marry me
out of principle.

ARTHUR (*Sits down, dazed*)   When?

ALA   This morning.

ARTHUR (*To himself*)   I see . . .

ALA   I didn't think you'd care. I thought . . . Look, I'm ready for the
wedding. (*She puts on her veil.*)   How do I look?

ARTHUR (*Gropes his way clumsily off the table*)   Wait a second, wait . . .
You? You did that to me?

ALA (*With affected nonchalance*)   I forgot to tell you. You were so
busy . . . We can go now. Should I wear my gloves? They're a bit
tight. You like the way I've done my hair?

ARTHUR (*Bellowing*)   You did that to *me*?

ALA (*Affecting surprise*)   You still going on about that? I didn't think
you'd even be interested. Let's change the subject, shall we?

ARTHUR (*In a state of collapse, gropes his way around the table; he seems to
have lost control over his movements; in a plaintive monotone*)   How could
you . . . how could you?

ALA   But you said you only needed me to help you with your plan.
Don't you remember? I didn't misunderstand you, did I? Yesterday,

when we were talking and you said such clever things, I was impressed. Really. Eddie could never have spoken like that.

ARTHUR (*Bellowing*) Eddie!

ALA Eddie's something else again.

ARTHUR (*Plaintively*) Why did you do that to me?

ALA What's got into you, darling? I've told you, I didn't think you'd care. Frankly, I'm surprised at you, making such a fuss over nothing. Now I'm sorry I even told you.

ARTHUR But why?

ALA Oh, my stubborn darling! I had my reasons.

ARTHUR (*Shouting*) What reasons?

ALA Let's forget about it. You're just getting yourself all worked up.

ARTHUR Tell me!

ALA I only wanted to . . .

ARTHUR Go on. Your reasons . . .

ALA (*Frightened*) Oh, the stupidest, silliest little reasons . . .

ARTHUR Go on!

ALA I won't tell you. You always get mad.

ARTHUR Oh God!

ALA If you want, we'll never say another word about the whole thing. Is it all my fault?

ARTHUR (*Goes up to Stomil and Eleanor*) Why are you all against me? What have I done to you? Mother, did you hear that?

ELEANOR Ala, I warned you.

ARTHUR (*Clinging to Eleanor*) Mama, tell her she mustn't do such things. Do something, help me, I can't live like this. Tell her . . . How can she treat me like this . . . (*He bursts into tears.*)

ELEANOR (*Tearing herself away from him*) Get away from me, you silly child.

ARTHUR (*Repulsed, staggers to the center of the stage; tearfully*)   I wanted to save you. I was so close . . . And now you've ruined it all. Ah, the world is evil, evil, evil.

ALA   Come to me, Arthur! (*She goes toward him.*)   Oh, my poor boy, I feel so sorry for you.

ARTHUR (*Shoving her away*)   You! Sorry for me? You dare to pity me? I don't need anyone's pity. You don't know me yet . . . but you're going to now. All right. You've rejected my idea. You've trampled me underfoot. (*To Ala.*)   And you besmirched the noblest idea in all history, you goose! Oh! What blindness! You can't even begin to imagine who it is you've lost. And who did you do it with? With this half-witted punk, this garbage dumped out by our times. I'll go away, but I won't leave you behind in this world. You don't know what you're living for anyway. Where is he, your darling lover? Where's that rotten beer belly anyway? I'll fix that early bird's guts! (*He runs desperately around the room, looking blindly for something on the tables and on the sofa.*)   The revolver! Where can it be? It's impossible to find anything with all this damned order! Mama, have you seen the revolver?

Eddie creeps up from behind, takes the revolver from his breast pocket, and, taking a wide swing, hits Arthur in the back of the neck with the butt. Arthur sinks to his knees. Eddie tosses the revolver aside, pushes Arthur's head deftly forward so that it hangs down, clasps his hands and, raising himself on his tiptoes, swings his hands down on Arthur's head like an ax. Arthur falls over, hitting the floor with his forehead. This scene must look very realistic.

ALA (*Kneels beside Arthur*)   Arthur!

ELEANOR (*Kneels on the other side of Arthur*)   Arthur! My son!

EDDIE (*Steps aside, looks at his hands, with surprise*)   Hm, that was hard.

AUTHUR (*Slowly and softly, as though amazed*)   Strange . . . everything's disappeared . . .

ALA   But I didn't want . . . It's not true!

EDDIE   Ha ha ha!

ARTHUR (*Still with his face on the floor, very softly*)   I loved you, Ala.

ALA   Why didn't you tell me before?

EDDIE "I love you and you're sound asleep."

ELEANOR (*Runs to Stomil and shakes him*) Wake up. Your son is dying!

STOMIL (*Opening his eyes*) Can't you people spare me anything?

He stands up with difficulty and, leaning on Eleanor, approaches Arthur. Eleanor, Stomil, and Eugene stand over him. Ala kneels. Eddie to one side makes himself comfortable in an armchair.

ARTHUR (*Stretching out on the floor*) I wanted . . . I wanted . . . (*Pause*)

ALA (*Stands up; matter-of-factly*) He's dead.

EUGENE Perhaps he's better off. He nearly murdered his uncle.

STOMIL Forgive him. He wasn't happy.

EUGENE (*Magnanimously*) Oh, I don't bear him any grudge. He can't hurt me now.

STOMIL He tried to overcome indifference and mediocrity. He lived for reason, but lived too passionately. He died because his thought had betrayed his feelings.

EDDIE He meant well but he was too high-strung. His kind never gets old.

All turn toward Eddie.

STOMIL Hold your tongue, you scoundrel, and get out of my house. You ought to be glad to get off so easy.

EDDIE Why should I leave? I'll say it again: He meant well. I'm staying.

STOMIL Why?

EDDIE It's my turn now. Now you're all going to listen to me.

STOMIL We listen? To you?

EDDIE Sure, why not? You've seen that I pack a wicked punch. Nothing to worry about so long as you keep quiet and do what I say. You'll see. You won't have to worry. I'm a regular guy. I like a joke, I like a good time. But get this: There's got to be order.

EUGENE We're in for it now.

EDDIE You know, you talk too much. Take my shoes off, for me, will you?

EUGENE   I submit to brute force. But I'll despise him in my heart.

EDDIE   Go ahead and despise me, but now take my shoes off, and quick.

Eugene kneels in front of him and takes off his shoes.

STOMIL   I've always thought we were slaves of abstractions but that someday humanity would take its revenge. Now I see that it's only Eddie.

ELEANOR   Maybe it won't be so bad. He certainly won't mind if you diet.

EUGENE (*Holding the shoes*)   Should I shine them, sir?

EDDIE   No, you can have 'em. I'm changing anyway. (*He stands up, takes off Arthur's jacket, puts it on, and looks at himself in the mirror.*)   A little tight, but not bad!

STOMIL   Come, Eleanor. We're only a poor old couple now.

EDDIE   Don't go too far, and be ready to come running when I call.

ELEANOR   Are you coming with us, Ala?

ALA   I'm coming. He loved me, nobody can take that away from me.

STOMIL (*To himself*)   We may as well assume it was love.

ALA   Did you say something, Father?

STOMIL   Me? No.

Eleanor and Stomil go out, holding hands. Ala follows. Eddie takes various poses and expressions before the mirror, thrusts out his lower jaw, puts one hand on his hip. Eugene runs up and down with Eddie's shoes, finally stops beside Arthur.

EUGENE   I've got the feeling, Arthur, my boy, that nobody needs you anymore.

He stands there meditating. Eddie goes out and comes back with a tape recorder. Puts it on the table and plugs it in. Immediately the tango "La Cumparsita" resounds very loud and clear. It must be this tango and no other.

EDDIE   Well, Uncle Eugene, would you like to dance?

EUGENE   Me? With you . . . Oh, all right, why not?

Eugene puts down the shoes beside Arthur. Eddie puts his arm around him. They take the proper position, wait out one measure, and start dancing. Eddie leads. They dance. Eugene still has the red carnation in his buttonhole. Eddie in Arthur's jacket that is too tight for him, his powerful arms protruding from the sleeves that are too short. He has taken Eugene by the waist. They dance all the figures of the tango. The curtain falls. "La Cumparsita" is still heard. As the light goes on in the theater, the tune issues from numerous loudspeakers throughout the house.

VATZLAV

❦

Translated by Ralph Manheim

CHARACTERS

VATZLAV

MR. BAT

MRS. BAT

BOBBIE

THE LACKEY

QUAIL

SASSAFRAS

THE GENIUS

THE GUIDE

JUSTINE

THE OFFICER

GENERAL BARBARO

OEDIPUS

THE EXECUTIONER

SOLDIERS

VOICES

The stage, consisting of a platform inclined toward the audience, is empty. The indications "right" and "left" are always from the audience's point of view.

SCENE ONE

Half-light. Thunder and lightning. VATZLAV *appears upstage and climbs up on the platform. He is a powerfully built man in his forties with blond hair. He is wearing a white collarless shirt of coarse material and trousers with frayed edges reaching halfway between his knees and ankles. He is barefoot. He steps forward and speaks to the audience.*

VATZLAV   I was a slave and now I'm shipwrecked. An outcast slave and now a castaway. Condemned to slavery, set free by a shipwreck, finding, when all was lost, my freedom, yet too lost and battered to enjoy my freedom . . . Maybe a rest would help. (*He sits down on the ground.*)   In the storm today, a slave ship foundered off the coast. I don't know what coast this is, but it must be far from my country. Taking advantage of the disaster, I swam ashore—well, to tell the truth, the sea threw me up on the sand. Everyone else drowned.

MAN'S VOICE   (*Offstage, right*)   He-elp!

VATZLAV   Not all of them, apparently! Hey! You alive?

MAN'S VOICE   I'm drowning!

VATZLAV   Just what I said. He's drowning like the rest. Me, I'm saved. By decision of Providence. If there is a Providence. There must be, because if there's been a decision, it must come from somewhere. If it was a decision. Forget it. It's facts that count, and the fact is I didn't drown.

MAN'S VOICE   I'm drowning . . .

VATZLAV   Quit bragging. You should've seen me when I was drowning.

MAN'S VOICE   Help!

VATZLAV   I'd help him if there was a Providence that meant me to save the poor bastard. But it doesn't look like it. On the contrary. It looks as if Providence had made up its mind to let him drown, and who am I to meddle with its decision? Assuming, of course, that there is a Providence, and in this case I'll bet money there is.

MAN'S VOICE   Oh! . . . Oh! . . .

VATZLAV   That proves it. The man's in trouble.

MAN'S VOICE   Countryman!

VATZLAV   Countryman? Yes, he's from my country. I could save him if
Providence weren't against it. Suppose I bucked Providence? Then
what? I'd have a witness to my slavery. Wherever I went, his eyes
would say to me: "I remember, old friend." Once freed, a single slave
can forget. A second slave won't let him. Conclusion: Providence
wants the second to drown so he can't interfere with the first.

MAN'S VOICE   Friend!

VATZLAV   Friend? If you're my friend, leave me alone. Does a friend
stand in a friend's way? What kind of a friend is it that keeps
reminding you that you were once a slave? You're no friend of mine
and you're no friend of freedom if you insist on living and poisoning
other people's freedom. If you were a real friend, you'd realize that I
don't need you. (*He stands up.*)   New life, I salute you!

MAN'S VOICE   Traitor!

VATZLAV   Traitor? Whom have I betrayed? Did I promise anyone not
to escape if I could? No. My guards swore I'd never escape. If I've
escaped, it's the guards who haven't kept their word. Or did I swear
to my fellow slaves that I'd drown with them if the ship was wrecked?
No. There was no such agreement between us. Whom could I betray?
Only the Providence that has chosen me. That I will never do. I will
go to meet my destiny, and I will say . . .

MAN'S VOICE   I'm dying!

VATZLAV   Here I am. Destiny, you want me to be free . . . But come to
think of it, what for? What can you do with freedom? . . . I'd better
think this over. (*He paces the stage.*)   What do free men do? (*He counts
on his fingers.*)   They make money, they win honor and glory. They've
done it since the beginning of the world. Slaves are the only ones who
don't because they're forbidden to. I see. Providence is showing me the
way. Providence wants me to be rich, powerful, and happy. And you
think you can prevent me, you envious hunk of fish bait? (*He raises one
arm toward heaven as though to grasp a hand that is extended to him.*)   Okay,
it's a deal. (*He raises three fingers and swears.*)   Providence, I swear to

you, you will not be disappointed. You can count on me. (*Thunder and lightning.*)   There's the answer. That's our pact.

MAN'S VOICE   Save me!

VATZLAV   Try to see it my way, pal. I've sworn an oath. (*He listens. Silence.*)   He's caught on. No more witness. No one to prevent me from starting a new life. Nobody knows me here. If anybody asks me who I am and where I came from, I'll introduce myself as a traveler of noble family. Isn't it my right? Suffering ennobles. After all they've put me through, I've got the makings of several princes with enough left over for a good-sized duke. In our country they say all foreigners are of noble family. It must be true, because in our country there's nothing but riffraff. Since foreigners aren't us, they must be rich and noble.

Vatzlav's double, a dummy rolling on the ground as if tossed by waves, appears upstage.

VATZLAV (*cont.*)   You still here? Get away! You belong in the ocean.

The double rolls up to Vatzlav's feet.

VATZLAV (*cont.*)   Is he stubborn! (*Kicks him.*)   If he's dead, why doesn't he sink? Why doesn't he lie quietly on the bottom? What will people think if they see me in such company? A stiff! And a low-class stiff at that. (*He takes the dummy by the feet and draws him to the "shore."*)   How can I prove he's no relation? . . . Somebody's coming . . . Say, get a look at that rig. He must be a duke.

SCENE TWO

Enter left THE LACKEY *in violet livery and white stockings. He is carrying a tray with two glasses of champagne. Seeing Vatzlav and the drowned man, he stops.*

VATZLAV   Morning, Duke . . .

He bows very low; The Lackey bows, too. The Lackey looks at the drowned man (the dummy).

VATZLAV (*cont.*)   Look, Your Highness, look at the pretty seagull.

Vatzlav points to the sky and The Lackey raises his eyes.

VATZLAV (*cont.*)   Why look at the ground when the sky is so beautiful?

The Lackey looks down at the drowned man.

VATZLAV (*cont.*)   Look, Duke, I'm a great dancer.

Vatzlav performs a few leaps and dance steps. The Lackey watches him but soon turns his eyes toward the drowned man.

VATZLAV (*cont.*)   Hm . . . He prefers the stiff. Is the stiff better than me? What's so interesting about him? . . . Look, Duke, if you must look at the ground, look—a shell. Here . . . (*Vatzlav picks up an imaginary shell.*)   Isn't it lovely?

The Lackey bows, as does Vatzlav. The Lackey exits left.

SCENE THREE

VATZLAV (*Tosses the imaginary shell after The Lackey, then bows ironically*)   You call that a duke? He didn't rap me in the mouth. If he'd have kicked me at least, or insulted me. No, not a word. He's a fraud. I suppose they're all frauds in this country. They won't fool me again. I'll show 'em who's noble around here. (*To the drowned man.*)   You again? Split! Bury yourself! Heave ho! (*He draws the dummy to the shore and throws it into the water.*)

SCENE FOUR

Enter left MR. and MRS. BAT, both in their forties. Mr. Bat wears black evening clothes, top hat, white gloves, and spats. In one hand he holds a black cane with a white handle, in the other a glass of champagne. He is smoking a cigar. Mrs. Bat is ostentatiously beautiful. She wears a pink crinoline very low at the neck, a complicated hairdo, and lots of jewelry. In one hand she carries an open parasol, in the other a glass of champagne.

MR. BAT   Ho, my good man. Have you seen a corpse by any chance?

VATZLAV   A what?

MR. BAT   I hear a body has been washed up on the beach.

VATZLAV   Who?

MR. BAT (*To Mrs. Bat*)   He seems to be deaf.

MRS. BAT   Or drunk. Foreigners are often drunk.

MR. BAT (*To Vatzlav*)   A corpse. I wish to see it.

VATZLAV   See it?

MR. BAT (*To Mrs. Bat*)   If he's not deaf, he's crazy.

MRS. BAT   Quite possibly. Foreigners are often crazy.

VATZLAV   See it? Down on your knees. Kiss the dust and do homage. That's what you can do.

MR. BAT   I'm losing my patience.

MRS. BAT   My dear sir, my husband's question was prompted by pure kindness. If his words have upset you, do control your anger and answer politely. I, too, should like to know.

VATZLAV   He's fortunate in having a charming lady to intercede for him. I'd have strangled him. But now listen, both of you, pay close attention, or I won't bear the consequences.

He takes Mr. Bat's cigar and smokes it with obvious pleasure.

VATZLAV (*cont.*)   Our ship sank in the storm today. Do you know what a ship is?

MRS. BAT   We choose to ignore that question.

VATZLAV   You don't know. If you never saw our ship, you haven't any idea what a ship really is. Fifty masts. So many sails there was room for thirty winds at the same time, and no crowding. As for the guns, you couldn't even count them. Every day we tossed two or three of them overboard just for the hell of it, for the splash, and there were always plenty left. The prow was pure gold.

MRS. BAT   Gold?

VATZLAV (*Takes Mr. Bat's glass of champagne, drinks, and then returns it*)   It was a royal ship. It belonged to a king. Down on your knees! He was a big dictator.

MRS. BAT   How big?

VATZLAV   The biggest in the world. We sailed the seven seas and wherever nations saw our flag they bowed down to it.

MRS. BAT   Why did they do that?

VATZLAV   Because he liked it.

MRS. BAT   Where is he now?

VATZLAV (*Pointing to the ground*)   Here, in this tomb. Oh, poor Daddy!

MRS. BAT   Daddy?

VATZLAV   I am his son. O cruel sea! An orphan's tears are saltier than your waters and more abundant. I will drown you, O sea, in my ocean.

MRS. BAT (*To Mr. Bat*)   How bereaved he is!

VATZLAV   Thank you, ma'am.

MR. BAT (*To Mrs. Bat*)   He must be lying.

VATZLAV   Take care how you speak to the king's son!

MRS. BAT   But how did you escape?

VATZLAV   We fought the tempest, but in vain. The waves beat down upon the deck. I saw the ship was sinking. My first thought was for the king, my father. "Daddy, climb upon my back. I'll save you." Thus I leapt into the sea and like a dolphin I cut through the angry waves. (*Vatzlav makes swimming movements.*)   For me to swim ashore was child's play. "Daddy," I said, "alight." But he lay still. I turned my head. No, no. I can't go on . . .

MRS. BAT   But he couldn't have drowned. What happened?

VATZLAV   Poisoned.

MRS. BAT   Poisoned in mid-ocean?

VATZLAV   I was rocking and pitching. He took some seasickness pills. Alas, he took too many. Don't make me go on . . . It's too painful.

MR. BAT   And the ship?

VATZLAV   It sank.

MR. BAT   Such a magnificent ship. It doesn't seem possible.

VATZLAV   There was a hole.

MR. BAT   In such a beautiful ship?

VATZLAV   The most beautiful hole ever seen.

MR. BAT   (*To Mrs. Bat*)   What shall we do with him?

MRS. BAT   Give him a few coppers.

VATZLAV   What? Coppers for a king's son?

MR. BAT   You see, he refuses.

VATZLAV   Maybe if you said silver . . .

MRS. BAT   The poor man!

MR. BAT   (*Taking his wife's arm*)   I've given him my cigar . . . (*They move to the left.*)

VATZLAV   Hey! What about the bread?

MR. BAT   He can smoke it.

VATZLAV   (*Runs after them and bars the way*)   I'm not asking for any presents.

He holds out the cigar to Mr. Bat.

VATZLAV   (*cont.*)   Here, I'll sell it to you.

MR. BAT   Thank you, but I have more.

VATZLAV   Couldn't you give me a job?

MR. BAT   I don't employ persons of good family.

VATZLAV   I'm practically nothing on my mother's side. She was a cook.

MRS. BAT   Haven't you some little job for him?

MR. BAT   (*Stopping*)   What can you do?

VATZLAV   Everything.

MR. BAT   That's too much.

Mr. and Mrs. Bat again begin to walk away.

VATZLAV   No, no, not everything. I can do certain things.

MR. BAT   (*Stopping*)   For instance . . .

VATZLAV   I can cheer. (*He claps his hands.*)   Long live! Long live!

MR. BAT   Who?

VATZLAV   Anybody.

MR. BAT   What else?

VATZLAV   Or . . . (*He shouts.*)   Down with! Down with! . . . I can do that, too.

MR. BAT   Down with whom?

VATZLAV   You're the boss.

MR. BAT   Not interested.

Mr. and Mrs. Bat start off again.

VATZLAV (*Barring their way*)   I can imitate animals. (*He crows like a rooster.*)

MR. BAT   You're out of tune.

Vatzlav barks.

MR. BAT (*cont.*)   That's better.

VATZLAV   I can roar, too.

MR. BAT (*Stopping*)   Roar? Let's hear you.

Vatzlav roars.

MR. BAT (*cont.*)   Hm, not bad.

VATZLAV   You mean, maybe . . .

MR. BAT   I'll see what I can do . . .

Mrs. Bat whispers in his ear.

MR. BAT (*cont.*)   But will he make the grade?

VATZLAV   I'll make the grade. Don't you worry.

MR. BAT   Get down on all fours.

Vatzlav complies.

MR. BAT (*cont.*)   What do you think?

MRS. BAT   I think he's lovely.

MR. BAT   Trot!

Vatzlav trots on all fours.

MR. BAT (*cont.*)   Good. You're hired.

VATZLAV   Thanks, boss.

MR. BAT   From now on, you're a bear.

VATZLAV   I'd rather be a hound.

MR. BAT   I have a large pack, but there's nothing to hunt. I need game.

VATZLAV   You mean? . . . Exactly what will I have to do?

MR. BAT   Run around the woods like a bear . . .

VATZLAV   Nothing else?

MR. BAT   And roar from time to time . . .

VATZLAV   That's easy.

MR. BAT   To frighten the sheep.

VATZLAV   Leave it to me. They won't have a minute's peace. Is that all?

MR. BAT   That's all. (*He takes a coin from his pocket.*)   Here's an advance.

VATZLAV (*Examining the coin*)   What? Only one? For such a difficult animal?

MR. BAT   You'll get the balance later.

VATZLAV (*Pocketing the coin*)   Okay, it's a deal . . . By the sweat of thy brow . . .

MR. BAT   But remember, no talking. You're an animal now and mum's the word. Forget that you understand what people say. Forget you have a tongue.

VATZLAV (*Sticking out his tongue*)   Ahhh . . .

MR. BAT   Put it away and shut up. (*To Mrs. Bat.*)   Now we have a bear.

They exit left.

Scene Five

VATZLAV (*Sticking his tongue out at them*)   Ahhh . . . "Now we have a bear." Hear that, Daddy? Never thought I'd sink so low, did you? But it might have been worse. (*Boastfully.*)   I'm lord of the forest . . . all the other animals are my vassals. Now I'll visit my kingdom. Forest, watch your step; here comes your master. (*He exits left.*)

Scene Six

Enter right BOBBIE, a sturdy man in his twenties. He wears a little boy's sailor suit—much too tight for him—blue blouse with a wide collar, short blue trousers, white kneesocks, and black shoes. He is holding a hoop and a stick. He has a ring on one finger and around his neck hangs a gold watch suspended on a chain.

BOBBIE   Oh, when will Daddy and Mommy get back? I don't like it when they go off by themselves. I dreamed about Daddy last night. He was holding a fork in one hand and a knife in the other. Then Mommy came in with a frying pan. Daddy sharpened the knife on the fork and Mommy rubbed me with butter. They put me in the frying pan. "Daddy," I asked, "is it a surprise?" And Daddy said: "It needs marjoram." "Daddy," I asked, "why marjoram?" "You're too young, you'll understand later on." And before I could say "Jack Robinson," I was seasoned. With marjoram and other spices. "Look," said Mommy, "he's getting all red." "Splendid," said Daddy, "he tastes best when he's red."

Scene Seven

Enter right Mr. and Mrs. Bat.

BOBBIE   Oh, Mommy, Mommy!

He hugs Mrs. Bat.

MR. BAT   Why are you so red?

MRS. BAT (*Placing her hand on Bobbie's forehead*)   Your little face is on fire.

MR. BAT (*Aside*)   Red, in my house?

MRS. BAT   How pink you are . . .

BOBBIE Pink?

MRS. BAT As a red rose.

MR. BAT (*Aside*) Oh! A rose!

BOBBIE It's because I'm so glad to see you both again. (*Aside.*) Oh, my goodness, I've told a lie.

MR. BAT We're glad, too. (*Aside.*) Those ruddy cheeks arouse my desires. But heavens, he's my son. Oh, if only he were green.

MRS. BAT That flesh-and-blood color is so becoming to you . . .

MR. BAT Stop!

BOBBIE It's becoming to you, too, Mommy.

MRS. BAT Silly boy, I'm always so pale.

BOBBIE But now you're blushing.

MRS. BAT That's odd.

BOBBIE If I'm like a rose, you're like a . . .

MR. BAT Stop!

MRS. BAT What's the matter?

BOBBIE He's as white as a sheet.

MR. BAT I'm thirsty.

BOBBIE I'll get you some water.

MR. BAT Water? Ha, ha!

BOBBIE A glass of wine?

MR. BAT Wine? Ha, ha!

BOBBIE Or some sherbet?

MR. BAT Sherbet? Ha, ha! I want . . . raspberries!

BOBBIE I'll go get raspberries.

MR. BAT Don't bother.

BOBBIE I'll tell the butler to bring you a whole bowl of them.

MR. BAT   They've got to be fresh.

BOBBIE   I'll go to the woods.

MR. BAT   You stay here. We'll go.

BOBBIE   I'll go with you.

MR. BAT   No, we wish to be alone.

BOBBIE   Always by yourselves.

MR. BAT   Good-bye.

Mr. and Mrs. Bat exit left.

MR. BAT'S VOICE (*Offstage*)   Raspberries! Raspberries!

SCENE EIGHT

BOBBIE   Mommy and Daddy have a secret. They're hiding something. Who are they hiding it from? From me. Who am I? A child. So it must be a secret that's not for children. It must be a sin. What? Can it be that my parents are sinners? But it's sinful of me to think such thoughts. I'd better stop or I won't be a good boy anymore. But if my parents are sinners, how can I be a good boy? On the other hand, I could be the wicked child of good parents. Or worse! I could be the good child of wicked parents. In the first case, I would be wronging them. In the second case, they would be wronging me. Either way, you'd have injustice. Only a good boy of good parents or a wicked boy of wicked parents can meet the requirements of justice.

MR. BAT'S VOICE (*Offstage*)   Raspberries! Raspberries!

BOBBIE   What are they up to in the woods? I'll follow them. (*He exits left.*)

SCENE NINE

Enter right Vatzlav wearing a bear mask.

VATZLAV   Whew! . . . Why did I get mixed up in this bear business? You run yourself ragged. I wouldn't wish it on my worst enemy. A shoemaker or a tailor can sit by the fire and no one finds fault with his work. Suppose I sat by the fire. Oh no, a bear's got to roam the woods. Who ever saw a bear outside of the woods?

A VOICE (*Offstage*) Me.

VATZLAV Ho! Who dares to contradict me, the king of the forest?

SCENE TEN

Enter left QUAIL, *the peasant.*

QUAIL Your humble servant.

VATZLAV Poor devil, come closer. Do you know whom you are addressing?

QUAIL You bet. His Lordship, the bear.

VATZLAV Well spoken.

QUAIL His Worship, the bear.

VATZLAV You seem to be an intelligent animal. Who are you?

QUAIL Quail.

VATZLAV A low-class bird. A quail can't hold a candle to a bear.

QUAIL I'm not a bird. I'm a man.

VATZLAV Are you sure?

QUAIL Sure as shit.

VATZLAV A quail-man?

QUAIL Quail's my name. It runs in the family.

VATZLAV That doesn't prove anything. What do you do for a living?

QUAIL I work in the boss's fields.

VATZLAV Hm. A peasant. Never mind. The royal bear deigns to talk to the humble peasant. See here, Quail, did you say you saw a bear outside the woods?

QUAIL Well, not exactly. I've seen his skin, though.

VATZLAV   Is that a joke?

QUAIL   It's a funny thing about a bear and his skin. He's not always in it. Sometimes, you see, the skin's in one place and the bear's someplace else.

VATZLAV   Do they hunt much around here?

QUAIL   Yup. When there's game.

VATZLAV   Quail, dear Mr. Quail, take me with you.

QUAIL   God forbid. Your place is in the boss's woods. I'd be in a fine fix if the game warden found your skin in my hut. They're hard on poachers in these parts.

VATZLAV   That's not what I meant. I'll work for you, I'll milk your cows . . .

QUAIL   Oh, no.

VATZLAV   Mind the children, chop wood . . .

QUAIL   Can't be done. You belong to the boss.

VATZLAV   Tell me this, at least. Is he a hard master?

QUAIL   He's easier on bears than on people. (*He exits left.*)

SCENE ELEVEN

VATZLAV   (*Removes his bear mask*)   So . . . it could be worse. But it's pretty bad all the same. When there's game, they hunt. Better to be a slave than to lose my skin in freedom. Maybe prison isn't so bad. You keep warm, they let you breathe, even if the stench turns your stomach. Did a man ever die of disgust? No. But plenty of men have died because they were disgusted with disgust. Served them right. That's the sin of pride, thinking you're better than other people. "Maybe this is okay for other people, but, personally, I can't stand it." That's what they say. God gave all men a nose to smell with, so why rebel against equality? Where do you find more equality than in prison? If we're all equal by nature, nature must want us to be in prison and not free. Morality, too, because you can starve in freedom but in prison they always fed me. I'm beginning to think I didn't really appreciate prison. A peaceful life, a secure old age—that's what I gave up. The hunters will come and kill me. What good is freedom when you're not the hunter but the hunted? Down with hunters! Long live bears!

SCENE TWELVE

Enter right Mr. and Mrs. Bat.

MR. BAT   What's that again?

VATZLAV   (*Putting his mask on*)   Long live hunters!

MR. BAT   Your orders were to be silent. Why are you shouting?

VATZLAV   Oh, master, I was thinking what a beautiful thing the hunt is. Ah, the hunt. The horns . . . the hounds.

MR. BAT   You're to keep quiet. Understand?

VATZLAV   But I can't. The sound of horns in the early morning, the joyous cries of the beaters—the thought of it filled me with such delight, such love for the hunters, even for the hounds, I couldn't help shouting . . .

MR. BAT   Enough!

VATZLAV   Long live the hunt!

MR. BAT   Silence!

VATZLAV   I will be silent, but the rapture of my heart cannot be stilled. No one can prevent me from loving in secret. Oh, hunters, how long must I await you?

Mr. and Mrs. Bat exit left.

SCENE THIRTEEN

VATZLAV   (*Taking off the mask*)   Maybe I overdid it. What if they unleash the pack? Here they come. No, it's a little boy.

Scene Fourteen

Enter right Bobbie.

BOBBIE So here I am in the forest. I can't see three steps ahead of me. But I won't turn back. I don't know what's in store for me here; at home I know everything. There's no hope when you know everything.

VATZLAV He looks flabby and stupid.

BOBBIE O forest, forest, you've given me hope.

VATZLAV I'll bet he's a coward.

BOBBIE A hope of hope.

VATZLAV I'll scare him out of his wits. Good God! That's the only pleasure I have left.

He puts on the mask, bounds in front of Bobbie and roars.

BOBBIE Why are you roaring?

Vatzlav roars louder.

BOBBIE (*cont.*) Are you in pain?

Vatzlav roars louder still.

BOBBIE (*cont.*) Don't you feel well?

VATZLAV (*Removing his mask*) You little snot, can't you see I'm a bear?

BOBBIE Really? That's too bad. Then go ahead and roar.

VATZLAV Aren't you afraid?

BOBBIE Not at all.

VATZLAV But I'm a wild beast. Why aren't you afraid?

BOBBIE That's just it. I know who you are and when I know something, it doesn't frighten me.

VATZLAV What if I ate you up?

BOBBIE Then I'd be eaten. I'd be even less frightened than now.

VATZLAV You lack experience. I remember when even the dead were afraid because they didn't know whether they were dead or still alive. My father begot me in fear, my mother bore me in dread. The moment I was born, I tried to turn back. I knocked at her womb and begged her to let me back in. But she wouldn't take me back because there's a severe penalty for harboring guilty people. Sometimes, when I was a baby, I suckled a sword instead of my mother's breast, and then when she gave me her breast, I was afraid; I thought it was a sword. They sent me to school and I graduated with the degree of Doctor of Fear. And now I'll give you a piece of advice: Be afraid, little boy, be afraid.

BOBBIE No, my dear sir, I'm not afraid of you.

VATZLAV Ah, woe is me!

BOBBIE You've had an unhappy childhood, I agree. Try not to think of it.

VATZLAV O wretched fate.

BOBBIE You were unhappy, but now cheer up.

VATZLAV O misery, misery.

BOBBIE Let's be friends. (*He offers to shake hands.*)   Put it there.

VATZLAV Pity, oh, have pity.

BOBBIE Forget the past.

VATZLAV Forget the past? Those glorious days? No one was ever beaten like me. Understand? No one. I hold the world's record for beatings and I'm proud of it. You can search the world over and you won't find anyone who can boast such beatings. No one can take the glory of my martyrdom away from me. If anyone tells me he was beaten, I'll answer that I was beaten more.

BOBBIE I see. You want to build a monument to your degradation . . .

VATZLAV Down on your knees to it.

BOBBIE To make a virtue of your weakness . . .

VATZLAV Pray to it.

BOBBIE To find beauty in your humiliation . . .

VATZLAV Why shouldn't I?

BOBBIE   I don't see what you're complaining about. I believe you were made to walk on all fours. With all the pleasures you seem to get out of your misery, what more do you need to make you happy?

VATZLAV   I want to be feared! Is it fair that I should be afraid of everyone and that no one should be afraid of me? No, it's not fair. There will be no justice in the world until I've scared the shit out of someone. Can't you think of someone?

BOBBIE   You mean someone weaker than you?

VATZLAV   That's right.

BOBBIE   No, I'm afraid not.

VATZLAV   Not for my own benefit . . . It's for the principle!

BOBBIE   Oh, if it's for the principle, cheer up. We'll find somebody.

VATZLAV   I like you, kid. We foreigners are tenderhearted. We like to chat, to exchange ideas. We're not stones like the curious specimens around here who'd rather die than open their mouths. We may be uncouth, but at least we're sincere. Warmhearted folk who speak their minds . . .

BOBBIE   Tell me, have you seen a child's parents around here?

VATZLAV   Honest, kindly . . .

BOBBIE   (*Aside*)   Still patting himself on the back.

VATZLAV   Simple, friendly . . .

BOBBIE   I asked you a question.

VATZLAV   Come to my arms.

He embraces Bobbie.

VATZLAV   (*cont.*)   I'm so moved.

BOBBIE   Aren't you going to answer me?

VATZLAV   Brother, I love you.

BOBBIE   Then you've seen them?

VATZLAV   If that old skinflint and exploiter of bears is your father, I saw him going that way with his wife.

BOBBIE Take me to them.

They exit left.

SCENE FIFTEEN

Enter right Quail and SASSAFRAS.

SASSAFRAS They say something's going to happen.

QUAIL You think . . . *pss* . . . *pss* . . .

SASSAFRAS *Shh . . . shh . . .*

QUAIL I didn't say a word.

SASSAFRAS You didn't say a word, but you said it mighty loud.

QUAIL Scaredy-cat!

SASSAFRAS I'm no scaredy-cat, but I keep my bravery to myself.

QUAIL It seems they've seen a comet.

SASSAFRAS Heaven help us!

QUAIL With a long tail.

SASSAFRAS That looks like . . .

QUAIL *Shh . . . shh . . .*

SASSAFRAS I didn't say a word.

QUAIL But you were going to.

SASSAFRAS All right. No tail.

QUAIL Why no tail?

SASSAFRAS Don't contradict me, neighbor. (*Raising his voice.*) No tail!

QUAIL All right, all right.

SASSAFRAS (*Under his breath*) Well, what about that tail?

Quail whispers in his ear.

SASSAFRAS (*cont.*) I don't believe it.

QUAIL As true as I'm standing here.

SASSAFRAS   What do you think of that?

MR. BAT'S VOICE (*Offstage*)   Raspberries! Raspberries!

QUAIL   Of what, neighbor?

SASSAFRAS   I didn't say a word.

QUAIL   I thought you did.

SASSAFRAS   You think too much.

QUAIL   So do you.

They exit left.

SCENE SIXTEEN

Enter right Vatzlav and Bobbie.

VATZLAV   I'm telling you, pal, everybody loves me. The women most of all . . . The way they ran after me . . . I couldn't get rid of them . . . Some days, I remember, I used to shut myself up at home, just to be alone. I'm reading my paper and whistling—I'm musical, you see— when all of a sudden, bam! A broad flies in through the window. The poor thing was so crazy about me, she jumped right in with her eyes closed. Trouble, trouble. Cost me a fortune in windowpanes alone. The glaziers all knew me. When they passed me on the street they'd say: "At your service, sir, any windowpanes today?"

BOBBIE   Climb a tree and report.

Vatzlav climbs on Bobbie's shoulders.

BOBBIE (*cont.*)   What do you see?

VATZLAV   People.

BOBBIE   What kind of people?

VATZLAV   Scum.

BOBBIE   Just plain people?

VATZLAV   Oh, oh no. There's my boss and his wife.

BOBBIE   Let me up.

Bobbie climbs on Vatzlav's shoulders.

BOBBIE (*cont.*)   Good God, what're they doing? All tangled up with the people. Feasting on the people.

VATZLAV   You'll find out.

BOBBIE   On the body of the people. His suckers are clinging to the body of the people, he's strangling them with his awful tentacles . . . Oh, Father, oh my father . . .

VATZLAV   What about your father?

BOBBIE   He's drinking the blood of the people!

VATZLAV   Nice daddy you've got there. Congratulations.

CHORUS OF THE PEOPLE (*Offstage*)   Drink our blood, my lord!

WOMAN'S VOICE (*Offstage*)   I've got a baby here, a luscious baby. Help yourself, my lord!

CHORUS OF THE PEOPLE (*Offstage*)   Drink up, my lord!

MAN'S VOICE (*Offstage*)   I'm an old man bowed with age, bled since childhood, but there's still some left.

CHORUS OF THE PEOPLE (*Offstage*)   Drink up, my lord!

MAN'S VOICE (*Offstage*)   We haven't many red corpuscles left, but you're welcome . . .

WOMAN'S VOICE (*Offstage*)   We beg you . . .

CHORUS OF THE PEOPLE (*Offstage*)   Drink our blood, my lord!

BOBBIE   Oh, Father, Father, so that's your raspberries. You never told me about your loathsome meals, your lunches, your dinners, your snacks . . .

VATZLAV   It wasn't anything to brag about.

BOBBIE   Maybe breakfast, too.

VATZLAV   Very likely.

BOBBIE   You talked about raspberries and you drank the blood of the people.

VATZLAV   There you have it.

BOBBIE   My father! A bloodsucker!

They exit right. Bobbie remains on Vatzlav's shoulders.

SCENE SEVENTEEN

Enter left Sassafras and Quail.

QUAIL   Did they suck your blood, neighbor?

SASSAFRAS   Sure did.

QUAIL   The boss sucked me dry.

SASSAFRAS   The boss is nothing. The missus is worse. When she gets her suckers into you, heaven help you.

QUAIL   Oh, well, it's all in a day's work.

SASSAFRAS   They say Jake saw Justice.

QUAIL   Where'd he see her?

SASSAFRAS   Swimming in the pond over near Gloomy Glen.

QUAIL   Naked?

SASSAFRAS   You bet. Pretty, too . . .

QUAIL   You know what, neighbor? Suppose we go over Gloomy Glen way.

SASSAFRAS   Take a look at Justice?

QUAIL   Not at frogs . . .

SASSAFRAS   You in a hurry, neighbor?

QUAIL   If Jake can see her, why can't I?

They exit right.

SCENE EIGHTEEN

Enter right Vatzlav and Bobbie.

BOBBIE   (*Climbing down from Vatzlav's shoulders*)   I don't want to be Mr. Bat's little boy anymore.

VATZLAV What do you want to be?

BOBBIE A bear.

VATZLAV How're you gonna swing that?

BOBBIE Let's swap. Give me your skin.

VATZLAV What? Deny my shaggy parents? My dear old dad with his black nose and my four-footed mother? You've got the wrong guy.

BOBBIE Dear quadruped, give me your parentage.

VATZLAV I love them so . . .

BOBBIE Do it for me.

VATZLAV Let me think. Only an unworthy son renounces his parents. But an unworthy son never renounces his parents for nothing. That would be bad business. I can't let you have them for nothing, because only an unworthy son renounces his parents, and if I let you have them for nothing, I wouldn't be an unworthy son. Follow me?

BOBBIE I'll give you my watch.

He gives Vatzlav his watch.

VATZLAV That's different. I'm turning into an unworthy son. I can feel it.

BOBBIE Will that do it?

VATZLAV I'm not a hundred percent unworthy yet.

BOBBIE Take my ring.

He gives Vatzlav his ring.

VATZLAV That's for my daddy. What do I get for my mommy?

BOBBIE I haven't got anything else.

VATZLAV Oh, well, let's say I've sold all of Daddy and only part of Mommy. Maybe it's better that way. I'm not renouncing my family entirely.

He gives Bobbie his bear mask.

VATZLAV (*cont.*) Good-bye, bear. (*He exits right.*)

BOBBIE (*Putting on the mask*) Good-bye, Bat family! (*He exits left.*)

SCENE NINETEEN

Enter right THE GENIUS. *He wears an antique coat and has a bushy black beard. He is bald.* JUSTINE *runs in from the left. She is a beautiful girl wearing a white muslin dress with a wreath of daisies in her hair.*

JUSTINE (*Presses her head against The Genius's chest*)   Oh Father, Father!

THE GENIUS   What's the matter, child?

JUSTINE   I went to the meadow to plait a wreath.

THE GENIUS   No harm in that. It's most becoming.

JUSTINE   When I'd finished, I looked at my reflection in the pond.

THE GENIUS   All perfectly innocent, so far.

JUSTINE   While I was looking at myself, a peasant came out of the bushes and gaped at me.

THE GENIUS   You can't forbid an honest peasant to look at you.

JUSTINE   But he wasn't honest.

THE GENIUS   You mustn't say that. Only the rich are dishonest, the poor are always honest.

JUSTINE   This one wasn't.

THE GENIUS   How do you know?

JUSTINE   Because when I took off my dress . . .

THE GENIUS   Oh, you took off your dress?

JUSTINE   I was going to bathe.

THE GENIUS   And then?

JUSTINE   He took out a stick and threatened me.

THE GENIUS   With a stick?

JUSTINE   Or something like it.

THE GENIUS   And then?

JUSTINE   I thought he was going to hit me, so I ran away. I hardly had time to pick up my dress.

THE GENIUS That was naughty of you.

JUSTINE Should I have let him hurt me?

THE GENIUS He had no intention of hurting you.

JUSTINE He was shaking that cruel instrument . . .

THE GENIUS Because he was feeling happy.

JUSTINE Swinging it in all directions . . .

THE GENIUS Suppose he was. It's only human that when a poor devil is feeling happy and has something in his hand he shakes it.

JUSTINE Then he wasn't going to hurt me?

THE GENIUS Of course not.

JUSTINE But I thought . . .

THE GENIUS You mustn't have such thoughts, my dear.

JUSTINE Where do babies come from?

THE GENIUS What did you say?

JUSTINE I'm a big girl now, and I ought to know.

THE GENIUS You're right, child . . . Well . . . babies . . . from the head.

JUSTINE Really?

THE GENIUS By the workings of reason. The same as in nature. Look at the flowers, the little birds . . . Nature is reasonable.

JUSTINE You're making fun of my innocence.

THE GENIUS I begot you with my head . . .

JUSTINE (*Momentarily shocked*) Oh, Daddy!

THE GENIUS And bore you with my head. Or better still, with my reason. I am at once your father and mother.

JUSTINE I've had no experience with these things, but I don't see how . . . With the head, by the head . . . Is it hard to do?

THE GENIUS It all depends. Not for me, because I'm a genius, the inspired leader of mankind.

JUSTINE Of course. There's no one as wise as you, Father . . . Or should I say "Mother"?

THE GENIUS As you wish.

JUSTINE I suppose I'll have to believe you. And since you're the wisest of men, you must have created me for some purpose. Why did you bring me into the world?

THE GENIUS A pertinent question. I'm glad to find you so reasonable. It proves that you really are my daughter. Know, then, that injustice governs the world.

JUSTINE What does that mean?

THE GENIUS Some are rich, others are poor.

JUSTINE What has that got to do with me?

THE GENIUS Patience! We know that everything in the world has its contrary. Consequently, if injustice exists, justice must also exist.

JUSTINE That sounds reasonable. But does it?

THE GENIUS No.

JUSTINE What a shame.

THE GENIUS But justice must exist.

JUSTINE You just said it didn't.

THE GENIUS Have you forgotten reason? Thanks to reason, my child, everything can be set right, for the world is reasonable. Since justice does not exist, it must be invented. And that's why I created you, the fruit of necessity fertilized by reason.

SCENE TWENTY

Enter right Vatzlav. Bobbie's ring is on his finger and he wears Bobbie's watch on a chain around his neck. He eavesdrops on the conversation.

THE GENIUS You are Justice.

JUSTINE And what am I supposed to do?

THE GENIUS Exactly what you've been doing. Bathe in the pond, take your hair down at night and braid it in the morning.

JUSTINE   That's easy.

THE GENIUS   And when a poor peasant wants to look at you, let him look.

JUSTINE   His eyes were so strange . . .

THE GENIUS   And don't swaddle yourself in superfluous clothing.

JUSTINE   I always take my clothes off to bathe.

THE GENIUS   Take them off even when you're not going to bathe.

JUSTINE   Really? What for?

THE GENIUS   How shall I put it? . . . You are Justice. The sight of you arouses a noble desire for justice. Inflamed by this desire, the poor will turn against the rich and do great things. They will build a new order, and in that new order you will be queen.

JUSTINE   Queen? Oh, I'd like that.

THE GENIUS   Therefore, show yourself to the people.

JUSTINE   Oh, I will. I will.

THE GENIUS   Let them see you in all your beauty.

JUSTINE   Yes! Yes!

THE GENIUS   Until now, Mr. Bat has held the stage with his ugliness. Now, your beauty will take over.

Justine starts to undress.

THE GENIUS (*cont.*)   No! Don't fling off your clothes like a farm girl. Disrobe with circumspection; hesitate, make it clear that you are undressing not for the audience, but for yourself. Make some show of reluctance, as though fighting down your shame. Let your secret lewdness gain the upper hand, but very slowly. Your lewdness will be measured by the shame you overcome. Begin discreetly, unveil a little, then a little more. Stop from time to time. They'll think your reluctance is winning out, but all the while they'll be certain of the contrary. For remember this: Certainty is the strongest of lures.

JUSTINE   Don't worry. I'll drive them mad. They'll follow me to the ends of the earth.

THE GENIUS   Your frivolities will serve the cause. Meanwhile, I shall go abroad to gain allies. I shall proclaim your name to many people and they will join ranks with us. Await my return. Farewell, my daughter. (*He exits right.*)

JUSTINE   Good-bye, Father. (*She exits left.*)

SCENE TWENTY-ONE

VATZLAV   Justice? I've heard of her, but this is the first time I've seen her face-to-face. Well, let's see what's in it for me. (*He exits left.*)

SCENE TWENTY-TWO

Enter right Sassafras and Quail.

QUAIL   Say, where is this Gloomy Glen?

SASSAFRAS   It can't be far.

QUAIL   How do you know?

SASSAFRAS   'Cause if it's far, we've taken the wrong path.

QUAIL   You know what, neighbor Sassafras? Something tells me that if it's the wrong path we ought to turn around.

SASSAFRAS   Think so?

QUAIL   Why should we go the wrong way?

SASSAFRAS   All right, we'll turn around.

They do so.

SASSAFRAS (*cont.*)   Is it still far?

QUAIL   It depends. If we're going the right way now, it can't be far. If we're not, contrariwise.

SASSAFRAS   You know what, neighbor Quail? Something tells me we ought to turn around.

QUAIL   What makes you say that

SASSAFRAS   'Cause if one direction is wrong, the other must be right.

QUAIL   You've got something there.

They turn around again.

QUAIL (*cont.*)   Neighbor!

SASSAFRAS   What?

QUAIL   Supposing the other's right and this way's wrong?

SASSAFRAS   Holy mackerel!

QUAIL   I'll tell you what, Sassafras. Let's go arm in arm.

SASSAFRAS   What for?

QUAIL   'Cause supposing I was going the wrong way and you were
going the right way, you'd lead me the right way. And supposing I
was going the right way and you were going the wrong way, I'd hold
you back.

SASSAFRAS   Good idea!

They walk arm in arm.

QUAIL   This way.

SASSAFRAS   No, that way.

QUAIL   Neighbor, seems to me you're going wrong.

SASSAFRAS   It seems to me *you're* going wrong.

QUAIL   I'm right and you're wrong.

SASSAFRAS   You must be blind.

QUAIL   Who's blind?

SASSAFRAS   You.

QUAIL   Then you're a chipmunk.

SASSAFRAS   A chipmunk?

QUAIL   Well, if you're not a chipmunk, you're an ass.

SASSAFRAS   What's that again?

QUAIL   I say you're stupid, neighbor.

SASSAFRAS   And you're a baboon.

QUAIL   What?

SASSAFRAS   You heard me.

QUAIL   (*Imitates the braying of an ass*)   Hee-haw, hee-haw!

They rush at each other and fight.

SCENE TWENTY-THREE

Enter right Bobbie with the bear mask on his face. He carries writing materials.

BOBBIE   Have you seen the boss's son?

SASSAFRAS   I've seen a baboon.

He beats Quail.

QUAIL   I've seen an ass.

He beats Sassafras.

BOBBIE   They haven't seen me. That's fine. It proves my disguise is
effective and no one recognizes me. This is a new life. Oh, how
beautiful it is to begin a new life, to strip off the past. It's true I
haven't had much of a past, but what there was of it was so degrading
. . . Oh, there seems to be some disagreement between you two.
What are you fighting about?

SASSAFRAS & QUAIL   (*In unison*)   Justice!

BOBBIE   An excellent cause. Justice is worthy of every sacrifice. But
why should you fight?

QUAIL   (*Hitting Sassafras*)   Because he's an ass.

BOBBIE   I infer that you yourself are not an ass, because members of the
same family don't fight among themselves. That's why I've become a
bear, so I could fight the Bats. Who are you?

SASSAFRAS   (*Hitting Quail*)   Baboon!

BOBBIE   Are you hitting him because he's a baboon or because you're
an ass?

QUAIL   Hear that? Answer the gentleman, you ass!

SASSAFRAS   I'm hitting him because I'm *not* an ass.

BOBBIE   That's odd. I could see the point if you *were* an ass.

Quail gets the upper hand. He sits on Sassafras and beats him.

BOBBIE (*cont.*)   What about you? Why are you hitting him?

QUAIL   Because I'm not a baboon.

BOBBIE   Then maybe you're an ass and he's a baboon? Speak up. Let's get to the bottom of this.

QUAIL   No, he's an ass.

BOBBIE   Then you must be the baboon.

SASSAFRAS   See? What did I tell you?

QUAIL   I'm Quail.

SASSAFRAS   And I'm Sassafras.

They stop fighting.

BOBBIE   Then where are the animals you were talking about just now? Never mind. Weren't you headed for a certain place where Justice is said to have appeared?

QUAIL & SASSAFRAS (*In unison*)   Yes, sir.

BOBBIE   Then my advice to you is to get going. Don't waste your time arguing who's an ass and who's a baboon. Leave that to the bear, who has his own opinion. Hurry, because I'm confident that when you poor yokels reach your destination your lives will be changed. Justice will make men of you even if what Sassafras says of Quail and Quail says of Sassafras is true.

QUAIL   What do you think, neighbor?

SASSAFRAS   That's no ordinary bear. He's educated.

QUAIL   Yeah.

SASSAFRAS   He talks like a minister.

QUAIL   Yeah, he ain't the same bear. He wasn't so smart when I saw him the other day.

SASSAFRAS   Maybe he's been going to school.

Sassafras and Quail exit left.

SCENE TWENTY-FOUR

Enter right Vatzlav.

VATZLAV (*Seeing Bobbie in his bear costume*)   Oooh! (*He starts to run away.*)

BOBBIE   Wait!

VATZLAV   I'm not so dumb.

BOBBIE (*Removing his mask*)   Don't you recognize your old friend?

VATZLAV   Oh, it's you. Thank God. I thought it was me.

BOBBIE   Are you afraid of yourself?

VATZLAV   You can't imagine how terrifying I am. I know myself.

BOBBIE   But you sold me your skin. Don't you remember?

VATZLAV   I've been so upset.

BOBBIE   I can see that. What's wrong?

VATZLAV   Too much on my mind.

BOBBIE   What have you been doing with yourself?

VATZLAV   Not much. But I've got something cooking now. If it works out I'll buy you a drink.

BOBBIE   Buy me one now.

VATZLAV   It's not in the bag yet. (*He makes a move to leave.*)

BOBBIE   You're leaving?

VATZLAV   I'm in a hurry.

BOBBIE   I need you. Could you deliver a letter for me?

VATZLAV   I've got this deal . . .

BOBBIE   It won't run away.

VATZLAV   Business waits for no man. Be good. (*He exits left.*)

Scene Twenty-Five

BOBBIE (*Puts on his mask and writes*)   "Dear Mommy . . ." No, not Mommy. I'm a bear now. She's not my mother anymore. "Dear Madam. The writer of this letter was your son, but he was devoured by a bear. I am no longer your son, I am a wild, free, and independent bear. If you wish to see me, I shall be in the forest waiting for you. Your bear."

OEDIPUS (*Offstage*)   I watch . . . I watch . . .

BOBBIE   That's Oedipus, my father's flunky and spy. Luckily, he's blind. Yoo-hoo! Here I am!

Scene Twenty-Six

Enter right OEDIPUS, *curly beard, Greek toga, blind man's white cane.*

OEDIPUS (*Groping around with his cane*)   Where?

BOBBIE (*Taking him by the hand*)   Here.

OEDIPUS   What are you doing?

BOBBIE   Writing a letter.

OEDIPUS   To whom?

BOBBIE   My mother.

OEDIPUS   Let me read it. (*He takes the letter and turns it in all directions.*)   I don't see very well. Read it to me.

BOBBIE (*Takes the letter and reads*)   "Dear Madam, wife of my beloved father. I regret to inform you that I love him much more than I love you. Kindly assure him of my profound respect and affection. I belong to him alone. His obedient servant and son."

OEDIPUS   I will deliver it.

BOBBIE   I hate to inconvenience you.

OEDIPUS   Give me that letter right now!

BOBBIE   As you wish.

OEDIPUS   I watch . . . I watch . . . (*He exits right with the letter.*)

SCENE TWENTY-SEVEN

BOBBIE   Now he's sure to deliver my letter. (*He exits left.*)

SCENE TWENTY-EIGHT

Enter right Mrs. Bat wearing a rose corsage. She holds a fan and pulls a meticulously clipped black poodle—a toy dog on wheels—by a string. On its neck is a silver bell and a red bow; its paws are adorned with little red bows as is its tail; a red cap sits on its head.

MRS. BAT   Little cutesy. Pretty doggy-woggy. Tell me, little cutesy, do you love your mistress? Do you like her a teensy-weensy bit? No, little cutesy doesn't love her. Naughty, naughty, naughty. I'm angry with doggy-woggy. Bad, bad horrid doggy-woggy. Your mistress is angry. She's going to leave you. (*She goes to one side.*)   Is doggy-woggy sad now? That's what he gets for not loving his mistress. It's all his fault. Ohhh. Is little cutesy crying? (*She comes back to it.*)   Don't be sad. Your mistress forgives you. Look, she's right here. Please don't cry. You'll break her heart. Oh, please stop, it was all in fun. Come, little cutesy, come to Mommy. (*She rocks it in her arms.*)   Good little doggy-woggy. Mommy loves her good little, dear little doggy-woggy. Here, let me tickle you to make you laugh. Now what! Oh, you fresh thing! (*She puts the toy dog down.*)   Now listen to me! You belong to Mommy and you've got to do what she says. Come here! (*She pulls the dog towards her and puts the fan in its mouth.*)   Sit up! (*She threatens it with her finger.*)   You do as I say or it's all over between us. Did you think I'd let you get away with such insolence? (*She stamps her foot.*)   So, doggy-woggy thought he could get fresh with Mommy! (*Pause. She pets it.*)   Nice little doggy-woggy. Good little doggy-woggy. Cunning little doggy-woggy. (*Losing patience.*)   So pretty! So well-behaved! (*Angry.*)   Oh! Oh! So well-behaved! (*She screams.*)   Why are you so well-behaved? (*She bursts into tears.*)   Always the same, always the same . . . Obedient, polite, cunning. It's driving me crazy . . . (*Furious.*)   Why don't you say something? Stupid dog, why don't you say something?

SCENE TWENTY-NINE

Enter right Oedipus with the letter.

OEDIPUS Where are you, madam?

MRS. BAT I'm not here.

OEDIPUS I have a letter for you.

MRS. BAT Here I am! (*She takes the letter and reads it.*) Heavens!

OEDIPUS: Yes, madam, yes, yes. That's how it is. Now, what do you think? . . . I can't hear you, madam.

MRS. BAT (*To herself*) A bear?

OEDIPUS Who?

MRS. BAT Nobody. (*She exits left, pulling the toy dog.*)

SCENE THIRTY

OEDIPUS What bear? (*He exits right.*)

SCENE THIRTY-ONE

Enter right Sassafras and Quail.

QUAIL (*Limping*) If this goes on, neighbor, Justice can lick my ass. I got a blister on my left foot and I can feel one coming on my right foot if we don't find her pretty soon.

SCENE THIRTY-TWO

Enter left Vatzlav. He wears, over his shirt, a loud, yellow blazer with silver trimming, in glaring contrast to his shirt, ragged trousers, and heavy wooden clogs. He also wears a bowler, Bobbie's ring and watch.

VATZLAV Well, gentlemen, you've come to the right place.

QUAIL (*To Sassafras*) Gentlemen? Does he mean us?

SASSAFRAS Must be some mistake.

VATZLAV   No mistake. The customer's always right and that makes him a gentleman.

QUAIL   You're very kind, sir . . . Who are you?

VATZLAV (*Bowing*)   An artist.

QUAIL   Then you're a nice artist. But we're looking for a certain person that Jake saw by the pond in Gloomy Glen. Have you seen her?

VATZLAV   She's right here. Be seated, gentlemen.

QUAIL   Do you see her, Sassafras?

SASSAFRAS (*With dignity*)   Mister Sassafras!

QUAIL   I don't see a thing. Let us pass, sir. We got no time to lose.

VATZLAV   There she is. (*He points left.*)

Sassafras moves to the left.

QUAIL   Hiding right there? Who'd have thought it? God bless you, sir . . . Hey, where you going, neighbor Sassafras?

SASSAFRAS (*With dignity*)   Mister Sassafras.

QUAIL (*Barring the way*)   Let me go first.

SASSAFRAS (*Haughtily*)   Beg your pardon, Quail. I go first.

QUAIL   I go first.

They jostle each other.

VATZLAV   Don't push, gentlemen. Pay your money and there'll be room for everybody.

QUAIL   Money? Jake saw her for free.

VATZLAV   Because if you pay, we all stand to gain. If it's free, nobody gains but you. And justice means equal gain for all. Don't be unjust when you're looking for justice.

SASSAFRAS   She was supposed to be in Gloomy Glen, down by the pond.

VATZLAV   Ah, rustic simplicity. Do you think justice grows in the swamps like rushes? Do you think she wades knee-deep in water like a heron? No, my simpleminded friends. Justice is a product not of nature but of reason. She is a delicate creature prone to pneumonia. And just for your convenience you want her to appear under the open sky, in the wind and rain, in ice and in snow? And for nothing! You ought to be ashamed of yourselves! Good-bye!

QUAIL Do we pay, neighbor?

SASSAFRAS Maybe he'll give us a discount.

VATZLAV You still here?

QUAIL He won't come down.

SASSAFRAS All right, we'll pay.

They pay Vatzlav.

VATZLAV (*Pocketing the money*) You're in luck. I'm giving you the last two seats.

Vatzlav, Sassafras, and Quail exit left.

SCENE THIRTY-THREE

Enter left Mrs. Bat pulling the toy dog which holds her fan in its mouth.

MRS. BAT (*To the dog*) I dreamed I was going through the woods. Suddenly you jumped out of the bushes. Your jaws were wide open and you had terrible, white fangs. I ran away and came to a clearing. In the clearing there was an enormous spit. My husband was turning it. He was wearing a chef's hat and he said: "He's turning red. He tastes best when he's red." And you were on the spit. I didn't want to eat you, but you came running after me. I'm lost, I thought, unless I can escape into my own belly. Then . . . (*Screams.*) How dare you suspect me? Take it back! You're nasty, disgusting, shameless. Do you realize what you're accusing me of? Is that what you've been thinking? At last I've had a glimpse of your sick brain. You vicious little brat. How dare you be jealous of your own fiendish imagination? You've insulted me. That's enough. Not another word. I won't listen to your ravings. I forbid you. Think what you please, but leave me out of it . . . I'm not talking to you. (*She turns her back to the toy dog.*) Oh, no. Certainly not. (*After each*

sentence she pauses, as if listening to the toy dog's answer.)   Really? . . .
That's odd . . . As you wish . . . No . . . No, I don't know him . . .
I've never laid eyes on him . . . Ah, what's that? . . . What bear? . . .
Well, what of it? . . . Do you want me to swear? . . . As you wish
. . . All right, I swear. Now are you satisfied? . . . Starting in again?
. . . I've just told you . . . What more do you want to know? . . .
I've told you everything . . . That's enough . . . I'm tired . . . Oh,
leave me alone . . . Stop, stop . . . I've had enough . . . What *do* you
want? . . . I refuse to answer. You bore me . . . What? . . . You've
been spying on me . . . You're vile, vile. You dared! . . . Serves you
right. It's your own fault . . . Yes, yes, yes, can I help it if you're not
a bear? . . . I love him! . . . Since when? From the very first moment
. . . No, go away. It's all over between us . . . No, it's no use . . .
Ha, ha! You, a bear? Don't even try. You're pathetic . . . Don't beg
me, don't apologize, you're wasting your time . . . You won't?
Then don't! (*She snatches her fan from the toy dog's mouth.*)   I'm going
away. (*She takes a few steps, pulling the toy dog along.*)   Don't follow
me . . . You still here? . . . You threaten me? . . . Brute force? . . .
Let me go! . . . Take your paws off me! . . . Nothing can stop me!
. . . I never want to see you again, understand? Nasty beast! (*She
kicks the toy dog and drops the leash.*)   But don't forget the beauty of
the fading rose. I'll leave you a memento. (*She takes a rose from her
corsage and throws it at the toy dog.*)   Be faithful to it. (*She exits right.
A moment later the toy dog is slowly pulled after her.*)

SCENE THIRTY-FOUR

*A drum is heard. A small curtain drops from the flies. Vatzlav enters right
beating a drum hanging from his neck. Quail and Sassafras follow.*

VATZLAV   Here we are. Be seated, gentlemen, be seated. In a few
moments Justice will appear.

*Quail and Sassafras sit down side by side in front of the small curtain with their
backs to the audience.*

VATZLAV (*cont.*)   Anyone else? Anyone else? A golden opportunity.
Step in, step right in.

Scene Thirty-Five

Enter right Mr. Bat.

MR. BAT I want a seat in the orchestra.

VATZLAV (*Running up to him, eagerly*) Certainly, Your Excellency. We have the best seat in the house for you.

He leads Mr. Bat toward center stage and kicks Sassafras and Quail.

VATZLAV (*cont.*) Hey, you, a seat for His Excellency!

Sassafras and Quail get down on all fours, side by side, facing the audience. Vatzlav wipes off their backs with his sleeve, as though dusting a chair.

VATZLAV (*cont.*) Here you are, Your Excellency. I think you'll be comfortable.

QUAIL What about us?

Sassafras puts his hand over Quail's mouth. Mr. Bat sits down on them facing the curtain, his back to the audience.

VATZLAV Your attention, please!

He beats his drum. The curtain rises just enough to show Justine in the costume of a striptease artist.

VATZLAV (*cont.*) Men are born and always continue free and equal. Civil distinctions, therefore, can be given only for public service.

QUAIL Can you see anything, neighbor Sassafras?

SASSAFRAS Nope.

QUAIL Me neither.

VATZLAV (*Stops beating the drum*) What's the disturbance?

QUAIL It ain't us. We're chairs.

VATZLAV I beg your pardon, Your Excellency. That chair squeaks.

Vatzlav goes over to Quail and kicks him. He beats his drum and continues his declamation while Justine undresses in the classical striptease style.

VATZLAV (*cont.*) The end of all political associations is the preservation of natural and unalienable rights of man. And these rights are liberty, property, security, and resistance of oppression . . .

QUAIL   Say, man's got it good.

SASSAFRAS (*Sighing*)   Yeah, wouldn't you like to be him?

VATZLAV   Liberty consists of the power to do whatever does not injure others. The exercise of the natural rights of every man has no limit other than those which are necessary to secure to every other man the free exercise of the same rights . . .

QUAIL   Punch me in the jaw, neighbor.

SASSAFRAS   Why, neighbor?

QUAIL   So I can punch you back.

SASSAFRAS   Oh, that's different.

Sassafras punches Quail; Quail punches Sassafras.

VATZLAV   The law ought to prohibit only actions harmful to society. What is not prohibited by the law should not be hindered . . .

Sassafras picks his nose.

QUAIL   Sassafras, take your finger out of your nose!

SASSAFRAS   It's my nose, ain't it? Is it hurting you?

QUAIL   It don't hurt me none, but it looks bad.

SASSAFRAS   It's my right.

VATZLAV   And no man can be compelled to do what the law does not expressly prohibit . . .

QUAIL   But nobody's making you.

SASSAFRAS   All right, I'll stop. (*He stops picking his nose.*)

VATZLAV   The law is an expression of the will of the community. All citizens have a right to concur, either personally or by their representatives, in its formation. It should be the same to all, whether it protects or punishes; and all, being equal in its sight, are equally eligible to all honors, places, and employment . . . No man ought to be molested on account of his opinions, not even on account of his religious opinions, provided his practice of them does not disturb the public order.

SASSAFRAS   Shit!

Vatzlav stops beating the drum and Justine stops undressing.

VATZLAV (*Severely*)   Is that a thought or an opinion?

SASSAFRAS   We-ell . . .

QUAIL   He didn't really mean it.

VATZLAV (*Resumes beating the drum*)   The unrestrained communication of thought and opinion being one of the most estimable rights of man, every citizen may speak, write, and publish freely. (*He stops beating. To Sassafras.*)   If it's a thought or an opinion you're expressing, okay. But if it's just plain shit . . .

QUAIL   Which is it, Sassafras?

SASSAFRAS   Shit.

VATZLAV (*To Quail*)   Is he an anarchist?

QUAIL   Hell, no. He's cracked.

VATZLAV   We'll see about that.

He continues beating the drum as Justine resumes her striptease.

VATZLAV (*cont.*)   Every man is innocent until proven guilty. But if jail is necessary, all unnecessary discomfort and severity should be prohibited by law.

Justine completes her striptease and takes her final pose. Mr. Bat applauds. The curtain falls, concealing Justine. Vatzlav bows as if the applause was meant for him. Mr. Bat exits right.

SCENE THIRTY-SIX

Sassafras and Quail rise, holding each other up. Quail limps.

SASSAFRAS   What's the matter, neighbor Quail?

QUAIL   I've got blisters.

VATZLAV   The rights to property being inviolable and sacred, no one ought to be deprived of them except in cases of clear public necessity, legally ascertained, and on condition of a previous just indemnity.

Sassafras and Quail exit right. Quail limps along. The small curtain disappears into the flies. Vatzlav follows the peasants. Justine exits left.

Scene Thirty-Seven

Enter right The Genius and THE GUIDE.

THE GUIDE   This is as far as I can go.

THE GENIUS   Lead me to the other side of the hill. I can find my own way after that.

THE GUIDE   No, I can go no farther.

THE GENIUS   Why not?

THE GUIDE   Because the crest of the hill is the border. On the other side, they have orders to castrate all camels.

THE GENIUS   But you're not a camel!

THE GUIDE   It's obvious that you're a stranger to these parts. First they castrate, then they look to see if you're a camel.

THE GENIUS   Why was such an order given?

THE GUIDE   Because it's easier to cut things off than to make them grow.

THE GENIUS   They're right. A camel's possessions are his private property and private property is the curse of society.

THE GUIDE   That's it, sir. And once deprived of his private property, the camel is able to hit high notes he would never have attempted before.

THE GENIUS   Then, surely, he sings hymns to the glory of justice.

A solemn cantata is heard sung by men with high falsetto voices.

THE GUIDE   Here they come. (*He runs off left.*)

THE GENIUS   I will follow those voices. Guide my steps, sweet music. (*He exits right.*)

SCENE THIRTY-EIGHT

Enter right Mrs. Bat carrying an earthenware pot.

MRS. BAT   I'm in love with the bear. There's no cure for it and I don't want one. If I had a cure, I'd throw it away. I'd burn this whole forest if it contained a balm that could heal my heart. I myself am my sickness. I would die if I were cured. My conscience sermonizes me, but I've left it at home. It's a conscience for home use, and this is the wilderness. What is forbidden in the city is permitted in the forest. The forest is without sin. How can there be sin where there are no men but only bears?

OEDIPUS   (*Offstage*)   Wait for me, madam.

MRS. BAT   He's found me, after all.

SCENE THIRTY-NINE

Enter right Oedipus.

OEDIPUS   Where are you, madam?

MRS. BAT   Here. (*She walks to the other side of the stage.*)

OEDIPUS   (*Goes to where she was before; he pokes around with his cane.*)   You're not here at all.

MRS. BAT   Not there. Here.

Oedipus goes toward the voice. Mrs. Bat goes back to where she was before.

OEDIPUS   She says here when she's there. And when I go there, she's here.

MRS. BAT   Not there.

She takes Oedipus by the hand and leads him to where she was before.

MRS. BAT   (*cont.*)   Here!

OEDIPUS   Oh, here.

MRS. BAT   Here. (*Surprised.*)   Why, yes, I must have been mistaken.

OEDIPUS   (*Tapping the pot gently with his cane*)   What have you got there, madam?

MRS. BAT (*Hiding the pot behind her back*)   Nothing.

OEDIPUS   In that little pot?

MRS. BAT   Nothing.

OEDIPUS   Then what do you need the pot for?

OEDIPUS   It's a pot full of nothing.

MR. BAT   Let me taste it.

MRS. BAT   But it's a bitter nothing.

OEDIPUS (*Menacingly*)   I wish to taste it, madam.

She offers him the pot. He puts his finger into the pot and licks his finger.

OEDIPUS (*cont.*)   Mmm . . . it's sweet.

MRS. BAT   It's bitter.

OEDIPUS   It's honey, madam.

MRS. BAT   Oh. Then it must be sweet.

OEDIPUS   Taking honey to the forest? That's dangerous.

MRS. BAT   Who would harm me?

OEDIPUS   The bears.

MRS. BAT   Who're they?

OEDIPUS   They love honey.

MRS. BAT   Really? I didn't know.

SCENE FORTY

Enter left Bobbie wearing his bear mask. He is not seen by the others.

OEDIPUS   What is the reason, madam, for this strange excursion?

MRS. BAT   I wanted to take a walk.

OEDIPUS   All alone?

MRS. BAT   Do you know someone who can do my breathing for me?

OEDIPUS   At this time of day?

MRS. BAT   I need air at all hours. It's best at dusk.

OEDIPUS: It will soon be night.

MRS. BAT (*Retreating slowly to the left, on tiptoe*)   Night? What's that to me?

OEDIPUS   Don't trifle with darkness, madam. The forest is always dangerous, but it's most dangerous at night.

MRS. BAT   I fear neither the forest nor the darkness. Why should I?

OEDIPUS   Because in the darkness good is indistinguishable from evil.

MRS. BAT   That's fine. If I can't see evil, it won't tempt me.

OEDIPUS   It's not fine at all. In the darkness you can sin without knowing it.

MR. BAT: I don't want to know. (*She exits left.*)

SCENE FORTY-ONE

OEDIPUS   Oh, madam, madam. I once sinned without knowing it. I was punished with blindness.

BOBBIE   Why were you punished if you didn't know?

OEDIPUS   Because the law is the law. Because I had eyes and I acted like a blind man, I was made blind. Now I'm the guardian of the law.

BOBBIE   What's the good of the law?

OEDIPUS   To safeguard morality.

BOBBIE   What's the good of morality?

OEDIPUS   Our morality is the basis of our civilization.

BOBBIE   But supposing it were the other way around. Suppose our civilization is the basis of our morality.

OEDIPUS   Our morality would be a necessity, hence all the more justified.

BOBBIE   Then it's moral for my father to drink the blood of the people in broad daylight. If that's morality, the civilization it's based on should rot. No, the morality such a civilization is based on should rot. Or, damn it, let them both rot.

OEDIPUS   What's that you're saying, madam . . . Is that your voice?

BOBBIE   No, it's mine.

OEDIPUS   Oh. Then it's a voice that resembles another as a mother's voice resembles a child's.

BOBBIE   Tell me how you sinned.

OEDIPUS   I killed my father and committed incest with my mother.

BOBBIE   Good for you. (*He exits left.*)

SCENE FORTY-TWO

OEDIPUS   Who said that? (*He gropes around with his cane and exits left.*)

SCENE FORTY-THREE

Enter right Sassafras and Quail carrying Vatzlav in a litter made up of an ornate armchair slung on two long poles. Quail limps.

VATZLAV   These damn woods. They may be all right for animals but not for honest citizens who've made a little money by the sweat of their brows. What do you find in woods like these? Bears and bandits. The former set a bad example because they don't work and own no property. That's how they show it's possible to get along without doing anything or owning anything. As for the bandits, let's not tempt fate by even mentioning them. There've been a lot of strangers hanging around here lately, tramps from God knows where, attracted by the wealth and freedom of our country. Runaway slaves. Looking for freedom. That's what they say. But I say each man gets only as much freedom as he deserves. Why were they slaves in their own country if they deserved better?

Quail stumbles.

VATZLAV (*cont.*)   Watch your step!

QUAIL   My foot hurts.

VATZLAV   Who cares?

QUAIL   Don't say that, boss. If all men are equal, my foot's as good as yours.

SASSAFRAS   You've got to be nice to us because we're "the people."

VATZLAV   What makes you so smart all of a sudden?

SASSAFRAS   It was in the paper.

VATZLAV (*To Sassafras*)   That's the times for you. Now that they've invented justice, everybody's talking about Quail. Quail is suffering, so you've got to suffer, too. You can't even sleep or eat in peace. If you sleep they tell you: "Don't sleep, Quail isn't sleeping." If you eat, they say: "Don't eat, Quail isn't eating." The sun sets. "Don't set, Mr. Sun, Quail isn't setting." A tree blossoms. "Stop blossoming, Mr. Tree, Quail isn't blossoming." To hell with you and your blossoms.

QUAIL   Don't curse, sir. I don't mind, but if society heard you they wouldn't like it.

VATZLAV   I'm not afraid of the truth. A fish used to be a fish, a poor man used to be a poor man. When you ate fish, the poor man stood and watched you. Now it's all mixed up. The fish is still a fish, but the poor man is a bone and he sticks in your throat.

SASSAFRAS   That's not the whole of it, boss. They say the fish will eat us all soon, you and us and them.

VATZLAV   The fish? What fish?

SASSAFRAS   The fish Leviathan.

QUAIL   The end of the world.

VATZLAV   When? Now? Just when business was beginning to look up?

Sassafras and Quail, carrying Vatzlav, exit left.

SCENE FORTY-FOUR

Enter right Mrs. Bat with her pot of honey.

MRS. BAT   My idiotic conscience has warned me of the night. What difference does it make whether I see what I'm doing? Besides, I have no intention of sinning. If I were going to sin, I'd feel ashamed, I'd hide. If I had evil thoughts, I'd hide my honey. But I'm not hiding it and that means I'm above suspicion. If I had anything to hide, I wouldn't cry aloud in the forest; I wouldn't tempt the hungry bear. But instead, I shout: "Honey! Honey! Come and get it!" (*She exits left.*)

Scene Forty-Five

Enter right Quail and Sassafras carrying Vatzlav in the litter.

VATZLAV   How can you tell when it's the end of the world?

SASSAFRAS   First it gets very dark.

VATZLAV   It's getting dark now.

QUAIL   It's not really dark now. The moon is rising.

VATZLAV   That's good news.

SASSAFRAS   There'll be plenty of light.

VATZLAV   Give me darkness. I wish the moon would go out.

QUAIL   It's not really light, boss. That's not the moon. It's somebody coming with a candle.

Scene Forty-Six

Enter right Oedipus with a lighted candle.

OEDIPUS   Night has fallen. Anything can happen in the darkness. I've lighted my candle to prevent conscience from falling asleep. Because I know by sad experience how easy it is to sin even with seeing eyes. In the dusk it's easier still, and for sinning the black night is the best time of all.

VATZLAV   A bandit. All shaggy . . . with evil in his eyes . . .

Sassafras and Quail drop the litter and fall on their knees before Oedipus.

SASSAFRAS & QUAIL (*In unison*)   O saint!

VATZLAV   A saint? Damn near broke my neck with his saintliness. Looks more like a beggar to me. Hey, you! No begging around here!

QUAIL (*To Oedipus*)   Your blessing.

VATZLAV   Forget it.

OEDIPUS (*Walks slowly to the left, tapping his cane on the ground*) I can tell by the voices that here are two pious men and one cheapskate. But none of these voices is the voice of that wicked man or that godless woman. I will go my way.

SASSAFRAS (*Rising from his knees*) He won't give us his blessing.

VATZLAV He walks like a blind man. But why should a blind man carry a lighted candle? (*To Oedipus.*) Hey! What are you doing with a candle if you're blind?

OEDIPUS This candle, sir, protects us all against evil.

VATZLAV Either he's pretending to be blind, and then he's a crook, or he's really blind, and then he's off his rocker.

OEDIPUS Woe betide us if it goes out.

VATZLAV We'll see about that! (*He blows out the candle.*)

OEDIPUS Shine, candle, shine! (*He exits left.*)

SCENE FORTY-SEVEN

VATZLAV A lunatic. I knew there were bandits and bears in these woods . . . I'd forgotten about lunatics. What's the matter with you two? You look like doorposts.

SASSAFRAS (*Genuflecting*) You blew the saint's candle out!

VATZLAV So what?

QUAIL (*Genuflecting*) Woe is us!

VATZLAV Have you both gone crazy?

Quail and Sassafras run out right.

VATZLAV (*cont.*) Hey . . . stop . . . wait for me . . . Is everybody nuts? (*He hoists the litter on his back and runs after them.*)

SCENE FORTY-EIGHT

Enter left Mr. Bat followed by The Lackey.

MR. BAT What seems to be the trouble?

THE LACKEY   In the first place, madam is very much upset.

MR. BAT   And in the second place?

THE LACKEY   It seems that the bear is stirring up trouble. He's been speaking to the peasants, inciting them to rebel.

MR. BAT   Tell the foresters to get ready for the hunt. Tell them to round up the hounds and load the guns.

The Lackey exits left.

Scene Forty-Nine

Enter right the toy dog.

MR. BAT   What do you want, you toady? Can't you keep an eye on your mistress? Do you think I feed you to run loose like a mutt? Go find her or I'll make you a watchdog, and all you'll get to eat is what you can bite out of trespassers. Where's your mistress? You're plotting something, you black bastard. What woods? . . . Why in the woods? . . . *Shh* . . . Not so loud . . . Dog, curly courtesan, quadruped page, flatterer, tail wagger, loathsome mongrel! If your perfumed snout isn't lying, I'll reward you with his bones, and a bear has plenty. You'll be gnawing on them all winter. And his skin, I'll give you his skin for a bed. But if you've lied . . . (*He picks up the toy dog and shakes it.*)   You'll be sorry, Iago.

He tosses the dog off stage right. He claps his hands and The Lackey enters.

MR. BAT (*cont.*)   Call the hunt!

Mr. Bat and The Lackey exit left.

Scene Fifty

Enter right Quail and Sassafras looking at the sky.

SASSAFRAS   That's funny. Not a cloud in the sky and it's dark. It's a long way till night and the stars are shining.

Quail blows his nose loudly. A flash of lightning.

SASSAFRAS (*cont.*)   Better cut that out, neighbor.

QUAIL   What did I do?

SASSAFRAS   I dunno. Maybe you're only blowing your nose, but maybe you're thundering, too, and that makes for lightning.

Quail blows his nose twice. Two flashes of lightning.

SASSAFRAS (*cont.*)   Cut it out!

QUAIL   Man!

SASSAFRAS   What did I tell you?

QUAIL   Beats the shit out of me.

SASSAFRAS   Don't worry. There's plenty left.

QUAIL   You know what, neighbor? I'll try it again.

SASSAFRAS   No, don't.

Quail blows his nose once. They wait. No lightning.

QUAIL   Hey, no lightning.

SASSAFRAS   Nope.

QUAIL   But it's getting darker.

A violent flash of lightning followed by three claps of thunder. Quail and Sassafras run to the other side of the stage and hold their ears.

SASSAFRAS   Quit it, neighbor.

A fourth explosion, louder than the others.

SASSAFRAS (*cont.*)   Cut it out, I tell you.

QUAIL   It ain't me. It's him up there.

SASSAFRAS   I don't believe you. I'll never believe you again.

Quail and Sassafras run out left.

SCENE FIFTY-ONE

A pack of dogs barking, seemingly getting closer. Vatzlav runs in from the right with the litter on his back. His violent movements indicate that he is being attacked by the pack. He struggles, kicks, rushes forward, snatches first one of his legs and then the other from the imaginary dogs.

VATZLAV Get away! Don't touch me! It's all a mistake, Mr. Hound. I'm a law–abiding citizen . . . I pay my taxes . . . Ouch! Let go, you mutt . . . That's my leg. Why does the government hire such stupid mongrels? . . . Ouch! . . . Ouch! . . . I was joking, nice dog. Hunting's all right with me if you hunt the right people. I'm all for it . . . Get away, you mutt, beat it . . . No, he won't . . . Not my ears! Please stick to my legs . . . Ouch! . . . Ouch! . . . Get away, you mutts. No, I didn't mean you, you noble descendants of the great whale . . . I'll put in a complaint. You'll see . . . I've got witnesses . . . I've got friends . . . I've got justice on my side! . . . Ouch! . . . Ouch! . . . I've got children! (*He runs out left as the barking recedes and dies away.*)

SCENE FIFTY-TWO

Enter right Oedipus and Bobbie. Bobbie is wearing his bear mask. Oedipus is walking backward. Bobbie is holding the point of his sword at Oedipus's throat.

BOBBIE Defend yourself!

OEDIPUS If you have a conscience . . .

BOBBIE Defend yourself!

OEDIPUS I will not defend myself, sir, I will defend the law . . .

BOBBIE Defend yourself!

They assume the stance of fencers. Oedipus awkwardly crosses his white cane with Bobbie's sword. Bobbie could easily strike the cane from the blind man's hand but he seems to derive pleasure from his superiority. He repeatedly allows Oedipus to recover his guard, then attacks again and knocks the cane aside, laughing. Still fencing, they exit right.

SCENE FIFTY-THREE

The barking of dogs is heard. Vatzlav runs in from the right with his litter on his back. He is out of breath. He puts the litter on the ground and sits down in the chair to catch his breath.

VATZLAV Come to think of it, they're right. Animals are smart. They smelled a foreigner. Who should they bite? Not one of their own people! If I were in their place, I'd start with myself, too, and leave the natives for later. But that's no help because I'm not in their place. (*The barking gets louder.*) Christ, here they come again. (*He puts the litter on his back and runs off left.*)

SCENE FIFTY-FOUR

Enter right Bobbie wearing his mask, and Mr. Bat. They fight violently with their swords. Mr. Bat is obviously the stronger of the two and Bobbie retreats. They exit left, fighting.

SCENE FIFTY-FIVE

Enter right The Lackey, running.

THE LACKEY   Master! Master! (*He runs out left.*)

SCENE FIFTY-SIX

Enter right Mrs. Bat dressed as a comic-opera gypsy. She holds a tambourine, which she shakes during her speech.

MRS. BAT   I'll teach my bear to dance and we'll go everywhere together. We'll go from city to city. The good folk won't refuse us their charity. We'll go to baptisms and weddings, dances and fairs. But we'll keep away from funerals, fires, and public executions. We'll steer clear of churches, cathedrals, and convents because the Church doesn't approve of us. We'll avoid legislatures, judges, court houses, and district attorneys, in short, all people and institutions engaged in making laws or enforcing them. We'll avoid devoted mothers, stern fathers, and obedient children, because, out of hatred for their own devotion, sternness, and obedience, they'd be only too happy to turn us over to the aforementioned institutions. We'll distrust those doctors who busy themselves with mental health. They would try to convince us that we're sick. And poets. They would want to make us believe in tragedy. Yes, we'll distrust poets, priests, and doctors, because if we reject sickness, tragedy, and sin they'll call the police. To repeat: If we stay away from doctors, poets, judges, legislators, the clergy, mothers, fathers, and children, not to mention divine, human, and natural morality, nothing can happen to. us. We'll be happy! (*She exits left.*)

SCENE FIFTY-SEVEN

Enter right Vatzlav with his litter. He looks around, cups his ear, and listens intently. He puts the litter down, climbs up on the chair, looks around, and listens again.

VATZLAV   I don't hear them anymore. Where are they? I don't get it. What's going to happen now? Yes, they took a few chunks out of me, but at least they protected me against the thieves, peddlers, and agitators who are always trying to make off with what you've earned by your honest work. I'd rather be bitten now and then than go without their protection. Yes, little puppies, where are you? If it weren't for you, wild boars, raccoons, and all sorts of forest riffraff would multiply like rabbits. Maybe they won't be gone for long. Let's not give up hope. But in the meantime, let's try to find a safe place for our property. (*He loads the litter onto his back and exits left.*)

SCENE FIFTY-EIGHT

Enter right Bobbie and Mr. Bat. They are still fighting, but now it is Mr. Bat who retreats. They exit left, fighting.

SCENE FIFTY-NINE

Enter right The Lackey, running with a limp. His face is black, his clothes are torn.

THE LACKEY   Master, oh, master . . . (*He exits left.*)

SCENE SIXTY

Enter right Quail and Sassafras carrying bundles containing all of their worldly possessions.

SASSAFRAS   All this on account of your cold.

QUAIL   I'm feeling better now.

SASSAFRAS   Sure, now that my house has burned down.

QUAIL   Mine's burned down, too. Fire's bad.

SASSAFRAS   Yeah, fire's bad, but it's nothing like a good flood.

QUAIL   Or hail.

SASSAFRAS   What do you think of the plague?

QUAIL   You're so picky and choosy. I take what I get.

SASSAFRAS   'Cause you're ignorant.

They exit left.

SCENE SIXTY-ONE

Enter right Mr. Bat and Bobbie fighting fiercely. Bobbie retreats. They exit left, fighting.

SCENE SIXTY-TWO

Enter right The Lackey, staggering. He crosses the stage slowly, falls, crawls a few feet, stops, and dies. Enter right two SOLDIERS *and* THE OFFICER. *They wear helmets with wide brims, coats of mail, tight-fitting breeches. The Soldiers carry lances; The Officer carries a sword.*

THE OFFICER   Remove this body.

The Soldiers carry The Lackey out left; The Officer follows.

SCENE SIXTY-THREE

VATZLAV'S VOICE (*Offstage*)   Fire! Fire! Help! Help!

VATZLAV (*He enters right, dragging his litter.*)   Oh, my years of bitter toil . . . Oh, my property! (*He takes off his hat and beats the chair as though to put out a fire.*)

SCENE SIXTY-FOUR

Enter right GENERAL BARBARO *in helmet, golden coat of mail, wielding a sword. Behind him, a Soldier carrying the mummified Genius at the end of his pole. The Genius points the way with one finger of his upraised hand. His face is waxen, two red circles adorn his cheeks, his lips are heavily rouged, and around*

his neck hangs a wreath of paper roses. A gold halo shines above his head.
Drummers and dancers follow behind him. The troop stops. Vatzlav puts on his
hat and hides under his litter.

GENERAL BARBARO   That does it, men. The war's over. I always said
these degenerates would be a pushover.

SCENE SIXTY-FIVE

Enter left Quail and Sassafras escorted by Soldiers who prod them in their backs
with lances.

SASSAFRAS   How's it going, neighbor Quail?

QUAIL   I've got shooting pains in my back.

SASSAFRAS   I've been having little twinges myself.

QUAIL   We must have caught cold.

GENERAL BARBARO   Who are you?

QUAIL   I'm Quail. This is Sassafras.

GENERAL BARBARO   I didn't ask for your names. Are you rich or poor?

QUAIL   We're poor, boss.

GENERAL BARBARO   Lucky for you. We have come to liberate you. To
help the poor, destroy the rich, as our beloved leader has taught us.
(*He bows low to the mummy.*)   May he live forever!

He raises his hand as if to strike the Soldier holding the mummy.

GENERAL BARBARO (*cont.*)   Is that a way to hold him?

Frightened, the Soldier raises the pole higher.

GENERAL BARBARO (*cont.*)   That's it. (*To Quail and Sassafras.*)   Well,
what do you think of him?

QUAIL   Pretty.

SASSAFRAS   But kind of stiff.

GENERAL BARBARO   I beg your pardon?

SASSAFRAS   Kind of lifeless.

GENERAL BARBARO (*Putting his sword to Sassafras's throat*)   I didn't quite get that.

SASSAFRAS   Lively, that's the word. Bless my soul, I never saw anyone looking so lively.

QUAIL   In the pink.

GENERAL BARBARO (*Lowering his sword*)   That's better. (*He picks his ear with his finger.*)   Sometimes I'm deaf in my left ear . . . He's lively, all right, and what's more, he's alive. We've just embalmed him a little to keep him from spoiling. The surface may be a bit shiny but it keeps out the rain. In all other respects he's in good health, better than you . . . And smart! He knows everything. (*To the Soldier.*)   Higher, you jackass!

SCENE SIXTY-SIX

Enter left Mr. Bat, unarmed, escorted by a Soldier.

GENERAL BARBARO   Who's this?

SOLDIER   Mr. Bat, the capitalist. He sucked the blood of the people.

GENERAL BARBARO (*To Quail and Sassafras*)   Is that true?

QUAIL   Yes, sir, he sure did.

SASSAFRAS   An all-day sucker, that's what he was.

GENERAL BARBARO   Hang him.

SASSAFRAS   Long live!

GENERAL BARBARO   The capitalist?

QUAIL   Of course not, boss. He meant the hangman.

GENERAL BARBARO   Oh, that's different.

QUAIL   He knows the score. Don't you, Sassafras?

SASSAFRAS   Sure thing. No use long-living a man with a rope around his neck.

GENERAL BARBARO   Hmm, you seem to have a head on your shoulders.

SASSAFRAS   That's right, boss. We're the people. That's the wisdom of the people.

QUAIL   Comes with our mother's milk, boss.

GENERAL BARBARO   Go in peace. And never forget that you've been liberated by the liberators.

QUAIL (*Bowing*)   Thanks, boss.

SASSAFRAS (*Bowing*)   Thank you kindly, boss.

GENERAL BARBARO (*To a Soldier*)   Take this man to the gallows.

Soldier exits with Mr. Bat.

QUAIL (*Aside to Sassafras*)   Let's get out of here, Sassafras. From now on we'll just have to suck our own blood.

SASSAFRAS   Got to keep up with the times.

Quail and Sassafras exit left.

SCENE SIXTY-SEVEN

GENERAL BARBARO (*To Soldiers who brought in Quail and Sassafras*)   Hang those fellows, too . . .

Soldiers make a move to leave.

GENERAL BARBARO (*cont.*)   But cut the rope. That'll teach them gratitude. First you hang them, then you cut the rope. They're too smart. That'll take them down a peg.

Soldiers exit left.

SCENE SIXTY-EIGHT

Enter left two Soldiers escorting Bobbie who wears his bear mask but is no longer armed.

GENERAL BARBARO   Who are you?

BOBBIE   The bear.

GENERAL BARBARO   I say you're a camel.

BOBBIE   Have I got a hump?

GENERAL BARBARO How do I know? Maybe you haven't. And maybe you have. If you have, you must be hiding it, because I don't see it. In that case you're circumventing the authorities. And if you haven't got a hump . . . how do I know you wouldn't have hidden it if you had one? In either case, you're guilty because now everybody's circumventing the authorities—or trying to. So to be on the safe side, we'll put you down as a camel.

BOBBIE I am a wild, free, and independent bear, and I recognize no authority.

GENERAL BARBARO That proves you're a camel.

BOBBIE I serve no man.

GENERAL BARBARO A camel if ever there was one.

BOBBIE Down with authority.

GENERAL BARBARO Definitely a camel! (*To the Soldiers.*)   Cut off his camelhood. This camel's voice is too deep.

Two Soldiers lead Bobbie out left.

Scene Sixty-Nine

Enter left Oedipus led by two Soldiers.

OEDIPUS I wish to register a complaint.

GENERAL BARBARO Go ahead, old man, I like denunciations.

OEDIPUS A young man wants to kill his father and violate his mother.

GENERAL BARBARO Must be full of beans.

OEDIPUS Which is contrary to divine, human, and natural law.

GENERAL BARBARO Wait a minute. Who are you?

OEDIPUS I am the exemplar of divine, human, and natural law.

GENERAL BARBARO That's quite a mouthful. (*He makes himself comfortable in the chair under which Vatzlav is hiding.*)   Hmm . . . You must be a VIP.

OEDIPUS Yes, indeed. An indispensable model for all mankind.

GENERAL BARBARO   An official personage, so to speak . . .

OEDIPUS   Upon my shoulders rests the order of the world.

GENERAL BARBARO   Are you as important as a king?

OEDIPUS   I was a king but I renounced my kingdom to become the guardian of the law. It follows that my office is the highest of all human dignities.

GENERAL BARBARO (*Leaning back in the chair*)   You mean you're more important than me? Holier than our beloved leader?

OEDIPUS   No one is holier than I.

GENERAL BARBARO (*To the Soldiers*)   Boys, take care of this senior citizen. Teach him the realities of life . . . Let's go, boys, I want to see teamwork!

OEDIPUS   What does this mean?

GENERAL BARBARO   It means they're going to screw you.

OEDIPUS   I am Oedipus Rex!

GENERAL BARBARO   We don't care if you're Santa Claus. With God's help we've fucked better people than you. Haven't we, boys?

SOLDIERS   Hooray!

GENERAL BARBARO   See? Don't worry. They'll fix you up.

OEDIPUS   Violate me? Me? An old man?

GENERAL BARBARO   That's the way it is, chum.

OEDIPUS   Will the heavens not take pity? Will the sun not go out and darkness fall upon the earth? . . . Between you and me, what pleasure . . .

GENERAL BARBARO   Who said anything about pleasure? Take a look at yourself. We're doing it for the glory of the flag and to demonstrate our virility, which shrinks from nothing, not even from you. We fear no sacrifice. We'll screw you with tears in our eyes, but we'll screw you. Right, boys?

SOLDIERS   Hooray!

OEDIPUS   Why this sacrifice?

GENERAL BARBARO To humble your pride. (*He stands up.*)   So you were a king? An exemplar? A VIP? Good. I'm glad you're not some poor bastard. A venerable patriarch? That's perfect. Today my soldiers are going to screw you. A hero of art and culture? They'll screw the culture and art out of you. A guardian of the law? The conscience of mankind? A good stiff cock up your ass will knock that out of you. Show you who's running things around here. (*He sits down.*)   Okay, boys, take him away.

OEDIPUS Woe is me!

Drums. Two Soldiers grab Oedipus under the arms and drag him out left. The entire troop follows them as the drums roll and the procession ends with the bearer of the mummy. General Barbaro, seated in Vatzlav's litter, stretches, yawns, and falls asleep without dropping his unsheathed sword.

SCENE SEVENTY

Vatzlav issues cautiously from his hiding place under the chair. He looks around, on all sides. He stops in front of the sleeping General Barbaro.

VATZLAV He's asleep. Made himself comfortable . . . In my chair. I bet he feels pretty good. I wonder what he's dreaming about. Before he took my place he could dream about taking it. What can he dream about now? About losing it? Conclusion: He had pleasanter dreams before. I could feel sorry for him except that he's having his bad dreams sitting down while I'm making a good speech standing up.

General Barbaro moves restlessly in his sleep and sighs.

VATZLAV (*cont.*)   All right, sigh. Your conscience must be torturing you for taking my chair. A nightmare. It must be killing you. I'd give it a hand, except you might wake up, the nightmare would vanish, and I'd be left holding the bag. But the more I look at your crooked mug, the more I want to fix it for you. I'd better look at something else. Another minute and I won't be able to resist. (*He turns his head, then looks at General Barbaro, then looks away again.*)   No, a little patience. (*He looks again.*)   I can feel myself slipping. (*He turns his head.*)   Don't look . . . Don't look . . . (*He looks.*)   Or I'll bash his head in . . . (*He turns away and covers his eyes with his hands.*)   Don't look . . . Don't look . . .

Vatzlav looks and raises his hand as if to strike. General Barbaro shifts his position. Frightened, Vatzlav jumps back. General Barbaro continues sleeping.

VATZLAV (*cont.*)   Whew! Narrow escape I had there. Oh, well, maybe it's good he's asleep. He's not nice when he's awake. I'll let him sleep, just take back my property. But how? First I'll disarm him, then we'll see.

He touches General Barbaro's hand and tries to take the sword. General Barbaro grunts in his sleep. Vatzlav jumps back.

VATZLAV (*cont.*)   All right, all right. I'm not interested in your property. Just return mine and we'll call it square. Nothing to get sore about. Come on . . . Hell, he won't listen to reason.

He takes General Barbaro by one leg and tries to pull him off the chair. Each time General Barbaro moves or grunts, Vatzlav stops, puts a finger to his lips, and tries to soothe him as if he were a child having bad dreams. Finally, half off the chair, General Barbaro moves so violently that Vatzlav gives up.

VATZLAV (*cont.*)   Is he stubborn! Oh, no, my fine-feathered friend, don't think you can get rid of me so easily. Hanging people, cutting things off people, okay, that's your business. But my property is my property. Give it back!

Vatzlav approaches the chair from behind, seizes the ends of the poles, raises the litter with General Barbaro in it and drags it to the right like a wheelbarrow. General Barbaro slips to the ground. Suddenly General Barbaro jumps up with his feet together and immediately assumes a fencer's stance. But he doesn't know where his adversary is and does not see Vatzlav.

GENERAL BARBARO   Ho, guards!

Three Soldiers run in, two from the left, one from the right with lances lowered. They surround Vatzlav, touching him with their lances. Vatzlav raises his hands. General Barbaro approaches him and examines him attentively.

GENERAL BARBARO (*cont.*)   Are you one of us?

Vatzlav shakes his head.

GENERAL BARBARO (*cont.*)   Where do you belong?

VATZLAV   I'm a foreigner.

GENERAL BARBARO   He's too thin to be from here, but too fat to be one of us. With the new regime, of course, the natives will get thin and we'll get fat, but then he'll be too fat for a native and too thin for one of us. I'd better hold him until tomorrow. If by then he hasn't definitely gained or lost weight, we'll hand him over to the executioner. Because a man has got to belong somewhere.

He sits down in the litter. Two Soldiers pick it up. To avoid being encumbered by their lances, they pass them along the poles of the litter or sling them over their backs. They exit left, carrying General Barbaro. Vatzlav follows, escorted by the third Soldier.

SCENE SEVENTY-ONE

Enter right Quail and Sassafras, each with a rope around his neck. The ropes are of equal length and trail on the ground.

SASSAFRAS   All this talk about equality. And now your rope is longer than mine.

QUAIL   That's impossible.

SASSAFRAS   Why is it impossible?

QUAIL   Because yours is longer than mine.

SASSAFRAS   I'd give you the shirt off my back, but if they hang us equal they should cut us down equal. It ain't right your having more rope.

QUAIL   I don't know about that. What bugs me is having less.

SASSAFRAS   Give back the difference.

QUAIL   You give back the difference.

SASSAFRAS   If that's the way it is, if you won't do what's right, I'll complain to our liberator. Good man, he'll string us up equally.

QUAIL   Good idea. He'll cut your rope down to size.

SASSAFRAS   He won't let me get the short end.

QUAIL & SASSAFRAS   (*In unison*)   He will do justice.

They exit left.

SCENE SEVENTY-TWO

Enter right Vatzlav. He is dressed in the shirt and tattered pants that he wore in scene one. He has neither his blazer nor bowler nor watch nor ring, but he still has his clogs. He is followed by THE EXECUTIONER *in red tights, his face covered by a red hood, carrying a large double-edged sword pointed upward.*

VATZLAV   Somebody hasn't kept his word in this deal. It could be Providence or it could be me. No, come to think of it, that's not it. We made a pact. We both did what we were supposed to, and nothing came of it. I wanted to be free, rich, happy, and I haven't really succeeded, though no one could deny I've had my freedom, that I've had money off and on and been happy from time to time. So I can't find fault with Providence, but I've nothing much to thank it for, either. I've been free as often as not, glutted as often as hungry, happy as often as sad. For a time I was young and now I'm old. I've gone in and out of the house an equal number of times. I've been awake and I've slept, done a certain amount of loving and a certain amount of hating. All in all, it's time to break up my partnership with Providence, because it hasn't done either of us any good, and retire from business because the debit cancels out the credit. Altogether, living is an ungrateful profession. And now they want me to be a professional corpse. But taken as a profession, death is just as stupid as life. What I'd like is amateur status. I wouldn't mind dying now and then, any more than I'd mind living. What I object to is sinking my whole capital into either one of them. These new bosses seem to attach a great deal of importance to my execution. They're determined to have me for a partner. But dying to order doesn't appeal to me . . . it would tie me up for all eternity. So I'll turn down their offer and clear out of this shop where I don't want to buy anything and have nothing to sell.

He takes out a cardboard jumping jack, pulls the string, and the jumping jack moves. He shows it to The Executioner, who looks at the toy with interest and laughs good-naturedly. He holds out his hand and Vatzlav gives him the jumping jack. The Executioner holds it by the top string because the sword in his other hand prevents him from correctly operating the toy. Eager to oblige, Vatzlav helps him; the jumping jack moves. The Executioner laughs. He gives Vatzlav his sword and operates the jumping jack with both hands. Vatzlav sneaks off to the right, turns, and then runs out. The Executioner continues playing with the jumping jack but suddenly stops and realizes that his victim is gone. He stops laughing. With an inarticulate shout of rage, he dashes off in pursuit of Vatzlav.

SCENE SEVENTY-THREE

Enter right Mrs. Bat in deep mourning. She leads Bobbie, in his bear costume, by the hand. Little red bows and silver bells are attached to his hands and feet. Mrs. Bat beats time on a tambourine as Bobbie performs an awkward bear dance. Vatzlav runs in from the left with the sword over his shoulder.

MRS. BAT (*Holding out the tambourine to Vatzlav*)   Alms for the poor bear and his keeper!

Vatzlav stops, digs into his pockets, and tosses a coin into the tambourine before running out right. Mrs. Bat moves left, shaking the tambourine as Bobbie dances beside her. Enter left The Executioner holding a noose.

MRS. BAT (*cont.*)   Alms for the poor bear . . .

Paying no attention, The Executioner runs out right. After a moment, Mrs. Bat and Bobbie exit left.

SCENE SEVENTY-FOUR

Enter right Sassafras and Quail with their ropes around their necks. Vatzlav runs in from the left with the sword over his shoulder.

QUAIL   Hey, boss.

SASSAFRAS   Wait, boss.

Vatzlav stops running.

QUAIL   Settle our argument.

SASSAFRAS   Who's got the longer rope?

QUAIL   Him!

SASSAFRAS   Him!

VATZLAV   Since you both think the other's rope is longer, swap ropes and don't bother me. I'm in a hurry. If I waste time on your ropes I'll get one all my own and I won't even have time to see if it's longer than yours.

SASSAFRAS   What's that? Longer?

QUAIL   Longer than ours?

SASSAFRAS Oh no, you don't.

QUAIL Get him, neighbor.

They pounce on Vatzlav, throw his sword to the ground, and beat him. The Executioner enters left with his noose. Vatzlav tears himself away from the peasants and runs out right with The Executioner hard on his heels. Quail and Sassafras exit left, shaking their fists at Vatzlav.

SCENE SEVENTY-FIVE

Enter left Vatzlav breathing heavily; his hand is on his heart.

VATZLAV Whew! I've shaken him off. That's not surprising . . . I've had more training running away than he has. High time. I can't go another step. When I think of all the running away I've done in my life! But this time my training won't help me because here I am back on the beach. The waves dash against the shore, the gulls cry, not a ship in sight. But what good is all this empty space if I can't go on? (*He sits down facing the sea upstage. He places his hands over his eyes and views the horizon.*)

SCENE SEVENTY-SIX

A woman is heard moaning and weeping to the left. Enter Justine. She has lost her wreath, her hair is in disarray, her dress is dirty and torn. She carries a baby. She moves right.

VATZLAV Hey!

Justine stops, turns toward him, and stops crying.

VATZLAV (*cont.*) Say, I know you. Aren't you the daughter of that old codger who invented justice?

JUSTINE No.

VATZLAV What do you mean, no? He gave you the name of justice and made you exhibit yourself in public. I made a pile of money on it.

JUSTINE It wasn't me.

VATZLAV Maybe not. You didn't have a baby then. (*He approaches her but she looks away.*) Let's see. Don't be ashamed. Hm . . . he reminds me of somebody, too. Who's the happy father?

JUSTINE The father is happy, the mother is miserable.

VATZLAV Really? Why?

JUSTINE I don't want to be a mother.

VATZLAV Then how come . . .

JUSTINE I didn't know where babies came from.

VATZLAV Where did you think they came from?

JUSTINE The head.

VATZLAV The head?

JUSTINE By the workings of reason.

VATZLAV (*Aside*) The poor girl is off her rocker.

JUSTINE Daddy told me to watch the birds and the flowers . . . "It's the same with them . . . Nature is reasonable . . . I begot you with my head and bore you with my head . . ." I was going to be a queen. (*She weeps.*)

VATZLAV Come on, take it easy . . . (*Aside.*) That's it, she's cracked.

JUSTINE (*Weeping*) The world is reasonable . . .

VATZLAV Reasonable? The world?

JUSTINE That's what I thought . . . (*She weeps.*)

VATZLAV Poor thing . . . Where are you going with the fruit of your father's wisdom?

JUSTINE To see the little fishies.

VATZLAV You're going to drown it?

JUSTINE The little fishies are reasonable, too. They won't do her any harm.

VATZLAV Give the bastard to me!

He grabs the baby as Justine moves away.

VATZLAV (*cont.*) Hey! Where are you going?

JUSTINE I'm going to tell the little birdies my troubles. (*She runs out left.*)

Scene Seventy-Seven

VATZLAV   Birdies and fishies! . . . What am I going to do with this brat?
I've got nothing for him to eat. And, besides, I hate kids. (*A police
whistle is heard on the left.*)   Maybe I could tell them I'm a nursing
mother? The benefits of progress, I'll tell them. See, I've had a baby.
Why wouldn't they believe me since they believe in progress, reason,
and justice? Except that they'll kill me, kid and all. (*He goes upstage,
stops, faces the sea, and addresses the baby.*)   See the other shore? . . .
Neither do I. But if we could get there you might grow up to be
somebody. Not here. (*A second blast from the police whistle.*)   I've heard
that a whole people passed through the sea and reached the other
shore without getting wet. (*A third blast of the police whistle. Holding the
baby in one arm, he takes off his shoes and rolls up his trousers. He picks up
his shoes and walks to the far end of the platform with the motions of a man
entering the water.*)   Brr . . . it's cold . . . (*He stops. Visible from the waist
up, he turns to the audience.*)   You wait here. If I don't come back,
you'll know I've made it. Then you can follow. (*He slowly disappears
behind the stage.*)

EMIGRANTS

❦

Translated by Henry Beissel

CHARACTERS

AA
XX

Gray, dirty walls with large blots and stains. A basement. A naked bulb hangs from the ceiling. The light is glaring. On the right wall at the back there is a door. (Note: Right and left are always right and left as seen from the audience's point of view.) There is no window. Along the two walls on the right and left there are two iron bedsteads. Above the bed on the right there is a nail, from which hang a coat as well as a wooden coat rack.

There is an old sink or basin, mounted directly on top of a drainpipe, against the back wall, about a quarter of the way from the left. The cracked enamel of the sink has turned yellow with age. The drainpipe is covered with rust spots. Above the sink, a bronze tap. Above the tap, a very ordinary shelf. Two toiletry cases, one very cheap, the other more fancy. Above the shelf, a fairly large mirror of bad quality hangs from a nail. A towel hangs from a nail on either side of the sink. Near the back wall, a little farther to the right, an old screen in a very dilapidated state. Also, there are all kinds of pipes of different sizes as well as electric cables running along the back wall right through the whole room.

Stage center, directly under the bulb, a table covered with newspapers. On the table there are two dirty plates, two spoons, two plastic tumblers, two open cans of food, one empty beer bottle, and one box with tea bags.

Cigarette butts. Two chairs on opposite sides of the table. On the chair on the right side, a pair of light gray trousers. Over the back of it, a tweed jacket and a silk tie. Under the chair, a pair of shoes. A man, badly shaven, in a dressing gown, is stretched out on the bed to the left. He is wearing socks and points his feet to the audience. He is a lean man in his thirties. His hair is thinning slightly. He wears glasses with dark plastic frames. He is reading.

On the bed on the right, a huge plush dog in vivid colors. A man is sitting on the chair on the right. He wears an old-fashioned black suit cut from a thick material, a little like the sort of suits worn on Sundays by the peasants of certain countries or certain regions. A white shirt, a tie in garish colors. His shoes are very pointed and carefully polished. The man is portly, built like a wrestler. He has enormous hands. His chubby face is clean shaven. Lots of hair, sideburns. He is sitting with his profile to the audience, looking at his partner stretched out on the bed. The two are about the same age.

For a few moments, the first (AA) reads, stretched out on the bed; the second (XX) remains seated watching him.

XX   It's me! (*AA doesn't react. Pause.*)   I got back.

AA (*Without interrupting his reading*)   One says: "I *am* back," not "I got back."

XX (*Scratching his calves*)   Got a cigarette? (*Without interrupting his reading, AA reaches under his pillow and brings out a package of cigarettes, which he holds out to XX, who gets up and hobbles over to the bed. He takes a cigarette. AA goes on reading. XX slips the cigarette into his pocket and takes a second one. After a moment's hesitation he takes a third cigarette after slipping the second into his pocket as well. He puts the third cigarette in his mouth.*)   That's it. I've helped myself. (*AA continues to hold the package of cigarettes at arm's length without taking his eyes off his book. Pause.*)

AA   Put them back . . . (*XX takes one cigarette out of his pocket and puts it back in the package. He turns around and walks away. AA still holds up his package of cigarettes, his arms outstretched, and goes on reading.*)   Put them back . . .

XX   I put one back.

AA   You took three. (*XX takes the second cigarette from his pocket and puts it back in the package. AA, who goes on reading, slips the package under his pillow. XX goes back to the middle of the room. He takes a box of matches from his pocket, opens it, takes out a match and is about to strike it when he stops his movements and looks in the direction of AA. Seeing that he is still reading, XX puts the match back in its box and slips the box back in his pocket. He goes to the chair on which the tweed jacket hangs. He feels the pockets, finds a box of matches, and takes it out. He lights his cigarette and slips the box of matches into his left pocket. XX seats himself in the same chair and in the same position as at the beginning. With obvious pleasure he inhales the smoke of his cigarette. He scratches the calves of his legs, unbuttons his shirt collar, undoes his tie, takes off his shoes. His socks are riddled with large holes. He blows on his shoes, which shine, as though he were removing invisible specks of dust, then he puts them delicately by the side of his chair. He stretches his legs with satisfaction and wiggles his toes.*)

XX   I went to the bus terminal.

AA (*Without interrupting his reading*)   So what?

XX   Nothing. Loads of people. (*Pause.*)   I had a beer.

AA (*Incredulous*)   You did?

XX I'm telling you. (*Pause.*)   Two beers. (*Pause.*)   In the bar.

AA Well!

XX They got public phones.

AA So what?

XX Nothing. People telephone.

AA Hmmm.

XX I didn't use the phones. I said to myself: What's the point of calling anyone? . . . So I just stood next to them.

AA Good. (*Pause.*)

XX There's newsstands too.

AA Oh?

XX They sell newspapers. But lots of other things as well.

AA So what?

XX Nothing. People were buying papers.

AA Really?

XX And they read them . . . I didn't read any. I said to myself: What's the point of reading a newspaper?

AA Of course.

XX So, I just stood next to the racks of papers. (*Pause.*)   They've got wickets. (*Pause. AA doesn't react.*)   I said, they've got wickets.

AA What?

XX For selling tickets.

AA Tickets?

XX People were buying tickets. (*AA whistles in admiration.*)   I didn't buy one. I just stood next to the wickets.

AA You were right.

XX Then I said to myself: I'm gonna take a walk on the platform.

AA Why?

XX   Because it's free. Back home you've got to buy a ticket to go on the platform, but here they let you pass for nothing. They're stupid.

AA   (*Distracted*)   Who is?

XX   Them. —So I went on the platform.

AA   Aha. Then what?

XX   Nothing. A whole row of buses. And it was blowing.

AA   What was blowing?

XX   The wind. So I said to myself: I'm going back in. Just then there was an announcement over the loudspeaker. So I decided to stay. And I stayed. But the wind was cold. Just as I'm going to go back in, what d'you think I see pull into the station?

AA   A bus.

XX   How did you know? (*Pause*)   That's right. A bus. International, the bus. It had six number plates and a big dog on the side. And me, I don't move, I just light a cigarette.

AA   Did someone offer you one?

XX   I had my own. Anyways, I don't move and I say to myself: Here, come here, my pet . . . here. You're not going any farther, this is the terminal. Come on! —And so the bus comes closer and closer till . . .

AA   . . . it came to a stop.

XX   How did you know? (*Pause.*)   It came to a complete stop. So I said to myself: You see? I told you you wouldn't go any farther.

AA   (*Turning a page in his book*)   And the bus?

XX   Nothing. It just stood there.

AA   Is that all?

XX   Right away people got off the bus. They got cold waiting for their luggage. Beautiful luggage: suitcases, bags . . . Me, I don't move. I just smoke very calmly. I said to myself: I'm gonna finish my cigarette and then I go. By this time they'd all gotten off. Just as I'm about to flick away my butt, there, right in front of me, a woman gets up in the bus. She's waiting inside, where it's warm. Not bad, eh?

AA   Interesting.

XX   Oh my God! She had hair down to here, she must've been an actress. So I said to myself: I'm gonna wait just a little longer till she's off. My butt was burning my fingers. I passed it from one hand to the other. And I said to myself: She's got to get off.

AA   And then?

XX   (*Triumphant*)   She got off.

AA   You were lucky. (*Long pause.*)   Finished already? (*XX laughs.*) Why are you laughing? (*XX continues to laugh.*)   What's so funny in all this?

XX   Well, I . . . followed her. (*For the first time AA looks up from his book at XX.*)

AA   You what?

XX   Well . . . (*He laughs.*)

AA   Stop laughing!

XX   You're just jealous . . . If you knew how she . . . and I . . .

AA   Where?

XX   In the washroom.

AA   What?

XX   Well, yes! In the ladies' washroom. She went in first, then I . . . hop hop, unseen is unknown—two times! (*AA closes his book.*)   She wanted more, but I didn't feel like it. (*AA takes off his glasses and puts them in the pocket of his dressing gown. He turns to lie on his side, supported on his elbow, and looks at XX.*)

AA   And after that?

XX   Nothing.

AA   What do you mean *nothing*?

XX   Nothing. Like I told you, I didn't feel like it anymore. Her, she wanted more, but I didn't feel like going on.

AA   All right. But afterward?

XX Afterward? Oh well, I left.

AA And she?

XX She too, she left.

AA You didn't get her address?

XX No. She wanted to give it to me, but I said to myself: What for? . . . And then there's always the risk that I'd lose it . . .

AA But she wanted you to take it, her address I mean.

XX Yes, she insisted. (*Pause.*)   An ambassador came to pick her up. I think it was her husband. In a big car with a little flag.

AA Aha. (*He fetches his package of cigarettes, takes a cigarette, searches for matches in the pocket of his dressing gown, gets up, goes over to the chair to search the pockets of his jacket, but can't find any matches.*)

XX A light? (*AA goes over to him; XX produces matches from the left-hand pocket of his jacket and gives him a light. AA picks a pair of trousers off the chair and throws them on the bed. He sits down and inhales deeply from his cigarette.*)

AA You want to know what happened?

XX I just told you.

AA No, no. I mean do you want to know what really happened?

XX If you know better than me . . .

AA But of course I know better than you. Let's begin at the beginning. It is true that you went to the bus terminal. But not directly. This morning, when you got up and looked in the mirror to shave, as you do every Sunday, you didn't have the slightest intention of going there. When you had put on your suit and your pointed shoes . . . I've often asked myself why you wear those shoes, considering that they cripple your feet. Do you really think those pointed shoes conceal your peasant trotters? . . .

XX (*Piqued*)   Those shoes cost a lot of money.

AA Certainly. —Now, where did you go? Into the street. Everyone is free to go there. But those looks! . . . From a mile away people know who you are. Yes, you have the right to walk there, but they have the right to look at you. And to recognize your foreign mug. Because you're part of our people. Your flesh and blood belong to our people. And in this respect you are the pride of our idealists, even if very probably you don't know anything about it. You are something holy for our patriots, the sacred host of our national communion . . .

xx Don't blaspheme!

aa I'm speaking in metaphors.

xx I don't give a damn, but I'm not going to let you insult religion.

aa Let's go back to your walk. As you were passing the cinema you told yourself that you'd enjoy going in there.

xx I love films.

aa Of course. In the cinema nobody can look at you. Everybody is looking at the screen. You too. You watch something move, images, you don't understand anything that's being said. But that's of no importance. The essential thing is that you are there and that you feel safe. Unfortunately, the cinema has one flaw: You have to pay to get in.

xx I never go to the cinema.

aa That's right . . . But not all is lost. There are still parks, galleries, the railway station . . .

xx And the bus terminal.

aa Of course. The bus terminal. Given the choice, you take what is closest. So, you dash straight off to the terminal. And there everything is just right for you. First of all, the entrance is free. Secondly, there you are no longer a stranger. There are no strangers at a station, precisely because it has been made for strangers. At such a station your foreign ways are completely at home. In fact, at an international bus terminal, it's the locals who look like foreigners. And besides, a bus terminal is well lit, well heated . . . there are newsstands, public telephones, wickets . . .

xx (*Dreaming*) A restaurant . . .

aa And a bar . . . as well. So you hung around the newsstand, the public telephones, the wickets . . .

xx I had a beer.

AA That I have my doubts about. A beer one has to pay for. On the other hand, I have no doubt that you went to the toilet . . .

XX What about the platform?

AA Let me finish! I'll get around to that.

XX At first I went on the platform.

AA Exactly. Physically, you first went on the platform and only afterward to the toilet. But mentally, you elaborated the story of the platform after you'd been to the toilet, and there the urinal played an important, I'd even say a fertile, role; it inspired you . . .

XX Are you trying to say that I never went out on the platforms?

AA But of course you did. And there were buses lined up on the platforms, one was just arriving, an international bus with a dog on the side, the passengers got off. All that is true. And it is equally true that a young woman, beautiful, elegant, got off last . . .

XX See what I mean?

AA Yes, all that you've seen, all right. And afterward you went to pee. Because it's free and because you can't get over the fact that here the toilets are cleaner than our baptismal fonts.

XX Don't blaspheme! The urinal was blocked.

AA It's true, on holidays the service is rather lax.

XX The bowl was full of cigarette butts.

AA There you are! So you contemplated the butts bobbing in the torrent of urine. There you find men reaching into their trousers with religious awe, each rummaging in his own trousers, each by himself and yet joined together in a sort of communion of promiscuous evacuation. You inhale those reassuring fumes. They don't disgust you. On the contrary. Do you know any other place where your neighbor finds himself in exactly the same situation as you? Where else does such incomparable equality exist? Nowhere. Naturally, you are incapable of comprehending that this is an equality of debasement. Such nuances escape you. To you, what is coarse is authentic. —So, you stayed there a long time. . . . Unfortunately, you couldn't stay there forever. Once you had finished your business, when you had stopped pretending you were still at it, and after you had run your comb through your hair—by the way, it's remarkable to observe the extent to which, in your case, urology is connected with cosmetic care—so then you left your little cubicle, and it was at this point that the idea was born in your head— remarkable, too, the extent to which cosmetic care stimulates your brain functions: One wonders if the action of the teeth of the comb on your cranium has something to do with it—anyway, it was then that this naive and stupid little lie was born in your heart about your amorous adventure with the woman who got off the bus last . . .

XX   I followed her . . .

AA   Nonsense. Oh, you stood by the bus all right and burned your fingers. But that cigarette butt is the closest you've ever come to freedom. Apart from that, you know only desire, hatred, envy, hero-worship, humiliation. . . . Of course you daydream of women, but they remain a terrible mystery to you because your sexuality has never developed beyond its primary functions. Which is why the toilet was precisely the place to stimulate your sexual fantasies to dream up an imaginary—

XX   Stop it!

AA   Why? Isn't that the way things happened?

XX   No!

AA   Don't worry. Next week you can go back to the bus terminal. (*XX takes an empty bottle of beer that is standing on the table, breaks it at the edge of the table, and brandishes the jagged neck of it. Both AA and XX get up.*)   All right, all right. You had her, you made love to her. She gave herself to you, she threw herself at your feet, she kissed your hands, she kissed your feet, she embraced your pointed shoes, she groveled before you, she adored you, you and your pointed shoes. She . . . the ambassador, and even the ambassador's limousine with the little flag! The ambassador bowed to you and they're going to have fireworks in your honor . . . and afterward they'll buy you an ice cream. Because you are beautiful! The whole world admires you. Are you content? Feeling better? Is that enough? (*XX sits down and puts the broken bottleneck on the table. Pause.*)   You want some tea? (*Conciliatory.*)   I can make you some tea.

XX   Do you have to spoil everything?

AA   Are you angry?

XX   What do you want with me?

AA   You are upset because what I said was true.

XX   You're always after me. I've never done you any harm . . .

AA   What do you want, my dear? I am merely helping you wake up to our situation, because on your own you're incapable . . .

XX   What situation? I went to the bus terminal.

AA   That demonstrates your situation.

XX   I wanted to feel good.

AA   That's it. It's always like that with us: We embellish the facts, we take our dreams for reality, we're full of pious hopes . . . A falsified present produces a sick future. History takes its revenge.

XX   What history?

AA   Ours, the history of our people.

XX   I went to the bus terminal.

AA   Right. And that's part of history. A small part, it's true. You *went* to the bus terminal—past tense, therefore history. History consists of such small individual incidents. There's no history in the abstract. Only idealists think so. They treat history as though it were a new god. But I'm not a Hegelian. Everything depends on how we interpret your little story. Are we going to examine it in the light of facts? Or are we going to examine the facts in the light of history?

Suddenly a loud gurgling sound issues from the pipes that pass through the room. AA makes a resigned gesture and sits down, thoughtfully, on his bed. XX stretches and yawns.

XX   I'm hungry.

AA   Eat, and leave me in peace.

XX   There's nothing to eat.

AA   What about the canned stuff?

XX   There aren't any more cans.

AA You've wolfed them all down?

XX Haven't you got any?

AA Yes, but I'm not giving you any more.

XX Why not?

AA For didactic reasons.

XX Mmmm. (*Pause.*) What's that supposed to mean?

AA It means that you're always wolfing down my cans of food.

XX That's not true. Mine as well.

AA Yours and mine. It's time you acquired a little order, discipline, loyalty . . .

XX Okay, but first I want to have something to eat.

AA Not from me.

XX Nothing?

AA Nothing.

XX It doesn't matter. (*Pause.*) Weren't you talking about tea?

AA You'll have to make it yourself. (*XX gets up, takes off his jacket, and hangs it over the back of his chair after having carefully dusted it. He disappears behind the screen. One hears him busying himself. He puts water on to boil. He returns and sits down. Pause.*)

XX Tell me, why aren't there any flies here?

AA (*Jolted from his dreams*) What?

XX I'm asking you why there aren't any flies.

AA Where?

XX Here, in this room.

AA (*Still a little distracted*) I don't know.

XX There aren't any out in the hall either, none at all. (*Pause*) Nowhere. (*Overexcited by his discovery.*) You tell me, have you seen any, around here, flies I mean?

AA   I don't think so. Not in winter anyway.

XX   Well, I'm telling you there aren't any. Neither in here, nor outside. There are no flies at all. Why aren't there any flies?

AA   I have no idea. Perhaps they've been exterminated. For hygienic reasons.

XX   Pity.

AA   But why do you need flies?

XX   It makes you feel better. You can catch them. You can watch them . . . it makes the time pass quicker. At home, we had flies. In the summer . . . (*Pause.*) There were always flies. And flypaper. I remember, we used to hang it by the light. They looked as if they were covered with honey, but it wasn't honey. Anyway, they stuck to it and they buzzed. And when the flypaper had been up a long time there were so many of them it was just one loud buzz, like music. Some had a deep buzz, some a high one, because for instance when you had a wasp or a hornet . . . No, the hornets worked themselves free, they were too strong . . . I remember . . . I remember—

AA   I remember, I remember, I remember! —I remember nothing!

XX   (*Sincerely surprised*)   What d'you mean? You don't remember?

AA   (*Jumps up from his bed and begins to walk up and down*)   No, I remember nothing, and I don't want to remember! It's always the same story: "You remember this? You remember that? . . ." Always, eternally, forever, after all these years! Now it's flies, you and your flies . . .

XX   Well . . . there were lots of them.

AA   Stop it!

XX   What d'you mean? You want me to say there weren't any when there were?

AA   There were flies, there were . . . So what? Does that mean that till the end of my days I have to remember a lot of stupid flies. I have other things to think about.

XX   You see. Now you admit there were flies.

AA   Oh shit! I never said there weren't any. Listen. The issue is not whether there were flies or not. There were, there were, and now they're gone. Period. That's all. Now, there are other things.

XX   What, for example?

AA   How do you mean "what"?

XX   Yes, what? Perhaps you can tell me what other things . . .

AA   Everything! . . . Ehm . . . The world, its problems.

XX   What?

AA   I'm talking about ideas, phenomena, events . . .

XX   (*Scornful*)   Eeeh . . .

AA   Social, economical, political processes, cultural currents, the prodigious bustle of a humanity at the crossroads, a civilization in the midst of a profound change. The universal problems . . .

XX   But there are no flies.

AA   Fortunately. In fact, that's an apt metaphor. The flies symbolize the pettiness of the problems to which we were condemned back home. All those local problems, those petty problems . . . The petty chauvinisms, the petty reforms—all little nothings by little people in a little country. Here, at last, one can unfold one's wings.

XX   Like a little fly . . . Bzzzz . . .

AA   Confront the big problems! It's only in meeting great challenges that greatness is born. There's no victory without risk . . . Yes. You have to think big. On a big scale. It's true, for me there are no flies anymore. Thank God!

XX   For me there are.

AA   Where? Here?

XX   (*Triumphant*)   No, back home, in the old country. Don't you remember?

AA   Oh no! Here you go again. (*A whistling sound is heard behind the screen.*)

XX   The water's boiling. (*He gets up and goes behind the screen. He returns* *carrying an aluminum water kettle. He pours the water into a plastic tumbler and then drops a tea bag into it.*)

AA   You could make me one too.

XX   Are you contributing the sugar?

AA   But I have already bought the tea.

XX   Yes, but there's no sugar. (*AA fetches a leather suitcase from under his bed; he produces a small key from his pocket, opens the suitcase, and brings out a package of sugar; he closes and locks the suitcase, then puts the key back into his pocket and the suitcase under his bed. He puts the sugar on the table. He sits down at the table. XX tips the kettle over AA's plastic tumbler.*)   There's no water left.

AA   Boil some more. (*XX slouches over to the tap. He turns it on, without result.*)

XX   There isn't any more.

AA   Without me you can do nothing. (*He goes to the sink and turns the tap on fully.*)   You're right. There isn't any more water.

XX   There isn't any because none comes out.

AA   None comes out because there isn't any, imbecile.

XX   It's not my fault, is it? (*AA returns to the table and stands there. XX puts sugar in his tea.*)

AA   Are you going to drink that tea? (*XX nods.*)   All by yourself? (*XX nods more vigorously.*)   That's what I call solidarity. I thought that when your friend has nothing to drink . . . (*XX takes more sugar.*)   That's too much sugar.

XX   I love sugar. (*He takes a little tea on his spoon, tastes it, adds more sugar, and stirs his tea. AA takes a coin from pocket.*)

AA   We are going to toss for it.

XX   What?

AA   To see who is going to drink the tea?

XX   Why?

AA   Because there is only one cup of tea, and we are two.

XX   But it's my tea.

AA   But I bought it.

XX   And I made it.

AA   All right. Let's say the two of us have equal rights to it. —Heads or tails?

XX   Heads. (*AA throws the coin high into the air.*)

AA   Tails!

The coin falls on the floor and rolls under the bed on the right. Both of them get on the floor to look under the bed. It doesn't matter where the coin falls. The actors look for it as if it had rolled under the bed.

XX   Have you got it?

AA   Not yet. (*Puts his hand under the bed.*)

XX   (*Pushing him away*)   Let me.

AA   Wait a minute! (*Brings out from under the bed a can of food.*)   What's that?

XX   That? . . . A can of food.

AA   Is it yours? But you have just finished telling me that you have no more cans . . . (*XX doesn't react.*)   All right. In that case, since it doesn't belong to anyone, I'm going to take it.

XX   No! (*Snatches the can out of AA's hand.*)

AA   You should be ashamed of yourself. To lie like this. (*Sits down on the chair to the right and reaches for the cup of tea.*)   Are you so afraid of having to share with me? Your avarice is stronger than your gluttony. As if I needed your canned food. (*XX hides the can under his bed.*) There's no need to hide it. Your secret is out. You can happily indulge your vice now. Go ahead! Satisfy your savage and bestial appetite. No, not bestial. Animals never eat any more than they need. Your appetite is monstrous, pathological.

XX   You want any of it?

AA   No, thank you. Your canapés don't appeal to me. (*He drinks a mouthful of tea and immediately spits it out.*)   Urrk! . . . It's too sweet!

xx   Well, I guess I'll eat a little . . .

AA   Bravo! You've conquered your avarice. There's some good in my method. Although it's debatable whether, in view of your avarice, your gluttony can be considered a virtue or vice versa.

xx   I'm going to eat.

AA   Eat, eat! I hope you enjoy it.

xx   Where's the can opener? . . . (*He gets very excited looking for the can opener.*)

AA   Tell me, why do you eat so much?

xx   Have you seen the can opener?

AA   Let's try and examine the question. There can be no doubt that in your case epicurism has nothing to do with it. So, what is it?

xx   It's disappeared. (*He disappears behind the screen.*)

AA   It's probably a question, quite simply, of the act of absorbing. We must assume that the absorption of food has a symbolic character. In absorbing nourishment, in the form of food, you absorb the surrounding environment. You absorb the world.   (*XX emerges from behind the screen. He has an ax in his hand. He sits on the left side of the table opposite AA and tries to open the can with the ax.*)   Yes, that's an attractive hypothesis. An act of substitution—or else . . . a magic act— that is to say, an act that realizes, in an arbitrary fashion, elements that are in fact, scientifically speaking, not identical. It's not so much a matter of food taking the place of everything else but of becoming reality itself. It would be interesting to compare my observations with certain data of contemporary anthropology concerning primitive civilizations. I'm afraid that the results of such a comparative study would establish a painful parallel between ritual cannibalism and—

xx   (*Having finally succeeded in hacking open the can of food with brute force*)   There!

AA   What d'you—?

xx   Take it! Eat!

AA   Why?

XX So that you stop talking.

AA You haven't understood what I said. Besides, I warned you beforehand, I don't want any. I feed myself in a balanced, rational manner.

XX If you don't want any, there's no need to jabber on. (*XX reaches for the can of food.*)

AA (*Taking the can*) Wait! What is this?

XX Meat. First-grade.

AA Where did you buy this?

XX In a store.

AA What store?

XX A regular store. —Give it back to me.

AA (*Putting on his glasses*) This is a can of dog food.

XX What d'you mean—dog food? (*AA reads the label.*)

AA "*Non Plus Ultra*. The All-Purpose Food for Domestic Animals. Healthy and Tasty . . . Prepared in our laboratories under the supervision of qualified veterinaries. A balanced diet consisting of all the necessary vitamins, proteins, and minerals. Contains no harmful preservatives. A natural product, artificially colored. Nutritious without producing side effects like indigestion or obesity. Try it on your friend and watch the expression of love and loyalty grow in his eyes. *Non Plus Ultra*—a Gift of Happiness for your four-legged friends!"

XX Well, all the same.

AA "All the same" what?

XX It says it's very good.

AA Good—for dogs!

XX It says nothing about dogs, it says "friends" . . .

AA "Your four-legged friends"—that means "dogs." It might include "cats."

XX Impossible.

AA Why "impossible"?

XX Because it's meat. One doesn't give dogs meat.

AA There's nothing contradictory in that. Dogs are animals, supreme carnivores.

XX They've made a mistake somewhere.

AA Of course not. Look, here, on top, it says clearly: "The All-Purpose Food for Domestic Animals" . . . And a little farther down, look, they mention veterinaries . . . You are not convinced?

XX Let me see. (*XX takes the can and scrutinizes it very closely. AA takes off his glasses and puts them back in the pocket of his dressing gown.*) No, I don't believe you.

AA Who speaks foreign languages here—you or me?

XX You're saying all this only to annoy me.

AA All right. Look at the can. You see that picture? A dog, smiling, in front of a rising sun—the picture of happiness and satisfaction.

XX So?

AA What d'you mean "so"? The dog is smiling because he is going to eat a can of this product. Even an illiterate can understand a picture like that.

XX A picture is only a picture. There are all kinds. Back home we had one in the parlor with a deer in a meadow and a sunset. The deer looks happy. So, is that supposed to mean it has come to devour the meadow?

AA Perhaps.

XX Never. A picture alone doesn't say anything. Pictures are for decoration. Yes. And this one tells you that the food in this can is very good. With such a nice picture—

AA Naturally. —I presume you bought this can because of its price. You bought the cheapest can of food in the store.

XX Finest quality.

AA For dogs.

XX Ultra-Super.

AA Yes, of that I'm sure. We must keep our dogs happy.

XX Well, anyway, I'm going to eat it!

AA Am I stopping you?

XX Just try.

AA Why should I? It hasn't done you any harm so far. (*Pause.*)   So, why don't you eat? (*XX in a fit of temper, throws the can of food into a corner. He sulks. Pause.*)

XX Because I'm not a dog.

AA No?

XX No!

AA As you like. (*Pause. XX gets up and goes to pick up the can.*)

XX Say . . . You tell me this is for cats too?

AA Yes. "Domestic friends"—that includes cats.

XX For sure?

AA Definitely. But what difference does that make?

XX Ah . . . Because if it's for cats, I can eat it. But if it's for dogs, no, out of the question! Do you think I'm a dog that I should eat dog food?

AA You are going to answer that right now.

XX No, you tell me, you tell me yourself—am I a dog? Eh? Am I a dog?

AA No. You're not. No man is a dog. Or at least, he shouldn't be.

XX There you are! That means, if it's for cats I can eat it. Cats, that's a different matter. Cats are not dogs. Eh, tell me, can I eat it or not?

AA You can . . . possibly . . .

XX You sure I can?

AA You can, you can . . . (*Suddenly he starts to shout.*)   Jesus fucking Christ! Eat what you want!! What difference does it make to me!

XX That means I can? (*He starts to open the can with his ax.*)

AA   Leave it.

XX   But you've just told me I can eat it. (*AA pulls his suitcase out from under his bed. He unlocks it with the key and gets out a can of food. He slides the suitcase back under his bed, but without locking it. He puts the can of food on the table in front of XX.*)   For people?

AA   For people.

XX   Well, that's different.

XX starts to open the can. There is the noise of people climbing stairs above their heads. Male voices, female laughter. AA puts his ear to one of the big pipes that passes vertically through their room.

AA   They're going up to the first floor. (*He moves away from the pipe.*) There's nothing like living in a basement. You hear absolutely everything through these pipes. The least noise, however quiet or intimate. Drainpipes, water pipes, the pipes for the central heating, the air-conditioning, the sewage . . . I hear it all. I hear people come and go, prepare to go to bed, and get up again. I hear them wash, flush the toilet. I hear them ventilate, relieve themselves, and propagate. However, up to now, I haven't heard anyone die yet. (*In the meantime XX has opened the can and begun to eat.*)

XX   I guess they must be pretty healthy.

AA   Sometimes I have the impression we live in their stomach. Like microbes. No? Look at these pipes. Don't they remind you of bowels?

XX   They're pipes that look like pipes.

AA   Well, they remind me of intestines. We live like two bacteria in the interior of another organism. Two foreign bodies. Two parasites. Or worse still—what if we are two pathogenic microbes? The agents of decomposition in a healthy organism? Germs, Kock's bacilli, viruses, gonococci? I—a gonococcus! I, who have always considered myself a precious cell, a cell of highly developed cerebral matter, in fact, a particle that is no longer matter only, that is already superior to matter—and here I am: a gonococcus in the company of a protozoan!

XX (*Suspicious*)   You talking about me?

AA   And on top of that, I can't stand basements! I hate them. Like all things subterranean. Everything that's underground gets on my nerves.

It affects my psychology. I need sun, air, space. I'm a head person . . .
And the head has to be held high in order to function normally. And
as a superior link in the evolutionary process, I wasn't made for caves.
I've always lived on top floors and I've always had large vistas. From
my windows. Here, there isn't even a single window.

XX   So much the better. You just get drafts from windows.

AA   Walls, nothing but walls and more walls!

XX   Yes, but at least they're warm. There are no drafts.

AA   The musty smell of basements.

XX   Nobody has ever died from that. But outside, in the fresh air, you
can catch a cold. My father (God rest his soul), he lived in a basement,
and he lived a long time.

AA   What did he die of?

XX   Pure air. One night he came home drunk and froze to death on the
road.

AA   Well, can you survive down here?

XX   Why not? It's quite a decent apartment. It's warm here. And it's
not expensive . . .

AA   That's true. And what's more it's me who pays the rent. Which
reminds me, yesterday I paid another two months. November and
December. And you owe me two months already. Altogether that
makes four months.

XX   I haven't got a penny.

AA   You have only just been paid.

XX   But I don't have any money.

*On the floor above, the doorbell rings. The new arrivals are received with shouts
of joy. The door is slammed.*

AA   I don't understand what you do with your money. You must be
earning at least as much as any average foreign laborer in this
country. In fact, you earn one and a half times as much, seeing that
you work twice as much. You're probably paid a special bonus, as

well, for the dangerous work you do. So, even if you are exploited and you're paid only half of all that, your earnings must still be well above the average income of a laborer. Yet, you live in the worst slum one can imagine, and since you live with me you pay only half the rent, which is minimal to begin with. And you don't even pay that: When I ask you to pay what you owe me, you tell me you have no money.

xx   It's true. But you have some.

AA   I beg your pardon?

xx   You always have money.

AA   (*After a pause, icily*)   Do you realize what you are saying?

xx   Well what? Isn't it true?

AA   Do you realize that I might finally lose patience?

xx   Well, if you pay you've got to have money, no?

AA   Do you realize that I've already lost patience?

xx   Why? (*AA puts on his trousers; XX stops eating.*)   You getting dressed? (*AA takes off his dressing gown and puts on his jacket.*)   Where you going?

AA   I am moving out.

xx   (*Relieved*)   Hmmm . . . it's not the first time. (*Reassured, he goes back to his can of food.*)

AA   (*Tying his scarf in front of the mirror*)   Up to now I have pitied you, but this time you've gone too far. You have just added chutzpah to plain dishonesty. I have had enough! I ask myself why I have put up with you for such a long time. How could I have endured your boorish manners, your egotism, your filth? Even when you sleep you get on my nerves. Your snoring prevents me from sleeping and your carbon monoxide gives me migraines. I pitied you, but now even pity won't stop me, because I have none left. Let me tell you, I've had enough of your company. Yes, enough! Up to here! I'm leaving!

xx   The key is under the mat.

AA   What did you say?

XX   I said the key'll be under the mat . . . In case you're coming back late . . .

AA   I'm not talking to you anymore. (*He puts on his coat, stops next to XX, and turns to face him as he buttons his coat.*)   You think I'm going to come back again? (*XX doesn't reply. He continues to chew his food calmly and pays not the slightest attention to AA. Getting no response, AA shrugs his shoulders and makes for the door. He puts his hand on the doorknob.*)

XX   Your shoes.

AA   What?

XX   You've forgotten to put on your shoes. You're not going to go out in the street in slippers, are you?

AA   I don't need your advice. (*AA returns to the middle of the room, puts on his shoes, goes back to the door, and puts his hand on the knob. Pause.*)   What makes you think I'd come back, if you don't mind my asking?

XX   Your bags.

AA   I beg your pardon.

XX   You've left your bags.

AA   So?

XX   It's obvious. If you were really moving out, you'd take your luggage.

AA   I admire your intelligence. But you're mistaken. I'm taking nothing with me.

XX   Exactly. That means you're not moving out.

AA   Oh yes? Well, I'm moving out. But I am taking nothing. I am leaving, that's true. But without taking anything. I am leaving everything behind although I am moving out. And despite the fact that I am going, I am taking nothing. I am simply leaving. I am moving out without taking anything. Now, is that clear?

XX   And your towels, your bedding, your clothes?

AA You know very well that material objects, clothes and things, are nothing in my eyes. I can do without them. I belong to the postconsumer society—unlike you.

XX You're leaving everything? You're leaving everything for me?

AA Ehm . . . perhaps not everything, come to think of it, maybe I'll take a little something as a souvenir . . . No, not everything. I'm going to take one thing, just a little thing that isn't worth much. (*He seems to be thinking.*) Now what could I . . . Let me see . . . That's it, I know! (*AA goes over to the bed on the right and takes the mascot, the dog Pluto, a stuffed animal.*)

XX No! (*XX rushes at AA.*)

AA But why not? This innocent mascot will remind me of the times we spent together. It'll ease my nostalgia . . .

XX You leave that alone.

AA You're not fair. I'm leaving you everything I possess. In exchange I'm asking nothing but this little knickknack as a souvenir; and you . . .

XX Give it back to me!

AA Let's go away from here, my pretty doggie. This gentleman is mean. This gentleman is nasty. This gentleman doesn't love us . . .

XX Are you going to give it back to me or not?

AA Come, my pet, let's leave this gentleman here. We'll go far away from here, far away . . . (*XX tries to snatch the stuffed dog, but AA succeeds in evading him and escaping to the other side of the table. They chase each other around the table.*) Wow! Wow! Look! . . . See how furious the gentleman is! Wow! Wow! Waw! Waw! (*He barks like a dog. The chase continues.*) Don't let him catch you! Run away! (*The moment XX is on the left of the table and AA on the right, XX jumps onto the table and grabs AA by the throat. But only the scarf remains in his hands. AA jumps aside but trips over the chair and falls to the ground with the chair. XX throws himself on top of him. AA holds Pluto up in the air with one hand. XX tries to catch it. AA changes the dog-mascot over into the other hand and throws it far behind himself. The two get up and rush after the mascot like two rugby players after the ball. They throw themselves violently on top of the dog.*)

At this moment, the water starts to run from the tap, which had remained turned on.) Ah! The water! *(AA leaves his partner who clasps the dog-mascot covetously to his chest; AA goes over to the tap and turns it off.)* At last! Now I can make myself a decent cup of tea. *(AA takes the kettle from the table, fills it from the tap, and disappears behind the screen. XX hasn't taken his eyes off him while clutching Pluto very tightly to his chest in an apprehensive attitude. AA emerges from behind the screen.)* What are you doing down there? . . . You praying or something? *(He takes off his coat and hangs it up.)* Come on, that's enough . . . It's time you got up . . .

XX You staying?

AA Only because of the tea. Where else can you make a decent cup of tea if not at home. Ah, home, sweet home! *(XX gets up and hides the stuffed dog under his pillow, i.e., on the bed to the right. He sits down on his bed. AA picks up his scarf and puts it over the back of the left chair; then he picks up the overturned chair on the right.)*

XX I'm going to pay you back as soon as I've got the money.

AA Ah, you want to discuss the rent?

XX Word of honor!

AA It's a small matter. Not really worth talking about.

XX Next month.

AA There's no rush.

XX Well, next week then.

AA But no, please, don't think about it.

XX Okay, the day after tomorrow.

AA Oh!

XX Is that all right, the day after tomorrow? . . . Or even tomorrow. You want it tomorrow?

AA No, really, I assure you. It's of absolutely no importance. Between friends . . .

XX Right now I can't. Word of honor . . .

AA   Aaah! How pleasant it is to be surrounded by all this furniture again
. . . (*He prepares to take off his jacket. XX rushes to help him take it off.*)

XX   Shall I hang it up?

AA   Don't bother. It isn't worth it. Just put it over the chair. (*He seats
himself comfortably in the chair on the left. XX hangs his jacket neatly over
the back of the chair.*)   In return, if you wouldn't mind . . . That light
tires my eyes. It's been troubling me for a long time, but I didn't want
to say anything since it didn't seem to bother you. Quite frankly, that
naked bulb is atrocious. Forgive me if I appear to be criticizing your
interior decorating, but couldn't you make some sort of shade? From
paper or something . . . I'm afraid I've never been particularly good
with my hands.

XX   I'll make one for you.

AA   Perfect. You're really quite unique. Look, there are some magazines
by my bed, use any of them. Unless you prefer ordinary newspaper.
(*XX picks up a magazine from the floor by the bed on the left.*)

XX   I need scissors.

AA   They're on the shelf. (*XX fetches the scissors from the shelf above the
sink. Then he climbs onto the table, unfolds the magazine, and tries to fasten
it around the bulb. AA watches him, shading his eyes with one hand.*)   This
doesn't bother you?

XX   What?

AA   Can you look at the bulb without the disconcerting feeling that
you're going blind?

XX   The bulb?

AA   The light. Doesn't it blind you?

XX   No.

AA   Doesn't it hurt your eyes?

XX   No.

AA   It doesn't make you cry?

XX   No.

AA Your eyelids don't burn? And you don't see little black spots dancing before your eyes? (*A pause.*)

XX No. (*AA climbs on the table. He raises XX's eyelids with his fingers, like a doctor examining a patient's eyes.*)

AA The other one. (*He looks into the other eye.*) Incredible! (*AA comes down from the table. XX continues to busy himself with the shade and the bulb. AA paces back and forth.*) Perhaps it's not so incredible after all. We know there can be considerable deviations from the norm. Both among those with hypersensitivity and those suffering from almost total apathy. It's the same with the speed of reflexes. From the ends of the nerve fibers to the center of the brain. Everything depends on the individual. (*Suddenly he stops.*) Have you ever been interrogated?

XX What?

AA (*Dry, brutal*) By the police?

XX I haven't done anything.

AA I'm not asking you if you've done anything. I'm asking you if you've ever been interrogated.

XX No.

AA (*Resumes a normal tone*) What a pity! You would've made a perfect subject. Not from the point of view of the police, of course. Your insensitivity would've enabled you to endure things that would've broken others. It's a pity, a real pity. You would've made an excellent political prisoner.

XX For me, politics—

AA I know, I know, you keep out of politics. That's what you were going to say, right? One can always dream. (*XX is evidently interested in an ad in the magazine he is using for a shade. He licks his finger, turns the page and looks. . . .*) What eyes! It wouldn't be easy to extort a confession from you. That is, if you had anything to say . . . Too bad. The talent is wasted on you. It's always like that. Those who shouldn't say anything, talk. And those who would be able to keep their mouth shut, have nothing to say.

XX Can I cut this out?

AA   What?

XX   This section here, with all the colors.

AA   You haven't listened to a word I was saying.

XX (*Showing him an ad in full color*)   If I could cut out this ad—just this one . . .

AA   Oh, my God! I keep asking myself if the God of my forefathers was the same as the one yours worshipped.

XX   I'm going to cut it out then.

XX climbs down from the table and sits on the chair to the right, facing the audience. He cuts out the ad. From above we hear music.

AA (*Puts his head between his hands and covers his ears.*)   That's all we need! (*He looks at his watch.*)   Four o'clock? That's impossible. (*He puts his watch to his ear.*)   Just as I thought. It's stopped. Say, what time d'you think it might be?

XX   Around nine o'clock.

AA   That means they've only just started. They're going to celebrate for at least eight hours . . . It's *their* party!

XX   Perhaps they're going to stop early.

AA   No, not tonight. They're. not going to stop. They're going to have fun till dawn. It's New Year's Eve. (*The water kettle whistles behind the screen.*)   Ah, the water! (*AA disappears behind the screen and returns with the kettle. He sits on his chair, pours the water into his plastic tumbler, and drops the tea bag into it. XX drops his arms, the scissors in one hand, the magazine in the other. Above them, the music fades. AA fishes the tea bag out of his tumbler, puts sugar in his tea, and stirs. XX lets the scissors and the magazine drop to the floor. He gets up slowly and walks like an automaton over to his bed (on the right). There he drops down on his back and stares at the ceiling. AA stops stirring his tea and looks attentively at XX.*)   What's the matter with you? . . . Don't you feel well? (*He stirs his tea, then stops again.*)   Are you ill? (*XX doesn't react. AA gets up and approaches him.*)   Hey—why don't you answer? (*He shakes XX by the arm, whereupon he rolls over to face the wall, turning his back to AA. AA appears to give up. He picks up the scissors and the magazine and goes back to XX.*)   Hey, you haven't finished. . . . Here! It's all yours. Take it, cut, cut as much as you want—the fridges, the vacuum cleaners, the cars and motorcycles, the transistor radios and outboard motors, the telephones and intercoms, the TVs and VCRs—it's stupid, but I'm not stopping you. Go ahead, cut all you like! . . . It goes without saying that you may do as you please . . . You have my permission . . . D'you hear? What's the matter? Are you annoyed or something? (*He sits down on the bed.*) If you want me to, I'll cut them out for you . . . Say something! D'you want me to cut them out for you? (*He cuts the color ads out of the magazine and then puts the scissors on the floor.*) Well, there it is . . . It's done. They're nice, don't you think? (*He holds the ads at arm's length and looks at them with a grin.*) Hey, look at them! . . . (*Enraged.*) You might at least look! Who d'you think I've cut them all out for? . . . Why don't you answer? . . . Are you manic-depressive? (*For a moment he sits without moving. Through the pipes we hear "Stille Nacht, Heilige Nacht," or "Minuit Chrétien," sung by a children's choir. Abruptly, XX buries his head in his pillow.*) Aha . . . so that's it! (*AA gets up and looks around. He is evidently considering something. Then he makes a decision. He takes everything that's on the table and puts it on the floor close to the wall. He empties the tea into the sink and rinses the tumblers. He goes to his bed, takes the pillowcase off his pillow, and spreads it across the table like a tablecloth. Then he fetches a bottle of cognac from his suitcase and puts it on the table. He places a package of cigarettes, which he had hidden under his pillow, next to the bottle. He puts the tumblers alongside. Then he dons his jacket. During that time the music has slowly faded.*) It's ready! . . . Hey! Wake up! . . . It's ready!

XX (*Sticking his head out from under his pillow*) What is it?

AA (*Solemnly*) The New Year. (*XX covers his head again with his pillow. AA pulls it away.*)

XX Leave me in peace!

AA Out of the question! I'm not going to drink by myself.

XX (*Defending himself*) I don't want any tea.

AA Who is talking of tea? I have something better, for such an occasion.

XX (*Seeing the bottle, he sits up.*) Where did you get that?

AA Never mind! I am treating you . . . Put on your jacket!

XX What for?

AA Because this is a festive occasion . . . A feast, a ball, a ceremony, a celebration, a cult, a custom, a ritual! Our good-bye to the year that's passing away . . . We welcome the New Year, a new era, a new life, everything is new. Alleluia! You are not going to stay in your shirtsleeves for such an elegant party, are you? . . . Come on! Get up, move, enjoy yourself! . . . (*He forces XX to get up and leads him to the table. He takes the jacket which hangs over the chair on the right and gives it to XX.*)   Straighten your tie! Button up! Comb yourself! After all, you don't want the New Year to be sick at the sight of you, do you?

XX You don't have a tie.

AA Me? . . . Yes, that's true.

XX So then?

AA Yes, but it's different in my case. I never wear a tie. It's not my style. (*XX takes off his jacket, hands it to AA, and goes back to his bed.*)   Wait. (*XX lies down on his bed again.*)   Is it really necessary? Really? Do I have to?

XX If it's a party, it's a party . . .

AA Very well. (*AA goes to his bed; on the way he hangs the jacket of XX over the chair on the right. He fetches his suitcase from under his bed, opens it, and brings out a tie. He puts on the tie in front of the mirror. XX watches him, then gets up and goes to sit on the chair to the right. He pulls a handkerchief from his pocket and uses it to polish his shoes. AA turns to him with his tie.*)   Is that all right now?

XX (*After taking a long look*)   When is the last time you shaved?

AA I don't remember.

XX Yes, exactly. You need a shave.

AA Ah, no! You're not going to ask me to shave right now.

XX If I can do it, you can do it too, no?

AA Nowadays it isn't necessary to shave anymore.

XX Not every day, no. But a holiday is different . . .

AA Okay, I'm prepared to shave. But on one condition.

XX What?

AA That you change your socks.

XX (*Looks with astonishment at his feet; he is wearing socks full of holes.*) Why? They're still quite clean . . .

AA It's either that or nothing.

XX If I put on my shoes, you can't see anything.

AA It's an ultimatum.

XX Okay, okay . . . (*XX gets out a suitcase made of pressed paper from under his bed and brings out a pair of socks. He takes off his old socks and puts them in the suitcase. He puts on the new pair of socks—they have at least as many holes as the old ones. During that time AA takes off his jacket and hangs it over the chair on the left. He stops in front of the mirror and starts to shave. Waiting for AA to finish his shave, XX remains seated, without moving. He continues to watch AA. He smiles.*) I can't wait till it's spring.

AA Why?

XX Because, I tell you, in spring some women go without panties.

AA Here we go again.

XX It's true, I'm telling you . . . We're digging ditches now, laying sewage pipes.

AA I don't see the connection.

XX Come on. When one of them walks by up above, you can get a look from below.

AA So that's how the common man gets his kicks.

XX Just now we're working in a ritzy district. Working in the east end isn't worth the effort. You see few people, and the women are either ugly or old. But where we are now we get the elegant ones . . . in fur coats and such. One of us is always on the lookout. He gives us a signal when a juicy one is coming. The best place is outside a department store, near the lingerie section. Or by a ladies' hairdresser. One time, I remember, we were laying cables in front of a chic restaurant . . . the ideal depth—five feet. Up above there was only a small plank . . . Oh, my God! I thought I'd twist my neck. That was a fine place to work . . . You should come some day.

AA   No, thank you. I have other possibilities.

XX   The worst was when we worked outside an army barracks. For two whole weeks we saw nothing but uniforms.

AA   Does your wife go to the hairdresser?

XX   No, of course not.

AA   To the restaurant?

XX   What d'you think? Where I come from you eat at home.

AA   She goes shopping then.

XX   Yes. (*A pause.*)   But back home, in our village, there are no sewage pipes or water mains.

AA   But there's an army barracks.

XX   Yes. How d'you know?

AA   It's easy. Back home there are army barracks everywhere. —So, perhaps she walks past the barracks.

XX   Yes?

AA   Your wife. (*A pause.*)

XX   What's that supposed to mean?

AA   Nothing. I've finished. (*Rinses his face and then dries himself with his towel.*)   Now, let's celebrate! (*XX gets up. Facing each other, they put on their jackets simultaneously, AA to the left and XX to the right of the table. Then they sit down at the same time. AA opens the bottle and fills their glasses.*)

XX   Were you married?

AA   Twice.

XX   How so?

AA   I was divorced . . . Cheers!

XX   Children?

AA What children? —Oh, no, I have no children.

XX So, why did you get married?

AA What d'you mean—"why"? For love . . . Because our minds met—is that good enough? Come on, drink! (*They drink. AA takes a cigarette and offers XX the package. XX takes a cigarette, too. AA searches his pockets for matches. XX gets a box of matches out of his right pocket, but puts it back right away. He gets another box out of his left pocket, gives AA a light, and then lights his own cigarette. He puts the box of matches back into his left pocket. The two of them inhale. Pause.*)

XX Tell me, why did you run away?

AA (*His thoughts interrupted*) What?

XX Why did you run away from the Old Country? Weren't you well-off there? You had two women, a home in the big city . . . You made a good living, you moved in the best circles, lots of VIPs, I bet . . . And here?

AA One doesn't run away toward something . One runs away from something.

XX Exactly. But back home you were better off than here.

AA One day I was walking in the park. There were children having fun on the playground. Suddenly I saw a boy a little older than they, hiding behind a lilac bush. He was picking up stones and throwing them at the children and then quickly hiding again behind the lilac bush. He gave me the impression of someone sneering at the world. He was perfectly content doing that, even cheerful. A strapping boy, strong clever . . . Each time he threw a stone he hid behind the lilac bush. (*A pause.*)

XX How old was he?

AA Probably around ten or twelve.

XX (*Moved*) Same age as mine.

AA Yes. It could've been your son. (*A pause.*)

XX And after that?

AA Nothing. That's all.

XX   Sure, sure . . . And now tell me the truth.

AA   That is the truth.

XX   You're not going to tell me that you emigrated because some brat
threw stones in a park. He didn't even throw them at you. So, out
with it. You can talk to me like a brother.

AA   Well, let's say . . . let's say I always had a problem with diction. For
instance, the word "generalissimo" . . . It's too difficult for me. I've
never succeeded in pronouncing it correctly.

XX   You? But you've got an education.

AA   Well, yes. Maybe it's not so much a question of diction as of
intonation, of the right note . . . I always sang out of tune.

XX (*In a low voice, confidentially*)   Are you . . . a political refugee?

AA   You could call it that. (*XX gets up from the table.*)   You mean you
never had any idea? (*XX goes toward the door and stops, turning his back on
AA.*)

XX   And you tell me that only now?

AA   I thought it was clear from the beginning. (*XX half opens the door
with infinite care, furtively sticks his head out, closes the door, and comes back
to the table.*)

XX   Are you on the list?

AA   Probably. (*XX remains standing, undecided.*)   What are you standing
for?

XX (*Siting down*)   I was a fool! (*Hits his forehead with his fist.*)   Still, from
the beginning I thought there was something suspicious about you.
He does nothing; he doesn't go to work; he lies on his bed all day
long, reading. And those soft hands, well groomed . . . An intellectual!

AA   How do you know I don't do anything? Because you think that
work consists only of digging ditches with a pneumatic drill?

XX   Okay, you tell me what you do on that bed?

AA   I think.

XX (*Irritated and scornful*)   Yeah . . . What about?

AA You, for instance. I ask myself if you would be capable of being an informer.

XX A what?

AA That is to say, could you denounce me? Not now, of course, and not here. But back home in the Old Country . . .

XX Back home we wouldn't have known each other.

AA You think one can only denounce people one knows, or friends? No. Listen. Let's assume you are in prison and I come to suggest that you escape. Or better still, I come to you with a plan to free all the prisoners. What would you do? Would you call the guards and hand me over to them?

XX In what prison?

AA In a prison where you're not that badly off. Maybe better than outside, free. Where you have enough to eat, where you're never cold.

XX I've never heard of a prison like that.

AA But a prison where one thing is forbidden, one single thing. It is forbidden to use words that start with the letter *P*. All words that start with a *P* are forbidden. Both in spoken and in written language.

XX Why?

AA So that nobody can write or speak the word "prison." You can have recourse to allusions or to synonyms. But the word "prison" is forbidden. It's forbidden to say it, to write it, even to think it.

XX That's not a prison.

AA Well, if I were to propose to you . . .

XX (*Jumps up*) What in hell d'you want from me?

AA I don't want anything! I merely ask myself what would have happened if I had actually proposed to . . .

XX I have a wife and children!

AA And I, I've . . . I've . . . Come to think of it, what do I have? Let's say I have my words . . . my dear, my beloved words, words that begin with all the letters of the alphabet. No, I am not proposing anything, I am not suggesting anything to you . . . Come on, sit down, and let's drink! You are not in any danger with me. I am a political refugee all right, but I am not an agitator. (*XX sits down. AA pours drinks.*)   Here you are! A toast to common sense and simple minds! Prosit! Skoal! Cheers! Down the hatch! *Tchin-tchin!* (*XX doesn't drink.*)   Don't be afraid! I'm just a dishrag. A coward. And perhaps, from a normal, simple human point of view—a bastard. . . . Come on, drink! . . . We're by ourselves. (*XX puts his glass down.*) Why aren't you drinking? (*XX is silent.*)   I understand. Now you think I'm a government agent.

XX   Eh, no!

AA   Admit it. I said I was a bastard, so you conclude I must be a government agent, right? (*XX is silent. AA raises his glass.*)   Shall we drink? (*XX doesn't react.*)   Well, well. You know, if you take a dislike to a loyal servant of your government, that raises certain doubts in your loyalty to the regime. That's bad, that's very bad, my friend. What if I really were a government spy?

XX   I never said that.

AA   But you thought it. So why not say it out loud? What harm would it do? (*XX remains silent. A pause.*)   Hmm. I'm beginning to understand. You've decided that if my mission is secret, you as a loyal citizen must not let on that you have any knowledge of it. Very good. A loyal subject should always pretend to suspect nothing. Bravo! Now you should also make my task a little easier by attacking the government a little. A few seditious ideas? A little criticism of the regime? How about it? . . . Don't feel constrained on my account. In the presence of a government agitator, a loyal citizen must not be too loyal, precisely to prove his loyalty.

XX   I don't understand what you're talking about.

AA   That's not important. I appeal to your common sense. Drink with me!—to prove that you're on the side of the regime! Remember I can report you to the authorities if I'm a secret government agent.

XX   I don't want to drink with you.

AA   Careful! I represent the state . . . the government . . . the regime . . . political power—

XX It's not because of that.

AA But why then?

XX Because you said you were a bastard.

AA Exactly. So what?

XX Well, that's all, it's because of that.

AA You mean you don't want to drink with a bastard?

XX Oh, why shouldn't I? Of course I can drink with a bastard. That's not the point. It's because you said we're among ourselves here. That means that I too am a bastard.

AA So, then, you don't consider yourself a bastard?

XX No.

AA Which means you think you're better than I.

XX That's not true. It's just that I don't see why I should be a bastard. What have I done for you to treat me like that? Tell me, why do you treat me like a bastard? (*AA is silent.*) If you don't know why, you should shut up instead of insulting me. One doesn't go around insulting people without reason. (*A pause.*)

AA All right. Let's say I exaggerated a little.

XX In that case, it's different. That means we're not among ourselves here.

AA Let's say—not quite.

XX (*Delighted*) But that changes everything. I can drink with you now.

AA That suits me fine.

XX (*Relieved*) So, let's drink.

AA We've settled our differences.

XX Right. (*They clink glasses and drink.*)

AA You know, it's strange . . . I wonder why I'm the only one of us who could possibly be a government agent?

XX Oh, stop it!

AA   Which means that only I could ever be suspected. The idea of suspecting you of being a government agent would never enter my head.

XX   Will you stop it, please!

AA   All right. I shan't insist.

XX   How long is it till midnight?

AA   I don't know. My watch has stopped.

XX   Maybe we could ask somebody.

AA   No. It's not worth the trouble. They're going to drink champagne upstairs. We will hear the corks pop at midnight.

XX   Yeah . . . And at home, they're waiting for me. Like every year. The children are waiting for me, they're hoping I'll come back . . . And once again I won't be there. Ah, what a life . . . what a life!

AA   But why haven't you gone back for a visit? You can . . . You're not a political refugee. You could go home for your vacation.

XX   Vacation? Me? I never get a vacation.

AA   But you could ask for one.

XX   Good God! You think I'm here to have a vacation? I'm here to make money. I shall take a vacation when I get back. A whole week. I shall wrap myself in a blanket, lie down in the orchard, and I shall sleep. I won't as much as move a little finger. Now and again I'll open one eye to make sure the sky is still there and then I go back to sleep. There'll only be the wife to bring me food. And after . . .

AA   Well, after that?

XX   After, I'll get up and get dressed. In style. Nothing but clothes from abroad.

AA   Why?

XX   What d'you mean "why"? Because it'll be my birthday.

AA   Your birthday?

XX   Sure. My birthday happens to be in May. I'll invite the whole village. Oh, I don't mean everybody. There are some I don't like;

they don't get invited. That'll teach them. —We'll kill a pig, a calf, or maybe a cow. . . . And I'm going to buy plenty of liquor . . . enough for everybody, and even to have some left over—I want them to have a good time, enjoy themselves, so they know I've come back from abroad. We'll spread everything out in the hall. For everybody to see. But not to touch, mind you. Just to look at. I'm going to ask my brother-in-law to watch things. Not that you can trust him, either.

AA You could get a dog.

XX A dog?

AA Yes, a watchdog. He wouldn't let anyone touch a thing. You'd tie him up, of course, so that he couldn't steal what he was supposed to guard.

XX That's a good idea. —After that, we'll have a party that lasts three days.

AA That I don't doubt.

XX And when the party is over, you know what I'm going to do then?

AA Obviously, you're going to clean up after the guests.

XX Like hell I will. My mother-in-law'll do that. No. I'm going to build my house.

AA No?!

XX Yes. A beautiful house. In stone. Two stories. And with central heating.

AA You must be joking.

XX The most beautiful house in the village. With my own money.

AA That's going to take a while.

XX Several years. But when I'm finished, we're going to move out of our in-laws' place and go live by ourselves. In our own house. Eh? So what d'you think of that?

AA It's a fine project . . . (*He gets up and raises his glass.*) Well . . . To your house!

XX To my house! (*They drink. Suddenly, the hand in which XX holds his glass begins to tremble.*)

AA   Watch out! You're going to upset your glass. Hold on, goddammit, you're going to spill half of it! What's the matter with you? (*XX is unable to hold his glass and puts it on the table. He sits facing the audience, turning his profile to AA, who puts his glass on the table too and goes over to XX.*)   Let me see your hands. (*XX puts his hands in his pockets.*)   Let me see your hands! (*Reluctantly, XX takes his hands out of his pockets.*) Show me! (*XX stretches out his arms, clenching his fists.*)   Not like this! Straighten them! (*AA forcibly opens his fists. XX turns away his head as he holds out his arms in front of AA. His hands shake in jerks. AA turns aside without looking at him. XX puts his hands back into his pockets.*)   Have you had this for long?

XX   A year.

AA   Often?

XX   No. Just every once in a while.

AA   More and more frequently? (*XX is silent.*)   I am asking you if this happens more and more frequently. (*XX is silent. AA takes his glass, goes to stand behind him, and with his left arm gives him a twist that forces him to tilt his head backward. He pushes the glass against his mouth. XX drinks the contents of the glass. AA replaces the empty glass on the table and picks up his own full glass. He empties it in one gulp and then puts it back on the table.*)

XX   (*Coughing and spitting*)   Thanks very much.

AA   Why don't you learn the language? (*XX goes on coughing, though now deliberately, in order to gain time.*)   I am asking you why you don't learn the language?

XX   What language?

AA   The language people here speak.

XX   (*Takes his hands out of his pockets and looks at them: They are still trembling.*)   It's going to go away soon. (*Puts his hands back in his pockets.*)

AA   Are you going to answer me or what?

XX   You mean why don't I speak their language?

AA   You know damn well what I mean. You're an illiterate in this country—worse, a deaf-mute!

xx I don't want to learn their language.

aa Why not? You live in this country. You eat here, you drink, you walk the streets like people here—so why don't you want to speak like them? You could get a better job . . .

xx They're not people.

aa No?

xx No. They're not human. There aren't any real people here.

aa And where, according to you, are these real people?

xx Back home.

aa Ah, yes.

xx (*Takes his hands out of his pocket and looks at them*)   It's over. (*Puts his hands back into his pockets.*)

aa Do you know what happens to people who work with a pneumatic drill for too long?

xx They age more quickly.

aa Not only.

xx They go a little deaf. (*He takes one hand out of his pocket and puts a finger in his ear.*)   After a while I get a buzz in my ear. I don't hear very well anymore.

aa That's normal. But there are other things.

xx (*Takes his finger out of his ear and his other hand out of his pocket.*)   It's over now. (*Puts his hands back into his pocket.*)

aa The buzzing?

xx No . . . My hands.

aa That's nothing. And the noise in your ear is nothing either. There's worse to come. As a result of exposure to the vibrations for ten hours a day, certain modifications occur in the conjunctive tissue, that is to say, in the tissue by which the flesh is attached to the bone. How long have you had this?

xx (*Looks at his outstretched arms*)   They've stopped shaking.

AA   I'm asking you how long you've been working with this machine.

XX   Three years.

AA   These modifications of the conjunctive tissue constitute a process of degeneration. In other words, the flesh begins to detach itself from the bones . . . The consequence is, of course, a total incapacity to work.

XX   Are you serious?

AA   Sickness and disability. It's a question of medically established facts. It's a terrible occupational disease.

XX   (*He's afraid*)   Eh, don't give me all this bullshit. You're just trying to scare me.

AA   (*Seizing XX by his lapels*)   You think you're a man, don't you? Well, you're nothing but an animal. You're not a human being at all. Not even a bastard! You're neither man nor dog, that's for sure! . . . A calf. Worse, an ox! A dull, helpless, stupid ox! A complete ox. Good only for pulling a plow till the moment you drop dead . . . Pulling a plow—that's what makes you happy! And you can't get enough of it! . . . You're happy, right? You're happy, no? (*He shakes XX.*)

XX   Don't shake me!

AA   (*Shakes him*)   I'll shake you till you wake up from your bovine dream. Because when you don't work you sleep . . . or you chew the cud. I shall go on shaking you and shouting at you till I've made a man of you. And I won't stop till I've achieved that. Because as long as you remain an ox, I'll be a bastard. The one goes with the other. The ox and the bastard. And I'll be the vilest of bastards so long as you're an ox in his yoke. There's no other way.

XX   (*Menacing*)   Don't shake me! I'm warning you! . . .

AA   You are going to defend yourself? It doesn't make any difference. Someday you're going to understand . . . and then you'll be grateful to me. Because it's not possible for only one of us to be a man. It's either both of us or neither. (*He launches into a lyrical flight of speech, partly under the influence of the alcohol he's drunk. He continues to hold XX by the lapels.*)   And when at last both of us can stand on our own two feet, we shall stand upright. We shall raise our heads. And then we shall see above us a branch, gently swaying. A branch bearing fruit.

The forbidden fruit! And the wind that moves that branch is the wind of history. And we hold out our hand and . . . (*XX slaps his hands. AA drops his jacket and staggers back.*)

XX   Don't you touch me! (*He gets up.*)   Who are you raising your hand against? Who? Eh?

AA   Don't you understand?

XX   What? You raised your hand against me! Against me! (*Furious, he goes toward AA.*)   You goddamn louse, you asshole, you son of a bitch! . . . You're going to see . . .

He raises his arm, ready to strike AA. The light goes out. Total darkness. Up above we hear people exclaim in chorus: the typical "aaah" of surprise that people produce when it suddenly turns dark. Then the sound of a trumpet and of whistling. At the same time a clock strikes twelve. In the distance bells begin to toll.

AA (*Voice only: in the dark*)   Midnight!

XX (*Voice only*)   Why has the light gone out?

AA   They turn them off at midnight on New Year's Eve. That's the custom here. (*A pause.*)   You have any matches? (*XX strikes a match. AA goes behind the screen and returns with a candlestick. He lights the candle with the match XX holds. He puts the candle on the table and turns to XX.*)   Good.

XX (*Scratches his neck with an embarrassed air*)   Ehm well . . .

AA   Now then, we could . . .

XX   As you like . . .

AA   In that case . . .

XX   Yes . . . ehm . . .

AA   Of course . . .

XX   Why not . . .

AA   Certainly . . .

XX   Sure . . .

AA   Well, let's drink . . . (*He pours new drinks.*)   To the New Year!

XX (*Raising his glass*)   To the New Year! (*They clink glasses and empty them. They are still a little stiff, embarrassed, uneasy. They sit down, AA on the chair to the left, XX on the right.*)   Listen to the bells!

AA Church bells.

XX Well, I wish you . . .

AA Likewise . . .

XX The past . . . is the past.

AA Let's forget all that . . . (*Offers XX his hand.*)

XX Well then. . . . I guess we should . . . (*Extends his hand to AA.*)

AA All the best . . .

XX Happy New Year! (*They shake hands across the table. They light their cigarettes, as before, following the same scenario, with one difference: XX does not go through his number with the two boxes of matches. They make themselves comfortable. From that moment on they are visibly under the influence of alcohol, especially XX.*)   Eeeh . . . New Year—how time passes! . . . Everything passes . . . I remember . . . it's a long time ago, I was still a boy, I tended the cows. I used to climb trees to take the eggs out of the crows' nests . . . I went to school barefoot. But only in the fall. In the spring there was too much work in the fields. And in the winter it was too cold. Then my father left for the city. But my grandparents stayed. Old people are funny. They prefer to stay. It was a wretched life, but they stayed. I guess they must've loved all that misery, eh?

AA That's not for me to judge.

XX Well, I didn't love it. (*Strikes his forehead.*)   And no one's ever going to make me say that I loved it.

AA Who, in his right mind, loves misery?

XX My father didn't either. He loved it so little that he drank away all the money he earned. And after that he loved it even less. So he went on drinking . . . But me, I don't drink.

AA That's good.

XX Because I hate poverty. I like having things. When I hold

something in my hands then I have it. And when I let it drop . . .
well, then I haven't got it no more, right?

AA That's right.

XX I work my ass off, but I get paid for it. And when I've gotten paid
. . . I'll be rich . . . So it pays off . . . Right?

AA It makes sense.

XX Only, sometimes I wonder what's the use of it all?

AA "All" what?

XX Well, all I've got . . . I can't take it with me when I die. They
won't let me get into paradise with it . . . and there's nothing I can do
with it in hell. So why do I slave like this?

AA It's you who wants it that way.

XX Sure, but what do I get out of it? I'm ruining my health . . . And I
don't have any pleasures. I don't drink . . . I don't smoke . . . except
when you offer me one . . .

AA (*Offers him his package of cigarettes*) Go ahead, help yourself! Please!

XX God bless you. (*He takes a cigarette but then throws it back on the
table.*) Tell me . . . what's the use. Eh? Why?

AA What about your children? You're going to build a house. You can
leave that to your children when your time is up.

XX And they, who're they going to leave it to?

AA Their children.

XX Ah . . . (*Pause.*) And how is it going to end?

AA It doesn't end. Why d'you want it to end?

XX Just like that, eh? . . . It doesn't end. You mean it'll never end?

AA That's right—never.

XX Hm . . . So you say there's no end . . . But how can that be seeing
there was a beginning?

AA You're asking some pretty difficult questions. Schopenhauer already
wrestled with them.

XX Who?

AA Schopenhauer.

XX A Jew?

AA Not necessarily.

XX Well, I don't like any of this. If there's a beginning there ought to be an end. If not, you can't have a beginning either . . . A hopeless beginning . . . And all this time I do nothing but slave and slave and slave. Never any pleasures . . . I never go to the cinema . . . I never go to any tarts . . You think that's easy, do you?

AA I never said it was.

XX To bitch, like you, that's easy! But if you ever tried to live like me . . . (*He succumbs increasingly to self-pity.*) You know how I live? . . . Like an animal! Like a dog!

AA No, you exaggerate a little.

XX (*Striking the table with his fist*) Don't you go contradicting me! Yes, like a dog! You said that yourself!

AA If you remember, I was talking of an ox.

XX (*Bending close to AA, confidentially*) Come here. I'm going to tell you something.

AA I'm listening.

XX Closer . . . (*He puts his hands on AA's arms and pulls him closer to himself until their foreheads seem to touch. He whispers something with passion but discreetly.*) And . . . and you were right. (*They return to their previous positions.*)

AA (*With an exaggeratedly polite tone; upper-class*) But no, my dear boy . . .

XX (*Putting his index finger to his lips*) Hush! . . . (*He cries.*) Like a dog! . . . Dogs live better than I do. At least they don't have to work so hard . . . what sort of a life is this, eh? Tell me, you call that living?

AA From a strictly biological point of view . . .

XX Yes or no—is that what life is about?

AA It depends.

XX (*Settling the question*) No. That's no kind of life . . . Pour us a drink!

AA Perhaps we've had enough for now.

XX No, it's not enough! This is the first time I've had a drink since I came here. It's well deserved, don't you think?

AA Without any doubt. (*AA refills the glasses. They drink.*)

XX Ah, that feels good . . . I'm going to give you a riddle.

AA Go ahead!

XX Here it is: has, but has not.

AA Wait a minute: "has . . ."

XX . . . but has not. (*He laughs.*)

AA "Has, but has not . . . Has, but has not . . ."—I have no idea.

XX Guess!

AA I can't. it's too difficult for me. (*XX strikes his chest with his fist.*) You? . . .

XX Me.

AA "Has . . ."

XX . . . but has not! That's good, isn't it? (*He bursts out laughing.*)

AA What is it that he "has"?

XX (*Stops laughing; in menacing tone*) 'Cause you don't think I have anything?

AA Do you?

XX You think I'm a have-not? My father was a have-not, my grandfather was a have-not, but not me! Okay, I'm gonna show you . . . (*He tries to get up, supporting himself heavily on the table.*)

AA Never mind. It's not necessary. (*He puts his hands on XX's arms and pushes him down again. XX pulls away violently.*)

XX I can afford it! Waiter! (*He makes a grand gesture across the table.*) This is my round.

AA　He is drunk . . . (*Pause. XX falls silent and lowers his head. AA inspects the bulb in the lamp.*)　What's the matter with the light? (*Pause. XX gets up and staggers to the sink.*)

XX　Turn it on.

AA　It is turned on.

XX　Ah . . . (*Pause. XX is looking for the sink in the half-dark.*)　What's turned on?

AA　The light.

XX　Aha . . . Now, if it's turned on, why are we in the dark?

AA　Because it's switched off. (*XX finally finds the sink. He puts his head under the tap and lets the water run.*)　. . . Having said that, I ask myself why it is switched off. It should have come back on.

XX　(*His head still under the tap*)　The New Year! The New Year!

AA　Yes, but it's taking a little too long.

XX　Maybe it's the bulb . . . (*AA picks up the candle and climbs on a chair. He inspects the bulb, using the candle to give him light.*)

AA　No. The bulb is all right. (*He climbs down from the chair, goes to the door, and opens it. He takes a quick look outside along the hall.*) Everybody is in the dark. Perhaps it's a short circuit, or a power failure . . . (*He closes the door again and puts the candle back on the table.*)　That's going to be the end of the candle.

XX　(*Trying to parody him*)　"That's going to be the end of the candle." . . . if you push down my cock like a handle.

AA　(*Irritated*)　Very funny . . .

XX　(*Turns off the tap and dries his face vigorously with his hand.*)　You don't like that?

AA　No.

XX　Maybe you don't like me either.

AA　No.

XX　Well then what are you doing here, with me? (*Pause.*)

AA　That's a fundamental question.

xx   I didn't ask you to come here.

AA   True.

xx   You invited yourself. (*Pause. XX sits down, this time in the chair on the left of the table.*)   Eh! Tell me, really, what in hell d'you want here with me?

AA (*Sitting down on the chair to the right.*)   Now? At this table?

xx   I'm not talking of the table. I want to know what you're doing here with me in this shitty place. (*AA shrugs his shoulders.*)   What are you doing here?

AA   The same as you.

xx   That's not true. I have no choice. I'm a complete ox, an illiterate, an animal . . . But you, you've got an education, you speak foreign languages . . . You don't have to stay here.

AA   That's correct.

xx   You can make out anywhere. You can be successful anywhere— "Spic Ingliche" and all that . . . So what are you doing here? What are you looking for?

AA   Nothing.

xx   No, you're looking for something from me. Occasionally I ask myself questions: I am nothing to you, a stranger. You give me food to eat, you lend me money . . . You bitch about it, but you lend it to me . . . If you're not happy, what are you doing here with me? I'm not holding you back. Eh! What d'you want from me?

AA   Nothing.

xx   Don't treat me like an imbecile! I may be a brute, but I'm not an imbecile . . . You can tell me everything. After all, we're drinking together. Eh! Why are you drinking with me?

AA   To atone.

xx   Atone for what?

AA   For the sins of my forefathers. Our forefathers never drank together.

XX Is that a sin?

AA Yes, that's a sin. A national sin.

XX You're pulling my leg.

AA You don't believe me?

XX No.

AA You're right. You have the sound instinct of our people. In that case, I say to hell with our forefathers. Today, it's me, all alone . . . me . . . going to the people, fraternizing with the people, you understand? I am a *narodnik,* a populist.

XX A what?

AA A *narodnik* . . . That's a nineteenth-century word. The idea, too, comes from the nineteenth century . . . It says that we must go back to the people, because our strength comes from the people . . .

XX That's a lot of bullshit.

AA Here we have the natural scepticism of the people. You have so many good qualities: a sound instinct, a sense of truth, the capacity for self-criticism . . . Well . . . I may be a philosopher, rationalist, and progressive, but you—you are the locomotive of history, the vanguard of humanity. So what is so strange about my drinking with a locomotive? What is so surprising about my preparing a plate of fried eggs for the vanguard of humanity? That I walk in my drawers in the same room with it and that I wipe my mouth with the same napkin as it? Have you ever thought of that? Eh?

XX Bullshit.

AA All right. Let's forget about mystical sentiments of guilt and atonement for sins committed by past generations. Let's forget about nationalist dreams. Perhaps I am a socialist.

XX Never.

AA Why?

XX Because I know socialists. We've got one that comes to the yard. Very polite. He never insults us. On the contrary. He's all smiles, he flatters us and brings us pamphlets, he explains things to us . . .

AA I don't, eh?

XX No.

AA I suppose I insult you?

XX And how! You're never content. This isn't right and that isn't right . . . And you keep on insulting me with your criticisms. One can see right away you're a gentleman, not a socialist.

AA I see that one cannot fool you.

XX That's for sure. I'm much too clever for that. I can see what's what right away. A socialist? I can smell them a mile away. But you, what could you possibly be, I mean seriously . . .

AA All right, what about a political agitator?

XX Eh? . . . No, never. I'm small-fry. The authorities aren't interested in me. It's the same here as in the old country. I'm good for nothing but hard work. If you were an agitator you wouldn't be staying here with me. You'd be somewhere else, with more important people— professors, people who think.

AA Do you never think?

XX Doesn't matter what I think . . . You want to know what I think? . . . I think of making money, of my children . . . of my good wife . . . Sometimes I think of tarts, too. That's natural. Everybody thinks of that. The authorities aren't interested in that sort of thing. So long as I don't try to be a smart aleck, so long as I stay quietly in my corner and do my work, the authorities don't care a damn what I think. They wouldn't bother sending an agitator here.

AA Have you never thought about freedom?

XX Meaning what?

AA Well . . . to be free.

XX How d'you mean?

AA Well, for example, to say what you think.

XX I already told you what I think. And I can repeat it for you. I can say it over and over from morning till night and from night till morning. Nobody stops me from saying what I think.

AA   But have you never thought about thinking any further?

XX   Think about thinking?

AA   You could put it like that . . .

XX   Certainly not. I'm not that stupid.

AA   There is nothing stupid about thinking.

XX   That depends. Back home in my village, we had an idiot. He never did anything because he was no good at anything. He wasn't even good enough to look after the cows. He lived alone in a house, only from what people gave him. Well then, what was he doing when he did nothing? What was he thinking? What could he think about when he didn't know how to do anything and when he didn't do anything. He thought only about thinking, he thought about nothing else but his thoughts. And do you think he was intelligent? No, he was stupid . . . He was a lunatic.

AA   But he was free.

XX   Now I understand. You're a priest.

AA   A priest? Don't make me laugh.

XX   Yes. You're a priest of freedom. That's it. I should've known right away. When you shook me by the collar. A priest with his catechism! A priest who comes and says: Beware of the power of the devil! Don't serve Satan! Serve Jesus Christ! But who is your Jesus Christ? Where is he? Show me? Is your God freedom? Then show me your freedom! Where is it? What is it? . . . I know only one kind of freedom—the freedom not to have to go to work. On Sundays, that's when I'm free. Give me seven Sundays a week and I shall kiss your feet as if you were Jesus himself. Seven Sundays— but paid!

AA   And if I were to take away from you even that single Sunday?

XX   You? What can you do? You can do nothing. You can give nothing and take nothing away from me. All you can do is lie on your divan and make up sermons. You're a divan apostle!

AA   You're right, I can't do anything. But the authorities can.

xx Which means that one must be on the right side of the authorities. Because if they can take things away, they can also give things. But you—you don't like the authorities, do you?

aa I don't exactly dote on them.

xx That's why they don't like you. And you want to know why you don't like them?

aa I can't wait to find out.

xx Because, before the authorities, you're no better than me—with all your books and studies . . . You don't like that, eh? You think you're smarter than me when it comes to dealing with the authorities, don't you? . . . Well, when there's only one authority we're all equal, because we're all equally shit-scared! In a dictatorship we're all the same.

aa Like in a public urinal.

xx Why not? I'm not squeamish.

aa Hear, hear! Come, let me embrace you.

xx What for?

aa Because you didn't let me down. I was right to count on you. I need precisely somebody like you. An ideal slave.

xx And you don't think you're a priest?

aa No. —All right, I confess there were times when an evangelizing fancy took me. But that was before I understood . . . You don't have to be afraid that I'll try to convert you. The impulse has died. It was a passing foible, a momentary temptation. In fact, I'm not at all cut out to be a missionary. And besides, evangelizing is not my cup of tea.

xx So you side with the authorities?

aa Wrong again. No, I'm a very special case. I need a slave. Not for purposes of practical exploitation, of course. No. I need you as a model . . . You're indispensable to me as a landmark . . . Especially here.

xx You're talking bullshit again.

aa I'm not talking bullshit. You asked me to tell you who I really am and what I'm doing here with you. Now I'm going to tell you: I am the knight of the last chance—and do you know who my last chance is? You!

XX   I'm what?

AA   My only and my last chance . . . my muse . . . my inspiration . . .

XX   Hey, don't tell me you're homosexual.

AA   Listen. You are right, in a dictatorship all people are equal. Fear creates that equality. It took me a long time to reach that truth. And with what ease you made that discovery, with what simplicity you expressed such a fundamental fact! . . . I envy you. Sometimes simple humility is more insightful than intelligence.

XX   I told you before that I'm not as stupid as that.

AA   It leaves me speechless to see how a man, an intelligent man at that, like me, can refuse to see the most obvious truth when that truth hurts his pride. I behaved like a monkey in a cage. I swung back and forth from my tail, I took running leaps from the pole to the wire fencing and back again to the pole, or when somebody threw me a nut I tried to get into the shell, all in order to feel the master of infinite spaces. It took me a long time to lose all my illusions, to reach an extremely simple conclusion: namely that I was a monkey in a cage.

XX   They're amusing, monkeys are. I've seen them in the zoo.

AA   You are right. Monkeys in a cage can be very amusing. When I finally realized that I was a monkey in a cage, I began to laugh at myself, and I laughed and laughed . . . till that laughter caught me by the throat and gave me the hiccups, till it turned into tears that drenched my monkey gob. That's when I realized that my antics weren't funny—except to the spectators and the keepers of the zoo: They never tired of throwing me nuts and candies, but the candies made me sick and I couldn't get inside the nutshells. That's how I learned that there's no way out for a monkey—first of all, he has to admit that he is a monkey . . .

XX   Yes, yes, sure . . .

AA   Secondly, having established his condition as a monkey or a slave, he must, without pride, derive at least some wisdom and some strength from it.

XX From a monkey?

AA Yes, my dear, from a monkey, from a monkey . . . Hasn't man descended from the monkey?

XX No.

AA That is your opinion. But science claims the contrary. Now, if man has descended from the monkey, then I, who am a monkey, am an aristocrat of humanity. It is in me, as humiliated and caged monkey, in my condition of imprisonment, that all knowledge about man finds expression. A pure knowledge, a knowledge untouched as yet by the vicissitudes of evolution or the hazards of freedom. A primal knowledge. So I decided to take advantage of the opportunity, in other words, I, the caged monkey, decided to write a book about Man.

XX A monkey can't write.

AA Especially when he is in a cage. Exactly. But I didn't understand that until later. For the moment I was stunned by these new perspectives. I decided to write a book about Man in his pure state, that is to say about Man as a slave, that is to say about myself—the work of my life, unique of its kind, the first in the world. The excrement, the nutshells, and all the other refuse that fouled up my cage suddenly turned into glittering diamonds. Such riches! I said to myself: We have nothing, but we do have our slavery. That's our treasure. What do others know about it? People here, for instance? They have written books about it, they've read all about it, but they haven't understood the essence of it. All literature about slavery is either dishonest or false. It's either the work of missionaries or of liberators, or, at best, of free individuals or slaves who dream of freedom—that is to say, of slaves who are no longer entirely slaves. What do they know about the integrity of slavery, a self-sufficient state of being that doesn't seek transcendence? About a slavery that feeds on itself? What do they know about the joys and sorrows of slavery, its mysteries, beliefs, and rituals? About the philosophy and cosmology of slavery, about its mathematics? They know nothing about it at all. But I, I know. So I decided to write about it.

XX And have you written your book?

AA No.

xx   Why not?

AA   Because I was afraid. (*Pause.*)   Are you not going to ask me what I
was afraid of? (*Pause.*)   You're right. I'm talking to a compatriot . . .
my Siamese twin . . . Anyway, the fact is that I was afraid, and that in
order to write I had to stop being afraid. So, in order to escape fear, I
fled the country.

xx   And now, you're writing?

AA   No, not at the moment.

xx   Why not?

AA   Because I'm not afraid anymore.

xx   You're never satisfied, so . . .

AA   It's a vicious circle. In order to take advantage of my only chance, I
lost it. In fleeing I stopped being a slave. I dissolved myself in
freedom, scattered myself in it. I lost my subject, and what is worse, I
lost the need for my subject . . . Theoretically, I still knew what I
wanted, but I no longer had either the will or the need. And then,
fortunately, I met you.

xx   What have I got to do with all that?

AA   Oh, you . . . You are exactly what I was when I ceased to exist.
You are like a comet that fell to the earth and buried itself deeply in
it. Immutable, unchanged, unaffected by your environment. A being
from another world, a mineral from another planet. You, fortunately,
are still a slave.

xx   I'm not going to sit here and let you call me names!

AA   But of course, of course you are a slave. And your vehement protest
doesn't change anything. You are heaven-sent, like a model, like an
inspiration. I am reborn in you as a slave. You've restored to me my
true self and my desire for self-determination. Thanks to you, I can at
last write my great work. —Now do you understand why I need you?

xx   That's not the reason at all.

AA   Do you believe that I would stay here, of my own free will, with
you, in this "shitty place," as you called it—if I were not moved by a
great project like that, imbued with a sense of mission?

XX And I'm telling you that's not the reason.

AA In that case, why am I here with you? Why, in your opinion? Come on, out with it—you tell me, if it's not asking too much.

XX Because you like talking.

AA I beg your pardon? What did you say?

XX Yep. That's all. You like talking to me.

AA And what could you and I talk to each other about?

XX For instance, about flies. About flies and . . . and flypaper . . . of life back home, in the Old Country . . . Of the past . . . Just talk about it, remember the good old days . . . That's normal, isn't it? It's human, no? And who d'you want to talk to, if not to me? To them? (*He points to the ceiling.*)

AA No!

XX Of course not. What do they know about anything? But one fellow countryman always understands another. What are you trying to tell me with your stories about slaves? You simply want to talk, discuss things . . . It's normal . . . About summer and winter. About what we eat back home, what we drink . . . It's normal, no? . . . Among roommates . . .

AA It's not true! I have a great idea . . . a great project . . . a great work . . .

XX Great work, my ass! . . . You think I don't see how you squirm when I receive a letter from home? You go to your corner and pretend to read a book—upside down! . . . I really feel sorry for you then . . . Because you never receive any mail.

AA Because I don't need any . . .

XX That's it . . . You don't receive any because nobody writes to you. You have nobody to write to, and nobody writes to you . . . You can talk, but write a book . . . You'll never write a book in your life, even if you know how to write . . . in several languages. Maybe it's just as well, because what would you want to write a book about, eh?

AA About you.

XX Come on. You'll just produce some sort of rubbish. And what good is that to anybody?

AA I'll write for everybody.

XX People have enough on their hands with their own trash; they don't need yours as well.

AA People are always in need of the truth.

XX Yes, but not any truth as disgusting as yours . . .

AA Ah! You're afraid I'll write the shocking truth about you.

XX You're going to write nothing.

AA Why?

XX Because you spend too much time lying on your divan.

AA At the moment I'm organizing my thoughts, I'm studying, I'm weighing the pros and the cons . . .

XX That's right . . . Always weighing things . . .

AA But I'm going to start soon. Okay, why not tomorrow?

XX Not tomorrow, nor the day after tomorrow . . . I know you well . . .

AA In a year or two, then—what does it matter? It's important that the work is allowed to mature. Then it will bear fruit . . .

XX You don't have that much time.

AA We have all the time in the world. I shall stay with you for as long as it will take.

XX Maybe you'll stay, but I won't.

AA You are not going to move out . . . Who would pay the rent for you?

XX Never mind, I'm moving back in.

AA Where?

XX Where d'you want me to go back to? Home, of course! I have somewhere to go back to, and I shall go back. But you, you'll stay here. Without me. Because you can't go back. You'll never go back. (*Pause.*)   So? You still feeling smart-assed? Eh? (*Pause.*)

AA   When?

XX   Anytime I want to. I'm going to stay here a little longer. I'm going to save a little more money and then—Good-bye! You won't see any more of me . . . I can go back home whenever I want.

AA   No, you can't. You'll never go back either.

XX   Me? Why not? . . . What's to stop me? I'm not a political refugee.

AA   At this time you're not.

XX   I'm not afraid. They can't accuse me of anything.

AA   Are you sure?

XX   And what should I be afraid of? You have reason to be afraid. But I, I have nothing on my conscience.

AA   You say that I don't write letters. That's true. You say that I shall never write a book. Maybe. But there is something that I could write.

XX   And what is that?

AA   A denunciation. (*Pause.*)

XX   I have never done anything against our government.

AA   Is that so? And who associates with a traitor, a renegade, a degenerate, an enemy of the regime, that is to say—me? Eh? It wouldn't happen to be you, would it?

XX   No.

AA   What do you mean—"no"? You live with me, in the same room . . .

XX   Nobody knows.

AA   Are you sure? What if I were to write to the authorities? A few words are enough, even anonymously . . . You know how little it takes. And then—good-bye to your house, good-bye to your garden, good-bye to wife and children . . .

XX   Why?

AA   There you have it! You're still asking me why. That's proof of your political depravity. It's not surprising, it's my influence . . . Tell me who you associate with and I tell you who you are . . . Have you already forgotten that it's enough to breathe the same air as a degenerate like me to be contaminated yourself? And on top of that, you have talked to me, you have drunk with me . . . Who knows what you talked about . . . There was no witness. Do you think that when they gave you permission to go abroad, it was in order to associate with an anarchist?

xx   You're not going to do that to me!

AA   And why not?

xx   I've got a wife! And kids.

AA   Really? . . . Well, it was I who thought of them first. Yes, you have a wife and children, and that's why you will never go back to them. You wouldn't want to endanger their lives, would you? (*Pause.*)   So, are you going to stay with me? (*Pause.*)   Yes, you are staying, you're staying. I feel that you are going to stay. We are going to stay here together. You will send gifts to your children. For Christmas. They like that. As for your wife . . . Are you sure that she really needs you?

xx   No . . .

AA   You see, the pieces fit . . .

We hear the sound of a rapidly approaching siren.

xx   There's a fire.

AA   I hope it's not here. (*The sound of the siren is coming closer still.*)

xx   There's nothing burning here . . .

AA   No, but it's going to burn. Have you ever heard of Nero?

xx   No. Who's he?

AA   He was a Roman emperor. He burned down his city because he was bored.

xx (*Suddenly interested*)   He set fire to it?

AA   Of course. He could allow himself to do it because he was the only free man of his time. So you can imagine how bored he was. The whole freedom of the earth for a single human being, that's terrible. Not surprising that he wasn't able to resist doing it, the poor man . . .

(*XX walks rapidly about the room, feeling the table and chairs with his fingers.*)   And now, let's return to our own time. Here, in a democracy, everybody has a little freedom, less certainly than the emperor, but a good deal more than the emperor's subjects. So everybody is bored, in proportion to the amount of freedom he has. What is worse, everybody is bored with the boredom of the others who are bored . . . —What are you looking for?

xx   Nothing. Nothing.

AA   The sum total of boredom therefore always remains the same. Conversely, the risk of arson provoked by boredom increases in proportion to the number of free people. If, once upon a time, that risk stood at one chance in a million, it's a million in one today. In other words, fires are inevitable . . . —What are you doing?

xx   (*Has just brought his large suitcase out from under his bed; puts his pillow in his blanket*)   I'm getting my bags ready.

AA   What for?

xx   Well, there's got to be a fire here, no?

AA   Not here! You don't understand. The fire starts on the upper floors where the free people live. Down here, there are only the emperor's subjects.

xx   That's the same thing.

AA   Not at all. It is not our fire. It's their fire.

xx   It's all the same.

AA   No! This is not an imperial fire. This is a democratic fire.

xx   If that's the way you want it . . .

AA   Let's not get mixed up in things that don't concern us. We have no right to this fire. At most we could go and sit out in the hall under the stairs and watch it from below, as befits slaves. The view from below has its advantages too. For instance, women run from fires. An opportunity you wouldn't want to miss! But beyond that, what does it have to do with us? It's neither our house nor our freedom. Come on, don't worry, leave your things alone. (*AA pours himself another cognac. Glass in hand, he walks across to the left of the stage and turns to face* *the proscenium with his profile to XX. XX deposits his suitcase, his bundle, and the stuffed dog near the door and turns to AA.)* I drink to the health of all who don't have the right to immolate themselves and who must wait for the emperor to use his privilege. There they wait in silence and darkness, in the cold and in pain, for the Promethean magic to illumine and to warm them; they wait for the last fight, the sumptuous gift of the emperor. Yes, Gentlemen! Until we are illumined and warmed. Because nothing will illumine or warm us loyal subjects better than a fire prudently set. To our brothers!

He raises his glass. In the meantime the siren has reached its maximum intensity. XX extinguishes the candle. For a moment there is total darkness onstage. Abruptly, the bulb lights up, throwing a raw, violent light on the scene. On the floor above we hear a series of joyous exclamations, the "aahs" of satisfaction and joy, as is normal in similar circumstances when the light reappears after a long period of darkness in a place where numerous persons have gathered. AA and XX find themselves face-to-face, AA is holding his glass in the air, XX is brandishing an ax. They remain motionless for several seconds. AA goes closer to XX and offers him his glass. XX lets his arm with the ax drop and accepts the glass.

AA (*cont.*) They are gone.

XX There's no fire.

AA It wasn't necessarily a fire engine. It could have been the police, for example.

XX You said there was a fire.

AA An educated guess. It could also have been a strike.

XX At the power station?

AA At the water works or the power station. Maybe that's why there wasn't any water earlier. (*Pause.*) Did you intend to kill me? (*XX nods.*) I understand. You expected there would be a fire. And that the fire would burn up my corpse and destroy the evidence. I would have disappeared in the flames of a conflagration. Well, well . . . I must say, I underestimated you. (*He refills the second glass which stands on the table.*) But tell me, did you really believe everything I said about fires? Did you take me seriously? Did you believe this house was on fire?

XX No.

AA Well then? (*XX takes a box of matches from his pocket and throws it into the air several times. Then he puts the box back into his pocket.*) Ah! It's getting better and better. Not only murder but also arson. (*He raises his glass.*) To my health! (*They both drink.*) So then, if I understood correctly, you believed that I . . . —Do you still think me capable of writing that denunciation?

XX Why not? (*He sits down on the chair to the left.*)

AA Perhaps you're right. God alone knows what men are capable of. You can't be sure of anything. But I would not have written that denunciation. And not at all because I wouldn't know how; but quite simply because it would be superfluous. Since you are not going to go back. —Do you still need that ax? (*XX is silent.*) Even if you had killed me out of fear that I would denounce you, you still would not go back. So why should I bother to write that denunciation? Don't worry! I am not going to write it.

XX No?

AA No. Give me that. (*He gets up and takes the ax out of XX's hand. He goes to put it in a corner.*) You can thank heaven you failed. What would you do here, without me, all alone? . . . Isn't it better that we stay together?

XX I'm not going to stay here.

AA But of course you're going to stay, even if you don't realize it yet.

XX I want to go back.

AA Sure you do. I believe you. You are here precisely because you want to go back. Your return home is your sole raison d'être. Without that, you wouldn't stay here another minute, you'd go mad . . . or you'd kill yourself.

XX So who's going to stop me leaving?

AA (*Turning to the right, to where XX has left his bags and the dog Pluto*) Pluto! Here, Pluto! . . . How stubborn that dog is! (*He heads for the door and picks up the dog.*)

XX (*Getting up*) Leave that alone!

AA I'm not going to murder it . . . You see, little doggie—this gentleman is jealous. Your master is jealous of you. He never lets me play with you . . . Such a deep attachment to a dog isn't normal. To a plush dog at that.

XX   Put it down!

AA   Why? Don't I have a right to caress it? Why are you always so jealous of this dog? That's odd. It's strange. It's suspicious.

XX   I'm not jealous at all. (*He sits down again.*)

AA   Ah! How well you look after him! . . . It looks as if he were going to burst—he's so fat. What do you give him to eat?

XX   Nothing. He is stuffed.

AA   Yes, of course. But with what? What is there inside him?

XX   There's nothing.

AA   Maybe it's a secret.

XX (*Gets up*)   Are you going to leave it alone or not?

AA   Let's get to the bottom of this! (*He picks up the scissors from the floor and before XX can stop him he cuts open the stomach of the plush dog: Out tumble bundles of money.*)   Ah!—so that's it! Now I understand.

XX   It belongs to me! Give it back to me! (*He grabs the money from him.*)

AA   I understand everything. That's why you never have any money.

XX   Give it back to me, you thief!

AA   Watch what you say. If I had wanted to rob you, I could have done so a long time ago. You think I never saw you put away that money?

XX   You were spying on me, eh?

AA   At first, it was only a matter of suspicion. People like you don't keep their money in the bank. And then, one evening . . .

XX   You saw me.

AA   Yes. I saw how you stuffed your dog with money. It happened quite unintentionally, I assure you. But we intellectuals are light sleepers.

XX   Thief! (*He sits at the table, on the chair on the right, and begins to count his money.*)

AA   You can check . . . I haven't taken a penny. Mind you, I could have . . . And I even had a right to . . .

XX   What right? It belongs to me!

AA   You owe me quite a lot of money . . .

XX   It's not for me . . .

AA   I know. I know. It's for your wife and children. But what do I care who you are saving your money for? What matters to me is that you are a miser. For me that's the best guarantee that you will never leave me. Because you'll never let go of your money—isn't that right?

XX   You think I'm going to leave it to you? You can wait a long time . . .

AA   I've never thought that. I'm not even going to ask you to pay me back your debts. —So, you propose to take it back home with you, do you?

XX   It belongs to me! It's mine! I'm not giving it to anyone.

AA   You have no idea how I love to hear you say "me" and "my" and "mine" . . . You pronounce these words with such conviction, such passion. But have you considered that over there you'd have to spend all this money which it has taken you so much trouble to amass? Back home you can neither make money nor save any . . .

XX   That's exactly why I've been saving up over here.

AA   That's it—"here"! Over here and not over there . . . Here you save a little more money every day, you lie on your bed thinking how tomorrow you'll have a little more money, the day after, still more, and in a year's time lots and lots more. You have a goal in life that grows more seductive the further removed it is. Have you already saved enough for a little house with a little garden? So, why not try to save some more until you can afford a bigger house with a bigger garden? It's quite simple. All you have to do is to postpone your return for a month or two. And then, why not an even bigger house with an even bigger garden? . . . And so you keep on postponing your return because the more money you have the more you want to have. The years pass and you're forever setting a new date for your return home, forever working and saving—for later on! . . . Hey, you've stopped. Why? It's so pleasant to watch you count your money . . .

xx   Why are you telling me all this?

AA   So that you understand that it isn't me who is holding you back. It isn't necessary for me to write a letter of denunciation to make you stay . . . You are going to stay here of your own free will. That's why I'm telling you all this. And also to make sure you don't take it into your head to play with an ax again.

xx   I'm not going to go back home?

AA   Never. Even though you'll always be under the impression that it's just a matter of days, that soon . . .

xx   Never?

AA   Why make so much of it? You have a good life, full of hope, nostalgia, and illusions. Not everybody is so lucky.

xx   But why "never"?

AA   I've already told you. Because you are a slave. Over there you're a slave of the state. Here you're a slave of your own greed. Whatever happens, you'll always be a slave. There's no possible liberation for you. Freedom means to be master of oneself. But in your case there's always someone else or something else that is your master. If it's not people, it's things.

xx   What things?

AA   The things you want to own, possess—things you can buy with your money. To be a slave of things is a form of slavery much more perfect than the best slavery you can get in prison. A truly ideal slavery—because there are no external restraints, not a single restriction. Your slavery is solely the creation of a slavish spirit thirsting for slavery. You have the soul of a slave, and that's why you interest me, on account of my work about the nature of slavery, a work I have every intention of writing . . .

xx   You know where you can stick your work . . .

AA   I couldn't care less what you think about my research. A scientist pays no attention to what the insect thinks of the microscope. I observe you, and I describe you—that's all.

XX   Who? Me?

AA   Yes, you. And what you think of that is of no importance at all. The only thing that matters is that you cannot stop being a slave any more than an insect can stop being an insect.

XX   Can't I?

AA   No, you can't. Because you can't change your nature. You can't because you would have to become someone else . . . and that's impossible. You can't because you can't stop being a son of a bitch, any more than you can stop dreaming of your return home, any more than you can help the fact that you never will . . . go back.

XX   I'll go back home.

AA   You won't.

XX   I will!

AA   And what about that? (*He points to the bundles of money.*)

XX   I'll go back! I'll go back! I'll go back! (*Each time he bangs the table with his fist. Then, suddenly, he begins to tear up the money.*)

AA   What on earth are you doing?! That's your money!

XX   I'm a slave! . . . I'm an insect! . . . (*AA tries to stop him, but XX pushes him away. He tears the bills into little pieces which he scatters all around himself.*)

AA   That's your money!

XX   My money . . . my hard-earned pennies . . . my savings . . . It's mine . . . mine! (*He goes on tearing up his money. AA tries to subdue him, but XX pushes him away so violently that AA staggers, stumbles, and falls to the ground. XX completes his work of destruction.*)

AA   You've gone mad. (*Moving on all fours, he picks up the torn bills from the floor.*)   Maybe one can stick them together again . . .

XX   You think so?

AA No. (*Throws the money on the floor and gets up.*)

XX Now what am I going to do?

AA How do I know? . . . You can do what you like . . . You are a free
man now.

XX What in hell came over me?

AA Why are you complaining? You have delivered yourself from the
condition of slavery, you have rebelled against the tyranny of money.
You have proven that you can afford the luxury of freedom. You
should be happy . . .

XX But now I won't be able to go back home.

AA You couldn't have gone back before, either. So, what's the
difference?

XX It's all your fault.

AA Did I ask you to tear up your money? All I did was to indulge in
theoretical speculations, but you—you had to go and play Spartacus . . .

XX Me? I didn't want anything! All I wanted was to go back home . . .
that's all.

AA Too late. (*He fetches his suitcase from under his bed and gets out several
sheets of manuscript. He sits down at the table on the chair to the left. He
begins to tear up the pages methodically.*)

XX What's that?

AA Plans, outlines, sketches, drafts. I was going to write a great work.

XX So, why are you tearing it all up?

AA Because I am no longer going to write it. I have come to realize
that the ideal slave doesn't exist, since even a convict like you has his
moment of freedom . . . You were a model for me, an inspiration, a
thesis, and a certainty. In one instant you have destroyed the fruit of
my experiences and my reflections. You have nipped a great work in
the bud. You're nothing but a vandal, a hooligan—

XX Hey . . . shut your fucking mouth!

AA Well, of course you don't give a damn! Because of this act of
yours, this one stupid act, humanity has suffered an irreparable loss—

and you don't give a damn! My work was going to make an important contribution to world culture . . . But of course, what is that to you? . . . One of the most original contributions! . . . And you don't give a damn!

XX (*Gets up and takes off his jacket, which he hangs over the back of the chair. He climbs up on the chair and then onto the table.*) Move over.

AA To think that you were such a fine slave! . . . You have ruined everything. You think only of yourself. (*XX takes off his tie and makes a noose of it. This he attaches to the electric wire near the socket with the naked bulb.*) Are you going to hang yourself?

XX Don't tell me I haven't got the right to do it.

AA Of course you do . . . You have every right. Suicide is the supreme right of the free man, the ultimate affirmation of freedom.

XX So, move!

AA (*Moving the papers to the edge of the table*) In fact, if would be the logical consequence of your previous action. Since you have begun to be free, one can't refuse you anything anymore. Although, I should warn you, it's better not to go overboard . . .

XX (*Pulling the tie to test its strength*) That should hold . . .

AA Excess and exaggeration are in bad taste. But bad taste is a characteristic trait of all people of the lowest social classes. Say, you wouldn't consider dropping it, would you?

XX (*Putting his head through the noose*) Move!

AA Why?

XX Because I'm going to kick away the table.

AA If you insist . . . That's what I call the greed of the opportunist.

XX I told you to get out of the way.

AA Rude and stubborn . . .

XX Are you going to goddamn move or not?

AA Do you really have to be so vulgar? Don't blaspheme!

XX Okay. I'm still going to kick that table.

AA Wait! What is your last word?

xx You can go and f—. . .

AA Hold it! Don't go on! Leave me with the memory of a man with a refined soul, even though of common origin . . . I know what you wanted to say, but that was intended for me. Now what about your family?

xx My family?

AA Have you forgotten that you have a family? After all, you owe them a few words. (*Pause.*)

xx They can't hear me.

AA Write to them!

xx Now?

AA Sure, right now! You are going to hang yourself, so you won't have another opportunity.

xx It's too late.

AA I'll write for you. All you have to do is dictate. Come on! Move over! (*He takes the last sheet of paper, which is not yet torn up, and turns the blank side up. He gets his pen out of his pocket.*)   Okay, go ahead!

xx My dear wife, my dear children . . .

AA (*Writes, mouthing the words*)   . . . my . . . dear . . . children . . .

xx I'm writing to let you know that I'm in good health . . .

AA . . . in . . . good . . . health . . . Hm! . . . Well, let's go on. (*He writes.*)   What's next?

xx I hope you are doing as well as I . . .

AA Maybe you'd better not say that.

xx Why?

AA It's not quite the thing to say. (*He moves his forefinger across his throat and sticks out his tongue.*)   It's true . . . but you'd better not. . . . (*AA reading it back:*)   ". . . to let you know that I'm in good health." Period. What's next?

XX   . . . and that I am doing quite well.

AA (*Writing*)   In heaven . . .

XX (*Goes on mechanically*)   As on earth . . . (*He corrects himself.*) Why "in heaven"?

AA Surely you'll go to heaven.

XX That's none of your business. Cross that out!

AA All right. Next?

XX I don't know.

AA You want me to write on your behalf?

XX Go ahead! Write!

AA (*Writing*)   I-miss-you-and-the-children . . .

XX Good.

AA And that's why I want to hang myself.

XX What?

AA Hang myself.

XX No, not that. Don't write that . . .

AA But it's the truth.

XX That's got nothing to do with it.

AA Okay. (*He writes.*)   . . . I'm going to hang myself because I don't miss you at all.

XX No!

AA You mean you don't like that either?

XX Not like that! . . . What kind of an intellectual are you who can't even write a letter!

AA So, go ahead! . . . How would you phrase it?

XX I don't know . . . I'd make it shorter.

AA I'm going to hang myself. With all my love. Your father and husband. —Sign! (*He holds out to XX the sheet of paper and his pen. XX* *skims the text, crumples up the paper, and throws it on the floor. He takes his head out of the noose and comes down from the table.)* So, you don't want to write anymore? (*XX turns his back to walk over to the right.*) Hey! My pen! (*XX gives him the pen and lies down on his bed, on the right, turning his face to the wall.*) As you like. (*He climbs on the table and removes the tie from the lamp. He throws the tie on the chair to the right.*) You are right, not everything is lost. I'm not talking of myself, but of you. You can start from scratch.

Up above, we hear a door slam, people going downstairs, laughter, voices.

AA (*cont.*) You'll see how happy your wife will be. And your children? They're waiting for you. They're expecting you. Your wife is waiting for you too . . . She longs for you to return . . . Imagine the explosion of joy! Everybody will turn out to welcome you, the whole village! Who knows, perhaps there'll even be a band. (*A last burst of laughter on the stairs. Silence, XX doesn't reply.*) And the presents, just think of the presents! By God! All the nice things you'll be bringing them. A present for everybody. And you know exactly the right thing to bring to each one. You'll buy to your heart's content. Whole suitcases full of all kinds of nice things. How jealous people will be! I can see it from here. (*XX doesn't reply.*) Everyone will envy you, you'll see. (*He goes to the right where XX has left his things, picks up a blanket, and covers XX with it. He goes to the left and lies down on his bed, on his back with his hands under his head.*) And then, you're going to build a house. A beautiful house. Large, and made of freestone. Not some kind of shack. And you'll have your flies, too . . . (*Pause.*) You'll send your kids to school . . . Give them an education, let them go places! Give them a chance to be somebody! It'll be a good school, a real school . . . And then everything will be good and true . . . Work will provide bread, and the law freedom, because freedom will be the law and the law will be freedom! Isn't that what we are looking for? What we are all aiming for? And if we all have a common goal, if we all want the same thing, what prevents us from creating a community, a healthy community, wise . . . You'll go back home and you'll never again be a slave. Neither you, nor your children . . .

XX starts to snore very noisily. AA turns on his side to face the wall. After a while another sound is heard over the snoring of XX, a sound that begins quietly and gradually becomes louder: sobs, poignant, heartrending sobs!

THE HUNCHBACK

✤

Translated by Jacek Laskowski

AUTHOR'S NOTE

Even though stage directions such as "the croaking of frogs" or "crickets chirping" may tempt one to think in terms of a sentimental melodrama, the piece—and that includes the scenery, props, costumes, and acting style— must not exaggerate pastiche, parody, or the grotesque. If these elements are there in the text, then they will emerge naturally and to the right extent only if the interpretation is unforced and bereft of all intentions of parody. This is the key to providing an interpretation with the right tone: Ignoring it will only lead to falsifying the author's intentions.

It is unacceptable to look for or present any nuances of homosexuality in the Baroness-Onka pairing and, whereas it is allowable to suggest the very slightest of nuances of homosexuality in the Stranger-Student relationship, it must be done with the greatest discretion and it must come exclusively from the Stranger. In fact ambiguity would be preferable even to a nuance.

A note to translators: There is no need to translate the names Onek and Onka [literally Little He and Little She—translator's note]. They should be left as they are in Polish. They sound well phonetically in all languages. They may be changed only if there is an extraordinarily precise and—and this is very important—equally well-sounding equivalent in a given language.

CHARACTERS

ONEK, a man in his thirties

ONKA, a woman in her late twenties

BARON, a man of forty

BARONESS, a woman in her thirties

STUDENT, a young man in his early twenties

HUNCHBACK, a man in his early thirties

STRANGER, a man in his late forties

ACT I

The front of a house seen obliquely on the right of the stage. There is a balcony with two columns. The house's entrance is double-fronted: The outer door—all wood—is slightly ajar; the inner door, part glass, is closed. There is a rocking chair on the left of the balcony and an ordinary chair on the right. A bellpull is hanging by the door.

There are two windows, both shuttered and closed, one on the left and one on the right of the front door. The facade of the house is a pastel pink, the window shutters a pale blue. There are a few steps leading down from the balcony onto the grass in front of the house. The lawn is closely cropped. Downstage, on the right, stands an oval-shaped table covered by a rustic, blue-and-white checked tablecloth. Placed around it are four chairs like the one on the balcony. Downstage left, positioned parallel to the footlights, is a stone, backless bench. Upstage, on the left, a bower, which is to say a small, horseshoe-shaped bench situated under a roof supported by slender columns. The house is surrounded by trees. There are trees and bushes in the background around the bower.

It's morning in early July. The atmosphere is sunny and azure: sunlight, greenery, light, and shadow. The left of the stage is brightly lit, the right is in the shade—indicating that east is to the right and west is to the left—the shadows slanting away from the trees, the house. Birds can be heard chirping.

SCENE ONE

ONEK *and* ONKA *enter left. Onek is short, rotund, plump, florid, vigorous. Clean-shaven. He is wearing a checked sports jacket, a "sporty" cap—with a peak—and plus fours. He is carrying a traveling bag. Onka is a pretty, petite blonde dressed in an enormous hat and a light-colored, long dress. She is carrying a delicate lady's umbrella which is unfurled.*

ONKA   Oh, what a pretty blue house.

Onek puts the hold-all down on the ground, goes up to the house, takes a pince-nez from his pocket, and puts it on his nose. He scans the house for a while.

ONEK   Pink.

ONKA   Green shutters . . .

ONEK Blue.

ONKA . . . and the trees! So, so, so . . .

ONEK Green.

Takes off his pince-nez. Onka turns her back on him, takes a handkerchief from her handbag, and puts it to her eyes.

ONEK (*cont.*) Green? Green?! That's the way it seemed to me. At a cursory glance . . . but I'm not insisting.

Onka doesn't respond.

ONEK (*cont.*) What a brute I am! I see they're green so I just come straight out with it like some yokel: "Green." I don't know what I'd give just to be able to see the world through your eyes, really I don't.

ONKA There's no need for all this, you know.

ONEK I see things any old how, I see any old things. I never stop to think. Whereas you artists . . . You have an entirely different sensibility. Ordinary mortals like me should learn from artists like you.

Goes up to her and stands by her; her back is still turned to him.

ONEK (*cont.*) Please forgive me.

Onka turns to him and stretches out her hand. He kisses it.

ONKA I forgive you. The trees are green.

ONEK No they're not.

ONKA They are green.

ONEK No, no, no! You're just saying that to bring yourself down to my level.

ONKA But they really are green.

ONEK I appreciate your sacrifice but I really don't deserve it. Stay where you are now—above me. I'll never ask you for anything other than that.

ONKA (*Stamping her foot*) The trees are green! Green, green, green!

ONEK If you insist.

ONKA Don't you dare talk to me in that tone of voice.

ONEK But I was only agreeing.

ONKA Don't!

ONEK Aren't they green, then?

ONKA No they are not!

ONEK That's a shame. I thought they were green. Hello there! Anybody there?

Goes up onto the balcony. Tries the doorknob, but the door is locked. Taps on the glass, presses his forehead against it, and peers inside. Then he pulls the bell-pull several times. The rope swings violently; the bell rings stridently. Onek stops ringing and waits. No one comes.

ONEK (*cont.*)   This is intolerable. I informed them of our arrival.

Comes down from the balcony.

ONEK (*cont.*)   Let's take a look around the back.

Goes right.

ONEK (*cont.*)   I sent a telegraphic communication.

Leaves right, followed by Onka. The hold-all remains onstage.

Scene Two

BARON *enters left. He is tall, forty, dark-haired, and sporting an exuberant, well-tended pair of whiskers. Dressed in an ivory-colored summer suit and a broad-brimmed felt hat of the same color, a white cravat, white shoes, and white gloves, he is carrying a cane with a heavy knob and he is smoking a cigar. He enters slowly, looking around meticulously and exhaling clouds of cigar smoke. Walks over to the right, lifts the corner of the tablecloth with his cane. His movements are controlled: Beneath the assumed indifference there is an obvious concentration and care. BARONESS enters right. She is a tall, slim brunette in her thirties, wearing an elegant costume including an ankle-length skirt and a dainty hat. In her wake comes a figure scarcely visible beneath the pieces of luggage it is carrying. The STUDENT, in his early twenties, is slim, pale, and sporting a pair of black gloves, which he'll not remove throughout the entire play except for just one scene. He is weighed down by suitcases and hatboxes; one suitcase is tattered; the rest are extremely elegant.*

BARONESS   Put them down, please.

Student piles the cases and boxes on the left; it seems miraculous that he could have lifted them all.

BARONESS (*cont.*)   Do you see that individual there?

She points to the Baron. Student is out of breath. He takes off his cap and wipes his forehead with his sleeve.

BARONESS   Kindly slap his face!

STUDENT   You're joking.

BARONESS   Far from it. That individual is my husband.

Smoking his cigar, Baron watches them. Student bows, Baron acknowledges this with a slight bow.

BARONESS (*cont.*)   Didn't you hear what I asked you to do?

Student fidgets with his cap.

BARONESS (*cont.*) (*Stiffly*)   In that case . . . you may leave.

She offers the Student her hand, but he merely bows and she withdraws her hand. Student picks up his miserable-looking little case from the pile of luggage and moves toward the house.

BARONESS (*cont.*)   One moment.

Student, not knowing what is wanted of him now, stops. Baroness goes up to him, throws her arms around his neck, and kisses him passionately. He is totally passive. Baroness bends him back; his cap falls off. Baron watches this and taps the ash off the end of his cigar. Eventually, Baroness frees Student from her embrace and, taking no further notice of him, looks straight at Baron. Student picks up his cap from the ground, knocks the dust off it against his knee, bows to Baroness, and walks hurriedly toward the house. However, Baron is in his way. Student stops, then describes a large semicircle to avoid him. As he does so, Baron watches him without moving. Student accelerates and runs up onto the balcony. He tries the doorknob but the door won't give. Student runs down the steps and off right. As he leaves, Baron half turns so that he is facing Baroness again.

BARONESS (*cont.*)   Why did you leave me on my own?

Baron turns away from her, walks to the right, and sits on a chair. Baroness sits on the bench, left. Baron gets up and leaves, right. Baroness jumps up and follows him off. The luggage brought in by the Student remains onstage.

SCENE THREE

The front door opens. HUNCHBACK *comes out onto the balcony. He is short, sturdy, crew-cut, and hunchbacked. Dressed in a coarse cloth shirt, cloth trousers clipped below the knees, thick, gray, homemade woolen knee-high socks and slippers. Apart from his hunchback, he is hale and hearty. He has a canvas apron in his hands. He stretches, rubs his eyes, and yawns. He puts on his apron and comes down the steps, picks up a few pieces of luggage, and carries them into the house.*

SCENE FOUR

Onek and Baron enter, right; Baron no longer smoking, Onek gesticulating vigorously as he speaks.

ONEK It's scandalous that no one came out to meet us. I informed them: I sent a telegraphic communication.

BARON That's possible, too.

ONEK My wife is an artist—she paints pictures.

BARON I find that not too difficult to believe.

ONEK You surely noticed that she is very sensitive.

BARON Indeed . . .

ONEK Ours is a perfect marriage. She is its soul and I am its flesh. She gives me heaven and I give her the earth. Although I must admit there is the occasional difference of opinion.

BARON But of course.

ONEK If you want my opinion I think that God created Man and Woman to complement one another. A woman has intuition, she's sensitive, has artistic talent—whereas I—I am blessed with some little knowledge and a grain of common sense.

BARON Is that so?

ONEK It's a natural attribute in a man. But if it weren't for her I would be simply pedestrian: shallow and bestial. She makes me noble. My strength and my common sense are at her service: which is as much as to say that they are at the service of goodness, of beauty, and of art. I protect her from life's prose.

BARON And you're right to do so.

While they were talking, they crossed the stage from right to left, and now they leave it left, at a leisurely pace in time with their conversation.

Scene Five

Onka and Baroness enter, right.

ONKA He works far too hard. I'm so glad he'll be able to relax at last.

BARONESS He has ideal conditions to do so.

ONKA Will you be staying long?

BARONESS That depends on my husband's whims. My husband is, unfortunately, a very whimsical man.

ONKA My husband is totally different. He can be relied on. He's responsible, reliable . . . Next to him, I feel such a child . . . Though there are times when it's he who behaves childishly.

BARONESS You mean in bed?

ONKA I beg your pardon?

BARONESS *Passons.*

ONKA Yes. Sometimes he cries in his sleep.

BARONESS But he does sleep.

ONKA He's exhausted. My husband is a very successful lawyer. We're even thinking about moving to the capital. And what about you?

BARONESS I'm financially independent.

ONKA No, I meant what about your husband . . .

BARONESS He plays cards.

ONKA Oh!

BARONESS And he always wins.

ONKA You're an extraordinary woman.

BARONESS Far from it.

ONKA In that case . . . could it be that I'm an extraordinary woman?

BARONESS I think not.

Pause.

ONKA (*Hurt*) And yet there is something extraordinary about you.

They cross the stage and leave, left. Hunchback comes out of the house, picks up the next few pieces of luggage, and carries them into the house.

SCENE SIX

They all enter stage left, Onek and Baroness forming the first pair, Baron and Onka the second.

ONEK It's an honor to be here in your company. A happy holiday is so dependent on the right company.

ONKA I hear that you study life.

BARONESS You have such a positive approach to the world . . .

BARON That is an exaggeration. I'm a dilettante. But you, it seems, you paint.

ONEK I know about people. Don't forget that I am in the legal profession.

ONKA Only in an amateur fashion.

BARONESS Quite. And yet there's not the slightest trace of cynicism. That is magnificent!

BARON Professionalism is repulsive to real art.

ONEK I believe in Man. I won't try to hide the fact that I come from a very poor background and that I've achieved everything through my own efforts.

ONKA And what about real life?

BARON There's no such thing.

BARONESS (*Turning to Baron*) Did you hear that?

BARON (*To Baroness, politely*) Unfortunately, no . . .

BARONESS This gentleman is a born optimist. It's so pleasant to find oneself in the company of such a healthy, generous nature . . .

BARON (*Nodding slightly*) My congratulations . . .

Student enters right, carrying his suitcase.

SCENE SEVEN

BARONESS Ah, there you are! Where have you been?

Student bows awkwardly.

BARONESS (*cont.*) He's our new friend. He's staying here with us all.

ONKA Really? Are you on holiday too?

ONEK Welcome! Welcome!

ONKA I'm pleased to meet you.

She stretches her hand out to him, but Student merely bows. Onka withdraws her hand.

BARONESS This gentleman's a student.

ONEK Very good! We need well-educated young people. Doctors, engineers—the iron railroads have a colossal future, you know.

STUDENT I'm studying philosophy.

ONEK Yes, well, we need those too. We need a contemporary Plato, that's what we need.

STUDENT I disapprove of the idealistic tradition.

ONEK Yes, but you do have ideals, don't you?

ONKA Stop interrogating the gentleman, dear.

Hunchback appears on the balcony.

SCENE EIGHT

ONEK   I say, you there . . .

ONKA (*Warning him*)   Onek, dear . . .

HUNCHBACK   Good morning, ladies and gentlemen.

Comes down from the balcony for the luggage.

ONEK   Are you a member of this household, my good man?

HUNCHBACK   Yes, sir, I am.

ONEK   Good. In that case call the proprietor, there's a good fellow. Inform him that his guests have arrived. Tell him that they have been waiting an hour even though I informed him of our impending arrival by means of a telegraphic communication.

HUNCHBACK   I'm afraid I can't do that, sir.

ONEK   Why not?

HUNCHBACK   Because I am the proprietor.

ONEK   Impossible!

ONKA (*Warning him*)   Onek, dear!

ONEK (*Thinking better of it*)   But of course. It's perfectly possible.

HUNCHBACK   Please come inside, ladies and gentlemen.

Goes into the house with the rest of the luggage.

ONEK   Did you see that?

BARONESS   I fear it was difficult not to see.

ONEK   Well, what are you going to say about that?

ONKA   Poor man.

ONEK   Poor man? Poor man?! It's a swindle. There was no mention in the advertisement of the fact that the proprietor is abnormal.

BARON   A hunchback.

ONEK   Yes, a hunchback, which is as much as to say abnormal. He should be prosecuted for this. He put in a normal advertisement while himself being abnormal. He's a swindler!

ONKA   Onek, dear, don't take on so.

ONEK   As members of society we must protect ourselves against this confidence trickery. If we don't take steps to protect ourselves we'll be back in the caves in next to no time.

BARON   He had every right to withhold the fact that he is a hunchback. There is, of course, quite a difference between a hunchback and someone who is not a hunchback, but the proprietor of a pension has the right to be a hunchback or not, and a hunchback has the right to be a proprietor of a pension or not.

ONEK   But holidays with a cripple!?

BARON   As far as I can recall, he didn't actually claim he wasn't a cripple. He simply refrained from making any kind of statement on the matter.

ONEK   But it's intolerable. This is the first time anything like this has happened to me.

BARON   I'll be the first to grant that it is more often the case that the proprietor of a pension is not a hunchback than that he is a hunchback. But what of it?

ONEK   What do you mean—what of it? It's intolerable!

BARON   But why is it?

ONEK   Are you prepared to tolerate it?

BARON   Allow me to repeat my question: Why exactly is it intolerable?

ONEK   I propose we issue him with an ultimatum: we leave immediately unless . . . unless . . .

BARON   Unless what? Unless he straightens himself out immediately? You know as well as we all do that isn't very realistic.

ONEK   In that case we'll leave.

Leaving his suitcase onstage, Student detaches himself surreptitiously from the group and moves right.

BARON (*Bowing to Onka*)   Madam.

Goes up onto the balcony and disappears into the house. Student vanishes right.

ONEK (*To Baroness*)   Please exert what influence you can on your husband.

BARONESS   I very much regret . . .

Follows Baron into the house.

SCENE NINE

ONKA   But Onek, dear, why do you want to leave?

ONEK   Why? Why? You think that that Quasimodo should get away with this?

ONKA   It's so beautiful here . . . I've always wanted to stay somewhere like this.

ONEK   That is the whole point. That monstrosity is in discord with nature. I'm all for nature, but I won't stand for aberration.

ONKA   But what about the ethics of the situation?

ONEK   The ethics are straightforward. My moral duty is to protect you from the sight of him. You're far too sensitive and delicate to have to look at that.

ONKA   Let's not be selfish. It's not his fault he's a cripple. I'm sure he suffers because of it. Don't let's make his suffering greater by showing him he repels us. Besides, you have paid a deposit.

ONEK   You're an angel. A real angel!

ONKA   And we won't be able to catch a train now, will we?

ONEK   On the one hand ethics, on the other aesthetics. A true dilemma.

ONKA   Besides, where could we go now? It won't be easy to find a decent pension at the height of the tourist season.

ONEK   We'll stay.

ONKA   You're wonderful.

ONEK   He can go to the station for our luggage.

Onka kisses him on the forehead. Blackout.

Scene Ten

Early afternoon, sunny; the right of the stage is in the sun, the left in the shade. The window shutters are open. Baron is sitting at the table. He is wearing meticulously pressed white trousers and a navy blue blazer. Student is sitting on the bench reading a book. Onek comes out of the house. He is wearing a shirt, unbuttoned vest, and slippers. He descends the steps and goes up to Baron. Sits down at the table, sprawling in the chair.

ONEK   You don't mind if I join you, Baron?

Baron, by means of a silky-smooth gesture, invites Onek to sit on the chair he already occupies.

ONEK (*cont.*)   Unbelievable. That trout in almonds was unbelievable.

BARON   Yes, indeed. The cuisine here has turned out to be surprisingly good.

ONEK   Good? My dear Baron, I never tasted anything like it. That . . . what was it called . . . that Finnish omelet?

BARON   Norwegian.

ONEK   It was delicious, anyway. Who would have thought he could cook like that?

Baron takes out a box of cigars.

BARON   Cigar?

ONEK   No, thanks, I don't smoke.

Baron lights his cigar.

ONEK (*cont.*)   Do you know why I don't smoke?

BARON   You don't enjoy it.

ONEK   Not at all. It's a matter of principle. Everyone should have a principle guiding them through life. My principle is: no smoking. It's a principle that's never let me down. Never to partake of tobacco.

BARON   I understand. You're a man of principle.

ONEK   Smoking weakens the mind and lowers the quality of life right down. And I want to preserve all my mental and physical faculties, to live naturally, vigorously, like a flower. Or like a plant.

BARON   Like a flower, which is to say a plant.

ONEK   Take now as an example. I came out because I think it's criminal to stay inside when it's so beautiful outside. My wife herself suggested I go for a walk. You have to take advantage of every opportunity.

BARON   And how is your wife?

ONEK   She has a migraine.

BARON   Your wife is a charming woman.

ONEK   She's color-blind.

Hunchback comes out onto the balcony. He is carrying a half-full decanter of liquor and two glasses, on a tray. Goes up to the table and pours the liquor. Onek refuses with a gesture.

BARON   You don't drink?

ONEK   Never!

Baron raises his glass, takes a sip, gives a nod of approval to Hunchback, who bows and withdraws, leaving the tray on the table.

ONEK   Do you know why I don't drink, Baron?

BARON   A matter of principle.

ONEK   You knew . . . ?

Hunchback goes into the house; Onek follows him with his eyes.

ONEK (*cont.*)   I don't trust him.

BARON   As a chef, valet, and maître d' he is irreproachable.

ONEK   Precisely. He must be hiding something.

BARON   What could he possibly be . . . ?

ONEK   You don't know hunchbacks.

BARON   I wouldn't have thought he'd be hiding anything. A hump on one's back is a particularly public thing, not easily hidden. If only on account of its absolute and unambiguous convexity . . . In fact, it's quite surprising how a hump is always convex and never concave. Bulging out, never in. Extrovert and never introvert. But even a concave or negative hump would scarcely be something one could hide.

Student raises his eyes from his book and starts to listen to their conversation.

ONEK　You're not letting yourself see the man for the hump, Baron. What is important is the man and what's inside him. His soul, that is to say his psyche.

BARON　Go on.

ONEK　He has a hump on his back whereas our backs are straight. We're healthy, strong, handsome, full of life's joys, whereas he is a cripple. He must dislike us for that.

BARON　I haven't noticed anything.

ONEK　Precisely. He resents us, but he won't show it. Hunchbacks are secretive, deceitful, vicious . . . Why, everyone knows that.

BARON　Let us assume you're right. What conclusions can we draw from the present circumstances? After all, he's feeding us, looking after us, and we pay him for his services. The benefit is mutual.

ONEK　(*Shaking his head*)　You're naive, Baron. Hunchbacks are vindictive.

BARON　Are you suggesting he may want to harm us?

ONEK　There's no doubting it. I advise you to be on your guard, Baron.

BARON　I see. What you're suggesting is that he's hatching a plot against us.

ONEK　Don't trust him, Baron. Be very careful and watch him all the time.

BARON　Thank you for bringing it to my attention. But if you're right, isn't it too late to do anything about it?

ONEK　It's never too late.

BARON　And yet it is—too late.

ONEK　Too late? How do you mean . . .

BARON　It's quite simple, really. It is literally too late. Let me explain: The easiest way for him to harm us is to poison us, to add something to the food. And since we have just finished eating lunch . . .

ONEK   You're not serious. Are you?

BARON   I'm merely developing your track of thought along logical lines. You don't feel any discomfort, do you?

ONEK   No . . . What about you, Baron?

BARON   No, I don't either. But that's no proof. After all, if he were using poison he would hardly use anything that took effect immediately. If we all suddenly died it would look very suspicious. Besides, it wouldn't pay him to get rid of his customers like that. No, if he's poisoning us, he's doing it gradually by giving us small doses of poisons that are killing us slowly. The first symptoms will be minor, almost imperceptible: a slight headache, a little tummy upset from time to time . . . The final result is obviously calculated to be delayed in its effect. Death will certainly occur after we have left this pension. Who knows? It might not come for years . . . What is the matter?

ONEK   I don't feel very well.

He stands up.

BARON   Are you going?

ONEK   I think I'll just lie down for a while.

BARON   What a shame, I was really enjoying our little chat. We shall meet at dinner, shall we not?

Onek walks into the house. Student gets up off the bench and walks right. As he passes Baron he slams his book shut much more loudly and violently than necessary, and walks into the house. Baron sips his liquor.

Scene Eleven

Baroness comes out of the house. She stops behind Baron then walks left. She turns to Baron pretending she has only just noticed him.

BARONESS   Oh, it's you . . . I didn't see you there.

Stands waiting for a reaction from him which would provide a clue as to how she should proceed.

BARONESS (*cont.*)   Are you having a rest?

Taking his silence as a sign of encouragement, she goes up and sits at the table.

BARONESS (*cont.*)   The last few days were so nerve-wracking . . . We've both been so on edge.

Baron makes a gesture of impatience.

BARONESS (*cont.*)   I admit I find it hard to control myself sometimes.

Pause.

BARONESS (*cont.*)   I think I have good reasons for it.

Baron rises from his chair as if he was about to leave.

BARONESS (*cont.*)   But perhaps it's just my nerves. You try to find an explanation and you end up blaming everyone else.

Baron resumes his chair.

BARONESS (*cont.*)   I am glad we came here. A new environment, a new way of life . . . I mean, this time we really are in the country.

Pause.

BARONESS (*cont.*)   And alone together. I mean, you can't really count those funny people, can you? That lawyer fellow is so strange . . . What do you think of her?

Baron says nothing.

BARONESS (*cont.*)   She's a bit excitable, but she's very nice. Do you know what she said when we were alone? She said: "Your husband is remarkably like the heir to the throne, only slightly smaller." Slightly smaller . . . I don't know what she could have been thinking of . . .

Pause.

BARONESS (*cont.*)   She was very interested in our marital life. I think she's a bit hysterical.

Pause.

BARONESS (*cont.*)   Have you noticed that you can see the ruins from our window? We'll have to go there some time. We could go to the lake, too.

Pause.

BARONESS (*cont.*)   Our first day in the country. It's so perfect, fresh, joyful—just like the first day of creation. Don't you feel that we could start afresh here? Start again just one more time?

Baron is silent. Baroness gets up.

BARONESS (*cont.*)   I think I'll go for a walk.

She takes the path upstage, past the bower. Baron sips his drink. Onka comes out of the house.

SCENE TWELVE

ONKA   Oh, it's you, Baron . . . I didn't realize . . . I'm not interrupting, am I?

Baron gets to his feet and bows.

BARON   Your company will give me the greatest pleasure.

Onka sits down: She is somewhat ill at ease.

BARON   Do you and your husband go away on holiday every year?

ONKA   Yes . . .

BARON   So do we. Abroad, usually.

ONKA   Italy?

BARON   We do go to Italy from time to time, yes.

ONKA   I've always wanted to visit Italy. My husband said that next year . . . When he gets a job in the capital.

BARON   And how is your husband feeling?

ONKA   Not very well.

BARON   Perhaps he needs something. Could I be of any assistance?

ONKA   That's very kind of you, but really . . . He's just lying down for a moment . . .

Pause.

ONKA   I wanted to stay with him but he pleaded with me to go out and enjoy the fresh air. He thinks only about me.

BARON   I do hope it's nothing serious.

ONKA   I think it's just a touch of indigestion.

BARON   Ah, yes. Well, this unhappy addiction he suffers can be ruinous to one's health, can it not?

ONKA   Addiction?

BARON   This predilection for alcohol.

ONKA   What do you mean?

BARON   You know better than I do.

ONKA   My husband never touches a drop.

BARON   I see . . . In that case, I'll not say another word.

ONKA   Are you suggesting . . .

BARON   I think we should change the subject. I was under the impression that you knew. But in view of the fact that you are not aware . . .

ONKA   My husband . . . partakes of . . . ?

BARON   Partakes! . . . What an exquisite euphemism. I tried to restrain him, but . . .

Points to the decanter.

ONKA   My husband drank?

BARON   Only he. I drink in moderation.

ONKA   Now I understand why he didn't want me to stay with him.

BARON   He preferred to conceal his state from you.

ONKA   He drinks in secret?

BARON   So it seems.

ONKA   How long has he been drinking, do you think?

BARON   Judging by the speed with which he became inebriated he has been drinking for some time. His body is weak; particularly as he smokes so heavily.

ONKA   My husband smokes?!

BARON Far too much. He took all my cigars.

ONKA He can't have been deceiving me all this time—can he?

BARON He didn't want you to worry. That is a point in his favor.

ONKA I can't credit it.

BARON Don't think about it, please.

ONKA But if it's true . . .

BARON Let's change the subject.

ONKA What can I do?

BARON The most important thing is not to let him know that you've discovered anything. The knowledge that you are aware of his weakness could drive him to a despair, which is but one step away from suicide.

ONKA No!

BARON I advise you to act as if you knew nothing at all. Treat him exactly as you have done hitherto. If he realized you've lost your confidence in him he might not survive it.

ONKA Baron, you're terrifying me!

BARON You must be brave. It's a disease that wounds but doesn't kill. Well, not immediately.

ONKA What do you mean by "wounds"?

BARON Tones down the quality of life.

ONKA Tones down the quality of life? What does that mean?

BARON I cannot be literal . . .

Pause.

ONKA My husband is very highly regarded . . . Could I ask you for a favor, Baron?

BARON I'll do anything you ask of me.

ONKA I won't let him know I've found out, of course. Since it might kill him.

BARON It would kill him undoubtedly.

ONKA I also get the impression he's hiding his addiction not just from me but from everyone.

BARON That's hardly surprising. After all, he has a position of some responsibility.

ONKA I don't mind, for myself. I can understand and forgive. But people . . . public opinion . . . and especially now, when we're supposed to be moving to the capital . . .

BARON I agree that the situation is a tricky one.

ONKA That's why I'd ask you not to mention it to anyone.

BARON You can count on my absolute discretion.

ONKA How will I ever be able to thank you, Baron?

BARON Your confidence in me is the only reward I could wish for.

ONKA Oh . . .

Pause.

ONKA I'll go and see what's happening to him.

She gets up. Baron also rises. Onka goes up to the balcony. She places a finger on her lips as a sign of enjoining silence. Baron reciprocates with the same gesture.

Blackout.

Scene Thirteen

Summery dusk. Frogs croaking and crickets chirping. It is after dinner. There are four chairs near the table downstage right: Onka, Baroness, and Baron are sitting on three of the chairs; the fourth is vacant. Onek is sitting on the bench left, facing the audience. He is thinking somber thoughts. Student is on the balcony, rocking himself rhythmically in the rocking chair. There is a samovar and a china tea set on the table. Hunchback is pouring and distributing the tea. Onka is laughing loudly and artificially. Baron has just finished telling an anecdote.

ONKA Onek, dear, did you hear that?

Onek doesn't react.

BARON (*To Baroness*)   Amusing, don't you think?

BARONESS   No. But I'm pleased to see you in such good spirits.

ONKA   Didn't you find it funny, Baroness?

BARONESS   Very funny. But only because I've heard it already. Many times.

Hunchback goes up to Baron, who takes a cup and sugar from the tray. Both women are already holding cups in their laps.

ONKA   You don't take sugar, Baroness?

BARONESS   No, I don't.

Hunchback goes up to Onek and offers him a cup of tea. Onek waves it away.

ONKA   Onek, dear, do have some tea.

Hunchback goes up to the Student and gives him a cup of tea, which the Student, too, drinks without sugar.

Hunchback goes into the house. Baron takes a small, leather-bound, antique-looking book out of his pocket.

BARON   I discovered something interesting about this region. This is a guide written in verse. I think the author was a local parish priest. It was published about half a century ago.

BARONESS (*To Onka*)   You may not know this, but my husband is also a poet.

ONKA   Really? He didn't mention that.

BARONESS   Why didn't you tell this lady you were a poet?

Baron leafs through the book.

BARON   Descriptions of the local beauty spots: The steam mill—steam machines were an innovation in those days—the island in the lake . . . but the most fascinating thing of all is the description of the hill where the witches' sabbaths were held.

ONKA   Really? Can you see it from here?

BARON   We could ask our host, I suppose. But I'm afraid it might be somewhat tactless. You see, the hill is called Hunchback's Peak.

ONKA   What a bizarre name!

BARON   The locals have called it that from time immemorial and that's the name the author uses. Needless to add he condemns and ridicules the superstitious belief in witches, which makes me think how curious is the change in the Church's position on this question. After all, the Inquisition sprang from a profound belief in the existence of witches and magic practices. And yet our worthy author claims that these practices were simply quite contemptible pagan nonsense. But I wouldn't like to wager on the salvation of his soul. The descriptions of those satanic conclaves, though he does put them in quotation marks, are altogether too colorful and convincing.

ONKA   What did they do at these meetings?

BARON   They performed multiple and multifarious sexual acts. Could you pass the sugar, please?

ONKA   Oh . . .

She passes the sugar to Baron.

BARON   Thank you. Numerous witches, with the devil.

BARONESS   What a fascinating book.

STUDENT   It's all rubbish.

BARON (*Turning to Student*)   You don't believe in magic?

STUDENT   It's sheer nonsense.

BARON   I understand. You don't believe it's possible for one man to deal with all the witches on his own, assuming, of course, that we can discount any suggestion of supernatural powers being involved. What do you think, madam?

ONKA   I . . . I'm afraid I don't know what you're talking about.

BARONESS   If I know my husband, he'll explain it to you.

BARON   What I meant was . . .

Student gets out of his rocking chair and goes up to Baron with fists clenched. After a moment he turns and runs off, upstage, past the bower.

BARON   As I was saying . . .

Baroness gets up, as does Onka. Baroness goes into the house. Onka turns to her husband.

ONKA   Take me to our room.

Onek, without taking any notice of her, slaps himself on the cheek, killing a midge. He inspects the dead insect and squeezes it between finger and thumb. Unable to get a reaction from him, Onka turns away and goes out into the house. Baron sips his tea. Onek gets up and goes up to Baron.

ONEK   Baron, lend me that book.

Blackout.

ACT II

SCENE ONE

The same kind of sunny day as in act one. Birds are chirping. Baron and Onek are playing croquet in front of the house. They are both in shirtsleeves: Baron in a batiste shirt with wide sleeves and frills; Onek in an unbuttoned shirt that is not particularly clean. During their dialogue they walk about the stage following the croquet balls as they are hit through the miniature hoops by the men's croquet mallets.

ONEK   I disagree. We can't be passive about this. We have to do something. We must take a stand.

BARON   I can see no possibility of doing anything. Of course as far as stands are concerned we can take one.

ONEK   You do agree that a hump is an unnatural phenomenon.

BARON   Statistically speaking, yes. But statistics aren't nature, statistics are arithmetic. A hump is a living organism, a creation of nature. It is, therefore, a natural phenomenon.

ONEK   You're prepared to accept that?

BARON   It's impossible to refuse to accept nature. Your shot.

ONEK   All right, it's a natural phenomenon, according to you, that is. But that merely means that we, as members of society, have no right to remain passive. After all, society sprang from the struggle to tame nature.

BARON   Are you saying you would like to eliminate him, physically?

ONEK   Who? Me?

BARON   That is the only way I can interpret what you have just said. That you are proposing the extermination of the crippled, the handicapped, the biologically inferior, and the weak. I shall refrain from passing any moral judgment: But even if one were to grant your premise, I don't see our hunchback as a weak or infirm person. Quite the reverse. As far as his intellectual powers are concerned, he is by no means subnormal.

ONEK You must have misunderstood what I was saying. I'm not a barbarian: I don't advocate a return to savage and bestial solutions; I believe in progress. Looking for a solution I do so within the terms of our civilization, in the name of our civilization. Everyone has the right to live.

BARON Ah, well, in that case you won't find a solution. The removal of the hump by way of an operation is out of the question. Medicine can't help you.

ONEK That's not what I was thinking of. Although it would be the best solution, if it were possible. All I want is to make this unnatural phenomenon . . .

BARON This abnormal phenomenon.

ONEK What?

BARON We have agreed, have we not, that the phenomenon itself is natural. So let us refer to it as abnormal. Natural, but outside the norm. The statistical norm.

ONEK It doesn't matter what you call it. The problem is that this preternatural . . .

BARON This abnormality.

ONEK This abnormality has to be integrated, civilized, so to speak, since it cannot be removed. Civilization is created by people who are normal, standardized; it follows, therefore, that the hunchback cannot be included in civilization. And yet here he is, sticking in civilization's very womb like a thorn, Baron, like a thorn. And this paradox is pregnant with tragic consequences.

BARON Indeed? What consequences?

ONEK You can't be serious!

Glances around and lowers his voice.

ONEK What about the poisoning?

BARON The poisoning . . .

ONEK Come, come, you said yourself he was poisoning us.

BARON That was merely a conclusion I drew from your basic premises, a logical construction. And besides, I noticed that you ate your breakfast this morning.

ONEK Only because a man has to eat. But that poison struck in my craw, I can tell you.

BARON We have no evidence.

ONEK Even if he's not poisoning us, he could, couldn't he? Or do something else. Burn us alive, or kill us in our sleep . . . how should I know what he'll come up with?

BARON Then what do you propose we do?

Onek puts his mallet to one side and takes Baron by the arm as if his arguments might be reinforced by physical pressure. He walks across the stage with Baron, gesticulating with his free hand.

ONEK We must tame him. Make him forget about his defect. Bring him back into society. Then he won't resent us. As things stand at present there's every danger that he'll turn against us. Tomorrow, if not today. He's a dangerous element, Baron. A destructive force that might explode at any moment. And if it exploded, what could we do? There'll be destruction, annihilation, and the unbridling of negative forces. But only if we do nothing to prevent it.

BARON. But what can we do?

ONEK We must behave in such a way that he starts to feel that he is as good as us. I've always been a democrat so my beliefs are in accord with the necessary social prophylactics. Ideology is in harmony with pragmatism. If we make him see we treat him as our equal, that there is no difference between him and us . . .

BARON But what about the hump?

ONEK What hump?

BARON He is a hunchback. You can't have forgotten about his hump.

ONEK The hump is unimportant. It doesn't exist.

Baron frees himself from Onek's grasp.

BARON That is a novel point of view, and a thoroughly dubious one at that. It is your opinion, but will it be his opinion, too?

ONEK   If we give him an example from above, so to speak . . .

BARON   I doubt if even then he'll be prepared to change his opinion of himself. After all, to have one's own opinion, especially about oneself, is a democratic right.

ONEK   Surely you don't imagine he'll persist in his opinion that he's a hunchback, do you? Even if we tell him that he isn't?

BARON   I'm certain of it. Being a hunchback without a straight back he has more chance than someone straight-backed but with a hump.

ONEK   More chance? More chance of what?

BARON   More chance to be himself.

ONEK   Why, the ungrateful so-and-so!

BARON   I can see only one way out.

ONEK   There is no way out.

BARON   Far from pretending he isn't a hunchback, we must emphasize the fact at every step, making it something to be proud of, a virtue, a distinct advantage. We must persuade him that a hump is one of nature's masterpieces and that hunchbacks are the most beautiful people in the world. We must let him see that compared with him it is we who are handicapped, we who are malformed and ugly . . . That we are worse than he is in every respect simply because we have been deprived of a hump. That we are abnormal . . .

ONEK   What? But he's the one who's a hunchback!

BARON   Can't you understand that what I'm suggesting is the only way to neutralize his enmity, the enmity you fear so much? Instead of feeling resentful, he'll be fired by a spirit of tolerance: He'll treat us with condescension, it's true, but at least it will be condescension untainted by hatred. He may treat us with disdain but at least he won't harm us.

ONEK   But I could never agree to a hunchback being better than me. The very idea!

BARON   As you wish. If you'd rather be poisoned, burned alive, or murdered in your sleep . . . I was only pointing out the alternative.

Hunchback appears on the balcony. He is carrying a letter and newspaper.

HUNCHBACK (*To Onek*)   A letter for you, sir.

Onek takes the letter and rips open the envelope. Hunchback put the paper on the table and leaves by going into the house. Having glanced cursorily at the letter, Onek moves toward the house.

BARON   What about our game?

ONEK   I concede.

Onek goes into the house. Baron takes the paper from the table, goes up onto the balcony, sits on the rocking chair, and starts reading the paper. Baroness and Onka enter upstage, beyond the bower. Onka is carrying a large bunch of freshly picked wild flowers and a lady's umbrella.

SCENE TWO

ONKA   He's handsome but I'm not attracted to him. He's a bit strange.

BARONESS   But he did behave like a real man, a real gentleman . . .

ONKA   You think so?

BARONESS   Well, perhaps he wasn't very subtle, but his intentions were very honorable. Which is more than you could say about my husband.

ONKA   I get the feeling that they don't like each other.

BARONESS   Nobody could like my husband.

ONKA   What about you, Baroness?

BARONESS   I asked that there should be no formalities between us, didn't I?

ONKA   I'm sorry . . . What about . . . you?

BARONESS   My husband? I don't like him either.

ONKA   How can you say a thing like that?

BARONESS   I love him.

They stop at the bower. Pause.

ONKA   I don't know what to say.

BARONESS   Let's sit down.

They sit in the bower, removing their hats. Onka folds her umbrella and lays the flowers next to her on the seat.

BARONESS   Haven't you guessed? Don't you suspect anything?

ONKA   Suspect?

BARONESS   Can't you tell from the way I behave, the way he behaves . . .

ONKA   You behave? He behaves?

BARONESS   I thought it was obvious. I thought everyone could see.

ONKA   I really don't know what you're talking about.

BARONESS   Don't lie to me! I really couldn't stand that.

Pause.

BARONESS (*cont.*)   I'm being frank with you, so you have no right to pretend that you don't know anything. Your hypocrisy is revolting . . .

Pause.

BARONESS (*cont.*)   I'm sorry. Don't be angry with me. Tell me the truth . . . Haven't you noticed . . . anything?

ONKA   Well, just a little something. Perhaps.

BARONESS   Of course. You see, that's why I'd rather speak openly about it to you than make the best of a bad job. If I look ridiculous then at least everyone will know that I'm the first to see just how ridiculous I am.

ONKA   I'm so sorry . . . Of course I'm not in the same situation myself but I can see how terrible it must be.

BARONESS   Don't pity me. I don't need your pity.

ONKA (*Hurt*)   Of course.

Pause.

ONKA (*cont.*)   I didn't mean to intrude.

Pause.

ONKA (*cont.*)   I have no reason to.

Pause.

BARONESS   You know, I have no illusions about him.

ONKA   Now I understand why you're so scathing about him.

BARONESS   Oh, no, you're quite wrong there. I know him better than anyone else can and I assure you that revenge doesn't come into the reckoning. I may be ridiculous but I'm not stupid, thank God. Oh, yes, I know him only too well. Perhaps that's why he treats me the way he does. He knows I'm the only person who sees through him.

ONKA   But in that case, why . . .

BARONESS   Exactly! Why indeed? I don't know. I'd give a lot just to find out why. If I only knew then perhaps I could free myself. But I really don't have a clue—though apart from that one thing I do know everything. I know he's evil and he doesn't love me; I bore him. But I can't stop myself trying. Despite everything. Despite so many failures . . . Trying again and again. I know everything about him that can be known but there is one thing I do not know: Why do I love him?

ONKA   Maybe that's because you don't really understand him. Maybe he needs more tenderness.

BARONESS   More what?

ONKA   More unselfish friendship . . .

BARONESS   My husband?

ONKA   Maybe a different approach . . .

BARONESS   Are you certain you're not attracted to him?

ONKA   Well, really! . . . I'm married.

BARONESS   To that sack of potatoes?

ONKA   What do you mean?

BARONESS   Not "what" but "who." Your husband, of course.

ONKA   How dare you!?

Gets up and puts on her hat.

BARONESS Sit down!

Takes Onka by the hand and forces her to sit down again. Onka is on the verge of tears.

ONKA You don't understand, you can't understand that there are happy marriages . . . marriages like . . . marriages that are . . . marriages where . . .

She can no longer control herself and starts to cry in earnest. Baroness removes Onka's hat and starts to stroke her hair. Gives her a handkerchief.

BARONESS I didn't mean to upset you. We all have our troubles. It's only natural. But you know about my troubles, so why don't you tell me about yours? Why do you want to hide anything from me?

ONKA I'm not hiding anything.

BARONESS My dear child, why pretend? For my benefit? We're both unhappy . . .

ONKA I'm very happy . . . (*She is crying.*)

BARONESS I see. And what about that sack of potatoes?

ONKA Stop it, please.

BARONESS So, you thought you'd pull a fast one, did you? You thought you'd hear me out and then you'd just go away without saying a word but feeling so very superior, is that it? "Look at what other women have to suffer . . . but not me. I'm better than she is. I'm on the greener side of the hill." Well, you can't play games like that with me, sweetie.

ONKA It's not true!

BARONESS What's that? You're not trying to wriggle out of it, are you? If you're not careful, my dear, I'll tell you something . . .

ONKA You're just being spiteful because . . . because . . .

BARONESS You're jealous of me.

Onka edges away violently.

ONKA Who, me? Jealous of you? That's too much, that really is!

BARONESS   You are too. Jealous. You'd exchange the whole of your potato existence just to be able to feel what I feel. To feel anything.

ONKA   This really is too much!

BARONESS   I may be unhappy, but I am alive; whereas you're unhappy and you're dead. Which of us two is better?

Onka springs to her feet, puts on her hat, and runs out of the bower.

BARONESS (*cont.*)   Your flowers!

Onka turns back. Baroness hands over the flowers and the umbrella. Onka snatches the flowers from her and runs onto the balcony. She stops next to Baron, who raises his eyes from the paper. She throws the flowers onto the table in front of Baron and runs into the house. Baron watches her go with amazement. Baroness goes up to the balcony, opens the umbrella out and twirls it, making it spin like a top.

BARON   What's the matter with her?

BARONESS   Oh, nothing. She's fallen in love with you, that's all.

Blackout.

SCENE THREE

Afternoon: Right of the stage is in sunlight, the left in shadow. Baroness is sitting in the rocking chair on the right, reading a book. Student, still wearing gloves, enters left, past the bower. Baroness raises her eyes from the book and watches him go up to the balcony without noticing her.

BARONESS   Good afternoon.

Student stops.

STUDENT   Good afternoon.

BARONESS   You weren't in for lunch today.

Student makes vague gesture.

BARONESS (*cont.*)   Weren't you hungry?

STUDENT   No.

BARONESS   I've noticed you hardly eat anything. Do please sit down.

Student sits on the vacant chair. He clenches and unclenches his fists.

BARONESS (*cont.*)   Why is that? Is something troubling you?

STUDENT   No.

BARONESS   Then why? At your age . . .

STUDENT   It repels me.

BARONESS   Food does?

STUDENT   Food, yes. And everything.

BARONESS   Everything?

STUDENT   I am repulsive.

BARONESS   What on earth are you saying? You're young, healthy, strong . . . Now, if you were a cripple . . . if you had a hump or something, I'd understand.

STUDENT   It makes no difference.

BARONESS   Come, even you will admit that it does make a difference, surely.

STUDENT   On the surface, perhaps. But not here . . .

Indicates his stomach.

BARONESS   Where? I can't see.

STUDENT   Inside.

BARONESS   Forgive me, but I still can't see. You're hermetically buttoned up.

STUDENT   Anyway, it's not visible.

BARONESS   Even if you undressed?

STUDENT   Even then.

BARONESS   Fascinating. Then where can it be seen?

STUDENT   In the dissecting room.

BARONESS   What you're saying is very strange. Are you by any chance cold?

STUDENT   No. Why do you ask?

BARONESS   You're always wearing gloves.

Student puts his hands behind his back.

BARONESS (*cont.*)   Do you suffer from eczema?

STUDENT   Of course not. But it makes no difference.

BARONESS   On the contrary: Eczema is an illness, whereas you're quite well. Or so at least you assure me.

STUDENT   It all depends on your point of view.

BARONESS   Really? So you do suffer from eczema?

STUDENT   No, I don't. But that isn't important.

BARONESS   You mean eczema isn't an illness, is that it?

STUDENT   From an all-embracing point of view it's not—no. The cells of tumors are cells in just the same way as so-called healthy cells. It's all the same.

BARONESS   In that case why won't you take off your gloves? Even if you do suffer from eczema?

STUDENT   I told you why.

BARONESS   Remind me.

STUDENT   They repel me.

BARONESS   Your own hands repel you?

STUDENT   My own hands most of all.

BARONESS   Why most of all?

STUDENT   Because they're mine. I can't free myself of them.

Leans across the table confidingly.

STUDENT (*cont.*)   They stalk me.

BARONESS   Do show me, please.

STUDENT (*Confidentially*)   I don't know that they'll want to just now.

BARONESS   Can't you stretch your hand out?

STUDENT   Sometimes I can't.

BARONESS   You amaze me more and more. I mean, you're not paralyzed, are you?

STUDENT   No. But sometimes my hands are separate.

Stretches his hands out and puts them on the table.

STUDENT (*cont.*)   They prance about like two rabbits in a field . . . or like something different . . . I don't know . . . some kind of creatures. I watch them . . . There, do you see that? They're off again.

His hands start to move about on the table.

BARONESS   Please take your gloves off.

STUDENT   What for?

BARONESS   I want to see for myself that you're not lying about not having eczema.

Student takes the glove off his right hand, stretches the hand out to Baroness, turning his head away as he does so. She takes his hand in hers.

BARONESS   Well, you were right.

STUDENT   What do you see?

BARONESS   Nothing. Your skin's completely clear. The nails, it's true, aren't exactly . . .

STUDENT   The skin, yes! But what about beneath the skin?

BARONESS   Beneath the skin?

STUDENT   Filth! Tendons, flesh, lymph, blood . . . all the same as . . .

BARONESS   The same as what? Do express yourself more clearly.

STUDENT   The same as what's on the plate.

BARONESS   Oh. You mean the food.

STUDENT   Tripe, brains, lungs, livers, kidneys—in me and in front of me. All slimy . . .

Baroness strokes his hand.

BARONESS   You have nice hands . . .

Student pulls his hand away sharply and replaces his glove.

STUDENT   We fool ourselves. We imagine we're clean, geometrically pure as an idea! But it's not true, Baroness. We are a heap, a stinking, pulsating plasma . . . or rather we are rotting, but even that's all the same. There's no difference between living and rotting—it's all a question of bacteria: Multiplying and dying is all the same bacteria, microbes, matter, filth . . .

BARONESS   We are rotting? Who is this "we"?

STUDENT   Each and every one of us.

BARONESS   I, too?

Student says nothing.

BARONESS (*cont.*)   Then what, according to you, is clean?

The sounds of piano music coming from the house. A classical—not romantic—piece is being played.

STUDENT   Music.

BARONESS   Do you play an instrument?

STUDENT   Unfortunately not. Though I'd like to be able to very much. I have no ear for music.

Pause as they both listen to the music.

STUDENT (*cont.*)   Who is it playing?

BARONESS   My husband.

Student gets up.

BARONESS (*cont.*)   Don't you want to listen?

Student leaves left. Blackout. The music continues to play.

SCENE FOUR

Lights up. Somewhat later that same afternoon. The shutters on the right are closed. Piano music coming from the house: a different piece from the one in the previous scene. Onek and Onka come in left riding a tandem bicycle: Onek is in front. There is a dead rooster with ruffled feathers across the handlebars. They cycle around the stage and stop in front of the balcony. Onek leans the bicycle against one of the balcony pillars. He picks up the rooster by the wing. He pulls the bellpull. The music stops. Baron appears in the doorway.

BARON Can I help you?

ONEK Oh, it's you.

BARON You rang.

ONEK Yes, but not for you.

BARON You don't need me either, madam?

ONKA We thought that . . . that . . . Onek, dear, apologize to the baron.

ONEK We were ringing for some service.

BARON What do I see there? You've been out hunting.

ONEK Hunting? No, of course not. We went on an outing. That's right, isn't it?

ONKA Yes. We visited the ruins, and we went to the lake . . .

BARON (*Pointing to the rooster*) Then what about that?

ONEK That? That was an accident.

ONKA We were cycling through the village and . . .

BARON (*To Onek*) I see . . . You ran over a rooster.

ONEK What do you mean I ran over a rooster? We both ran over it.

BARON (*To Onka*) Really? You, too, madam? I can't credit it. It's too cruel.

ONKA I . . . I didn't mean to. (*To Onek.*) You were in front.

ONEK That's right! Blame it on me. It's all my fault, I suppose. Anyway, no one ran it over. It just ran out under the wheel.

BARON (*Bowing to Onka*) Lady Macbeth . . .

Onek pulls the bellpull again. The right-hand shutter opens and Baroness appears in the window.

BARONESS   What's happening?

BARON   Lord and Lady Macbeth have just returned from an expedition.

BARONESS (*To Onka*)   Oh? Where did you go?

ONKA   We went to the lake and then we went to see the ruins of the old mill and this roo— . . .

BARONESS   I'll be right down.

She disappears from the window. Baron comes down from the balcony and goes up to Onek.

BARON   Are you sure it's dead?

ONEK   Why don't you check for yourself?

Baron stretches out his hand and touches the ruffled feathers. Baroness appears on the balcony.

BARON   Poor Don Juan. And you were such a good fellow. This is indeed a just punishment: death under a matrimonial cycle.

ONKA   It wasn't me! It wasn't my fault!

BARONESS   Control yourself. (*To Onek.*)   And take that garbage away. Why did you drag it here anyway?

ONEK   What do you mean "why"? You can make broth out of this.

BARONESS   Are you hungry then?

ONEK   No, but there's no point wasting it . . .

BARONESS   And why are you making such a racket?

ONEK   I was ringing for the hunchback. I wanted to send this to the kitchen.

BARONESS   Take it away at once. And throw it into some bushes somewhere. The farther away, the better.

ONEK   But . . .

BARONESS   And stop arguing. (*To Onka.*)   And you come inside.

Onka goes into the house obediently, Baroness letting her go in first and then following her in. Baron spreads his arms out as if to say: "What can I do?"

ONEK Where is that hunchback?

BARON He's not in. He went to the post office.

ONEK Why didn't you say so before?

BARON I thought you enjoyed ringing.

Onek turns around and leaves left, carrying the rooster. Baron watches him go until Onek disappears. Then he sits down in the rocking chair and starts to rock to and fro. Blackout.

SCENE FIVE

Dusk, the same light as at the end of act one: the croaking of frogs and the chirping of crickets. Sitting on the four chairs, which are arranged in a semicircle around the table, right: Baroness, Onka, Baron, and Onek. Student is sitting on the bench, left, facing the audience. Hunchback is busy as usual preparing the tea: seeing to the samovar, setting out the cups, etc.

Silence.

Suddenly, Onek starts to speak, loudly and adopting a note of false offhandedness.

ONEK Does anyone know the name of that hill?

Nobody answers. The company isn't very talkative this evening.

ONEK *(cont.)* It's called Hunchback's Peak.

Silence. When Hunchback isn't looking, Onka signals to Onek to stop.

ONEK *(cont.)* Does anyone know what Hunchback's Peak is named after? It's named after a hunchback.

BARON Is that a fact?

ONEK It certainly is. What do you think of that?

Silence. Hunchback starts to serve tea, starting with the women.

ONKA Exceptionally fine weather we're having, don't you think?

BARON What connection do you think there could be between the name of the hill and a . . . how would one put it . . . a . . .

ONEK Hunchback?

BARON Exactly so. Would you be good enough to clarify that for our benefit?

BARONESS Here we go.

ONKA (*Quietly*) I beg you, Baron, please stop.

ONEK How do you mean: What connection could there be? Hunchback's Peak. That is to say, the peak of the, or a, hunchback. Someone who is, or was, a hunchback. And the hill was named after him. The hunchback. It's really quite straightforward.

Hunchback appears to be oblivious to all this: He passes Baron some tea.

BARON I hadn't thought of it in that light but you may well be right.

ONKA Could we not talk about something else?

ONEK Why should we? Some people may regard it as unpleasant but I would venture to disagree with them. Personally I consider that a hunchback is better than an ordinary back.

BARON Now that is an interesting theory. But can you justify it?

Onka stirs her tea, rattling the spoon loudly against the side of her cup.

ONEK Indeed, I can. Take, as an example, the contrast between a hill and a plain. Now what is interesting about a plain? Nothing. It's either flat or very flat. But hills are altogether different: Some hills are higher, some are lower; the eye has something to dwell on. A hunchback makes a far better landscape than we do. There isn't a painter who would disagree. Isn't that so, Onka?

ONKA Kindly leave me out of this.

BARON Insofar as landscapes are concerned, you may well . . . but if one takes into account other considerations, it surely cannot be preferable to be a . . . how did you describe it?

ONEK A hunchback?

BARON Exactly so. After all, if one considers the proportions of the human body, the aesthetic canons formulated by the Greeks, the statue of the Belvedere Apollo to name but . . .

ONEK Do you know why the Greeks did not carve statues of hunchbacks, Baron?

BARON What an extraordinary question!

ONEK Because they were straight-backed themselves but they wanted to be hunchbacks.

BARON You amaze me, sir! The Greeks, you say, wanted to be hunchbacks?

ONEK But of course they did. Why should you be amazed by it? Everyone would like to be a hunchback.

ONKA If you don't stop this at once . . .

BARONESS Be quiet!

BARON I fear I still can't see how this superiority you impute manifests itself.

ONEK You don't like hunchbacks; is that it, Baron?

BARON You're changing the subject.

ONEK What do you have against hunchbacks?

BARON Nothing at all. I'd simply like to know what you have in their favor.

ONEK You should be ashamed of yourself, Baron.

BARON You still haven't answered my question.

ONEK I like them. Some of my best friends are hunchbacks. And I'm not ashamed to say that to your face, Baron.

BARON But my dear sir . . .

ONEK It's high time the matter was brought out into the open and we all admitted that a hump is a thing of beauty. That we should all have a hump.

ONKA He's completely drunk.

Student gets off the bench and walks right; he stops next to Onek and starts listening intently.

BARON Would you like to have a hump, sir?

ONEK   Who—me?

BARON   If we should all . . .

ONEK   Unfortunately, I've been deprived. By nature. It's a gift, Baron, a
gift from God—a blessing, something rare . . . You have to be born
with it, Baron. It's like . . .

STUDENT   Sssshhhh . . .

*Onek breaks off in midsentence. Everyone turns to the Student who has put a
finger to his lips, enjoining silence. Involuntarily, they also all start to listen.
Student, leaning across nearer to Onek, cups his ear with his hand.*

STUDENT   Your stomach's rumbling.

*Straightens himself out like a doctor who has just delivered his diagnosis. Baroness
bursts out laughing. Student returns to the bench and resumes his place on it.
Onek leaps to his feet.*

ONEK   How dare you?!

BARON   May I have the sugar, please?

*Hunchback passes him the sugar bowl. Onek sits down. Baroness contrives to
stifle her laughter. Nobody looks at Hunchback during the silence, during which
he becomes the focal point. Finally, Hunchback leaves, going into the house.*

SCENE SIX

ONKA   How could you?

ONEK   What did I say?

ONKA   You really are stupid, aren't you?

ONEK (*To Baron*)   It's all your fault. Why on earth did you drag the
Greeks into it?

ONKA   I've had enough.

Gets up.

ONEK   I didn't mean any harm.

Onka turns away from him and moves upstage. Onek gets up to follow her.

ONEK (*cont.*)   Wait! Look, just a minute . . .

BARON (*To Baroness*)   You don't happen to know where my cigars are, do you?

BARONESS   No, I do not!

She gets up and follows Onka and Onek upstage. Baron gets up and walks toward the house. Onka stops just short of the wings.

ONKA   Who is that?

As Onek catches up with her, she grabs his arm for protection.

ONKA (*cont.*)   There's somebody there!

Baron stops and stares at Onka and Onek.

ONEK (*Uncertainly*)   You're imagining it . . .

A deep and politely toned voice comes from the wings.

STRANGER   Good evening.

Scene Seven

Onek and Onka edge back. It has grown murkier. Out of the bushes and the darkness beyond the bower comes STRANGER. *He is an impressive-looking individual with a pointed, twirled mustache. He is wearing a bowler hat and a black suit. There is a gold watch chain visible across his vest. He walks toward the center of the stage past Onka, Onek, and Baroness. He is carrying a cane. Student gets off the bench as soon as he sees Stranger, who takes off his hat and repeats in his rich, polite voice.*

STRANGER   Good evening.

Pause.

ONEK (*Hesitantly*)   Good evening . . .

STRANGER   I'm glad to see you have dined already, ladies and gentlemen. I wouldn't have wanted to interrupt you.

They watch him in silence.

STRANGER (*cont.*)   Do please sit down, ladies and gentlemen. Let us not stand on ceremony. I'll just sit . . .

Looks around.

STRANGER (*cont.*)   Aaaah! . . .

Goes up onto the balcony, picks up the fifth chair, and carries it to the center of the stage, placing it so that the back is pointing into the wings left and so that he will be able to see all the other chairs.

STRANGER (*cont.*)   Here.

He is about to sit down when, realizing that nobody else has made a move, he draws himself up to his full height and, with a polite but emphatic gesture, invites the women to sit down. The women, acting a little as if they have been hypnotized, sit down, and Stranger follows suit, his back turned left. Onek sits, too. Baron and Student remain standing.

BARON   I don't believe we've had the pleasure, sir.

Stranger takes a small medicine bottle out of his pocket, removes the stopper, and places the bottle to his nose. He inhales deeply several times, replaces the stopper, and puts the bottle back into his pocket.

STRANGER   Please forgive me: I suffer from hay fever.

ONEK   The best thing for hay fever is camphor oil.

STRANGER   Really? I'll have to try it. But there's only one true and rather radical remedy and that is to change one's environment.

BARON   I can perceive no obstacle to that.

Student turns and moves toward the exit, left.

STRANGER   I must confess I'm not very fond of the countryside. All those herbs, flowers, grasses . . . To you, ladies and gentlemen, they are a source of pleasure and even of health. But where I'm concerned . . .

Turns in his chair.

STRANGER (*cont.*)   Surely you're not leaving us.

Student stops and stands at the exit, his back to the others. Pause. Stranger's eyes remain fixed on him. Student turns back and sits down on the bench again. Stranger turns back to the others.

STRANGER (*cont.*)   . . . Where I'm concerned they are quite simply a source of suffering. Well, and are you enjoying your vacation, ladies and gentlemen?

ONEK   Oh, very much. Thank you.

STRANGER (*To Onek*)   It is beautiful here, is it not? So peaceful. Quiet and relaxing.

ONEK   Yes, it is.

STRANGER   I'm sure you've been on an outing or two, have you not? It's a beautiful region for outings.

ONEK   Certainly it is.

STRANGER   And cycling trips . . .

ONEK   Cycling?

STRANGER   Yes, cycling.

ONEK   Why cycling?

STRANGER   Wonderful exercise, cycling. But it can cause accidents. Why only today a cyclist ran over a rooster in the village. But you've heard about that, haven't you?

ONEK   I haven't, no, but perhaps my wife . . .

STRANGER   Well, to add to the misfortune the cyclist simply took the victim of the accident and ran away. Instead of paying the owner compensation.

BARON   How do you know that?

STRANGER   The owner made a formal complaint.

BARON (*With no trace of irony now, politely, though not quite humbly.*)   Allow me to introduce myself, sir.

STRANGER   There's no need for that. No need at all.

Baron sits.

STRANGER (*cont.*)   Besides, the incident is trivial. The peasants don't know what they want. No, seen globally, this incident is meaningless. I simply mentioned it because we were talking about cycling.

ONEK   Even so, we should . . .

STRANGER (*Interrupting him sharply*)   I said it was meaningless!

Onek shuts up like a clam.

STRANGER (*cont.*)   There are far more important things happening. You must have read today's newspapers. Have you?

BARON   Yes.

STRANGER   And what do you say have to say about it?

BARON   About what?

STRANGER   Isn't it obvious?

BARON   I'm afraid I have to admit that it's not, though I read the paper from cover to cover. But then I might have overlooked it.

ONEK (*Leaping to his feet*)   I'll bring the paper out here.

STRANGER   There's no need for that. No need at all. I'm sure you would have noticed. It's possible that for certain reasons it wasn't announced publicly. It might have had a disastrous effect on people, given a bad example . . .

ONEK (*Resuming his seat*)   That's very true.

STRANGER   Nevertheless, the facts themselves cannot be altered, and therefore, they have to be taken into account. This is the back of beyond here, it's true, but that is precisely why one should be on one's guard all the more here. Why one shouldn't trust appearances. Indeed, one should mistrust everything and everyone. Do you trust me, ladies and gentlemen?

ONEK   In view of the fact that we are all loyal subjects . . .

STRANGER   Yes, of course. But how do you know who I am?

ONEK   Would you care for some tea? I'll ring for the . . .

Leaps from his chair.

STRANGER (*Very emphatically, with a trace of impatience*)   No, thank you!

Onek sits.

BARON   You'll permit me to remind you that it was I who first asked you to identify yourself, sir.

STRANGER . . . And you received no reply. And shall I tell you why? Because it would have meant nothing. Even if I had come here in uniform—and believe me, ladies and gentlemen, the uniform I might have appeared in would have been no ordinary uniform—it would have meant nothing because when all is said and done anyone can dress himself up in an uniform. Even if I had presented my credentials—and I might just mention that the signature on such credentials would have had a very profound effect on you, ladies and gentlemen, far more profound than you can even imagine—those credentials could just as easily have been forged. And even if they were genuine how could anyone be sure that I wasn't a wolf in sheep's clothing? Unfortunately, instances of infiltration are becoming increasingly frequent, and that includes the highest levels. And yet even all this is but the tip of the iceberg. Let us assume that everything is aboveboard: I am in a position of authority—and let us be clear that it is no subordinate position, though I prefer not to be more specific than that for the moment. I might just mention that in view of my record I have the unqualified support and confidence of the very highest authorities.

ONEK (*Leaping to his feet*) Your Excellency!

STRANGER Sit down!

Onek sits.

STRANGER (*cont.*) Yet despite all this, ladies and gentlemen, please be good enough to ask yourselves how one can be sure that after a long and brilliant career, after years of loyal service and blind obedience, I am not being gnawed by doubts? Chewed by the worm of skepticism? That, in short, I am not being devoured by the hyena of treachery?

ONEK Oh, no, Your Excellency, I'm sure you're not.

STRANGER (*Irritably*) Of course I'm not! (*Controlling himself.*) I simply wanted to provide you with an example, ladies and gentlemen. In the times that are coming upon us the question of identity, ladies and gentlemen, becomes increasingly difficult to resolve satisfactorily.

Turns to Student.

STRANGER (*cont.*) But why are you skulking in the corner like that? Do please join us. Please . . .

Student gets up off the bench reluctantly and walks across the stage, watched by Stranger. He walks up onto the balcony and sits in the rocking chair.

ONKA We really had no idea . . . This is such an honor.

BARONESS Are you staying long?

ONKA You will stay here with us, won't you? There is a room vacant in the house.

STRANGER That's very thoughtful of you, madam, but unfortunately I can't. Though I would dearly like to. Despite the hay fever . . . But I shall be in the area for a time. I have an assignment that will detain me here.

BARON If I have followed your argument correctly, sir, we are undergoing a crisis of confidence—a lack of confidence in our institutions, and ourselves. What do you advise we do in this situation?

STRANGER To disbelieve more than ever.

BARON Disbelieve? Disbelieve to regain confidence? But surely that is an irreconcilable contradiction.

STRANGER Not at all. If we disbelieve consistently and conclusively, we shall be certain in the knowledge that our faith is not being abused, and, thereby, we shall be able to regain our faith and our confidence.

ONKA But I need to have faith in someone!

STRANGER You are a woman, madam, and a wife. Marriage is in the same category as other institutions like the Church, the throne, and the monarchy . . . It belongs to the world of order. Institutions are what they are and nothing more. They acquire their identity by proclaiming it. But now we are being confronted by a different world: a world of antithetical identity. Our enemies are too weak to be capable of fighting us in the open. So they pretend to be what they are not. Not being us they pretend to be us. In other words, they are taking advantage of our faith. We shall be helpless unless we employ the same weapon against them: the weapon of antithetical identity.

BARON Do you mean that we are to pretend to be our own enemies?

STRANGER Precisely. We must pretend to be our own enemies in front of each other just in case we come across our enemies who are pretending to be us. It's the only way we can win their confidence and bring them out into the open.

BARON So despite everything it is a question of confidence.

STRANGER Yes, but not of our confidence. The struggle will be resolved when we know whose lack of confidence will overcome whose. Unfortunately we are not allowed the choice of weapons but now that the weapon has been forced upon us we must prove ourselves stronger than our enemies in its use.

BARON But in this situation it's impossible to know who is who!

STRANGER At first glance it is indeed impossible.

ONKA But that's terrible.

STRANGER I sympathize with your feelings, madam. But perhaps you do not fully appreciate the situation we're in. Perhaps you can't see what might happen if we do not take the appropriate steps and take them decisively. I may well be behaving indiscreetly if I tell you that we find ourselves on top of a volcano, but I shall tell you nevertheless.

ONKA You see, being here we don't know anything. Life here is so peaceful . . .

STRANGER . . . and meanwhile the volcano is erupting, bubbling beneath our feet. We are being poisoned by conspiracies, secret societies, plots . . .

ONEK It's true! The hunchbacks are plotting!

STRANGER The hunchbacks? What . . .

ONKA My husband doesn't feel very well. Please take no notice.

STRANGER As I was saying, there are terrorists. Mostly young people who believe that the real world can be replaced by a world of ideas. I don't deny that their motives are noble but they are ready to be bathed in a mire of vile, blood-soaked deeds for the sake of an abstract ideal. They are quite ready to disguise everything for the sake of honesty: They are even prepared to enslave the mind for the sake of freedom, freedom from people and things.

STUDENT   Are you accusing us of something?

They all turn to him as he stands up.

STUDENT (*To Onek*)   I demand to be given legal protection. Is it lawful for people to go around making insinuations? Either we are being accused of something, in which case we are entitled to a defense—and if that is so then I want you to be my lawyer—or we are free of any taint of suspicion.

ONEK   I'm afraid I specialize in probate law . . .

STUDENT   In that case I refuse to be put in a legally ambiguous situation. Good night.

Bows curtly and exits along the path, past the bower.

ONEK   In my opinion he is a highly suspect character.

STRANGER   Come, let's not exaggerate. He's young, that's all . . . Are you well acquainted with him, ladies and gentlemen?

BARONESS   Indeed we are.

STRANGER   And?

ONKA   He's a little strange.

BARONESS   There's nothing at all strange about him. And, furthermore, I do not consider it appropriate for us to be conducting a conversation of this kind.

STRANGER   In that case, I won't take up any more of your time, ladies and gentlemen.

Stands.

STRANGER (*cont.*)   Please do not lose heart. Get plenty of rest. Enjoy your vacation to the full, ladies and gentlemen, and let me advise you to take lots of gentle exercise.

Baron and Onek stand up. Stranger bows to the women, nods to the men. Baron returns the nod briefly and correctly while Onek bows from the waist.

STRANGER (*cont.*)   Take walks, go cycling . . .

Onek stretches out his hand but Stranger ignores it as he puts on his bowler hat and moves to the exit through which he made his entrance.

STRANGER *(cont.)*   Well, ladies and gentlemen, I'm afraid I'll be seeing you again shortly.

Leaves by the path. Onek moves after him hurriedly but Stranger disappears past the bower and into the dusk, which has grown murkier. Onek returns to center stage.

ONEK   What did he want?

Blackout.

ACT III

Late morning. The weather has changed: There is none of the brightness, none of the light-and-shade of the first two acts. The light is a dull, consistent white with neither shadows nor sheen. Baron and Onek are sitting at the table, right, Baron to the right of the table with his back to the wings, Onek opposite. They are playing chess. Baron moves a piece on the board.

BARON Check.

Pause. Onek meditates over the chessboard.

BARON (*cont.*) You seem to find it difficult to concentrate this morning.

ONEK I didn't sleep at all well last night.

BARON Yes, I heard you walking about on the stairs in the middle of the night.

ONEK That wasn't me.

BARON Wasn't it?

ONEK No, it wasn't. Who was it?

BARON It wasn't me, either.

Onek moves a piece.

BARON (*cont.*) Careful. I'll take that with my bishop.

Onek takes the piece back. Meditates.

BARON (*cont.*) Do you lock your door at night?

ONEK What about you?

BARON I did yesterday. But I do have a gun, you know.

ONEK Really?

BARON Well, I hadn't thought there was much danger, but after your performance yesterday . . .

ONEK It was your idea.

BARON But the way you implemented it was disastrous. You certainly didn't overdo the finesse, did you?

ONEK Why didn't you do anything yourself? It's easy to be wise in hindsight . . .

BARON I suspect I wouldn't have been able to do much myself, either. He's far too intelligent.

ONEK Didn't I tell you hunchbacks are crafty? I pleaded with you. I warned you . . . It was like beating my head against a brick wall. Now we've got a real mess on our hands.

BARON It could still work. But it would have to be done by someone else.

ONEK Who, for instance?

BARON A woman.

ONEK You mean: Make him feel superior to a woman?

BARON I mean make him feel himself our equal.

ONEK Impossible.

BARON When all is said and done, any handicap is, first and foremost, a handicap in one's relationships with women. If he could be persuaded that where women are concerned he is not handicapped at all, then he'll stop feeling handicapped in our company.

ONEK Could you explain that?

BARON Look, it's quite simple. If you, or I, tell a hunchback he's beautiful there's no reason for him to believe us. But if a woman told him . . . if, moreover, a woman demonstrated it to him . . .

Pause.

ONEK Women don't like hunchbacks.

BARON Are you quite sure of that?

ONEK But he's a dwarf. A hunchbacked d— . . .

Claps his hand to his mouth and stares at the balcony. Hunchback has appeared: He is wearing a leather apron and carrying a huge, curved gardening knife. He goes to the table, stops. Pause. Onek slowly starts to rise from his chair.

Scene Two

HUNCHBACK   I've found you at last, sir.

ONEK   You have?

Hunchback passes the knife to his left hand and takes a letter out of an inside pocket with his right. He gives it to Onek and moves away, left. Onek stands stock-still holding the letter.

BARON   What about the paper?

Hunchback stops.

HUNCHBACK   No paper, Baron.

BARON   Why not?

HUNCHBACK   It wasn't delivered, Baron.

Leaves left. Onek collapses onto the chair.

Scene Three

ONEK (*In a whisper*)   Did he hear?

BARON   Did he hear what?

ONEK (*Glancing around his shoulder*)   What I said about his being a dwarf.

BARON   I can't be sure.

ONEK   Maybe he didn't hear.

BARON   But I must say I didn't like his tone of voice.

ONEK   Resentful, wasn't it?

BARON   Worse than that.

ONEK   Defiant?

BARON That, too. But there was a trace of something else there.

ONEK Do tell me, for God's sake.

BARON There was something in his voice, something sort of . . . something kind of . . .

Pause. Onek takes out a handkerchief and mops the sweat from his forehead.

ONEK Do you think it would work, Baron?

BARON Do I think what would work?

ONEK You know. With a woman.

BARON There's no doubt it would. It's the last and only way.

ONEK I'm not a woman.

BARON Exactly. That's why there's no point discussing it.

ONEK No point at all.

BARON Let's not think about it anymore. Your move.

Blackout.

Scene Four

Onka and Baroness are downstage waiting, while Hunchback hangs a garden swing up from a branch by the bower.

BARONESS Why don't you leave him?

ONKA He needs me.

BARONESS For what?

ONKA You look at these things far too unequivocally, far too simply. Please don't take offense but you really don't understand what it means to be needed by someone.

BARONESS It's true. I'm afraid I don't.

ONKA I am with him and, by being with him, I help him cope with life. I agree he's not a strong man, but that's exactly why he needs me. Especially now.

BARONESS   Why especially now?

ONKA   Now that I found out he drinks.

BARONESS   Didn't you know?

ONKA   No. He hid it from me, the poor man. That's the best proof I could have that he really does love me.

HUNCHBACK   It's ready.

The women go upstage and sit on the swing, facing the audience. Hunchback pushes the swing and they start to move to and fro.

ONKA   What about you? Have you tried?

BARONESS   Tried what?

ONKA   Tried to leave.

BARONESS   I've longed for nothing else. But you know only too well why I can't.

ONKA   I didn't mean it like that.

BARONESS   Oh, you mean taking a lover.

ONKA   You're always so . . .

BARONESS   Well, what did you mean . . .

ONKA   You know . . .

BARONESS   Are you sure you want me to tell you?

ONKA   Not if you don't want to.

BARONESS   No.

ONKA   No?!

BARONESS   I don't want to.

ONKA   Do tell me.

BARONESS   Certainly not.

ONKA   Please.

Baroness leans across and whispers something into Onka's ear. The swing starts to move faster.

ONKA No!

BARONESS Yes.

ONKA Really?

Baroness whispers again.

ONKA And?

BARONESS And that was it.

ONKA I don't believe it.

BARONESS Unfortunately, it's true. It's never happened to you, I take it.

ONKA To me? Of course it has.

BARONESS You're lying.

ONKA I swear it has!

BARONESS Seriously?

ONKA Well, not completely.

BARONESS What do you mean?

Onka leans over and whispers in Baroness's ear. Baroness bursts out laughing.

ONKA Stop laughing!

BARONESS But it's very funny.

ONKA I'll never tell you anything again.

BARONESS Just a minute. Do you mean . . .

Whispers.

ONKA Well, exactly!

BARONESS But then . . .

She whispers again. Onka bursts out laughing: Both women are now laughing. Baroness whispers something more.

ONKA (*Laughing*) Oh, no! Stop it, please!

BARONESS Well, don't you think so?

ONKA   Or then again . . .

Puts her arm around Baroness and whispers. A fresh burst of laughter. The swing takes them higher and higher as they laugh till they are almost crying. They put their arms around each other, holding onto their hats, which are in danger of being swept off their heads by the wind. Suddenly they stop laughing as Student appears on the balcony, then walks across stage, past the swing, taking no notice of them or Hunchback. The women's eyes follow him as, ascetic and lost in thought, he leaves left. Onka leans forward, watching him leave, then, puffing out her cheeks, she emits a vulgar and contemptuous sound. Both women burst out with cheerful and carefree laughter.

Blackout.

SCENE FIVE

Stranger is standing outside the house, observing it. The same bunch of wild flowers that Onka brought from her walk with Baroness and then presented to Baron flies out of the window on the right and falls at Stranger's feet. Surprised, Stranger picks up the flowers. Baron, wearing a dressing gown, appears in the window. Noticing Stranger with the flowers in his hand, Baron is about to withdraw, but is too late.

STRANGER (*Raising his bowler*)   Thank you very much.

BARONESS   I'm not . . .

STRANGER   I'm touched, but I don't really think I have done anything to deserve such a gift.

BARON   I'm afraid there seems to have been a misunderstanding.

STRANGER   Ah, in that case . . .

Goes up to Baron and gives him the flowers. Just as Baron is stretching his hand for them automatically, Onek appears left, carrying a fishing rod over his shoulder and a wicker basket with a lid. He stops, thunderstruck.

BARON (*Taking the flowers*)   Thank you.

ONEK   Excuse me . . .

Coughs to draw attention to himself. Stranger turns to him.

ONEK (*cont.*) Excuse me.

STRANGER What are you doing here?

ONEK I've just been fishing.

STRANGER Yes, of course. And are they biting today?

ONEK They certainly are.

STRANGER Yes, it is fine weather for fishing, is it not?

BARON A little humid.

STRANGER That's only to be expected before a thunderstorm.

ONEK (*Coming closer to the house*) What beautiful flowers . . .

STRANGER I'm afraid there's been a misunderstanding.

ONEK Did you pick them yourself?

BARON My wife was just doing some cleaning and . . .

STRANGER A coincidence.

BARON The gentleman was just kind enough to pass them . . .

ONEK I understand perfectly. Flowers can say more than words ever can.

STRANGER (*Sharply*) I trust you have a fishing permit.

ONEK Who, me?

STRANGER It is my duty to point out that fishing without a permit makes you liable to very severe fines.

ONEK But I didn't catch anything! I must have dozed off. Sitting by the lake. It's the weather . . .

STRANGER I must warn you that your record isn't exactly unblemished.

ONEK Thank you. I'm very grateful to you. I was just going. I'll just be off, then . . .

Backs away toward the balcony.

STRANGER One more thing.

ONEK I don't want to interrupt. I'll just . . .

STRANGER Be good enough to tell that young man that I should very much like to see him.

ONEK Yes, right away. He's a very pleasant young man.

STRANGER On a matter of great urgency.

ONEK Yes, of course. I understand. But he's not in.

STRANGER How do you know that?

ONEK I saw him by the lake.

STRANGER Then let me wish you both a very good afternoon.

Raises his bowler and leaves left.

ONEK I didn't realize you were so well acquainted.

Baron shrugs and withdraws from the window with his flowers. Onek takes a fish out of the basket and goes into the house. Pause. The sound of glass smashing comes from the other side of the window. The flowers come flying out through the window again and fall onto the ground.

SCENE SIX

Late dusk, night almost; therefore much darker than at the ends of acts one and two. Sounds of frogs croaking and birds singing. Right-hand window is open and lit, a beam of light coming out of the window's rectangle and falling onto the lawn. There is more light falling onto the balcony as it comes through the door, which is also open. There are a few Chinese lanterns hung over the table, colored paper balls containing burning candles stretched out over the stage on a wire. A waltz is being played on the piano in the house. The table is covered by a white tablecloth and on it is a silver champagne bucket containing a bottle of champagne. There are glasses, side dishes, and plates with small sandwiches and cakes, all of them started, on the table. Five chairs scattered around the stage. There are napkins, Onka's stole, and Onek's jacket on the chairs. It's clear the party has been going on for some time. A woman's voice hums the melody of the waltz though not in particularly good time: Occasionally, a man's voice joins in. Student is sitting in the rocking chair on the balcony: He is holding a bottle of champagne and rocking himself to and fro. The sound of Onka laughing and the waltz playing come from inside the house. Onka runs out onto the balcony. She is holding a glass of champagne. Onek follows her out. He is in shirtsleeves.

ONEK   You've had enough!

Onka, laughing, sits on the arm of the rocking chair.

ONKA   Please protect me!

ONEK   I beg you: You've had quite enough to drink already.

ONKA   I'm an enchanted princess and that is a dragon. I'll reward you handsomely.

Presses her glass against Student's lips and pours champagne into his mouth.

ONEK   I won't ask you again.

Student holds the bottle out to him, inviting him to drink.

ONEK (*cont.*)   And I thought you were a serious young man. And here you are joining in this distasteful orgy along with the rest.

STUDENT   I challenge you to a duel. Bang-bang!

Pretends to shoot Onek with his fingers as if they were a pistol.

ONEK   Silly games.

STUDENT   I'm not talking to you. You're dead.

Onka bursts out laughing.

ONEK   What are you laughing at?

ONKA   Ssshhh, you're dead. Haven't you noticed you're dead?

ONEK   No, I have not.

ONKA   I'm not surprised. You're drunk.

Student gets up suddenly, nearly causing Onka to fall off the chair.

ONEK   What charming manners!

Student withdraws upstage and stands with his back to the balcony. Takes out a watch and looks at it?

ONKA   Come on, let's dance!

Seizes Onek's hand and drags him off the balcony. Forces him to take a few turns of a waltz. The waltz being played on the piano breaks off suddenly. Onek and Onka fall onto a couple of chairs, panting. Baron appears in the doorway. He is holding a glass.

ONEK   Oh, welcome. Well–come. You're the one responsible for what's happening: You made my wife drunk.

BARON (*To Onka*)   Is that true?

ONKA   Take no notice of that hypocrite, Baron. He wants to pretend that he's faultless.

ONEK   What do you mean "pretend I'm faultless"? Was it me who ordered all that champagne for everyone.

ONKA   You? Order champagne? For everyone? Out of the question.

ONEK   Well, then.

ONKA   In-con-ceiv-able.

Baron goes down from the balcony, takes the stole from the back of a chair, and chivalrously puts it around Onka's shoulders. Then he takes the bottle out of the bucket. Onka proffers him her glass.

ONKA   More!

BARON   With the greatest pleasure.

Pours some out for her and for himself. Sits and raises his glass.

BARON   Let us drink to the geese!

ONEK   What geese?

BARON   The wild geese. Did you not know that the wild geese are migrating extraordinarily early this year? It seems that, though it's still July, a gaggle of geese was seen flying south only this afternoon.

ONEK   So what? Let them fly away if they want to.

BARON   It's an extraordinary phenomenon.

STUDENT (*Going up to Baron*)   Did you see them?

BARON   Not personally, no. But our host told me about them.

STUDENT   It's possible.

BARON   Are you a student of ornithology?

STUDENT   No. But it is possible.

BARON (*Shrugging*)   It is a fact.

STUDENT   Facts are possible, too.

BARON   I'm afraid I don't follow.

STUDENT   That doesn't matter.

BARON   You're not being overly polite, are you?

STUDENT   Especially as you're paying for my drink?

BARON   You do me the honor of accepting.

STUDENT   You're right there.

ONKA   Is our prince out of sorts, then?

Baroness appears on the balcony, waving a handwritten sheet of paper.

SCENE SEVEN

BARONESS   I found it!

ONKA   Come down here. Come down to us. Where have you been hiding so long?

BARONESS (*Going down to them*)   Do you know where I found it? In a shoe. Now isn't that a marvelous hiding place?

ONKA   A love letter!

BARONESS   Something much better than that. Poetry.

ONKA   Not poetry!

BARONESS   A poetic opus. A poem. Shall I read it to you?

BARON   No.

ONEK   I never heard of anyone hiding poems in shoes before.

BARONESS   Ah, but my husband does. I told you my husband is a poet, didn't I?

ONKA   Hurray!

ONEK   But why does he hide them—in shoes?

BARONESS   Because he's ashamed.

ONEK   What's there to be ashamed of?

BARONESS   My husband is very shy when it comes to his own poetry. He even hides his poems from me. Don't you, darling?

Baron is silent.

STUDENT   Well, well, well. Who would have thought . . .

ONEK   Really, there's no need to be shy . . .

STUDENT   Are they lyrical poems?

ONKA   Read them, read them!

ONEK   It will be a real pleasure to hear them.

Student draws up a chair and sits down next to Onka.

STUDENT   Read them, read them!

ONKA   Read them! Read them!

BARON   (*Quietly*)   I wouldn't advise you to.

BARONESS   Very well. Here, by public demand . . .

Stands beneath the Chinese lanterns in a mock-theatrical pose, holding the sheet of paper in one hand and placing the other hand on her heart.

BARONESS   (*cont.*)   First of all—the title.

Baron gets up.

BARONESS   (*cont.*)   "On the fortieth anniversary of my birth" . . .

Baron takes a couple of steps toward her and stretches his hand out for the sheet of paper. Baroness retreats the same number of steps, maintaining her posture and looking at the sheet. Onka becomes serious.

BARONESS   (*cont.*)   "On the fortieth anniversary of my birth" . . .

ONEK   We've had that already.

STUDENT   Do read on. Please.

Onka seizes the Student's arm, restraining him. Baron takes a few more steps forward with his hand outstretched. Baroness retreats but she is no longer posing. The hand which was on her heart has dropped. She repeats, but more softly this time.

BARONESS   "On the fortieth . . .

Baron clicks the fingers of his outstretched hand once. Baroness stops reading and raises her eyes to him. She lets the hand that is holding the sheet of paper drop to her side. Baron and Baroness look into each other's eyes. Silence. Onka tugs nervously at the ends of her stole. The silence becomes prolonged. Onka picks up a glass from the table and hurls it to the ground, smashing it. The sound of the breaking glass cuts through the silence. Everyone, including Baron and Baroness, turns to Onka.

ONKA   I'm sorry. I didn't mean to . . .

Onek bends down to pick up the broken glass, catches against Student accidentally; Student moves his chair a little; a minor commotion ensues. Baroness hides the sheet of paper in her cleavage and joins the rest of the company. Baron turns and goes back to the table. He sits down.

ONEK (*Picking up shards of broken glass*)   I did warn you, I asked you . . .

BARONESS   It's too dark. I can't read it.

STUDENT   What a shame. I'm very fond of poetry. Aaaagh!

Onka has kicked him on the ankle.

ONKA   I'm sorry, I didn't mean to.

ONEK   I don't know what's come over you, really I don't.

Baroness stands behind Onka, leans over, and kisses her lightly on top of her head. She puts her hands on Onka's shoulders, embraces her, pressing her cheek against Onka's. Onek gets up and puts his jacket on.

ONEK   Right. Time for bed!

BARON   Already? But the evening's only just begun.

Student looks at his watch. Hunchback comes out of the house carrying a bucket full of bottles. Seeing him, Onka starts to clap.

SCENE EIGHT

ONEK   Be good enough to take that straight back!

Ignoring him, Hunchback puts the bucket down on the table and starts opening a bottle.

BARON (*In a whisper, to Onek*)   That was said far too sharply.

ONEK   I didn't say anything

Baron stands up.

BARON   Ladies and gentlemen, I propose that our next toast should be
our host.

ONKA   Let's drink his health. Yes, let's drink!

Baron takes the bottle from Hunchback.

BARON   For once he'll be our guest.

ONKA   Long live our host!

STUDENT   It makes no difference to me.

*Baron opens the bottle: The cork shoots out, the champagne starts to froth. Baron
gives Hunchback a glass. Onka, Baroness, and Student go up to Baron with
their glasses. Baron pours, starting with Hunchback. Baron turns to Onek, who
is still sitting, away from everyone else.*

BARON   How about you?

ONEK   You know my principles.

BARON   What's that? You refuse to drink the health of our host?

STUDENT   Good shot.

ONKA   I told you he was a hypocrite.

STUDENT (*Pretending he's shooting from a gun*)   Bang-bang.

ONKA   You might at least have the courage . . .

BARON   This isn't very generous of you. Our host will have every right
to feel insulted.

Onek gets up.

ONEK   Oh, very well. Just this once.

STUDENT   Got him!

*Onek picks up a glass and joins the others. Makes a grimace, which is supposed
to be a smile, toward Hunchback. Baron pours. Student makes a sound imitating
hunting horns proclaiming a kill. Curls his hand into a trumpet and makes a
noise next to Onek's ear.*

STUDENT   Halla-lee . . .

Baron raises his glass.

BARON   Well, then, ladies and gentlemen . . .

STUDENT   Halla-lee . . .

ONEK   (*Waving Student away*)   Get off me, can't you?!

BARON   Your very good health, sir!

They all drink Hunchback's health. He becomes the center of attention. Then he, too, drinks.

BARON   (*cont.*)   All the way! Down the hatch!

Everyone, except Onek, obeys this injunction and empties his or her glass. Onek leaves his half full.

BARON   (*cont.*)   And now for a little surprise.

STUDENT   Fireworks and illuminations.

The stage is lit briefly as if by the glow of a distant fire. This is followed by a clap of distant thunder. They all fall silent for a moment, astonished.

ONKA   What was that?

ONEK   Thunder.

STUDENT   That wasn't thunder.

BARON   Are you a student of meteorology?

STUDENT   No. But it wasn't thunder.

ONEK   What was it, then?

STUDENT   Fireworks.

With the exception of Hunchback, they all laugh at the joke. The champagne is beginning to take effect.

BARON   And now for the surprise. We're going on a picnic.

ONEK   Are you completely crazy?

ONKA   (*Clapping happily*)   A picnic! A picnic!

BARON   A picnic, together with a sightseeing expedition. A visit to the greatest attraction of this region, to see unforgettable sights and experience a metaphysical enchantment. We're all going to the devil's hill.

ONEK   Now? In the middle of the night?

BARON   You seem to be unaware of the fact that one can see witches only at night.

ONKA   Are we going to see some witches?

BARON   With a bit of luck . . .

ONKA   Ooooh, I'm scared.

BARON   There's no danger for the ladies. As for the men . . . That depends on one's point of view.

ONEK   In the dark? Over those potholes?

ONKA   That's a point. Will we be able to find the place?

BARON   We have an excellent guide with us. Our host will show us the way. After all, he does know the region very well. Isn't that so?

Hunchback bows.

ONKA (*To Baroness*)   Will you go?

BARONESS   Of course.

ONKA   We're going! We're going!

ONEK   This is insane. I won't lift a hand to help . . .

STUDENT   A foot, surely.

ONEK   A foot? Why a foot?

STUDENT   Well, you're not going to crawl on all fours, are you?

ONEK   Ha, ha, very witty. I'm not going anywhere or anyhow. I've never heard a more insane idea.

ONKA   Why do you always have to spoil the fun?

BARON   Have you no *afflatus*?

ONEK   What!?

BARON   No spark of imagination?

ONEK   No, I do not. And I am not going anywhere.

BARONESS   Nobody's forcing you to.

ONEK   Nobody, eh?

BARONESS   Nobody. You can stay at home.

STUDENT   In bed.

BARON   We'd be very sorry, but if you really don't want to . . .

ONEK   In that case—good night!

ONKA   Good night.

ONEK   Who was that to?

ONKA   You, of course.

ONEK   But we are staying here.

ONKA.   You are staying here. I am going.

ONEK   On your own?!

BARON   But your wife is going with us.

ONEK   I forbid it!

Onka goes up to Baron and takes his arm. Baroness takes Student's arm.

BARON   Off we go!

Hunchback goes into the house. Both couples—Baron and Onka leading—turn to left. Baron hums the waltz he was playing earlier. Onka joins in. They both hum, recapturing the same mood of jollity with which the scene began.

BARONESS   Do you believe in witches?

STUDENT   It makes no difference to me.

BARONESS   You're not very polite, are you?

STUDENT   Your husband was good enough to draw attention to the same thing earlier.

BARONESS   You don't like my husband, do you?

STUDENT   I loathe him.

BARONESS   I know how you feel.

Both couples leave left. Onek stands dumbfounded.

Hunchback comes out of the house wearing a cloak that reaches down to the ground. He is carrying a basket and a lantern. Ignoring Onek he collects the bottles from the table and puts them into the basket. Leaves left. Onek walks left, slowly, pausing at almost every step. Suddenly, he turns around, rushes across to the table, with one gulp drinks what he previously left in his glass, and runs out right, following the others.

Blackout.

SCENE NINE

Overcast dawn, though the rain has fallen already. Onek, wrapped in a blanket, is sitting in the rocking chair on the balcony. He is dozing, his mouth open, his head pressed against his shoulder, one arm dangling helplessly down. His is the dramatic and immobile position of a passenger convulsively calcified after falling asleep at dawn following a tiring and uncomfortable nighttime train journey. From time to time he emits a snore. All around him are the remains of the previous night's feast just as they were left at the end of the previous scene. Baron comes out onto the balcony. He is wearing a smoking jacket and carrying a cup of hot tea without a saucer. He switches the cup from one hand to the other because the heat is scalding his fingers. He stops next to Onek and stares ahead, stirring the tea with a spoon.

BARON   Not back yet?

Onek wakes with a tempestuous snore.

BARON *(cont.)*   Not back yet?

ONEK   What?

BARON   You certainly do make a good sentry, don't you? Falling asleep on duty.

ONEK   What time is it?

BARON   Four o'clock.

ONEK Aren't they back yet?

BARON That's what I asked you.

Onek unwinds the blanket from around himself. Stands.

ONEK Where did you get the tea?

BARON From the kitchen.

Onek moves to the door of the house, changes his mind, and goes back; then he comes down from the balcony. Looks around.

ONEK It's stopped raining.

Goes back to the balcony.

ONEK (*cont.*) Maybe something's happened to them . . .

BARON I shouldn't think so. They're in good hands.

ONEK I'm sure they got lost.

BARON I doubt it. He's a local man.

ONEK Then why aren't they back yet?

Baron sits on the railings of the balcony and takes an enormous sip of tea. Onek sneezes.

BARON Have you caught a cold?

ONEK I wouldn't be surprised. I got soaked to the skin.

BARON You weren't the only one.

ONEK I told you . . .

BARON You're not starting that again, are you?

ONEK How on earth did we manage to lose one another?

BARON What's so surprising about that? The thunderstorm, the downpour . . .

ONEK It's all your fault. I told you we should have gone left . . .

BARON . . . and I said we should go right. How can you be so sure they turned left?

ONEK Well, they didn't turn right, did they?

BARON They might have gone straight on.

ONEK It was a terrible night.

BARON Romantic.

ONEK Rheumatic, you mean. I have pains . . .

BARON Yes, it was a trifle damp in the wood.

ONEK Damn it all!

BARON Your wife was in very good form, wasn't she?

Onek sits in the rocking chair again.

ONEK I can't understand what's keeping them so long.

BARON They're walking, picking wild strawberries, admiring the flora . . .

ONEK You do talk rubbish sometimes!

BARON Perhaps you have a better explanation. Do you?

Pause.

ONEK I think we should go out to look for them.

BARON A gentleman would never dream of doing anything like that.

ONEK But damn it—she's my wife!

BARON That is why.

ONEK What do you mean? What are you trying to say?

BARON I? I'm saying nothing. It's you who are . . .

Pause.

ONEK He's a hunchback.

BARON He certainly is.

ONEK A small hunchback. Disgusting. A nightmare on legs. Wouldn't you say so?

BARON I would. A monster.

ONEK (*Relieved*) I knew it. There's no more to be said.

BARON Do you know the story of Beauty and the Beast?

ONEK What's that?

BARON The thing takes place in romantic scenery—a wood. A beautiful woman comes across a beast. And do you know what happens next?

ONEK She runs away.

BARON Not at all. She falls in love with him. Totally and irrevocably.

ONEK Sheer nonsense.

BARON It's the attraction of opposites, you see.

ONEK I tell you it's absolute nonsense!

BARON Have it your own way.

Pause.

ONEK What time is it?

BARON Past four.

STUDENT (*Coming out of the house onto the balcony*) Twenty past four.

Student is fully dressed. He is carrying his battered case. When he appears he is just putting his watch back into his pocket.

SCENE TEN

BARON I thought you were asleep.

STUDENT No. I'm leaving.

BARON So suddenly?

STUDENT Do you have any objections?

BARON You know, you bore me.

STUDENT (*To Onek*) Well, and how is our game? Getting tender?

ONEK Go to hell!

STUDENT Good-bye. It was very well to make your acquaintance.

Goes down from the balcony and moves left. Onka and Baroness enter left, holding each other by the arm, both of them protected by the Hunchback's cloak. Hunchback, carrying the empty basket and the now extinguished lantern, follows them on. Seeing the women, Student stops in the center of the stage. Onek gets up. Baron doesn't move.

ONEK   Aaaaah, at long laaaast . . .

BARONESS (*To Student*)   Are you leaving us?

STUDENT   Yes. But that doesn't matter. Your welcoming committee is waiting for you.

Indicates Onek and Baron.

STUDENT (*cont.*)   I'm sorry I can't be present at the ceremony.

Hunchback walks past the women and Student. Goes up onto the balcony, bows to the two men as he goes past them, and disappears into the house. Onek glares after him and then stares at the door through which Hunchback went: His back is turned to Student and the two women. Baron sips his tea.

BARONESS   Nevertheless, I think you will be present.

STUDENT   I very much regret to have to tell you that you're mistaken. I have some important business to attend to.

BARONESS   I very much regret to have to inform you that you are staying. The police are not allowing anyone into the station . . .

STUDENT   How do you know . . .

BARONESS   We ran across some peasants on our way and they were just returning from the station and warning everyone. It looked as if the whole village was moving: children, livestock, and everything.

The two women move toward the house. Student follows them. The women go up onto the balcony. Onek turns around to them. They stop in front of him as he blocks their path.

ONEK   And now I think it's time for a little talk.

BARONESS   You're in our way.

Onek steps to one side. The two women go into the house.

STUDENT You will testify that I was with you both all night, won't you?

Baron and Onek do not react. Getting no response, Student goes into the house. Baron and Onek look at each other. Onek turns to the door and rushes into the house. Baron sips his tea.

Blackout.

ACT IV

Morning. Sunny weather again, as in acts one and two. The Chinese lanterns and all other traces of the feast have vanished. Onek and Baron are onstage.

ONEK You'll challenge him to a duel and shoot him like a dog.

BARON I can't. The laws of honor forbid me to duel with a cripple.

Pause.

BARON (*cont.*) But you could.

ONEK I could?

BARON I can lend you the weapons.

ONEK No . . . If you can't, then I can't either. The laws of honor, you know.

BARON My apologies. I did not wish to imply any slight.

ONEK But couldn't you . . . shoot him without a duel?

BARON I make a point of not shooting servants.

ONEK You could always make an exception in his case.

BARON Besides, I'm not in the least bit jealous.

ONEK You're not?

BARON Of course not. I believe that a husband should have complete faith in his wife. Didn't we swear we would be faithful to one another?

ONEK But . . .

BARON Besides, as a Christian I forgive my enemies.

ONEK I didn't know you were a believer.

BARON I wasn't. But I have become one confronted by the evidence. The existence of the hunchback is sufficient proof of the existence of God.

ONEK   How do you work that out?

BARON   It's clear only a superior being can create a being that is inferior.

ONEK   What about you and me?

BARON   I'm speaking only for myself, of course, but I don't consider myself sufficiently inferior to provide satisfactory evidence for the existence of God.

ONEK   So what you're saying is I can't rely on your help.

BARON   I'll serve you with good advice, but that is all.

ONEK   But why does it have to be a hunchback . . . a hunchback like him . . .

BARON   Third level.

ONEK   What?

BARON   You are suffering the third level of torment. I offer you my sympathy.

ONEK   Oh, really. And what, pray, is the first level?

BARON   The first level of torment comes when we are jealous of a rival who is our equal. In looks. The second level of torment is when we are jealous of a rival who is better-looking than us. In those circumstances we can always revert to hoping that we can become as good-looking as our rival. But the third level is the result of having an ugly rival of whom we are jealous. Then we don't even have recourse to wanting to be like him. After all, who wants to be ugly? It's not possible to want the impossible. Yes, my dear sir. Jealousy of beauty is hard to bear, but jealousy of ugliness is intolerable.

ONEK   He's a mere flunky!

BARON   Ah, so you're not a democrat after all.

ONEK   A hunchbacked flunky!

BARON   You're quite wrong to be angry. The only way to universal equality is through misalliances, through socially and biologically mixed marriages. When all the children of the world are partially hunchbacked then everything will become straightforward.

ONEK   I'll annihilate him!

BARON   Now that is not nice, not nice at all. On the other hand . . .
Who knows? Maybe, as a democrat and a liberal, you are right . . .
Let's analyze the problem. The ideal of democracy is universal
equality. It's such a magnificent ideal it's worth sacrificing a great deal
for it. But equality between a majority and a minority is impossible;
that's obvious from a definition of the two terms. So, it is necessary to
eliminate either the majority or the minority. Since we are democrats,
the elimination of the majority doesn't even enter into consideration.
Therefore, it is essential to eliminate the minority . . . Yes, you're
right.

ONEK   What are you talking about? All I said was . . . Look, when a
man's on edge he says all sorts of things he doesn't mean.

BARON   Yes, of course, I realize that it would be a utopia.

Pause.

BARON (*cont.*)   So do you want to borrow that pistol?

ONEK   Why should I . . .

BARON   To protect yourself. You'll feel safer.

ONEK   But he doesn't have anything against me now . . . now that . . .
you know what I mean . . .

Fidgets in a paroxysm of embarrassment.

BARON   You mean now that he feels himself to be your equal? Now
that there's no longer any inferiority complex?

ONEK   Precisely.

Wipes his forehead, tugs at his collar, etc.

BARON   You'll pardon me for saying this, but there is no proof that it
happened the way you think it did.

ONEK   What do you mean? You mean there was nothing between
them?

BARON   I can't say that, either. Not with any degree of certainty.

Onek runs up to Baron and seizes him by the arm.

ONEK What, then? How? What's happening? What did happen? Why don't you just tell me?

BARON One can never be sure of anything.

Onek lets go of Baron's arm.

ONEK I'll go mad.

BARON Maybe he feels superior to you now.

Hunchback comes out of the house, onto the balcony.

HUNCHBACK A letter for . . .

Before he can finish the sentence, Onek turns and runs out left.

SCENE TWO

HUNCHBACK Is the gentleman feeling unwell.

BARON I fear he is.

HUNCHBACK A letter for you, Baron.

Hands Baron a note. The letter is clearly very brief because Baron reads it in a couple of seconds.

BARON Did she ask for a reply?

HUNCHBACK No, Baron.

Pause. Hunchback turns to leave.

BARON (*Sharply, coarsely*) Hey, you—wait!

Hunchback turns back. Baron controls himself and speaks politely again.

BARON Please request her to come here immediately.

HUNCHBACK Very good, sir.

BARON I'll wait for her here.

Hunchback goes into the house. Baron sits on a chair facing the house and lights up a cigar.

Scene Three

Onka, wearing a dressing gown, comes out onto the balcony. Baron stands. Onka comes down from the balcony and sits on a chair. She crosses her legs. Baron continues to stand.

BARON   I'm glad to see you're feeling better now.

Pause. Onka inspects him closely as if seeing him for the first time.

BARON   I must admit that nocturnal episode was a little tiring.

Baron waits for a reply, according to the rules of polite conversation, but in vain. Only after a considerable time does Onka speak.

ONKA   Well?

BARON   I hope that as a result of it you don't think too badly of me.

ONKA   I'm listening.

BARON   I wouldn't want you to . . .

ONKA   You wanted to talk.

BARON (*Slightly irritated*)   I'm sorry, I don't understand.

ONKA   I'm waiting.

BARON   Excuse me for saying so, but it is I who am waiting. For my wife.

ONKA   She won't come.

Pause. Baron sits down opposite Onka. Onka studies her nails.

BARON   She won't come?

ONKA   No. She asked me to come in her stead. Only if I felt like doing so, of course.

BARON   Do you know . . . about this?

Shows her the note.

ONKA   Of course I do. She wrote it in my presence.

Pause.

ONKA (*cont.*)   And she asked me to find out if you had anything to say.

BARON   Am I to understand, then, that what I have to say doesn't interest her?

ONKA   Not in the least. She is not interested.

BARON   Well, well . . .

ONKA   Do you have anything to say?

BARON   Anything to say to you?

ONKA   I'll repeat it to her.

BARON   But if she's not interested . . .

ONKA   I don't have to repeat it to her. You can just tell me.

BARON   And are you interested?

Onka studies her nails.

ONKA   A little.

BARON   You're very kind.

ONKA   On the other hand, you could talk about something completely different.

BARON   And would that, too, interest you?

ONKA   More, even.

She swings the top leg rhythmically.

BARON   I appreciate that. I really do appreciate it.

ONKA   Why are you so conceited?

BARON   I? Conceited? I was simply expressing my gratitude.

ONKA   You're conceited. And you've no cause to be. Not now.

BARON   You think not?

ONKA   I know it. Now you're only worth as much as you're really worth.

BARON   And how much is that? How much am I worth, according to you . . .

Onka remains silent.

BARON (*cont.*)   Thank you. In which case I'll just continue to be conceited.

Gets up.

ONKA   Don't go.

BARON   I'm not going. I'm simply moving.

Onka gets up and goes up to Baron. She stands much closer than is necessary to conduct a conversation.

ONKA   Where to?

Baron doesn't reply. Onka gets very close to him and raises her head up to him. Baron stands stiffly, his arms held tight against his body. A motionless pause. Onka raises her hands and adjusts Baron's tie. Baron turns away from her and goes into the house. Onka watches him until he disappears, then walks slowly across to the bower and sits there, her back to the audience.

Student peers around a tree, looks all around, then starts walking left on tiptoe.

SCENE FOUR

As Student reaches exit, left; Stranger enters and they meet face-to-face.

STUDENT   I might as well tell you that I refuse to answer any questions.

STRANGER   I have no intention of asking any questions.

STUDENT   In that case we have nothing to say to one another.

STRANGER   I'll do the talking.

STUDENT   I don't want you to.

STRANGER   But I want to.

Student turns and goes toward the balcony. Stranger stands in his way.

STRANGER (*cont.*)   I'm asking you to listen. Please.

Student sits on a chair. Stranger removes his bowler and places it and the cane on the table, then sits down opposite Student, on the other side of the table.

STRANGER (*cont.*)   You're looking slightly unwell. Didn't you sleep well?

STUDENT   We went on an expedition.

STRANGER   We?

STUDENT   I have witnesses.

STRANGER   In that case you must have heard the explosion.

STUDENT   What explosion?

STRANGER   Last night the ruins of the old mill were blown up.

STUDENT   We did hear something. We thought it was a thunderstorm.

STRANGER   Who do you think could have done it?

STUDENT   I have no idea.

STRANGER   Let's consider it together. There's no question of sabotage, of course. Those ruins had been abandoned for a very long time indeed.

Student doesn't react.

STRANGER (*cont.*)   (*Sharply*)   Yes or no?

STUDENT (*Reluctantly*)   Yes, they were abandoned.

STRANGER   It has been suggested, therefore, that the explosion was to serve as a symbol: ruins blown up. Ruins. In other words something which exists but is of no use to anyone. What do you have to say about that?

STUDENT   I don't understand a word.

STRANGER   But you're a young man. You should understand it better than anyone. The explosion was a symbol of the revolution.

STUDENT   What's a revolution?

Stranger stands, walks around the table, draws up a chair, and sits next to Student.

STRANGER   I can appreciate that you don't trust me, but I'll prove to you that you are being unjust. So you know why I am here? Well, we have good reason to believe that a person we've wanted to meet for some time has been hiding in this region for a while. I took it upon myself to identify this person.

STUDENT   And what success have you had?

STRANGER   Oh, a great deal. Though the person is still at large we could arrest him at any moment.

STUDENT   What's holding you back?

STRANGER   I have given you proof that you can trust me, now what proof do I have that I can trust you?

STUDENT   You already do trust me. What you have told me is a state secret. If I were someone other than an ordinary student . . .

STRANGER   This is a question of the degree of confidence: I must have proof that I can trust you even more.

STUDENT   Why?

STRANGER   You're not interested?

STUDENT   No, I am not.

STRANGER   Never mind. I'll take a chance. You see, the reason I'm not arresting this person is because of the affection I feel for . . .

STUDENT   What? You, in your position?

STRANGER   It's a flaw, I know. But I'm only human. This person's youth persuaded me. You see, I'm not totally heartless.

STUDENT   And you're prepared to betray your God, your honor, and your country because of this affection.

Stranger puts his hand on Student's hand.

STRANGER   It's stronger than just affection.

Student withdraws his hand.

STUDENT   That's no excuse.

Stranger stands up.

STRANGER   I can see that you're not convinced.

STUDENT   No, I am not.

STRANGER   Then I will give you evidence that will appeal to your mind, since you have no heart.

Looks around the stage, then moves the chair so he is sitting opposite Student. They are now face-to-face.

STRANGER   I want to make a deal with this person. In return for not being arrested, this person will save my life.

STUDENT   You're asking for more than you can pay for.

STRANGER   Not at all. It's a fair deal. Being arrested is far worse than death to this person, believe me.

STUDENT   Very well. I believe you. But where do you come into all this? What can you be afraid of?

STRANGER   At the moment, nothing. But tomorrow I'll be in the same kind of danger as this person is in, or would be if I were to make an arrest today.

STUDENT   But this person is an unarmed fugitive! He can't do anything for you.

STRANGER   Not today, it's true. But tomorrow this person will be able to do the same for me as I am doing for him now.

STUDENT   How on earth . . .

STRANGER   Tomorrow this person will be what I am today and I will . . .

STUDENT   . . . and you will be what he is today. I understand.

STRANGER   It's perfectly obvious, isn't it?

STUDENT   Except for one thing. I don't see why you're telling me all this. You should be saying it to him.

Stranger stands up.

STRANGER   Are you refusing?

STUDENT   I'd dearly like to be able to help you, but I'm an ordinary, impoverished . . .

Stranger takes a watch out of his pocket and looks at it.

STRANGER   I'll give you time to think about it. I'll come here at five-thirty precisely.

Takes the bowler and cane.

STUDENT   It would give me great pleasure to meet you again. I really enjoy talking to you . . . but, unfortunately . . .

STRANGER   Listen to me, young man. You can do as you see fit. You can do whatever you please. Anything at all. But I advise you not to do one thing, just one thing. I advise you not to laugh at me.

STUDENT   And what if I am not laughing at you?

Stranger puts on his bowler and moves left.

STRANGER   Tomorrow will come tomorrow and not before.

Leaves left. Student gets up and moves left. Stops. After a moment's hesitation he leaves right.

SCENE FIVE

Baroness comes out of the house, followed by Baron.

BARON   When are you leaving?

BARONESS   Today.

BARON   As you wish.

BARONESS   His Excellency will give me a pass. After all, he is from our social sphere.

Pause.

BARON   I simply don't understand how it happened.

BARONESS   Nor do I. But I'm not interested.

BARON   So suddenly?

BARONESS   So much the better.

BARON   Forgive me for being tedious, but the psychological aspect of the case does interest me.

BARONESS   I'll gladly help in any way I can but I really don't know.

BARON   Are you revolted by me?

BARONESS   Why should I be?

BARON   For organizing that expedition last night.

BARONESS   You must be joking. Yesterday maybe I was . . . I really don't remember.

BARON   Can't you try to remember?

BARONESS   I don't want to.

BARON   Don't your emotions interest you?

BARONESS   Not all of them, no.

BARON   Do you hate me?

BARONESS   At this moment? Not in the least.

BARON   I understand. You're pretending to be indifferent. You imagine that that is the best way to get revenge.

BARONESS   Is that what you believe?

BARON   I know it for a fact.

BARONESS   Please yourself.

BARON   But you're wrong, you know.

BARONESS (*Not concentrating*)   What?

BARON   You're quite wrong if you think you'll hurt me by behaving like this.

BARONESS   I'm sorry. I was thinking about something else.

BARON   Don't you want to discuss it?

BARONESS   I'd love to but there really is nothing to discuss. And I have so many other things to think about at this moment. I have to pack, look up the timetables . . .

BARON   Are you taking everything?

BARONESS   But of course. Why do you ask? . . . Be honest, would you rather I stayed?

BARON   Since you're leaving I . . .

BARONESS   Thank God for that. I can't stand scenes.

BARON   Neither can I.

BARONESS   You know, it's interesting.

BARON   What is?

BARONESS   I'm not in the least upset by the fact that you're not upset.

BARON   Really? And what do you deduce from that?

BARONESS (*Stretches out her hand*)   Thank you.

BARON   What for?

BARONESS   For that. It means I really don't love you anymore.

BARON   Don't mention it.

They shake hands.

BARONESS   And now you really must excuse me but I don't have much time.

BARON   Of course.

Baroness goes up to the bower. Onka gets up. They both leave, past the bower. Baron watches them go.

Blackout.

SCENE SIX

It is five-thirty in the afternoon. Stranger is sitting on the bench, stiff as a ramrod. After a while he takes out his watch and glances at it. Puts it away. Gets up and leaves left.

Baron comes out of the house, picks up the rocking chair, and carries it down from the balcony. Places the rocking chair on the lawn, slightly upstage, near the balcony, from where he can observe the entire stage. Sits and lights up a cigar.

Hunchback comes out of the house. He is carrying a potted plant. Comes down from the balcony and moves left without seeing Baron. When he is in the middle of the stage two gunshots ring out, one immediately followed by the other. Hunchback stops and looks behind, right. Then he looks ahead, left. Looks behind once again. Then he leaves, left. Onek comes on, right, pince-nez on his nose. Goes to middle of the stage without seeing Baron.

BARON   You missed.

Onek turns around, astonished to see him.

ONEK.   Did someone shoot?

Baron stands up and goes up to Onek.

BARON   You missed.

ONEK   I heard a noise so I came to see what . . . Did you see anything?

BARON   No, I didn't see. But I do know. You missed, and you missed twice.

ONEK   Twice?

BARON   You're a terrible shot.

ONEK   What are you talking about?

BARON   Fancy missing at such close range. And twice, too.

ONEK   I really don't know what you're talking about.

Hunchback comes in, left. He no longer has the potted plant in his hands. Goes up to Baron and whispers in his ear. Baron and Hunchback leave hurriedly, left. Onek sits on a chair, removes his pince-nez. He is exhausted and apparently dazed.

Baron comes in, left, followed by Hunchback.

BARON (*To Hunchback*)   Hurry up!

Hunchback goes into the house. Baron goes up to Onek.

BARON (*cont.*)   I was mistaken. You didn't miss.

Onek stares at him, stupefied.

ONEK   Whaaa . . . ?

BARON   But it was someone else you hit.

ONEK   What's happened?

BARON   Come with me.

Onek gets up and follows Baron off, left.

Hunchback comes out of the house. He is carrying a spade. Goes out, left.

SCENE SEVEN

Onek comes in, left, followed by Baron. Onek is holding his head in his hands.

ONEK   Oh, my God, my God . . .

BARON   I hope you realize what the punishment for something like that is.

ONEK   But I didn't do it on purpose.

BARON   Can you prove that?

Onek takes his hands from his face.

ONEK   But it wasn't me. I swear it wasn't!

BARON   Then who was it?

ONEK   I only fired once.

BARON   But very successfully, I must say. Right in the temple.

ONEK   It was someone else. I was here . . .

Points right.

ONEK (*cont.*)   And this other person was . . .

Points left.

BARON   Very well, you only fired once. Let us assume for the sake of argument that I believe you. Let us assume, furthermore, that the police will also believe you. It is possible, of course, to ascertain which of the shots was the fatal one. But can you be sure it wasn't yours? Can you risk an investigation not knowing in advance what that investigation will reveal? Besides, how will you explain the fact that you were shooting?

ONEK   What can I do? What can I do?

BARON   I don't have a clue. You should know best.

ONEK   Please help me!

BARON Let's think about this logically. There are strange things happening. His Excellency's disappearance won't remain unnoticed for long. Search parties will be sent out very soon. When they fail to find him they'll realize that he has been assassinated. Massive manhunts will be set up and terrible repressions are bound to follow. Interrogations . . . You'll have a choice: Either you confess or you maintain that you saw nothing. If you confess, you'll be risking an investigation, the result of which could well be disastrous for you. Let us assume, then, that you don't confess. Only three of us know what really happened: the hunchback, you, and I. You, of course, won't say anything. I can speak for myself in this, but the hunchback . . .

ONEK Will talk!

BARON It's your choice. Will you trust him with your life?

ONEK My life?

BARON When I said there would be an investigation, I was, of course, referring to what would happen in normal times. But in such times as now an execution without benefit of trial would appear to be more probable if the hunchback simply denounces you without coming forward with any additional evidence.

ONEK In that case, I'm done for.

BARON You must run away immediately.

ONEK Where to?

BARON Abroad. But the most important thing for you is to leave this house immediately. Now. You don't have a moment to lose.

Onek runs frenetically toward the balcony. Stops.

ONEK What about my wife? What will I tell my wife?

BARON It would be best if she knew nothing at all about it.

ONEK You mean—go without saying good-bye?

BARON I know it's painful, but it's also essential.

ONEK Will you tell her . . .

BARON Anything you want me to.

ONEK   Will you tell her I have just received a very important message? Been called away on urgent business. A telegram.

BARON   Of course.

ONEK   And that I love her. And that I'll write a letter as soon as I can.

BARON   I won't forget. Rest assured.

ONEK   Or I'll send her a telegraphic communication.

Onek runs to the balcony.

BARON   One moment!

Onek stops in midflight. Baron stretches out his hand. Onek turns back to Baron, taking the gun out of his pocket as he walks, and gives it to him. Then, at last, he goes into the house.

Baron puts the revolver into the right-hand pocket of his jacket.

Student enters, left.

STUDENT   Good afternoon, Baron! What's new in aristocratic circles?

Baron reaches into his jacket and takes a revolver out of an inside pocket. It is exactly the same as the one he has just put into his right-hand pocket. He hands the revolver to Student.

STUDENT (*cont.*)   What's this? Why are you giving me this?

BARON   I'm returning it to its rightful owner.

STUDENT   Where did you find it?

BARON   In the dead man's hand.

STUDENT   What do you mean?

BARON   In His Excellency's hand.

STUDENT   His Excellency is dead?

BARON   He was shot just a moment ago.

Pause.

STUDENT   How do you know he was shot?

Baron shrugs.

STUDENT   Let's be logical about this. You found him with a gun in his hand, right?

BARON   That's right.

STUDENT   Well, then. He shot himself.

BARON   There's no certainty of that.

STUDENT   Why ever not?

BARON   Someone might have shot him and put the gun in his hand.

STUDENT   What on earth for?

BARON   To make it look like suicide.

Pause.

STUDENT   And you suspect me?

BARON   I do.

STUDENT   That's nonsense. What motive could I possibly have? You might as well suspect that lawyer fellow.

BARON   He's above suspicion.

STUDENT   Why is he? I happen to know he had a gun. You gave it to him.

BARON   The gun I lent him contained blanks.

STUDENT   Did he know that?

BARON   No.

STUDENT   You lent him a revolver and you didn't tell him it had blanks? Why?

BARON   I didn't want him to hurt himself. Or anyone else . . . He's of a nervous disposition; he doesn't know how to use a gun.

STUDENT   Then why bother to lend him a gun?

BARON   I was being kind to him. He had been suffering from a persecution complex lately and he asked me to lend him a gun. For self-defense, he said. So I acquiesced. I knew there was no danger.

STUDENT   Remarkable foresight.

BARON   And besides, I couldn't give anything but blanks. I never keep live ammunition in the house. My wife is subject to bouts of hysteria.

Pause.

STUDENT   What's going to happen to the body?

BARON   I've had it buried.

STUDENT   Without informing the authorities?

BARON   I considered discretion to be in all our interests.

STUDENT   I have nothing to hide.

BARON   In that case do you want me to inform the authorities?

STUDENT   No.

BARON   Excellent.

Student moves toward the balcony, then stops, turns back, and goes up to Baron. Stretches out his hand for the revolver. Baron gives it to him.

STUDENT   Are you sure you don't need it?

Baron takes the gun out of his right-hand pocket.

STUDENT   Blanks.

BARON   Not anymore.

Baron removes the magazine from the revolver and puts it into the right-hand pocket of his jacket. Then he reaches into the inside pocket and takes out another magazine. He lobs it up into the palm of his hand. He loads his revolver.

BARON   The same kind, you see.

Student checks his revolver and discovers that the magazine is missing. He puts the gun away and goes into the house without saying a word. Baron watches him go. Only when Student has gone inside does he put the revolver away in his inside pocket.

Hunchback enters, left.

HUNCHBACK   Ready, Baron.

BARON   It has to be covered by the turf.

HUNCHBACK   I've done that, Baron. There's no trace.

BARON   Let's just go and check, shall we?

Baron and Hunchback leave, left. Door of the balcony opens slowly. Onek appears, carrying a suitcase. Puts on his pince-nez making sure the coast is clear. Runs down the steps and slips out, right.

Blackout.

SCENE EIGHT

The rocking chair is back on the balcony. Baron is sitting in it, waiting. Baroness and Onka enter along the path by the bower. Baron gets up and goes to meet them.

BARON (*To Onka*)   I'd like to speak to you. (*To Baroness.*)   I assume you have no objections.

BARONESS   Of course not. I'll leave you to it.

Baroness goes into the house.

BARON   I'm leaving for Italy.

ONKA   I hope you have a pleasant journey.

BARON   I'll be visiting Venice, Sienna, Sorrento, not to mention Naples and Capri.

ONKA   It sounds wonderful.

BARON   And I'd like you to come with me.

ONKA   Could you repeat that, please?

BARON   I'm asking you to accompany me.

ONKA   I was mistaken, then.

BARON   I appreciate that this is unexpected but . . .

ONKA (*Emphasizing "me" and "Baron"*)   I thought it was you who wanted to accompany me, Baron.

BARON   Then we'll go together.

ONKA   But I've not agreed to anything.

BARON   But you do agree.

ONKA   Of course I don't.

BARON   You're refusing?

ONKA   Of course I am. What do you take me for?

BARON   You won't stop to consider?

ONKA   My dear Baron, I really don't think it would be proper for me to
enter into any discussions on the subject. I am amazed that a man
from your background should have made such a proposition. I am
amazed that you are amazed by my reaction to it, and I must confess I
am very disappointed. I had the highest regard for you but now I am
amazed to find myself still talking to you instead of leaving without
another word. In short, I am amazed and the only thing I can now do
is try to forget this rather distasteful incident, an incident that does
you no credit at all, Baron.

BARON   Why exactly does it do me no credit?

ONKA   You seem to forget that I am a married woman.

BARON   Come, come, we're not going to be flippant about this, are we?

ONKA   Really? Flippant? Meaning what, exactly?

BARON   Your marriage does not appear to be a happy one.

ONKA   This is incredible. How can you presume to pass judgment on
my marriage?

BARON   I have good cause to suppose . . .

ONKA   You have good cause! To suppose! You are forgetting not only
that I am a married woman but also the fact that there are husbands
whose wives do not leave them. But then in your case that's quite
understandable. I can only pity you.

BARON   There are, however, wives whose husbands leave them.

ONKA   Yes, but not me.

BARON   Indeed yes. You.

ONKA   This is the height of insolence.

BARON   Your husband has abandoned you.

ONKA   What do you mean . . .

BARON   Has left you. For ever. Without even saying good-bye. He took his things and left while you were out.

Onka sits down on a chair.

BARON (*cont.*)   I understand how difficult it must be for you to believe it but you must reconcile yourself to the facts. Even if you don't believe me, the facts are undeniable. You are an abandoned woman.

ONKA   But why did he . . .

BARON   Because he doesn't love you.

ONKA   You don't know that . . .

BARON   He told me. Personally. I was his confidant.

ONKA   And you knew about this when you suggested that . . .

BARON   Yes, I did.

ONKA   Why didn't you tell me right away?

BARON   That would have been indelicate of me.

Onka is silent.

BARON (*cont.*)   Nevertheless, my offer still stands.

ONKA   I don't want to talk about it just now.

BARON   There's plenty of time.

Onka goes into the house.

Blackout.

SCENE NINE

Late evening. Baron is sitting at the table on the left. Hunchback comes out of the house. He is loaded with suitcases, hatboxes, etc. He puts the cases down in front of the balcony. Baron watches him. Hunchback goes into the house for the next load of luggage. Then he leaves, right. Baroness and Onka come out of the house. Baron stands up. Onka stands to one side. Baroness goes up to Baron and stretches her hand out to him. They shake hands. Now Baroness stands to one side. Onka goes up to Baron and stretches out her hand. Baron doesn't offer his.

ONKA   Good-bye.

BARON   But you're staying.

BARONESS   No, she's leaving with me.

BARON   Where to?!

BARONESS   Venice, Sienna, Sorrento . . .

BARON (*To Onka*)   Is this true?

Onka confirms it with a nod.

BARON (*cont.*)   But that's impossible . . .

BARONESS   I'm taking her with me. It's the best solution in the present situation.

BARON   With you?

BARONESS   I need a lady companion.

BARON   Yes, but does she need you?

BARONESS   Of course she does. The wretch has left her penniless. Isn't that right, my dear?

Onka confirms it with a nod.

BARONESS (*cont.*)   Luckily I'll be able to take care of her.

BARON (*To Onka*)   You do have an alternative, you know . . .

BARONESS   There's no need for you to use euphemisms just because I'm here. The sweet little thing told me everything, didn't you, my dear?

Onka confirms it with a nod.

BARON   Then why . . .

BARONESS   You're behaving like a typical pig. You'll have to excuse me for using such an expression, but I can't think of another way to put it. How else can you describe a man who wants to take advantage of a woman who has been abandoned, to take advantage of her misfortune? Surely only in the way I've already described you, you will agree. Isn't that so, my dear?

BARON Ah, so that's how you interpreted it for her benefit, is it?

BARONESS It's my duty as a woman to make her see the vileness of your behavior. She is my friend and I shall not allow some male hyena like you . . .

Hunchback enters, right, pulling a cart. He stops in front of the balcony and starts loading the luggage onto the cart.

BARON Are you talking to me or to her now?

BARONESS To you, of course.

BARON (*To Onka*) Do you believe her?

BARONESS It's difficult not to believe what's obvious.

BARON I underestimated you.

BARONESS Thank you for the compliment, but I don't need it.

Baroness goes up to the cart and counts the pieces of luggage. Baron and Onka stand facing each other in silence.

BARONESS One, two, three . . . Where's my blanket?

ONKA In the big case.

BARONESS If I've told you once I've told you a hundred times I want it out.

ONKA I forgot.

BARONESS I forgot. I forgot. How is it that you forget everything I say to you?

Hunchback harnesses himself to the cart. Pulling the cart, he leaves, left.

BARONESS (*To Onka*) Come along. We're going. (*To Baron.*) Bye. Take care.

Baron straightens himself up, adjusts his tie, pulls his jacket down, and goes up to Onka. Stands in front of her.

BARON Will you be my wife?

BARONESS   What did you say?

Baron takes no notice of her, addressing himself straight to Onka.

BARON   I'm asking for your hand.

BARONESS   Her hand . . . He's asking for her hand . . .

Baroness starts to laugh, louder and louder. Onka and Baron are forced to turn away from each other and to look at her. Her laughter destroys the beauty and tension of the moment.

BARON   Stop laughing!

BARONESS   He's asking for her hand. The king of intriguers, the caesar of cheats, Baron von Bluff himself is declaring his passion. No, this is just too much. I can't take any more!

BARON   Please take no notice of her. I'm being serious.

BARONESS   Serious! No, stop it, it's just too funny to be true.

Baron turns away from Onka and goes up to Baroness, who is still laughing hysterically.

BARONESS   You're magnificent! This is incredible. Spare me, spare me. You're surpassing yourself.

Baron seizes her by the throat. Her laughter is cut short and the expression on her face changes. Onka turns and runs out, left. Baron lets go of Baroness and takes a couple of steps left, looking after Onka. Baroness feels her aching neck; she gives a short laugh that is difficult to distinguish from a sob and leaves, left.

Blackout.

SCENE TEN

Dusk. The croaking of frogs and singing of birds. There are five chairs around the table but only two of them are occupied by Baron and Student. They are both facing the audience. There is a samovar, a sugar bowl, and a plate with cakes on the table. Baron and Student drink tea in silence. After some time:

STUDENT   Why don't you play something. I like music.

Baron doesn't react. Student picks up the plate from the table and offers it to Baron. Baron doesn't react. Student holds the plate in front of him for a moment, then puts it back on the table.

STUDENT Didn't you always enjoy your food? Game, omelets, *vol-au-vent, sauce béarnaise, champignons à la crème* . . . you're a connoisseur, aren't you? A connoisseur of delicatessen. Are you sure you don't want anything? Are you quite certain . . .

BARON Would you do me the kindness of not speaking?

STUDENT Any reason why I should? Everyone has the right to speak at the table. Weren't you always the life and soul of the dinner party?

BARON (*Tired*) Shut your mouth!

STUDENT What's this I hear, and that from the lips of a man with impeccable manners.

BARON Why are you showing off?

STUDENT Who, me?

BARON Yes, you. There's no one here. So for whose benefit are you performing? We're alone here.

STUDENT That's exactly it. There's no one here: a melancholy remark. The plaint of an actor in an empty theater. The tragic fate of a performer who exists only on the stage—and now there is nobody left in the auditorium. They've all left and the lights have been turned off. So what's the point? Why bother? For whom? Of course, I don't count. You never did take any notice of me, did you?

BARON Poor, forgotten little boy . . .

STUDENT You old fraud.

BARON Unloved and therefore so angry, so very, very angry . . .

STUDENT You took everyone in, except me. Wonderful acting: They had tears in their eyes. Especially the women. Sobs, standing ovations for the darling . . . Our star, our one and only stage lover . . . But the performance is finished.

BARON And yet one does want to be loved . . .

STUDENT You're an impostor!

BARON   The revenge of the virgin.

STUDENT   You clown!

Baron turns slowly until he is facing Student. They look at each other in silence.

BARON   You're quite right, of course.

STUDENT   You don't love anyone.

BARON   Do you?

STUDENT   At least I do hate.

BARON   Whom?

STUDENT   You.

BARON   And does that make you feel better?

STUDENT   At least I'm not empty.

BARON   How long can one hate?

STUDENT   A lifetime.

BARON   You're young.

Student stands up.

STUDENT   But I won't live long.

Student goes into the house.

Blackout.

SCENE ELEVEN

Early morning. Sunny. Birds are singing. Baron is asleep, his head resting on his forearms, which are spread out on the table. On the table in front of him are the samovar, sugar bowl, two cups, the plates with cakes on it, and the empty bottle, with a glass. Hunchback, in his linen apron, is standing by Baron. He is holding a tray in one hand and shaking Baron gently with the other.

BARON   (*Still asleep*)   What?

Hunchback continues trying to wake him. Baron sits up in his chair.

BARON   Coffee.

He rubs his eyes.

HUNCHBACK   There is no coffee.

BARON   Mmmmm?

HUNCHBACK   It's finished.

BARON   What?

HUNCHBACK   They've stopped selling it.

Baron gets up. His clothes are crumpled and he is unshaven. Walks toward the balcony.

HUNCHBACK   Excuse me, Baron . . .

Baron stops.

BARON   What is it?

HUNCHBACK   I'm closing the place up.

BARON   What?

HUNCHBACK   It's no longer a viable proposition. Everyone has gone.

BARON   Everyone?

HUNCHBACK   Everyone. The young gentlemen has also gone. He took the bicycle.

BARON   I see. Couldn't I stay?

HUNCHBACK   Times are becoming uncertain . . .

BARON   Of course. What time is my train?

HUNCHBACK   The trains are no longer running.

BARON   Not running? The trains?

HUNCHBACK   The ladies left on the last train.

BARON   Order some horses.

HUNCHBACK   There are no horses.

BARON   No horses? In the country?

HUNCHBACK   No horses.

BARON   Tell the peasant I'll pay well.

HUNCHBACK   There are no peasants.

BARON   I see.

Baron walks into the house. Hunchback puts the samovar, sugar bowl, cups, plate, bottle, and glass on the tray. Puts the tray on a chair. Takes the tablecloth, shakes it out, and folds it. Puts the folded tablecloth on the table, puts the tray on the table, takes the chairs onto the balcony, and arranges them in a corner into a pyramid shape. He is putting the last chair onto the pile when Baron comes out onto the balcony. He is wearing a long coat and a wide-brimmed hat. He is carrying a suitcase in his left hand and a cane in his right. He walks past Hunchback without taking any notice of him, as if he didn't exist. He doesn't so much as turn his head, even though he comes very close to him and Hunchback stops working to look at Baron. Baron walks down from the balcony. Hunchback watches him, then turns and walks into the house. Baron walks left without looking around. He stops in the middle of the stage, puts the suitcase down, transfers the cane from his right to his left hand, and picks up the case with his right hand. Hunchback comes out of the house. He is holding a pair of lady's slippers. Stands on the balcony and calls after Baron.

HUNCHBACK   One moment, sir. One moment!

Baron turns around and waits. Hunchback runs down the steps and goes up to Baron. He holds the slippers out to him.

HUNCHBACK   The lady forgot her slippers.

Baron turns and walks out, left.

Hunchback stands for a moment holding the slippers in his hands, then turns and goes up to the table. Puts the slippers on the tray, next to the samovar, sugar bowl, cups, plate, bottle, and glass. Puts the folded tablecloth across his forearm, picks up the tray and, carrying it before him with both hands, goes into the house.

FOUR ONE-ACT
ANIMAL PLAYS

FOX HUNT

❦

Translated by Jacek Laskowski

CHARACTERS

FOX

ROOSTER

INVALID

HELPER

MASTER OF HOUNDS

FIRST HOUND

SECOND HOUND

EX-KING

EX-COUNT

The scene—almost a dump. Strips of old newspapers, orange peel, empty cans. Upstage, slightly on the left, a leafless tree. Slightly on the right, a wooden bench, as seen in public parks, the green veneer matted and scratched.

SCENE ONE

Entering right: FOX *and* ROOSTER. *Fox is a tall man with a red, thin, turned-up mustache. Red hair. Wearing a capacious fox-fur overcoat reaching down to the ground. Rooster is a rather small man, neurotic. In an exotic brocaded and embroidered dressing gown of Japanese cut. Bedroom slippers on bare feet.*

ROOSTER I'm going no farther.

FOX And there's no need to. We're in the forest. (*Rooster looks around.*) Do you like it?

ROOSTER No.

FOX Truth to tell it's no longer the forest of my youth.

ROOSTER I want to go home.

FOX If it weren't for me you'd never stick your beak out of your yard.

Rooster sits on the bench.

ROOSTER My yard . . .

FOX Your small, limited world of poultry.

ROOSTER The yard can't do without me.

FOX Anyone can peck at grain.

ROOSTER What about the sun? Who'll wake the sun? Without me it'll be perpetual night.

FOX I envy you your megalomania.

ROOSTER It was I who woke the sun at every dawn.

FOX A blessed narrowness of horizons. Only in a small world are we great!

ROOSTER Without me there'll be no dawn. If I don't wake the sun, the sun will wake no one. The farmer won't go out into the field, his wife won't look after the livestock, and the livestock won't wake either. Perpetual night, perpetual sleep.

FOX   What could be better?

ROOSTER   No one will wake.

FOX   In which case nobody will notice your absence. Those who are absent in sleep won't know that you're absent.

ROOSTER   I cannot wake them because I am absent.

FOX   Neither present nor absent, from their point of view. In fact they don't have a point of view because they're asleep.

ROOSTER (*Getting up off the bench*)   Is that what you think?

FOX   To them you are beyond being and not-being.

ROOSTER   That's what you've brought them to.

FOX   Them? Don't you mean you?

ROOSTER   Unhappy things.

FOX   Stop pretending. You'd like to wake them only so they'll notice you. That's all you care about.

ROOSTER   Cock-a-doodle-do!

Jumps onto the bench. As he crows he waves his arms, billowing the sleeves of the kimono.

FOX   Rooster mentality!

ROOSTER (*Coming off the bench*)   What are you going to do with me?

FOX   Me? With you?

ROOSTER   I am in your power.

FOX   If you insist on dotting the *i*'s.

ROOSTER   When you stole into the henhouse I understood everything. But when, instead of behaving like a normal fox, you said, "Pssst . . . Good evening. Kindly follow me," I understood only that you are not a normal fox. I didn't even have time to dress . . .

FOX   You'd rather . . .

ROOSTER   No! But I'd prefer to know where we stand.

FOX   I will never cease to be amazed by the nature of living things. Scarcely have you escaped the worst and you're already dissatisfied.

ROOSTER   Because I don't know what awaits me.

FOX   And you're sure you would like to know . . .

ROOSTER   If it's something not too bad . . .

FOX   In keeping with nature again. And yet it's strange, strange . . .

ROOSTER   I don't understand your behavior.

FOX   I am a normal fox but in an abnormal situation . . .

ROOSTER   A fox who steals into a henhouse . . . That seems to me quite normal, unfortunately.

FOX   That henhouse again. Believe me, the world is bigger than your henhouse. I had in mind not that fragmentary situation in the henhouse but my situation generally, my existential . . .

ROOSTER   What's that to me . . .

FOX   Oh, hennish blindness! If not for my existential situation, its specificity, you would no longer be alive. Begging your pardon.

ROOSTER   Oh, in that case, it is I who beg your pardon.

FOX   That's all right. In brief, I am the foxes' end . . .

ROOSTER   Agreed, but why have an inferiority complex about it?

FOX   Not the end as a description of quality, you chicken, but of quantity. I am the only fox remaining in this forest. My species has been exterminated. I am the end of my species.

ROOSTER   Oh, really? That's sad news.

FOX   Your hypocrisy irritates me, but never mind. What's worse is that not only am I the last fox but also the last animal in this forest. All other species have been destroyed.

ROOSTER   May one ask how you survived, if you'll permit . . .

FOX   Exceptional personal qualifications. The best survive.

ROOSTER   I see.

FOX   You surely realize how difficult is the situation of the last animal in the forest. That's what I call an abnormal situation.

ROOSTER   Scary?

FOX   Sad. No one to talk to. That's why I decided to invite you to accompany me.

ROOSTER   It was kidnapping.

FOX   I behaved as best as I could in the circumstances.

ROOSTER   Does that mean you only want to talk? No more?

FOX   Are we not talking?

ROOSTER   So far . . .

FOX   Imagine yourself alone in the whole henhouse, alone in the whole yard.

ROOSTER   There's no danger of that.

FOX   Oh, no. Slaves increase, only the wild and the free animals die out.

ROOSTER   I call that civilization.

FOX   That's a point of view.

ROOSTER   That sardonic tone is out of place. Civilization creates higher values.

FOX   For example?

ROOSTER   Apparently everyone will soon have mechanical feeders. You just need to press the pedal and the grain pours itself into your beak. Without any limits.

FOX   Beautiful. And?

ROOSTER   You can't deny that we have made great progress. The times are long gone when you had to creep and search for some worm.

FOX   That's true. You are quite plump. Your granddad, rest his soul, didn't look this good. Though I have pleasant memories of him . . .

ROOSTER   You knew my granddad?

FOX   Fleetingly.

ROOSTER   So you won't deny that progress exists.

FOX   That would be dishonest of me.

ROOSTER   Morally, too, our system is better than yours.

FOX   Morally?

ROOSTER   You savages eat one another.

FOX   We—in the plural—are history. Did I not tell you that I am the last?

ROOSTER   But you live by plunder.

FOX   Besides, that "one another" signifies that at least there is as good a chance to eat someone as there is to be eaten. Whereas with you . . .

ROOSTER   We do not eat anyone.

FOX   And nobody eats you? (*Pause.*)   Go on, tell me: How is it with you?

ROOSTER   Cock-a-doodle-do . . . (*Crows, waving the sleeves of the kimono.*)

FOX   An evasive reply. (*The sound of a royal hunting fanfare.*)   The chase approaches. Let's move away.

ROOSTER   I'm staying.

FOX   You forget that you are my guest.

Seizes the resisting Rooster by the arm and pulls him off left.

Scene Two

Accompanied by the sound of the fanfare, a wheelchair comes onto the stage, pushed by a man in hunting costume. INVALID in the chair also in hunting costume. Both armed with rifles. Invalid covered by a blanket from the waist down. Apart from the fanfare, the distant barking of dogs is heard. The fanfare and barking go quiet.

INVALID   I am going no farther.

HELPER   Shush now! Sit quiet and hunt. Just see how we'll hit upon a fox.

INVALID   What fox? There are no foxes. I want to go home.

HELPER   Who said there aren't no foxes? Who?

INVALID   Everybody knows.

HELPER   Neo-Malthusians, reactionaries of various kinds. If you listen to reactionaries, Uncle, I won't take you hunting no more.

INVALID   Why should I go hunting? I have no wish to. (*Reaches into his pocket.*)   Here, take this . . . (*Gives Helper a coin.*)

HELPER   What's this . . . ?

INVALID   That's for a beer. Only let's go back. Home, yes? Homey . . . (*Helper looks around, hides the coin in his pocket.*)   We're going back!

HELPER   Not so loud . . . You want to give me away, Uncle?

INVALID   But we are going back, aren't we?

HELPER   Try to understand me, Uncle. You think it gives me pleasure? Everyone would like to go home.

INVALID   So why don't we go back?

HELPER   You can't right away. You have to shoot at least two or three times at a fox.

INVALID   But there are no more foxes . . .

HELPER (*Putting his hand over Invalid's mouth and looking around uneasily*)   You starting again, Uncle? (*Withdraws his hand.*)

INVALID   I'll stop. Only let's go home . . .

HELPER   You're just like a child, Uncle. Home, home. I told you, Uncle, everyone would like to. Take a shot, Uncle.

INVALID   What at?

HELPER   Just shoot straight ahead, anywhere, as if you had something to shoot at. Pretend, at a pretend fox, understand, Uncle . . . We'll say a fox appeared, Uncle took a shot but missed, and then we'll be able to go back home in peace.

Invalid fires. MASTER OF HOUNDS, *also in hunting gear, runs on, left, carrying a rifle.*

MASTER   Got him?

HELPER   No, he got away.

Takes the rifle from Invalid, opens it, takes out the spent cartridge, loads another bullet, closes the rifle, and hands it back to Invalid.

MASTER   Wretched luck . . . (*Suspiciously.*)   You saw him?

HELPER   Of course. Why else would Uncle shoot?

MASTER (*Approaching Invalid*)   Likes shooting, eh?

HELPER   Adores it.

MASTER   And it's healthy, eh?

INVALID   Very, only the dampness . . .

MASTER (*To Helper*)   What's he say?

HELPER   Says there's damp in the house. The forest is good for his rheumatism.

MASTER   Very true. And now follow me! The scent is fresh!

Turns and goes off left. Helper follows, pushing the chair.

INVALID   So aren't we going home?

HELPER   You saw for yourself, Uncle, nothing could be done.

INVALID   Oh, Jesus!

They disappear left.

Scene Three

Entering from right come FIRST HOUND *and* SECOND HOUND. *Dressed like petty officials: suits and ties. One of them, First Hound, is carrying a briefcase. Second Hound lies down on the bench. Master enters left followed by Helper pushing the chair with Invalid in it. Master, bent over the ground, is following the scent.*

MASTER   Can't seem to hear the dogs.

HELPER   Must have lost the scent.

MASTER   (*Spotting the dogs*)   What are you dogs doing?

First Hound shrugs his shoulders; Second Hound doesn't react at all.

MASTER   Why aren't you following the fox?

FIRST HOUND (*To Second Hound*)   Shall we bark?

SECOND HOUND   Tell him.

FIRST HOUND (*Takes documents out of the briefcase and spreads them out on his lap*)   By the terms of our contract . . .

MASTER   I asked you why you are not chasing the fox.

FIRST HOUND   By the terms of our agreement we are due a bonus.

MASTER   You'll get it.

FIRST HOUND   But we haven't had it yet.

MASTER   Let's talk about it later. You must bark and follow. The fox is nearby.

FIRST HOUND   We don't work day rates, we work piece rates. I barked (*Puts on glasses.*)   I have today already barked two thousand eight hundred and thirty-six times, that is to say three hundred and thirty-six times above the quota, counting from the last settling up, and my colleague . . .

MASTER (*Looking into his briefcase*)   What is that?

FIRST HOUND   A woof-woof meter. This is where the daily woof is recorded. And my colleague has barked two thousand six hundred and twenty times.

SECOND HOUND   Twenty-six.

FIRST HOUND   It's not written down.

SECOND HOUND   Then write it down.

FIRST HOUND (*Writing down*)   Twenty-six.

MASTER   Gentlemen, the fox is getting away from us!

FIRST HOUND   That may be; but what about the bonus?

MASTER   We'll settle all this later, I promise you. But now—after the fox!

SECOND HOUND (*To First Hound*)   What do you say?

FIRST HOUND   What about you?

SECOND HOUND   I'm not sure . . . We'll charge overtime.

FIRST HOUND   We've had overtime.

SECOND HOUND   Extra overtime then. And family allowance.

FIRST HOUND   Won't go down.

SECOND HOUND   Why not?

FIRST HOUND   Because we're not married.

SECOND HOUND   Everyone had a father and a mother.

FIRST HOUND   True.

SECOND HOUND   And a holiday bonus.

FIRST HOUND   It's not a holiday today.

SECOND HOUND   It is for me. It's my birthday.

FIRST HOUND (*To Master*)   Agreed. But it will cost extra overtime, plus family allowance and a holiday bonus.

MASTER   Gentlemen, you're ruining me!

FIRST HOUND (*To Second Hound*)   We're ruining him.

SECOND HOUND   If he won't agree tell him to bark himself.

FIRST HOUND (*To Master*)   My colleague says . . .

MASTER   All right, all right, only let's get started!

FIRST HOUND   Sign here.

Hands Master a pen. Master signs the document. First Hound puts the papers in the briefcase. Takes off his glasses and stands up. Second Hound stretches and yawns. Then First Hound and Second Hound stand next to each other in a line.

FIRST HOUND   Three . . . four!

FIRST HOUND AND SECOND HOUND (*Together*)   Woof-woof-woof, woof-woof-woof . . .

They leave left, barking with no conviction. It's more like reciting "woof-woof-woof" than imitating the barking of dogs.

HELPER   Aren't they charging too much?

MASTER   It means nothing. Everything is on credit.

HELPER   Oh, that's all right then.

MASTER   Onward! Now we'll get him.

HELPER   Sure to, sure to.

They all leave, left.

SCENE FOUR

Fox and Rooster enter, right. Fox is dragging Rooster.

ROOSTER   I understand why you have to run away. But why do I?

FOX   Solidarity.

ROOSTER   That's not entirely true.

FOX   If you already know, then why ask? Since you have to be with me at least make an effort to keep our relationship formally correct. The truth isn't sweet for you. And I also have no interest in underscoring it at every step.

ROOSTER   I hope that they catch you at last.

FOX   Tut, tut: Why this sincerity?

The passionless barking of dogs from the right.

ROOSTER   They're close already.

FOX   The distance has, therefore, to be increased. (*Approaches the left wings and stops.*)   Oh, not good.

ROOSTER   What?

FOX   Bad.

ROOSTER   Meaning good.

FOX   They're coming from this side, too.

ROOSTER   Hurrah!

FOX   Spare me the stupid remarks.

ROOSTER   Does this mean we're lost? (*Chants joyfully.*)   We are lost . . . We are lost . . .

FOX   Idiot. You don't yet know what a fox can do. (*Turns from the left wings and approaches the tree.*)   Come over here.

ROOSTER (*Coming up to Fox unwillingly*)   You want to use me as a hostage.

FOX   You overestimate yourself. A thousand roosters aren't worth one fox. They have a surfeit of poultry and they won't hesitate to shoot you just to get me. As a hostage you are useless to me.

ROOSTER   God be praised.

FOX   Get up.

ROOSTER   Where?

FOX   Up the tree. We'll hide in the tree.

ROOSTER   A fox in a tree?

FOX   That is my secret. I've survived so long because I taught myself to climb trees. They look for me down below while I am up above.

ROOSTER   Simple.

FOX   Ingenious. Up you go!

ROOSTER   But I don't know how.

FOX   As a bird you should know how to do it better than me. Birds live in the trees.

ROOSTER   But I really don't know how. I am a domestic bird.

FOX   Degenerate. But I will teach you.

Fox pulls a knife out. Rooster, clucking and waving the sleeves of his kimono, runs up to the tree and quickly clambers onto a branch.

FOX (*Putting away the knife*)   The instinct of self-preservation performs miracles. (*Climbs onto the tree clumsily.*)   Ooofff, I don't enjoy this.

Sits on the branch next to Rooster.

ROOSTER   They're coming!

FOX   Not one word!

Takes out a handkerchief and gags Rooster.

Enter left EX-KING and EX-COUNT. Both in hunting gear and with rifles.

EX-KING   And yet, dear Count, I am pleased that we once hunted our fill. The hunting was so different then.

EX-COUNT   And the forest was different then.

EX-KING   Do you remember that abundance of wildlife? Deer, stags, grouse, and even pheasants.

EX-COUNT   This was a forest where there were even trees . . .

Kicks at a strip of newspaper beneath his feet.

EX-KING   I admit that now I hunt only out of politeness. Not to hunt when everyone else hunts would mean setting myself apart, would show a contempt for our beloved fellow citizens.

EX-COUNT   Your Royal Highness . . .

EX-KING   Don't call me that. I am merely a citizen.

EX-COUNT   And yet Your Royal Highness himself addressed me just a moment ago as Count.

EX-KING   Old habits one needs to rid oneself of. We are but citizens among other citizens. Liberty, equality, fraternity . . .

EX-COUNT   First and foremost equality. As for the rest . . .

EX-KING   One has to start somewhere. Liberty and fraternity through equality.

EX-COUNT   Couldn't you have equality through liberty? Or through fraternity?

EX-KING   Apparently it can't be done. But it's not up to us to take initiatives. We are but relics of the past. We can but play the part of witnesses.

EX-COUNT   A witness is entitled to his own opinion.

EX-KING   That's up to the procurator. We mustn't defy fate and demand more than they're offering us. After all, we are not badly off. That is to say no worse than others. What am I saying? Equally well as others. I am pleased that I have rid myself of the prerogatives that were my exclusive property. It was a great burden.

EX-COUNT   Your Royal Highness . . . Citizen . . . will allow me to differ.

EX-KING   You forget that your privileges were only a part of mine, of my royal prerogatives. They were bestowed on you by me, you drew from my treasure chest. It was I who carried the greatest responsibility. Standing between you and the masses was I.

EX-COUNT   Yes, Your Royal . . .

EX-KING   Not royal, not royal. (*The barking of dogs.*)   Especially as our beloved fellow citizens are approaching.

The royal hunting fanfare resounds. From right come First Hound and Second Hound, barking. Behind them Master and Invalid in a chair and Helper. The hounds bark for another moment without passion, then sit down on the bench. First Hound takes out of his briefcase a thermos and sandwiches. The hounds set about eating their meal. They unpack the sandwiches, share the contents of the thermos, etc. The fanfare goes quiet.

MASTER   Hi there, hunters!

EX-KING   Hi there.

EX-COUNT   (*Reluctantly*)   Hi there . . .

CROWD OF HUNTERS   (*Offstage, an echo*)   Hi there . . . !

MASTER   The hunting is progressing satisfactorily.

EX-KING   (*Politely*)   Indeed.

MASTER   Is there anyone left who doesn't hunt?

CROWD OF HUNTERS   (*Offstage*)   Nooooo . . . !

MASTER   And that's how it should be. Gone are the times when the privilege of hunting was enjoyed only by the king. (*To Ex-King.*)   You don't resent me making the allusion, do you, Citizen?

EX-KING   No, not at all, don't hold back.

MASTER Everyone may pick up a rifle and hunt fox. More, everyone should. Taking advantage of privilege is the duty of every citizen.

INVALID Oh, Jesus . . .

MASTER What?

HELPER My uncle was saying: "Oh, Jesus, it's good!"

MASTER Look at this paralyzed old man. Even he, though paralyzed and sick, joyfully takes advantage of the privilege. His participation in the hunt is the best evidence of our achievements. Hunting is the right not just of the healthy and strong. Universal hunting, hunting for all without exception, that's what we've come to!

CROWD OF HUNTERS (*Offstage*) Hurrah . . . !

MASTER Allow me, on behalf of us all, to heartily congratulate our invalid. Long live the invalid!

CROWD OF HUNTERS (*Offstage*) Long live . . . !

Master goes up to Invalid and shakes his hand warmly. Then he takes out of his pocket a medal and pins it to Invalid's chest. The Crowd of Hunters, offstage, claps and sings.

CROWD OF HUNTERS (*Offstage, singing*) A-hunting we will go,
  The hounds all join in glorious cry,
  The huntsman winds his horn
  And a-hunting we will go.

INVALID (*To Helper*) What is it?

HELPER The Saint Hubert Medal. Just keep it, Uncle, and stop fussing.

MASTER And now—after the fox!

CROWD OF HUNTERS (*Offstage*) After the fox!

EX-KING I don't wish to butt in, but may I say something?

MASTER Of course, of course. Though you are an ex-king, Citizen, you are also a citizen. We're listening.

EX-KING The principle of universal hunting for everyone is, of course, just and proper. There isn't the slightest excuse for someone hunting and someone else not.

MASTER   True, very true. (*To Crowd of Hunters*)   Listen, men!

EX-KING   It's just a question of the game. The quantity of game is inversely proportional to the quantity of hunters.

MASTER   Where is this leading, Citizen Ex-King?

EX-KING   The more hunters, the less game. And it seems to me that in this respect we have reached the critical point.

MASTER   The what?

EX-KING   We have reached the point where everyone hunts but there is no longer anything to hunt.

MASTER   That is an observation which demonstrates that you, Citizen, have not cut yourself off from your past.

EX-KING   I am not defending the past. I am merely stating facts which can be proved objectively.

MASTER   Are you suggesting, Citizen, that universal hunting is harmful?

CROWD OF HUNTERS (*Offstage*)   Boooo . . .

EX-KING   Only in the sense that it's harming itself.

CROWD OF HUNTERS (*Offstage*)   Boooo . . . Boooo . . .

MASTER   Are you, Citizen, undermining the principle of universal hunting?

CROWD OF HUNTERS (*Offstage*)   Boooo . . . Booo . . . Booo . . .

EX-KING   Not at all. I am merely pointing out that the principle is undermining itself. You can have a privilege only when it is an exception. When everyone has the same right, then it's very laudable but you can't call it a privilege. Then it is a right and not a privilege. When everyone has a privilege, then no one is privileged. Also there is no game.

MASTER   We were a little too indulgent with you.

EX-KING   That's the logic of it, anyway. Now when it comes to the facts . . . (*Ex-Count tugs at his sleeve.*)   What?

EX-COUNT   We weren't going to interfere.

EX-KING   But this isn't subjective; this is objective. (*Turns to the presumed Crowd of Hunters.*)   I call on each one of you to bear witness: Who has seen any game? (*Crowd of Hunters is silent.*)   There we are. Everyone knows the forest is empty. Insofar as it can be called a forest.

MASTER   (*To Ex-King*)   A little private word.

Takes the Ex-King by the arm and takes him under the tree. Ex-Count sits on the bench, or rather attempts to sit on the edge of the bench, since the Hounds have no intention of making room for him though the bench is sufficiently large. After several vain attempts, Ex-Count resolves to fight and pushes First Hound toward the middle of the bench. First Hound pushes Ex-Count back, in other words past the edge of the bench. Ex-Count sits in the middle of the bench, between the two Hounds. Then Second Hound moves and sits between First Hound and Ex-Count. Then, with a joint effort, the Hounds push Ex-Count off the bench. Or again Second Hound does not change places but both Hounds move from both sides toward Ex-Count, squashing him between them until he goes red in the face. Throughout this the Hounds and Ex-Count pretend not to notice each other. It's a matter of creating background activity during the conversation of Ex-King and Master. Some action should also be given to Invalid and Helper.

MASTER   We can tell each other certain things but why do it in front of everyone else?

EX-KING   This thing affects everyone.

MASTER   No need to incite them. Everyone can see that life's not jolly.

EX-KING   All the more reason.

MASTER   There is no game. That is a fact. But what's the solution? I mean, we can't ban hunting. That would entail deleting the whole program. And we can't allow that.

EX-KING   Of course, it's unthinkable.

MASTER   It's easy to criticize, but it's harder to propose something concrete. If you were in my place . . .

EX-KING   You only have yourselves to blame. You unleashed desires and now you cannot satisfy them.

MASTER   At the beginning it wasn't that bad . . .

EX-KING At the beginning there was still some game.

MASTER Apparently there is still one fox left.

FOX There isn't!

MASTER Did you say something?

EX-KING Me? No. Did you?

MASTER I imagined it.

Fox removes his fur coat and turns it inside out. It is now a green cloak that could pass as hunting dress. Out of his pocket he takes a hunting hat with a feather—the same as all the other hunters are wearing—and presses it down onto his head. Performs all these actions while Master and Ex-King continue their conversation.

EX-KING Even if there is one fox left it won't be enough for everyone.

MASTER So what do you see as the way out? Go ahead, please, suggest something.

EX-KING I see no way out.

MASTER In that case say nothing.

EX-KING That's not a way out either. If it's not me, sooner or later someone else will say something.

MASTER No fear of that.

EX-KING The state of affairs cannot be concealed.

MASTER That doesn't mean it should be talked about.

EX-KING Everyone thinks the same.

MASTER But not saying it.

Fox gets down from the tree and sits between Ex-King and Master.

FOX Will you allow me, gentlemen, to join in this conversation?

MASTER Who are you?

FOX A hunter, a colleague, a companion. Straight from the ranks of brother hunters, modest and unknown and yet in my anonymity typical. *Vox populi,* ha-ha.

MASTER A hunter? So where's your rifle?

FOX Being repaired. Trigger isn't working, firing pin not functioning, bullets don't fit.

MASTER What do you want?

FOX By chance I heard a fragment of your conversation. Oh, only a fragment. You were speaking, gentlemen, of the developmental difficulties of universal hunting.

MASTER That was a private conversation.

FOX Of course, of course. That is why I overheard it only by chance. But the subject is close to all of our hearts. Mine, too, as a hunter.

MASTER A strange kind of hunter.

FOX Well, I agree with your analysis of the situation. The game is long gone and the rumors about there being one more fox in this forest are, unhappily, completely unfounded. However, I do not subscribe to the hypothesis that there is no way out. There is a way out, if you gentlemen will be kind enough . . .

MASTER I don't suppose that the first hunter who happens along can help here. This has exercised the finest minds.

FOX And yet, and yet . . .

MASTER The most outstanding experts in the field.

EX-KING Let him speak.

FOX Thank you, friend. Well, the solution is simple. If it's not possible to ban hunting, from which God preserve us, nor to restrict the number of hunters, from which God preserve us, too, then we need to try for more game.

MASTER Some solution!

EX-KING That's not new. That's what makes it so impossible.

FOX One moment. Though of course there is no more wild game, irrevocably and irredeemably gone, that doesn't mean there are no more animals.

MASTER What's he babbling about?

EX-KING Let's let him finish.

FOX   Wherein lies the problem? Not in the thing itself but in the fact that we're incapable of looking at it with fresh eyes. We persist with traditional solutions, which in a new situation really don't pass the test. Whereas we need to adjust the means to the end, synchronize targets and needs, mobilize our reserves, update, modernize . . .

MASTER   I'm losing my patience.

EX-KING   Could you not be clearer?

FOX   In brief: Wild animals need to be replaced with domestic animals. For example: with poultry. Then at last our hunting will emerge from the doldrums. Poultry is plentiful. More: It will find unlimited possibilities of development since the production of poultry will be unlimited. I recently heard about automatic feeders . . . Supply for demand, masses for the masses, each to his own for his own. Let's forget once and for all about the fox and start shooting the domestic hen.

In the tree Rooster tries desperately to say something through his gag but, of course, without success.

MASTER   But that has nothing at all to do with hunting!

FOX   Why not? The one is an animal and so is the other.

EX-KING   From a hunter's point of view there is a difference between a fox and a chicken.

FOX   But is it a difference worth insisting on?

EX-KING   You claim you're a hunter?

FOX   Of course.

MASTER   Just one little question, then: At which end of the rifle is the hunter?

FOX   Ha, ha, excellent joke!

MASTER   But I wouldn't joke about it. Your license, please.

Suddenly Hounds act as if they've scented something. They get up off the bench, stretch their necks out, and sniff. Ex-King puts a hand on Master's arm and points to the Hounds. Forgetting about Fox, Master and Ex-King carefully watch the Hounds' behavior.

EX-KING They've scented something.

MASTER Aha . . .

Checks the ammunition in his barrels.

Now the Hounds are very animated. First Hound hurriedly packs his breakfast in his briefcase. Surprised by this turn of events, Ex-Count watches them. Helper, too, watches Hounds. Only Invalid notices nothing. Fox, taking advantage of being left alone, retreats on tiptoe toward wings, left. Hounds leave hurriedly right. On the left, a long way away still, the ominous howling of a wolf. Everyone turns toward left and listens.

MASTER (*After a moment*) Imagined it.

General relief. The howl resounds again. Then a whole pack howls.

MASTER That's impossible . . .

EX-KING And yet . . .

MASTER Not here! There are none here!

EX-KING They've evidently come from elsewhere.

MASTER Where?

EX-KING From distant foreign parts . . .

MASTER All the way here?

EX-KING Evidently they're hungry. (*Howl of wolves.*) Very hungry.

Pause.

MASTER You'll forgive me, colleagues, if I withdraw from the hunt for a moment. I just remembered that I have something urgent to see to.

Leaves right.

EX-KING In which case I, too, will take advantage of this interval. As I mentioned, I hunt only for the company. What about you, dear Count?

EX-COUNT I am of the same opinion as Your Royal Highness. (*Ex-King and Ex-Count leave, right. Helper secretly distances himself from the chair. Invalid notices his ploy.*)

INVALID Hey, where are you off to?

HELPER   I'll be right back.

INVALID   Why are you leaving me?

HELPER   Because I'm in a hurry. (*Leaves right.*)

INVALID   What's this, why has everyone gone? . . . Hey!

Fox comes running in, left. As he runs he tears the hunting hat off his head and hurls it to the ground. Takes the coat off and turns it back with the red, furry, foxy side on the outside. Clambers up onto the tree. Hurriedly frees Rooster of his gag.

FOX   Wolves!

Rooster collapses into a panic, waves the sleeves of his kimono, crows, jumps up and down on the branch.

FOX   Quiet! This time it's serious.

ROOSTER   And what's going to happen now?

FOX   As long as we're up the tree we're in no danger.

From left, very close by now, the sound of a howling pack. Rooster dives into Fox's arms, hides his face in Fox's chest. Fox pats him on the shoulder, giving him courage. Invalid wheels himself around to face the wings, left.

INVALID   What is it? (*Pause.*)   I asked what is it, what does all this mean? Is there anybody here?

FOX   Wolves!

INVALID   Whaa . . . ?

FOX (*Making a megaphone with his hands by his lips*)   Wolves! ! ! ! !

INVALID   Wolf! Wolf!

Fires the rifle at the tree. Fox puts his hand to his heart and slowly, grabbing at the tree, slides down to the ground. Lies motionless.

ROOSTER   That was no wolf, you idiot!

INVALID (*In a panic*)   Wolf! Wolf!

Fires at the tree again. Rooster leans over to one side. Slides down, hangs from the branch, releases the branch, falls. Lies next to Fox.

INVALID   Well, praise be to God, I managed it.

Lays the rifle across the chair.

INVALID (*Sings*)   A-hunting we will go . . . A-hunting . . .

Humming the rest of the tune wordlessly he takes out a roll of mint candies, unwraps one of them, throws the wrapper onto the floor. Opens his lips in preparation for throwing the candy into his mouth. Howling next to him. Invalid freezes with mouth open and hand holding the mint aloft. His jaw drops. He looks into the wings, left, in profile to the audience.

SERENADE

Translated by Jacek Laskowski

CHARACTERS

FOX

ROOSTER

BLONDE

BRUNETTE

RED

Onstage the facade of a henhouse standing on a plank—the plank raised up on posts. Downstairs—three windows in a row. Upstairs—only one window positioned symmetrically above the middle window. (The surface of the facade—a triangle, or half an ellipse or wheel, on top of a rectangle.) The downstairs windows are in the rectangle. All the windows provided with wooden shutters, at present closed.

Leading from the plank to the ground is a primitive and narrow staircase, wooden, so steep it's almost a ladder leaning against the plank. The plank has no handrail and runs the length of the facade. It also runs along the sides of the henhouse if the side facades are visible. If not, in other words, if the sides of the facade go out into the wings (when the stage is too small for the previous version), then the plank goes out into the wings on both sides.

Night, but bright. The moon is shining though it is not visible. In front of the henhouse, back to the audience, sits FOX *in fox fur and a huge black Afro-style wig. He is sitting on a stool and playing a cello. The cello case, open, is lying on the ground close by. For a while Fox plays a quiet, beautiful cello piece.*

After a while the upper window opens. ROOSTER *appears in a Japanese kimono and a nightcap.*

ROOSTER   Hey, you, Ginger! Thief, layabout, crook-leg! Get out of here!

Taking no notice of him, Fox continues to play.

ROOSTER   Did you hear me? I give you two minutes to pack your box and split. And never come back here again!

Fox continues to play in unruffled peace.

ROOSTER   Get out! To your hole! To the wood!

The first window from stage left opens and BLONDE *appears. A young woman. Hair tied with a broad red ribbon.*

BLONDE   Why are you shouting?

ROOSTER   And why aren't you asleep?

BLONDE   What a question! How can one sleep when you're making so much noise?

ROOSTER   I'm making a noise? I am? It's this vagabond, schemer, road hazard!

Fox breaks off for a moment. Only in order to stand up and bow to the lady. After which he sits down and plays on.

BLONDE   Listening only to you. Can you not stop? Just for a moment? At midnight, at least. I've had enough of this yelling. All day long you're crowing and preening; we deserve some rest at night. Close the window and go back to bed. At once!

ROOSTER   I am fighting for public order!

The first window on the right opens. BRUNETTE *appears.*

BRUNETTE   What is going on here? I can't sleep. (*To Blonde.*)   Why are you screaming?

BLONDE   I'm screaming? It's this rooster.

BRUNETTE   It's you. Decent hens are asleep not carrying on in the night.

ROOSTER   Exactly.

BRUNETTE   Stop butting in! (*To Blonde again.*)   You think you're alone in the henhouse? (*Notices Fox.*)   Who is that gentleman?

Fox cuts off his serenade, stands up, and bows, after which he sits down and goes back to the cello.

ROOSTER   Gentleman? That is a lout.

BLONDE   Old witch!

BRUNETTE   Who's old?!

BLONDE   You are!

The middle window opens. RED *appears.*

RED   Are you off again?

ROOSTER   Oh, no! You at least could not butt in!

RED   I'm butting in? I am? I can't get a wink of sleep because of these bags and you say that I'm butting in?

BRUNETTE   Because of who?

BLONDE Because of what bags?

ROOSTER I meant don't get agitated.

RED Oh, excuse me, it's I who am to blame, I who get in your way, it is I who get you agitated.

BLONDE Oh, dear, oh dear . . .

ROOSTER Not me, you! I mean yourself . . . You agitate yourself.

BRUNETTE And me.

RED Torture me, torment me, by all means, if it gives you pleasure . . .

ROOSTER Go to sleep! All of you!

Red cries, or rather screams hysterically. Suddenly she cuts off her yelling. She observes Fox with interest.

RED Who is that?

Fox stands up, bows, after which he returns to cello.

ROOSTER Take no notice of him.

RED Your colleague?

ROOSTER Colleague? Do I look like his colleague?

RED No. He looks like an artist.

ROOSTER Artist? A bandit, swindler, and jerk!

RED So you do know him?

ROOSTER For some time now. I know him only too well. I know him like a bad penny. I know him so well I wish I didn't know him at all.

RED But I'm seeing him for the first time.

ROOSTER That's one time too many.

RED He must be a foreigner.

BLONDE He's dark.

ROOSTER He's pretending to be Italian but he can't fool me. I recognized him right away.

BRUNETTE   He's ugly.

BLONDE   Doesn't appeal to me.

ROOSTER   Quite right. And if you knew who he really is . . .

BLONDE   Too short.

BRUNETTE   Too tall.

RED   Neither this nor that.

ROOSTER   That's all immaterial. If you knew who you are dealing with here . . .

BLONDE   Single?

BRUNETTE   Married?

RED   Widower?

ROOSTER   Much more. This is a fox.

BLONDE   A fox!

BRUNETTE   A real fox?

RED   Truly? A fox?

ROOSTER   I didn't want to frighten you but it's better you should know and be on your guard.

BLONDE   I'm frightened!

BRUNETTE   I think I feel faint.

RED   I'm shivering.

ROOSTER   Don't be afraid, you're in my care.

BLONDE   I thought foxes were ginger.

ROOSTER   Dyed hair.

BRUNETTE   I thought they had beards.

ROOSTER   Not at all.

RED   Eeee, not much of a fox . . .

ROOSTER   And now that I've warned you, we're going to sleep. With me in the henhouse, you'll be safe. As long as you don't go out, till morning. In the daytime Fox won't dare to pillage in the yard. Therefore—to sleep, to sleep!

RED Good night, sisters.

BLONDE Bye, darling.

BRUNETTE Good night, sweetheart.

Red closes her shutter.

BLONDE Good night, dearest.

BRUNETTE Bye, little one.

Blonde and Brunette close their windows. Rooster stretches and yawns, winds up his alarm clock.

ROOSTER It didn't work, eh? (*Fox doesn't react.*) Good night, organ-grinder.

Rooster closes his shutter. Fox continues to play his cello.

As before, as throughout, the moon rises. Some nocturnal birds, some nightingales, a pleasant autumn night.

Behind the shutter the Rooster is snoring. The first window on the left opens slightly and a ribbon flies out of it. Fox stops playing. Stands, picks up the ribbon.

The window opens completely. Blonde appears, her hair undone. Pretends not to notice Fox.

FOX Did you lose something, madam?

BLONDE (*Simulating surprise and fear*) Oh . . .

FOX This ribbon, maybe? (*Blonde closes the window.*) Don't leave! (*Window opens again.*)

BLONDE I won't talk to you, sir. You are a bandit.

FOX Even a bandit doesn't deserve loneliness.

BLONDE A bandit, a robber, a brute! You should be ashamed of yourself.

FOX It's easy to accuse. But if you knew the circumstances . . .

BLONDE I don't know and I don't wish to know.

FOX Of course not. Always the same thing: contempt, condemnation, hatred . . . What madness to expect anything different.

BLONDE You've only yourself to blame.

FOX I know all that by heart. I should be used to it, but it does hurt . . . All that remains is music and loneliness.

BLONDE You love music?

FOX When I have no person to love . . . When everyone has turned against me . . . Music is the only thing I have left in my loneliness.

BLONDE And banditry!

FOX Who said I was a criminal by vocation?

BLONDE My husband.

FOX I thought women were capable of more understanding.

BLONDE That's true. Anyone who loves music can't be completely bad.

FOX Let's not talk about it anymore. Nobody will ever understand me.

BLONDE Why? We can talk. (*The increasingly loud snores of Rooster.*) As long as it's not too loud.

FOX Maybe you could come out onto the balcony?

BLONDE Not for anything in the world!

FOX It would be nearer from the balcony . . .

BLONDE Out of the question. So there are elements of good in you, sir?

FOX Destroyed, crushed by society.

BLONDE Society has to protect itself from the likes of you.

FOX The other way around. It was society that made me the way I am. But even now . . . If just one fraternal soul, if just one hand stretched out, just a fragment of feeling . . . But no, those are all hallucinations. I must be bad so I will be bad. I will play the part I am given.

BLONDE   You mustn't lose hope.

FOX   Too late.

BLONDE   It's never too late.

FOX   Maybe you will, after all, come out onto the balcony?

Rooster coughs in his sleep.

BLONDE   Pssst . . .

FOX   Why?

BLONDE   My husband . . . I'm afraid he'll wake.

FOX   Good-bye.

Moves away from window.

BLONDE   Where to?

FOX   The forest.

BLONDE   We were going to talk.

FOX   No. I must not put you at risk.

BLONDE   Why . . . If we were to talk more quietly . . .

FOX   (*Markedly more loudly than before*)   It cannot be done more quietly!

BLONDE   Pssst . . . Just wait a moment.

FOX   No. I will take my path to the end. I am lost.

BLONDE   One moment.

Vanishes from the window. Fox waits. Blonde appears on the plank, on the left. In a nightgown, barefoot.

FOX   I hate you.

BLONDE   Why? Have I done you any harm?

FOX   Yes. You do me wrong.

BLONDE   How am I to understand that?

FOX   You bring back hope to me but then disillusionment will follow and I will feel even worse, even lonelier, even more in pain . . . It is better not to have hope. You are playing with me.

BLONDE   And now it is you who do me wrong with such a, such a judgment.

FOX   Yours is a cruel game.

BLONDE   Do you not trust me?

FOX   So I hate you doubly. Awakening in me a hope that cannot be fulfilled, you inspire my hatred. So I hate you because I must hate you, whereas . . . whereas I . . .

BLONDE   What?

FOX   It doesn't matter.

BLONDE   Why don't you tell me?

FOX   Whereas I feel other feelings pressing up.

BLONDE   What feelings?

FOX   I must not name them.

BLONDE   Why not?

FOX   In any case, feelings that are the direct opposite of hatred.

BLONDE   Oh . . . (*Pause.*)   You're only tormenting yourself. If you could trust me just a little . . .

FOX   Trust . . . I had it once. I was a trusting, confident fox. But the world untaught me trust. And I said to myself: never again.

BLONDE   It's not my fault and you are accusing me.

FOX   To be able to trust one must have a minimum proof that one can trust.

BLONDE   Then it's no longer trust but certainty.

FOX   I'm not talking about certainty. I'm talking about a sign, a symbol, something tiny.

BLONDE   For example?

FOX   If you wished to come down lower . . .

BLONDE   Oh, no, not that!

FOX   There we are. So you don't trust me.

BLONDE   I trust you, but . . .

FOX   And yet you hesitate.

BLONDE   Surely I have reasons . . .

FOX   So where is the trust? You demand trust. But you? Do you trust me?

BLONDE   But you must admit that in my situation . . .

FOX   Farewell, hope.

BLONDE   All right. But not too close.

Gets onto the ladder and comes down a few rungs. At the same time, Fox comes closer to the foot of the ladder quickly. Blonde retreats two or three steps up. Pause.

BLONDE   Do you trust me now?

FOX   A little.

BLONDE   Only a little?

FOX   You're afraid of me.

BLONDE   You have such a terrible reputation.

FOX   You are afraid of me, which means that you still don't trust me.

BLONDE   That's true. But I, too, need a sign, if not proof . . .

FOX   Then I will give you more than a sign. I will give you proof that you can trust me completely.

BLONDE   I doubt if that's possible.

FOX   Here is the ribbon you lost. Please tie me up.

BLONDE   Tie you up?

FOX   Yes. Please tie my hands. Then not only will you be completely safe but I will be completely unarmed. I give myself up to you totally. Can there be a greater proof of trust?

BLONDE   I don't really know . . .

FOX   Please.

Offers her the ribbon.

Pause. Blonde stands on the ladder, undecided. Then she starts to step down the ladder slowly. Fox stands at the foot of the ladder holding in his hand, and stretching it upward, the ribbon. Blonde stretches her hand out. Between their two outstretched hands there's still some distance. Blonde stops.

BLONDE   No. (*Withdraws her hand.*)

FOX   You give up?

BLONDE   The ribbon is not enough. I need a bigger guarantee.

FOX   In that case I suggest we go to my place. I have handcuffs at home.

BLONDE   Really?

FOX   Handcuffs, chains, ropes, and even stocks.

BLONDE   And you'll let yourself be tied up?

FOX   Like a lamb. You'll tie me up from top to toe and along the hems. I'll be completely tied up.

BLONDE   Is it far?

FOX   In the forest, close by.

BLONDE   All right. I'll just slip something on. (*Steps up the ladder.*)

FOX   Must you?

BLONDE   It won't take long.

FOX   I'd prefer not to wait . . .

BLONDE   I'll be right back.

Blonde returns to the plank, sending Fox a smile as she goes. She exits along the plank, left. Fox watches her go then moves away from the ladder. Puts the ribbon into his pocket. Then he puts the cello into its case. Takes the stool and the cello, walks over to the ladder, where he stops and waits, expecting Blonde to appear at any moment. But the waiting becomes prolonged, so he puts the stool down onto the ground. It is a folding stool, so folding and unfolding it will vividly inform the audience of Fox's intentions. Sits down on the stool but he's constantly on the alert, holding the cello case on his lap.

The sound of female laughter. Fox, disconcerted, looks around, attempting to guess where the laughter is coming from. The window that is first from the right opens. Brunette appears, laughing.

FOX   May one ask what amuses Madam so much?

BRUNETTE   You do.

FOX   I see no reason.

BRUNETTE   A naive Fox—that's very funny. (*Fox shrugs his shoulders.*) Someone who waits, and waits, and waits . . . (*Fox puts down the cello, stands up, walks.*)   and waits, and waits . . . (*Fox whistles.*)   Waits and believes she'll come straight out. (*Fox stops whistling.*)

FOX   She won't come?

BRUNETTE   She will. Tomorrow at the same time.

FOX   She said she'll just slip something on.

BRUNETTE   And that only if you are in luck, sir. She'll certainly not finish any earlier.

FOX   Slipping on?

BRUNETTE   Painting herself, oh pale, naive Romeo . . .

FOX   Painting . . .

BRUNETTE   Standing in front of the mirror and improving her beauty. A hopeless undertaking in her case. Oh, and by the way, what is it you see in her? (*Fox looks at his watch.*)   I guess it's a result of the dark. If you were to see her in the daytime . . . What will you do with her?

FOX   An indiscreet question.

BRUNETTE   Forgive me, but I'm curious what one does with something like that. What can you do with something that has a complexion like hers, size nine shoes, and is twenty pounds overweight? Does one eat it?

FOX   You guessed.

BRUNETTE   Because I can't imagine the possibility of anything else.

FOX   But I don't intend to do anything else with her. Did your husband not tell you who I am?

BRUNETTE   A fox, but . . .

FOX   So what doubts can there be. A fox, therefore a murderer.

Pause.

BRUNETTE   What about the courtship? I heard everything.

FOX   I have to use subterfuge to entice my victims. I mean, I can't announce straight out: Madam, I wish to kill you. I have to say: Madam, I love you. I cheat. Women as such do not interest me.

BRUNETTE   And yet you were quite convincing.

FOX   A question of practice.

BRUNETTE   And was it always successful?

FOX   From the first to the last. And so there will be no misunderstanding: I am impotent.

Pause.

BRUNETTE   I wonder why you are so sincere with me.

FOX   Because you interest me.

BRUNETTE   As a woman?

FOX   Neither as a woman nor as a victim.

BRUNETTE   Not as a woman—I understand. That's because of your incapacity. But not as a victim—why? (*Fox is silent.*)   Have you not tried to treat it?

FOX   It's incurable.

BRUNETTE   How do you know?

FOX   I'd rather not go into details.

BRUNETTE   It could be you never came across the right woman.

FOX   It could be. But then, killing satisfies me completely.

BRUNETTE   Yours is a classic case. You kill because you're unable to love. You kill instead of.

FOX   No. I like to kill. It makes me feel good.

BRUNETTE   Do you have a spare moment?

FOX   Why?

BRUNETTE   I take an interest in psychopathy. I'd like to talk with you.

FOX   (*Looks at his watch*)   The fact is I have a date. But since you say she won't come right away . . .

BRUNETTE   No fear of that. (*Vanishes from her window. Reappears on the plank, right. In a nightshirt.*)   So I don't interest you as a victim?

FOX   I regret to say that you don't come into the reckoning.

BRUNETTE   But I'm just like all the others.

FOX   No.

BRUNETTE   What do you see in me that's different? (*Fox is silent. Brunette inspects her shoulder, her legs, her arms, her hip . . . Fox modestly averts his head.*)   At first glance at least . . . Exactly the same. Do you see a difference? (*Fox is silent.*)   Maybe one should take a closer look.

She makes a move as if she was about to remove her shirt.

FOX   No!

BRUNETTE   Ah, now, that gives me pause to think.

FOX   Let's change the subject.

BRUNETTE   You promised to talk to me. Have you ever seen a psychoanalyst?

FOX   I don't believe in psychoanalysis.

BRUNETTE   Pity. Psychoanalysis might have helped you. To explain many things.

She approaches the ladder.

FOX   Please don't come any closer.

BRUNETTE   Are you afraid of me?

FOX   No, but please don't come any closer.

BRUNETTE   Interesting, interesting . . . (*Sits on the plank, her legs hanging down front the plank.*)   I'm starting to believe that it is not incurable.

FOX   I give you my word of honor.

BRUNETTE   Your only problem is that you don't want to get cured.

FOX   What an idea!

BRUNETTE   Oh, yes. You fear a cure. You have created a defense complex. You tell yourself that being the way you are makes you happy. But it is untrue. You protect the delusion that you resolved to acknowledge as true. You defend that decision. Though at root you long for a cure, you long for it though you don't want to know about it.

FOX   That is a brash hypothesis.

BRUNETTE   It is a normal mechanism.

FOX   Risible. It's all speculation, pseudoscientific theories.

BRUNETTE   In that case why are you frightened of me?

FOX   I'm not at all frightened.

BRUNETTE   Okay, we'll see.

Brunette stands up and goes down the ladder. Fox retreats violently.

FOX   No, no, I beseech you!

Brunette stops at the ladder.

BRUNETTE   So you don't deny that you are afraid of me.

FOX   I don't deny it. Only don't come any closer to me. I beg you.

BRUNETTE   That's better. You no longer deny it. Now you only plead and beg. And so you do admit that you are afraid of me.

FOX   I admit it. As long as it's not too close . . .

BRUNETTE   Very well, I won't come close to you. But on one condition.

FOX   Whatever you command.

BRUNETTE Now confess to me why you are afraid of me.

FOX Do I have to?

BRUNETTE I'll come down.

FOX There's something different about you.

BRUNETTE Different from that stupid hen?

FOX Oh, there's no comparison! There's no problem with that one. In the presence of that one I feel nothing, whereas with you . . .

BRUNETTE In other words, something she doesn't have?

FOX Which no other woman I've met so far has. Something I'm feeling for the first time in my life. And that something arouses something in me . . .

BRUNETTE What?

FOX Fear.

BRUNETTE Only fear?

FOX No.

BRUNETTE What else?

FOX Something equally exceptional, hitherto unknown to me. . .

BRUNETTE I suspected as much.

FOX Something I fear and desire at the same time . . .

BRUNETTE Ah, you see, I was right.

FOX And that's why I ask you not to come close.

BRUNETTE You poor thing. (*Comes down the ladder.*)

FOX You were not supposed to come close!

BRUNETTE It's just for your own good.

FOX But I'm frightened.

BRUNETTE But desire it at the same time.

FOX No, I can't stand this!

BRUNETTE   It's only a moment and then you'll be well.

FOX   No, not!

BRUNETTE   I'll cure you.

On the left of the plank Blonde appears. She is wearing a hat and full makeup. At the same time the middle shutter opens with a bang. Appearing in the window is Red.

RED   There, there, both of them!

Blonde and Brunette stand still, one on the plank, the other on the ladder. Red bangs on the ceiling with a broom handle, waking Rooster. Her window is beneath his window. Brunette goes up the ladder quickly back onto the plank. The shutter at the top opens with a bang. Rooster, torn out of his sleep, appears.

ROOSTER   What, what, what is it . . . what's happening? (*Spots Blonde and Brunette on the plank.*)   What are you doing there?

BRUNETTE   Who, us?

BLONDE   Who, me?

ROOSTER   Yes, you!

BLONDE   You mean her . . .

RED   Both of them!

ROOSTER   You're not asleep either?!

RED   Both of them! The one and the other!

ROOSTER   One and the other, what . . . (*Notices that Blonde is wearing her outdoor clothes.*)   Where are you two off to . . . ?

BRUNETTE   For a walk. (*To Blonde.*)   Aren't we, darling?

BLONDE   Yes, for a stroll. Together.

Brunette and Blonde link arms.

RED   That's untrue. Each one separately.

ROOSTER   Each one separately what . . . ? (*Notices Fox.*)   Is he still here?

Fox sits down on the stool.

BRUNETTE Who?

BLONDE Exactly. Who?

ROOSTER Fox!

BLONDE What fox . . . Aaah, Fox! . . . So he is.

BRUNETTE Where, show me . . . That is Fox?

ROOSTER Both for a walk?! . . . When Fox . . . Have you gone mad, all of you together?

RED Not together, both separately!

ROOSTER I said both.

RED But both together! Separately!

ROOSTER Separately together?

RED No, both separately.

ROOSTER I don't understand any of it, but that doesn't matter. Going for a walk when Fox is waiting . . .

RED Not for a walk!

ROOSTER Not for a walk? (*To Brunette and Blonde.*) I thought you said that you were going for a walk.

BRUNETTE We? For a walk?

BLONDE What walk?

BRUNETTE Did you say we were going for a walk?

BLONDE Maybe you did . . .

ROOSTER Was it for a walk or not?

BRUNETTE Not for a walk at all. She wanted to show me her hat.

ROOSTER Now? At night?

BRUNETTE It's a night hat.

ROOSTER I don't like the look of any of this.

RED Not together!

ROOSTER   Quiet! Will you put an end to that?

BRUNETTE   It's all because of her. (*Points to Red.*)

BLONDE   She's hysterical.

BRUNETTE   Why isn't she asleep?

BLONDE   Why is she sitting in the window?

BRUNETTE   Why is she looking out of the window?

ROOSTER   Exactly. Why aren't you asleep? Why are you looking out of the window?

RED   But they, but Fox . . .

BRUNETTE   Oh-oh—what about Fox?

BLONDE   Why Fox?

RED   They and Fox . . .

BRUNETTE   Why's she on about Fox?

BLONDE   Fox on the brain.

ROOSTER   Enough of this! Off to bed this instant!

BRUNETTE   If that's what you want . . .

BLONDE   Very willingly.

BRUNETTE   By all means.

Brunette goes right, Blonde goes left.

ROOSTER   You, too!

RED   Why me?

ROOSTER   To bed! Now!

RED   But why?

Cries. Brunette and Blonde are now by the wings, Brunette on the right, Blonde on the left.

BLONDE   What about my hat?

BRUNETTE   Beautiful, darling.

Brunette vanishes right, Blonde left. Rooster vanishes from his window. Brunette and Blonde appear in their windows, Brunette in the right, Blonde in the left window. They slam their shutters simultaneously. Onto the plank, left, Rooster enters. He is carrying a chair.

ROOSTER (*To Red who is still sitting in the window.*)   What are you still doing here?

RED   It's not me, it's them . . .

ROOSTER   In the window again?

RED   Not me, them! (*Rooster closes the shutters; Red pushes them back.*) Not me! Not me!

ROOSTER   Sleep! We'll settle accounts later.

He closes the shutters despite Red's resistance. A short scream from Red on the other side of the shutters, then silence. Rooster sets the chair with a flourish on the plank, in the middle, next to the ladder. Sits on the chair and ostentatiously crosses his legs as if to say: "I am master of the situation." Pause.

ROOSTER   Well? (*Pause.*)   There's nothing for you here. The serenade is over.

Fox gets up from his stool.

ROOSTER (*cont.*)   Adieu, troubadour.

Fox stands.

ROOSTER (*cont.*)   You'll get nothing here even if you wait till morning. Go back to the forest.

Fox takes the ribbon out of his pocket. Rooster stands up.

ROOSTER (*cont.*)   Where did you get that ribbon?

Fox shrugs his shoulders, turns his back to Rooster, and faces the audience. Takes off his wig.

ROOSTER (*cont.*)   Did you hear what I asked you?

Fox ties a bow on the cello case. Then he folds the stool, and with the wig, the cello in its case, and the stool, he makes his way to the exit, left. Rooster watches him.

ROOSTER (*cont.*)   Hey, where are you going?

FOX   Back to the forest.

ROOSTER   But what's your hurry?

FOX   There's nothing for me here.

ROOSTER   What are you trying to say?

FOX   (*Stops, turns around.*)   And you?

Pause.

ROOSTER   Where did you get that ribbon?

FOX   I found it.

ROOSTER   You found it?

FOX   He who finds doesn't need to look.

ROOSTER   For a ribbon?

FOX   You can think what you like.

ROOSTER   Answer me this minute!

FOX   Really? But why?

ROOSTER   Because . . . Because I'm asking.

FOX   Some reason . . .

ROOSTER   I'm curious.

FOX   What do I care?

ROOSTER   I'm allowed to ask.

FOX   Of course, if done politely. (*Coming close to the plank.*)   So what's this about?

ROOSTER   What happened?

FOX   When?

ROOSTER   When I was asleep.

FOX   Oh, then . . . Nothing special.

ROOSTER   Still, I would like to know.

FOX   But nothing important.

ROOSTER   Nothing? Or nothing important?

FOX   Nothing important.

ROOSTER   What!

FOX   Nothing.

ROOSTER   If I don't find out I shall go mad.

FOX   (*Approaches the ladder*)   I could tell you . . .

ROOSTER   Yes, yes, tell me the truth!

FOX   . . . but in your ear only. Just between the two of us.

ROOSTER   All right, let it be.

FOX   It wouldn't do to say it out loud. (*Lowering his voice.*)   I can't in front of the ladies.

ROOSTER   The ladies? Why not?

FOX   Because . . . (*Covers his mouth with his hand and whispers something.*)

ROOSTER   What? How? I can't hear. (*Fox whispers again.*)   I can't hear anything!

FOX   Well that's a great pity.

ROOSTER   Repeat it one more time.

Kneels on the plank. Puts his hand to his ear and leans out so far he almost falls off. Fox whispers something.

ROOSTER   No, I heard nothing.

FOX   Regret it because it was interesting.

ROOSTER   I'll go mad.

FOX   Especially to you.

Rooster leaps to his feet, waves his arms, and crows.

FOX   But I do admit that from this distance you won't hear anything. Oh, too bad.

ROOSTER   And if came down lower?

FOX   Well, that would be different.

ROOSTER (*Feverishly*)   Then I will find out?

FOX   Then without a doubt.

ROOSTER   I'm coming right down. Coming!

Rooster runs down the ladder. When he is halfway down the ladder—blackout.
In the darkness the peaceful sound of the cello. A sonata . . . After a moment,
lights up. In the middle of the stage, back to the audience, sits Fox in his wig,
playing the cello.

The scene is brightly lit, the whole stage lit by sharp, even light. On the plank
the chair has gone and Red, Blonde, and Brunette are standing side by side. All
three are wearing black, with black veils, black hats, and black gloves. In other
words: in mourning.

Fox finishes the sonata. Red, Blonde, and Brunette applaud: the clapping muted
by the gloves. Fox stands up and bows. Then he turns to the audience and bows
again. Red, Blonde, and Brunette continue to applaud.

His face and hands are covered in blood.

PHILOSOPHER FOX

❧

Translated by Jacek Laskowski

BISHOP

FOX

ROOSTER

The scene—almost a dump. Fragments of old newspapers, orange peels, cans. Upstage, slightly to the right, a leafless tree. Slightly to the left, a wooden bench, as found in public parks, the green veneer old and chipped. Sitting on the bench is BISHOP in a distinguished bishop's costume, stiff-backed in a majestic pose, miter on head and crosier in hand. Upstage, a baby carriage on high wheels and with hood raised.

From left FOX enters, a man in a fox fur. He is carrying a large and heavy sack. Walks across right, stops, looks back at Bishop, turns back toward the bench. Puts the sack down on the ground, between the bench and the proscenium, straightens his arms out with relief. Sits on the bench, next to Bishop. Sits thus for a moment in silence. After a moment he speaks.

FOX Nice weather today . . . (*Bishop doesn't react.*) Comparatively. Autumns usually tend to be cooler. (*Bishop doesn't react. Pause.*) That is only my opinion, open to debate. (*Pause.*) And what is Your Excellency's view? (*Bishop doesn't react. Fox pulls out a cigar box from pocket.*) Does Your Excellency smoke? (*Bishop doesn't react.*) Nor do I. (*Fox puts the box back in his pocket. Sits in silence for a long while. Then he stands up decisively.*) Your Excellency will permit me to introduce myself. I am Fox. (*Bishop doesn't react. Fox stands for a while with outstretched hand that is not noticed by Bishop, then he sits down again.*) I'm very glad to meet you. There is no one to talk to here; I have in mind edifying conversation with someone of worth, someone on a some sort of level . . . Here everything has died off, there are no more quadrupeds even . . . nothing but worms. Does Your Excellency often visit the forest? It's pleasant here, isn't it? (*Pause.*) What news from the wide world? Apparently there are changes everywhere, reforms, new currents making their way through . . . Even in the bosom of the Church, they say this and that about it, that even in Church spheres ferment rules, a loosening of disciplines, differences of opinion, secularization . . . I'm only repeating. Is it true that secular progress is threatening spiritual tradition? I'd willingly hear something authoritative about it; Your Excellency is, so to speak, at the fount . . . (*Pause. Fox sighs.*) Well, I understand. It wouldn't be proper for Your Excellency to express a view. And yet since Your Excellency doesn't deny, there must be something in it. I know nothing about politics, but I'll be frank. As far as I'm concerned, I'm completely on the side of tradition and I guess that Your Excellency is, too. Please forgive me my temerity, but I see it by the costume, by these pontifical robes. Reformers do not dress like this. They discard the old robes just like they discard the old symbols and the old values. It goes together. Yes, Your Excellency certainly doesn't belong with them. I mean, how could Your Excellency belong with them when they are against the hierarchy, that is, against Your Excellency? (*Pause. Fox leans over and inspects the bishop's ring on the dignitary's finger.*)   Pretty ring. (*Pause.*)   Your Excellency will allow me to share some of my thoughts with him. Thank you, this is my only opportunity. I have often meditated on serious matters, but here there's no one to open one's mouth to, and spiritual persons are never to be seen. For instance, I think about martyrdom and the martyrs. Just the thoughts of a dilettante. But they prey on my mind. I feel awkward in front of an authority like Your Excellency, but I'm sure Your Excellency won't be angry. Well then, I noticed that martyrdom has played a large part in our history. First of all, the Christians were martyred for their faith, then they themselves martyred others for their faith. One way or the other, whichever way you look at it, without martyrdom you can't get started. Suffering was the way one measured the value of a belief, but today—what is the measure? Today convictions cost nothing because tolerance rules. Well, maybe not everywhere, but at least it does here and only things that happen in our land count. Today nobody cares if someone else believes in something or not: freedom of conscience. But in view of this how to measure conscience? Today nobody wants to martyr anybody and even if someone did want to be martyred for their faith, there is no opportunity for it. Suffering has been put to the service of pleasure in keeping with the tendency of our age. Suffering, which used to serve spiritual matters, now serves only the carnal exploits of perverts. That's right! Suffering has been banished from the kingdom of ideas and given to sadomasochists. But consequently can one still even talk about suffering? That noble substance has been so debased, it has stopped being itself because it has stopped being noble. The soul no longer ennobles it. So what is faith without suffering, and suffering without faith? (*Pause.*)   Your Excellency will tell me there is still plenty of suffering in the world even if we take away that part given over to perverts to transform into pleasure. Granted. There is still a lot of suffering which I would call ownerless. Who knows better than I do how much suffering there still is, of course, but it's suffering with no higher sense, with no direction or spiritual benefit. Unfortunately, being a fox I come across it every day. Your Excellency is aware that I am a bloodthirsty animal. (*Bishop turns his head to Fox for the first time since their meeting.*) Oh, I'm all right. That's how I was created. I mean, strictly speaking I'm not bloodthirsty, I just eat meat, I have to feed myself the meat of other animals to live, and to live I have to kill. (*Bishop raises himself slightly on the bench, still staring at Fox. Fox points heavenwards with his finger.*) Your Excellency should rather direct your gaze up there, not at me. At the master, not the servant. At the one who created me, not the creature. I didn't invent myself, it wasn't my project. If it was up to me I'd prefer to eat dairy products and vegetables, though eating eggs is suspect from the point of view of a respect for unborn life and the latest research suggests that plants aren't as feelingless as was thought earlier. (*Bishop sits down and once again stares straight ahead.*) It's not my fault that from time to time I have to catch some rabbit, or a hen, or a goose or . . . Your Excellency will allow me not to go into details. Yes, yes, the blind ruthlessness of nature . . . (*Pause.*) Your Excellency is against it? So am I. Factually I am in order, but morally I'm torn. One has to live, but can simple biological survival put the soul at ease? I often tell myself: "There you are, Fox, once again you have martyred some innocent creature just to satisfy your blind instinct. You were ordered to kill, that's true, but could you not season it with some ideal? Do you constantly have to kill with no spiritual sense, with no higher ideal and must your victims constantly have to die not for any noble cause but only to satisfy your boorish hunger?" Excellency, I have had enough of it and now, when I saw Your Excellency, I thought to myself: "He's been sent from above." I suspect that not only one can but one should say that . . . Excellency, I'll show you something. (*Fox gets up, approaches the sack.* ROOSTER, *who is sitting in the sack, appears. Rooster has a comb in his hand and is combing his hair.*) There you are, here is one of my victims. A rooster, beauty of life, vitality, reproductiveness in person. Just take a close look at him, Your Excellency: that expression, that posture, that bright eye . . . (*To Rooster.*) Bow to His Excellency. (*Rooster doesn't react.*) And yet he has to die. So much beauty and strength, so much joy of existence, all that will go, all that will be destroyed. Brutally, immediately, like a broken thread . . . (*Fox wipes away a tear.*) And for what, why, he asks, in the name of what cause? (*To Rooster.*) You do ask, don't you? And there is no reply. And I have to do away with him with my own hands. Why, where is the spiritual sense of that cruel deed I in turn ask. And there is no reply either. Both the executioner and the victim ask themselves the same question: "Why? Why am I dying? Why am I killing?" And the same silence is the reply to both of us. Is that how it should be? Is that fair? Can one live like this? (*Moved, Fox wipes another tear. Then he threatens Rooster, raising his hand.*)   Bow to His Excellency, I said! (*Under the influence of this threat, Rooster lowers his head in a bow to Bishop.*)   And what does Your Excellency say to that? (*Pause.*)   Get out! (*Helps Rooster get out of the sack and pushes him toward the bench. As he's moving, Rooster puts the comb into his pocket. They both stand in front of Bishop.*)   Excellency, from whom can we expect advice, help, if not from Your Excellency? Your Excellency is a spiritual leader par excellence. I understand that Your Excellency has found himself here in a, so to speak, private capacity: a park bench, fresh air . . . Of course. But problems are everywhere, even in the fresh air. (*Slides down onto his knees in front of Bishop and forces Rooster to do the same. Bishop stands up.*)   This can't go on like thus! Tell us what we are to do, how we are to live! Tell us how to kill and how to die. I don't mean how, I mean what for. What for, Excellency, what for! (*Bishop sits down again, sits looking into the distance, motionless and hieratic. Long pause.*)   Your Excellency is silent. (*Fox gets up, as does Rooster.*)   You disappoint me, Excellency. (*Puts a hand on Rooster's shoulder.*)   Come, my little martyr without faith. Your executioner takes you to the scaffold with the same lack of conviction as you go to it. Forgive him, for though he knows what he does, he doesn't know what for. You don't know what you are dying for, he doesn't know what he is killing you for. We are brothers in ignorance. (*Bishop leans forward, rests his elbow on his knee, puts a hand to his eyes. In the other hand he is holding the crosier. Fox packs Rooster into the sack and picks up the sack over his shoulder, puffing with the effort.*)   Adieu, Excellency. Pity. (*Goes right, stops.*)   If only Your Excellency would say one word! Do I not deserve that much? Is it not Your Excellency's duty? (*Puts sack on the ground.*)   Excellency, I am warning you. The Church is not the only institution to which I can turn. Someone else will willingly look after me, will not decline to help. Someone else is just waiting for the chance. Someone who will teach me the sense of living and dying, but will teach me in his own way. He will give me ideals, but they'll no longer be Your Excellency's ideals, oh, no! Quite the reverse. You catch my drift, excellency? (*Pause. Fox takes a few steps toward the bench.*)   Excellency,

either you speak to me at once or I shall go elsewhere. I'll go to the
devil himself and it won't be my fault. I will give myself to the devil
and God himself will acquit me but will demand an account from
Your Excellency. Excellency, I am waiting. (*Fox stands and waits. Then
he goes closer to the bench.*)   Is Your Excellency crying? (*Fox sits down
on the bench next to Bishop.*)   There, there, Excellency, I didn't mean
to upset you. I expressed myself a bit harshly, it's true, but is that
surprising . . . (*Pause.*)   I appreciate that it's not that simple. But if
Your Excellency could just try . . . Or maybe we could both try? . . .
Joint effort . . . I even have an idea. (*Looks around like a street-corner
trader about to suggest an illegal transaction. Lowers his voice, points to the
sack containing Rooster.*)   Why doesn't Your Excellency try to convert
him? No risk but it will pay off whatever happens. Either he'll agree,
in which case he'll die a Christian, or he won't agree and then I'll
throttle him for being a hardened pagan, in the name of the faith.
Either way, he'll die in the name of a higher worth, and not, so to
speak, bare-assed. Well? What do you say to that, Your Excellency?
(*Pause.*)   Excellency, this is a sound proposition. Do I have to set out
the benefits that will flow from this to Your Excellency? Either we'll
have one fewer pagan, or we'll have one more martyr. And you know
yourself, Excellency, that martyrs today are thin on the ground. I
mean, you need martyrs. Do I have to explain it to Your Excellency?
(*Pause.*)   Excellency, I am giving Your Excellency a beautiful
opportunity . . . for nothing. Your Excellency simply cannot not take
advantage. Your Excellency's predecessors would have given a lot for
something like this. To convert they had to make long journeys, they
traveled to savage peoples, with difficulties, discomfort, and even
risking their lives. But here—it's luxury. Your Excellency is sitting
here comfortably, breathing, resting, and the pagan invites himself
along. Just stretch out your hand, Excellency, and it's all ready.
(*Pause.*)   I understand: This is so advantageous that Your Excellency
simply cannot believe it and that's why you're hesitating. Your
Excellency is wondering what's in it for me, since I'm persuading
Your Excellency so forcefully. But did I not mention that I've had
enough of the mindless cruelty of nature, of the lack of ideals, of the
moral vacuum . . . (*Bishop takes his hand from his face and looks at
Fox.*)   Well, all right, all right. It's the honest truth but I can see that
Your Excellency still doesn't believe me. In which case . . . If Your
Excellency were to offer me the ring Your Excellency wears on his

finger . . . I would accept it to reassure Your Excellency. It would be proof of my selfishness if Your Excellency insists on having such a proof. Then Your Excellency will be reassured that there are no ulterior motives for my suggestion; my motives will become comprehensible to Your Excellency. It pains me but I'll do it for Your Excellency. I'll take it without even looking at it; I am confident that it's real.

The sound of an infant's crying. Bishop gets up and moves over to the baby carriage. Rocks the carriage to calm the child. Fox gets up from the bench.

FOX (*cont.*)   Your Excellency!

The child doesn't quiet down, but cries even more loudly. Bishop rests the crosier against the carriage, leans over, and picks up the infant in both hands. Rocks it in his arms but the infant screams. Fox approaches Bishop.

FOX (*cont.*)   Your Excellency, Your Excellency, do you hear me?

Bishop goes to the bench, sits, unbuttons the episcopal robe, and takes out a splendid woman's breast, which he offers the child to feed it. The Bishop is, in fact, a woman. Fox covers his eyes with a gesture of not quite embarrassment, not quite despair. The child sucks and stops crying. Fox uncovers his eyes in the hope that it was all an hallucination, but he sees again what he saw before, so he instantly covers his eyes again. At last he takes his hands from his eyes once and for all, but he no longer looks at the Woman-Bishop but aside and at the ground.

FOX (*cont.*)   Your Excellency . . . madam . . . I withdraw everything I said about progress and tradition. What I meant was that I've always been on the side of progress and against tradition, yes, always, especially as a child. Nevertheless . . . (*Confused, choking, puts a hand to his throat, swallows.*)   Madam, please forgive me this emotion. The rapidity of progress has outstripped my fondest expectations . . .

Takes out a handkerchief from his pocket and wipes the sweat from his brow. Meanwhile, having fed and quieted the child, Woman-Bishop hides her breast in her robe, gets up, goes to the baby carriage, and lays down the child inside it. Picks up the crosier again. Fox hides his handkerchief in his pocket and addresses the Woman-Bishop.

FOX   That does not mean, however, that we cannot continue. My offer still stands. I'm keeping it open. Yes, nothing's changed. I don't belong to those who defend the past at any price and accept nothing new. Oh, no! Everything is as it was! What I mean is that everything is as it is, new but at the same time old. That's right! New but old or, in other words, old but new . . . I can't express myself but what we're dealing with here is fundamental problems. As I have had occasion to remark . . . (*Woman-Bishop moves right with the carriage. Fox shouts to detain her.*)   Madam Excellency!

A short wail from the child. Woman-Bishop stops, turns to Fox, and puts a finger to her lips, enjoining silence. Then indicates the child with her finger, showing that the child should not be woken. Retreats finally right, pushing the baby carriage and majestically wielding the crosier. Fox stands for a moment stupefied, then goes to the bench and sits down in the posture of a crushed man. Rooster sticks his head out of the sack.

ROOSTER   What is it?

FOX   The end.

ASPIRING FOX

Translated by Jacek Laskowski

CHARACTER

FOX

The stage is dark. Only a lantern—a light placed in a lantern—lights a circle in which the following picture can be seen: a bench, and sitting on the bench a monkey (a dummy). The monkey is small. Its legs—or back limbs—do not reach the ground, stick out over the front of the bench as if a doll has been put on the bench. Monkey is dressed in a red jacket with silver buttons, epaulettes on the shoulders. On its head a cap, also red, of the kind once worn by jesters. On each of the three corners of the jester's cap—a bell.

The monkey is chained to a barrel organ—a brightly painted box on two wheels, standing close to the bench. The chain is long enough for the barrel organ not to obscure the bench (and monkey), but still within the circle of light. The bench is facing the audience, slightly to the left. The lantern is on the bench, on the left of the monkey. The barrel organ is slanted left from the monkey, closer to the proscenium than the bench. One end of the chain is fixed to an iron collar around the monkey's neck. Entering right comes FOX, initially difficult to make out as a character because that side of the stage is in darkness. Goes along the proscenium to the left as if he was intending to exit into the wings, left. But he stops and inspects the monkey. Fox is wearing a fox fur, reaching down to the ground. A ginger, pointed mustache, ginger slicked-down hair with a part.

FOX (*Softly, hesitating*) Who's this I see? (*Approaches the bench.*) At this hour? (*Stands in front of the bench for a moment, inspecting the monkey.*) May I rest?

Fox sits on the bench, on monkey's right. Between him and the monkey is the lantern. He sits turned toward the monkey anticipating a reaction which, naturally, doesn't come. Receiving no reaction, Fox turns to face the audience. For a moment Fox, just like the monkey—which does so throughout the performance—sits facing the audience in silence. After a while Fox turns decisively back to the monkey.

FOX (*cont.*) I really don't know how to act. Should I apologize for my boldness or my lack of it? It all depends on how you, sir . . . how you, madam . . . see our relationship. (*Pause. The monkey, of course, is silent.*) I understand. I admit it's hard to see it clearly. Or rather to resolve which side to look at it from. I mean, one can look at it from two sides. On the one hand, we both belong to the animal world. Fox and monkey are warm-blooded mammals, vertebrates, quadrupeds. If one of us was, say, a fish, then there would also be an affinity. I mean a fish is also not a plant nor is it a mineral. But it would be a lesser affinity. But the way things stand now, or rather we stand now, that is to say the way we sit now, here, next to each other, I could address you, sir, you, madam, as a brother. Or then again: sister. Depending on the sex. (*Pause.*)   Cool night. (*Pause.*)   Well, almost. I wouldn't want to exaggerate it but then again one cannot ignore what is, after all, a close affinity . . . (*Pause.*)   Then again, I'm not insisting. I'm only presenting the matter from one side, from one of two possible sides . . . But if we were to see our relationship from that particular side, which is dependent on agreement, then the certain lack of confidence with which I address you . . . sir . . . madam . . . the certain restraint would be out of place. It simply is not proper between relatives—this reserve bordering on coolness, this lack of familial feelings . . . Isn't that so? Indeed, I should rather shout: (*Fox stands up and throws his arms out wide.*)   Hi, there, monkey! Put it there! (*Goes still, noticing that the monkey doesn't react and that he may have committed a gaffe*)   Well, I didn't say that. (*Pause. Fox looks closely at the monkey.*)   Nice get up. (*Pause.*)   On the other hand, such familiarity wouldn't be completely appropriate. You, sir . . . madam . . . as a monkey are a being that is, if I may say so, ambiguous. Oh, by no means in any negative sense. Forgive me for having used such a word, but it's hard for me to find another that would better reflect the nature of the question. On the one side, the one I have already spoken from, you undoubtedly belong, madam—I will continue to address you thus not daring to ask your sex but preferring to accept that I'm dealing with the feminine element: It makes it easier, I can count on a certain gentleness, a maternal attitude which will facilitate understanding—on the one side, then, you, madam, undoubtedly belong to the animal world. Yes, but from the other side was it not your species, madam, that started humankind? You, madam, are the link joining animals to people. There is as much human in you as there is animal. And if we forget about your animality, madam, then we are dealing, madam, with your humanity. You can say the same things about you, madam, as you can about a human being. Humans' nature is half monkey and half angel. Monkey—half animal, half human. In other words, half and half again, though on a different rung, the difference is only in the level of sublimation whereas the principle of half-and-halfness is the same. I hope I haven't offended you, madam, through the comparison with the human being. A comparison from which a certain inferiority to man may be drawn. I just ask you to look down at all the lower species, at all the rungs

which you, madam, have already been through; look at me, for
instance . . . You'll instantly feel superior. Besides, what is there
standing in the way of further evolution? Once you possess the secret
of change, madam, you will be able to evolve upward at will. I guess,
madam, that you are not doing so at the moment for some personal
reasons. Maybe you are tired, madam, and you wish to rest awhile
here, on this bench, after the effort it indubitably required to get
yourself out of the purely animal nature. But in a moment you will set
off again, madam, on the triumphant march toward higher forms of
existence. Which I, unfortunately, cannot say about myself. I am only
an ordinary fox, in other words one hundred percent animal, with no
half-and-halfness, and therefore with no better prospects for the
future. And that is precisely why, if we take into account the second
side of your nature, that superiority of yours over me already achieved
and confirmed, as well as the way open to even higher regions of
being which are accessible to you, then I, a simple and irrevocable fox
can say only: I kiss your hand, madam! (*Rises from the bench to make the
bow that precedes the kissing of a lady's hand. But the monkey, of course,
doesn't react, so Fox collapses back onto the bench.*)   Besides, your very
appearance, madam, is evidence of the fact that as much divides us as
unites us. Your dress, madam, and the situation in which I find you.
They are not in the least animal. I have only my foxy fur, but you are
dressed in human costume and not just the kind that protects from
the cold and is merely a ready-to-wear supplement of biological
adaptation, an artificial extension of a natural function. Your costume,
madam, is symbolic, it expresses abstract ideas, in other words
exclusively human ones. Purple is the color of royalty and the color of
passion. Silver—of costliness, the epaulettes express nobility and
courage. Whereas your headdress, madam, symbolizes wit, in other
words a sense of humor, a trait that is evidence of humanness and is
completely inaccessible to us animals. This thing (*Touches the chain by
which the monkey is tied to the barrel organ.*)   is also human-made. It
expresses attachment, in other words a category which, though
known to some domestic animals, arose in the mind of man and was
applied to those animals by man. So they know it only in the passive
sense. Chains, knots, bars, and handcuffs are indubitable evidence of
spirit, since they are a conscious curtailment, a deliberate steering, a
targeted exclusion of freedom. And what are you tied to, madam?
Literally tied to, which literalness implies a higher purpose, expresses a

spiritual tie. You are not in the least tied to something utilitarian like, if you'll pardon me, a dog tied to its kennel to guard the yard, nor like a horse to a treadmill. You are tied to something outside utilitarianism and, as is well known, only someone who is not an animal may and is able to devote himself to something that has no use. You, madam, are tied to music. Excuse me, may I? (*Fox gets up and turns the handle. Mozart's Sonata in A Major plays.*)   Music, the purest of the arts, expressing nothing except itself. More refined than literature that, though it is no longer of the material world, is nevertheless still subject to its laws of the struggle for existence sublimated into the battle of ideas. More refined than painting or sculpture, which have to resort to shapes and pictures and are therefore not free of carnality. Music, the absolute art, in which the last traces of slavery vanish, free of pictures and words—those guardians of every consciousness— which, like prison officers, though they feed it also guard it so it won't slip off. It is when I listen to music that I am most conscious of being a mere fox. It awakens in me a longing for a perfection that is inaccessible to me; my sights are set high. But only my sights, unfortunately . . . (*Stops turning the handle; the sonata is silenced.*)   . . . and I cry. (*Sits down on the bench again. Pause.*)   Forgive me. But you can have no idea, madam, what it means to be stuck on a low level of evolution. Music makes me conscious of the abyss between me and creatures more advanced than me. Now I no longer doubt that more divides us than unites us. Yes, between me and you, madam, there is an abyss. You are already on the other side of the evolutionary leap. Whereas I am still only an animal. (*Pause.*)   Don't you feel cold? (*Pause.*)   You no longer remember what it's like to be merely an animal. And anyway, in the times when you were an animal it was still bearable being just an animal. Morally and materially. Nature was still the only reality, the only option. To be an animal then neither brought shame nor created difficulties in survival. Homo sapiens wasn't yet shining his superiority into our eyes and wasn't calling himself the king of creation, and his kingdom, which didn't exist then, wasn't depleting nature's resources. Today everything's turned for the worse for us animals. Civilization is displacing nature, increasingly curtailing the possibilities of our survival, and culture is giving us an inferiority complex. We all once started as equals, so why have some gotten so high and others stayed in the same place as billions of years ago? Why are you human-shaped, madam, and I am not? That is a question to which there is no answer. I wander through the nights, hunted and hunting for food, and in my head the same question sounds constantly: Why, why, why? . . . (*A rooster crows.*)   Soon it will start to dawn, but the night will not end for me. The night of limited being, the limbo of biological duration, the blind tyranny of instincts, the cursed circle of fear and hunger, running away and chasing. Not for me the dawn of the spirit, the divine spark of intellect, the light of consciousness appearing, super-consciousness and super-duper-consciousness. Not for me a soul. Soul! Why can I not have a soul? (*Fox gets up off the bench. For a moment he stands facing the audience. Then he turns back to the monkey.*)   Madam, you know the secret. You are halfway on the road between us, the proletariat of creation, and man, the ruler of this earth. You know what to do so as not to stay forever at the bottom. I beseech you, madam, divulge that secret to me. For the memory of our mutual past, for pity of an impoverished relative, for consideration also of the good of evolution. Is not evolution the only law, the only true religion, the only meaning of the universe? Is not progress, the march to perfection, rising higher and higher, the only aim, the only purpose of existence? And if it is, then, madam, you don't have the right to refuse me. We'll go together. You'll become a human being and I'll become a monkey. Then, when human beings take the place of angels, I will take the place of humans. And that's not even the end yet. It's possible there are other stages of evolution unknown to us yet. Archangels, archarchangels, and so on, and on to giddy heights. Can you not see it, madam? Does it not bring you joy? Just one word and you will become more than an ordinary monkey. You will become, madam, a messiah, the liberator of all creatures which till now are excluded from the march to the heavens. Will you tell me, madam? (*The rooster crows again. Fox leans over the monkey. Lowers his voice.*)   It's still night, but in a moment the sun will rise. What better opportunity, what more apposite moment to divulge the secret. The light you bestow on me, madam, will join as one with the rays of the rising sun. (*Fox takes the lantern and puts it out; the stage is now totally dark.*)   Darkness favors the animals and morning will be the state of revelation. We are alone, but in a moment the human will appear, your cousin, madam, impresario and guardian. The human is jealous of the secret. He prefers to remain the ruler of creation in accordance with the promise given him in Genesis: ". . . have dominion over the fish of the sea, and over the fowl of the air, and over every living thing that moveth upon the earth." Man doesn't want the fish, birds, reptiles, and all the animals to discover the secret of humanness. But of course you do know that secret, madam. There is still time to reveal it before the human comes and interrupts us. The human—jealous of his humanness. The human—acme of creation, the human—the highest form of being on this earth. Speak, madam. I want to become a human!

The rooster crows for the third time. The stage lights up and is now completely visible. On the ground are bits of old newspapers, empty bottles, and cans. Upstage and slightly on the right of the stage, a leafless tree. On the tree hangs the organ-grinder. (It is, of course, unacceptable for the public to guess sooner the presence of the hanged man in the background. If the lighting control is inadequate, then one may cover the hanged man with black gauze and raise it at the right moment.) A broad-brimmed hat covers his face. In a poor, worn, and colorless jacket. A long scarf of a somewhat livelier color covers the neck and hangs loosely along the lifeless body. Fox stands in front of the monkey, facing the hanged man. For a moment he looks at the hanged man. The light has, meanwhile, reached its full intensity and is not changing.

FOX *(cont.)*   Ah, then I'll just be on my way.

Goes out left.

ON FOOT

Translated by Jacek Laskowski

CHARACTERS

FATHER

SON

LADY

SUPERIUS

WOMAN

GIRL

LT. ZIELINSKI

RUFFIAN

TEACHER

FIDDLER

CLEOPATRA

ACT I

The stage represents a skyline, a horizon, and a field. It is empty save for the numerous medium- and small-bore cartridge shells scattered over the field.

SCENE ONE

FATHER, *aged forty, is standing in the middle facing stage left. He is wearing a threadbare overcoat and an old hat that were once "best" but have long since been relegated to everyday use. He is carrying a homemade knapsack made of gray canvas and his shoes are muddy.*

FATHER   You're a real pest, you are. I never saw anyone piss as much as you piss.

SON *comes on hurriedly, stage left. He is fourteen. He is wearing a navy blue coat that is too tight for him; he has grown out of it. There's a cap with earflaps on his head and he is carrying a knapsack just like his father's. He finishes buttoning up quickly and apologetically.*

FATHER (*cont.*)   It's probably fear. You're scared, aren't you?

SON   No.

FATHER   Getting across the highway will be the worst. Transports use the highway. There might be bombing.

SON   Do we have to cross the highway?

FATHER   There's no other way. (*Pause.*)   Or mines. There's mines everywhere now. Everything's been mined.

SON   Let's wait till night.

FATHER   You're talking rubbish. It's even worse at night. Bandits.

Son walks stage right.

FATHER (*cont.*)   Wait, what's your hurry?

Moves to wings, stage left.

FATHER (*cont.*)   Just wait for me here.

Father goes out, left. Son looks around anxiously, notices a cartridge on the ground, squats down, and looks at it closely. He picks up the cartridge, stands up, moves away from the place where he found the cartridge, stops, and inspects the cartridge in his hand. Father reenters, left, buttoning his fly.

FATHER (*cont.*)   Chuck that!

Son winds up to do what Father told him to do.

FATHER (*cont.*)   Don't chuck it! It could be a live shell!

SON   Then what am I supposed to do?

FATHER   I told you to put it down carefully, didn't I? Do you want it to rip your arm off? Or your leg?

Son stares at the cartridge in terror.

FATHER (*cont.*)   Put it back where you found it.

Son bends down to put the cartridge on the ground.

FATHER (*cont.*)   Is that where you found it?

SON   No. It was over there.

Indicates the place where he picked up the shell.

FATHER   I told you to put it back where you found it!

Son goes over to the place he previously indicated and bends down.

FATHER   Careful, careful . . .

Son puts the shell down on the ground. As he does so there is an explosion in the distance, intensified by its echo. They both listen.

FATHER (*cont.*)   Did you hear that?

SON   Yes, I did, Dad.

FATHER   Hell's teeth. (*Pause.*)   So what do you think?

SON   They're shooting.

FATHER   Hell's teeth. We should have stayed at home.

SON   So who is it, then: them or us?

FATHER   Us. (*Pause.*)   Or them. (*Pause.*)   So let's go.

They go out right. Blackout, during which the sound of distant shooting grows louder. It lasts as long as is needed to remove the spent shells from the stage.

SCENE TWO

The cartridge shells have vanished. Enter left SUPERIUS *and* LADY.

Superius is fifty-odd years old, handsome, with an unusual face and "hypnotic" eyes. He is wearing a fur coat with a beaverskin collar, and a wide-brimmed hat. On one foot he is wearing an elegant, knee-high, lace-up boot (of the kind worn by Europeans in Africa, or in automobile races in the twenties); the other leg is wrapped in thick rags. Superius is leaning heavily against Lady's shoulder.

Lady is a small woman, smaller than Superius, and aged between thirty and forty. She is wearing a coat with a fluffy red fox around her neck, and rubber, or Wellington, boots. Apart from the fact that she is supporting Superius, she is also carrying a sizable suitcase and a traveling bag containing toiletries. Although her double role of nurse and porter is crushing her, she plays it bravely.

LADY   It's not far now.

SUPERIUS (*Stops and thereby makes his companion stop, too*)   Whither? (*Pause.*)   Whither is it not far, actually?

LADY   Perhaps you'd like to rest.

SUPERIUS   Is that a suggestion or a supposition?

Lady puts the suitcase down on the ground.

LADY   Sit down.

Superius sits on the suitcase.

LADY   Does it hurt?

Superius stretches out the leg wrapped in rags and inspects it with distaste.

SUPERIUS   How much can this piece of offal weigh?

LADY   Don't think about it.

SUPERIUS   Have you ever considered how much a human leg might weigh? On its own, separately. Five kilos? Six? Ten? Why has it never aroused your curiosity?

LADY (*Tired, mechanically*)   Would you like something to eat?

SUPERIUS   It never aroused my curiosity, either. I regret it now. After all, I had the opportunity. There were so many lying in the trenches, between the trenches—arms, heads, legs—all separate. I could have collected the limbs and weighed them. As an officer I had the right to. An obligation, even. Maybe. Why did I not do it when I had the chance . . . ? Clearly, I was too young, too busy playing the giddy goat . . . I'm acting feverish, am I not?

LADY   No.

SUPERIUS   (*With a hypochondriac's irritability*)   Do you think I'm not feverish? Do you know how I am feeling? I am certain I have a fever.

LADY   Maybe a slight fever.

SUPERIUS   Not a slight fever! A huge fever. A magnificent, an extraordinary fever! A Renaissance fever. Early Renaissance.

LADY   Yes, all right. You have a Renaissance fever.

SUPERIUS   You think I'm insane, don't you?

The sound of an explosion, then its echo.

LADY   Don't you think we should get away from here?

SUPERIUS   Am I, or am I not?

Another explosion.

LADY   Let's go.

SUPERIUS   Let's go. For the time being.

She helps him get up and lets him lean on her. A third explosion. Lady picks up the suitcase. They move right.

SUPERIUS   (*cont.*)   Ten kilos at least.

Blackout. The wail of a siren.

SCENE THREE

Center stage, back turned to the audience, sits a figure with the close-cropped hair favored by army recruits and convicts, and wearing an army greatcoat devoid of insignia; it is khaki, covered in dust and well-worn. Father and Son enter left.

FATHER   . . . so I told him straight: Don't you talk to me like that, I said, you don't know who you're dealing with.

SON   And what did he say?

FATHER   Started apologizing but I wasn't having any of that. I said: You show me your authorization. I'm not even going to talk to you unless you have an authorization. Hand it over! Show us your authority to talk to me. Come on, let's see it!

Father becomes excited and waves his arms about. Then he notices the seated figure and stops.

SON (*Lowering his voice*)   Who's that?

FATHER   Quiet! Why are you shouting like that?

SON (*Even more quietly*)   What is he doing here?

FATHER   God only knows.

SON   Is he armed?

FATHER   Could be.

SON   Russian, is he?

FATHER   Can't tell.

SON   German?

FATHER   Can't tell.

SON   A bandit?

FATHER   How the hell am I supposed to know?

Pause.

SON   He can't see us.

FATHER   He could be pretending.

SON   He's not moving.

FATHER   So what?

SON   What are we going to do?

FATHER   We're leaving.

Father crosses himself and moves forward, followed by Son. When they are still some way from figure, Father stops and turns to Son.

FATHER If he asks you any questions, you don't know anything. Right?

Son nods. They go past the sitting figure, behind its back, coming between it and the audience. When they are a few paces past it, Son stops.

SON (*Whispering*) Dad . . .

FATHER (*Stops, turns back, and whispers*) What is it?

SON He's not asking any questions.

FATHER Isn't he?

SON Not a word.

FATHER Maybe it would be better if I talked to him first.

SON Do we have to?

FATHER He mustn't think we're running away.

SON What are we going to do, then?

FATHER It's best to say something. If he thinks we're running away, he'll start shooting.

SON What should I say?

FATHER Don't you say anything. I'll do the talking.

Goes up to the sitting figure.

FATHER (*cont.*) Excuse me, sir . . .

SON How about German?

FATHER And if he's a Russian? He'll think we're Krauts and he'll start shooting.

SON Russian, then.

FATHER You're stupid. He might be a German. Excuse me, sir . . .

The sitting figure remains perfectly still. Father takes a cigarette case out of his pocket, opens it, and holds it out.

FATHER (*cont.*) Cigarette?

Pause. Ingratiatingly.

FATHER (*cont.*)   Would you like a smoke, sir?

He touches the sitting figure on the shoulder. Figure leans back slowly and crashes to the ground, supine. Its face is crimson with blood, quite unrecognizable. Father moves back, with his cigarette case still held out before him. Son stands motionless, gazing at the corpse. Father stops, closes the cigarette case, and returns it to his pocket. He turns and moves towards the exit, right. As he approaches the wings he stops and turns round. He sees Son standing motionless and staring at the lying figure.

FATHER (*cont.*)   Let's go.

Son stares at the corpse quite hypnotized as if he hasn't heard Father calling. Father goes up to him, takes him by the shoulder, and leads him out, right.

Blackout. The sound of a crying infant.

Scene Four

A baby carriage, pushed by WOMAN, *comes on stage left. The carriage is full of goods, though they are covered from view by a piece of canvas sheeting. Woman is a peasant woman: She is stout and rough, not old, and she is wearing a shawl over her head and shoulders, a skirt, and knee-length military boots. She is carrying a bundle on her back.*

Following Woman is GIRL, *who is also carrying a bundle. Girl is pregnant; sufficiently far advanced for it to be evident.*

WOMAN   Sweet Jesus, I told you not to take deutsche marks. Nowadays deutsche marks aren't worth any more than prewar money. The war money's all crap, too. I told you to take bacon.

GIRL   He wouldn't give me bacon.

WOMAN   Then you should have taken tobacco.

GIRL   He wouldn't give me tobacco.

WOMAN   Wouldn't give me, wouldn't give me—but he took the booze, didn't he? You're stupid. I should never have sent you. I should never have had you. Sweet Jesus of Nazareth, all this pain, all this suffering I have to endure, will you not thunder against the injustice, sweet Lord above . . .

An explosion, followed by its echo. Woman comes to a halt.

WOMAN (*cont.*)   . . . have mercy on us women. Are we going through the wood?

GIRL   The wood's been burned down.

WOMAN   Then it's through Thirsting Meadow.

GIRL   All that way?

WOMAN   Stop complaining. Stop complaining or I'll give you something to complain about.

GIRL   Can't you see I'm coming?

WOMAN (*Points to Girl's belly*)   With your merchandise, right?

GIRL   What is it now?

WOMAN   Who's going to buy that off you?

GIRL   I got it for nothing.

WOMAN   Yes. Army surplus stores.

Blackout. The growing sound of galloping cavalry.

SCENE FIVE

A small wayside shrine in the middle of the stage. Father and Son enter stage left.

FATHER   In nineteen twenty we charged the bayonets. I came across a fellow about six and a half feet tall. I could see I was done for. And there was no running away. He was just about to run me through but then he only smacked me on the face and knocked me to the ground. And all the time he was bad-mouthing my mother. I was almost a child then, not much older than you are now. A volunteer.

SON   What was it like after the war?

FATHER   After the war times were hard.

Stops and takes an already somewhat empty flask from the inside of his coat.

FATHER (*cont.*)   What are you looking at me like that for? I have rheumatism . . . This will warm me up. It's medicinal, understand?

Takes a gulp from the bottle and grimaces.

FATHER (*cont.*)   It really is vile . . . But I have to drink it.

Puts his hand to his side.

FATHER (*cont.*)   I have these pains right here.

Turns his back on Son and takes another swig from the bottle.

FATHER (*cont.*)   There, that's better. I hate this stuff.

He screws up the bottle and puts it away.

FATHER (*cont.*)   It will be different after this war, you'll see. America will look after us.

SON   Will I go to high school?

FATHER   I should say so. It'll be a first-rate high school. Nothing but the sons of doctors, lawyers, and engineers. Do you remember Doctor Uziemblo?

SON   No.

FATHER   He was a smart man. And his father was a peasant.

SON   And will there be water?

FATHER   What do you mean—water?

SON   In the bathroom, so we don't have to fetch it from the well. And warm so we don't have to heat it up. Will there be a bathroom?

FATHER   Goes without saying. And you'll be able to walk along the street whenever you want. No police, no militia, no searches, no raids, no sending to labor camps or concentration camps. You just go out into the street and walk as if it was the most natural thing to do. If you want to, you go back home but if you don't want to, you go for a stroll. And if something upsets you, you just come straight out and say so, out loud, so everyone can hear. And nobody will get at you for it, there's no bugging, no denunciations.

SON   And will you be able to buy everything?

FATHER   Absolutely everything.

SON   And play football?

FATHER   Clubs will be quite legal. All sports. And theaters.

SON   Will we go to the theater?

FATHER   If you work hard at school then there's no reason why we shouldn't. On a Sunday, or the holidays . . . I'll come, too. We'll dress up and we'll go. I've been to the theater already.

SON   Do they have artists in the theater?

FATHER   They're all artists. And artistes . . .

SON   What else will there be after the war?

FATHER   Things will be good after the war.

VOICE   Halt!

Father and Son stand still and turn. A young man with a fair, closely trimmed mustache comes out from behind the shrine. He is well built and handsome in a coarse way. He is wearing a short sheepskin jacket with a belt, green breeches, and knee-high boots. He has a green fatigue cap on his head. There is a pistol in its holster at his belt. He summons Father and Son to him with a finger. They walk up to him slowly, then stop. The young man calls them up closer with a finger. Father and Son go up closer.

VOICE (*cont.*)   I am Lieutenant Zielinski. And who are you?

FATHER   Fellow citizens.

LT. ZIELINSKI   Don't you know Lieutenant Zielinski?

FATHER   No.

LT. ZIELINSKI *whistles, using his fingers. From behind the shrine comes* RUFFIAN *wearing a loose-fitting Wehrmacht uniform coat without a belt or insignia. He's wearing a peaked civilian cap and sporting an ax.*

LT. ZIELINSKI   They don't know Lieutenant Zielinski.

RUFFIAN   That cannot be.

LT. ZIELINSKI   Ask them, then.

RUFFIAN   Don't you know Lieutenant Zielinski?

FATHER   N ... No.

RUFFIAN   Who are they?

LT. ZIELINSKI   They say they are fellow citizens?

RUFFIAN   And they say they don't know Lieutenant Zielinski?

LT. ZIELINSKI   Exactly.

RUFFIAN   This is Lieutenant Zielinski. Don't you know him?

FATHER   We have been introduced.

LT. ZIELINSKI   Oh, no. You haven't been introduced properly.

RUFFIAN   Shall I introduce them?

Lt. Zielinski walks around Father and Son, inspecting them closely.

LT. ZIELINSKI   I think I know them from somewhere. (*Having completed a circle, at whose center stand the frightened Father and Son, he returns to his starting point.*)

LT. ZIELINSKI (*cont.*)   Don't we know them from somewhere?

RUFFIAN   Now you mention ...

FATHER   We were ...

LT. ZIELINSKI (*Interrupting*)   Quick march!

Father and Son move to the right.

LT. ZIELINSKI (*cont.*)   Halt!

Father and Son stop.

LT. ZIELINSKI (*cont.*)   Are you Jews?

FATHER   What? Us?!

LT. ZIELINSKI   Maybe you're Jews.

FATHER   Lieutenant Zielinski, sir!

LT. ZIELINSKI   Only if you are Jews ...

FATHER   Lieutenant, sir ... What are you saying, sir ... Lieutenant, can't you tell we're your own people, sir?

LT. ZIELINSKI   All right, you can leave. But watch yourselves, because if you turn out to be . . .

Father and Son exeunt right, watched by Lt. Zielinski and Ruffian.

Blackout. The sound of trucks and armored cars gets louder and drops by turns as if being recorded at a roadside where they are driven. This lasts as long as it takes to get the next scene ready.

SCENE SIX

Upstage, across the breadth of the stage, there is a railway track without an embankment. There are ripped wires hanging between telegraph poles. Downstage, slightly right, there is a bench, which can accommodate four sitters comfortably or five uncomfortably. Stage left, there is an empty tin drum, an old army petrol drum. There are two or three other drums, or smaller canisters, scattered around chaotically; they have been pierced and twisted out of shape. In addition, there are broken ammunition boxes, bits of fencing, empty cans. The middle of the stage is covered in straw, hay, old rags, and pieces of paper—in other words, general wartime detritus.

Sitting on the bench, facing the audience, are—from the left: Girl, Woman, and TEACHER, a man of about forty in a pathetic coat, a hat, and worsted earmuffs. Teacher's suitcase is next to the bench, on his right. Spread out on the bench between Woman and Girl is a newspaper and on it a loaf, already started, and a piece of bacon. Woman cuts the bread and the bacon with a penknife and eats; Woman's bundle is between Woman and Teacher; Girl's bundle is on the ground, next to the bench, on her left. The carriage, whose contents are covered by canvas, is upstage center. Sitting on the drum with his back to the group described above, facing the wings left, is Superius. He is bareheaded. Standing in front of him, and soaping his face in preparation for a shave, is Lady. She is holding a shaving brush in one hand and a bowl with soapy lather in the other. The traveling bag, opened, is on the ground.

SUPERIUS   I must have a bath.

LADY   In cold water?

SUPERIUS   I am covered in germs. There are germs perambulating over me in all directions.

LADY   We could light a fire. We could . . .

SUPERIUS (*Interrupting*) We, we, we. You're forgetting that we are not a married couple. My self has a separate existence. I suspect it is louse-infested.

LADY You're imagining it. You have too much imagination.

SUPERIUS Imagination is a prerequisite for transcendence. I wouldn't say it was a quality *an sich,* but as a faculty . . .

WOMAN Two liters for three kilos. How much does that make a kilo? (*Thinks.*) A kilo and a half for one liter . . . one liter is a kilo and a half . . . so one kilo . . . (*To Girl.*) Don't you know?

Girl says nothing. Pause.

WOMAN (*cont.*) 'Course you don't know. You're too stupid. Wait; I give three kilos for two liters . . . How much will that be for one kilo?

TEACHER Six million six hundred and sixty-six thousand six hundred and sixty-six ten millionths, to the first seven decimal places. The number goes on recurring to infinity.

Pause. Woman stares at Teacher, her mouth agape with astonishment.

WOMAN (*Suspiciously*) How do you know that?

TEACHER I was a teacher before the war.

WOMAN Not from these parts, then?

TEACHER Displaced. I'm getting back now.

WOMAN Everyone's going back now.

Meanwhile, Lady has finished lathering Superius's face and takes a razor out of the traveling bag.

SUPERIUS It's not sharp. Sharpen it.

LADY You keep telling me to sharpen this razor. What for?

SUPERIUS So that the razor disappears leaving only sharpness.

LADY Sometimes I can not understand you.

SUPERIUS You never can.

Lady puts the razor to one side and sits on the suitcase, turning her back to Superius. Pause. Superius puts his hand on her shoulder.

SUPERIUS   You know I have no one in the world but you.

LADY   Then why do you treat me like this?

SUPERIUS   That is precisely why. Whom else can I treat like this if I have no one but you?

Lady gets up and starts sharpening the razor.

WOMAN   Do you know any news?

TEACHER   It's not easy to get reliable information just now. Things are happening quickly but everything's disorganized. There is confusion everywhere, as is usual when the battleground is moving.

WOMAN   They say that Churchill has come down by parachute to see how things are here.

She looks around and lowers her voice.

WOMAN (*cont.*)   Maybe he's sitting in the bushes around here somewhere . . .

TEACHER   I doubt it.

Scene Seven

Enter Father and Son, left.

SON   Are the trains running yet?

FATHER   Even if they're not running yet they may be running still.

SON (*Noticing people at the train stop*)   People . . .

FATHER   They're waiting for a train.

SON   There'll be a crush.

FATHER   A crush is better than having to go on foot. Don't your feet hurt?

SON   N . . . no.

FATHER   You take after me.

SON   They hurt a little.

FATHER   My feet never hurt.

They go up to the group on the bench.

FATHER (*cont.*) Praise be to God.

WOMAN For ever and ever.

FATHER Can we sit down here?

WOMAN There's no room.

TEACHER By all means. We can move up.

Teacher moves across to the edge of the bench. Woman takes her bundle off the bench reluctantly.

FATHER (*Tips his hat*) Heartfelt thanks. We've been walking since yesterday. I can't feel my feet.

Sits down where Woman's bundle was, between her and Teacher. Son sits down between Father and Teacher.

WOMAN (*Faced by a fait accompli, more conciliatory*) And where is it that God is taking you?

FATHER To the wife. She was in hospital since the New Year but the front moved and they evacuated the sick somewhere. So we're looking for her. Me and my son. What about you?

WOMAN I go around looking for trade.

FATHER And them?

Indicates Superius and Lady.

WOMAN Some gentlefolk.

Meanwhile, Lady has finished sharpening the razor and started shaving Superius.

SUPERIUS Can you recall when we left home?

LADY A month ago.

SUPERIUS Which century? I feel as if we have been on the run for ages.

LADY We started running away in autumn.

SUPERIUS Which autumn? It is unimportant. All the autumns have passed by. In that respect, the last autumn is no different from the first. But whither are we running? Whence and whither? From the west to the east and from the east to the west. And thus the directions have annihilated each other and even our flight is an illusion.

LADY Keep still.

SUPERIUS When did this misunderstanding begin? Is there a greenwood tree somewhere still where tables are laid and beer is drunk? Where have the revelers gone and why? And why did they not drink their beer?

While he has been speaking Superius has not been entirely still, which makes it difficult for Lady to shave him.

LADY Stop moving about.

SUPERIUS You're right. That is probably the only way out: to stop moving. To be still. To attain the ultimate immobility. Immobility is closest to the absolute because every movement is relative.

LADY Oh, my God . . .

Superius touches his cheek with his finger, which he then inspects.

SUPERIUS Blood . . .

LADY It's not my fault. I told you to be still.

SUPERIUS You have spilled my blood?

LADY What's to be done.

SUPERIUS Iodize it!

In a panic Lady searches through the contents of the traveling case.

LADY There's no iodine.

SUPERIUS Disinfect it with eau de cologne.

Continues to inspect the speck of blood on his finger.

SUPERIUS *(cont.)* A bright scarlet, yet deep.

At the same time, Lady continues to search through the case.

SUPERIUS *(cont.)* In terms of color as well as metaphysics even one drop of blood seems to be unfathomably deep.

LADY There's no eau de cologne left.

SUPERIUS   What?

LADY   It's run out.

SUPERIUS   I will not accept that.

LADY   I told you to be more sparing with it but you wouldn't listen. I never saw anyone use so much eau de cologne.

SUPERIUS   I reject all your arguments. Do you hear me? I protest. I do not agree: vehemently and irrevocably not! Do what you like but I must be disinfected!

Lady looks around helplessly. Then she goes up to the group, stage right.

SUPERIUS (*cont.*)   Anything but germs.

LADY   Excuse me, could someone lend me some eau de cologne . . .

WOMAN   What?

TEACHER   I regret that I do not have any.

FATHER   I've run out, too. I had some first-class stuff.

Runs his hand over the stubble on his cheeks miserably.

SUPERIUS   Are you going to be much longer?

WOMAN   I have some moonshine.

SUPERIUS   I am bleeding!

Woman stands up, and from under the canvas sheet covering the carriage, she pulls out a little bottle with an improvised cork made out of a crumpled rag.

TEACHER   Hooch, or homemade alcohol.

LADY   Does it disinfect, too?

FATHER   And how!

LADY   What do I owe you?

WOMAN   That depends.

She goes up to Superius. Without taking any notice of him she squats down next to the traveling case and touches it, feeling the quality of the hide.

WOMAN (*Approvingly*)   Goatskin. (*Feels the suitcase.*)   Pigskin . . . (*Then she feels the fur coat on Superius, quite unembarrassed, as if there was no one* *wearing it.*)   Beaver fur. (*Turning to Lady.*)   From you I'll accept payment only in dollars.

LADY   We don't have any dollars.

WOMAN   Rubles, then; gold rubles.

LADY   We don't have any rubles, either.

WOMAN   All right, then: gold. By weight.

LADY   We haven't any gold.

WOMAN   Gentlefolk like you and you don't have any?

LADY   We're refugees, not princes.

SUPERIUS   Indeed, I am: I am the Prince de Ténèbres.

LADY   Stop that: This isn't the time for it.

SUPERIUS   And I possess innumerable treasures.

WOMAN   Didn't I say so?

SUPERIUS   . . . of the spirit. Gems of experience, diamonds of intelligence. For example: I can share with you, madam, a very interesting conversation I had once with the mistress of Lord Russell.

WOMAN   Do what?

SUPERIUS   Or I can reveal to you, madam, my own interpretation of Einstein's theories. It's A1.

WOMAN   Is he sick?

LADY   Please try to understand.

SUPERIUS   I can do all that and more. And yet I am bleeding like an animal.

WOMAN   I'll give you a liter for the fox.

Lady takes off the fox stole from around her neck and hands it to Woman, receiving in return the bottle of moonshine. Woman regales herself with the fox.

WOMAN (*cont.*)   And I'm selling at a loss.

SUPERIUS (*Shouts*)   Like an animal, do you hear?

LADY   All right, all right . . .

She runs over to him. Woman goes up to the bench. Father gets up off the bench.

FATHER   My, my, what a chic person!

WOMAN   It's true, isn't it?

FATHER   I didn't recognize you at first. Like a doctor's wife.

WOMAN (*Stroking the fur*)   It's prewar.

FATHER   A queen of beauty. It calls for a celebration drink, doesn't it, Professor?

TEACHER   We could drink to victory.

FATHER   To victory and beauty. I believe there is a drop of . . .

Approaches the baby carriage. Woman counters energetically by wheeling the carriage across stage right, away from the would-be celebrants.

WOMAN   There ain't, there ain't! There ain't nothing!

Meanwhile, Lady disinfects the cut on Superius's cheek with the moonshine.

LADY   Does it sting?

SUPERIUS   It stinks. Eau de Pologne.

Teacher gets up off the bench and approaches Superius.

TEACHER   Do you think that's funny?

SUPERIUS   Ah, I recognize this. "Defile not the hallowed ground."

TEACHER   You are mistaken. Defiling or hallowing are gestures and emotions. We have had enough of gestures and emotions. What we need now is thought.

SUPERIUS   A penny for them?

TEACHER   It's always the same in this land of ours. Anything to show off. Any way and in front of anybody, and in front of ourselves is best of all. It's easiest to do so with jokes.

SUPERIUS   If they're jokes at one's own expense . . .

TEACHER   Cheap jokes cost too much.

SUPERIUS   I can afford them.

TEACHER   There you go again.

SUPERIUS   Are you telling me to think? Me? I have had enough of thoughts, more than enough. I am sick of thoughts.

TEACHER   I find that hard to believe.

SUPERIUS   Shall I tell you why? Because no thought is the ultimate, the absolute superthought. There's only a rabble of thoughts, one thought breeding another, one thought substituting another, and all of them worth exactly the same—no more and no less. A hierarchy of thoughts is just one more illusion.

TEACHER   Clearly you're lacking a method.

SUPERIUS   And you no doubt have in mind some constructivist-positivist national or even socio-welfare geophysico-political and economic fornicating thought. Do you know what it is to desire the superthought? To be tormented by the inaccessibility of the ultimate thought, of the final formula? By the formlessness that is the deficiency of the absolute? By the insatiability?

TEACHER   You're a metaphysician?

SUPERIUS   You are a miserable cataloger. First you judge me to be a quipster and a fool, then a metaphysician. What else? You won't find yourself short of words and notions; you feel very much at home in the storehouse of French letters. You have them all arranged on your shelves.

TEACHER   You are being impolite.

SUPERIUS   Oh, you clerks of undergraduate logic, you axiom-grinders, you pensioners of the lexicon. Oh, you arrivistes of the intellect. You have climbed onto a mound of primitive abstraction and you are so out of breath that you claim the mound is the Himalayas. You're incapable of climbing higher, you beggars.

TEACHER   You're insulting me!

SUPERIUS   Then you can challenge me to a duel. As a person with a degree, you are qualified to participate in an affair of honor.

TEACHER   You're not a metaphysician. You are a quipster and a fool.

SUPERIUS   When the absolute is impossible and thoughts bore one, then only jokes remain. Feeble ones, I admit.

TEACHER   Oh, no, you won't resolve this with a joke.

SUPERIUS   I don't intend to.

TEACHER   And yet . . .

SUPERIUS (*Getting up*)   How do you know how I intend to resolve it? And not just this, not just these national dilemmas of yours. How can you possibly know that?

The sound of an accordion and two singing voices.

VOICES (*Singing*)   Some bugger is coming to kill me
Or coming to be killed by me,
With horror my thoughts do fill me,
And my palms with sweat are all slimy.

Enter stage left Lt. Zielinski and Ruffian, singing and tottering. Lt. Zielinski has his arm around Ruffian's shoulder; Ruffian is playing the accordion. Lt. Zielinski releases his hold on Ruffian and moves forward.

SCENE EIGHT

LT. ZIELINSKI   Greetings, countrymen! Attention, at ease, fall in, fall out. Welcome, dawn of liberty. All money and valuables to be given up for the fund of our liberated country, *aber schnell*. At my command you will stand in a row, hands up, pockets out. Anyone who doesn't donate gets done for treason. Eyes right! I am Lieutenant Zielinski, so fucking help me!

Superius limps up to Lt. Zielinski and stands up very close to him.

SUPERIUS   And I am General Fly-Rumba-Spankowski.

LT. ZIELINSKI   I don't know any general . . .

Whistles through his fingers. Ruffian takes the ax from under his coat—which he is able to do because the accordion is slung over his shoulder on a belt.

SUPERIUS   What is this? Insubordination?

For a moment it looks as if Superius's bluff might not work. Then Lt. Zielinski comes to attention and salutes.

LT. ZIELINSKI   General.

Ruffian puts the ax back in his belt.

SUPERIUS   I'll make you rot in Sing-Sing, I'll give you an auto-da-fé. I'll send you to the galleys you, you common-or-garden hooligan.

LT. ZIELINSKI   Yes, General.

SUPERIUS   I had better men than you impaled in Upper Persepolis, at the Nether Glacier in Galicia station, you creeping crackpot criminal, you crazy cripple of a cretinish cretinocracy, you cretonne crab, you.

LT. ZIELINSKI   I await your orders, General.

SUPERIUS   My orders?

Turns and walks aside, stops with his back turned to Lt. Zielinski. To himself:

SUPERIUS (*cont.*)   What orders shall I give . . .

Lt. Zielinski remains standing at attention. They are all waiting for "General" Superius's decision. Superius turns back.

SUPERIUS (*cont.*)   Drinks! Drinks for everyone. I proclaim a wake, a wedding, and a christening.

LT. ZIELINSKI (*Salutes*)   Yes, sir.

WOMAN (*Kneeling by her carriage and putting her arms around it*)   Sweet Jesus, they're going to requisition it!

ACT II

The same scene; a clear and bright night. The horizon is visible. The telegraph poles and wires stand out sharply against the light navy blue sky and the none-too-dark ground. Although the moon is not visible, the space is filled with the light of the galaxies.

Scene One

Center stage there is a fire built in part on a tin drum; it is burning the broken boxes, crates, and planks of wood, which were in the place. The bench has been moved and is now center stage, too, behind the fire. Sitting on the bench: Superius in the middle, Lady on his left, Teacher on his right. Left of the fire, facing it and sitting on canisters or other improvised seats, are Father and Son. Right of the fire are Woman and Girl. The pieces of luggage are placed accordingly. Ruffian is standing with the accordion in his hands. Stage right, where it was at the end of the previous act, is the baby carriage. Instead of bottles of moonshine, it now contains Lt. Zielinski. His legs, in knee-high boots, stick a long way out of the carriage, as do his arms. The canvas sheet is on the ground near the carriage, and there are numerous bottles standing—if full—or lying—if empty—all around the entire company. Ruffian is playing the accordion and everyone else, with the exception of Superius and Son, joins in the drunken choir. One of Lt. Zielinski's hands is hanging helplessly down. The other is holding a bottle and marking time, conducting the music.

ALL   How quickly pass the moments,
     They come and disappear.
     Next year, next day, next moment
     We will no more be here.
     And all our youthful years
     Will never come again,
     They leave us only tears
     And sighs, regret, and pain.

The singing comes to an end. Father claps and cries, "Hurrah, hurrah!" Ruffian performs a closing and emphatic coda on his accordion. Woman giggles excitedly. Teacher buries his face in his hands and sobs.

FATHER   What's wrong, Professor?

TEACHER   I don't know, really I don't. I apologize to you all, Ladies and Gentlemen. It just came over me.

SUPERIUS   We all know what "it" is. The rationalist's soul could not withstand the assault of mysterious powers. His stiff consciousness is being put into turmoil, pursued, as it is, by the ghosts of the subconscious. Our teacher has been consumed by longing, also known as the blues. Have another drink, Professor. You might as well.

TEACHER (*Sobbing*)   Regret and pain . . . So many regrets. So much . . .

FATHER   What is there to regret, Professor? After all, the war's coming to an end. We're all returning to our homes.

TEACHER (*Stops sobbing and speaks angrily, almost aggressively*)   What do you mean—"home"?! My wife left me for an artist.

SUPERIUS   Even if she hadn't left you . . .

FATHER   You don't say—she defiled the holy sacrament of marriage, did she? If she'd done that for an engineer, or a doctor . . .

LADY   When?

TEACHER   In nineteen thirty-nine itself. On the morning of September the first.

WOMAN   She certainly picked her moment.

TEACHER   Half an hour before the war she left a note on the table. "I'm leaving for a new life." And then the bombs started.

FATHER   She couldn't have foreseen that.

WOMAN (*Sighs*)   Yes, yes, that Hitler's to blame for everything.

LADY   Do you still love her?

TEACHER   Me? Not at all.

LT. ZIELINSKI   Then why the hell are you bawling?

TEACHER   Because I remembered.

FATHER   Well, forget it. We'll get you married off again.

WOMAN   You're a decent human being. I'd give you my own daughter in marriage, I would.

FATHER   Exactly. Do you want a brand new fiancée?

LT. ZIELINSKI (*Drunkenly*)   She's not exactly brand new, is she?

WOMAN   Have you got any objections?

LT. ZIELINSKI   Far from it. A fiancée with a child is even better than one without. (*To Teacher.*)   It'll come premade. You won't have to work at it.

WOMAN   What's he saying?

LT. ZIELINSKI   Only what everyone can see.

FATHER   Your daughter is in a delicate condition.

WOMAN   Delicacies like that are worse than poison.

FATHER   Why so? A child brings comfort and joy. There'll be a christening.

WOMAN   But there's been no wedding.

FATHER   And who is the lucky father, if I may be so bold?

WOMAN   Who can tell? First of all, some German military policeman forced her. After that, all sorts used to come around. They were supposed to be fighting one another, but there was no dispute about what they wanted from her. I hope they all hang.

SUPERIUS   Apropos.

FATHER   That means it's a war baby. But don't worry about that; it will be born after the war.

In the distance a scream, not human, not animal. It is inarticulate and from some distance away, but because the night is clear it is very audible.

WOMAN   What was that?

FATHER   Sounds spooky.

WOMAN   Don't say things like that. The place is full of corpses.

FATHER   But we are alive.

WOMAN (*Crossing herself*)   God preserve us! Argh!

She screams, terrified, as she sees, approaching from left, a figure in a military greatcoat that reaches all the way down to the ground; the collar is raised. The figure's head is close-cropped. It is the same figure that appeared in scene three of the first act, with the same indistinguishable face—the author suggests the actor wear a colorless, transparent stocking—but this time not bloodstained. He is wearing black glasses. In one hand he is carrying a stick, which he uses to find his way, and under the other arm there is a fiddle.

SCENE TWO

LT. ZIELINSKI   Halt! Who goes there?!

Tries to get up in the carriage but is too drunk and so falls back down again. Ruffian puts his accordion aside and goes up to the newcomer. He trains a flashlight beam on him.

RUFFIAN   It's okay, Lieutenant. It's some blind fellow.

He turns the flashlight off.

LT. ZIELINSKI   What's he want?

FIDDLER   I've come to the wedding. I heard the singing. I always go to weddings and play.

Superius gets up off the bench. FIDDLER sits at the fire, between it and the audience, with his back to the audience.

FIDDLER (*cont.*)   It can be a christening or a wake. To everyone according to his needs.

The scream from a distance is heard again.

FATHER   You've been on the road. Maybe you can tell us what's happening over there?

FIDDLER   What, that? They're hacking someone to pieces.

SUPERIUS   Whom?

FIDDLER   Someone they caught.

WOMAN   Sweet Jesus, it's not a human being, is it?

FIDDLER   A German military policeman. He was running away in civvies but they recognized him. They're having their fun with him by the bridge.

Screaming heard. Ruffian walks over to Lt. Zielinski and leans over him, speaking in a whisper.

RUFFIAN   If that's them already, Lieutenant, then we'd better go.

Lt. Zielinski tries to get up, but can't. He falls back and waves his hand to show he's giving up.

Superius walks over to the left and stands away from the others with his back to them, looking into the distance from where the screams are coming.

FIDDLER   They have blunt knives, so it's taking them some time. It's not the same as a razor.

Superius turns his head and looks at Fiddler. Then he looks into the distance again.

Girl gets up off the ground and moves diagonally across upstage left, toward the horizon, in the direction from which screams are coming.

WOMAN   Where do you think you're going?

Girl keeps walking straight ahead. Woman jumps up, catches Girl, and leads her back to the fire. She makes her sit down next to her and holds her hand. The scream comes again.

WOMAN (*cont.*)   Don't you listen.

FIDDLER   Why ever not? The bride must listen when the bridegroom beckons.

Starts playing a rustic wedding tune and sings.

FIDDLER (*Singing*)   When their touch's bewildering.
  Look up at the skies, girl,
  So all of your children
  Have those black, black eyes, girl.

Father gets up and walks over to Fiddler.

FATHER   Get out of here.

Fiddler takes no notice of him and continues to play the wedding tune. The sound of one last scream which breaks off suddenly.

FIDDLER   Well, they're finished now.

Stops playing.

WOMAN Lord have mercy on his soul.

Lady starts laughing. Suddenly, she stops, walks over to Fiddler, and speaks softly but emotionally, almost passionately.

LADY Play me something about love.

FATHER Not in front of the child.

FIDDLER (*To Superius*) Do you permit it?

They all look at Superius. Superius turns and goes back to the fire.

SUPERIUS I have nothing more to say on the subject. But if you're asking me . . . Do you know a different tune?

FIDDLER That will come in its own good time.

Superius takes the traveling case with the shaving tackle and sits on a wooden box, left. He takes out the razor and starts sharpening it.

FATHER But I do not agree to it!

TEACHER What harm will it do you?

FATHER Gracious lady, my late father only made us in the winter and then only to warm himself up because during the spring, summer, and autumn, he was too busy working, and during the dog days he didn't have any strength left. So what has love got to do with it, gracious lady?

TEACHER (*Gets up*) All this is irrelevant.

FATHER I turned out a success without anyone's help, so I married because you can't live without a wife and children. But where does love come into it, gracious lady?

TEACHER Stick to the subject.

FATHER Oh, yes, I have seen love, in the pictures, but I only rarely went to the pictures and never without the wife, but love at home? We never had any of that. No love, gracious lady, and that's why I won't allow it in front of the child.

LADY You're not from our set.

Father backs away in the face of such an incontrovertible argument. After waiting a moment, and having noted her crushing victory, Lady turns away from the defeated Father and addresses Fiddler.

LADY   About love. Please.

Fiddler starts to play a popular melody from the interwar years—and beyond— called "La Paloma." Lady turns to Teacher.

LADY (*cont.*)   Please dance with me.

Lady and Teacher start to dance.

FATHER (*Looks around helplessly*)   Not from her set . . . 'Course not. We're not royalty. (*Pause.*)   But everything was always decent at home! We had enough to eat and the wife kept the place clean . . . And it all came from my work. My son will testify to that. (*To Son.*)   Well, wasn't it like I said? Come here, tell the people.

SON   Don't drink any more, Dad.

FATHER   Come here, come here.

Drags Son to middle of the stage.

FATHER (*cont.*)   Show yourself. Tell the people how your father looked after you. Were you ever hungry?

SON   No, Dad.

FATHER   Did you go to school?

SON   Yes, I did.

FATHER (*Triumphantly*)   There, he went to school! (*To Son.*)   You were always warm, weren't you?

SON   Stop it, Dad!

Tears himself away from Father.

FATHER   What's this? You refuse?

Stands for a while as if he can't believe his eyes and ears. Then he calls on everyone sitting around to witness.

FATHER (*Piteously*)   Ladies and Gentlemen, do you see the gratitude I get for all my efforts, all my hardships . . . I never thought about

myself, it was always for the family . . . And what do I get for it all . . .
(*To Son.*)   Is this how you repay me for all my sacrifices?!

Goes up to Son and makes as if to strike him, but Son protects his face with his arm, turns, and runs away. Father is too drunk and now also too full of self-pity to give chase.

LADY   Now I feel as if I were on a barge of burnished gold. Like Cleopatra.

TEACHER   Gold is not a good material for boat building.

LADY   Don't say anything. Close your eyes, please.

TEACHER   I'm frightened I might trip.

LADY   Let's float, let's float . . .

FATHER   To my wasted life . . .

Ruffian walks up to him with a bottle, pats him consolingly on the shoulder, offers him the bottle. Father drinks, then Ruffian drinks. Together they walk over to Lt. Zielinski and offer him a drink. Lt. Zielinski drinks; they are on very friendly terms.

SCENE THREE

Son walks up to Superius.

SON   Excuse me, sir . . .

SUPERIUS (*Stops sharpening the razor*)   Ah, it's you, the future of the nation. What do you want?

SON   I'm scared.

SUPERIUS   What of?

SON (*Points to Fiddler*)   Of him. And my father.

SUPERIUS   Just wait a little longer and your father will be scared of you.

SON   When?

SUPERIUS   When you procreate. Or better still—when you kill someone. You were unlucky with this war, poor boy. It came too early. You got nothing out of it.

SON I don't understand what you're saying to me, sir.

SUPERIUS Doesn't matter. I'd rather not be understood at all than misunderstood. I always speak in monologues. But don't worry, your turn will come. You'll arrange your own little war.

Puts the razor away in the traveling case.

FATHER I'm with you fellows. What's past is past, now we're on top. What do I care about the family, I'll go with you, fellows, I'll join the army!

FATHER, RUFFIAN, & LT. ZIELINSKI (*Singing together*)
Meadow, meadow, lush green meadow
Who will scythe your verdant sward
When I have to wear this sword
Meadow, meadow, lush green meadow.

SUPERIUS Do you know my epic poems?

SON No, sir.

SUPERIUS What about my novels?

SON No, sir. But I will read them. I'll read everything after the war. I mean, the war's nearly finished.

SUPERIUS The war and everything else.

SON Everything's only starting now.

SUPERIUS Not my illusions.

Father and Ruffian help Lt. Zielinski out of the baby carriage and the three of them, with arms around each other, stagger into the middle of the stage, singing.

FATHER, RUFFIAN, & LT. ZIELINSKI (*Singing*)
We'll go, fellows,
Cut the trees down,
Get some money
Get our thirsts drowned,
Oh, can't you see it climbing,
Oh, can't you see it climbing,
Forest where the trees abound.

TEACHER You remind me of someone.

LADY   Who?

TEACHER   Cleopatra. In a barge of burnished gold.

SCENE FOUR

RUFFIAN (*Whistles through his fingers*)   Wahey! They're playing for us now!

Fiddler stops playing "La Paloma." Lady and Teacher stop dancing.

FIDDLER   Any requests, ladies and gentlemen?

RUFFIAN   One of our tunes!

Fiddler starts up a polka. Father moves away from his companions and removes his coat.

FATHER   Now it's my turn!

Father drags Woman to dance with him.

WOMAN (*Simpering*)   What are you doing?

FATHER   Let me live a little!

RUFFIAN   Yooo-hooo!

Father and Woman start dancing in a rustic-suburban manner. Son goes up to the dancing couple and stops nearby.

SON (*Timidly*)   Dad . . .

FATHER   I don't know you, you jerk. Can't you see that my time has come?

Son retreats back to Superius.

SON   Sir, please tell them to stop.

SUPERIUS (*Reciting*)   "And Noah drank of the wine and was drunken; and he was uncovered within his tent. And Ham saw the nakedness of his father . . ." Do you know it?

SON   Did you write it, sir?

SUPERIUS (*Points to the sky*)   No, it was him. And there is no mention of me in the story. Do you know what that means?

SON No.

SUPERIUS It means I mustn't interfere.

SON But he's my father.

SUPERIUS That's exactly why. This matter must be resolved between the two of you. There was no intermediary between Noah and his sons.

SON But he's . . .

SUPERIUS You can do as Ham did, or as Shem and Japheth did. There is a choice but you must make it on your own.

SON But I can't on my own.

SUPERIUS I'm sorry for you but I cannot help you. It is forbidden.

SON But he's so . . . he's so . . . now he's . . .

SUPERIUS At the very last moment your father is enjoying his last moment of freedom.

SON I . . . I don't know, sir.

SUPERIUS I shall explain it to you. Only war gives ordinary people their freedom. They stop being who they are, or who they're not. That depends on the specific class. Your father belongs to the first category. You see how they celebrate? But it will be all over tomorrow.

SON What about you?

SUPERIUS I was never ordinary. I didn't need the war. On the contrary. I am now rotting like a common-or-garden piece of offal.

WOMAN You're some dancer.

FATHER 'Cause I can feel the fire burning in you, madam. (*Puts his hand on Woman's behind.*)

RUFFIAN Stoke that fire!

SUPERIUS Simply rotting. Don't you understand that either?

SON You mean like everyone?

SUPERIUS (*Putting his hand on Son's head*) You're a bright boy. Now I feel truly sorry for you.

Superius puts the razor in the traveling case.

FATHER   Round and round!

WOMAN   Round and into the middle!

RUFFIAN   Yahoo!

Ruffian takes the accordion; now the accordion and fiddle are playing together.

FATHER (*Singing*)   Pretty Mary told me
    That she was afraid
    Of a certain soldier
    Standing on parade.

RUFFIAN   Yooo-hooo!

WOMAN (*Singing*)   I would give it gladly
    Gladly if I could,
    But my little treasure's
    Lost in some dark wood.

RUFFIAN   Oooo-weeee!

Son moves away from Superius. Superius hides his head in his hands. Musicians up the tempo. Ruffian, Lt. Zielinski, Lady, and Teacher form an audience around the licentious couple, whom Ruffian encourages with yelps and whistles. Music grows faster and faster until Father stumbles and falls, pulling Woman down with him. He keeps his arms around her; Woman squeals, pretending to try and free herself. They roll about on the ground; the "audience" laughs and claps.

Suddenly Woman stops fighting and squealing; the couple on the ground, Father on top, become quite still. At the same moment, the musicians break off their melody, and the "audience" stops laughing and clapping.

SCENE FIVE

Now everything takes place in a suddenly altered rhythm, in slow motion, as if with total concentration and anticipation. In the sudden silence—only Father's panting can be heard—everyone concentrates on the couple lying on the ground.

Father slowly raises Woman's skirt. Ruffian has laid the accordion aside and is shining the flashlight on the couple. Then Son runs up to Ruffian.

Another change of tempo, this time to one that is fast and violent. Son tries to snatch the flashlight from Ruffian's hand. A short struggle during which the light from the flashlight is thrown crazily in all directions. Ruffian pushes Son away. Son falls.

Son raises himself; he is on all fours. Ruffian turns the flashlight on him, then he walks over to him and kicks him. Son falls again.

Father gets up off Woman. Once again there is a change, a slowing down, of tempo.

FATHER (*To Ruffian, slowly, forcefully*) Did you strike my son . . . ?

Ruffian aims the beam of light at Father, straight into his eyes, blinding him. Despite this, Father approaches Ruffian slowly.

FATHER Did you strike my son, you motherfucker?

Ruffian takes the ax from his belt. Behind Father's back, Lt. Zielinski reaches into his holster for the revolver. Father continues to walk toward Ruffian, and raises his fist.

The unhurried, regular rattle of wheels on railway tracks becomes audible and gradually grows louder.

WOMAN It's coming!

Her cry breaks the tension. A change of tempo as everything speeds up. Ruffian switches the flashlight off and puts the ax back into his belt. Lt. Zielinski returns his gun to its holster. Son gets up off the ground. Woman makes for her luggage, ordering Girl to help. Son picks up Father's coat and helps Father into it. Lady runs over to Superius and breaks into his isolation. Superius takes his hands from his face. Lady start preparing him for the journey.

Everyone is packing and moving about; then they line up along the railway track, upstage, their backs to the audience.

Only Fiddler remains unmoved by it all.

SCENE SIX

Judging by the sound, the train should be in front of them, but it cannot be seen. It is an invisible train. The unhurried, rickety, heavily loaded good carriages rattle along the tracks slowly, monotonously, rhythmically, as Fiddler starts to play, very softly, "Little Town of Belz." The group gathered alongside the tracks stands motionless, frozen. The train goes farther and farther away, its sound becoming less and less audible though it can be heard for a long time. When it can no longer be heard the music stops simultaneously.

SCENE SEVEN

The people at the tracks turn around slowly, sleepily. As they walk toward the audience they start speaking softly, as though impersonally.

WOMAN   It wasn't ours.

RUFFIAN   You would have seen ours.

LADY   It wasn't us.

LT. ZIELINSKI   We were going but they took them.

TEACHER (*Matter-of-fact*)   A transport.

In the same slow and sleepy way, they prepare themselves for sleep around the fire. Only Son remains standing motionless among them.

They speak as they lie down, even more quietly and sleepily.

WOMAN   There's nothing coming.

RUFFIAN   Not a sound.

LT. ZIELINSKI   Imagined it.

TEACHER   Yes, an illusion.

Superius props himself up on his elbow.

SUPERIUS   An illusion?

LADY   Go to sleep, dear.

She tucks him up again next to her with the fur collar. They have spread themselves out and gone to sleep. Son continues to stand motionless among the supine figures. Fiddler is sitting as he has been throughout the act, next to the fire with his back to the audience. Now that he has stopped playing he, too, is motionless. The fire dies. After a moment Fiddler stands up, and without the help of his white stick but behaving as if he can see perfectly, he goes to where Superius is resting next to Lady. He stands over Superius.

Superius raises himself.

SUPERIUS (*Whispers*)   Is it time now?

Fiddler waits silently. Superius gets up carefully so as not to wake his sleeping companion. Fiddler starts to move toward exit, left. Superius picks up the traveling case where the razor is and follows Fiddler. He stops, turns around, and looks at Son who has been, and is, witness to this whole scene. For a while Son and Superius look at each other, then Superius turns away from Son and, without a word, follows Fiddler off, left.

When Superius has gone, Son goes up to where pregnant Girl is sleeping. He lies down next to her but not like a man—like a child. He presses himself up against her shoulder childlike, as if she were his mother.

Girl wakes and, finding herself in this situation, strokes his head protectively, as naturally as if she were mothering him.

SON (*Childishly, complaining*)   I don't want to, I don't want to . . .

Blackout. The sounds of the "Internationale" played on a fiddle for as long as it takes to remove the scenery from the stage.

EPILOGUE

SCENE ONE

A bright sunny day. The stage is empty.

Father and Son enter left, as at the beginning of Act I. Son is limping slightly.

FATHER I had a bad attack of flu yesterday. My head's still killing me now. How do you feel?

SON Fine.

FATHER You don't feel sick or anything?

SON No.

FATHER Isn't it funny how it'll get one person and miss another. That's likely because you're young. Disease gives young people a wide berth. Damn it, we're going to have to go on foot again.

SON Is it far still, Dad?

FATHER It can't be farther than nearer. Didn't I say the trains weren't running yet? We wasted so much time . . .

Casts a sidelong, contrite glance toward Son; he is feeling guilty.

FATHER (*cont.*) And then this flu on top . . .

SON It's all right, Dad.

FATHER (*Sighs with relief, though not entirely confident that everything has been settled*) Ah, well, these things happen . . .

They walk in silence for a moment.

FATHER (*cont.*) What's this? Are you limping?

SON What, me? 'Course not, Dad.

FATHER I can see, can't I?

SON It's nothing, Dad. Come on.

FATHER Nothing, indeed. You're hobbling. Your shoe is likely rubbing. Your shoes are too tight.

SON No, they're fine.

FATHER How can they be fine? You're a growing boy so you've grown out of them. We have to get you a new pair.

SON We don't have to, Dad.

FATHER I know what I'm talking about. We'll get you a pair of decent prewar shoes.

SON What do you mean—prewar? It'll be after the war . . .

FATHER It will be after the war, but they will be prewar. I mean, I'm not going to buy you any old rubbish.

They walk on. Father watches Son. Son is limping very obviously, even though he is trying to hide it. Father stops him.

FATHER (*cont.*) Sit down.

SON But we have to keep going.

FATHER Sit down when I tell you. You're not going to crawl around in pain. We have to think of something.

Son obediently sits down.

FATHER (*cont.*) Take it off.

Son takes the shoe off the foot he was favoring. Father sits down next to him and he, too, starts taking off his shoes.

FATHER (*cont.*) The other one, too.

Son takes off the other shoe. Father gives him his own shoes.

FATHER (*cont.*) Try mine.

Son puts on Father's shoes.

FATHER (*cont.*) Get up and walk about a bit.

Son gets up and walks up and down a few paces.

FATHER (*cont.*) All right? Come here.

Son goes up to Father and stands in front of him. Father presses the toes of the shoes with his fingers.

FATHER (*cont.*)   To a T.

Starts putting on Son's shoes.

FATHER (*cont.*)   See how you've grown. Your my size already.

Struggles with Son's shoes, which are too tight.

FATHER (*cont.*)   Fancy that! Yours fit me, too, on my word of honor . . .

SON   They must be too small.

FATHER   Not at all! My feet must be shrinking or something . . . Mine were beginning to be too big for me.

Finishes tying up the laces, stands up, and taps his foot, grimacing with discomfort.

FATHER (*cont.*)   Just right. There, see? Everything will be fine.

Lt. Zielinski and Ruffian enter, right.

Scene Two

Lt. Zielinski is wearing the same short sheepskin jacket as before, but without the belt and the gun. Instead of his cap, he is wearing a civilian hat.

Ruffian, wearing the same loose-fitting Wehrmacht coat without insignia, the same civilian peaked cap, and the accordion slung over his back.

LT. ZIELINSKI   Who is this I see?

Father bends down and picks up a stone. Shielding Son, he awaits the two newcomers as he holds the stone in his hand. Lt. Zielinski raises his hat to them.

LT. ZIELINSKI (*cont.*)   Good day, Gentlemen . . . What's this, don't you recognize me?

FATHER   Lieutenant Zielinski, I'd like to . . .

LT. ZIELINSKI   Lieutenant? You mean Citizen Zielinski. (*To Ruffian.*)   Do you know anyone called Lieutenant Zielinski?

Ruffian shakes his head.

LT. ZIELINSKI (*cont.*)   See?

FATHER   So you're no longer a lieutenant?

LT. ZIELINSKI   Lieutenant, indeed . . . (*To Ruffian.*)   Was I ever any kind of lieutenant?

RUFFIAN   You, Lieutenant? Never.

LT. ZIELINSKI (*Menacingly*)   What do you mean—Lieutenant?

RUFFIAN   What I meant to say was: Citizen Lieutenant Zie—

LT. ZIELINSKI   What do you mean—Citizen Lieutenant?

RUFFIAN   Mr Zielinski, sir.

LT. ZIELINSKI   Mr? Sir?

RUFFIAN   Citizen Zielinski.

LT. ZIELINSKI   At last!

RUFFIAN (*Coming to attention stiffly*)   Yes, sir!

LT. ZIELINSKI   You see? So what do you say—are you coming with us?

FATHER   To the army?

LT. ZIELINSKI   What do you mean—the army? Times have changed. We're going west.

FATHER   Far?

LT. ZIELINSKI   As far as we can.

FATHER   What for?

LT. ZIELINSKI   For a new life. (*To Ruffian.*)   Right?

Ruffian nods.

FATHER   What's going to happen to the old life?

Lt. Zielinski runs a finger across his throat meaningfully.

FATHER (*cont.*)   But me and my son . . .

LT. ZIELINSKI   You won't get anything by staying here. I'm advising you as a friend. This is no picnic.

FATHER   But what about my wife?

LT. ZIELINSKI   Don't you want a new life?

High above them in the sky, the sound of planes flying past. It is a monotonous growl. Father, Son, Ruffian, and Lt. Zielinski look up into the sky.

FATHER   They're flying.

LT. ZIELINSKI   Those are the last.

Pause. They look into the sky.

FATHER   It's very high . . .

They look into the sky for as long as the planes can be heard. Then they lower their heads, except for Father who continues looking into the heavens.

LT. ZIELINSKI   Well? Are you coming?

Father doesn't answer, just continues looking up into the sky.

LT. ZIELINSKI (*cont.*)   What's the matter with you, are you deaf?

Father stops looking into the sky.

LT. ZIELINSKI (*cont.*)   Are you coming with us or not? I won't ask again.

FATHER   I'm going back home.

LT. ZIELINSKI   Please yourself. It's none of my business. (*To Ruffian.*)   Onward, pioneers!

Lt. Zielinski and Ruffian leave, left.

SON   Won't they come back anymore?

FATHER (*Gruffly*)   Don't talk nonsense.

They move stage right. Lady and Teacher enter, right.

Scene Three

TEACHER   Ah, old friends!

Father raises his hat.

TEACHER (*cont.*)   Which way are you gentlemen headed? Because we are going to the capital.

FATHER   Aren't you going home?

TEACHER There is no return to the old dustbins. They have been swept away by the winds of history.

FATHER What do you mean? Has your home been blown down?

TEACHER I was speaking metaphorically.

LADY They probably don't know what a metaphor is. Do you know?

FATHER I think I've . . .

LADY Then you will learn. We have a colossal program for education, reeducation, and collaboration. (*To Son.*) We are relying especially on the young generation.

TEACHER Of construction, reconstruction, and superstructure. An enormous undertaking. Are you of the people?

FATHER Me? . . . that is . . . how can I put it . . .

TEACHER (*Shakes Father's hand enthusiastically*) I'm delighted. We're going to begin immediately to fill the centuries-old abyss between the people and the enlightened classes. Without a moment's delay.

LADY You should know, my good man, that you are the motive force of history. This gentleman will explain it to you.

FATHER But we're in a hurry . . .

TEACHER Of course you are. There has been a colossal acceleration of processes. We, the intelligentsia, are essential for the task of consolidating . . .

LADY Elevating . . .

TEACHER That's what I was saying . . . For the task of elevating, disseminating, and consolidating. We were underestimated by a political system based on the law of profit, of buying and selling; we, the intelligentsia, were forced into the background by a world of vulgar materialism, we, whose natural element is the world of ideas. But that is finished with.

LADY Forever.

TEACHER (*Rubbing his hands*) We're going to play our part, we're going to play our part . . .

LADY   A historic role.

SUPERIUS (*Entering stage right, behind Lady and Teacher*)   It's all quite true.

Scene Four

Superius is dressed just as he was when we last saw him in Act II except that there is no trace of the fact that his leg was hurt. He is accompanied by a beautiful woman in trailing and transparent robes decorated with sequins and jewels, like something out of a stage designer's dream of a Middle East operetta. Superius and she are arm in arm.

TEACHER   Are you here again?

SUPERIUS   Not entirely and not for long. I have other pastimes. I merely wanted to show my companion the land of my youthful years, my environment, so to speak, my background. She has never been here before; it's exotic to her. And to take the opportunity to see what is happening here now. (*To Bayadère.*)   You see, darling? Exactly as I predicted: the final, irrevocable triumph of mediocrity.

Bayadère nods in agreement. Teacher stares at Lady; Lady stares at Bayadère.

SUPERIUS (*cont.*)   I was right not to stay any longer with you people. It was the last moment.

LADY   Who is that hussy?

SUPERIUS   What's this, petal? Are you jealous? Now, when . . .

He looks meaningfully at Teacher.

TEACHER   Exactly, little petal; don't forget he did leave you and we do have a historic mission.

SUPERIUS   I did hope you would have forgiven me. I left for your own good since, as things transpired, we were not compatible. It was my fault, I admit. I was incapable of loving you as you deserved to be loved. I would have been an eternal debtor of your love.

LADY   What love . . .

SUPERIUS   Your love for me.

LADY   Ha-ha-ha; you call that egoism love?

SUPERIUS   The egoism was mine; yours was the love.

LADY   That exaggerated attention to the individual unit in total isolation from society and its consuming problems?

TEACHER   Aren't you exaggerating, petal?

LADY   That petty subjectivism? That wasn't love. That was a typical reflection of a system of production where the social means of production are in private hands.

TEACHER   And yet, little petal . . .

LADY   (*To Teacher*)   Shut up! (*To Superius.*)   If you think I loved you, then let me tell you that I never did—never!

SUPERIUS   It doesn't matter, petal. It doesn't matter.

LADY   That wasn't real feeling. I love only now!

SUPERIUS   (*To Teacher*)   Congratulations.

LADY   I love mankind, and particularly the masses.

Embraces Father.

FATHER   (*Resisting*)   There's no need, there's no need . . .

LADY   Only this is real love. True love. I feel that I was created for real love. There was nothing there before . . .

Changes her tone from the affected to the genuine: In other words, she shouts:

LADY   (*cont.*)   Who is that hussy?!

SUPERIUS   Your behaviour is unseemly. (*To Bayadère.*)   Take no notice, Cleo, try to understand . . .

TEACHER   You're not from these parts, then?

SUPERIUS   Who, Cleopatra? Of course not. We met as soon as I stepped out of the time-space continuum and we took a liking to each other immediately. That is the fundamental advantage of nonbeing: you can choose your company.

TEACHER   (*Bows to* CLEOPATRA)   It's an honor. You have come all the way from Egypt, have you?

LADY   (*Threateningly, warning him*)   Careful! . . .

SUPERIUS   Geography and history have no meaning outside the
time-space arrangement. All that counts there is the affinity between
personalities and temperaments, the general level, generally speaking—
the attraction of similar dispositions. Isn't that so, Cleo?

Cleopatra snuggles up to Superius who puts his arm around her.

TEACHER   Allow me to introduce myself, ma'am.

LADY   That's enough. Home!

FATHER   Aren't you going to the capital, then?

*Lady grabs hold of Teacher's arm and drags him forcefully back in the direction
from which they came, that is, stage right. Teacher follows her because he is being
dragged, but his head is turned toward Cleopatra and Superius. Before he is
pulled into the wings he raises his hat politely and Superius returns the gesture by
raising his own wide-brimmed hat. Lady and Teacher disappear stage right. A
short pause.*

SUPERIUS   Well, we are going back, too. We only dropped in for a
moment.

Raises his hat to Father.

SUPERIUS *(cont.)*   I wish you well.

*Father returns the bow; Son clicks his heels as boys used to be taught to do at
school.*

Superius and Cleopatra move left, arm in arm.

SON   Excuse me, sir . . .

SUPERIUS *(Stops)*   Yes.

Son points right.

SUPERIUS *(cont.)*   Thank you very much, boy, but in our situation
directions mean nothing.

*Cleopatra smiles at Son and waves good-bye to him. Superius and Cleopatra
leave, left.*

SCENE FIVE

FATHER (*Watching them go*)   What a polite gentleman.

SON   What a beautiful lady.

FATHER (*Sighs*)   There are such things in the world . . .

SON   What were they talking about?

FATHER   It's over our heads.

SON   But I'd like to know.

FATHER   Know what?

SON   Know everything.

FATHER   It's not that simple. You catch one end and the other end slips away. You catch the other end and you can't cope with the first end . . . Everything in life's like that.

SON   So what can you do, Dad?

FATHER   You have to grab it in the middle.

SON   How do you mean?

FATHER   I mean, has to be honest and that's all. Do you understand?

SON   I think so.

FATHER   There's no thinking about it. You either understand a thing like that or you don't. (*Pause.*)   Do you understand?

SON   Yes, I do.

FATHER   Are you sure?

Son walks up to Father and touches his hand. Pause.

SON   Yes, Dad, now I understand for sure.

Pause. Then Father takes out a large handkerchief. Son drops his hand. Father wipes his nose, trumpeting noisily. Then he puts the handkerchief back in his pocket.

FATHER   Right, then, let's go.

They move right, Father in front, limping in Son's tight shoes. After a few steps Father stops, looks up into the sky. Son also stops and also looks up, wanting to see what Father is looking at.

Father raises his arm and stretches out his index finger. He speaks as he points into the sky.

FATHER   They have it made.

Drops his head and his arm. Moves off left again, followed by Son.

FATHER   We, we have to go on foot.

Blackout.

A SUMMER'S DAY

Translated by Jacek Laskowski

CHARACTERS

SUX

UNSUX

LADY

ACT I

SCENE ONE

A bench. A tree next to it. UNSUX, a man of about thirty, is standing at one end of the bench; he has an unexceptional appearance and is wearing an old pair of trousers and a gaudy short-sleeved shirt. There is a rope attached to a branch of the tree. Unsux pulls at the rope several times to check the strength of the knot.

SCENE TWO

SUX, *a man of about forty, of striking appearance, enters stage right. He is wearing a lightweight, cream-colored summer suit and similar hat. He is carrying a light cane. He sits at the opposite end of the bench and looks straight ahead, into the audience, taking no notice of Unsux.*

Unsux looks down at Sux for a moment, then ties the loose end of the rope into a noose. He puts the noose around his neck, then looks at Sux again. Sux continues to ignore him. Eventually Unsux starts to speak.

UNSUX   Aren't you going to ask me anything?

Pause.

UNSUX *(cont.)*   This doesn't interest you, eh?

Pause.

UNSUX *(cont.)*   You don't give a damn about what I'm doing, do you?

Pause.

UNSUX *(cont.)*   You can see what I'm doing, but it makes no impression on you. Everyone has the right to do exactly what they like, right?

Pause.

UNSUX *(cont.)*   Especially in a public place, eh? You're probably thinking: "I'm not interfering with him, so why's he interfering with me?" You're probably furious with me, you think I'm imposing on you, that I'm downright rude because I'm disturbing you, whereas you're polite because you're not interfering with what I'm doing. But that's exactly it: Why don't you interfere? Why aren't you stopping me? Why don't you even talk to me? Why are you letting me . . .

Sux rises from the bench and walks right.

UNSUX *(cont.)*   No, wait, please don't leave!

Sux stops.

UNSUX *(cont.)*   I do admit I'm pushy, but you must understand that in my situation . . .

Pause.

UNSUX *(cont.)*   Please stay. I promise I'll keep a grip on myself. I'll speak calmly, more softly . . . Only please don't go away just yet.

Pause.

UNSUX *(cont.)*   I'll be quiet.

Sux sits back down on the bench.

UNSUX *(cont.)*   Well, I'm not actually capable of being completely quiet. But don't worry, I'll only talk about things generally, I promise. Nothing personal, nothing about my private life. Surely you can talk to me about general things.

Pause.

UNSUX *(cont.)*   The weather's nice today . . .

Pause.

UNSUX *(cont.)*   Though it's probably going to rain.

Pause.

UNSUX *(cont.)*   Not that either? You're right. I'm incapable of conducting a conversation on general topics. And do you know why that is?

Removes the noose from his neck, sits on the bench next to Sux, leans over to him confidentially.

UNSUX *(cont.)*   Because I'm useless at it. No, don't contradict me. Even in an ordinary social conversation on a general topic. I'm totally useless.

Now addressing not Sux but talking straight ahead.

UNSUX (*cont.*)   I can't do anything. Take this hanging, for example. I thought to myself: I have to put an end to everything once and for all. I was getting there, too, and then what? You came along, we started talking, and I'm still alive. It's the same with everything. If I were to tell you about my life . . . Shall I?

Pause.

UNSUX (*cont.*)   You agree, right? Did you say something?

Pause.

UNSUX (*cont.*)   You didn't say anything but I know what you were thinking. You were thinking: What do I care about his life? And if you had said something, if you'd been polite and said something to me, this is as much as you'd have said to me: "By all means, I'd be very interested to hear it, but some other time, some other place perhaps." That's what you would have said. And do you know how I know what you would have said if you'd said anything? From experience. Because I know it all. I know it backward. When it comes to me, it's always—as they say—some other time. And do you know what that means? Some other time means never.

Pause.

UNSUX (*cont.*)   Yes, never. Whatever I want, whatever I strive for, I never get it straightaway, only . . . well, when? Take a guess . . .

Pause.

UNSUX (*cont.*)   Yes, you guessed. Quite simply never. Whenever I try to do something, or have something, it always ends the same way. That is to say—it never ends at all because I'm always trying and wanting something and with what result? Yes, exactly—with no result whatever. Don't ask me why that's the way it is, because I don't know myself. Must be destiny or something . . . Can you swim?

Pause.

UNSUX (*cont.*)   Of course you can, one can tell just by looking at you. You can and you do it excellently. And I can't. Not because I didn't want to learn. I did, I wanted to very much. My youth, you could say, swam past with my efforts. I attended various swimming classes, I was very determined, and I never learned. I stay afloat for just a couple of

minutes and then I sink. Why? God only knows. I mean I have a
normal build, I have normal strength, I make the correct movements—
and nothing. It must be something inside me. Some fault or something
missing . . . Don't you think?

Pause.

UNSUX (*cont.*)   I only mentioned the swimming by way of an example.
The swimming itself is a trifle, but it's the same with everything.
Women, too. Women most of all. Just look at me. Am I
hunchbacked? Or cross-eyed? You must admit I'm not. Of course I'm
not as handsome as you, but apart from that I'm quite normal. And?
Nothing. I can't even say that women won't look at me. That would
be extraordinary; something, you might say, exceptional. Sure, one or
another woman might look, but she'll do it by looking through me, as
if she were looking into the distance, looking for somebody else to
arrive. And I can't even deny that I went out, as they say, with one or
another of them. Indeed, it did happen, but it always seemed as if I
was in the background. As if she was walking and I was behind her,
never the other way around. Not that I demand that it even be the
other way around: just to walk with her, side by side . . . And then
even that never lasted, they left me kind of naturally. No arguments,
in fact no anything special at all. They were simply there and then
they weren't there for no apparent reason. And it wasn't that they left
without saying a word—that would have been something, you
understand. Something I could have grabbed hold of and held on to.
Some evident misfortune, a deformity. No, they did say something to
me, only it was something so meaningless that I don't even remember
what it was. They weren't angry with me, they didn't reproach me,
they didn't pity me. Yes, sir, even pity would have been better than
this—how to describe it?—this nothing. So I'm not even worth
pitying or what?

Pause.

UNSUX (*cont.*)   I can't even claim to be tragic. There's not even
anything tragic about me. And it's all down to the fact that I'm
constantly wanting something very badly, I'm constantly trying for
something, and nothing ever comes of it. And all I have to show for it
is hope, nothing but hope, constant hope. My hope is that at least I'll
manage to hang myself . . .

SUX I envy you.

UNSUX What did you say?

SUX I said I envy you.

UNSUX You? Me?

SUX Yes.

UNSUX I don't think you've understood. You can't have been listening to what I was saying. Please allow me to say it again. Only this time, kindly listen carefully. The thing is that I never . . .

SUX There's no need. I heard and understood everything perfectly. You are a fortunate man.

UNSUX Are you mocking me?

SUX No. You're fortunate but you don't know that you are. And you probably wouldn't have found out if we hadn't met.

UNSUX But I still don't know. What do you mean, I'm fortunate? I am?

SUX Of course. You have hope, right?

UNSUX Exclusively and constantly.

SUX There you are, then. You have hope and it never stops. That's a treasure. You possess a real treasure.

UNSUX But I never succeed in anything!

SUX Well? After all, that's the only reason you can have hope. If you succeeded in accomplishing your aims, then that would be the end of hope. But as it is, you have an aim in life.

UNSUX But I never achieve it!

SUX If you did achieve it then you wouldn't have it anymore. And life without an aim is the worse thing that can happen to a man.

UNSUX What could be worse than my situation?

SUX My situation, sir. Your situation, compared with mine, is just a string of good fortune. Because in my life everything is the exact opposite of yours. I always succeed in everything.

UNSUX   Just as I thought.

SUX   Anything I aim for, anything I want—I achieve instantly. I can't even wait for achievement because it happens so quickly after the wish. I have everything I could possibly wish for.

UNSUX   Yes . . . And?

SUX   And that's what's so bad. When there is nothing left to achieve because everything has been achieved, the question arises: What's it all for?

UNSUX   I don't understand.

SUX   Of course you don't understand, you fortunate man. You cannot comprehend what it means to be confronted by such a question, and that's what makes you a fortunate man. Because it's a question that contains within it all the other questions and there is no answer to them. It's a question about the overall meaning of life.

UNSUX   And what kind of problem is that?

SUX   Not one for you, but a fundamental one. The result is that everything means something to you, and for me nothing does. You can find pleasure in any trifle—for instance, in going for a swim. Whereas I can't take pleasure in anything.

UNSUX   But I can't swim!

SUX   But you're telling yourself that you'd be happy if you could! And you'll never persuade yourself that it's not true. I am an excellent swimmer and I can tell you that it doesn't bring happiness. When I'm swimming I'm thinking: What's this swimming for, why is it I who am in the water, why this me, why this water?

UNSUX   I don't believe you. Just to swim, just one time . . .

SUX   What can I do to convince you that you are mistaken? Happily mistaken. What if I were to tell you that I, too, am aiming to commit suicide?

UNSUX   You?

SUX   Me, me most of all. I have more right to suicide and more reasons for it than you do. You don't like your own life, whereas I don't like life in general. And that is a big difference. Take a look at this.

Takes a gun out of his pocket.

SUX   I came here with the same intention as you did. Now you understand why your behavior seemed quite normal to me. I want to do the same as you.

UNSUX   You want to shoot yourself? Really?

SUX   That's the only reason I came here. The place is appropriate, out of the way . . . We both agree that suicide should be committed in solitude. You were quite right to remark that I wasn't pleased to find you here. This spot seemed to be mine in advance. You took it from me, so to speak.

UNSUX   I'm sorry. I didn't know.

SUX   You couldn't have known. You thought I was an ordinary passerby, didn't you? Particularly since, despite my displeasure, I kept myself under control and didn't reproach you; I just waited calmly for you to hang yourself.

UNSUX   That was nice of you.

SUX   I let you go first even though there's no way of telling which one of us has been meaning to kill himself longest.

UNSUX   Have you been thinking about it long, then?

SUX   From the moment I realized there was no other way out.

UNSUX   And will you succeed?

SUX   Succeed?

UNSUX   In killing yourself.

SUX   I succeed in everything. There isn't the slightest doubt.

UNSUX   Still, I wouldn't do it. I mean, if I was in your place . . .

SUX   But you're not. You're not in my place and I'm not in yours. Everyone's in his own place. Besides, even if we did change places, the result would be the same. We would both commit suicide except that you would do so for my reasons, which would be yours, and vice versa. So what's the difference?

UNSUX   None, I suppose. Only I would like, just once, to be inside the skin of someone who's doing well. Just to know how it feels, what it's like. Still, if I can't, then I can't. You're right, there's no point talking about it. I apologize once again for intruding. As for who goes first, I'll be only too pleased to give way.

SUX No need for that. A couple of minutes sooner or later makes no difference.

UNSUX The fact is I'd prefer it if you went first.

SUX Oh? Why?

UNSUX The thing is . . . you might consider this inappropriate, but I'd like to see someone who's been successful in life end tragically. That would be a comfort to me . . . You're not offended, are you?

SUX No, why . . . no, not at all.

UNSUX Because you see, really it's all the same to you as you said yourself, but it would give me just a little satisfaction . . .

SUX Really?

UNSUX Yes, believe me. And in fact . . . No, that would be too much.

SUX What's that?

UNSUX No, nothing . . . only it occurred to me that . . . No, you really would be offended.

SUX I assure you I won't be.

UNSUX What if I were to do it . . .

SUX Do what?

UNSUX You know, what if I were to shoot you instead of you shooting yourself, personally? What if I were to save you the trouble of doing it yourself; what if you let me kill you instead? It's unimportant to you whether you shoot yourself or someone else does it, but it would bring me solace. Killing you would be even more pleasant than watching you killing yourself. Considerably more pleasant. It would be my personal revenge for an unsuccessful life.

Pause.

SUX You're wrong.

UNSUX Why's that?

SUX   Because killing yourself is harder than being killed. Consequently, by doing it for me, you would merely be doing me a favor, thereby confirming one more time that I succeed in everything, that everything falls into place for me according to my wishes without any effort from me. So what kind of revenge would that be? Just think about it. It would be no kind of revenge for you, nor satisfaction; quite the reverse, quite the reverse.

UNSUX   Do you think so?

SUX   Isn't it obvious? You just need to think about it logically for a minute.

UNSUX   But I have no guarantee that you will shoot yourself!

SUX   I've already told you that every one of my aims is achieved. Don't you worry: I'll certainly kill myself.

UNSUX   But knowing my luck . . .

SUX   Don't you believe I will?

UNSUX   Course I do, but nothing I believe in has ever come true.

SUX   How can I convince you?

UNSUX   There is a way.

SUX   Go on.

UNSUX   You simply shoot yourself.

SUX   Now?

UNSUX   Now. It's the only way you'll convince me.

Pause.

SUX   Well, yes, you're probably quite right.

UNSUX   Unless you've changed your mind.

SUX   Not at all.

UNSUX   In which case there's no problem. Right?

Pause.

SUX   No, in principle there is none.

UNSUX   You shoot yourself here right now, in front of me, and it's all settled.

SUX   Yes. Settled.

Pause.

UNSUX   So what are you waiting for now?

Sux releases the safety catch. Pause.

UNSUX *(cont.)*   Do you still have some misgivings?

SUX   No . . . I have no misgivings.

UNSUX   So what are you still thinking about?

SUX   Just one thing. I don't yet know if I should go for the heart or the head.

UNSUX   I'd advise you to go for the head.

SUX   Why?

UNSUX   Because everything is in the head and everything comes from the head. Everything is the head's fault. The heart is innocent.

SUX   Is that what you think?

UNSUX   You know life as well as I do. Though from a different side.

SUX   Yes, it is the head.

Pause.

UNSUX   Well?

Sux puts the revolver to his head.

UNSUX *(cont.)*   I'll count to three. When I say "three"—you'll pull. One . . .

Pause.

UNSUX *(cont.)*   Two.

SCENE THREE

Attractive LADY, no older than thirty, enters stage right. Sux puts the gun in his pocket.

Lady walks across the stage. When she reaches stage right, she inadvertently drops a handkerchief and continues walking.

She leaves, stage right.

SCENE FOUR

UNSUX   Did you see that?

SUX   See what?

UNSUX   What a beautiful woman . . . I've not seen one like her in my whole life. What about you?

SUX   Often.

Unsux rises from the bench and picks up the handkerchief.

UNSUX   She lost her handkerchief.

SUX   She didn't lose it. She dropped it on purpose.

UNSUX   How do you know?

SUX   I know about these things.

UNSUX   But why? Why would she lose a handkerchief on purpose?

SUX   So that one of us would pick it up, catch up with her, and say: "Madam, you lost your handkerchief. Allow me. Are you going out for a walk by any chance? What a strange coincidence. So am I. Perhaps we could walk together. What are you doing this evening?"

UNSUX   Are you sure?

SUX   There's nothing more certain.

UNSUX   I'm going after her!

Unsux goes right, stops.

UNSUX *(cont.)*   No, I haven't the courage.

SUX   What do you mean "courage"? Don't be so childish. It's quite simple.

UNSUX   For you—but not for me. With my bad luck . . .

SUX   Bad luck has nothing to do with it. Only calculation. Hers, not yours. She's counting on you, not you on her. All you have to do is answer her call.

UNSUX   But I mean . . .

SUX   Why are you still hesitating? Go after her, go after her now!

UNSUX   . . . I mean we don't know which one of us she is summoning.

SUX   Quite so . . . That's something you can never be sure of.

UNSUX   Because if it's not me, I'll only make a fool of myself.

SUX   That's a risk we always have to take, we men.

UNSUX   Because if it wasn't for me she dropped the handkerchief, then it was for you . . . Yes, it certainly wasn't for me. I mean, I don't appeal to women.

SUX   I repeat: That's something you can never be sure of. You never know whom they like or why. So don't be discouraged.

UNSUX   What should I do?

SUX   Try. I see no other way.

UNSUX   Go after her?

SUX   If she means anything to you.

UNSUX   And how! I think I'm in love. But on the other hand . . .

SUX   If you're in love there is no other hand.

UNSUX   There is, because if I don't appeal to her . . . I know! Let's go together.

SUX   But why?

UNSUX   Just in case. We'll find out which one of us she chose, and I won't be risking anything.

SUX   But what if it was you she chose? Then my presence there will be inappropriate.

UNSUX   But then you won't be risking anything either. Coming with me, you have an alibi and, going with you, I have one, too. As you so rightly say, we can't be certain so we need to take out an insurance policy. Which one of us is the chosen one? It seems to me that it's you, but I hope that it's me. Experience tells me that it's not me, that it's you, but hope . . . Hope says what she wants. Let's go together, the question will resolve itself, and I'll make less of a fool of myself if it transpires that hope has cheated me again. Let's go!

SUX   You forget that I have an important matter to attend to here.

UNSUX   Later, later.

SUX   What do you mean—later? This was supposed to be my final moment.

UNSUX   It will be your final moment later, too. And you'll be doing me a favor. A big favor.

SUX   Do you insist?

UNSUX   I'm asking you. Please.

Pause.

SUX   So be it. I'll do it for you.

UNSUX   Let's go then, let's go!

He goes right. Sux follows him. They exit right. Blackout.

ACT II

A garden café, a small table, and three chairs—white enamel. Lady, Sux, and Unsux are sitting at the table. Lady behind the table facing the audience, Unsux on her right, right profile to the audience, Sux on her left, left profile to the audience. In front of each one of them is a glass of colored lemonade with a straw.

UNSUX Beautiful weather today.

Pause.

UNSUX (*cont.*) Though rain isn't out of the question . . .

Pause.

UNSUX (*cont.*) Though it might not rain.

LADY (*Turning to Sux*) Your friend is not a decisive man.

SUX On the contrary. He is a very decisive man. He decides to accept everything simultaneously.

LADY (*To Unsux*) Is that true?

UNSUX It's untrue. I'd only like to . . .

SUX Exactly. He'd like to. He loves life which means he has many and various desires. He therefore worries constantly that his desires will not be fulfilled.

LADY I understand that perfectly.

SUX And these desires are frequently mutually contradictory. Hence his apparent indecisiveness.

LADY And you? Do you desire anything?

SUX No.

LADY Why?

SUX I see no need to.

LADY Does that mean you have no wishes? Even with regard to the weather?

SUX   None.

LADY   Terrible situation. Neither of you gentlemen want to help me resolve things, though each one of you for a different reason. (*To Unsux.*)   Perhaps you could express a firm opinion: Will we have rain or shine?

UNSUX   Shine.

LADY   In that case we'll go to the beach.

UNSUX   To swim?

LADY   Of course. What else does one do at the seaside in beautiful weather?

SUX   In that case, maybe it will rain.

LADY   You've disappointed me.

SUX   Please forgive him, my friend has trouble with preferences. As a lover of life and its charms he would prefer the sun, but for certain reasons known to him he avoids water sports, particularly in the company of women before whom he doesn't wish to be compromised. That is just one of his contradictions. He desires the sun but he avoids the beach and so he forecasts rain.

UNSUX   That's not the reason at all.

LADY   (*To Sux*)   I'm no longer asking for your opinion because I know you have none. But do you at least know how we could pass a rainy afternoon?

SUX   We could go to the theater.

LADY   Here, at this seaside resort—there's no theater.

SUX   I saw them hanging out posters. A touring company, a summer season. Two famous actors are appearing; one's a comedian, in other words a clown, and the other is a tragedian.

LADY   So let's go and see the comic. I prefer comedy. (*To Unsux.*)   How about you?

UNSUX   OK.

LADY   OK or yes you'll come?

UNSUX   I'll come.

LADY   At last. So that's decided. We'll see the comedy.

SUX   Not necessarily.

LADY   Why not? Do you prefer tragedy? Haven't we established that it's all the same to you?

SUX   I just wanted to say that we have no choice. The comic and the tragedian are appearing in the same show.

LADY   Together?

SUX   That's the nature of the show. The clown is funny because he's always trying to achieve something and he never succeeds. Meanwhile the tragic hero performs the deeds that the other one fails to perform.

LADY   What's tragic about that?

SUX   The ending. It transpires that it was only worth intending to perform those deeds. The consequences are very different from the intentions.

LADY   To my mind, it's the clown who's the tragic one and deserving of sympathy. To want, to try, and to fail—that's not funny but sad.

UNSUX   Madam, you are absolutely right.

SUX   It's sad but only from his point of view. Whereas from the point of view of the audience, it's very funny. People laugh at it.

LADY   And do women, too?

SUX   People do.

LADY   I don't laugh at it.

UNSUX   Quite right, too.

SUX   Am I to understand that the tragic hero makes you laugh?

LADY   Of course he does. If he's funny . . .

SUX   In what circumstances do you mean?

LADY   When he regards himself as a tragic hero.

SUX   I know this actor and I assure you that he's excellent. The public admires him. Wherever he appears, all the tickets are sold out.

Unsux rises from his chair.

UNSUX   I'll go then.

LADY   Where to?

UNSUX   To buy the tickets. I might be in time.

SUX   Excellent idea.

LADY   No, you stay here.

UNSUX   But it will be too late.

SUX   My companion is right. Please don't delay him. Otherwise we really do run the risk of not getting into the theater.

LADY (*To Sux*)   In that case, you go and book our places.

SUX   Me?

LADY   Yes, you.

SUX   But my companion has already expressed the wish . . . I wouldn't want to deprive him of his initiative.

LADY (*To Unsux*)   You won't mind if your friend takes your place, will you?

UNSUX   No, but . . . I wanted to do it for you.

LADY   That's very nice of you, but it will be even nicer if you keep me company. (*To Sux.*)   Meanwhile you will go and reserve our places. You'll also do it . . . for me.

SUX   If that's your wish . . .

Stands, bows, and goes out right.

SCENE TWO

LADY   Why are you standing? Do sit down.

Unsux sits on his chair.

UNSUX   I don't think he was very pleased.

LADY   Have you known each other long?

UNSUX   An eternity.

LADY Since childhood, then.

UNSUX No, but I've always thought about him, even before we met. I always wanted to be like him.

LADY And are you thinking about him now?

UNSUX No, now I'm thinking only about you.

LADY Please tell me something.

UNSUX What about?

LADY About your friend.

UNSUX Are you thinking about him?

LADY Not at all. It's just idle curiosity. A subject of conversation to kill time.

UNSUX Maybe I should just go.

He gets up from his chair.

LADY *(cont.)* Do sit down. How many times must I repeat myself? (*Unsux sits back down.*) What a terrible person you are.

UNSUX You're right. I'm useless.

LADY If you're thinking only about me, as you said you are a moment ago, then why are you thinking so much about yourself?

UNSUX Because I'm thinking I'm not worthy of you. Although . . . No, I don't even dare say it.

LADY It doesn't matter: Just say it.

UNSUX It occurs to me that maybe I'm not all that useless since you agree to spend time with me.

LADY Is that it? And didn't I ask you to keep me company? Did you notice that?

UNSUX Exactly. If such a beautiful, intelligent woman as yourself isn't revolted by me, then maybe I'm not all that bad.

LADY That's not enough. In your place I wouldn't be so modest. Please remember that the more you value yourself, the more valuable are your compliments.

UNSUX Right, then. So if an exceptionally beautiful, the most beautiful, most sensible woman in the world wants me to spend time with her, then not only am I not all that bad but . . . I'm quite OK. No, I can't believe that.

LADY Why ever not?

UNSUX Because this is the first time in my life it's ever happened to me.

LADY What's strange about that? This is the first time we've met.

UNSUX Exactly. Why didn't we meet earlier? How different my life would have looked.

LADY Better, I hope.

UNSUX Better? Madam, it has been no life at all. It's only now that I'm beginning to live.

LADY Even if you're exaggerating it's nice to hear.

UNSUX I'm not exaggerating. If I were to tell you the story of my life . . . Shall I?

LADY I'll gladly hear it but . . . will we have time? Is it a long story?

UNSUX I can sum it up: You have saved me.

LADY Really?

UNSUX Yes. If not for you I wouldn't be alive now. You arrived at the precise moment I was about to commit suicide.

LADY And I prevented it?

UNSUX Seeing you I wanted to live again. I thought to myself: Life is you. And I went after you.

LADY But not by yourself.

UNSUX It just so happened that I was with a colleague. Pure chance. As it happens he didn't want to . . .

LADY He didn't?

UNSUX That man's finished. Spoiled by success. Nothing interests him anymore. Do you know what he's looking for?

LADY   I cannot imagine.

UNSUX   A metaphysical answer to the question of being.

LADY   Fancy that . . .

UNSUX   Yes. Besides, he's had everything, experienced everything, and he's bored by everything. That's the one thing he's missing. So aside from a metaphysical answer to the question of being, he's not interested in anything.

LADY   Anything and anyone?

UNSUX   Absolutely nothing and no one. He barely consented to become acquainted with you.

LADY   Yet he did consent.

UNSUX   Because I persuaded him to. He did it for me.

LADY   You persuaded him? Why was that?

UNSUX   'Cause . . . 'cause I didn't have the courage to.

LADY   And you still don't have any courage. You haven't the courage not to mention it. You're constantly looking for insurance. You're constantly begging. What do you expect from me? Charity?

UNSUX   Please . . . I know I'm a coward. I have an inferiority complex and that irritates you. But at least I'm honest.

LADY   That's true.

UNSUX   I don't dissemble. When I admit to cowardice, it's the truth. But when I say that I love you, that, too, is the truth.

LADY   You love . . .

UNSUX   Yes, from the first moment I saw you. It's the love of a coward . . . and, as you say, a beggar. Agreed. But it is love.

LADY   Real love?

UNSUX   You won't find one more real. Someone who honestly confesses his beggary and cowardice, even though they're not traits that flatter him, can certainly be believed when he confesses his love. 'Cause after all it's no disgrace.

LADY   Disgrace? Why of course not. It's . . . brave.

UNSUX   It's not brave at all. To confess one's love.

LADY   It is brave—very brave if the feeling is sincere.

UNSUX   It's not brave as far as I'm concerned. It's a need and a great joy.

LADY   You are a remarkable man.

UNSUX   I am?

LADY   An exceptional, very brave man. I've never till now known anyone like you.

UNSUX   What? Has no one ever told you he loves you?

LADY   Oh, many times. But they always expected something from me in return. "I love you and so for that you owe me something, I deserve something for it." As if it was some kind of debt that I never incurred and that I never wanted.

UNSUX   What do you mean—debt? It is I who am in your debt. I owe you gratitude, I owe you everything, everything for that one exceptional feeling that I'm experiencing thanks to you.

LADY   And you want nothing from me?

UNSUX   Only that you consent to being loved. Even from a distance.

LADY   And you won't commit me to anything else? You don't expect anything else, demand anything?

UNSUX   How could I presume to? It's you who can demand everything from me. I even ask you to demand, I beg you to demand. After all, it is I who love you; you don't love me.

LADY   And you confess it so straightforwardly?

UNSUX   How else could it be?

LADY   And you're not afraid?

UNSUX   Of what?

LADY   The consequences.

UNSUX   I long for the consequences.

LADY   So I was right. You are a remarkable man.

UNSUX   Are you being serious?

LADY   I couldn't be more serious. You have impressed me.

UNSUX   But I didn't mean to.

LADY   I'll go even further. You move me.

Unsux jumps from his chair.

UNSUX   I don't know how to say this but . . . this is . . . this is . . . the most beautiful day of my life, the first day of my life. And I'm certain the sun will shine!

Lady stretches her hand out to him. Unsux takes it in both of his and kisses it. Sux returns stage right and witnesses the scene.

SCENE THREE

Unsux releases Lady's hand. Sux approaches them, sits down, takes a cigar out of his pocket, and lights it. He blows out a cloud of smoke. Pause.

LADY   What news?

SUX   At your request I have reserved seats at the theater.

LADY   You've done excellently.

SUX   Unfortunately, they're for the evening performance.

LADY   It doesn't matter.

SUX   And also, equally unfortunately, only two seats.

LADY   And why is that?

SUX   Because they were the last two seats in the entire theater. As I said, the show is very popular because of the great tragedian's talent.

LADY   That doesn't matter either.

SUX   I would even say: all the better. The show really is worth seeing.

LADY   I meant that it doesn't matter that there are only two seats.

SUX   I hope so.

LADY   Because two seats are better than no seats at all. I would have been distraught if there'd been no seats at all.

SUX   So would I have been.

Unsux, who hitherto has been standing motionless, sits down and speaks equally decisively.

UNSUX   So would I.

Lady and Sux look at him. Unsux puts one leg over the other and crosses his arms across his chest with a sudden and ostentatious self-confidence. Pause.

LADY   As it happens, I don't know if I want to go to the theater.

Unsux instantly changes position: He is now taken aback, confused, and unsure of himself.

UNSUX   What do you mean?

Sux blows out a cloud of smoke.

LADY   I'll think about it. If I change my mind, then you gentlemen won't have lost anything by it. You'll even benefit by it. You'll be able to go to the theater. Together.

Sux and Unsux stand up simultaneously and look at the Lady.

LADY   (*cont.*)   But there's no rush. The show doesn't start till this evening, and besides I haven't decided anything yet. We have the whole afternoon in front of us. And it's sure to be sunny. (*To Unsux.*)   Isn't it?

Unsux nods by way of agreement. Lady gets up from her chair. Goes left.

LADY   (*cont.*)   So we'll meet on the beach.

Waving good-bye to both men, she leaves left. Sux and Unsux sit down slowly, simultaneously. Pause.

SCENE FOUR

SUX   Now what?

UNSUX   Let's introduce ourselves.

Sux lets out a cloud of smoke. Blackout.

ACT III

A blue sky-scape, marine horizon. Roar of the sea, the squawking of seagulls. Two deck chairs and a parasol. On one of the deck chairs, Sux in a dark blue beach robe is reading a newspaper. Next to him is a beach bag. The other deck chair is folded up.

SCENE TWO

Unsux comes in left, dressed as before. He is carrying a rolled-up swimsuit under his arm. Sux stops reading.

SUX   I was beginning to think you wouldn't come.

UNSUX   Would you have wanted that?

SUX   It's all the same to me, but after what you told me about yourself . . . (*Stands up and goes up to Unsux, folding his newspaper.*)   I mean, you can't swim.

UNSUX   I can a bit.

SUX   If I understood you correctly, you stay afloat for a few moments and then you sink. Isn't that so?

UNSUX   That was before.

SUX   Before what?

UNSUX   Before I met her.

SUX   What's changed?

UNSUX   I've acquired faith in myself.

SUX   But that doesn't mean you've learned to swim.

UNSUX   No, but I've acquired a confidence in my own potential. It was a lack of confidence in my own potential that caused me not to learn to swim, not the other way around. Before, I was convinced that, since I didn't learn to swim, it must have been because of a lack of potential, so I stopped believing in it. But now I see that it's a lack of faith in myself, which I predicated in advance, that was the cause of all my failures.

SUX   That's still only a theory.

UNSUX   Not entirely. A start has already been made in practice.

SUX   What kind of start?

UNSUX   It's transpired that I have a chance with her.

SUX   Really?

UNSUX   Yes. It was enough for me to believe in myself just a little and everything turned out to be easier than I'd thought. And that, in turn, allows me to believe in myself even more, which brings in even better results. If things carry on like this, this very evening I shall be happy.

SUX   Hope again?

UNSUX   No. This time it's certainty. Almost . . .

SUX   I see. Almost.

UNSUX   I am in love. That's certain.

SUX   But that's not everything.

UNSUX   But I do have grounds to suppose that it's not unrequited.

SUX   Congratulations. I wish you success. But to return to the subject of swimming . . .

UNSUX   Where is she?

SUX   Our lady friend? She's not here yet.

UNSUX   Surely she hasn't changed her mind?

SUX   I couldn't say.

UNSUX   Surely she'll come, won't she?

SUX   Judging by what I've just heard from you—you shouldn't have any doubts. I mean, she arranged to meet you on the beach.

UNSUX   Well, then, I'll go and get changed. (*Walks left.*)   If she comes in the meantime, tell her I'll be right back.

SUX   Certainly.

Unsux goes out left.

Scene Three

Sux carefully folds the newspaper, fans himself with it for a moment. Then he puts the newspaper aside and starts doing exercises, moving his arms, bending, etc. He does them slowly, efficiently, and with no comic effect; the exercises should be aesthetic.

Scene Four

Lady enters right, dressed differently than before, carrying a beach bag. For a moment she watches Sux with evident pleasure.

LADY   Bravo.

Sux stops exercising and bows like an acrobat acknowledging applause.

LADY *(cont.)*   Bravo, excellent. Especially for a tragic hero.

SUX   That wasn't intended for public consumption.

Bends down; picks up and unfolds the deck chair. Lady approaches him.

SUX *(cont.)*   Have you made your decision yet?

LADY   Not yet.

SUX   Time's passing.

LADY   It's a long time till this evening. Besides, before I make my decision I'd like to have some more data. Could you facilitate that for me?

SUX   With pleasure.

LADY   If I'm to go or not go to the theater, I'd like to know some more about the show you mentioned.

SUX   But of course. I'm at your service.

LADY   Surely I'm entitled to.

SUX Indubitably.

Sux indicates the unfolded deck chair. Lady sits or rather half-reclines on it.

LADY To begin with, as I mentioned, I don't like tragedy. Though you assure me that in the program there is a clown who amuses everyone because he fails at everything, that actually doesn't make me laugh; it saddens me. So my first question is: Are you sure that he succeeds at nothing?

SUX I confess I don't know the ending.

LADY How so? You said you did know it.

SUX What I meant was I knew the tragic figure.

LADY About whose tragic nature I have my doubts. To my way of looking, anyway. As I've already mentioned, the tragic figure tends to make me laugh if it takes itself too tragically. So there is a chance that if I went to the theater tonight, I might laugh and not just cry even if the clown makes me sad. But you assured me that the actor in the tragic role plays the part magnificently and that one can only interpret it tragically and cry. Do you stand by your assurance?

Meanwhile, Sux has stretched himself out on the other deck chair.

SUX Unfortunately I must. He is a great actor.

LADY Pity. So I can only count on the clown not making me too sad. In other words, that he doesn't meet only with misfortunes.

SUX For that to happen he would need to stop being a clown.

LADY But maybe in the end something will work out for him. What do you think?

SUX That doesn't depend on me.

LADY So there is a chance that I will like the show. Isn't there?

Pause.

LADY (*cont.*) In that case, let's assume I will go to the theater. But we have only two tickets to get in with. That means that one of you gentlemen will have to withdraw. Would you withdraw?

SUX If you wished it . . .

LADY   We're not talking about my wishes at the moment, but yours. Ah, I forgot; after all, you don't have any wishes . . .

Pause.

LADY (*cont.*)   Or maybe in this case you do have a wish, oh quite exceptionally of course, just this one . . .

Pause.

LADY (*cont.*)   Or is it still all the same to you . . .

Pause.

LADY (*cont.*)   No reply?

SUX   I . . . the decision's not mine.

LADY   Neither yes nor no. Good. In that case, let's talk about your friend. Would he withdraw?

SUX   I can't speak for him.

LADY   But what do you think?

SUX   No, he wouldn't.

LADY   Why?

SUX   Because he's fallen in love with you.

LADY   Whatever next!

SUX   That's why I am of the opinion that you should go with him and not with me.

LADY   So! At last I hear you express an opinion of your own.

SUX   Only on a subject that doesn't affect me directly.

LADY   An impressive impartiality.

SUX   Neither he nor I can accompany you without your consent. And that means that you must choose one of us.

LADY   Must? Not at all. I may.

SUX   Nevertheless . . .

LADY   The freedom to choose is my privilege.

SUX Well, then, I consider it to be your obligation to choose him and not me.

LADY What obligation?

SUX A social one. He, unlike me, has been socially disadvantaged by nature. By fate. Nature is blind and has no concept of justice. Whereas we, as a society, govern ourselves by that very concept. So you, as a member of society, ought to put right the wrong done him by nature, and choose him and not me. To correct inequality—that is an obligation you may not ignore.

LADY I may not?

SUX If you were to choose me it would be acting against the ideals of humanism.

Pause.

LADY You're right.

SUX From the standpoint of social justice, there is no alternative.

LADY I completely agree with that. Particularly as, in choosing you, I would not only be making the injustice done him by fate worse, but I would also be injuring you.

SUX Me? In what way?

LADY I would deepen your metaphysical unease. You succeed at everything in life, so if you were to succeed this time, too, you would be confronted by the question of the transcendental meaning of life. Which question is, apparently, your fundamental problem since you have no other worries. A further success would cast you even further into metaphysical misery. No, I cannot lend my hand to such a thing.

SUX Let's not exaggerate.

LADY . . . even if I wished to very much.

SUX Even then?

Lady gets up, goes up to him, puts a hand on his shoulder.

LADY Particularly . . .

Touches his cheek with a fingertip.

LADY (*cont.*)   . . . then.

Sux raises his arm to embrace her. Lady releases herself from him suddenly, turns away from him, and withdraws. Sux gets up from the deck chair. Lady stands with her back to him. Pause.

SUX   I'm asking for some metaphysical misery.

LADY   In return for . . .

SUX   Yes, in return for.

LADY   But would it be worth it?

Sux takes two, three steps toward her.

SUX   I'm asking.

LADY   I want to hear that again.

SUX   I'm asking.

LADY   Louder.

SUX   I'm asking!

Lady turns to face him.

LADY   And I'm asking you to take a close look at me.

SUX   I've already done that.

LADY   And you can see what I look like?

SUX   From the moment of our first meeting. Even when you are absent.

LADY   Well, then. In that case tell me: Do I look like Karl Marx?

SUX   Like who?

LADY   Karl Marx. Or like Robin Hood, at least.

SUX   No. Most certainly not.

LADY   Precisely. And I'm not in the least bit interested in putting right social injustices or in any other kind of charitable activity. Nor do I care about your metaphysical problems. Not even a little. And whenever I choose anything or anyone, I always do so only how I choose to.

SUX How? Or who?

LADY They are independent of each other. I like you very much indeed and if my choice were dependent only on "who" then I would choose you without hesitation. But there is the "how" to consider.

SUX If it's "very much" . . .

LADY How is not a question of "very much," "a little," "more or less." How is also about how all this makes me look. How it makes me feel. What I might expect to get if I chose you. What I would be for you. One more trifle, one more successful encounter, one more successful event. But no more than that. But I want to be more than that. I am more than that.

SUX To him?

LADY Yes, to him. To him I mean so much that it makes me mean a lot to myself. Or at least as much as I need to. Thanks to him. He will return what I can give him and even more, a hundred times more than you could ever be capable of doing.

SUX You're choosing him?

LADY No, I'm choosing myself. The self that I prefer, the self that suits me. You, he—what nonsense. He's thinking: you. You're thinking: him. Him, you—you're always thinking like that and you can't think in any other way. But I'm thinking: me.

SUX In other words: she.

LADY Yes, she. But neither he nor you can comprehend that.

SUX I understand.

LADY The only thing you understand is that you've lost.

SUX In this situation—that's enough.

LADY Since you mention the situation, I do hope you'll know how to behave when the three of us are together.

SUX You can count on me.

Pause.

LADY Are you angry?

SUX   Not at all.

LADY   I'm so sorry . . .

SUX   No need to be.

LADY   Will you . . . forgive me?

SUX   You can rely on my friendship and my deepest respect.

LADY   Respect?

SUX   And genuine admiration.

LADY   And is that all?

SUX   No. Please also accept my gratitude for this moment of immeasurably fascinating conversation.

LADY   All right then . . . but I'd rather we didn't exaggerate. We'll see each other in a moment. I'm going to get changed.

SUX   Well, good-bye for now then.

Lady goes out right.

SCENE FIVE

Sux folds the deck chair that he'd earlier set out for the Lady and lies down on the deck chair that remains folded out. He closes his eyes. The squealing of seagulls, the rhythmic roar of the sea. Unsux enters from the left.

SCENE SIX

Unsux is wearing a one-piece swimsuit that stretches down to the elbows and the knees. It is hooped and calls to mind the costume of a vaudeville clown.

UNSUX   Did she come?

SUX   No.

UNSUX   Isn't she here yet?

SUX   Well, since she hasn't come . . .

UNSUX   I can't understand what could have happened.

SUX   She'll be late. That's normal.

Unsux walks along the beach impatiently. Sux watches him.

SUX *(cont.)*   It's even better for you.

UNSUX   Why is it better?

SUX   Because while she's away, you can check out your swimming.

UNSUX   But why?

SUX   Surely you don't want to make a fool of yourself in front of her.

UNSUX   You want me to get into the water twice?

SUX   In your place, I'd practice a little before she comes. When was the last time you practiced?

UNSUX   Swimming? Twenty years ago.

SUX   And you haven't practiced swimming since then?

UNSUX   Not once.

SUX   And you intend to risk it in her presence? With no preparation?

UNSUX   It's not a risk. Her presence alone gives me strength. With her here I can do anything. It's a miracle.

SUX   It may be a miracle but it's not technique.

UNSUX   You can't know anything about it.

SUX   Not about miracles, no. But I know a lot about technique. I was an instructor.

UNSUX   A swimming instructor?

SUX   I also have a certificate in lifesaving. That was before I won the district championship in the two-hundred-meter freestyle.

UNSUX   Championship?

SUX   Several championships. I have various cups and medals.

Pause.

SUX   What's happened to you?

UNSUX   Nothing.

SUX   You're out of sorts. You were in a much better mood a moment ago.

Unsux stops at the edge, looks into the distance. Pause.

SUX   (*cont.*)   I also took part in high-diving competitions.

UNSUX   And?

SUX   And what?

UNSUX   What about the high dives?

SUX   Nothing. Second place.

UNSUX   Only second?

SUX   Yes. In the national championships.

UNSUX   I see.

SUX   . . . and only because I scored the highest marks for artistic merit. It's not worth mentioning.

Pause.

UNSUX   Maybe I should try after all.

SUX   What?

UNSUX   Well . . . to practice a bit . . .

SUX   On reflection I think you shouldn't.

UNSUX   Why not?

SUX   Because you could get discouraged and then you'll get your complex again. With technique you never know, especially after such a long break, but miracles happen all the time. At least in your case, they do. It'll be best if you wait for her. I mean, for the miracle.

UNSUX   No, I think I will try after all.

SUX   As you wish. It's all the same to me.

Sux spreads out his newspaper and starts to read, taking no notice of Unsux. Unsux makes arm movements as if he were swimming.

UNSUX   I think this is how it's done . . .

Sux continues to read his newspaper.

UNSUX   Watch.

Sux tears his eyes away from the paper and watches Unsux.

SUX   Yes, not bad.

UNSUX   Right, then, I'm off to the water.

Goes into the water. In other words, he steps down beyond the edge of the stage. He's up to his knees in the water.

UNSUX   (*cont.*)   Brrr . . . it's cold.

SUX   That's because you're not used to it. Not surprising after twenty years.

Unsux bends down and splashes his face with water.

UNSUX   I think it might even be twenty-one.

SUX   Twenty-one?!

UNSUX   Yes, I think so.

SUX   You said it was only twenty.

UNSUX   I made a mistake.

SUX   In that case you've no time to lose.

Sux stands up, looks into the wings, right. Unsux walks even deeper into the water.

UNSUX   Oh, I don't like this at all.

Sux walks up to the edge.

SUX   Hurry up!

Unsux is now visible only from the waist up. He stops and turns to Sux.

UNSUX   I'd like to ask you a favor.

SUX   What is it?

UNSUX   If anything happens please rescue me.

SUX   There's nothing to worry about.

UNSUX   I wouldn't want to die just now.

SUX   But of course.

UNSUX Now that I've met her . . . You do understand.

SUX You don't need to explain that to me.

UNSUX I want to live.

SUX Because you're in love.

UNSUX Precisely.

Unsux goes farther and farther into the water until he vanishes.

Scene Seven

Sux stands at the edge looking out to sea, so with his back to the audience. The rhythmic ebb and flow of the waves are louder than before. Sux folds his hands behind his back. He continues standing. The loud roar of the sea, the squawking of seagulls. This continues for a long time. Theatrical time more and more prolonged. Finally, when the anticipation and the lack of action have become intolerable, Sux turns away from the edge. He goes up to the folded deck chair and unfolds it. Then he takes out of the beach bag a box of cigars and, out of the box, a cigar. He lights a cigar, blows out a cloud of smoke. He lies down on the deck chair, smoking a cigar.

Scene Eight

Lady enters from right. She is wearing swimwear similar to that worn by Sux, except that hers is white. Seeing her, Sux puts out his cigar.

LADY Isn't he here yet?

SUX No.

LADY That's strange.

SUX A little strange, I agree.

LADY I mean, we clearly arranged to meet on the beach, all three of us.

SUX And I had the impression that this meeting was very important to him.

Lady puts her bag down next to the other deck chair, goes up to the edge of the sea. She stands on the edge and looks out to sea, thus with her back to the audience.

SUX (*cont.*)   Unless I was mistaken.

Lady returns from the edge and sits down on the deckchair.

LADY (*To herself*)   I wonder what excuse he'll make.

SUX   So do I.

LADY   You're not entitled to say anything on the subject!

SUX   Then let's change the subject.

Pause.

LADY   I was thinking about that metaphysics of yours.

SUX   And . . . ?

LADY   It's nonsense. I don't believe in any of your suffering.

SUX   Shame.

LADY   You made it all up just to make yourself appear more interesting.

SUX   But, as I see, without success.

LADY   But even if there is something in it, you're very attached to it.

SUX   To what?

LADY   To that metaphysical misery of yours, which you've invented for yourself.

SUX   And how do you know that?

LADY   Yes. You wouldn't let anyone take it away from you for anything in the world. That makes it mean that it's just made-up misery.

SUX   So is it just made-up or is there something in it?

LADY   Both the one and the other. First of all you made it up and then you believed in it yourself. You can recognize real misery by the fact that a person would gladly get rid of it. Whereas he wants to keep made-up misery at any price. And that's how it is in your case.

Pause.

SUX   And I don't believe in your feelings toward this person.

LADY   Toward you? Of course I don't have any.

SUX   I didn't mean me, I meant him. Whatever you feel toward him is also made-up.

LADY   I told you, you are not entitled to . . .

SUX   Indeed I am. I'm paying you back in kind. You're ridiculing my misery, so I'm entitled to tell you what I think of your feelings. I think they're made-up.

LADY   I forbid you!

SUX   Too late. Now I'll finish what I was saying. You made them up because you needed them. If my torment isn't real, then your feelings aren't either. You can tell real feelings by the fact that they are of themselves and independent of our wills, whether or not we need them. The most real are those we don't need at all, those we don't want, those we resist . . .

LADY   I think I no longer wish to remain in your company.

SUX   Very well. In that case I'll withdraw.

Sux gets up.

LADY   No, I'll withdraw.

Lady gets up.

SUX   You're no longer waiting for him?

LADY   No. If he wants me, he knows where to find me.

SUX   In the theater.

Lady picks up her beach bag and moves to the right.

SUX   (*cont.*)   I have a certain proposition.

Lady stops.

SUX   (*cont.*)   If you intend to withdraw and I do, too, then . . . let us withdraw together.

Pause.

LADY   That wouldn't be sensible.

SUX   But it would be logical.

LADY   In that case . . . But only because that that's how things have panned out. For no other reason.

SUX   Of course. There is no other reason.

Sux folds both deck chairs. A pause in the dialogue.

LADY   And yet it makes me slightly uneasy.

SUX   But why? This is about logic and nothing else.

LADY   I wasn't thinking about us but about why he hasn't come yet.

SUX   Ah, about that. There's nothing to worry about there, either. It's safe here, peaceful . . . A small seaside place, a sunny summer's day . . .

LADY   He confessed to me that, before he met me, he wanted to commit suicide.

SUX   That's possible. But that was before he met you.

LADY   Didn't he mention it to you?

SUX   Yes, he did. But that was long ago.

Sux finishes folding the deck chairs, furls up his parasol, picks up his beach bag, and joins the Lady. They both make their way right.

LADY   And have you ever thought about suicide?

SUX   Oh, yes. I even came close to doing it.

LADY   And what saved you?

SUX   I realized that there's always time to do it.

LADY   Always?

SUX   Yes. One can kill oneself even half an hour before death.

LADY   I'd like to get to the hairstylist if there's time.

SUX   Even five minutes before . . .

They are at the exit into the wings.

SUX   (*cont.*)   Yes. It's a reassuring thought.

They go out right.

BIBLIOGRAPHY

Works by Mrożek

Plays

1. *Profesor* (The Professor). Produced 1956, published 1968.
2. *Policja* (The Police). 1958.
3. *Męczeństwo Piotra Oheya* (The Martyrdom of Peter Ohey). 1959.
4. *Indyk* (The Turkey). Published 1960, produced 1961.
5. *Na pełnym morzu* (Out at Sea). 1961.
6. *Karol* (Charlie). 1961.
7. *Striptease* (Striptease). 1961.
8. *Zabawa* (The Party). Published 1962, produced 1963.
9. *Kynolog w rozterce* (A Dog Fancier in a Dilemma). Published 1962, produced 1963.
10. *Czarowna noc* (The Enchanted Night). 1963.
11. *Śmierć porucznika* (Death of a Lieutenant). 1963.
12. *Tango* (Tango). Published 1964, produced 1965.
13. *Krawiec* (The Tailor). Written 1966, published 1977, produced 1979.
14. *Poczwórka* (The Foursome). Published 1967, produced 1968.
15. *Dom na granicy* (Home on the Border). Published 1967, produced 1978.
16. *Testarium* (The Prophets). Published 1967, produced 1968 (West Germany), 1982 (Poland).
17. *Drugie danie* (Repeat Performance). Published 1968, produced 1968 (West Germany), 1977 (Poland).
18. *Vatzlav* (Vatzlav). Published in English 1970 (New York), in Polish 1982 (Paris). Produced 1970 (Switzerland), 1979 (Poland).
19. *Szczęśliwe wydarzenie* (Blessed Event). Published 1971 (Paris), 1973 (Poland). Produced 1971 (West Germany), 1973 (Poland).
20. *Rzeźnia* (The Slaughterhouse). Published 1973, produced 1975.
21. *Emigranci* (Emigrants). Published 1974, produced 1974 (Paris), 1975 (Warsaw).

677

22. *Garbus* (The Hunchback). 1975.
23. *Serenada, Polowanie na lisa, Lis filozof* (Serenade, Fox Hunt, Philosopher Fox). 1977.
24. *Lis aspirant* (Aspiring Fox). Published 1978, produced 1979.
25. *Pieszo* (On Foot). Written 1979, published and produced 1980.
26. *Ambasador* (The Ambassador). Written 1980, produced 1981, published 1982 (Paris).
27. *Letni dzień* (A Summer's Day). 1984.
28. *Alfa* (Alpha). Published 1984 (Paris), produced 1984 (New York), 1989 (Poland).
29. *Kontrakt* (The Contract). 1986.
30. *Portret* (The Portrait). 1987.
31. *Wdowy* (Widows). Published 1990, produced 1992.
32. *Miłość na Krymie* (Love in the Crimea). Published 1993, produced 1994.
33. *Wielebni* (The Reverends). Written 1996, published 2000, produced 2001.
34. *Piękny Widok* (A Beautiful View). Written 1998, published 2000.

Fiction

Opowiadania z Trzmielowej Góry (Stories from Bumble Bee Hill). Warsaw, 1953.
Półpancerze praktyczne (Practical Half-Armors). Kraków, 1953.
Maleńkie lato (The Small Summer). Kraków, 1956.
Słoń (The Elephant). Kraków, 1957.
Wesele w Atomicach (A Wedding at Atomville). Kraków, 1959.
Ucieczka na południe (Flight to the South). Warsaw, 1961.
Moniza Clavier (Moniza Clavier). Warsaw, 1967.
Opowiadania (Short Stories). Kraków, 1964 and 1974.
Donosy (Denunciations). London, 1983.
Małe prozy (Small Prose Works). Kraków, 1990.

Satirical Drawings

Polska w obrazach (Poland in Pictures). Kraków, 1957.
Postępowiec (The Progressive). Warsaw, 1960.

Przez okulary Sławomira Mrożka (Seen through Sławomir Mrożek's Glasses). Warsaw, 1968.
Rysunki (Drawings). Warsaw, 1982; Kraków, 1990.

Essays

Dwa listy i inne opowiadania (Two Letters and Other Stories). Paris, 1970; Kraków, 1974.
Małe listy (Little Letters). Kraków, 1982.
Dziennik powrotu (Journal of a Return). Kraków, 1996.

Autobiography

"Sławomir Mrożek," in *Contemporary Authors: Autobiography Series,* Vol. 10. Detroit, 1989.

Films

Rondo, principal actor, 1958.
Wyspa róż (Island of Roses), scenario, 1975.
Amor (Cupid), scenario and direction, 1978.
Powrót (The Return), scenario and direction, 1979.

Selected Critical Studies

In English

Drama at Calgary (Special Mrożek Issue), III, 3 (1969).
Esslin, Martin. "Eastern Absurdist: Sławomir Mrożek—Poland" in *Brief Chronicles,* pp. 150–61. London, 1970.
Gerould, Daniel. "Contexts for *Vatzlav.*" *Modern Drama,* XXVII, I (March 1984), pp. 21–40.
———. "Introduction," in *Twentieth-Century Polish Avant-Garde Drama,* pp. 13–95. Ithaca, 1977.
———. "Mrożek Revisited," in *Slavic Drama: The Question of Innovation,* pp. 27–40. Ottawa, 1991.

————. "The Mrożek Festival: Cracow, Summer 1990." *Soviet and East European Performance,* 3 (1990), pp. 12–8.

Goetz-Stankiewicz, Marketa. "Sławomir Mrożek: The Molding of a Polish Playwright," in W. J. Stankiewicz, ed., *The Tradition of Polish Ideals: Essays in History and Literature,* pp. 204–25. London, 1981.

Grol-Prokopczyk, Regina. "Sławomir Mrożek's Theatre of the Absurd." *The Polish Review,* XXIV, 3 (1979), pp. 45–57.

Kłossowicz, Jan. *Mrożek.* Warsaw, 1980.

Kott, Jan. "Mrożek's Family," in *Theatre Notebook, 1947–1967,* pp. 135–40. New York, 1968.

Mrożek Festival. Cracow 15–29 June 1990. Kraków, 1990.

Stephan, Halina. *Transcending the Absurd: Drama and Prose of Sławomir Mrożek.* Amsterdam, 1997.

Sugiera, Małgorzata. "Mrożek's Dramatic Triptych: *The Hunchback, On Foot, Portrait,*" in *Forum Modernes Theater,* Bd. 6/2 (1991), pp. 133–44.

Wirth, Andrzej. "Dramaturgy of Models," in *Theatre Byways: Essays in Honor of Claude L. Shaver,* ed. CjnStevens and Joseph Aurbach, pp. 102–4. New Orleans, 1978.

In Polish

Błoński, Jan. *Wszystkie sztuki Sławomira Mrożka.* Kraków, 1995.

————. "Mrożek i Mrożek," "Mrożka droga do komedii," "Mędrek cham I jednoaktówka," "Dramaturgia modelów," "Wniebowstąpienie," in *Romans z tekstem,* pp. 161–269. Kraków, 1981.

Kelera, Józef. "Mrożek—Dowcip wyobraźni logicznej," in *Kpiarze i moraliści,* pp. 86–114. Kraków, 1966.

Morawiec, Elżbieta. "Pieszo znaczy uczciwie," "Przypowiastki Mrożka," "Portret indywidualny i zbiorowy," in *Seans pamięci,* pp. 108–30. Kraków, 1996.

Mrożek: Utwory Sławomira Mrożka na scenach polskich i zagranicznych. Kraków, 1990.

Nyczek, Tadeusz. "Obrona tradycji," in *Emigranci,* pp. 70–85. London, 1988.

Stephan, Halina. *Mrożek.* Kraków, 1996.

Sugiera, Małgorzata. *Dramaturgia Sławomira Mrożka.* Kraków, 1996.

Teatr (Special Mrożek Issue) No. 3, 1989.